EFFECTIVE COMMUNICATION IN BUSINESS

SHIRLEY KUIPER, Ed. D.

Management Department
College of Business Administration
University of South Carolina

MORRIS PHILIP WOLF, Ph.D.

Formerly of the University of Houston
and Louisiana Tech University

10TH EDITION

SOUTH-WESTERN PUBLISHING CO.

Credits:

Managing Editor: Karen Schneiter
Developmental Editor: Susan Freeman
Production Editor: Karen E. Davis
Designer: Elaine St. John-Lagenaur
Production Artist: Steve E. McMahon
Associate Photo Editor/Stylist: Mike O'Donnell
Marketing Manager: Colleen Thomas

Copyright © 1994

by SOUTH-WESTERN PUBLISHING CO.

Cincinnati, Ohio

Library of Congress Cataloging-in-Publication Data

Kuiper, Shirley.
    Effective communication in business / Shirley Kuiper, Morris Philip Wolf. — 10th ed.
       p.   cm.
    Wolf's name appears first on the earlier edition.
    Includes bibliographical references and index.
    ISBN 0-538-70545-0
    1. Business communication.   2. English language—Business English.   I. Wolf, Morris Philip.   II. Title.
HF5718.K84   1994   92-5765
651.7—dc20   CIP

Whatever your career goals may be, you can benefit personally and professionally from *Effective Communication in Business,* Tenth Edition.

PURPOSE AND SCOPE

The purpose of this Tenth Edition is to provide ethical as well as profitable concepts, methods, and guides for developing your awareness of—and your success with—the business of communication. Like its nine predecessors, this edition is both traditional and innovative. It is traditional in perpetuating principles and techniques which—tested by trial, error, and expertise—continue to affect business activities constructively. This edition is innovative in that it reflects recent contributions of science and technology to the ethical, profitable exchange of goods and services in a multicultural environment.

As with its previous editions, this book is written for postsecondary students of diverse ages, backgrounds, interests, and experiences. Those students include people who elect or who are required to complete a business communication course at senior colleges and universities, at community and junior colleges, or at continuing-education centers. *Effective Communication in Business,* Tenth Edition, offers such students many opportunities for awakening and developing a sense of useful, constructive wonder; a sense of wonder about themselves and about billions of other people, throughout the world, whose lives, cultures, and careers are directly or indirectly influenced by the business of communication.

SPECIAL FEATURES

The Tenth Edition of *Effective Communication in Business* is a complete instructional package, a unified teaching-learning system, with these special features:

1. *Concept-and-practice approach.* Communication theories are merged with applications throughout the text.
2. *Global contexts.* The contents set the study of business communication in interpersonal, organizational, multicultural, and worldwide contexts.
3. *Empirical insights into business as communication.* Traditional approaches and experience-based approaches to goals, skills, and criteria of successful business administration through effective communication are explained.
4. *Innovative methods and techniques.* Innovative, as well as traditional, methods and techniques are represented by updated exercises; communication-process models; communication-by-objectives approach; whole-into-parts message planning; collaborative and solo communication strategies; uses of logic, psychology, language, and metacommunication to help the student achieve ethical, profitable goals.
5. *Revised contents.* The text provides current relevant information, discussion questions, applications, and case materials. New exercises enhance the end-of-chapter activity assignments.
6. *Standard chapter organization.* Every chapter opens with an outline for preview and, later, review. The chapter outline is followed by statements of learning objectives, by a unifying decisions case, and by a context statement. Every chapter closes with review, transition, and communication activities.
7. *Abundant end-of-chapter activities.* The instructor has flexibility in varying assignments from class to class and from term to term with an abundant supply of discussion questions, applications, cases, multicultural communication exercises, and follow-ups to the unifying decisions cases.
8. *Attractive design.* These design elements elicit the student's attention: easy-reading layout, color contrasts for emphasis and variety, wide margins for notes, marginal questions to highlight important

ideas while developing interest, and numerous illustrations to complement explanations throughout the text.

TEXT AND CHAPTER ORGANIZATION

Effective Communication in Business, Tenth Edition, has 22 chapters arranged in six major parts followed by eight appendices.

Part 1, Communication Awareness (Chapters 1–5), elicits student attention to interpersonal and organizational relationships through communication as an active, purposeful process instead of an accidental or static "thing." Part 1 identifies achievable communication goals, relevant skills, and recognizable standards for evaluating message effectiveness. Part 1 also introduces students to the multicultural, technological, and collaborative nature of the contemporary business communication environment.

Part 2, Communication Readiness (Chapters 6–8), provides transitions between theories and practices. Part 2 prepares the student to plan, organize, and develop goal-oriented business messages enhanced by appropriate tone and appearance.

Part 3, Message Patterns (Chapters 9–13), applies the Part 1 and Part 2 information to receiver-oriented methods of recognizing message categories and to composition techniques for individual messages within those categories. Part 3 focuses student attention on favorable, neutral, unfavorable, mixed-news, goodwill, and persuasive messages.

Part 4, Visual and Oral Media (Chapters 14–15), reminds the student that effective writing, although extremely important, is not the only means of conveying business messages. Part 4 applies information from Parts 1–3 to the visual, oral, and nonverbal aspects of business communication.

Part 5, Communicating with Reports (Chapters 16–20), develops student skills with multimedia production, transmission, and evaluation of reports for managerial decision making. Part 5 describes report purposes and functions, planning and writing processes, research methods, and transmission procedures.

Part 6, The Employment Process (Chapters 21–22), integrates student communication skills for marketing personal and professional skills. Part 6 identifies data sources and their uses in personal, career, and employment-opportunity analysis. Part 6 describes preparation, presentation, and follow-up procedures for *curricula vitae,* personal data sheets, and interviews.

Eight appendices supply additional, detailed information to support the six major parts of *Effective Communication in Business,* Tenth Edition.

INSTRUCTIONAL MATERIALS

The following instructional materials enhance the package for *Effective Communication in Business,* Tenth Edition:

1. *Study Guide and Supplement.* This student aid reinforces information presented in the text and gives students additional opportunities to apply what they learn. Each chapter contains a study guide and exercises. Answers and the study guide are grouped at the end of the supplement and permit immediate reinforcement. Suggested solutions for the exercise are provided in the *Manual.*

2. *Instructor's Manual.* A comprehensive teacher's manual, packaged in a three-ring binder, includes:
   a. teaching suggestions for the entire course
   b. teaching suggestions for each chapter
   c. solutions to the end-of-chapter activities
   d. solutions to *Study Guide and Supplement* exercises
   e. a set of 138 transparencies with suggestions for their use
   f. a miniquiz for each chapter to reinforce basic language skills
   g. a test bank with pretest, a test for each part, and a final exam
   h. solutions for each miniquiz and test bank

3. *MicroSWAT III.* Computerized diskette versions of the test bank are provided. MicroSWAT III eases test preparation by enabling the instructor to:
   a. generate complete tests from the test bank
   b. select individual questions from the test bank
   c. have the computer randomly select questions

Microcomputer knowledge is not essential for using MicroSWAT III; the program prompts the instructor at every step.

ACKNOWLEDGMENTS

Many people—each in his or her special and valuable ways—have earned our gratitude. We acknowledge our indebtedness

►   to students, those we assist personally in the classroom or workplace and those whom this book allows us to serve throughout the world

►   to business practitioners—entrepreneurs, corporate executives, staff members, and other dedicated workers—especially to those who recognize that business *is* communication

►   to researchers, who disclose what had been unperceived or forgotten—especially to those who communicate their insights effectively and ethically

►   to instructors—especially to those who teach people rather than subjects and who, thereby, continually learn about themselves

The Tenth Edition reflects suggestions from those who have used its predecessors—suggestions from students, employers, employees, researchers, and instructors. We thank these reviewers, particularly, for their comments:

Dr. Laurence Barton, University of Nevada—Las Vegas, Las Vegas, Nevada
Dr. Marsha Bayless, Stephen F. Austin State University, Nacagdoches, Texas
Ms. Donna Cox, Monroe Community College, Rochester, New York
Mrs. Lindsay Kerr Danahy, Clermont General and Technical College, Batavia, Ohio
Dr. R. Neil Dortch, University of Wisconsin—Whitewater, Whitewater, Wisconsin
Dr. Earl A. Dvorak, Indiana University, Bloomington, Indiana
Dr. Marie E. Flatley, San Diego State University, San Diego, California
Mrs. Gwyndolyn E. Fouche, Florissant Valley Community College, St. Louis, Missouri
Dr. Garth Hanson, Brigham Young University, Provo, Utah
Dr. Lorene Holmes, Jarvis Christian College, Hawkins, Texas
Dr. Carol Larson Jones, California State Polytechnic University
Dr. Karen Lee Kothenbeutel, Southwest Missouri State University, Springfield, Missouri
Dr. Sandra McKee, DeVry Institute of Technology, Decatur, Georgia
Dr. Glynna E. Morse, Memphis State University, Memphis, Tennessee
Mr. Keith Mulbery, Bowling Green State University, Bowling Green, Ohio
Dr. Rodney L. Smith, University of Dubuque, Dubuque, Iowa
Dr. Taggart Smith, Purdue University, West Lafayette, Indiana
Dr. Lorrie Steerey, Eastern Montana College, Billings, Montana
Mrs. Jacqueline B. Stowe, McMurry College, Abilene, Texas
Dr. James E. Suchan, U.S. Naval Post-Graduate School, Monterey, California
Dr. Louis Perry Trahan, Blinn College, Brenham, Texas
Dr. Janet L. Williams, The University of Georgia, Athens, Georgia

Believing that effective communication is a reciprocal process, we invite your comments concerning *Effective Communication in Business,* Tenth Edition, and your recommendations for the next edition.

Shirley Kuiper
Morris Philip Wolf

CONTENTS

PART 2   COMMUNICATION READINESS

PART 3 MESSAGE PATTERNS

PART 6 THE EMPLOYMENT PROCESS

P
A
R
T
1

COMMUNICATION AWARENESS

More than ever before, communication bridges are necessary. Rapid changes in national and international business arenas require that businesspeople communicate effectively, not only in their native cultures but also across cultures. Consider these facts:

▶ In the early 1940s, the United States and Japan were at war; in the early 1990s, the United States and Japan exchanged over $130 billion annually in goods and services.[1]

▶ In the early 1950s, the United States and the Soviet Union were engaged in an ideological battle over the merits of capitalism and communism; by the early 1990s, the USSR had been dissolved, and its former member states were converting to free-market economies.

▶ In the early 1960s, Taiwan was considered a Third World economy; in 1989 it had a growth rate of 7 percent and had become the world's leading exporter of semiconductors.[2]

▶ In the early 1970s, U.S. investment in private enterprises abroad was

[1] *Economic Report of the President* (Washington, DC: U.S. Government Printing Office, 1991), p. 405.

[2] Massoud M. Saghafi and Chin-Shu Davidson, "The New Age of Global Competition in the Semiconductor Industry: Enter the Dragon," *Columbia Journal of World Business,* vol. 24, no. 4 (Winter 1989), p. 60.

approximately $75 billion;[3] by 1990, that figure had risen to over $300 billion.[4]

▶ In the early 1980s, approximately 18 percent of U.S. elementary and secondary schools had microcomputers for student use; by the end of that decade, over 97 percent of U.S. elementary and secondary schools used microcomputers in their instructional programs.[5]

Changes of such magnitude could be accomplished only by building communication bridges to span cultural and technical gaps. Communication bridges help people in this complex modern world to work together, to exchange products and services, and to achieve their objectives profitably. The goal of this book is to prepare you, as a business communicator, to meet the communication challenges of today's business environment.

This book challenges you to answer these questions:

▶ What communication skills do I need to succeed in business—locally, nationally, and internationally?

▶ How can I acquire and refine these skills?

---

[3]U.S. Bureau of the Census, *Statistical Abstract of the United States: 1981,* 102d ed. (Washington, DC: U.S. Government Printing Office, 1981), p. 836.

[4]U.S. Bureau of the Census, *Statistical Abstract of the United States: 1990,* 110th ed. (Washington, DC: U.S. Government Printing Office, 1990), p. 797.

[5]Ibid., p. 145.

1

INTERPERSONAL AND ORGANIZATIONAL CONCEPTS

OBJECTIVES

After completing this chapter, you should be able to:

1. Describe the communication process.
2. Explain the functions of internal (vertical, horizontal, diagonal) and external organizational communication.
3. Demonstrate communication by objectives (CBO) through planning, organizing, directing, and controlling your messages.
4. Identify the major characteristics of the business communication environment in which you will spend your career.

DECISIONS CASE

Andy Warren, a management trainee at World Enterprises, enters the training center early on the first day of the World Communication Seminar. Waiting for other trainees to enter the room, Andy muses: "This is as good a place as any to start. I suppose we'll hear all about World's communication policies and procedures. That's good. I want to get started on the right foot—do everything just as expected."

As other trainees arrive, Andy makes an important observation: The trainees apparently represent several nationalities and cultures. "World communication!" thinks Andy. "Maybe there's more to this session than I anticipated. What is communication? What is world communication? What is communication at World Enterprises? How can I communicate effectively with these trainees? with the people I will supervise? with my superiors? with our customers?"

Additional questions about this decision-making case are stated at the end of this chapter. Study the chapter before answering those questions.

CHAPTER CONTEXT

Businesspeople confront challenges daily—challenges that require constant adjustment to changes in people and the environment. Renewed consumer demands for quality, new national and international competitors, and changes in political or economic environments are some of the hurdles that businesses encounter as they move toward their goals.

You are preparing to meet the challenges of a modern business career, and no part of your preparation is more significant than your education as a communicator. What you do, say, and write will influence many lives and careers, including but not limited to your own. The following chapters deal with *how* to meet the challenges of effective communication. This chapter directs your attention mainly to *what* is involved and *why*.

THE COMMUNICATION PROCESS

Communication involves more than neat memos and letters, more than clear speech and gestures. Words, gestures, memos, and letters are parts of a complex process.

A Model of the Process

People have been trying to define communication for more than 2,000 years. The Greek philosopher Aristotle identified three elements of communication: speaker, speech, and audience. Current communication theory models call these three elements *sender, message,* and *receiver.*

What is communication?

Communication is the process whereby sender and receiver exchange messages. Although sender, message, and receiver are the primary elements of communication, they are not the only elements in the process. A modern view of the communication process also acknowledges *encoding, transmission* via a *medium, decoding,* and *feedback* as essential parts of that exchange process. Visualize the process as shown in Illustration 1-1.

What is a message?

A **message** is a representation of ideas and feelings. Someone who originates a message is called the **sender.** The communication process begins when the sender is motivated to share ideas or emotions with another person. However, one individual can never experience directly what another experiences. Only *evidence* of the experience, not the experience itself, can be shared. That evidence is provided through symbols.

What is encoding?

A **symbol** stands for or suggests something else. Your school's mascot, for instance, stands for the school. Symbols may be words, gestures, emblems— even unarticulated sounds or deliberate silence. **Encoding** is the act of choosing and using symbols to represent ideas or feelings. Selection of appropriate

Illustration 1-1   THE COMMUNICATION PROCESS

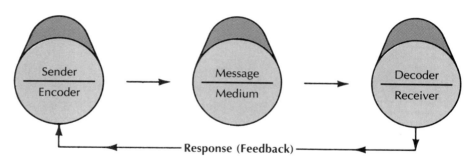

symbols is essential for effective communication. The sender must use symbols that accurately represent the information to be conveyed. Moreover, the symbols must be sufficiently familiar to the receiver to convey the intended message. The sender becomes an **encoder** by speaking, writing, using gestures, assuming a particular stance, or signaling with facial expressions.

The most carefully encoded message communicates nothing until it is received and decoded. The **medium** conveys, or transmits, the message through written, oral, nonverbal, or electronic means to a decoder/receiver. The **decoder/receiver** interprets the symbols. If the decoder interprets the symbols as the encoder intended, communication may occur.

Since effective communication requires evidence that the message has been conveyed, the receiver's response is essential. That response, **feedback,** may take the form of words, deliberate silences, gestures, facial expressions, postures, actions, or the like. When the decoder/receiver responds, that person becomes, in turn, a sender/encoder; and the communication process continues.

Noise (distraction, irrelevance, or interference) can impair the communication process at any point. During the encoding phase, a sender may use symbols that are ambiguous or unfamiliar to the receiver. That noise, often called a semantic barrier, prevents the receiver from decoding the message accurately. Some senders encode and transmit irrelevant, excessively detailed information. That practice may create **information overload,** a situation in which the receiver is unable to process all stimuli or to separate important information from unimportant information. In addition, use of an inappropriate medium may create physical or psychological interference in the transmission and reception stages. Finally, a receiver's limited experience or restricted vocabulary can block the decoding and feedback stages.

Communication is always a two-way process. Although some people speak of one-way communication, a better term for that activity is **expression.** When you express, you provide evidence of your ideas and feelings. Your concern, however, is with delivery (release) of those thoughts or feelings, not with interaction between yourself and other people. For example, if you stub your toe while climbing the stairs, you may groan or cringe in pain. You are probably not interested in audience response; in fact, you may have no audience. Expression does not require response.

Unlike expression, communication does require response. When you communicate, you *exchange* with other people the evidence of ideas and feelings. Response is necessary for you and other people to know that communication has actually occurred. Consider again the toe-stubbing situation. A friend may hear you groan or see you cringe, rush to you, and offer assistance or soothing words. That *response* is evidence that you have communicated.

What is decoding?

What are examples of noise?

How does expression differ from communication?

Characteristics of Messages

What are the
characteristics of
messages?

To comprehend more fully the complexity of the communication process, consider these facts about messages:

▶ Messages may be verbal or nonverbal.
▶ Messages usually have two dimensions.
▶ Messages may be intentional or unintentional.
▶ Messages themselves have no meaning; meaning is in people.

Recall your first communication effort today. Perhaps it was a "good morning" to a family member or a friend. You probably accompanied that verbal (worded) message with nonverbal (nonworded) symbols, such as posture and gestures—maybe a brisk step and a hug, or a shuffling gait and a shrug. A nonverbal message can complement and reinforce a verbal message, or it can contradict the verbal message. A shuffling gait and a shrug may suggest that you don't find anything good about the morning, in spite of your words. When nonverbal and verbal messages conflict, the receiver tends to accept the nonverbal as the more authentic message.

Verbal messages may be spoken (vocal) or written (nonvocal). Both spoken and written messages are affected by nonverbal characteristics. If you write "good morning" on a note and place it at the receiver's breakfast plate along with a flower, the nonverbal accompaniments reinforce the written message.

What is paralanguage?

Nonverbal messages may also be vocal or nonvocal. **Paralanguage** is the *vocal* modification of messages through changes in vocal tone and accompanying sounds, such as laughs, sighs, or groans. *Nonvocal* components of nonverbal messages include posture, gestures, facial expressions, touching, uses of distance, uses of material objects. For example, if the receiver of your note and flower laughs or sighs contentedly, that vocal yet nonworded response conveys acceptance and understanding of your message. If the receiver turns to you, raises an eyebrow, and discards the note and flower, those nonvocal acts communicate rejection of your message.

What is
metacommunication?

Most messages have two basic dimensions, the content dimension and the relational dimension. The content dimension conveys information about the world of the sender and the receiver. The relational dimension offers information about the sender-receiver relationship. That dimension is often called **metacommunication**. Metacommunication (*meta*, "beyond") goes beyond the content dimension. Consider this message: "I won't be home for dinner this evening." Verbally, the message transmits content about the sender's plans for the evening. The existence of the worded message also suggests something about the relationship between sender and receiver—

that they often share dinner. Nonverbally, however, the tone of voice, the speaker's posture, and the timing of the message may convey even more significant information about the relationship. The nonverbal messages go beyond the verbal message to suggest mutual respect and concern or—perhaps—selfishness, indifference, or anger.

The preceding examples also demonstrate two more facts about messages. First, messages may be intentional or unintentional. Second, meaning is within people, not within messages. Consider again the words "good morning." Assume your spouse or roommate enters the room while you are reading the morning newspaper. You absentmindedly mutter "good morning" but do not raise your head or acknowledge that person in any other way. Maintaining your interest in the newspaper, you may unintentionally convey lack of interest in someone who is, in fact, very important to you.

What is the message? Is the morning "good"? You may think it is and that all is going well. If you are fortunate, the receiver will agree, recognizing your usual interest in the morning's news. If you are less fortunate, the receiver may perceive you as an insensitive oaf. Meaning is within people. A message is effective only if the meaning assigned by the receiver is similar to the meaning intended by the sender. As the preceding discussion of message characteristics suggests, both reason and emotion influence communication.

Reason and Emotion

All people, including you, are emotional-rational beings. Although capable of reason, people sometimes act irrationally. When their emotions take control, normally rational people may experience conflict within themselves, with others, and with environments and circumstances.

As you try to satisfy your physical and social needs, your brain enables you to create ideas. However, as you interact with your environment, which includes actions and messages of other people, you generate emotions as well as ideas. You modify your ideas with fear or courage, hatred or love, egotism or generosity. You not only think; you feel. So do the people whom your actions and words touch.

How do reason and emotion affect communication?

How do these insights pertain to you as a communicator? Words and messages are tools for influencing human behaviors in business and your personal life. When you write a letter, compose a report, or use nonverbal communication, you affect people, not just things. Your personal and professional success requires messages that produce appropriate responses. You can compose effective messages if you consider not only the rational but also the emotional components of communication.

Insights about the communication process will assist you as you prepare for a business career. Understanding communication within an organizational context further promotes career success.

COMMUNICATION IN ORGANIZATIONS

An **organization** is any group of people committed to a common goal and ready to share information and resources in pursuit of that goal. Organizations could not exist without communication because communication is necessary both to form and to operate an organization.

Only through communication can people become aware of mutual goals, decide how to reach those goals, and assign duties and responsibilities. To achieve organizational goals, organizational members must interact effectively with people outside the organization as well as those within. **Organizational communication** is the process of sharing information between and among organizational members (**internal communication**) and with people outside the organization (**external communication**).

What is internal communication? external communication?

Internal Communication

Internal communication enables managers and subordinates to accomplish the tasks required for organizational success. Internal communication is influenced by organizational structure. Many organizations evidence a hierarchical structure consisting of multiple levels of superiors (such as executives, managers, and supervisors) and subordinates. In this structure, authority and responsibility are defined by one's position in the hierarchy. Within a hierarchical structure, organizations typically practice division of labor. Under division of labor, each person is responsible for specific tasks, but all individuals and tasks must be coordinated to achieve the goals of the organization.

Exercise of authority, fulfillment of responsibilities, and coordination of diverse efforts require that messages flow in many directions, as shown by Illustration 1–2. **Vertical communication** (subordinate-to-superior or superior-to-subordinate communication) generally follows the hierarchical chain of command. **Horizontal communication** (peer-to-peer communication) is essential to accomplish effective division of labor. In contemporary businesses, many tasks are handled by groups whose members come from various units and different hierarchical levels (such as committees or quality circles). Both horizontal and **diagonal communication** (communication across units and different hierarchical levels) are required for effective functioning of such groups.

Illustration 1–2   ORGANIZATIONAL COMMUNICATION AS A
RECIPROCAL, MULTIDIRECTIONAL PROCESS

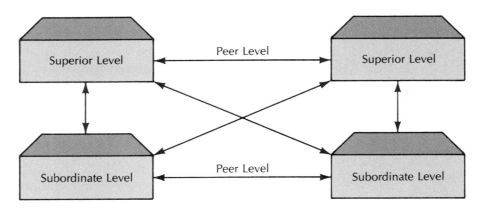

Vertical Communication. Vertical communication moves both upward and downward, reinforcing the hierarchical chain of command. **Upward communication** consists of messages from subordinates to superiors. When you communicate with superiors, your primary job is to supply information for making decisions. The purposes of upward communication are to report progress or achievement, to report problems (current or anticipated), to propose improvements, and to convey feelings and attitudes about organizational practices. By effective upward communication, you help supervisors, managers, and executives perform their tasks. To ensure communication accuracy, you should verify information before including it in your message. Be sure your data are valid, reliable, timely, and pertinent. If your data are not correct, you may hinder managerial decision making and administration.

To ensure proper transmission, you should send your message through recognized organizational channels and use an appropriate medium. Media differ in their ability to transmit information. Lengel and Daft[6] classify media as rich or lean on the basis of three criteria: ability to transmit multiple cues, ability to facilitate rapid feedback, and ability to provide a personal focus. The richest medium is face-to-face communication because it meets all three criteria. Impersonal media, such as fliers or bulletin board announcements, are lean. They can accommodate few cues, allow for delayed feedback only, and have no personal focus. Memos, letters, and reports tailored for a specific

What is your job in subordinate-to-superior communication?

---

[6]Robert H. Lengel and Richard L. Daft, "The Selection of Communication Media as an Executive Skill," *The Academy of Management EXECUTIVE,* vol. 2, no. 3 (August 1988), pp. 225-232.

What is a rich
medium? a lean
medium?

receiver are richer than bulletins because they have a more personal focus, even though they do not permit immediate feedback. Interactive media, such as the telephone or interactive computers, are richer than memos or letters. Interactive media permit both a personal focus and immediate feedback, but they cannot accommodate the nonverbal cues that are part of face-to-face communication.

The medium affects both message transmission and message reception. Research has shown that using lean media for communicating about routine management problems and richer media for nonroutine problems contributes to communication effectiveness. (See Illustration 1–3.) To ensure proper reception, remind yourself constantly that other messages compete with yours for the executive's attention. Use the techniques described in this book to make your messages complete but brief, courteous, and clearly related to your receiver's purposes. Provide what your superior has requested and anticipate what that person will need.

Downward communication consists of messages from superiors to subordinates. It is used to provide information about general policies and procedures, to give specific instructions, to solicit information needed in decision making, to motivate, and to provide feedback about performance. As with

Illustration 1–3 MEDIA EFFECTIVENESS

MANAGEMENT PROBLEM

	Routine	Nonroutine
Rich	*Communication Failure* Data glut. Rich media used for routine messages. Excess cues cause confusion and surplus meaning.	*Effective Communication* Communication success because rich media match nonroutine messages.
Lean	*Effective Communication* Communication success because media low in richness match routine messages.	*Communication Failure* Data starvation. Lean media used for nonroutine messages. Too few cues to capture message complexity.

MEDIA RICHNESS

SOURCE: Robert H. Lengel and Richard L. Daft, "The Selection of Communication Media as an Executive Skill," *The Academy of Management EXECUTIVE*, vol. 2, no. 3 (August 1988), p. 227. Reproduced with permission.

upward communication, the medium influences the effectiveness of downward communication. (Review Illustration 1—2.)

When you communicate with employees at levels subordinate to yours, your job is to share information related to their concerns about work requirements, organizational policies, and organizational success. From a subordinate's viewpoint, pertinent communication questions include these:

What is your job in
superior-to-
subordinate
communication?

1. *What* are the effects of my work? *Where, when, why,* and *how* does my work benefit my employer and me?
2. *What* are the effects of cooperation with my employer? *Where, when, why,* and *how* does cooperation benefit our company and me?

Your messages should enable your readers or listeners to identify *themselves* within the context of what you write or speak. Use your words to bring yourself and your receiver together by sharing organizational values and objectives.

Emergencies, of course, may postpone immediate answers to key communication questions. Urgent matters may require direct orders without explanation. However, you should be mindful of these guides:

1. Appropriate explanations, which identify reasons for direct orders, sustain loyalty.
2. Direct orders, even without explanation, are effective with loyal personnel.

Those guides reinforce each other. In business, as in other planned activities, one person tells another what, where, when, and how to do something. In contemporary business, however, the mind of the clerk as well as that of the president asks why? In a democratic society, people expect reasons for the use of their energies and talents. People expect to have their humanity acknowledged and their dignity preserved. Let that insight guide you when you communicate with subordinates or others.

Horizontal Communication. When you exchange messages at organizational levels like or equal to yours, you facilitate the horizontal flow of information within your firm. Peer-to-peer communication is used to coordinate activities, share feelings, and influence or persuade others at the same level of the organization. Your horizontal messages should enable peers to identify *themselves* with what you write or say to them. Expect your peer receiver to interpret basic communication questions and answers from his or her viewpoint as follows:

What is your job in
peer communication?

1. *What* are the effects of my work? *Where, when, why,* and *how* does my work benefit my peer and me?
2. *What* are the effects of cooperation with my peer? *Where, when, why,* and *how* does cooperation benefit our company and me?

Diagonal Communication. In today's complex business environment, effective organizations require diagonal as well as vertical and horizontal communication. Groups often complete a specific task that requires a variety of expertise. Group members may be drawn from different departments and levels in the organization. To complete the work, group members must communicate outside the traditional hierarchical chain of command.

For example, a major manufacturer of computer software for the insurance industry typically assigns responsibility for a specific client to a team. A team may consist of a sales representative, a systems analyst, a technical specialist, and a trainer. The group is responsible for determining client needs, integrating the new software into the client's system, and training the client's employees. Although the formal organizational chart may show the individual members reporting to specific supervisors or managers within the hierarchy, the group itself may be responsible to another individual for successful implementation of a project. Upon completion of the project, the individual members are assigned to different teams and are responsible to new team leaders. Therefore, communication often crosses the traditional chain of command. Effective diagonal communication requires understanding of and commitment to organizational goals, not only to unit or department goals.

The Grapevine. **Formal communication** flows through official channels, following the chain of command or authorized lateral and diagonal routes. In contrast, **informal communication** flows outside official channels, showing little regard for organizational structure. Individuals involved in informal communication may represent many different organizational levels or work units. The informal network is often called the **grapevine**.

In a classic study of the grapevine, Keith Davis identified four types of communication chains: single strand, gossip, probability, and cluster. (See Illustration 1–4.)[7] In a **single-strand chain**, A tells B, who tells C, who tells D, and so on. In each repetition, the message may be filtered or distorted, eventually resulting in great inaccuracy. In a **gossip chain**, one individual passes a message to several others, but the receivers do not continue the chain of communication. In a **probability chain**, a sender communicates randomly

---

What is your job in diagonal communication?

---

[7]Keith Davis, "Management Communication and the Grapevine," *Harvard Business Review,* vol. 31, no. 5 (September–October, 1953), pp. 43–49.

Illustration 1–4   COMMUNICATION CHAINS

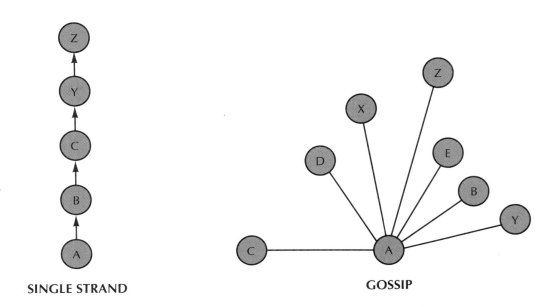

SINGLE STRAND   GOSSIP

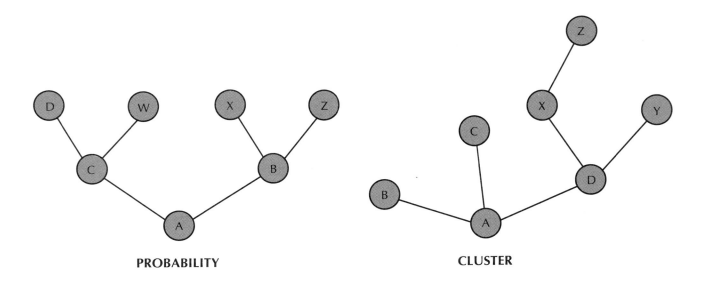

PROBABILITY   CLUSTER

with two or three receivers who randomly pass the message along. In a **cluster chain**, the initiator of the message tells a few selected individuals who in turn pass the message to a few selected individuals. People who pass on messages are known as **liaisons**.

According to Davis, the grapevine is most commonly a cluster chain. That fact accounts for some of its characteristics:

What are
characteristics of the
grapevine?

1. *It is selective.* Senders and transmitters of grapevine messages tend to select their communication partners in terms of the nature of the message and its importance to those individuals.
2. *It is fast.* A cluster communication chain operates more rapidly than a single-strand chain because it is not dependent on sequential transmission. Transmitted by informal, face-to-face conversations, telephone calls, and even computer messaging systems, grapevine messages tend to move more rapidly than those transmitted through formal, chainlike channels.
3. *It is accurate.* As shown in Illustration 1–4, a message passed through a cluster chain passes from A to Z by going through only a few liaisons. Therefore, the potential for distortion is less than if the message were passed through a single-strand chain. Research has shown the grapevine to be 80–90 percent accurate. However, the 10 percent of error in a message could be the most important part of the message.
4. *It can be used for managerial purposes.* By identifying liaisons, management can place into the grapevine information that it wishes employees to receive. Managers have successfully used the grapevine to counteract rumors, to test how contemplated actions will be received, and to obtain feedback about employee morale.

The climate of an organization influences the kinds, accuracy, and impact of messages transmitted through the grapevine. The grapevine serves employees by satisfying their social instincts to communicate. It can also satisfy employees' needs for information about their work and job security. Davis suggests the following guides for effective use of the grapevine:

How can managers
effectively use the
grapevine?

1. Tell people what will affect them.
2. Tell people what they want to know, rather than simply what you want them to know.
3. Tell people soon.

This book provides specific suggestions and guides for communicating with individuals and groups within your organization. Your career will also require that you be skilled at external communication.

External Communication

What is the role of external communication?

What company can long afford to ignore customer demands? What company can succeed if it does not maintain satisfactory relationships with its suppliers? The disturbing loss of business to foreign competitors during the 1970s caused many U.S. companies to renew their commitment to customer satisfaction and improved vendor-buyer relationships. External communication plays a major role in satisfying customer needs and obtaining satisfactory goods or services from suppliers.

A free enterprise economy is based on freedom of choice, and informed choices require valid information. Therefore, accurate, timely communication between a business and its public is essential. External communication includes a wide range of customer communication, such as customer surveys, media and direct mail advertising, direct sales, and responses to adjustment requests. External communication also includes exchanges of information with suppliers, such as orders, requests for proposals, acceptance of proposals or bids, and requests for adjustments.

As you prepare external communication, realize that a primary purpose of such communication is to provide information to guide informed choices. Remember, too, that you may persuade but you cannot compel a customer or supplier to act. Of the many ways to persuade, probably the surest is to serve the public—and to communicate that service—well.

Whatever your position or title in the organizational structure, your career success will be influenced by how well you function as a communication manager.

YOUR ROLE AS A COMMUNICATION MANAGER

Management is a systematic process in pursuit of a common goal. That process includes planning, organizing, directing, and controlling an organization's activities and resources.[8] Traditionally those activities were called managerial functions, implying that only managers performed them. Today, however, many organizations expect employees at all levels to plan, organize, direct, and control their work.

The management functions apply also to communication. They operate when someone decides on and achieves communication goals through proper planning, organizing, directing, and controlling of messages and media. The

[8]Ramon J. Aldag and Timothy M. Stearns, *Management* (Cincinnati: South-Western Publishing Co., 1991), p. 13.

Who participates in
communication
management?

process described here may aptly be called **communication management**. All employees, not only employees who are called supervisors or executives, participate directly or indirectly in communication management. Since each employee's job requires communication, each employee should act as a **communication manager**. (See Illustration 1–5.)

Planning

To the extent that you design messages and actions for achieving your justifiable goals, you fulfill the communication manager's function of planning. **Planning** defines goals along with methods and resources required to reach those goals. Planning leads to systematic progress.

Your life and your career will be influenced by what you or others say, write, and do. With this awareness, you will not take communication for granted; you will treat it with care. You will establish communication goals

Illustration 1–5   FUNCTIONS OF A COMMUNICATION MANAGER

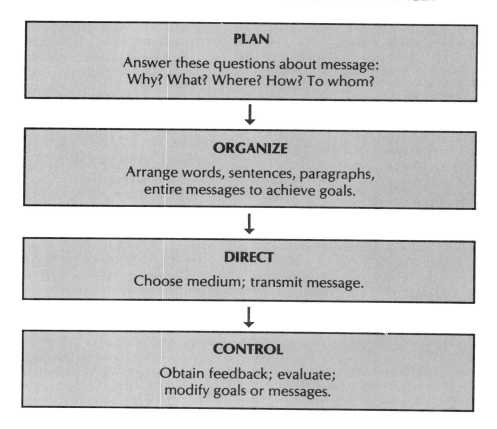

PLAN
Answer these questions about message:
Why? What? Where? How? To whom?

↓

ORGANIZE
Arrange words, sentences, paragraphs,
entire messages to achieve goals.

↓

DIRECT
Choose medium; transmit message.

↓

CONTROL
Obtain feedback; evaluate;
modify goals or messages.

Why are planning and
organizing necessary?

and plan your messages and actions according to those goals. You will learn to answer this basic communication question: "*Why* should I say *what—when, where,* and *how—*to *whom?*"

Organizing

Built upon plans, **organizing** is the work of bringing together people, equipment, materials, processes, and goals. As a communication manager, you must familiarize yourself with your company's goals, structure, operating methods, and use of authority and responsibility. Based on such knowledge, you will organize words, sentences, paragraphs, and entire messages to achieve your communication goals. Chapters 6 through 22 provide specific suggestions and guides for planning and organizing letters, memos, reports, and oral presentations.

Directing

Directing activates people to apply skills, energies, and values to what has been planned and organized. In communication management, the directing (or activating) function is accomplished by transmitting appropriate messages. As your career advances, you will perform the directing function by stimulating coworkers and directing the activities of subordinates. Directing requires communication of what you and your coworkers expect of one another, such as honesty, reliability, creativity, cooperation, and efficiency.

As a communication manager, your job will be to transform ideas and emotions into relevant, productive actions. You probably will find that instructions and directives have greatest value when you explain them in terms of employee benefits associated with employer goals. Also, you will recognize personnel as individuals who often need explicit guidance and encouragement, tactful supervision and correction.

Why are directing and
controlling necessary?

Controlling

Effective planning and organizing produce action. Action, however, does not complete a communication manager's task. Planning, organizing, and directing (transmitting) messages are not enough. You will need also to assess the results and to revise your ongoing communications.

Controlling is the art of using feedback to modify plans and influence human behavior. As an effective communication manager, you will use evaluation to measure performances against standards, to remedy deviations from company goals, or to set new standards and goals. You will evaluate your own performance in terms of what your messages and actions produce.

Feedback, or response to what you communicate, will be your major instrument of control.

As a communication manager, you will recognize the need for objectives. The next section describes the communication-by-objectives approach to controlling communication quality.

COMMUNICATION BY OBJECTIVES (CBO)

Peter Drucker introduced **management by objectives (MBO)**, an approach that emphasizes achieving results instead of being merely busy.[9] MBO is intended to generate systematic progress toward achievable goals. Using the MBO approach, managers and subordinate employees set performance goals reached through discussions at all levels of an organization.

In the 1980s, many U.S. corporations adopted **total quality management (TQM)**. The TQM movement was stimulated primarily by an effort to close the quality gap that Japanese companies had filled and to restore confidence in U.S.-made products. The chairman and CEO of the H. J. Heinz Co. stated the goals of TQM in this way: "Our goal is to do each job right the first time, to reduce the price of non-conformance, and to meet or exceed the specifications of our internal and external customers."[10] Under TQM, employees at all levels are involved in establishing quality goals and monitoring performance to ensure that those goals are met. Quality is always defined in terms of customer needs, preferences, and expectations. A customer may be an external purchaser or a person or group within the organization who receives the production output.

Both MBO and TQM emphasize the importance of goals. TQM goes beyond MBO by insisting that quality be the primary goal. Moreover, TQM emphasizes that quality must be proactive, not reactive. Doing it right the first time instead of paying to correct errors is a fundamental goal of TQM. Major firms such as Texas Instruments even rank their top-level managers in terms of quality performance and distribute pay increases and bonuses accordingly.[11]

The emphasis on total quality is not limited to the manufacturing sector.

---

[9]Peter F. Drucker, *The Practice of Management* (New York: Harper & Brothers, 1954). See also Jan P. Muczyk and Bernard C. Reimann, "MBO as a Complement to Effective Leadership," *The Academy of Management EXECUTIVE,* vol. 3, no. 2 (May 1989), pp. 131–138.

[10]Anthony J. F. O'Reilly, as quoted in "O'Reilly Supports Total Quality Management at Heinz," *Beta Gamma Sigma Newsletter,* Summer 1991, p. 1.

[11]"Quality: The U.S. Drives to Catch Up," *Business Week,* November 1, 1982, p. 68.

Quality is a growing concern in office work, too. Although factory productivity in the United States has risen 51 percent since 1973, productivity of office workers dropped 7 percent during that time. Consequently, many companies have initiated quality control programs for white-collar workers. Companies such as Metropolitan Life Insurance Co., Corning Inc., AmEx, and First National Bank of Chicago experienced dramatic improvements in customer service—and increased business—after introducing quality control programs based on measurements of quality as perceived by customers.[12]

Both MBO and TQM demonstrate this fact: In the business world, you are likely to be rewarded for what your effort achieves—for the goals that you attain—but not for your effort alone. Incorporating the concepts of management by objectives and total quality management, this book proposes that you adopt a **communication-by-objectives (CBO)** approach to your work. The CBO approach emphasizes the need to determine and achieve appropriate communication goals. When you communicate, you must recognize that your letters, reports, and other messages are not merely composition exercises. These messages are instruments to fulfill your own objectives and those of your employer. Moreover, a message will achieve your objectives only if it also satisfies the receiver's needs and expectations. Whether or not you are called a manager, your messages affect the total organization of which you are a member.

The communication manager who practices CBO effectively seeks answers to these questions: *Who? What? Where? When? Why? How?* For example:

> ► *Who* are the senders and receivers of this message?
> ► *What* is the purpose (goal, or objective) of this message? *What* is the **corethought** (key idea, main point, or gist) of this message?
> ► *Where* in the communication process are sender and receiver relationships reinforced?
> ► *When* was the message sent (or when will it be sent)? *When* was the message received (or when will it be received)?
> ► *Why* was the message (or why will it be) sent?
> ► *How* does the message use data sources and information? How does the message satisfy sender and receiver needs? How was the message (or how should it be) worded? How was the message (or how should it be) transmitted?

What is the key idea of CBO?

---

[12]"Quality Is Becoming Job One in the Office, Too," *Business Week,* April 29, 1991, pp. 52–53+. See also Bruce Lloyd, "Office Productivity—Time for a Revolution?" *Long Range Planning,* vol. 23, no. 1 (February 1990), pp. 66–79.

Use the preceding questions and their answers as guides to managing your communication inside and outside your company. They apply to interpersonal communication as well as organizational communication.

THE CONTEMPORARY BUSINESS COMMUNICATION ENVIRONMENT

What are major characteristics of the contemporary communication environment?

The business communication environment for which you are preparing is substantially different from the business communication environment of 10 or 20 years ago. You will work in a business environment that is becoming increasingly multicultural, technological, and collaborative.

A Multicultural Environment

The closing decades of the 20th century were marked by significant changes in the international business community. Consider these examples:

▶ In 1957, Japan's Honda Motor Co. (already well known for its motorcycles) first manufactured four-wheel vehicles. That company began automobile production in the United States in 1982. When its founder, Soichiro Honda, died in 1991, Honda Motor Co. was the third-largest auto producer in Japan and the fourth-largest in the United States.[13]

▶ In 1990–91, over one million new private businesses opened in Poland, Czechoslovakia, and Hungary.[14]

▶ In 1990 and 1991, significant business news included the U.S.–Mexico free-trade pact and increasing privatization of industry in Eastern European countries.[15]

To communicate effectively in this multicultural business environment you must be aware of and sensitive to cultural diversity. Chapter 3, "Cultural Aspects of Business Communication," should help you begin to develop that awareness. In addition, each chapter contains a section called "Multicultural Insights," questions to stimulate your thinking and class discussion about cultural differences and similarities.

---

[13]"Honda Founder Dies at 84," *The State* (Columbia, SC), August 6, 1991, p. 5B.
[14]See "Reawakening, A Market Economy Takes Root in Eastern Europe," *Business Week,* April 15, 1991, pp. 46–50.
[15]See "The Mexico Pact: Worth the Price?" *Business Week,* May 27, 1991, pp. 32–35.

A Technological Environment

Rapid advances in computer technology have changed the nature of office work, from clerical to managerial levels. One writer asserts that if the automobile industry had advanced since 1981 as rapidly as the computer industry, a Rolls-Royce would cost $2.70 and get two million miles to the gallon. Personal computer manufacturers shipped more than eighteen times as many personal computers in 1990 as they did in 1981.[16]

You will undoubtedly use electronic communication technology in your career. Chapter 4, "Electronically Assisted Communication," looks at some challenges of working in an electronic communication environment. Many applications and cases in this book remind you of the pervasiveness of electronic communication tools in today's business world.

A Collaborative Environment

Quality team, project group, committee, task force—these and other terms demonstrate an important fact about the business communication environment: You will often work and communicate as a member of a group, not only as one individual to another. Effective communication within and between groups requires adaptation of your individual speaking and writing skills to the needs of the group. Chapter 5 discusses skills for collaborative communication. Several applications and cases in Chapters 6 through 22 ask you to apply those skills.

REVIEW AND TRANSITION

You have been introduced to business communication as an interpersonal, organizational, and worldwide activity involving profitable exchange of goods and services. Associated with the communication manager theme, you have explored the communication process, the scope of business communication, and the contemporary business communication environment. As you use this book to develop your communication expertise, apply the CBO approach—plan, organize, direct, and control your messages to achieve your personal and organizational objectives. You will gain further insight to the goals and skills of effective communicators as you study Chapter 2.

YOUR DECISIONS FOR CHAPTER 1

Review the Decisions Case that introduced this chapter. Now that you have studied Chapter 1, what answers do you give to Andy's questions? Which of those answers are tentative? Why?

---

[16]Ron Wolf, "The PC Boom," *The State* (Columbia, SC), August 11, 1991, p. 1G.

Before reading Chapter 1 you probably had preconceptions about business communication. What were those preconceptions? Why did you have them? Which ones do you still have? Why? Which ones are you beginning to change? Why?

DISCUSSION QUESTIONS

A. Within the context of Chapter 1, what are appropriate definitions and examples for these terms?

1. communication
2. encoder
3. message
4. decoder
5. medium
6. metacommunication
7. communication manager
8. CBO

B. What are the interpersonal and organizational implications of the following statements?

1. Messages themselves have no meaning; meaning is in people.
2. Although capable of reason, people sometimes act irrationally.

C. Why should you concern yourself with messages *and* their effects upon people?

D. How are the Chapter 1 guides for subordinate-to-superior communication adaptable to other communication levels?

E. From your own experience with superior-to-subordinate communication, what real incidents show the following to be complementary?

1. Appropriate explanations, which identify reasons for direct orders, sustain loyalty.
2. Direct orders, even without explanation, are effective with loyal personnel.

F. From your own experience with peer-to-peer communication, what real incidents show the need for answers to these questions?

1. *What* are the effects of my work? *Where, when, why,* and *how* does my work benefit my peer and me?
2. *What* are the effects of cooperation with my peer? *Where, when, why,* and *how* does cooperation benefit our company and me?

G. From your own experience with grapevine communication, what real incidents demonstrate the characteristics of the grapevine as given in Chapter 1?

H.   What ideas and emotions are associated with your responses to the following:

1.   *Why* should I say *what—when, where,* and *how*—to *whom?*
2.   In the business world, you are likely to be rewarded for what your communication effort achieves, for the goals that your communication effort attains—but not for your effort alone.

I.   In what specific ways is awareness of a communication manager's functions likely to influence your written messages? your oral-visual messages? your nonverbal messages?

J.   What is the relationship of CBO to the functions of a communication manager?

K.   From your experience, what evidence confirms the characteristics of the contemporary business communication environment described in Chapter 1?

APPLICATIONS

1.   To provide a writing sample for your instructor to evaluate, select several of the preceding discussion questions and compose paragraphs that answer them.

2.   In a written message of not more than two pages, introduce yourself to your instructor and to your classmates. State these data about yourself:

a.   name and birthplace
b.   educational background
c.   work experience (paid or unpaid)
d.   community participation (civic, professional, social, or other public service)
e.   educational and career goals
f.   hobbies and special interests

3.   Write an explanation of how you applied the communication manager functions to your message of introduction (Application 2). Explain how you planned, organized, directed, and controlled your communication activity.

4.   Using your library resources, write a summary of major contributions to communication or management theory by any of the following: Abraham Maslow, Douglas McGregor, Peter Drucker, David Berlo, Claude Shannon and Warren Weaver, Wendell Johnson, Neil Postman, Keith Davis, or other individuals suggested by your instructor.

5.   Study at least two consecutive issues of the *Journal of Business Communication,* or the *ABC Bulletin* (both are published by the Association

for Business Communication), or the *Journal of Business and Technical Communication* (published by Sage Publications). Then write answers to these questions:

a. What communication topics are discussed?
b. Why do those discussions merit publication?
c. What communication insights do you gain from reading them?
d. How do those insights pertain to your development as a communicator and manager?

Your instructor may ask you to report your findings orally as well as in writing.

6. Write an explanation of why the following statements do or do not represent effective communication. Then write appropriate revisions of the defective items.

a. To cash in on a big savings on maintainance costs, go buy youre nearest Car Mart Service Center now.
b. The advertizing copywritter asked, "Is this new food produck microwaveable?"
c. Expert communicators consider themselves and other people as unique but interdependent persons.
d. Business effects evryone directly, or indirectly.
e. Is comunication a exchange of evidence representing ideas, and feelings?
f. Does communication feedback include deliberate silences, as well as, actions, and words.
g. Expression does not require feedack, communication requires feedback.
h. Eficient organizations are networks of interdependent interacting parts tyed together by infomation.
i. Use you're messages as tools for acheiving you're goals.
j. As a businessperson communication is essential to your career advancmeant.
k. Illumination must be extinguished before departure by you from this work area.
l. The invoice for those supplys were paid last Wensday.
m. To locate the employment office turn left right there.
n. Having replaced the ribbon that computer printer makes clear copies.
o. Is either Kane or Gomez here?
p. They're distributions centers are in Austin, Texas, Dayton, Ohio, and Tampa, Florida.
q. Those contracts are dated March 3, 1989; March 8, 1990; and April 5, 1991.
r. Do you have a record of whom recieved the shipment?

MULTICULTURAL INSIGHTS

Chapter 1 introduced you to the multicultural business communication en-vironment. Each chapter in this book concludes with a set of questions to help you gain insights to the multicultural dimensions of business communication.

What should you do if your class does not have students from countries other than the United States? If international students are not enrolled in your class but are attending your college, your instructor may ask you to meet and interview them through an appropriate campus organization.

If no international student attends your college, use the following questions as role-playing exercises. Imagine, as realistically as you can, that *you* are such a student. Answer these questions—and others headed "Multicultural Insights" in the following chapters—as you think an international student would answer them. Then explain *why* you think so. The resulting discussions will help you heighten your awareness of your communication environment as well as that of another person whose experiences may differ greatly from yours.

If your class *does* have international students, you and they may answer the following questions through formal or informal discussions, conferences, reports, and the like. As the communication course progresses, international students should invite native U.S. classmates to respond, thereby exchanging facts, opinions, ideas, and feelings about the communication process.

1. Some people who speak and write only one language assume that all languages are structured like their own. That assumption often contributes to communication problems in business. What sounds are in American English and are also in your native language? What sounds are in one of those languages but not in the other? In what ways do the grammar and syntax of American English resemble and differ from those of your native language?

2. Some people assume that all languages have alphabets (letters that can be arranged in various patterns to produce words). Those people do not realize that patterns of language influence patterns of thinking. When we reason, the language we are using affects the ways in which we arrange our thoughts before we speak or write. In what ways do the elements and structural patterns of your native language compare with or contrast to those of American English? Does your native language have an alphabet composed of letters like those of American English? What symbols or signs are used in your native language to represent ideas, feelings, and sounds? to convey formality, informality, courtesy? Is your native language written from left to right? from right to left? vertically? Is it traditionally written with a pen? drawn with a brush? recorded with another instrument? What traditional devices are used with your native language to represent numerical calculations? What marks are used for emphasis or punctuation? How many types are needed for keyboarding your native language?

3. What traditions, customs, and values influence the ways in which your native language is used? What traditions, customs, and values do you perceive to be associated with uses of American English?

4. What aspects of American English are difficult for you to use in business messages? Why? In what ways could your instructor and your classmates help you overcome those difficulties? How can you help yourself to overcome those difficulties?

5. What dialects are associated with using your native language? What dialects have you discovered among users of American English? In your experience, what are the effects of dialects on business communication?

6. What nonverbal symbols—gestures, facial expressions, postures, movements—help you to communicate with people who use your native language? What nonverbal symbols help you to communicate with people who use American English?

7. In what ways is American English different from other kinds of English that you have encountered (for example, British English, Canadian English, Australian or Asian English)? In your experience, how do those differences affect business communication?

8. Suppose that one of your classmates (someone for whom American English is a native language) decides to study business communication as used with your native language. What would that person need to learn besides grammar and punctuation?

9. What educational experiences have acquainted you with the uses of American English? How have those experiences prepared you for your course in business communication?

2

COMMUNICATION GOALS, SKILLS, AND CRITERIA

OBJECTIVES

After completing this chapter, you should be able to:

1. Identify the basic goals of effective business communicators as inquiring, informing, persuading, and gaining goodwill.
2. Improve the perceptual skills of observing, reading, and listening.
3. Improve the interpretive skills of analysis and synthesis while minimizing fallacies.
4. Compose sentences and paragraphs (later on, complete messages) that are attractive, accurate, coherent, clear, concise, and courteous.

DECISIONS CASE

R. B. Harris, a recent college graduate and a new employee of your firm, has been assigned to the Customer Services Department. Although sincere and enthusiastic, Harris seems to alienate people after speaking to them for more than a few minutes. You read a memo that Harris has prepared. The spelling, punctuation, and grammar are correct, but the message is so wordy and vague that its corethought eludes you.

Harris asks you for guidance. "I know I need to improve myself as a communicator," Harris says earnestly. "But how can I tell when my messages measure up to what they should be?"

What do you say to Harris?

Additional questions about this decision-making case are stated at the end of this chapter. Study the chapter before answering those questions.

CHAPTER CONTEXT

Privately and in business, people communicate according to what they perceive, how they interpret what they perceive, and how they use their interpretations. Motives, values, and customs influence perceptions; perceptions influence interpretations; and actions or reactions are based on interpretations. To communicate effectively, you must:

a. Define the basic goal of each message.
b. Interpret data accurately and logically.
c. Present your data and interpretations attractively, accurately, coherently, clearly, concisely, and courteously.

BASIC GOALS

Effective business communicators achieve these goals:

1. Gain goodwill.
2. Inquire.
3. Inform.
4. Persuade.

Business **goodwill** is appreciation that a firm or a person acquires beyond the value of what is sold. Goodwill is essential to achieving the other three basic goals of an effective business communicator.

Almost every business communication opportunity can be used to establish or reinforce goodwill. Your inquiries should do more than request information. They can reinforce rapport with the receiver by courteously acknowledging that person's expertise or ability to help you. Your messages to inform should do more than convey data. The timing and tone of informative messages can strengthen a valued sender-receiver relationship. Persuasive messages should do more than stimulate someone to act as you desire. You can build goodwill while persuading if you demonstrate that the requested action benefits the receiver as well as you.

What communication skills will help you to establish goodwill, inquire, inform, and persuade effectively?

How is the goodwill
goal related to the
other basic goals?

FUNDAMENTAL SKILLS

To reach your communication goals, you must develop—and continue developing—your perception, interpretation, and application skills. Those skills are analogous to the *input, process,* and *output* phases of information processing. Illustration 2–1 shows the relationships of perception skills (input), interpretation skills (process), and application skills (output).

Observing, reading, and listening are input skills; they enable you to *perceive* data. Analyzing and synthesizing are processing skills; they enable you to *interpret* what you perceive. Writing, speaking, and using silent language (gestures, facial expressions, and other nonverbal signals) are output skills; they enable you to *communicate* your interpretations to other people.

Perceptual Skills

Through your physical senses of sight, hearing, touch, etc., you obtain data about yourself and your universe. You extend your physical senses by using tools such as telescopes and microscopes, earphones and amplifiers, meters

Illustration 2–1   FUNDAMENTAL SKILLS OF EFFECTIVE COMMUNICATORS

Perception Skills Observing Reading Listening	→	Interpretation Skills Analyzing Synthesizing	→	Application Skills Writing Speaking Doing
INPUT		**PROCESS**		**OUTPUT**

and gauges. With those tools you enlarge the quantity, quality, and variety of stimuli that activate your brain. This process of detecting stimuli, of inputting data to the human being, is **perception**.

Like other processes, perception has limitations. Your sensory organs and their mechanical extensions are imperfect. There are "sights" and "sounds" that people and machines do not detect. Furthermore, your mind defensively screens and sifts stimuli. In effect, except for stimuli whose force is irresistible, your mind admits only the data you *choose* to recognize.

What is the benefit of acknowledging that you cannot perceive every aspect of a person, an object, a process, or a message? The admission of imperfection can improve your communication ability. Ineffective communicators unnecessarily restrict perception by sometimes assuming that what they do not detect is undetectable. Awareness of the fact that you may easily miss important details of a communication event can put you on guard; and that awareness will help you become a careful observer, reader, and listener.

Do you expect other people to have your traits and attitudes? Do you reject contradictions of your biases or habits? Such human tendencies limit what and how you perceive. Someone else may not perceive what seems obvious to you—and vice versa. For example, if you enjoy the study of accounting, you are apt to learn more about it than would someone who is interested in another field. Your senses input and your mind processes accounting data that other people, who do not have your motivation, may exclude from themselves. You may be disappointed because they do not see accounting as you do. But you, in turn, may not share their appreciation of an advertising layout, a textile design, a symphony, or a poem.

Through our perceptions and our interpretations of what we perceive, all of us create our own realities. As Milton wrote many years ago, "The mind is its own place and in itself/Can make a heaven of hell, and a hell of heaven."[1]

---

[1] John Milton, *Paradise Lost*, Book I, lines 254–255.

What is the role of
perception in
communication?

If you enlarge your experience, your perception can improve and your world
will expand. As a business communicator, you can enlarge your experience by
observing, reading, and listening.

Observing. A successful communicator is someone who has become an expert observer. Consider the conversationalist or writer who interests you.
That person uses many references to historical and contemporary events or
ideas. By contrast, consider people whose conversation topics are so restricted that you become bored. Often those people show little awareness of
people and events around them. At best they *express* themselves, but they do
not *communicate* with you.

To improve yourself as a communicator, observe your own actions and
those of other people. Notice the *who, what, when, where, why,* and *how* of
events in your environment. Observe messages as well as actions. Recognize
that worded and nonworded messages are stimuli for, parts of, or responses
to actions. Realize that written or spoken messages can be effective only if
you and other people carefully read or actively listen to those messages. Reinforce your observations by active reading and active listening.

How can you improve
your observation
skills?

Reading. When you observe an event, you perceive stimuli as they exist in
the real world outside yourself. When you read, however, you perceive stimuli that *stand for* (*represent*) actual events or objects. For example, when you
read the word *computer,* you perceive a set of ink marks on paper. What you
then see in your mind's eye is the machine that is represented by those
marks. Your mind's eye may see a mainframe computer, a microcomputer, or
both, depending on your previous observation, reading, or listening. You can
enlarge your mind's eye if you use the following suggestions:

How can you improve
your reading skills?

1. To improve your reading, become aware of the rate, or speed, at
     which you detect the stimuli (ink marks). The reading experiment in
     Application 2 of this chapter will help you.
2. If you read slowly, your eyes probably stop, or fixate, more often than
     necessary on a line of words. To read faster, fixate your eyes only
     three times on a line (near the beginning, at the middle, and near the
     end of the line). Your reading rate will accelerate, and with continu-
     ing practice, you will understand what you read at the faster rate.
3. Try to avoid moving your lips and your throat muscles as you read. If
     you silently pronounce or whisper the words, you will slow your read-
     ing rate. With deliberate practice you can reduce and then eliminate
     lip-reading or vocalizing tendencies.
4. Vary your reading techniques according to your particular purposes.

Three of those techniques—skimming, scanning, and study-reading—are described here:

a. *Skimming.* Is your purpose to identify general topics rather than details? to review what you have already read? or simply to be entertained by amusing literature and personal correspondence? Then *skim.* Read quickly, but use these aids to your comprehension: headings and subheadings; introductions, transitions, and summaries; corethought statements. Other aids, especially for skimming a book or a report, are title pages, prefaces, tables of contents, illustrations, appended materials, and indexes.

b. *Scanning.* Is your purpose to discover or to verify a specific item—for instance, a name or an address? a date? a word, statistic, or fact? Then *scan. Scanning* is skimming with a specific target of information in mind. First skim the message to locate the section(s) pertaining to your purpose. Then read those particular lines attentively.

c. *Study-Reading.* Is your purpose to absorb virtually all of a message? every fact and implication? every nuance of style as well as of data? Then skim, scan, and *study-read.* Summarize the message, and its parts, in your own words. Test your summaries, notes, and comments against evidence in the message itself. Ask and answer appropriate questions concerning the evidence, its presentation, your perception, and your interpretation. For example, are you perceiving words and numbers as they actually appear in the message? Are you reacting to the message itself? to your impressions of the writer? to the appearance and format of the message? to data presented by the message? to data within yourself but not presented by the message?

What is skimming?

What is scanning?

What is
study-reading?

To read effectively, use the guides in Illustration 2–2. Seven of them concern the written or printed message. Six of them concern you as you interact with that message.

Reading and listening are complementary skills that pose these questions:

1. What are the main ideas of the message?
2. What evidence supports the main ideas?
3. What is implied as well as stated?
4. What response does the message elicit?

Listening. As reading is an application of vision, listening is a use of hearing. To listen effectively is to *understand* what you hear. Effective listening re-

Illustration 2–2   READING GUIDES

Concerning the Message	1.	Notice the name of the sender and the date of the message.
	2.	Observe structural devices (letterhead, subject or reference line, headings, table of contents, etc.)
	3.	Read quickly to identify the core-thought of the message.
	4.	Notice emphasis signals (indention capitalization, underlining, italics, lists, illustrations, colors).
	5.	Note mentally, or in writing, the data that you receive from the message.
	6.	Underline or circle key units of the message, if permissible.
	7.	Write marginal summaries of the data and of your response to those data, if permissible.
Concerning Yourself	1.	Focus your full attention on the message you are reading. You deceive yourself if you think you can simultaneously speak and read or listen and read.
	2.	Read silently. Avoid shaping your lips into sounds.
	3.	Read progressively. Do not begin a new line and then look back at the preceding line.
	4.	Focus on word *groups* rather than on individual words.
	5.	Guard against seeing only what you expect instead of what is actually written.
	6.	Concentrate on your reading. Minimize interruptions as you read. When necessary, ask not to be interrupted.

quires control of speech as well as hearing. When everyone talks, few hear and none listen. You cannot talk and listen simultaneously; no one can. Compulsive talkers, people who constantly monopolize speech, block effective listening and valuable response. Such talkers defeat themselves by obstructing the exchange of information that they and others can use. Do not follow their example. Instead, speak when necessary and appropriate for you to do so.

When others speak meaningfully, give them what you expect for yourself: attention. By focusing your full attention on meaningful speakers, you can develop an *active listening attitude,* an attitude to help you grasp as well as absorb information. Your attitude affects what you perceive; therefore, your attitude affects what you hear.

Develop an active listening attitude by following these suggestions:

1. Give deliberate and complete attention to the oral message and the speaker. Strive to keep your personal prejudices from screening out what the speaker actually says.
2. Respond with pertinent questions or comments about the data and their interpretation.
3. Participate appropriately in the communication event. Instead of being passive, respond visually, vocally, in writing, or with thoughtful silence. The more active your participation as a listener, the more informative your listening is apt to be.
4. Attend to data and style of presentation. Both data and style acquaint you with needs, desires, interests, and values of the speaker.
5. Look for the speaker's nonverbal cues. Use those cues to supplement your perception of the verbal message.

To improve your listening, use the guides in Illustration 2−3.

You perceive data by observing, reading, and listening. But what happens to data after you perceive them? How are data processed, or interpreted, by your mind?

Interpretive Skills

Interpretation is the assignment of meaning. Interpretation requires logical reasoning, which involves analysis and synthesis of data.

Analysis. When you analyze, you identify elements; you separate a whole into its parts. Analysis provides ingredients for interpretation. For example, when you try to identify the ingredients of an unfamiliar dinner entree, you

How can you improve your listening?

How does analysis differ from synthesis?

Illustration 2–3   LISTENING GUIDES

Concerning the Message	1. Anticipate what you may hear next. Make pertinent notes. Since thought is faster than speech, your mind may wander from what is being said. Use the time lag; review what you hear.
	2. Detect whether the speaker goes from general statements to specific examples or vice versa. Identifying message structure helps you to listen.
	3. Determine the main ideas. Note transitions; often they signal changes of data and restatements of main ideas.
	4. Notice changes of volume, resonance, intensity, and rate. They are signals of emphasis.
Concerning Yourself	1. Observe the speaker's facial expressions, gestures, and other mannerisms, when possible. During telephone conversations, try to visualize the speaker. Your listening will improve as you mentally perceive the *person* who is speaking instead of a disembodied voice that you happen to hear.
	2. Discern the speaker's patterns of breath groups, sounds, and pauses. They are the punctuation of speech.
	3. Guard against hearing only what you expect instead of what is actually said. Ask the speaker to clarify what you may have misheard.

engage in analysis. When you analyze a message, you identify the elements of structure, format, and tone.

Synthesis. When you synthesize, you combine elements into a significant pattern. After using analysis to identify the ingredients in the new dinner entree, you may try to replicate that dish by combining the ingredients you have identified. That is synthesis.

In communication, you are often confronted by apparently miscellaneous parts (words, punctuation marks, ideas, and feelings) instead of an organized presentation (a complete message). Your job then is one of synthesis—to combine words, punctuation marks, ideas, and feelings into a message.

Analysis and synthesis are complementary. They are tools of interpretation through logical reasoning.

Logical Reasoning. These are the basic styles of logic:

How does induction differ from deduction?

▶ *Induction.* **Induction** is reasoning from particular instances (from specific examples or specific facts) to a generalized conclusion. Induction helps you *synthesize* data.

▶ *Deduction.* **Deduction** is reasoning from generalizations to a particular instance. Deduction helps you *analyze* data.

Induction and deduction are complementary; the results of induction can become the **premises** (assumptions) of *de*duction. Here is an example of how induction and deduction work in a business situation.

Assume your employer asks you to participate in a market survey to determine women's preferences for clothing styles. You will use questionnaires to collect data. To construct the questionnaire you must use deduction. You will break down your major question (What clothing styles do women in our target market prefer?) into many questions about color, fabric, skirt length, etc. When completed questionnaires are returned, you must perceive before you can interpret the data. That is, first you will notice the responses on every questionnaire that is properly completed. Then you must use induction to synthesize the data, using particular instances (individual responses to questionnaire items) so that you can derive a general summary and conclusions from those data. You reason from the specific answers of Ms. A, Mrs. B, Miss C, Ms. D, and the others to this generalization: "The responses indicate that we should market these products, but not those." You have used *in*duction.

What are the three parts of a syllogism?

Deduction is often stated in another form, the **syllogism**, which has three basic parts:

1. **Major Premise** (large assumption): Something stated as being generally true. Usually the words *all, every,* or their equivalent are stated or implied in the major premise.

2. **Minor Premise** (little assumption): Something stated as being true in

a particular, not a general, instance or case. In its elementary form, the syllogism has one major premise and one minor premise.

3. **Conclusion:** Not just an ending, but a logically inescapable *inference* derived from the premises.

Here is an example of deductive reasoning in the form of a syllogism:

1. *Major premise.* All of our travel club members get discounts on air fares.
2. *Minor premise.* You are a member of our travel club.
3. *Conclusion.* You get a discount on air fares.

If the premises of a syllogism are true, the conclusion will be true. If, however, even one of the premises is false, the conclusion must also be false. Syllogistic reasoning may be logically correct but untrue, as in this example:

1. *Major premise.* Every car owner should buy tires from us.
2. *Minor premise.* You own a car.
3. *Conclusion.* You should buy tires from us.

You may use a syllogism to persuade as well as to inform, but you should use it carefully and ethically. It can have a powerful effect upon people. When used accurately, a syllogism can clarify a difficult concept or persuade someone to act. If people detect a faulty syllogism, however, they may discount the validity of your entire message.

For business communication and other forms of human behavior, logic imposes order upon data. **Logic** is a system of thinking, a method for interpreting what you perceive. But logic is not necessarily truth. What you choose to do with logic may lead you, and those whom your messages influence, to truth.

Logic is a communication aid. Use logic carefully and ethically. Otherwise, you and your readers or listeners may become victims of **fallacies**, which are false or erroneous forms of logic. Recognize these fallacies when they are used to influence you—or when you are tempted to use them in persuading other people:

1. name-calling
2. bandwagon appeal
3. time and cause-effect confusion
4. detouring[2]

What is logic? What are fallacies?

---

[2]Scholars identify the first four fallacies on this list as follows: *argumentum ad hominem* ("argument to

Identify seven
common fallacies.

5. begging the question
6. self-contradiction
7. hasty generalization

Name-calling exploits prejudices by attaching emotion-arousing labels to people, actions, or ideas. As a form of stereotyping, name-calling assigns to all members of a group the characteristics that may be true for some members of that group. Name-calling shifts attention from issues to personalities associated with those issues.

> We need a new night manager for our 14th Street Hasty-Mart. Hearst looks good on paper. He's done this kind of work before and has good recommendations. But he's only 18 years old. You know how undependable teens can be. He'd probably have his friends hanging around most of the time. Let's hire someone who's more reliable.

> This purchase request was submitted by Ethel Levy. You know that women just like to buy things. We probably don't even need those supplies. Her purchase request is bound to cost our company more than we need to spend. Turn it down.

Bandwagon appeal exploits the fear of isolation. Bandwagon appeal shifts attention from facts or issues to the desire for group approval.

> Every retailer in town is having a July 4 sale. If we don't have one, people will question our patriotism. Come on! Let's have an Independence Day sale.

> Maybe Terry should get this promotion, but everybody expects Carmen to move up. Let's recommend Carmen.

Time and cause-effect confusion asserts or implies that changes occur simply because time passes. Someone who uses time and cause-effect confusion insists, without proof, that just because Event A precedes Event B, B must be the result of A.

> We didn't have these personnel problems before Stanislavsky was hired. He must be causing them.

> For years this company was losing money. Then I became general manager. We're making a profit now. The reason is obvious, but I'm too modest to mention it.

---

the man"); *argumentum ad populum* ("argument to the people"); *post hoc, ergo propter hoc* ("after this, therefore because of this"); and *non sequitur* ("it does not follow"). With current emphasis on sex-fair terminology in the United States, perhaps *argumentum ad hominem* should be renamed *argumentum ad personam* ("argument to the person").

Detouring states as fact something that is not proved by the given information. Detouring provides premises and then states a conclusion that does not fit them.

> Yes, we need to increase sales; and this is the best advertising proposal I've seen, so it will do the job for us. Let's adopt it right now.

> You've been a computer programmer for five years, and your work has been excellent. Therefore, you should become Manager of Information Systems.

Begging the question offers restatement or repetition as an inadequate substitute for information. Begging the question is sometimes called circular reasoning. Defining a word by repeating that word is one example of begging the question. Here are others:

> Your work is inferior because it's shoddy. Since it is inferior, it's not satisfactory. This unsatisfactory work is unacceptable. I can't pay for unacceptable work.

> We should adopt this policy because it is what we need. Since this policy is exactly what we need, let's go with it.

Self-contradiction is a fallacy that asserts incompatible data. The ideas presented are such that if one is true, another must be false.

> To receive a sample at no cost to you, please return your completed request form with $6.95 for handling and shipping.

> I never eat fish, but the Venetian flounder sounds so good, I'll try it.

Hasty generalization, or *jumping to conclusions*, is also a fallacy. It asserts that what *may* be true of a few cases *must* be true always or almost always.

> Olsen left the office early yesterday. Kahn and Montez left early today. They're all in the Warehouse Division. Warehouse employees rarely put in a full day's work.

> On June 7 and 14 we wrote Brown about his overdue payments. He didn't pay us then. What makes you think he'll pay if we ask him again?

Name-calling, bandwagon appeal, time and cause-effect confusion, detouring, begging the question, self-contradiction, and hasty generalization often create communication problems. At best, such fallacies cause confusion; at worst, they disrupt personal and professional relationships. When you use analysis and synthesis to interpret what you perceive, guard against fallacies. They introduce inaccurate, irrelevant, or incomplete evidence. Fallacies are emotion-stirring substitutes for reasoning.

Application Skills

By your perceptual skills you input data for communication; by your interpretive skills, you process data for communication. The application or output skills—writing, speaking, and doing—enable you to convey your interpretations to others. Most of this book focuses on development of application skills, which begins by establishing and applying criteria for effective messages.

CRITERIA FOR MESSAGE EFFECTIVENESS

As defined in Chapter 1, a message is a representation of ideas and feelings. After perceiving and interpreting information, you generate ideas and feelings. To share those ideas and feelings with others, you must encode them into messages to be conveyed or transmitted through a medium.

An effective message achieves its purpose. Feedback provides evidence of whether that purpose actually has been achieved. Even before you receive feedback, however, you can predict whether your message is apt to be successful. You can make such predictions realistically by applying effectiveness criteria as you plan, organize, develop, and transmit your message. Illustration 2–4 identifies six **criteria** (evaluation standards) that often are used in the United States and other cultures to measure the completeness of messages and, therefore, their effectiveness.

Appearance is listed as the first criterion because it tends to tune in or tune out your receiver. Other criteria are accuracy, coherence, clarity, conciseness, and courtesy. Obviously, a message with attractive appearance but insufficient or inaccurate information is defective. An unclear message based on accurate information, also, is defective. Likewise, a coherent, clear, concise, but discourteous message is defective. The common defect in such examples is that they are incomplete; they do not meet *all* of the effectiveness criteria.

An *effective* message fulfills all of the criteria discussed in this chapter. To be effective, your message needs an appearance that attracts its receiver's attention to accurate and adequate information conveyed by coherent, clear, concise, and courteous statements. Thus, the criteria are not independent of one another; they are *inter*dependent. They do not operate separately; they interact.

Appearance

First impressions are easier to reinforce than to change. Rightly or wrongly, business communicators and business messages are judged partly, sometimes

Illustration 2–4   CRITERIA FOR COMPLETE, EFFECTIVE MESSAGES

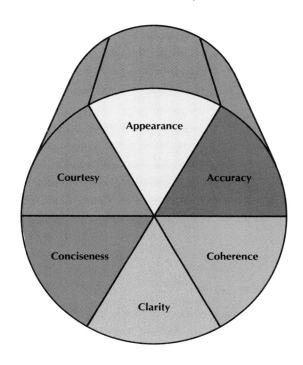

Do your messages
distract? attract?

largely, by their physical appearance. As a business *speaker,* you defeat your communication purposes when your physical appearance distracts from your message. As a business *writer,* you get a similar result when your message— even if it meets other criteria—departs from expected standards of format, layout, legibility, and neatness.

Distracting Appearance	Attractive Appearance
Wearing a jogging suit in a traditional business meeting with a major client.	Wearing clothes that convey a desired image of the firm.
Wearing distracting jewelry while giving an oral presentation.	Wearing jewelry that complements your outfit but does not draw undue attention to you or the jewelry.
Sending mistyped, smudged, or wrinkled memos and letters.	Sending written messages that are clean, properly formatted, and error free.

Appearance influences the receiver's perception and interpretation of your message. Message appearance may be the first impression the receiver gains of you, your message, and your firm. Use message appearance to promote positive first impressions.

Accuracy

Accuracy complements the proper appearance of a message. Many people produce messages that may be understood, but effective business communicators produce messages that are not misunderstood. To ensure accuracy, ask yourself these questions:

▶ Is the information valid, reliable, sufficient?
▶ Are word choice, grammar, spelling, and punctuation appropriate?

Inaccurate	Accurate
A $35.00 price discounted by 10 percent is $32.50.	A $35.00 price discounted by 10 percent is $31.50.
Of 480 questionnaire respondents, 40 percent, or 129 people, had seen the Tyler Company television commercials.	Of 480 questionnaire respondents, 40 percent, or 192 people, said that they had seen the Tyler Company television commercials.
Management, and communication is inseprable.	Management and communication are inseparable.

Are your messages inaccurate? accurate?

An attractive, accurate message may not yet be effective. Another standard—coherence—must be met.

Coherence

Coherence is an integration of diverse elements. A coherent message demonstrates systematic, logical connections of its many parts. To make your messages understandable, unify the sentences and paragraphs into a whole. You can achieve that coherence through planning, emphasis, spelling and punctuation, complete sentences, transitions, modifiers, and parallelism.

Planning. Coherence begins with planning. Do you design a sentence so that every word pertains to the sentence corethought? Does every sentence in every paragraph support the paragraph corethought? Does every paragraph reinforce the corethought of the entire message? Subsequent chapters of this book present message-*planning* techniques in detail.

Do you plan before you write or speak?

Planning for coherence includes deciding what data to emphasize and which emphasis techniques to use.

Emphasis. Here are ways to emphasize a written item:

1. Place the item in a prominent position.
2. Support the item by balance, comparison, or contrast.
3. Repeat or restate the item.
4. Compose independent clauses for major data and dependent clauses for minor data.
5. Use—but do not overuse—typographical and other mechanical aids.

Do you use
purposeful emphasis
techniques in your
messages?

Emphasis by Word Order. The beginnings and endings of sentences, paragraphs, and whole messages are emphatic positions. Those positions attract special attention unless they are filled by needless words. Word order and word choice reinforce each other, as shown by these examples:

Unemphatic	Emphatic
It will be appreciated if you complete and return the enclosed form immediately for prompt processing of your claim in this manner.	Please complete and return the enclosed form immediately. As soon as we receive the form, we will process your claim.
I have the pleasure of informing you of your selection as Salesperson of the Year, Lee, and of offering my congratulations on this auspicious occasion.	Congratulations, Lee, you are Salesperson of the Year!

Emphasis by Balance, Comparison, Contrast. When you **balance**, you emphasize items equally. When you **compare**, you emphasize similarities. When you **contrast**, you emphasize differences.

Balance. Michael Jordan is a basketball star; Michael Jackson, a rock music star.

Comparison. What Jordan is to basketball, Jackson is to rock music.

Contrast. Whereas Michael Jordan is a basketball star, Michael Jackson is a rock music star.

Emphasis by Repetition and Restatement. With **repetition** you emphasize by presenting an item verbatim at least twice. With **restatement** you emphasize by presenting an item and then using synonyms to present it again.

Jackson—not Jordan—is the musician. Remember, please: Jackson is the star of rock music.

Jordan is the basketball star, the hero of the hoops.

Emphasis by Subordination. Sentences may present data of equal rank or value. Often, however, a sentence emphasizes one item more than another. Major data are usually conveyed by *independent clauses*; minor data, by *dependent clauses*. A compound sentence presents data of equal rank or value by using two or more independent (coordinate) clauses. A complex sentence subordinates some data by using at least one dependent clause along with one or more independent clauses. If you consistently use compound sentences or a series of simple sentences, all data appear to be of equal value. To achieve appropriate emphasis, subordinate minor data.

Coordinate and Unemphatic	Subordinate and Emphatic
Flag sales were brisk, and Joni reordered.	Because flag sales were brisk, Joni reordered.
The job offer was attractive, but I decided to go to graduate school.	Although the job offer was attractive, I decided to go to graduate school.
Sales of the Jeffers KB Turbine doubled, for Jeffers had modified the KB six months earlier.	Six months after Jeffers had modified its KB Turbine, KB sales doubled.

Emphasis by Typographical and Visual Aids. This book displays mechanical aids for emphasizing typewritten or printed messages. Those aids include variations in formats and layouts; different sizes and styles of type; headings and subheadings; italics, and boldface print; capitalizations of whole words or of word groups; varied spacings, margins, and indentions; and colored ink or paper. Emphatic visual aids include illustrations and columnar copy.

Computer technology facilitates variations in typographical and visual aids. Be cautious, however, as you use those mechanical aids for emphasis. When too many items are emphasized, nothing gets appropriate emphasis. Planned emphasis improves message effectiveness; haphazard emphasis distracts the reader.

In addition to planning and emphasis, correct spelling and punctuation contribute to message coherence.

Spelling and Punctuation. English spelling is difficult for many people. English has 26 symbols (alphabetical letters) that represent about 45 sounds. American English spelling reflects the influence of Noah Webster, whose publications changed many British English spellings (*flavour* to *flavor*, *centre* to *center*, etc.) supposedly to match spelling with pronunciation. Other phonetic reforms of American English spelling (for example, *tho* for *though* and *tuf* for *tough*) have not been generally accepted. English tends to have several spellings for one sound (e.g., the vowel sound in *to, two, too, shoe, flew, flu, flue, lieu*). And one spelling often represents more than one sound (e.g., *ough* in although, bough, ought, rough, through).

Like other aspects of a dynamic language, spellings and pronunciations change, sometimes quite rapidly. Up-to-date dictionaries are therefore necessary writing tools. In today's computerized writing environment, many writers also have access to dictionary software that checks spelling or finds synonyms with a simple keyboard command. Appendix G contains a list of frequently misspelled or misused words. Effective communicators use such aids without hesitation.

At best, incorrect spelling or word choice is distracting. At worst, it destroys message coherence and sender credibility. Observe the effect of the following spelling and usage errors:

Do you verify your spelling and punctuation?

Incorrect, Incoherent	Correct, Coherent
There cite is more apropriate then hours.	Their site is more appropriate than ours.
Your order is already to be shiped.	Your order is all ready to be shipped.
This dinning room suit is offerred at a 30 percent discount.	This dining room suite is offered at a 30 percent discount.

Like correct spelling, proper punctuation helps to make a written message coherent. Notice how easily punctuation changes the interpretation of the following sentence.

Version A	Version B
Send this report to Lynn Ray.	Send this report to Lynn, Ray.
Raise the gear-release lever.	Raise the gear. Release lever.
I think so; do you?	I think. So do you.

Punctuation marks are communication signals that improve message coherence. Appendix B reviews those signals in detail. In addition, grammatically complete sentences contribute to message coherence.

Complete Sentences. A completely stated sentence requires at least one independent clause. Incomplete statements, called **sentence fragments** or

fragmentary sentences, may be common to informal writing and to speaking, but they can cloud communication. For coherence, do not write dependent clauses as if they were complete sentences; for example:

Fragmented	Complete
The Jeffers order? The one I mentioned to you yesterday afternoon?	When did you receive the Jeffers order that I mentioned to you yesterday afternoon?
This collection procedure is customary. Although you can modify when necessary.	Although this collection procedure is customary, you can modify it when necessary.

Do you avoid sentence fragments, run-on sentences, and run-together sentences?

A comma placed between two main clauses *not* joined by a coordinating conjunction is a **comma splice** or **comma fault**. A sentence with a comma splice is called a **run-on sentence**; for example:

Your work is excellent, therefore you will receive a bonus.

I finished the report, then I went home.

Main clauses joined without a coordinating conjunction or proper punctuation produce a **run-together** or **fused sentence**; for example:

Your work is excellent therefore you will receive a bonus.

I finished the report then I went home.

Run-on and run-together sentences are corrected in any of these ways:

1. Connect the two main clauses with a comma and a coordinating conjunction.

    Your work is excellent, and you will receive a bonus.

    I finished the report, and then I went home.

2. Replace the comma with a semicolon.

    Your work is excellent; therefore, you will receive a bonus.

    I finished the report; then I went home.

3. Make a sentence of each main clause.

    Your work is excellent. You will receive a bonus.

    I finished the report. Then I went home.

4. Change one of the main clauses to a subordinate clause.

Because your work is excellent, you will receive a bonus.

After I had finished the report, I went home.

Planning, emphasis, correct spelling and punctuation, and complete sentences contribute to message coherence. So do transitions, modifiers, and parallelism.

Transitions. "To transit" is to go from one point to another. Use transition words, phrases, sometimes even whole paragraphs, to move readers from one unit to the next in your message. Here are some useful transition techniques:

1. Repeat key words and key phrases

    You've tried. You've tried to find *a home.* But *have you tried to find your home* at *New Town? New Town,* conveniently located where Jordan Highway crosses West Road, offers spacious *garden apartments* and townhouses. The *garden apartments* are . . .

2. Use link words and link phrases

    Plant 3 employs 1,137 people. *Moreover,* new contracts probably will require at least six additional machinists and eight additional office workers at Plant 3 during the next quarter. Plant 4, *however,* can meet its quarterly production schedule with its present work force of 1,750 employees. Supporting data are presented in the next section of this report.

Modifiers. Modifiers are words, phrases, and clauses that influence interpretation of other sentence elements. For coherent communication, you must generally place modifiers next to the element you intend them to affect. Notice that you change the meaning by shifting the position of a modifier in the following sentence:

Only you have invested $8,500 in Project X. (You alone have put that sum into the project.)

You have *only* invested $8,500 in Project X. (You've participated financially but in no other way.)

You have invested *only* $8,500 in Project X. (You've put neither more nor less than that sum into the project.)

You have invested $8,500 in Project X *only.* (You've put that amount into no other project.)

Place modifiers so that they relate logically to other sentence elements.

Do you use
transitions, modifiers,
and parallelism
effectively?

Illogical, Incoherent	Logical, Coherent
Arriving ahead of schedule, it was necessary for the cartons to be stored. (Did *it* arrive early?)	*Arriving ahead of schedule, the cartons* had to be stored.
Schwab put a fabric on the cutting table *which was a blend of silk and wool.* (Was the *table* really made of silk and wool?)	Schwab put a *silk and wool fabric* on the cutting table.
Tired from a long day of work, the bed looked good to me. (Was the *bed* tired?)	*Tired from a long day of work,* I welcomed the sight of my bed.

Parallelism. Grammatical **parallelism** (stating two or more parts of a sentence in identical grammatical form) contributes to coherence. Through parallelism you signal that at least two parts of a sentence have the same logical relationship to the main thought.

Nonparallel, Incoherent	Parallel, Coherent
Atkins enjoys *writing* and *to illustrate* sales brochures. (*Writing* is a gerund; *to illustrate* is an infinitive. The construction needs two gerunds or two infinitives.)	Atkins enjoys *writing* and *illustrating* sales brochures. (Two gerunds.)
	Atkins likes *to write* and *to illustrate* sales brochures. (Two infinitives.)
These guides are useful *for coherence* and *to enhance clarity.* (*For coherence* is a prepositional phrase; *to enhance clarity* is an infinitive phrase. The construction needs two prepositional phrases or two infinitive phrases.)	These guides are useful *for coherence* and *for clarity.* (Two prepositional phrases.)
	These guides are useful *to achieve coherence* and *to enhance clarity.* (Two infinitive phrases.)
The job includes *scheduling mechanical maintenance* and also *the dispatch of the delivery vans.* (*Scheduling mechanical maintenance* is a gerund phrase; *the dispatch of the delivery vans* is a noun modified by a prepositional phrase. The construction can be made parallel by two gerunds or by two grammatically identical clauses.)	The job includes *scheduling mechanical maintenance and dispatching delivery vans.* (Two parallel gerunds in one phrase.)
	In this job *you schedule mechanical maintenance, and you dispatch delivery vans.* (Two grammatically identical clauses.)

Clarity

Meaning is within people rather than within words, sentences, or paragraphs. The previous criteria for message effectiveness (appearance, accuracy, and coherence) contribute to ensuring that the meaning in the receiver's mind corresponds with the sender's intended meaning. A fourth criterion, clarity, contributes to message effectiveness. Use the following guides to compose messages that convey your meaning unmistakably.

Word Choice. When you choose a term that is new to your receiver, explain what *you* mean by using the term. Do likewise when you use a common term in a special way. For example, *hard rock* signifies one thing to an oil well driller but something else to a popular music fan. A business communicator may use *feedback* as a synonym for any response to a message. But to an acoustical engineer, *feedback* stands for noise or electrical interference. For clear communication, choose your words according to what you understand about your receiver's personality and experience as well as your own.

Complete Wording. To reinforce clarity, include every word that is necessary for understanding your sentences.

Incomplete	Complete
Engine 44A uses less fuel. (Less than what? How much less? To do what?)	Engine 44A uses 15 percent less fuel than does Engine 43B in operating a 3,000-pound standard-shift car.
WBI's Flight 319 is thirty minutes faster. (Faster than what?)	WBI's Flight 319 is thirty minutes faster than ACA's Flight 535.
Their Atlanta office is at 423 Peachtree. (Street? Road? Avenue? Place?)	Their Atlanta office is at 423 Peachtree Street, NE.
Your flight reservation has been confirmed for 9:45 tomorrow. (a.m.? p.m.?)	Your flight reservation has been confirmed for 9:45 tomorrow night.
Just sign the enclosed card. (Then what?)	Just sign and return the enclosed card.

How can you improve
message clarity?

Grammatical Consistency. Clarify your messages by consistent grammar. For example, if the grammatical subject of a sentence is singular, the main verb must be singular. If the sentence subject is plural, the main verb must be plural. The subject need not be the first word of the sentence; therefore, be especially diligent when the sentence begins with a modifier, a verb, or an expletive. An **expletive** is a word or phrase that occupies the customary position of the subject and delays the identification of the subject. (Example: *Here* are two things you should consider.)

Subjects and verbs must agree in grammatical number. Pronouns and their antecedents (words to which pronouns refer) must agree in number and in person.

Grammatically Inconsistent	Grammatically Consistent
Unless you plan your messages, *it* wastes time and money.	Unless you plan your messages, *you* waste time and money.
Do this *computer cost* $950?	*Does* this *computer cost* $950?
Here *is* the *contract and* your memo.	Here *are* the *contract and* your memo.
When *was* those *circuits* tested?	When *were* those *circuits* tested?
Schools for all sorts of training *is* needed.	*Schools* for all sorts of training *are* needed.
ABC Corp. announced *their* merger with XYZ.	*ABC Corp.* announced *its* merger with XYZ.
Management must retire when *they* reach age 70.	*Managers* must retire when *they* reach age 70.

You should also make antecedents obvious when you use pronouns. Avoid using whole clauses, sentences, or paragraphs as antecedents.

Unclear Reference	Clear Reference
When *Duval* discussed that decision with *Gates, he* emphasized production schedules. (*Who* emphasized?)	When *Duval* and *Gates* discussed that decision, *Duval* emphasized production schedules. (Noun repeated for clarity.)
	When *Duval* discussed that decision, *he* emphasized production schedules to Gates. (Pronoun clearly represents Duval.)
Van Dorn requested a special *discount, which* arrived after the goods had been billed. (Does *which* refer to *discount* or the clause that begins with *Van Dorn*?)	Van Dorn's special-discount *request* was late; *it* arrived after the goods had been billed. (Pronoun clearly represents request.)
Analyzing your receiver's needs is necessary if you wish to communi-	Analyzing your receiver's needs is necessary if you wish to communi-

cate effectively. That is sometimes difficult. (What is difficult?)

cate effectively. Determining those needs is sometimes difficult. (Noun restated for clarity.)

Clarity requires complete statement of data and complete comparisons. Clarity may even require restatement of a noun to avoid an unclear pronoun reference. However, complete statement does not justify wordiness. A fifth criterion for message effectiveness is conciseness.

Conciseness

How does conciseness differ from brevity?

People sometimes use many words to mask a lack of information. In contrast, some knowledgeable people speak or write with such brevity that they omit data their receivers need. Conciseness is not mere brevity. **Conciseness** is the statement of complete data in as few words as necessary.

Many wordy terms can easily be condensed into concise equivalents; for example:

Wordy	Concise
1. at all times	1. always
2. at the present time	2. now
3. at this point in time	3. now
4. at that point in time	4. then
5. costs the sum of	5. costs
6. despite the fact that	6. although, despite
7. due to the fact that	7. because, since
8. enclosed herewith for your information you will find	8. . . . is enclosed
9. for the period of a year	9. for a year
10. the month of June	10. June
11. for the simple reason that	11. because, since
12. in conjunction with	12. with
13. in the event that	13. if
14. in the near future	14. soon
15. in the recent past	15. recently
16. in view of the fact that	16. because
17. it will be appreciated if you do	17. please do
18. to the effect that	18. that
19. until such time as	19. until
20. we would ask that you	20. please

Do such condensations omit data? See for yourself:

Verbose		Concise	
1.	At all times be courteous.	1.	Always be courteous.
2.	Sales are rising at the present time	2.	Sales are rising now. *Or:* Sales are rising.
3.	Sales are rising at this point in time.	3.	Same as Item 2.
4.	Sales rose at that point in time.	4.	Sales rose then.
5.	This camera costs the sum of $185.	5.	This camera costs $185.
6.	Despite the fact that sales are rising, we should economize.	6.	Although sales are rising, we should economize.
7.	Due to the fact that your work is excellent, you are being promoted.	7.	Because your work is excellent, you are being promoted.
8.	Enclosed herewith for your information you will find our current brochure.	8.	Our current brochure is enclosed.
9.	The Alaska assignment is for the period of a year.	9.	The Alaska assignment is for a year.
10.	Here are the cost figures for the month of June.	10.	Here are the cost figures for June. *Or:* Here are the June cost figures.
11.	I've phoned you for the simple reason that I don't understand your memo.	11.	I've phoned because I don't understand your memo.
12.	The sale begins in conjunction with the opening of our new store.	12.	The sale begins with the opening of our new store. *Even more concisely:* The sale begins when our new store opens.
13.	In the event that I'm not there, please wait.	13.	If I'm not there, please wait.
14.	Production will start in the near future.	14.	Production will start soon. *Or:* Production will start May 23.
15.	Production began in the recent past.	15.	Production began recently. *Or:* Production began May 23.
16.	In view of the fact that you've surpassed every quota, here is a bonus.	16.	Since you've surpassed every quota, here is a bonus.
17.	It will be appreciated if you reply immediately.	17.	Please reply immediately. *Or:* Please reply by August 30.
18.	They reported to the effect that sales had declined.	18.	They reported that sales had declined.

19. Use that machine until such time as the new one is installed.	19. Use that machine until the new one is installed.
20. We would ask that you review this contract.	20. Please review this contract.

Another form of wordiness is use of unnecessary connectors. Use conjunctions and conjunctive adverbs only when they are needed to complete a thought.

Unnecessary	Necessary
This collection procedure is customary; but you can modify it, yet only when justified.	This collection procedure is customary, but modify it when justified.
Send two cartons to Metz and also to Morales and, in addition, two to Stern today or tomorrow afternoon.	By tomorrow afternoon send two cartons apiece to Metz, Morales, and Stern.

Be frugal with your words. Thrifty word choice saves money and time for dictation, transcription, keyboarding, reading, and filing; conserves supplies and postage; and is cost effective for telephone services, interviews, and conferences. By combining complete information with thrifty word choice, you can make your messages clear rather than vague or cluttered. By being concise, you can conserve your own and your employer's resources.

Courtesy

What is the relationship of empathy to courtesy?

The best advice for developing communication courtesy may be this: Empathize with your receiver. To **empathize** is to project yourself psychologically into another person's circumstances without surrendering your own identity, needs, and obligations.

While recognizing your own needs and desires, constantly try to anticipate, to perceive, and to interpret those of your receiver. Your time and effort are precious; so are your receiver's. But you respond negatively to curtness; so does your receiver. Whether you convey satisfying, disappointing, or neutral information, do so courteously. Which style, curt or courteous, would you prefer if you received these messages?

Curt	Courteous
You don't need to keep reminding us about your claim.	Thanks for following up on your claim.

I'm too busy to talk to you about that refund now. Call back at 4:30 p.m.	Your refund request deserves my full attention. Please call back at 4:30 p.m.
There's no way for you to be promoted if you stay with us; so get a job elsewhere.	To advance your career, perhaps you should consider opportunities elsewhere.

Discourtesy evidences itself in many ways. Withholding necessary information, transmitting unneeded information, and timing messages inappropriately are discourtesies. Courtesy involves genuine awareness of your receiver's needs, purposes, attention span, and time.

Business communicators are sometimes advised, "Write as you speak." Consider this probability, however: Unless your oral communication meets the criteria cited in this chapter, your writing—like your speaking—may be ineffective. In your oral and your written messages, strive for attractive appearance, accuracy, coherence, clarity, conciseness, and courtesy.

REVIEW AND TRANSITION

To gain goodwill, to inquire, to inform, and to persuade are a business communicator's basic goals. Those goals can be attained by skillful *perception,* which requires purposeful observing, reading, and listening. They can be attained by skillful *interpretation,* which requires careful analysis, synthesis, and use of logic. They can be attained by skillful application, which requires efficient speaking, writing, and nonverbal behavior.

In computer-analogy terms, perception is *input;* interpretation is *process;* application, as evidenced by effective messages, is *output.* Message effectiveness is gauged by the standards of appearance, accuracy, coherence, clarity, conciseness, and courtesy.

Communication skills are not inborn. They are learned, practiced, and adapted with many variations inside and among the many cultures of this world. Awareness of cultural similarities and differences is necessary for effective business communication today. Chapter 3 explores answers to this question: How do cultural patterns affect business communication—and business communicators?

YOUR DECISIONS FOR CHAPTER 2

As noted in the Decisions Case for Chapter 2, the spelling, punctuation, and grammar of Harris's memo are correct; but the message is wordy and vague. What basic goals should Harris attempt to achieve with the memo? What fundamental skills were not applied? Of which communication criteria should you make Harris aware? Why? What communication techniques will help Harris to fulfill those criteria?

DISCUSSION QUESTIONS

A. Within the context of Chapter 2, what are appropriate definitions and examples for these terms?

  1. goodwill
  2. analyze
  3. synthesize
  4. induction
  5. deduction
  6. fallacies
  7. criteria
  8. parallelism
  9. sentence fragment
  10. run-on sentence

B. To gain goodwill, to inquire, to inform, and to persuade are goals of an effective business communicator. Why is goodwill necessary to attain the three other goals?

C. From your experiences, what are examples of business *mis*communication resulting from *mis*perception? from *mis*interpretation? What words or actions might have improved communication in those examples? Why?

D. Is logic truth? What evidence justifies your answer to that question? As someone who is striving to become an effective business communicator, why should you use logic—but carefully?

E. Besides the examples given in Chapter 2, what are illustrations of the following?

  1. name-calling
  2. bandwagon appeal
  3. time and cause–effect confusion
  4. detouring
  5. begging the question
  6. self-contradiction
  7. hasty generalization
  8. false premise for a syllogism

F. What are the criteria of effective business communication? What examples, besides those in the text, illustrate or violate the criteria?

G. What is the relationship of Chapter 2 to Appendices A–C of this text? How do you plan to use those appendices as you study Chapters 3–22?

H. In what ways are these statements related to the goals and skills of effective communicators?

1. In effect, except for irresistible stimuli, your mind admits only those data that you choose to recognize.
2. Meaning is within people rather than within words.
3. The best advice for developing communication courtesy may be this: Empathize with your receiver.

APPLICATIONS

1. Misperceptions can produce misinterpretations as, for example, when one term is mistaken for another. Demonstrate your ability to perceive and to interpret appropriately.

    a. Pronounce the following terms to a classmate or your instructor. Ask for feedback about the accuracy of your pronunciations.

        (1)   access, assess, excess, asked, axed
        (2)   advice, advise, adviser
        (3)   affect, effect, reflect, reflects, reflex
        (4)   all together, altogether, all to gather
        (5)   as, like, identical to, similar to
        (6)   assistance, assistants
        (7)   ate, eight, eighth
        (8)   buy, by, good buy, goodbye
        (9)   capital, capitol
        (10) cite, sight, site
        (11) complement, compliment
        (12) elicit, illicit
        (13) except, accept
        (14) for, fore, four, forth, fourth, forty, fortieth
        (15) idea, ideal, idol, idle
        (16) incidence, incidents, instants, instances
        (17) interest, interested, disinterested, uninterested
        (18) it's, its
        (19) lay, lie, lye
        (20) loose, lose, Lou's

    b. Write sentences that appropriately place the preceding terms in business contexts.

2. To discover the kind of reader you are, try the following experiment. You will need a book, a desk or table, a mirror, a stopwatch or a clock with a second hand, and a partner.

    Sit at the desk or table. Place the mirror against one page of the open book, but read from the opposite page. Have your partner stand behind you. Ask your partner to arrange the mirror so that he or she observes your eye movements as you read. By looking at the mirror, your partner can count the number of eye fixations that you make per line. Read for one minute and record your reading rate (words per minute). Also record the number of eye fixations you made per line, as reported by your partner. Exchange places with your partner. Test your partner's reading habits in the same way (reading rate and number of eye fixations per line). Use a new page of the book for each test. Keep retesting to increase reading speed. To determine comprehension, you and your partner should discuss the corethought and supporting details of what each of you has read.

3.   Use a reading diary to summarize your next study assignment. Submit the summary to your instructor for review and comment. Include this information in the diary:

> ► *Message:* Identifying information such as title, date, and pages.
> ► *Author/sender:* Name, other relevant information about message originator.
> ► *Corethought:* One-sentence summary of main idea.
> ► *Details:* Brief outline of supporting information.
> ► *Response:* Your response (or intended response) to the message.

4.   Use a listening diary similar to the reading diary in Application 3 to summarize your next class discussion. Submit the summary to your instructor for review and comment.

5.   Write appropriate revisions of these illogical statements:

a.   Celebrities endorse this product. You want to be like a celebrity. You should buy this product.
b.   Communicating is when you communicate the evidence of ideas and feelings.
c.   Profits have decreased for the simple reason that they are less than they were last year.
d.   Although I was absent from four of the five scheduled tests, I am sure that I communicate well; therefore, I should pass this course easily.
e.   This report is late, but you should give me full credit because I finally completed it.
f.   Carla hasn't missed any work time. Her absence yesterday was an exception.
g.   We lost the Ryan account after we assigned it to Kristy. Therefore, don't blame me. Blame Kristy.
h.   Entry-level employees are all the same—unreliable.
i.   Since we moved Hurst to the production unit, our output has doubled; so Hurst deserves a big bonus.
j.   Our branch offices are open until 5 p.m. daily. They close at noon on Wednesdays.

    k. Everyone else likes my idea; you should like it, too.
    l. As I entered the conference room, everybody stopped talking. What have I done wrong now?

6. Find an advertisement, a sales promotion letter, or other business message that has a fallacy. Identify the fallacy and appropriately revise the fallacious message.

7. Write a business-related paragraph that demonstrates inductive order.

8. Write a business-related paragraph that demonstrates deductive order.

9. Many people produce messages that may be understood. Effective communicators try to produce messages that cannot be misunderstood. Using a business context, compose a paragraph (of at least four sentences) that you believe cannot be misunderstood.

10. Rewrite the following items to illustrate conventional American English spelling, punctuation, and grammar:

    a. Whitney Corporation a major manufacturer of home applyences offers atractive career oppurtunities.
    b. Become a productive member of the Whitney team, and enjoy competive income exellent benefits and strong growth potentual.
    c. We provide an industry leading benifets package of medical and dentel insurace sick leave and payed holidays.
    d. If you are a college educated busness specialist join HRH Finacial Services, and particpate in this chalenging fast growing industry.
    e. Invest in Woods Hill a new, residential, comunity of 425 homecites and 85 acers of recrational facilitys.
    f. "For your convience" the sales representive said "we have a 24 hour toll free telephone number"
    g. "Is this recomendation your's, or her's" Stacy aksed.
    h. If any of our employees have a sugestion they usualy make them during prodtivity revues.
    i. Was the Grady contracks negotated by you and he?
    j. Kelsey a senior busness student intrested in entrepreneurship is all ready developing a business plan for obtaining start up capital.

11. Illustrate coherence by transition in the following ways:

    a. Write a paragraph that demonstrates transition by appropriately repeating key words or key phrases.
    b. Write a paragraph that demonstrates transition by appropriately using link words or link phrases.

12. Rewrite the following to demonstrate coherence by modification:

    a. As a college student majoring in business, many career opportunities are available to you.

    b. Before boarding the corporate jetcraft, is it necessary to inspect carry-on luggage?

    c. Having updated that computer program, data retrieval be improved.

    d. When requesting maintenance or repair, it is necessary to process Form 5A.

    e. Has the contract already been issued about which you asked?

    f. People have excellent employment prospects who communicate effectively.

    g. While preparing for employment interviews you can understand why Dana researched the job market.

    h. Those sales representatives are here to see you who scheduled appointments to see you this morning.

    i. Is your office now open where you process employment applications?

    j. Before presenting this marketing proposal, surveys were conducted that were nationwide.

13. Rewrite the following sentences to demonstrate coherence by parallelism:

    a. Anna Chung is intelligent, ethical, and does her work efficiently.

    b. She is a fine employee not only because of her technical knowledge, but also her communication skills are effective.

    c. Ways of increasing profits include reducing costs and to improve quality control.

    d. I'd rather limit our product line than sacrificing quality.

    e. Successful business students learn the skills of how to communicate, accountancy, and management.

    f. Loan officers usually welcome entrepreneurs who have realistic goals and with documentation to support them.

    g. Sloan's work involves executive speechwriting and to improve media relations.

    h. Sumter, Inc., has career opportunities for managers, accountants, and also in marketing.

    i. Vera decided to accept neither the Clary offer nor working at Winfield.

    j. Blake designs office systems that are up to date and which are reliable.

14. Write three sentence fragments. Explain how those fragments may be clearly understood in oral–visual communication (for example, as parts of a conversation or of a television commercial). Then revise the fragments into complete statements for a written message.

15. Rewrite these verbose items into concise equivalents:

a. Our trend of sales for the fiscal years of 1990 in addition to 1991 is encouraging.

b. It is not without pleasure that I wish to take this opportunity to express to you my gratitude.

c. With respect to the request submitted by you for a special discount if you double your previous order, the answer is affirmative.

d. Prior to the Diaz conference I shall appreciate it if you provide me with copies of the Transco proposal and the Cheung contract as well as the Gibbs report.

e. Lubov as well as Larkin and also Schuyler have been awarded contracts by us.

f. The success of Weller Industries with competition in global markets is without a shadow of a doubt definitely attracting attention which is favorable on the part of investors.

g. We would ask that the questionnaire which is enclosed be completed and returned by you by April 5 at the very latest.

h. It goes without saying that it will be appreciated if these estimates are reviewed by you.

i. In the event that you find that you need additional information, please do not hesitate to call me.

j. In view of the fact that a safety defect has been discovered, it is necessary that New Star products be recalled by their manufacturer without any loss of time.

16. Rewrite the following items to demonstrate courtesy by empathizing with the receiver:

a. [Telephone pickup] "Beta, Inc.; hold on."
b. Don't bother me now. I'm busy.
c. You're wrong about that date; it's May 14.
d. You failed to initial that memo.
e. I can't do that now; I'm on my coffee break.

MULTICULTURAL INSIGHTS

1. Which of the goals and skills discussed in this chapter apply to business uses of your native language? Which do not apply? Describe the cultural similarities and the differences associated with use or with nonuse of those goals and skills.

2. Which patterns of logic and of fallacies, described in Chapter 2, exist also with use of your native language? To what extent do business messages (advertisements, for example) communicate the evidence of ideas and of feelings?

3. Which of the communication criteria described in Chapter 2 apply to business use of your native language? Which do not apply?

4. If you can conveniently do so, bring to class several examples of business messages (including advertisements) written in your native language. Using those messages as visual aids, discuss their similarities to and differences from their American English counterparts.

5. Which of the criteria for message effectiveness are easy for you to fulfill with American English? Why? Which are difficult for you to fulfill with American English? Why?

3 CULTURAL ASPECTS OF BUSINESS COMMUNICATION

CHAPTER OUTLINE

I. Communication Skills as Learned Behaviors
II. Business Communication and Cultures
    A. Culture-to-Culture Communication Model
    B. Terminology of Culture-to-Culture Communication
III. Communicative Behaviors and Cultural Values
    A. Cultural Uses of Language
    B. Cultural Uses of Metacommunication
        1. Space
        2. Time
        3. Gestures and Facial Expressions
IV. Review and Transition

OBJECTIVES

After completing this chapter, you should be able to:

1. Recognize cultural influences on the global marketplace and on your career.
2. Describe the interrelationships of business, communication, and culture.
3. Explain typical stages in culture-to-culture communication.
4. Be sensitive to verbal and metacommunication differences in culture-to-culture communication.

63

5. Participate effectively in culture-to-culture communication on campus or at work.

DECISIONS CASE

With the assistance of his state development board, your friend John Duncan has identified a potential new market for his popular gas grills. Executives of one of Japan's largest companies have arrived at Duncan's plant to discuss an agreement to distribute the grills in the Pacific Rim. Besides Japan, the executives anticipate marketing the grills in South Korea, Taiwan, and Thailand.

Although Duncan Corp. controls more than 60 percent of the domestic gas grill market, this is its first venture into the international market. While enthusiastically describing the opportunities, Duncan also voices some concerns: "I know how to sell to U.S. distributors, but I'm not sure how to approach the Japanese. After the first firm handshake, what do I do? Coffee in the cafeteria—that should break the ice. Then a tour of the plant so that I can point out the features of the grill and the manufacturing process. Then to the conference room for the audiovisual presentation that we give to all potential distributors. I'll have a proposed contract ready for them to look at. We can start our negotiations before lunch . . ."

"Wait," you interrupt. "I'm not sure that will work."

What would you advise Duncan to do differently? Why?

Additional questions about this decision-making case are stated at the end of this chapter. Study the chapter before answering those questions.

CHAPTER CONTEXT

As you studied Chapters 1 and 2, you learned about the roles of perception, interpretation, and application in the communication process. You were reminded that people perceive, interpret, act, and react differently from one another. What one person assumes or notices may be undetected by someone else—sometimes with unprofitable results for business. Awareness of that fact is especially important for success in the international business arena.

Because economic interdependence has become worldwide, awareness of *diversity* in human heritages is essential to your education as a business communicator. Your career affects and is affected by the actions and messages of other people who compete and cooperate with you, directly or indirectly, in a global marketplace. Their life-styles may differ from yours, yet you and they need to communicate effectively. Chapter 3 provides insights to fulfilling that need.

Why study other cultures as well as your own?

COMMUNICATION SKILLS AS LEARNED BEHAVIORS

Business communication students are sometimes told to write and speak "naturally." But what is natural? *Capacity* for language may be inborn for humans, but communication *skills* are not inborn, not natural. Communication skills are systems of *acquired* techniques that you and other people can learn, practice, evaluate, and adapt to business careers.

What is the significance of this statement: "Communication skills involve learned behaviors"?

You mislead yourself, however, if you assume that all communication customs are identical to yours. Communication skills involve *learned* behaviors, which vary greatly throughout the world. The differences make business communication a fascinating, challenging, and often rewarding activity, especially when it bridges gaps among cultures.

Why do we perceive differently?

How you perceive is determined largely by how and what your culture teaches you to notice. How you interpret is determined largely by how your culture teaches you what your observations mean. For example, U.S. businesspersons often conclude an exchange with "thank you." Some cultures consider it rude to say "thank you," because that expression suggests to them the end to what should be a continuing flow of give and take. You may consider it intrusive for a stranger to sit next to you on a bus or subway car when empty seats are available; but in many countries, it would be considered an insult if that stranger sat elsewhere.[1]

BUSINESS COMMUNICATION AND CULTURES

A **culture** is a system of shared values, beliefs, and behaviors that influence and are influenced by communication. The word *culture* denotes the total way of life for a people, all—says Edward Hall—"of their learned behavior patterns, attitudes, and material things."[2]

How do cultures, communication, and technology interact?

Today, divergent life-style systems are finding new ways of communicating through domestic, international, and multinational business enterprises. With unprecedented speed and impact, modern technology enables people throughout the world to communicate diverse values, attitudes, and beliefs. That diversity, in turn, affects profit or loss in exchanging products and services.

---

[1]Sondra Thiederman, *Bridging Cultural Barriers for Corporate Success: How to Manage the Multicultural Work Force* (Lexington, MA: Lexington Books, 1991), p. 3.

[2]Edward T. Hall, *The Silent Language* (New York: Doubleday & Co., 1973), p. 31.

A Culture-to-Culture Communication Model

Assume that, for mutual economic gain, members of two cultures, A and Z, perceive the need to do business with each other. Illustrations 3−1 through 3−5 depict a basic model of communication stages through which those cultures must pass to accomplish mutually beneficial business exchanges. In that model, Culture A is represented by a circle, and Culture Z is represented by a hexagon.

Illustration 3−1 shows the two cultures at a precommunication stage. They are separated from each other by their diverse life-styles.

Despite profound differences in life-styles, A and Z communicate to narrow the cultural gap between them, as shown by Illustration 3−2.

Illustration 3–1   TWO CULTURES AT A PRECOMMUNICATION STAGE

Illustration 3–2   TWO CULTURES WITH ECONOMIC INCENTIVES TO COMMUNICATE

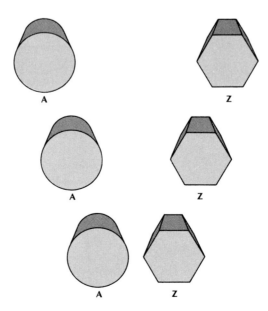

What does this model suggest about culture-to-culture communication?

Although retaining their separate identities, A and Z narrow the communication gap (G), as shown by Illustration 3–3.

If A and Z permeate each other, a new culture, AZ, might result. (See Illustration 3–4.)

Instead, however, A and Z probably would retain their identities while establishing and reinforcing a culture-to-culture environment of communica-

Illustration 3–3 TWO CULTURES NARROWING A COMMUNICATION GAP

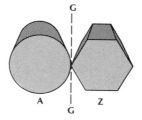

Illustration 3–4 NEW CULTURE FORMATION

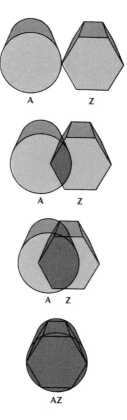

tion for mutual economic gain. That communicative environment, CE in Illustration 3–5, enlarges as both cultures become increasingly sensitive to their differences and similarities. Both cultures profit materially and socially from the expanded communication environment.

Illustration 3–5   TWO CULTURES ESTABLISHING AND REINFORCING A COMMUNICATIVE ENVIRONMENT

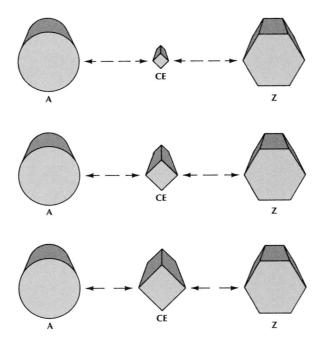

The theoretical model depicted by Illustrations 3–1 through 3–5 suggests various cultural relationships. Effective study of those relationships begins with precise use of terminology.

Terminology of Culture-to-Culture Communication

As you begin your study of the cultural aspects of business communication, you should be aware of these terms:

1. **Cultural** pertains to the total life-style of a people. **Intracultural** refers to components of that life-style.
2. **International** refers to relationships between and among sovereign states (nations) that have recognizable political and geographic boun-

daries. Cultures, however, may be contained within—or may extend beyond—those political and geographic boundaries.

3. **Intercultural** refers to relationships between cultures. **Cross-cultural** and **transcultural** pertain to the bridging of gaps among cultures.

4. **Bicultural** pertains to two cultures. **Multicultural** refers to more than two cultures.

5. **Culture-to-culture communication**, as used in this chapter, includes aspects—but avoids semantic restrictions—of other terms in this list. Culture-to-culture communication, for example, includes attempts to bridge communication gaps between people within a national boundary as well as among people of different nations.

What is culture-to-culture communication?

COMMUNICATIVE BEHAVIORS AND CULTURAL VALUES

Communicative behaviors reflect cultural values, which differ throughout the world. Behaviors that people of one culture value as outgoing, confident, and informal may be devalued as blatant, boastful, and insensitive by people of another culture. For example, businesspeople in the United States are often trained to be candid, frank, and direct. But if your behavior emphasizes those values when you try to deal with people of Mediterranean, Latin American, or Asian cultures, you may be (mis)perceived as being tactless, insensitive, or rude. If you demonstrate time-is-money-so-I'm-always-in-a-hurry behavior, you might break rapport with a customer and lose a sale.

Religious heritages provide an even more fundamental example. Although the United States is a religiously diverse country, U.S. managers tend to be influenced by the Protestant work ethic, which promotes honesty, integrity, hard work, and diligence. That ethic demonstrates faith in individuals and their ability to influence their environment. Members of many other cultures, however, feel that their lives are controlled by a higher power. Consequently, those people fatalistically accept success or failure, wealth or poverty.[3] You may assume that everyone places high priority on deterministic tools such as economic forecasts and production-distribution schedules derived from those forecasts. But if that assumption governs your behavior when you try to do business with people of other cultures, you may fail. Such failure is possible not because your product or service is inferior but because millions of people,

[3]Eva S. Kras, *Management in Two Cultures: Bridging the Gap Between U.S. and Mexican Managers* (Yarmouth, ME: Intercultural Press, 1988), pp. 30–31.

In what ways do
communicative
behaviors reflect
values?

including perhaps your prospective customer, believe that such forecasting and scheduling are intrusions upon the will of God.[4]

The preceding examples suggest a basic insight into cultural aspects of metacommunication. What people of one culture consider unimportant behavior may be perceived and interpreted as highly significant to people of other cultures. To ignore cultural values is to believe mistakenly that business consists solely of products and services—or that communication consists only of words. Business and communication involve people. People are cultural beings, and appreciation of cultural diversity is required of successful business communicators today.

As you continue developing your communication expertise, recognize that people view one another and the world in different ways. Those ways are evidenced by differing cultural uses of language and of metacommunication.

Cultural Uses of Language

David Berlo, a noted communication theorist, suggests that people think about only what they can name (with words or other symbols). Berlo asserts that the "ways in which we think are determined in part by the ways in which our language is structured."[5] Berlo's insight discloses one kind of communication gap—the linguistic gap—which businesspeople try to bridge.

The Japanese language, for example, is capable of delicate nuances of states of mind and relationships. It contains layers of "soft" language with various degrees of courtesy and respect. "Plain" or "coarse" language is considered improper.[6] Reflecting cultural values, traditional Japanese business correspondence tends to be more formally structured, more modest and ceremoniously polite, less direct, and less concise than is U.S. business correspondence.

Nigerians distinguish levels of familiarity by their form of address. Although friends will call one another by their first names, older brothers and sisters are rarely addressed by first names. As a sign of respect for seniority and age, an older brother is addressed as N'da Sam ("my senior Sam") and an older sister as N'se Sarah ("my senior Sarah"). Nigerians always use "sir" and "ma'am" when addressing a businessperson, government official, someone older, or someone in a position of authority.[7]

---

[4]Hall, p. 11.

[5]David K. Berlo, *The Process of Communication: An Introduction to Theory and Practice* (New York: Holt, Rinehart & Winston, 1960), p. 70.

[6]Philip R. Harris and Robert T. Moran, *Managing Cultural Differences,* 3d ed. (Houston: Gulf Publishing Company, 1991), p. 41.

[7]Ibid., p. 524.

What are concepts?

Thus, cultures convey ways of viewing the world by conventions of language and action. Do Americans and other users of English consider, for example, what the very structure of the language may imply to others? Linguist Mario Pei observes: "English is the only language that capitalizes 'I' in writing, whereas many languages capitalize 'you,' and this has been interpreted, rightly or wrongly, as a sign of an exaggerated ego. . . ."[8]

Differing concepts of familiar U.S. business phenomena can impair international business communication. For example, Professors Jeremiah J. Sullivan and Naoki Kameda caution that U.S.–Japanese business negotiations for joint ventures can be blocked by differing concepts of profit. Whereas North Americans view profit mainly as personal gain for corporate owners, Japanese conceive of profit as social *and* corporate gain.[9] Kras contrasts Mexican and U.S. concepts of work and leisure. The prevalent views among Mexican managers is that a person works to live and leisure is essential for a full life. In contrast, many U.S. managers live to work and perceive leisure as a reward for hard work.[10]

The idiom, slang, and jargon of a language are especially difficult for nonnative speakers to master. American business English is filled with ritualistic phrases like "Let's do lunch sometime" or "I'll talk with you again soon." Few Americans expect a response to the greeting, "How are you?" But the Dutch expect the inquirer to stop and listen.[11] Even within a culture, several words may signify the same objective reality. For example, in U.S. English the words *fired, terminated, released, let go, laid off,* and even *riffed* (from *r*eduction *in f*orce) are all used to indicate that a person has lost her or his job. Imagine the difficulty a person from another culture could have with those words!

Cultural use of language also includes the etiquette of interruptions, silence or pauses, spontaneity of speech, and volume of speech. In many Far Eastern cultures, interruptions are considered extremely rude. In contrast, French, Italian, and Arabic cultures regard interruptions as expressions of enthusiasm and commitment to the conversation. Many Americans feel awkward if a conversation is suddenly interrupted by a pause, but an Asian might interpret silence as the listener's contemplation of what has just been said. Many people in U.S., Italian, or French cultures regard spontaneity as evidence of creativity and enthusiasm. Asians, however, tend to speak only after careful deliberation. In the United States, individuals are expected to use

---

[8]Mario Pei, *The Story of Language* (New York: The New American Library, 1960), p. 69.

[9]Jeremiah J. Sullivan and Naoki Kameda, "The Concept of Profit and Japanese-American Business Communication Problems," *The Journal of Business Communication,* vol. 19, no. 1 (Winter 1982), p. 38.

[10]Kras, p. 72.

[11]Thiederman, p. 131.

What examples
demonstrate that
language conveys
cultural diversity?

moderate volume—neither too loud nor too soft. The southern European or Middle Easterner who tends to speak more loudly may be perceived as aggressive, crass, and pushy; and the soft-spoken Asian may appear meek and retiring.[12]

The communication lesson is clear: Americans doing business with members of other cultures need to develop communicative awareness of themselves as well as of other people. Moreover, that awareness must extend beyond the cultural uses of language to culturally diverse forms of communication.

Cultural Uses of Metacommunication

To exchange evidence of ideas and feelings, people use more than words. People use time, space, gestures, facial expressions, postures, clothing, cosmetics, jewelry, etc., as signals of meanings. **Metacommunication** (*meta,* "beyond") is a technical term for the use of such signals.

What is
metacommunication?

Metacommunication conveys messages *about messages* through handshakes, smiles, frowns, and other cues that *transcend* words. Metacommunication can confirm, contradict, or substitute for words. In Western cultures, for instance, agreement may be confirmed by a down-up nod of one's head or contradicted by a side-to-side shake of the head, whatever words may or may not be used. In Mexico and the Middle East, "no" is signified by a back-and-forth movement of the index finger. That gesture unmistakably indicates disagreement, no matter what words may be used.[13]

Metacommunication reflects cultural values, particularly with respect to use of space, use of time, and use of gestures and facial expressions.

How may cultural
values be conveyed by
metacommunication?

Space. The space we maintain with our bodies suggests a desire to control closeness. Ideas about what constitutes closeness differ among cultures and with circumstances. Thiederman[14] observes these cultural variations:

▶ *0-18 inches:* Middle Eastern males, eastern and southern Mediterraneans, and some Hispanic cultures.
▶ *18 inches-3 feet:* Mainstream Americans and Western Europeans.
▶ *3 feet or more:* Asians (Japanese, the farthest) and many African cultures.

[12]Ibid., pp. 127−130.
[13]Ibid., p. 140.
[14]Ibid., p. 132.

How does culture
affect use of space?

Circumstances may alter the use of space. Since much U.S. business is conducted across an office desk or in a conference room, space for interpersonal business communication may be extended several feet beyond the norm. However, for confidential or personal communication, the space between speaker and listener tends to be reduced.

In contrast with Latin American and Middle Eastern cultures, the United States is a noncontact society. Whereas Latin Americans and Middle Easterners require relatively close physical proximity during a conversation, a North American tends to consider such closeness an invasion of personal space.[15] The usual *business* spacing for interpersonal business communication in Latin America is like that of *confidential* spacing in the United States. Except for Mexican people, most North Americans tend to back away from such closeness. However, backing away often suggests to Latin American businesspeople and others that United States counterparts are aloof or unfriendly.

In the United States, space and location often connote status. An American executive's office tends to be large and frequently is located on the top floor of a building. In the Middle East, however, the size of an office seems to convey little significance; in France, a manager is apt to be located amid subordinates so that the manager can exercise control conveniently.[16]

Time. Many North Americans and North Europeans segment time. People of other cultures tend to flow with time. To U.S. businesspeople, five minutes is a significant unit of time—the point after which one may justifiably be offended or irritated if kept waiting. In France, fifteen minutes is perceived as a significant delay.[17] In Latin America and the Middle East, however, long waiting periods are customary in business. They enable visitors literally to visit, to socialize with one another in a business setting, and to associate business relationships with a total rather than segmented life-style.

Cultural differences regarding time are often evidenced in contract negotiation and fulfillment. In Japan and elsewhere, delays of months or even years may not signify loss of interest in negotiating an important business contract. In contrast, most North Americans view such delays as serious hindrances. In the Middle East and elsewhere, the imposition of due dates and deadlines suggests inconsideration, even rudeness, and thereby seems to justify ignoring such schedules. U.S. businesspeople who overlook such cultural conventions

How does culture
affect use of time?

---

[15]Harris and Moran, p. 41.

[16]R. Wayne Mondy, Robert E. Holmes, and Edwin B. Flippo, *Management Concepts and Practices* (Boston: Allyn & Bacon, 1980), p. 385.

[17]Thiederman, p. 142.

of communication may suffer large losses before learning that "delay is often a highly effective negotiation tactic when used on impatient Americans."[18]

Gestures and Facial Expressions.[19] Cultures vary widely in how they use the hands and the face in communication. Although the handshake is an almost universal business greeting, its strength and form differ across cultures. (See Illustration 3–6.) You should avoid most other uses of the hand (touching, pointing, beckoning, etc.) unless you are well acquainted with the culture. Many commonly used United States gestures are considered offensive or obscene in other cultures, including the American "OK" signals (thumbs up, and V for victory) and the silence signal (index finger to the lips while making a "shh" sound).

Many people think the smile universally communicates goodwill and cheerfulness. However, a smile does not have the same meaning throughout the world. Americans tend to use the smile freely as a representation of friendliness, goodwill, and optimism. Middle Easterners might use a smile to placate a colleague and avoid conflict, and many Asians smile to cover discomfort, embarrassment, or anger.

Similarly, the use of eye contact varies among cultures. (See Illustration

How does culture affect use of hand gestures and facial expressions?

Illustration 3–6   HANDSHAKES: CULTURAL DIFFERENCES

Americans: Firm

Germans: Brusk, firm, repeated upon arrival and departure

French: Light, quick, not offered to superiors, repeated upon arrival and departure

British: Soft

Hispanics: Moderate grasp, repeated frequently

Middle Easterners: Gentle, repeated frequently

Asians: Gentle; for some, shaking hands is unfamiliar and uncomfortable (an exception to this is the Korean, who generally has a firm handshake)

SOURCE: Reprinted with permission of Lexington Books, an imprint of Macmillan, Inc., from *Bridging Cultural Barriers to Corporate Success* by Sondra Thiederman. Copyright © 1990 by Sondra Thiederman.

---

[18]Mondy, Holmes, and Flippo, p. 385.
[19]All examples in this section are derived from Thiederman, pp. 131–143.

3–7.) Complicating cultural differences are differences among subcultures. For example, in the United States Anglo-Americans tend to seek eye contact when the other party is speaking but may let their eyes wander when they themselves are speaking. African-Americans tend to do the opposite. Unfortunately, the difference can lead an Anglo-American to feel that an African-American is aggressive when speaking but uninterested in what the other party has to say.

The preceding examples illustrate that communication is more than the use of grammar and vocabulary. Communication includes nonverbal uses of time, space, and related cultural characteristics that many American busi-

Illustration 3–7 VARIATIONS IN EYE CONTACT

Very direct eye contact

Groups: Middle Easterners, some Hispanic groups, the French

Misinterpretation: Hostility, aggressiveness, intrusiveness, bossiness

Correct interpretation: A desire to express an interest, a desire to communicate effectively

Moderate eye contact

Groups: Mainstream Americans, northern Europeans, the British

Misinterpretation: Lack of interest in what is being said

Correct Interpretation: A desire not to appear aggressive or intrusive

Minimal eye contact

Groups: East Asians, Southeast Asians, East Indians, native Americans

Misinterpretation: Lack of interest, lack of intelligence, dishonesty, lack of understanding, fear, shyness

Correct interpretation: A desire to show respect, a desire to avoid intrusion

SOURCE: Reprinted with permission of Lexington Books, an imprint of Macmillan, Inc., from *Bridging Cultural Barriers to Corporate Success* by Sondra Thiederman. Copyright © 1990 by Sondra Thiederman.

nesspeople assume to be the same as their own. That assumption is fallacious and may be costly in personal as well as business communication, especially in today's culturally diverse business environment.[20]

REVIEW AND TRANSITION

Culture, the total life-style of a people, affects perception and interpretation of what is perceived. Communication *capacity* may be inborn, but communication *skills* are systems of acquired techniques that vary from culture to culture.

The syntax and grammar of languages differ from culture to culture, and linguistic differences often represent different cultural values. Metacommunication, which can confirm, contradict, or substitute for words, also varies from culture to culture.

The Multicultural Insights exercises throughout this book are designed to heighten your awareness, appreciation, and profitable use of culture-to-culture communication. As you study the following chapters, which deal primarily with American business communication practices, recognize that business practices—like cultures themselves—vary throughout the world.

Chapter 4 identifies and describes recent technological developments and their impact on domestic and cross-cultural business communication.

YOUR DECISIONS FOR CHAPTER 3

When you first read the Decisions Case at the beginning of this chapter, what suggestions were you prepared to give to Duncan? Why? Now that you have studied Chapter 3, what procedures would you recommend to ensure that Duncan communicates effectively with his Japanese visitors? What are your reasons for the similarities or differences between those two responses?

DISCUSSION QUESTIONS

A. Within the context of Chapter 3, what are appropriate definitions and examples for these terms?

1. culture
2. international
3. intercultural
4. intracultural
5. cross-cultural

---

[20]For additional insights to cross-cultural communication, see the following: Geert Hofstede, *Culture's Consequences, International Differences in Work-related Values,* abridged ed. (Beverly Hills, CA: Sage Publications, 1984); and Larry A. Samovar and Richard E. Porter, *Intercultural Communication: A Reader,* 4th ed. (Belmont, CA: Wadsworth Publishing Company, 1985).

6. transcultural
7. multicultural
8. transcend
9. diversity
10. metacommunication

B. What are cultural aspects of business communication? Why should you concern yourself with them?

C. Within your own culture, what are characteristic attitudes toward the following?

1. competition and cooperation
2. education and training
3. employed persons and unemployed persons
4. personal debt and national debt
5. work habits, including punctuality and absenteeism
6. job security and career opportunities for men and for women
7. standards of productivity and quality
8. young employees and elderly employees

D. With what culture other than your own are you most familiar? How did you become familiar with that culture? What are its characteristic attitudes toward the eight factors listed in Discussion Question C?

E. Why should you, as a businessperson, continue developing your awareness of metacommunication and of culture-to-culture communication?

APPLICATIONS

1. Provide writing samples for your instructor to evaluate. Select several of the preceding discussion questions and compose paragraphs that answer them.

2. Look again at the writing samples you provided for Application 1. How many times do the words *I, me, my,* or *mine* appear in those samples? What cultural values does the frequency of first-person pronouns in your message convey?

3. With your instructor's supervision (and, if your instructor permits, with the help of your classmates), revise your writing samples. Replace first-person pronouns with words referring to your reader and to the topics of your writing samples. What cultural values do your revisions—and your feelings about revising—convey?

4. In a two-page written message (or in a five-minute oral presentation), describe culture-to-culture communication opportunities at your col-

lege. Identify academic courses, campus organizations, or college-sponsored events that emphasize those opportunities.

5.   Identify the words that best describe businesspeople of your culture. (*Note: Monolingual* pertains to knowing only one language; *bilingual,* two languages; *multilingual,* more than two languages.)

active	illogical
aggressive	impulsive
bilingual	individualistic
boastful	law-abiding
calm	logical
competitive	loyal
confident	materialistic
considerate of old people	modest
considerate of poor people	monolingual
cooperative	multilingual
courteous	passive
decisive	philosophical
dependable	pragmatic
dependent on others	proud
easygoing	religious
emotional	self-assertive
enthusiastic	self-centered
ethical	self-motivated
family-oriented	self-reliant
friendly	serious
generous	thrifty
goal-oriented	truthful
group-oriented	unemotional
hardworking	unreliable
honest	youth-oriented

6.   Look again at the words that you have identified. What consistencies and inconsistencies do they disclose? What do the inconsistencies suggest about how you perceive members of your own culture? How may those inconsistencies affect your communicating with people whose culture differs from yours? Orally or in writing, share with your instructor and classmates your answers to those questions.

7.   Business communicators are often required to summarize information, and many executives restrict summaries to as few words as necessary. Begin to practice the art of summarizing. Citing evidence from the text, do the following:

   a.   Review the outline given at the beginning of Chapter 3. Summarize Topics I, II, and III.

   b.   Revise your writing so that you have one summary paragraph for each topic.

    c.   Summarize the resulting three paragraphs into one paragraph.

    d.   Compare your single paragraph with the chapter outline. Revise the paragraph as necessary to reflect fully, yet succinctly, the content of Chapter 3.

MULTICULTURAL INSIGHTS

1. Review your responses to the Multicultural Insights exercises at the ends of Chapters 1 and 2. In what ways has your study of Chapter 3 confirmed or contradicted your previous responses?

2. What traditions and customs associated with business uses of your native culture pertain to speaker-listener spacing? to attitudes concerning time? to courtesy and mutual respect?

3. How does metacommunication affect business transactions in your culture? in other cultures with which you are familiar?

4. What aspects of your native culture would probably make communication easy (or difficult) for someone familiar with another culture? Provide suggestions for bridging culture-to-culture communication gaps, especially those involving business transactions.

5. Language and culture interact. What aspects of the American English language make communication easy or difficult for you? What aspects of U.S. culture make communication easy or difficult for you?

6. Orally and in writing, translate the following words, phrases, and sentences into your native language. With your instructor's guidance, present the items and their translations to your fellow students.

a.	career goals	m.	business transactions
b.	products and services	n.	payment authorization
c.	management decisions	o.	Thank you very much for your assistance.
d.	a marketing proposal		
e.	employment procedures	p.	You're welcome; please call on me again.
f.	profit and loss		
g.	price reductions	q.	How may I help you?
h.	financial reports	r.	When will the conference begin?
i.	job security		
j.	business associates	s.	Please repeat the question.
k.	contract negotiations	t.	Shall we resume this discussion tomorrow?
l.	cost estimates		

ELECTRONICALLY ASSISTED COMMUNICATION

OBJECTIVES

After completing this chapter, you should be able to:

1. Describe the role of electronic media in business communication.
2. Assess likely consequences of using various electronic communication media.

3. Use communication criteria to evaluate all electronically assisted communication.

DECISIONS CASE

A major airline is looking for more efficient ways to schedule flight crews. Crew scheduling is done in its Kansas City, Missouri, office. Because the airline serves major airports worldwide, its pilots and flight attendants are located throughout the world. Those employees or their supervisors must call the crew-scheduling department for daily flight assignments.

Handling those incoming calls—about 7,000 per month, averaging one minute per call—is costly. In what ways can electronic technologies help the company communicate crew schedules more efficiently and effectively?[1]

Additional questions about this decision-making case are stated at the end of this chapter. Study the chapter before answering those questions.

CHAPTER CONTEXT

In recent years, computers have drastically changed the work environment. Tasks that once required many hours of laborious hand labor are now done with the ease of a few simple keystrokes.

To perform effectively and efficiently in today's businesses, you must be skilled in using electronic communication media. Using electronic media, however, does not guarantee communication success. Electronically mediated messages must satisfy the traditional communication criteria: appearance, accuracy, coherence, clarity, conciseness, and courtesy.

THE IMPACT OF ELECTRONIC TECHNOLOGY

During the decade of the 1980s, the computer became recognized as an essential tool at work and at school. In 1980 the ratio of computer terminals to white-collar workers in U.S. businesses was one to seven; in 1985 that ratio was one to three.[2] By 1990 nearly every white-collar worker had a computer at her or his workstation.

---

[1]Based on a case cited in Gail Siragusa, "Voice Mail Takes Off," *Administrative Management*, vol. 47, no. 4 (April 1986), pp. 43–48.

[2]Michael Lewis, "Computerization of the Workplace," *The State* (Columbia, SC), March 30, 1986, p. G1.

During the 1980s schools began preparing students for an electronic work environment. In 1983 the ratio of microcomputers to students in U.S. public elementary and secondary schools was 1 to 92.3; in only five years that ratio had changed to 1 to 26.9.[3]

Electronic technology has an impact on both written and oral communication. Coupled with advances in telecommunication transmission and networking capabilities, computer-processing capabilities affect all phases of the communication process: encoding, transmission, decoding, and feedback.

Encoding requires less dependence upon the traditional sender-assistant relationship. Instead, senders may use electronic dictation equipment to compose messages for later transcription by office support personnel. An emerging trend, however, is that message originators—salespersons, engineers, supervisors, and even managers—now compose and edit documents at a microcomputer equipped with word processing software, using little or no administrative support.

Message *transmission* relies heavily on electronic technology. Whereas transmission of written messages once was accomplished primarily by traditional postal systems, written messages can now be sent electronically throughout the world. Transmission of oral messages once consisted primarily of face-to-face and telephone communication, but oral-message transmission now includes teleconferencing and videoconferencing as well as systems to store voice messages for later reception and decoding.

Decoding of written communication now includes reading messages displayed on computer screens, often in nontraditional formats. In contrast with face-to-face communication, decoding of electronically mediated oral messages is affected by reduced access to nonverbal cues.

The capacity of electronic communication media to store as well as transmit and receive messages according to the needs of senders and receivers also affects communication timing and *feedback*. Although the speed of electronic communication can hasten message transmission and feedback, storage options permit delayed reception and feedback. Communication problems may arise when one party expects immediate feedback, but the other party uses delayed feedback.

Potential communication opportunities and hazards are identified in the following discussion of electronically assisted oral and written communication. Avoiding potential hazards, you can enjoy the advantages provided by electronic communication technologies.

In what ways can electronic communication technologies affect message encoding, transmission, and decoding?

How may feedback be affected by electronic media?

---

[3]U.S. Bureau of the Census, *Statistical Abstract of the United States: 1990,* 110th ed. (Washington, DC, 1990), p. 145.

ELECTRONICALLY ASSISTED ORAL COMMUNICATION

Many new techniques for communication by telephone and in conferences have entered the business communication environment. These techniques include voice messaging and electronic conferencing.

Voice Messages

Although the telephone has long been used in oral business communication, you have only a 17 percent chance of reaching a businessperson on the first phone call.[4] Electronic advances, however, improve telephone efficiency by permitting both concurrent and nonconcurrent telephone communication. **Concurrent telephone communication** occurs when a sender and a receiver participate during the same time frame. **Nonconcurrent telephone communication** occurs when a sender's oral message is transmitted, stored, and later forwarded to a receiver. Storage and forwarding functions may be performed by a recording device connected to the receiver's telephone (an answering machine) or by a company's voice mail system.

Voice mail (sometimes called **voice store-and-forward**) is an electronic message system operating through integration of a minicomputer with a company's telephone exchange. The minicomputer receives voice messages from the phone system, converts them to digital codes, and stores them on magnetic disks. The system's storage capacity is partitioned into "mailboxes" for its users. The computer transmits the messages according to the sender's instructions or holds the messages until the receiver asks for them. The most advanced systems offer these features:

1. *Message-waiting indication* alerts the user that a message is waiting.
2. *Call forwarding, direct mailbox* lets users forward all incoming calls to their mailboxes when they do not want to be disturbed. This feature may also permit transfer of calls to another number.
3. *Transfer to an operator* allows a caller to talk to an operator instead of leaving a message in the mailbox.
4. *Hard-copy retrieval* allows the receiver to retrieve the message at a computer terminal as well as by using a voice terminal.

Voice mail enhances productivity while retaining some conversational warmth. Telephone tag (telephone users repeatedly missing one another as

What is concurrent telephone communication? nonconcurrent?

What are the major features of voice mail?

---

[4]*Business & Economic Review,* vol. 37, no. 1 (October–November–December 1990), p. 43.

they place and return calls) and the extraneous information that accompanies many telephone calls can be virtually eliminated. Yet vocal emphasis and tone, often lost when an assistant writes a brief note to summarize an incoming call, are retained. Although some systems permit hard-copy retrieval, many receivers do not generate a hard copy. Therefore, voice mail is most effective when messages are concise.

Many businesses use voice mail to improve communication between traveling employees and their home offices. Other companies have found that voice mail enhances communication between major customers and sales representatives[5] and among supervisors of different shifts.[6]

Effective use of voice mail can yield substantial savings of time and money. Cost savings from reduction in number of calls, length of calls, rates for calls, and personnel time have been estimated at $45 to $195 per month per user.[7] Using those estimates, a company with 100 users could save from $4,500 to $19,500 monthly by using voice mail.

When you engage in concurrent telephone communication, immediate feedback and sender-receiver interaction contribute to your message clarity and completeness. However, when you use a nonconcurrent mode, such as voice mail, you must take extra steps to ensure those qualities.

As you give instructions to incoming callers, follow these steps:

1. Minimize background noise that could distort your message.
2. Identify yourself adequately.
3. Describe the kind of information the caller should leave.
4. Explain how the caller should use the system.

When leaving a message to be stored and forwarded, follow these steps:

1. Control background noise or distracting speech habits that can distort the message.
2. Listen to and follow instructions for leaving the message.
3. Identify yourself adequately.
4. State the purpose and time of your call.
5. Indicate the feedback, if any, that you desire.
6. State how, when, and where the message receiver can best reach you.

How can you improve communication clarity and completeness when using voice mail?

---

[5]Joseph V. Arn and Beverly Oswalt, *Office Automation* (Boston: Boyd & Fraser Publishing Company, 1988), p. 126.

[6]Raymond W. Beswick and N. L. Reinsch, Jr., "Attitudinal Responses to Voice Mail," *The Journal of Business Communication,* vol. 24, no. 3 (Summer 1987), pp. 23–35.

[7]Siragusa, "Voice Mail Takes Off," p. 44.

Besides changing one-to-one telephone communication, electronic technologies affect conference modes.

Electronic Conferences

Improved technology and rapidly declining costs have made electronic conferences increasingly attractive during the last decade. Whereas the cost of a fully equipped videoconference meeting room was $500,000 in the early 1980s, that cost was about $75,000 at the end of that decade. The cost of one hour of two-way, cross-country transmission declined from $1,000 to $500 during that time. By 1990 there were an estimated 1,250 videoconference facilities in dozens of countries, and the number was growing by 30 percent a year.[8] As a business communicator, you need to know how to use this medium effectively.

A **teleconference** is a concurrent telephone conversation among three or more people at different locations. Conferees are often alone at their respective telephones. But conference rooms equipped with special-purpose microphones and speakerphones also permit a group of people to assemble at one location to confer with another group elsewhere. If the room is also equipped with a computer terminal and screen for display of computer graphics during the conference, the meeting becomes an **audio-graphic teleconference**.[9]

In a **videoconference** (also called a **video teleconference**), both video transmission and audio transmission support concurrent communication among people at two or more locations. For greatest effectiveness, videoconferencing requires multiple television cameras and viewing screens, special sound systems for audio transmission and reception, appropriate lighting, and seating arrangements to complement camera angles. (See Illustration 4–1.)

Equipment requirements and the cost of video transmission make videoconferencing more expensive than teleconferencing. However, since videoconferencing permits transmission of both nonverbal and verbal cues, many managers justify the added cost as the price of a superior communication medium. Moreover, rapid cost reductions for equipment and transmission are making this medium increasingly available to businesses.

A major advantage of electronic conferencing is that communicators can save much of the travel time and expense required to reach remote conference locations. One user estimated that the $10,000 cost for three days of

In what ways are teleconferences and videoconferences alike? different?

---

[8]Charles Lunan, "Reduced Costs Are Helping Video Teleconference System Take Off," *The State* (Columbia, SC), September 16, 1990, p. 4-H.

[9]Larry R. Smeltzer and Charles M. Vance, "An Analysis of Graphic Use in Audio-Graphic Teleconferences," *The Journal of Business Communication*, vol. 26, no. 2 (Spring 1989), pp. 123–141.

Illustration 4–1   USING VIDEOCONFERENCE TECHNOLOGY

Photo courtesy Hotel Inter-Continental, New York

face-to-face meetings was reduced to $2,500 for two hours of video teleconferencing.[10] Freed from the need to assemble conferees in one location, managers gain scheduling flexibility. Regularly scheduled short conferences meet many normal conference needs, and emergency conferences can be convened quickly.

The efficiencies of electronic communication are not limited to oral messages. Electronic technology has also changed the written communication process.

ELECTRONICALLY ASSISTED WRITTEN COMMUNICATION

In the business environment, many written messages contain both verbal and numerical information. Therefore, a complete electronic communication system consists of subsystems that enable efficient compilation and transmission of both verbal and numerical information. A typical electronic system

---

[10]Lunan, loc. cit.

today includes word processing, database, spreadsheet, and graphics capacity, as well as equipment for electronic transmission of messages.

Word Processing

A major element of an electronic communication system is **word processing**, the application of computer technology to the production of written messages. Word processing saves time in message production, particularly during the revision and editing stages. Word processing can also economize on document storage, because completed messages (and their many versions before completion) can be stored on electronic media that occupy considerably less space than their printed counterparts.

From an individual perspective, word processing is a communicator's use of an electronic typewriter or microcomputer programmed for text manipulation. From a systems perspective, however, word processing is the integration of electronic hardware and software, technically trained people, and appropriate procedures for creating and processing written messages.

A basic word processing system includes microcomputers or typewriters with electronic processing and storage capacity. The electronic memory permits the user to store, retrieve, revise, and reproduce textual material with little effort. Advanced word processing systems integrate several electronically controlled communication tools—dictation units, typewriters, computers, information storage-and-retrieval equipment, telecommunications—for efficient production of written messages.

Word processing systems are designed to accommodate three major message modes: correspondence, narrative and statistical documents, and form messages. Letters and memos, normally one page in length, comprise the largest word processing volume. In the 1980s, machine dictation and longhand were the most common inputs for letters and memos, but keying (typing) by the originator is rapidly becoming the primary input.

Narrative and statistical documents, such as operating reports, budgets, and policy manuals, depend on analysis and synthesis of data from several sources. Such documents, which may require revisions or special formatting, are especially amenable to word processing production. The original data, either verbal or numerical, are entered into the system by keyboard or by transfer from database, spreadsheet, or graphics files. The originator or an assistant then proofreads and edits the copy. Production time is saved because only the copy changes need be keyed as the document is revised.

Identical or nearly identical messages, based on a master draft or sent to more than one person, are called **form messages**. The growth of word processing systems has increased the business uses of form messages when per-

What does word processing encompass?

sonal correspondence is not necessary. Form messages are often used for these purposes:

1. to represent single sales messages, series of such messages, and units in a follow-up system
2. to answer inquiries and requests
3. to acknowledge orders and payments
4. to handle simple claims and adjustments
5. to serve as units in collection procedures

A form message has two notable advantages over an individually prepared message:

1. *It multiplies skill.* An expert communicator can prepare master forms, adapt them to a specific situation, and give precise instructions for their use. Then less experienced communicators, guided by the originator's expertise and by proper supervision, can use the forms efficiently for numerous business situations.
2. *It saves cost.* One master draft of a form letter can be reproduced, virtually without limit, at relatively low unit cost. Individually prepared messages are expensive.

Form messages involve use of these communication aids: guide forms, complete forms, and paragraph forms.

A **guide form** consists of a detailed outline and/or a model message based on an outline. A communicator uses the guide form as a reference for message content and format. For example, suppose you ask your instructor to write an employment recommendation on your behalf. Yours may be one of many similar requests that your instructor receives every year. To expedite communication, your instructor may compose a message guide form identifying the teacher-student association, the length of that association, the number and nature of courses involved, your performance in each of those courses, and other appropriate data for recommending you to a prospective employer. Using the guide form would ensure that every recommendation written by the instructor includes those categories of information, but the particular data used for the letter recommending *you* would apply to your circumstances specifically.

A **complete form**, however, is an entire message sent without adaptation or revision. A complete form may be reproduced on letterhead by a copy process or by word processor. If a complete form is to be reproduced individually, the form often is given a code number. A communicator specifies the code and identifies the addressee. An assistant then produces the already prepared message.

A **paragraph form** consists of a group of related sentences that can be combined as units of a message. The paragraphs can be fitted so closely to particular needs that they give the effect of personalized dictation. Using careful judgment, a communicator can join paragraph forms into almost limitless patterns that suit differing circumstances.

Paragraph forms and complete forms often are grouped in a booklike collection called a **dictaform**. The paragraphs are grouped under subject headings—for example, headings for sales promotion, credit approval or rejection, and collection. Each subject heading may have a certain number of pages reserved in the dictaform, as shown by this example:

<aside>
Describe the most commonly used types of form messages.
</aside>

```
                    DICTAFORM INDEX


          Subjects                        Pages

Administrative Reporting...........  2-14

Acknowledging Customer Orders......  15-20

Promoting Sales....................  21-33

Following Up on Sales..............  34-42

Responding to Credit Requests......  43-52

Responding to Adjustment Requests..  53-61

Enforcing Collections..............  62-75

Goodwill Messages for Special

    Occasions......................  76-85
```

Each page of a dictaform presents a group of paragraphs. Each paragraph is designated A, B, C, etc. The dictator scans the dictaform, selects the paragraphs needed, and constructs a complete message by jotting down the symbols; for instance, 7A, 9C, 11D, 12K, 14E. An assistant then copies the paragraphs in the order indicated.

Assume that you wish to construct a sales-promotion message from the dictaform index. You would turn, in this illustration, to "Promoting Sales," pages 21–33 of the form book. Pages 21–24 offer paragraphs for attracting your reader's attention; perhaps you select 21A (paragraph A from page 21):

> To meet your requirements for rapid and reliable investment services, Foster & Schuyler offers you a new commodity section geared to prompt, personalized attention.

Pages 25–27 of the form book show a group of paragraphs designed to develop your reader's interest; maybe you select 26F:

> These Foster & Schuyler investment aids are at your disposal:
> --detailed briefings on markets with notable potential
> --weekly summaries of trading patterns and price outlooks
> --modern telecommunication equipment for up-to-the-second data

Pages 28–30 present paragraphs for stimulating and reinforcing your reader's desire; you choose 29C:

> With Foster & Schuyler, you can monitor exchange developments as they occur. With Foster & Schuyler, you can share instantaneous reports from worldwide news services. With Foster & Schuyler, you can profit from the advice of professional account executives who have experience and insight.

Pages 31–33 provide paragraphs for eliciting favorable response, "action-getting" paragraphs; you select 31J:

> Because speculation in commodity futures can be risky, you need sufficient capital to offset possible reverses. And you need current information...which F&S is ready to supply. For that information, please visit our office or telephone (608) 555-2874.

Having chosen your paragraphs from the dictaform, you give their index symbols (21A, 26F, 29C, 31J) to your assistant, who turns to the dictaform, locates those paragraphs, and writes them in the order you indicated. A word processor can be programmed to do the job in seconds.

An example of the result appears in Illustration 4–2. (*Note:* The index symbols would not appear on the letter. They are shown to illustrate the result of dictaform composition.)

Database, Spreadsheet, and Graphics Applications

Many business messages require input, analysis, storage, and retrieval of quantitative data. In today's computerized office, managers use microcomputers equipped with database, spreadsheet, and graphics software for analysis and presentation of quantitative data.

Database software enables the computer to act as an electronic filing cabinet for both verbal and numerical data. For example, customer names, addresses, and telephone numbers can be stored along with product numbers, quantities, and prices of purchases. Users can sort the data to meet their management and communication needs: by customer, sales territory, product, etc.

In addition to maintaining private databases, increasing numbers of companies subscribe to commercial or government database services. Such database services satisfy a wide range of information needs. For example, *Population Index* gives demographic data and the *Official Airline Guide* consists of flight schedules. One of the newest data bases, TIGER (Topographic Integrated Geographic Encoding Reference), combines 1990 census data with U.S. Geological Survey geographic coordinates. When used with mapping

What are communication uses for database software?

Illustration 4–2   COMPLETED DICTAFORM LETTER

FOSTER & SCHUYLER INVESTMENT SERVICES
618 Washington Avenue, West
Madison, WI 53703-2219
608-555-2874

April 17, 19--

Mrs. Margaret A. Wilson
100 Baynard Court
Madison, WI 53715-7199

Dear Mrs. Wilson

21A   To meet your requirements for rapid and reliable
       investment services, Foster & Schuyler offers you a new
       commodity section geared to prompt, personalized
       attention.

26F   These Foster & Schuyler investment aids are at your
       disposal:

       -- detailed briefings on markets with notable
          potential

       -- weekly summaries of trading patterns and price
          outlooks

       -- modern telecommunication equipment for up-to-
          the-second data.

29C   With Foster & Schuyler, you can monitor exchange
       developments as they occur. With Foster & Schuyler,
       you can share instantaneous reports from worldwide news
       services. With Foster & Schuyler, you can profit from
       the advice of professional account executives who have
       experience and insight.

31J   Because speculation in commodity futures can be risky,
       you need sufficient capital to offset possible reverses.
       And you need current information . . . which F&S is
       ready to supply. For that information, please visit
       our office or telephone (608) 555-2874.

       Sincerely yours

       Gerald Sherlock
       Investment Counselor

software, TIGER enables businesses to do highly detailed market mapping and data analysis.[11]

In a fully integrated system, quantitative data stored in database files can be transported into spreadsheet files for analysis. Verbal information from a database or spreadsheet analysis can be imported into a word processing file for use in letters and reports.

Spreadsheet software allows users to analyze quantitative data quickly and easily. The data may be keyed directly into the spreadsheet or transferred from a database file. Such software is used widely for calculating the results of operations and forecasting results under assumed or "what if" conditions. Both numerical data and mathematical formulas can be entered into a spreadsheet. By changing data or formulas, managers can quickly see the financial impact of changed business conditions.

Graphics software enables managers to visualize the results of quantitative analysis. Most spreadsheet programs include simple graphics programs that generate line, bar, and pie charts based on data derived from a spreadsheet. With fully integrated software, those charts can be transferred into a word processing application for use in a written document. More complex software, sometimes called **presentation software**, permits production of sophisticated graphics and presentation of visual aids by computerized projection techniques.

New communication technologies have brought about major changes in the production of written business messages. Message transmission has also experienced dramatic changes.

Electronic Message Transmission

When you must transmit a written message quickly, telecommunication services can help you. **Telecommunication** refers to systems for transmitting voice, written, and data messages over short and long distances. Telecommunication integrates telephone, telegraph, radio, and electronic technologies into worldwide relay systems operated by public service telephone companies.

One of the important functions of telecommunication technology is to link different kinds of equipment into networks for efficient information exchange. An individual computer user can expand her or his communication network with a **modem**. This input/output device connects a microcomputer with the telephone system. A modem converts computer-generated signals

What are communication uses for spreadsheet software?

What are communication uses for graphics software?

What is the role of telecommunication technology?

[11]Paul H. Lewis, "Is There a TIGER in Your Library?" *Business and Economic Review,* vol. 37, no. 3 (April–May–June 1991), pp. 23–27.

to audio signals, thereby allowing the computer to be connected via telephone lines to other modem-equipped microcomputers or larger computers.

Another linkage system is the **local-area network (LAN)**, a privately owned network within a geographical area bounded completely by private property. For example, several microcomputers linked by wire or cable to a mainframe computer in one building form a LAN.

If a network connects computers in offices on one side of the street to computers in offices on the opposite side of the street, it is no longer a LAN, because the linkage crosses public property. The network is then called a **wide-area network (WAN)**. A WAN links information processing equipment in geographically distant areas. Using telephone lines, microwaves, and satellites, a WAN can link equipment as near as across the street or as far as the other side of the globe. Consequently, a WAN is also called a **global network**.

What is electronic mail?

What does facsimile transmission contribute to an electronic mail system?

Electronic mail is the integration of privately owned (or leased) electronic transmission devices with telecommunication services provided by the public utilities. Many computer users refer to computer-to-computer message transmission as electronic mail or **E-mail**. However, office systems experts use *electronic mail* to signify a system that may include facsimile transmission systems, computer-based message systems, and communicating word processors, as well as telegram or Telex II (**TWX**) services provided through Western Union. Selection of an electronic mail service depends on need for feedback, speed desired, editing requirements, length of message, and cost.

A **facsimile transmission system (fax)** combines electronic copying technologies with telecommunication transmission. With such a system, a communicator places a document into a scanner-transmitter at the sending location, and an identical document is printed by a receiver-recorder at another location. The system makes an electronic image of the entire document. Thus, it can transmit graphs and pictures as well as words and numbers.

One of the newest fax products is a very small portable machine engineered to ensure reliable transmission over cellular phone lines.[12] Equipped with a small portable fax machine and a cellular phone, a user can transmit written messages from an automobile or a remote field site.

Facsimile transmission time depends on the quality of the system and the amount of information on a page. Some units can send letter-size copy anywhere in the world within 30 seconds. Facsimile transmission is sometimes used during a teleconference or videoconference to send documents among conferees.

A **computer-based message network** allows users to enter messages via

---

[12]Pictured in *The State* (Columbia, SC), September 30, 1990, p. 3-H.

What is a computer-based message system?

keyboard input at computer terminals. Those messages are sent to designated recipients' electronic mailboxes. The sender and receiver need not be in concurrent communication. When users access their mailboxes, messages are displayed on a computer video screen. After reading a message, the receiver can erase it, store it, or print a copy of it.

Computer-based messaging is used extensively for interoffice communication, and in some businesses it is rapidly replacing the written interoffice memorandum for certain kinds of communication. Studies have shown that this electronic medium is used primarily for sending and receiving production-oriented information but less frequently for resolving disagreements, negotiating, or exchanging confidential information.[13]

Computer-based messaging has generated new formats and protocols for interoffice communication. Messages are typically short, direct, personal, and sometimes even jovial.[14] Messages are single spaced, as are written memorandums; but some software does not permit double spacing between paragraphs because depressing the Enter key signals the computer to transmit the message. The simplified memo format described in Chapter 8 is more efficient than the traditional format for this medium because the simplified format omits the extraneous words *To, From, Date,* and *Subject.* Even that format can be simplified with some systems. If the log-on and transmission processes automatically identify the sender and receiver, their names need not be keyed into the message. (See Illustration 4–3.)

Sometimes network users exchange several messages about a single topic. This use of a computer-based message network is called **computer conferencing**. In computer conferencing, receivers display and evaluate messages from several senders simultaneously. In contrast with videoconferencing or teleconferencing, computer conferencing is nonconcurrent and all messages are written. Moreover, the nonconcurrent communication mode lets participants examine issues at length before responding. Because messages are written and nonconcurrent, this medium is more appropriately considered a form of electronic mail than a conference mode.

A **communicating word processor** can exchange information with another word processor. The communication link may be by LAN or WAN hookup. This system permits keying of a message at one location with editing and printing at another location. Since some receiving units operate unattended, users can send messages at night when telephone transmission rates are low.

---

[13]John Sherblom, "Direction Function, and Signature in Electronic Mail," *The Journal of Business Communication,* vol. 25, no. 4 (Fall 1988), pp. 39–54.

[14]J. A. Turner, "E-Mail Technology Has Boomed, but Manners of Its Users Fall Short of Perfection," *The Chronicle of Higher Education,* April 13, 1988, pp. A1, A16.

Illustration 4–3   COMPUTER-BASED MESSAGING (E-MAIL)

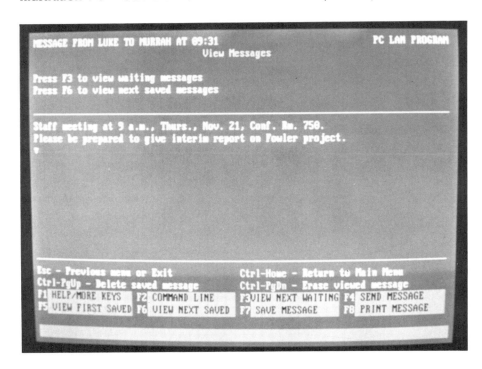

A communicating word processing system is used less between companies than within companies because hardware and software are frequently incompatible. The system is, however, highly functional within a company with widely dispersed offices. For example, a national insurance company with home offices in Jacksonville, Florida, can process insurance policies for agents throughout the nation and transmit the documents to agents' offices for printing and delivery to clients.

The new electronic communication technologies have created many challenges for communication managers. Although the hardware and software can facilitate communication, electronic technology may impair communication if it is used thoughtlessly.

How do communicating word processors contribute to information processing?

CHALLENGES OF ELECTRONICALLY ASSISTED COMMUNICATION

Maximum benefits from electronic technology depend upon effective management of the system, applying criteria for effective communication to all electronically produced messages, and using the system ethically.

What managerial
challenges does
information
processing present?

Managerial Considerations

Firms that have successfully implemented electronic communication systems emphasize clear, complete communication within the firm while planning, organizing, and controlling the system.

Planning. Objectives of the planning process should be to determine needs for data processing, word processing, and transmission services and to identify hardware and software that will satisfy those needs. Managers responsible for planning information processing systems use several internal communication media, including memos, problem-solving groups, conferences, and surveys of employees, to meet those objectives.

Organizing. Communication of policies and procedures is essential to organize and activate the system. Training sessions, conferences, procedures manuals, and job descriptions are examples of communication media used for the organizing and activating functions.

Controlling. For system control, users must communicate needs and expectations to support personnel. For example, a user must communicate clearly how long a document or file, such as a letter or an address list, is to be retained. The originator should also assume responsibility for updating, revising, or requesting deletion of files that have been stored. A system user who faces a time constraint should communicate that need clearly and courteously to the support personnel and monitor progress on the task.

The popularity of facsimile transmission has created new control problems for managers. Procrastinators tend to delay writing messages and then send them by fax instead of using less-expensive mail services. Broadcast or bulk fax services have also arisen, resulting in increasing volumes of junk fax—messages that are useless to the receiver. Since the receiver supplies the paper to print a fax message, high volumes of junk fax add to operating costs. Moreover, unauthorized fax use can tie up the equipment and delay receipt of desired messages. Businesses experiencing such problems have resorted to protecting fax numbers as carefully as they protect computer access codes.

Communication Considerations

What communication
challenges does
information
processing present?

A major communication challenge is capitalizing upon the efficiencies of electronic technology while retaining the goodwill of message receivers. Word processing capabilities, for example, permit a communicator to use well-composed—or poorly composed—messages repeatedly. Storing forms, paragraphs, or complete texts of letters or reports for later use saves time and money. But if stored materials are used thoughtlessly, goodwill may be sacrificed. Some word processing users attempt to personalize messages by inserting the receiver's name into otherwise impersonal text. However, if a company erroneously places 30-year-old Ms. Watson on a mailing list for a letter to be sent to retirees, personalizing the letter will do little to gain Ms. Watson's goodwill.

Effective word processing users consider the message context before deciding which word processing feature to employ. As shown in Illustration 4–4, the context governs the level of personalization, suggests goodwill implications, and directs the communicator toward effective decisions.

Senders must also evaluate the length and tone of messages transmitted electronically. Readability and transmission costs are directly related to document length. Since multiple-page documents are more difficult to read from a computer screen than from hard copy, receivers may prefer computer-based messages that fill no more than one computer screen. Longer messages are often transmitted by fax; but lengthy documents are expensive for the sender, who pays telephone transmission costs, and for the receiver, who pays paper costs. Attempting to make electronically transmitted messages brief, some senders become curt. Effective communicators, however, recognize that a courteous, empathetic tone can be maintained along with conciseness.

Effective communicators are also cautious about transmitting sensitive information electronically. Empathetic communicators often rewrite sensitive messages several times before transmitting them. To ensure confidentiality and adequate revision, writers of sensitive messages may do well to use traditional transmission modes instead of computer transmission.

Ethical Considerations

What ethical considerations affect use of electronic communication technology?

Along with advances in electronic communication tools have come new ethical concerns. Message senders must respect the privacy and property rights of message receivers. For example, when a customer or supplier gives you a voice-mail access code or a fax number, the intent is to facilitate business communication. Your ethical responsibility is to use access information for the intended purposes, not to clog the receiver's communication system with irrelevant messages. Moreover, releasing access codes or passwords to unauthorized users betrays the confidence others have placed in you.

The volume of junk fax has given rise to legislation restricting unsolicited fax messages. In Connecticut, people receiving unsolicited messages may seek up to $200 damages from the sender. In Maryland, a sender attempting to sell goods, services, or real estate by fax without first contacting the recipient is liable to fines up to $1,000. In Oregon, anyone sending faxes to a customer

Illustration 4–4 MESSAGE CONTEXT GUIDE FOR WORD
PROCESSING DECISIONS

Context	1. Receiver is unique; in a unique situation.
	2. Receiver is one of a narrowly identified group.
	3. Receiver is one of a mass audience.
Examples	1a. Response to complex question asked by a client.
	1b. First notice of an overdue account.
	2a. Mass mail advertisement of a new product.
	2b. Special request.
	3a. Announcement of a special sale to selected customers.
	3b. Announcement of a change in office hours.
Goodwill and Personalization Considerations	1. Personal message required; possible loss of goodwill if impersonal.
	2. Personalized form message may promote goodwill.
	3. No goodwill loss if impersonal; possible sacrifice of goodwill if personalized.
Word Processing Decisions	1. Use machine dictation for personal, individualized message.
	2. Use form message, personalized by inserting receiver's name.
	3. Use undisguised, mass-produced message; no names inserted.

who asks not to get them may be fined up to $25,000.[15] It appears that legislatures and courts are prepared to protect businesses from unethical users of communication technology.

---

[15]"Legislation Affecting Faxes," *Public Relations Journal,* vol. 46, no. 4 (April 1990), p. 12.

REVIEW AND TRANSITION

As a business communicator in the 1990s and beyond, you will use many electronic tools—voice mail, microcomputers, electronic conference facilities, electronic mail services—for message origination and transmission. You will use those tools as routinely as your business communication predecessors used pencils, pens, typewriters, paper, telephones, and postal systems.

Effective users of electronic communication media consider the purpose of each message and the context in which it will be received. Be guided by your receiver's—and your own—information needs, time constraints, cost constraints, and attitudes toward electronic technology as you choose an appropriate communication medium for each message. Be guided also by your ethical obligations to others in a complex communication environment.

Many of your business communication responsibilities will be conducted in collaboration with other employees. Electronic communication media facilitate collaborative communication, which is the topic of Chapter 5.

YOUR DECISIONS FOR CHAPTER 4

Review the Decisions Case for Chapter 4. Which, if any, of the electronic communications media did you suggest before you read Chapter 4? In what ways, if any, would you change your recommendations now? Why?

DISCUSSION QUESTIONS

A.   Within the context of Chapter 4, what are appropriate definitions and examples for these terms?

   1.   nonconcurrent telephone communication
   2.   voice mail
   3.   teleconference
   4.   videoconference
   5.   form messages
   6.   electronic mail
   7.   facsimile transmission system (fax)

B.   In what ways have electronic communication technologies already affected you? How will those technologies affect you as a business communicator?

C.   In what ways do nonconcurrent and concurrent telephone communication differ?

D.   How can voice mail facilitate business communication?

E.   What are the advantages and disadvantages of face-to-face conferences? teleconferences? videoconferences?

F. What are advantages and disadvantages of form messages?

G. What is word processing? What examples of word processing have affected you as a student? as a consumer? as an employer or employee?

H. What are advantages and disadvantages of electronic mail?

I. How are goodwill and word processing related?

J. What ethical issues, besides those cited in the text, confront users of electronic communication technology?

APPLICATIONS

1. Select any communication medium listed in Discussion Question A. Interview someone who uses that medium in her or his work. Discuss the person's positive and negative experiences with the medium. Orally or in writing present a summary of your interview results.

2. Select any communication medium listed in Discussion Question A. Using books and business journals, learn more about that medium and its current use in business. Orally or in writing, present a summary of your findings.

3. If a computer-based messaging service (E-mail) is available on your campus, interview students and faculty who use the service. Identify the service(s) available and the positive and negative aspects of those forms of E-mail. Orally or in writing, present your findings.

4. Rewrite the following items to demonstrate the business communication criteria of accuracy, coherence, clarity, conciseness, and courtesy:

   a. The genral manger is responsible for administeration of company policys and proceedures in acordence with state laws, and fedral regulations.

   b. Anders Corporation rewards employees who are loyal, productive, and have communication skills.

   c. This vehicle is available with a five speed transmission 90 HP 12 valve fuel injected engine and three year 36000 mile bumper to bumper warranty.

   d. Morgan writes reports that are accurate, clear, and without unnecessary words.

   e. T. Y. Chen whom is president of this firm earned a masters degree at you're college didnt she?

   f. Needless to say, it is incumbent upon us to implement economies at this present point in time.

   g. Priced at only $35,000 I can assure you that this property is a good buy.

    h.   What computer software do you recommend with the capabilities we require?

    i.   The insurance coverage can begin immediately which you inquired about.

    j.   Enclosed herewith for your information is the summary of sales by GroCorp for Region 5.

    k.   The fire department's main responsibility is to provide manual fire suppression in the event of fire.

    l.   Because of physical and organizational separation, access of one group to another is often hindered.

5.   You are a communication specialist employed by Silva, Inc., a producer of household products. Your customer services department has asked you to compose form messages for use in responding to customer inquiries or complaints.

    a.   Write three different paragraphs from which a correspondent may select a letter beginning. Identify the context for which you recommend use of each paragraph.

    b.   Write three different paragraphs for use as the final paragraph of a letter. Identify the context in which you recommend each be used.

6.   As communications director for Reliable Casualty Company, you participate in this lunchroom conversation:

    CARMEN: I dictate all correspondence. I refuse to give up the personal touch. Every client deserves personal attention.

    EMI: I use form messages most of the time. They make me more productive; that's what word processing is all about—productivity.

    BRANTLEY: [Looking at you] I certainly wish we had some guides for deciding when to use form messages and individually dictated letters. Sometimes form messages don't say what I want to say, but I don't want to spend time dictating a message. Will you prepare some guides for us?

    YOU: That's a great idea, Brantley. I'll have them on your desks tomorrow morning.

Write a set of guides for appropriate uses of form messages. Include guides for personalizing those messages. As directed by your instructor, use a format that will facilitate your readers' use of the guides.

7.   Some Reliable Casualty Company employees use its recently installed facsimile transmission system for all written communication from branch offices to corporate headquarters. Others never use it. As communications director, write a set of guides for use of the system. As directed by

your instructor, use a format that will facilitate your readers' use of the guides.

8. You are the manager of the London office of Global Gifts, Inc., which has its headquarters in Minneapolis, MN, USA. Global Gifts is a mail order company specializing in unique—but expensive—collectible items garnered from around the world. The company markets its upscale merchandise by catalog to carefully selected customers.

   Global has offices in London, England; Paris, France; Madrid, Spain; Amsterdam, the Netherlands; Geneva, Switzerland; and Oslo, Norway. Each office has a manager and two or three field agents who are responsible for locating and purchasing high-quality merchandise that will appeal to Global's mail order customers.

   Because of volatile exchange rates and the competition in the collectibles market, field agents often must decide quickly whether to purchase specific items. However, independent purchasing decisions have contributed to an imbalanced inventory for the company. For example, agents from the Madrid, Amsterdam, and Oslo offices bought similar silver chafing dishes, resulting in an overstock of chafing dishes.

   You think that Global Gifts can solve this problem with an information processing system. If necessary, conduct library research or interview businesspeople to learn more about specific ways in which an information processing system could meet Global's needs.

   Write a message to J. P. Wilson, president of Global Gifts, Inc. For this message, use a format recommended by your instructor. In the message propose the following:

   a. Establish a computerized inventory data base in the Minneapolis office. (Add details based on your research.)
   b. Install facsimile transmission equipment and computer terminals in all European offices and in the Minneapolis headquarters. (Add details.)
   c. Provide field agents with portable laptop computers and portable fax machines equipped with modems. (Add details.)
   d. Train field agents to use the equipment for verifying inventory and communicating with other agents about potential purchases.

MULTICULTURAL INSIGHTS

1. Do communicators who conduct business in your native culture tend to use word processing equipment more or less extensively than do communicators in the United States? Why? Give evidence from your readings, observations, or experience to support your position.

2. What communication protocols, if any, would encourage or discour-

age the use of word processing by communicators who conduct business in your native language?

3. Besides word processing, what electronic media, if any, are used among business communicators of your native culture? What economic or cultural factors account for the differences in use? Cite evidence from your readings, observations, or experience to support your position.

COLLABORATIVE COMMUNICATION

CHAPTER OUTLINE

OBJECTIVES

After completing this chapter, you should be able to:

1. Promote effective collaboration by perceptive use and interpretation of nonverbal symbols.
2. Participate effectively in small problem-solving groups.
3. Exercise the responsibilities of conference leader or conferee.
4. Contribute to planning, organizing, directing, and controlling a collaborative writing project.

DECISIONS CASE[1]

"Listen to this," says Donna, your lunch companion. "I volunteered to work on the technical manual for the XL-92 computer. I know the hardware well and thought this would be a welcome change of pace, but I'm beginning to wonder what I got into."

You raise your eyebrows questioningly, encouraging her to continue.

"You wouldn't believe the people I have to work with. We have a guy with a degree in journalism—he should be pretty good at writing, and he knows the product. Then there's a woman who spends her evenings playing percussion in a jazz band! I don't know why she volunteered. She hasn't shown much interest in anything we've tried to do during our first week. Add to that two women who know nothing about the hardware. They do seem eager to contribute to the project, but they're short on technical skill. Finally, there's the real technical wizard, but he has difficulty communicating his expertise to other group members."

You nod sympathetically.

"I'm the one who tries to get things started every day, but we haven't made much progress. You did some group projects at the university, didn't you? What do you think I should do? How can we become a functional group?"

What experiences have you had with task groups? What advice can you give Donna about working in such groups?

Additional questions about this decision-making case are stated at the end of this chapter. Study the chapter before answering those questions.

---

[1]A situation similar to this is reported in Charles H. Sides, "Collaboration in a Hardware Technical Writing Group: A Real-World Laboratory," *The Bulletin of the Association for Business Communication*, vol. 54, no. 2 (June 1991), pp. 11–15.

CHAPTER CONTEXT

Increasingly, career success requires the ability to interact harmoniously with members of a task group. In the world of work, major decisions with serious consequences are often made by groups. Project teams, quality circles, committees, task forces, meetings, conferences—all of these work groups require cooperation and collaboration among members. Communication skills essential for group participation range from accurately perceiving and interpreting nonverbal signals to writing reports in collaboration with other group members.

THE COLLABORATIVE COMMUNICATION ENVIRONMENT

What are business examples of collaborative communication?

To **collaborate** is to work with others to achieve an objective. In the business environment, collaboration is required to achieve many organizational goals. For example, the introduction of a new product requires collaboration among personnel in research and development, finance, purchasing, marketing, manufacturing, and human resource administration.

Collaboration is not limited to work within an organization. Today, many businesspeople unite with individuals or groups outside of their organizations to address common problems. For example, in recent years many communities have formed business-education task forces to investigate ways to improve education for business. Similarly, a group representing a community's residents, businesses, and governing bodies may collaborate to formulate a community development plan.

Those examples demonstrate important facts about collaborative work groups. They are comprised of individuals who have diverse values, attitudes, abilities, and goals. Yet those individuals share a problem and depend upon one another for its satisfactory solution. To collaborate effectively, group members often must subordinate personal feelings and goals to the group objective.

What are the characteristics of four collaborative communication modes?

For many people, *collaboration* evokes the image of a face-to-face problem-solving group. However, in today's international and technological business environment, group members may represent various cultures and may be physically separated from one another. Therefore, contemporary decision groups use several modes of collaborative communication. (See Illustration 5–1.)

Collaborative modes differ on several dimensions: message flow, participant locations, communication signals, and technical mediation. In face-to-face, teleconference, and videoconference modes the participants are in concurrent communication (immediate, continuous oral interchange). In a teleconference or videoconference, however, the participants are at multiple sites,

Illustration 5–1   COLLABORATIVE COMMUNICATION MODES

MODE	CHARACTERISTICS			
	Message Flow	**Participant Locations**	**Communication Signals**	**Technical Mediation**
Face-to-Face	Concurrent	Single	Oral Nonverbal Written	Nonmediated
Teleconference	Concurrent	Multiple	Oral Restricted nonverbal Limited written	Telecommunication (oral)
Videoconference	Concurrent	Multiple	Oral Restricted nonverbal Limited written	Telecommunication (oral/visual)
Computer conference	Nonconcurrent	Multiple	Written	Computer network (LAN or WAN)

thereby limiting the use of supplementary nonverbal or written signals. Users of electronic conferencing technology sometimes supplement oral messages with written messages sent by postal services or facsimile transmission. A videoconference can also accommodate visual transmission of written messages. In a teleconference, users have no access to visual cues, thereby limiting nonverbal communication. Videoconferencing also partially restricts visual cues because participants are often seated, thereby limiting natural movements. In contrast, computer conferencing is a nonconcurrent mode of collaboration. This medium permits participants to ponder, look up information, and edit messages before responding to other members of the collaborative group.

As you can see, collaboration requires effective oral, written, and nonverbal communication. In addition, some collaborative efforts rely on multicultural understanding and technical communication skills.

Nonverbal communication has a role in some modes described by Illustration 5–1. Therefore, you should consider how nonverbal signals add to or distract from verbal messages.

NONVERBAL COMMUNICATION IN THE COLLABORATIVE ENVIRONMENT

In a study of the impact of nonverbal communication in organizations, 92 percent of the respondents (505 business persons ranging from line workers to executives) rated nonverbal aspects important or very important in group conversations, such as committee meetings and department meetings.[2]

By definition, nonverbal communication is wordless. It may be transmitted by touch (the gentle pressure of a friendly hand on your shoulder can communicate encouragement). It can be conveyed by taste (flavors of food can communicate loving, careful preparation) or by smell (aromas or odors can signify savory foods or pleasant surroundings). It can also be conveyed by hearing (a horn may signify the approach of a vehicle). Most often, however, nonverbal communication is perceived visually and is transmitted by appearances, timings and distances, body language (postures, movements, gestures, and facial expressions) and vocal tones.[3]

How is nonverbal communication transmitted?

Appearances

The way someone or something looks can create or bridge communication gaps. For instance, the appearance of a job applicant or an employee may be interpreted as evidence of personal values, attitudes, and abilities. Appearance is so significant in business that corporations and individuals sometimes employ wardrobe engineers for advice about professional dress. A wardrobe engineer uses research data to manipulate a person's clothing and accessories for desired effects. A major outcome of wardrobe engineering research is the recognition that audience characteristics influence reactions to appearance. For example, doctors, Wall Street brokers, and blue-collar workers react differently to a pin-stripe suit.

Some generalizations about appearance can be made, however. Soiled, crumpled, or ostentatious clothing; poorly groomed hands or fingernails; heavy cosmetics or colognes; superfluous jewelry or accessories—these and other facets of personal appearance can block communication. Rightly or

---

[2]Gerald H. Graham, Jeanne Unruh, and Paul Jennings, "The Impact of Nonverbal Communication in Organizations: A Survey of Perceptions," *The Journal of Business Communication,* vol. 28, no. 1 (Winter 1991), pp. 45–62.

[3]Chapter 3 presented some cultural differences in nonverbal behaviors. The discussion in this chapter relates to life-styles in the United States primarily. For additional insights, see J. Vernon Jensen, "Perspective on Nonverbal Intercultural Communication," in Larry A. Samovar and Richard E. Porter, *Intercultural Communication: A Reader,* 4th ed. (Belmont, CA: Wadsworth Publishing Company, 1985), pp. 256–272.

How may appearance
affect
communication?

wrongly, observers take appearances as cues, as indications of care or carelessness toward oneself, toward other people, and toward responsibilities.

Timings and Distances

Effective communicators observe protocols for use of time and space. United
States businesspeople tend to segment time into five-minute periods. A person who arrives less than five minutes late for an appointment seldom apol-
ogizes. At five minutes a brief apology is expected, but communication usually
continues. Beyond 10 or 15 minutes, however, the latecomer risks facing
communication barriers.

A person's observance or abuse of time expectations can profoundly affect
the climate for collaboration. For example, when you deliberately place a telephone call so that it is received very early in the morning or very late at
night, your timing may convey urgency. An unimportant telephone call received at dawn or at midnight is unlikely to please your listener. When you
honor established meeting times—beginning and ending—you also show respect for your collaborative partners.

How may timings
and distances
influence
collaboration?

An appropriate distance between collaborative partners depends upon
previous relationships, level of intimacy, communication purpose, and available physical space. Informal or business conversational distance is usually
just outside easy touching range. When you lean close to someone during a
face-to-face conversation, you may imply that your message is confidential. If
you approach a face-to-face listener too closely, however, he or she may in-
stinctively move away from you, thereby breaking rather than reinforcing
rapport. Unless obviously justified, deviations from space norms tend to
make one or all parties to the communication uncomfortable.

Body Language and Vocal Tone

Body and facial positions or movements, along with vocal tone, are also nonverbal communicators. Unless deliberately distorted, these nonverbals tend to
complement one another and give clues about the communicator's feelings.

Facial characteristics seem to be the most accurate nonverbal communicators
in honest communication. When visual cues contradict audio cues, decoders
tend to be influenced more by the visual, except when extreme discrepancies
exist. When there is a great difference between vocal and facial cues, decoders
tend to suspect the sender is lying; decoders then are influenced more by tone
of voice, considering it more likely to reveal the truth than the more controllable facial cues.[4]

How do body and
facial gestures
influence
communication?

---

[4]Graham, et al., op. cit.

Several postures, movements, or expressions are used quite consistently in Western cultures. Examples of such behaviors and their interpretations are given in Illustration 5–2.[5]

Illustration 5–2   NONVERBAL BEHAVIOR

Nonverbal Behavior	Interpretation
brisk, erect walk	confidence
standing with hands on hips	readiness
sitting with legs crossed, foot kicking slightly	boredom
arms crossed on chest	defensiveness
walking with hands in pockets, shoulders hunched, shuffling gait	dejection
hand to cheek	evaluation, thinking
touching, slightly rubbing nose	rejection, doubt, lying
rubbing the eye	doubt
hands clasped behind back	anger, frustration, apprehension
locked ankles	apprehension
head resting in hand, eyes downcast	boredom
rubbing hands	anticipation
sitting with hands clasped behind head, legs crossed	confidence, superiority
open palm	sincerity, openness, innocence
pinching bridge of nose, eyes closed	negative evaluation
averted eyes	deception, inattention, lack of trust
smiling too much or too little	deception

---

[5]See Gerald I. Nierenberg and Henry H. Calero, *How to Read a Person like a Book* (New York: Hawthorne Books, 1971); *Meta-Talk Guide to Hidden Meanings in Conversations* (New York: Simon and Schuster, 1973); and Judee K. Burgoon, "Nonverbal Signals," in Mark L. Knapp and Gerald R. Miller, eds., *Handbook of Interpersonal Communication* (Beverly Hills: Sage Publications, 1985).

Effective communicators read nonverbal behaviors of others wisely. Clues that your listener is bored, doubtful, or defensive should alert you to act—illustrate, clarify, explain, encourage—to overcome communication barriers. However, nonverbal signals must be interpreted cautiously. Rubbing the eyes or touching the nose does not always indicate doubt or lying. The listener may have sore eyes or an itchy nose!

As a participant in collaborative groups, you will use many languages including words, numbers, appearances, timings and distances, body language, and vocal tone. Using complementary verbal and nonverbal languages and observing how others use those languages will increase your communication effectiveness.

PROBLEM SOLVING IN SMALL GROUPS

Businesses often use small groups, generally defined as four to ten people, to generate ideas or solve business problems. Your career success may well be influenced by your ability to contribute effectively to such groups.

Judgments about what constitutes an effective group are highly subjective. Group effectiveness is often measured by outcomes, such as productivity, member satisfaction, and group cohesiveness. Those outcomes tend to be interrelated. Although a group is assigned a specific task (productivity), the group is unable to achieve its goals without some degree of group cohesion; and members often derive satisfaction from both task completion and relationships within the group. One thing is certain: Each group in which you work is unique, requiring that you adapt to the task, the context, and the people. One scholar describes an ideal group as "one that can, if not welcome internal and external change, at least accept and adapt to it; that can make the most of what it has in the way of its resources, human and otherwise; . . . that can be open to new ideas and ask for assistance when necessary."[6] This section presents the following topics to help you adapt to different task groups: communication behaviors, stages of group development, and patterns of decision making.

Communication Behaviors

Communication behaviors evidenced in small groups fall into three categories: task-oriented, process-oriented, and dysfunctional behaviors.[7] Effective group

---

[6]Susan Jarboe, "What We Know About Individual Performance in Groups: Myths and Realities," in Gerald M. Phillips, ed., *Teaching How to Work in Groups*, (Norwood, NJ: Ablex Publishing Corporation, 1990), p. 37.

members demonstrate constructive task-oriented and process-oriented behaviors and avoid dysfunctional behaviors.

Task-Oriented Behaviors. You can contribute to task accomplishment by demonstrating one or all of these behaviors:

What is task-oriented behavior?

1. *Initiating discussion:* "This looks like an interesting project. Let's begin."
2. *Seeking information:* "How many customers returned the completed questionnaire?"
3. *Giving information:* "Forty percent of our policyholders are under age thirty."
4. *Coordinating:* "Laura's best customers are recent college graduates, but Mario's sales to that market have been slow. Let's look at their sales strategies."
5. *Evaluating:* "The major difference seems to be the timing of their calls."
6. *Summarizing:* "Midafternoon seems to be the best time to call for an appointment. Does everyone agree?"

Process-Oriented Behaviors. By following these behaviors, you will help a group function as a cohesive unit:

What is process-oriented behavior?

1. *Encouraging:* "That's helpful information, Sandy. Have you observed other differences?"
2. *Harmonizing:* "Joan, your suggestion for a time-management seminar is good. Could we combine it with Paul's suggestion for a program on selling by telephone?"
3. *Opening gates:* "Barbara, you seemed ready to say something."
4. *Acting as a liaison:* "I'll get that information from accounting before our next meeting."
5. *Setting standards:* "We'll start at 9 a.m. tomorrow. Does everyone agree?" (And follow through by starting on time the next day.)

Dysfunctional Behaviors. The following actions tend to prevent group unity and delay task accomplishment:

What is dysfunctional behavior?

1. *Blocking*—using tactics such as criticism or interruption to prevent

---

[7]This classification comes from the seminal study of group behaviors: Kenneth D. Benne and Paul Sheats, "Functional Roles of Group Members," *Journal of Social Issues,* Spring 1948, pp. 41–49.

the group from reaching agreement: "Look, Joan, forget about time management. Nobody's interested."

2. *Seeking recognition*—clowning, bragging, or monopolizing the discussion to focus attention on oneself instead of group objectives: "Hey! Did I tell you about the time management seminar the company sent me to last year? It was at a resort on Hilton Head Island, and . . ."

3. *Competing*—expressing different views simply to gain attention or to attack individuals: "What we really need is a one-week conference, not a measly two days."

4. *Withdrawing*—acting bored and indifferent; refusing to participate or accept responsibilities: "Whatever you want is OK. I probably won't attend anyway."

5. *Repeating*—using one or two ideas repeatedly: "As I said earlier, I still think a time management seminar is a waste of time."

To promote effective communication in a group, participants must observe nonverbal and verbal cues. Defensiveness, impatience, and boredom impede communication. Recognizing nonverbal clues to such attitudes, a skillful group leader or participant acts to change the communication environment. Appropriate changes should result in cooperation, acceptance, and enthusiasm.

However, cooperation, acceptance, and enthusiasm are not immediate. Groups need sufficient time to progress through the normal stages of group formation, including conflict.

Stages of Group Development

Individuals bring to groups multiple goals, values, attitudes, and skills. That diversity can be an asset that contributes to goal achievement, or it can be a liability that distracts from performance.

Experienced group members do not expect immediate productivity. They recognize the need to progress through four stages of group development: orientation, formation, coordination, and formalization.[8]

Orientation. During the orientation stage, group members assess their relative skills, explore their understandings of the group task, and evaluate what

---

[8]This classification is offered by Albert C. Kowitz and Thomas J. Knutson, *Decision Making in Small Groups, The Search for Alternatives*, (Boston: Allyn and Bacon, 1980). Other scholars identify as few as three and as many as six stages.

each person can contribute to task achievement. Members also begin to establish acceptable and unacceptable interpersonal behaviors.

The orientation stage is characterized by uncertainty and caution. While exploring the task parameters, some group members make tentative or ambiguous comments; others seek clarification. Contributors may jump from one topic to another. Various decisions may be proposed, but members are not ready to strongly support one position. Members tend to be more agreeable during this phase than in later stages.

By exploring the task, members also learn much about one another. They learn what skills, knowledge, and outside contacts each possesses. They learn who is task oriented, who is process oriented, and who may be dysfunctional. The orientation stage concludes when the group has defined the task and individuals have formed their impressions of group members.

Formation. During the formation stage, group structure develops and the group agrees on a strategy for reaching its goal. This phase is often characterized by competition, argumentation, and conflict.

To fulfill its task, the group must develop its strategy: establish specific objectives, agree on procedures for fulfilling the objectives, and define each member's role in achieving those objectives. During this stage, members begin to specialize in the things they do best. Some are good at generating ideas, others at obtaining information, others at synthesizing and harmonizing, etc.

The most critical role decision the group must make is the selection of a leader. During the orientation phase, quiet, uninformed, or unskilled individuals are often tacitly excluded from the leadership role. Potential leaders usually have strong views about the group task and strategies for its accomplishment. A leader emerges (by consensus, negotiation, or election) as the members discuss alternative positions and choose the most acceptable approach. Conflict is likely—and can be healthy—during strategy development and leader selection. Conflict avoidance may divert the group's attention from important issues. Such avoidance can result in choice of an unsatisfactory leader or an inappropriate strategy. Unresolved conflicts often result in information loss and lack of commitment.

When the group settles on its structure and direction, it is ready to progress to its major work period.

Coordination. Coordination is often the longest, most task-oriented of the four group-development stages. Member roles have been defined, the patterns of interpersonal relationships have been established, and specific duties have been assigned. Members now make a concerted effort to collect and interpret the information needed to reach the group's goal. Although the

What are the stages of group formation? What are the characteristics of each stage?

group strategy has been defined and accepted, conflict may still arise. At this stage conflict usually centers around interpretations of data. Conscientious group members, however, share information, evaluate data objectively, and avoid emotional argumentation. The quality of the group's decision depends on the willingness of its members to examine alternatives objectively.

Formalization. The fourth stage is characterized by supportive, accepting participation. In this stage the group produces and accepts the content and form of its final product (i.e., decision, proposal, report, etc.). Group members reinforce one another with compliments and mutual congratulations. A sense of comradeship pervades the group, and celebration parties are not unusual.

To progress efficiently and effectively through the four stages of group development, group members must be able to exercise various patterns of decision making.

Patterns of Decision Making[9]

Different circumstances require different decision-making styles. Task groups must be able to adapt their decision-making styles to the task and context. Although consensus is desirable in many contexts, circumstances may necessitate negotiation or voting.

Consensus. Consensus decisions reflect the views of all group members. Ideally, all members contribute to the discussion, expressing and justifying their preferences. Members listen respectfully to alternative views, and they evaluate proposals by criteria that promote the group's objective. To avoid conflict, members may have to tone down the expressions of their opinions and surrender some individual goals for the sake of a group decision.

Consensus decision making takes time, but it is particularly important for groups that must continue to work together for an extended period. The task-oriented behaviors (initiating discussion, seeking information, giving information, coordinating, evaluating, and summarizing) contribute to achievement of consensus. So do the process-oriented behaviors of encouraging, harmonizing, and opening gates.

Negotiation. Like consensus, negotiation incorporates the views of the members; but negotiation results in an agreement that includes the minimally acceptable requirements of opposing groups. Negotiated decisions are

What are three patterns of decision making? When is each appropriate?

---

[9]Based on Julia T. Wood and Gerald M. Phillips, "Teaching Groups Alternative Patterns of Decision Making," in Phillips, op. cit., pp. 50–65.

usually reached through a series of tradeoffs among members. Often no member is completely satisfied, but all find enough value in the decision to support it.

Negotiation may be necessary when group members are dependent on the group but hold potentially antagonistic views on an issue. It is a time-consuming process because conflicting factions typically begin with greater demands than they are eventually willing to accept. However, members who are committed to the process and to preservation of the group can reach a negotiated compromise that synthesizes the expectations of all factions.

Voting. Voting is a democratic process. It protects the rights of minorities to be heard, but it does not guarantee that minority ideas will be incorporated into the final decision. To protect members' rights, voting must be conducted by rules established in advance or during deliberations, and results must be honored.

Voting may be necessary when time is limited and negotiation seems likely to fail. However, voting presumes there will be winners and losers. Losers tend to become apathetic and withdraw—physically or psychologically—from the group.

The three decision patterns—consensus, negotiation, and voting—may be used in small problem-solving groups and in other collaborative settings, such as conferences.

CONFERRING

Conferences are oral exchanges of data and opinions, intended to inform participants or to solve problems. Oral communication skills, group problem-solving skills, and the ability to respond to nonverbal cues contribute to conference effectiveness.

Conference modes include face-to-face conferences, teleconferences, and videoconferences.[10] Evidence exists that conferring skills can be applied as effectively in a videoconference as in a face-to-face meeting. Studies comparing those two modes have shown videoconferences to be equal to or superior to face-to-face conferences on these variables:

How effective are videoconferences?

1. accuracy of transmitted information
2. rate of transmission
3. participants' perception of accuracy

---

[10]Review Chapter 4 for descriptions of teleconference and videoconference technology.

4. participants' perception of personal productivity
5. participants' satisfaction
6. participants' performance in complex problem solving[11]

A successful conference requires preparation and distribution of an agenda prior to the conference; effective leadership; and prepared, actively involved conferees.

The Conference Agenda

The conference leader is generally responsible for preparing an **agenda**, a list of topics to be discussed and things to be done during a conference. Agenda preparation involves these steps:

1. Determine the conference purpose. Is it to inform? Whom? What? Why? When? Where? How?
2. Identify the conference topics, the people who will present them, and the amounts of time needed for discussion.
3. List the conference topics according to their significance for the meeting (No. 1, most important; No. 2, second in importance; and so on). Give priority to the items that need immediate attention.
4. Review the topic list. If necessary, adjust the priority of topics and the designation of speakers as well as times.
5. Determine the time anticipated for the entire conference.
6. Correlate the topic list with the total available time. Compose supplementary lists for use if the main agenda takes more time or less time than planned.
7. Place the items in logical sequence. For example, if a conference is to deal with personnel requirements of a revised production schedule, it would be logical to discuss the production timetables before focusing on personnel changes.
8. Separate main topics into their parts. For instance, the production schedule may be discussed in terms of departments, impact upon other units of the organization, logistics, and quality control.
9. Predict probable responses from the conferees. A conference needs conversational give-and-take to be effective. Allow time for questions, answers, and comments from the conferees.

---

[11]Donald K. Rosetti and Theodore J. Surynt, "Video Teleconferencing and Performance," *The Journal of Business Communication,* vol. 22, no. 4 (Fall 1985), pp. 25–31.

10. Confirm availability of the conference room (including necessary furniture), note-taking supplies, and audiovisual equipment, if warranted. Confirm availability of the conferees as well.
11. Edit and proofread the agenda into its final form.
12. Have the agenda and its proposed distribution approved by the appropriate authority within your organization.
13. Reproduce copies of the authorized agenda. (See Illustration 5–3.)
14. Distribute the copies. Allow the conferees sufficient time to study the agenda before the meeting.

In addition to preparing an agenda, the conference leader is responsible for ensuring that the conference runs smoothly.

Illustration 5–3   MEETING AGENDA

```
                        AGENDA

           PROJECT EC48 PRODUCTION TEAM

          Thursday, July 5, 1992, 1:30 p.m.

                         in

               CONFERENCE ROOM E73


      PRESIDING:  Karen S. Linton, Marketing
                         Manager

      1.  Call to order
      2.  Correction and approval of minutes,
          June 18, 1992, meeting
      3.  Committee reports
          a.  Market analysis
          b.  Production planning
      4.  Progress report:  Search for sub-
          contractors
      5.  Unfinished business:  Software
          selection
      6.  New business
      7.  Adjournment
```

Responsibilities of the Conference Leader

As a conference leader, your responsibilities are to organize and control the group discussion. Your tasks are to elicit participation, allow and often reconcile divergent opinions, bring people to agreement, and move people to propose actions or to accept decisions. As an effective leader, you will use many of the process-oriented and task-oriented behaviors for small-group problem solving. These are your basic leadership duties:

What are a conference leader's responsibilities?

1. Communicate the conference purpose.
2. Introduce participants or ask them to introduce themselves.
3. Detect directions to which the discussion tends. Tactfully minimize irrelevant talk.
4. Identify significant ideas and give due credit for them. Stress their relevance to the conference purpose.
5. Emphasize elements of agreement. To achieve major agreement, you may decide to compromise on minor issues. Perhaps you will restrict or postpone controversial discussion that blocks the business of the meeting.
6. Invite recommendations from the conferees, especially when leading discussions of alternative proposals. List all proposals on a visual aid, such as a chalkboard or a flip chart. Encourage adequate discussion to reach unanimity or consensus. Remember that, although you serve as conference leader, you may retain the privilege of other members in the discussion group. Like them, you may remain neutral, you may speak directly for or against a proposal, you may support conferees who advance a proposal you prefer, or you may support conferees who criticize a proposal you do not favor.
7. Summarize conference results, or ask a participant to do so. Prepare a conference report and distribute it to authorized receivers.

As with any conference, the effectiveness of an electronic conference relies upon thorough preparation. Before scheduling an electronic conference, leaders should be able to answer "yes" to these questions:

1. Is the medium suitable for the conference communication requirements? Consider nonverbal aspects as well as costs. Teleconferencing is less expensive than videoconferencing. But a *video*conference may be necessary for complex problem solving, which relies heavily on visual cues that a *tele*conference cannot provide. A teleconference, however, may suffice for information exchanges that do not involve visual cues.

What guides can help a manager decide whether to hold an electronic conference?

2. Is an electronic conference more economical than a face-to-face meeting? Consider both monetary and human costs. Human costs include stress and time loss associated with travel.

After deciding to hold an electronic conference, the leader has further preparation duties:

1. Establish a limited agenda. Conferees tend to tire easily in an electronic conference, perhaps because they lack the freedom of movement and the interpersonal stimulation available in a face-to-face meeting. Therefore, the number of topics and conference length should be limited.
2. Brief the participants. A preconference briefing includes all information that will enhance effective communication. Include information about other participants, the agenda, suggested participant roles and preparation, procedures for conducting the conference, and system operating instructions. For videoconferences, diagrams of room layouts and suggestions about appropriate camera dress are also useful.

Responsibilities of Conferees

What are the conferees' responsibilities?

As a participant, you will contribute to conference effectiveness by fulfilling these responsibilities:

1. Study the agenda and prepare for the meeting.
2. Familiarize yourself with the audio-visual equipment before the conference begins, especially for an electronic conference.
3. Introduce yourself, or respond appropriately when introduced by the leader. During a teleconference, identify yourself each time you speak, unless the participants are so few that they can readily identify your voice.
4. Avoid side conversations or extraneous noises that interfere with communication. For electronic conferences, avoid behaviors that may interfere with message transmission, such as manipulating equipment or shuffling papers.
5. Listen and speak carefully. Also observe nonverbal cues, if possible. In a teleconference, recognize that listening must compensate for loss of visual cues. As speaker, do not expect listeners to interpret nonverbal cues they cannot see.

Some problem-solving groups and conferences are conducted with minimal written input or output. The meeting agenda and minutes may be the only written messages associated with the collaboration. However, in other instances the collaborative group uses several documents as information sources and generates others during the fact-finding and decision stages. Since groups may also be responsible for production of a substantial written report, today's business communicators must possess collaborative writing skills.

COLLABORATIVE WRITING

Your job responsibilities will almost surely include collaborative writing. In a study of on-the-job writing, 73.5 percent of the respondents reported that they sometimes write with one or more persons. Most respondents said that at least 10 percent of their writing was done collaboratively, but the average for all respondents was 25 percent.[12]

A collaborative writing group has a specific writing task, and the group's productivity is measured by the quality of that document. Groups of employees are often assigned to write a product user's manual, documentation for computer software, a company's annual report, a business plan, or simplified forms. A problem-solving group may also be required to prepare a comprehensive report of its work. In that report the group defines the problem, presents and interprets data, and recommends action.

A collaborative writing group can expect to experience the usual orientation and formation stages before it enters the coordination and formalization stages. All stages can contribute to productivity, however, if group members practice communication by objectives (CBO) and incorporate the traditional managerial functions: planning, organizing, directing (activating), and controlling.

How does CBO relate to collaborative writing?

Planning

Planning begins during the orientation stage. While becoming acquainted with one another, group members should determine individual strengths and weaknesses, as well as preferences or dislikes as they affect the task. Effective planning for collaborative writing includes the following:

1. Clarify the task—define the problem, the project objective, and subtasks that must be completed to reach that objective.
2. Identify potential data sources and other necessary resources.
3. Develop workable procedures.

---

[12]Lester Faigley and Thomas P. Miller, "What We Learn from Writing on the Job," *College English*, vol. 44, no. 6 (October 1982), pp. 557–569.

4. Set goals for the project.
5. Define criteria to evaluate whether goals are accomplished.

Organizing

To organize the group's work, members—by consensus, negotiation, or voting—must distribute responsibilities and resources. Specifically, the group must agree on the following:

1. *Leadership.* Will one person be designated leader? Will leadership rotate, with different individuals assuming that role for various phases of the project? For example, one person may coordinate the fact-finding stage; another person, the writing stage.
2. *Task assignments.* What are each person's responsibilities? What resources and authority does each individual have to fulfill those responsibilities? Under what circumstances may a person act independently? What actions require group approval?
3. *Schedules.* When, where, how (face-to-face or electronically) will group meetings be held? What are target dates for completion of specific phases of the project? What is the agenda for the next meeting?

Directing (Activating)

Many of the group's tasks will be conducted outside regularly scheduled group meetings. As the leader of a project—or any phase of it—you must ensure that members fulfill their responsibilities. Records of decisions or assignments are useful tools for directing a project. Regularly scheduled meetings with clearly defined agendas help the group resolve problems and sustain its momentum.

Activating the group requires each member to fulfill conscientiously her or his tasks—research, writing, editing, etc. As you perform your group-writing tasks, follow the guides presented in the remainder of this book for planning and organizing messages, conducting research, formatting reports, etc.

Controlling

To control a collaborative writing project, members must review progress regularly. Some groups do this in face-to-face meetings; others use electronic conferencing to stay in touch with one another. At those meetings each member should report progress on her or his part of the project and define goals to be accomplished before the next meeting. Progress-review meetings are appropriate times to discuss difficulties encountered and to seek assistance in resolving problems.

Collaboration is a reality of today's business world. In all collaborative efforts members should be able to ask and answer questions, solicit and give opinions, comment gently and succinctly, manage tensions, stay on an agenda, and keep track of what is going on.[13]

REVIEW AND TRANSITION

Collaborative communication is common in today's business environment. Collaborative communication modes include face-to-face meetings and mediated conferences, using either concurrent or nonconcurrent communication flows. Work groups may include problem-solving groups, conferences, and collaborative writing teams.

Nonverbal communication influences the collaborative environment. Effective encoders use nonverbal symbols that complement and reinforce their verbal messages. Effective decoders attend to verbal and nonverbal symbols, but interpret nonverbals cautiously.

Task-oriented behaviors (initiating discussion, seeking information, giving information, coordinating, evaluating, and summarizing) and process-oriented behaviors (encouraging, harmonizing, opening gates, acting as a liaison, and setting standards) contribute to effective communication in problem-solving groups, conferences, and collaborative writing groups. Dysfunctional behaviors (blocking, seeking recognition, competing, withdrawing, and repeating) distract from group cohesion and goal achievement.

Task groups should expect to experience four stages of group development: orientation, formation, coordination, and formalization. During those stages, many decisions will be reached by consensus; but the context may require negotiation or voting on some issues.

Your collaborative communication skills will serve you well in your educational and business careers. Your instructor for this and other courses may require that you complete some of your course requirements as a team member, and your employment will almost surely place you into collaborative assignments.

Chapter 6 directs your attention to planning, organizing, and developing business messages. As you study the principles and guides presented in that chapter, consider how they apply to group as well as individual writing tasks.

YOUR DECISIONS FOR CHAPTER 5

What task- and process-oriented behaviors has Donna alluded to in her description of the technical writing group? What dysfunctional behaviors appeared to exist? Should Donna continue to assume the leadership role? Why

---

[13]Gerald M. Phillips, "Theoretical Basis for Instruction in Small Group Performance," in Phillips, op. cit., p. 290.

or why not? If Donna continues as group leader, what should she do to forge a production group?

DISCUSSION QUESTIONS

A. In the context of Chapter 5, what are appropriate definitions and examples for the following terms?

1. collaboration
2. nonverbal communication
3. task-oriented behavior
4. process-oriented behavior
5. dysfunctional behavior
6. consensus

B. Through your education or employment, what has been your experience with collaborative communication? What successes? What discouragements?

C. What collaborative communication modes are you likely to encounter in business? What are the major characteristics of each?

D. How may nonverbal communication promote or impede collaboration?

E. What are the stages of group formation? What are the characteristics of each stage?

F. In what ways are small-group communication behaviors applicable to conferring and collaborative writing?

G. How is communication by objectives applicable to the following?

1. problem solving in small groups
2. conferring
3. collaborative writing

APPLICATIONS

1. Form a four-student team to discuss one of these Chapter 5 topics: problem-solving in small groups, conferring, or collaborative writing. Each group should apply small-group problem-solving techniques to prepare and deliver an oral report to your classmates on selected aspects of your chosen topic. (Report length will be assigned by your instructor.) These are your tasks:

   ▶ select the broad topic
   ▶ define the elements of the topic to be reported by your group

▶ assign roles and responsibilities to group members
▶ gather supplemental information
▶ rehearse the presentation
▶ deliver the presentation

2. As directed by your instructor, form teams of four to six students. Rewrite the items in one of the following sets (as assigned by your instructor) to demonstrate the business communication criteria of accuracy, coherence, clarity, conciseness, and courtesy.

SET A

a. Employment intraviews were held this morning by Granby Enterprises which included more than 150 applicants of which I was one.

b. Protective clothing must be worn by you in this area this area contains volatile chemicals.

c. Questions are asked by one member of the survey team, the other records responses.

d. As the visitors watched computer keyboards clicked video screens flashed every employee worked with maximum efficiency.

e. Norton Corporation lead it's competitors last year however this year Norton is losing sales.

f. "This is your new office" said the manager "you've been promoted"

g. The market was erratic last quater, nevertheless we are optimistic about long term results.

h. There was a moment of silence, then the CEO made an unexpected anouncement.

i. When Nora was a college sophmore she enjoyed studying stastistics now she plans to become a finansial anilyst.

j. Before Kirk requested employment interviews, he researched at least fourty compnies; with regard to they're entry level job requirments.

k. "Patel Corporation a leader in it's field is a progressive firm" the recruiter assured Lynn.

l. "I worked at Patel last Summer" Lynn replyed "and hope to join it full time after graduation"

m. It is my belief that Myra Kim, who joined the Rand Agency last month has grate potential.

n. Here as you requested Ms. Burke is the current production reports.

o. After skiming several issues, Dale decided the Employment Oppurtunitys Magazine would be a useful data sauce.

p. Three people are competing for promotion Benz Garcia and Van Buren.

SET B

a. Above skyscrapers soared below people crowded the streets, that city was an exciting place in which to work in.

b. "Where are you at" Lib asked "and when can you deliver those documens"

c. Casey's international business studies includes management systems, busness communication, and european as well as asian languages.

d. Here's the latest figures on market trends and profitable conclusions can be drawn by you from them.

e. Our products are as good if not better than theirs.

f. Riverside Village offer convient country living at it's best award winning schools and as described in the enclose broshure state of the art security services.

g. Does Vera work for the Clary Company or either for Winfield Industries?

h. Will Kim be travling with you, and I to Chicago, and Denver in Febuary.

i. It would behoove you not to fail to be prompt.

j. Considering the increase in competition, the time for us to explore new marketing strategies is now.

k. This venture is planned to be financed by Corby, Inc., in association with Morita Corporation.

l. In order to get this project off the ground, so to speak, an initial investment in the neighborhood of approximately 25 million dollars is anticipated.

m. These contracts are ready for Rosa's signature which she planned to mail today.

n. Inception of the group should commence promptly.

o. It is common to witness two of the groups pursue solving the same problem simultaneously.

p. The current structure of the fire protection system necessitates much attention.

3. Refer to Application 2. Form groups of 6 to 12 students by combining a Set-A Group with a Set-B group. Each subgroup should present and defend its revisions to its partner group.

4. Write a summary of your own perceptions and evaluations of each team member's performance in the small-group meeting and during the larger-group exchange. Identify the task-oriented, process-oriented, or dysfunctional behaviors practiced by team members with whom you worked as you completed Application 2. What behavior changes, if any, occurred when you formed the larger group (Application 3) to share results of the small-group problem solving?

MULTICULTURAL INSIGHTS

1. What insights to nonverbal communication can you add to those described in Chapters 3 and 5? How may nonverbal behaviors affect your working collaboratively with people of another culture?

2. Is group problem solving used in your native country? Why or why not? How common in your country are the other types of collaborative communication discussed in Chapter 5? What cultural values account for the similarities and differences in uses of collaborative communication?

3. Which of the topics presented in Chapter 5 or in the other chapters of Part 1 would you like to discuss further with your instructor and your classmates? Why?

Cases

Communication is a decision-making process. To emphasize that fact, Chapters 1–5 opened and closed with descriptions of decision-making situations involving perception, interpretation, and application skills.

Here at the end of Part 1—and at the ends of other major parts in this book—are case scenarios that offer additional opportunities to recognize, reason about, and profit from your own, as well as other people's, communication behaviors. Use these cases to bring together your knowledge and skills as you continue improving your communication proficiency. These case materials may be recycled, with you and your peers changing roles, circumstances, interpretations, or outcomes. Guided by your instructor, you may rewrite the cases or improvise your own to illustrate business communication themes.

Following each case are questions to help you develop insights concerning the communication process and people who participate in that process, including yourself.

CASE A: KEN, FRANKLIN, AND MEDIA SPECIALISTS, INC.
(Perception, Interpretation, Oral and Nonverbal Communication)

A year ago, after completing his college degree, Ken joined the small but dynamic advertising firm of Media Specialists, Inc. (MSI). Ken's salary is less than he expected, but MSI offers excellent advancement opportunities. The MSI founder and president, Merle Franklin, is an innovative and energetic leader. Franklin excels at stimulating, guiding, and rewarding employee achievements.

This morning Ken is suddenly called to the MSI executive suite. The furnishings, especially those in President Merle Franklin's office, quietly but clearly connote success. Somewhat uneasy about this unexpected, private conference with the president, Ken feels stressful. His fingers quiver slightly, and his throat is dry. But Merle Franklin smiles and, with a friendly gesture, invites Ken to sit on a large chair in front of the president's desk. Touching the leather armrests of the chair, Ken's fingers release some of the tension he feels.

"Ken," says Franklin, "you know I don't take people for granted."

"Yes," Ken agrees. "You're noted for your attention to every employee's performance record. You acknowledge effort, but accomplishment is what you really reward."

"Right, Ken. And when someone proves that he or she is ready to move up, I like to convey the good news myself. That's why you are in my office this morning. Your work has earned you some very good news."

Ken relaxes. His fingers rest comfortably on the armchair as he returns Franklin's smile.

"As of this moment, Ken, you have been promoted."

Ken's smile widens. His eyes seem to enlarge and sparkle.

"You are now a full-fledged media coordinator," Franklin announces impressively. "Congratulations!"

Responding to the news, Ken adjusts his position. His toes flex. His shoes tap the deep pile carpet. His breathing quickens.

"And," Franklin continues, "your salary is doubled."

Joyfully, Ken springs to his feet. Franklin also rises and says: "This promotion isn't a favor or a gift, Ken. Continue the excellent quality of your work, and you'll be an account executive next. Then—who knows? You may become a vice president. Eventually, perhaps, you will be *president* of MSI."

There is a long, emphatic, thoughtful silence while Ken thinks of his present achievements and his future possibilities. He grins; career prospects at MSI are great!

Franklin ends the happy silence with: "Well, young man, speak up. What do you say?"

Ken steps forward, moves around the desk, hugs Merle Franklin, and replies, "Thanks, Mom."

INSIGHTS

Do you sometimes notice what you *expect* to observe instead of what actually occurs? Do you sometimes leap to inappropriate conclusions because of your preconceptions? Test your perception and interpretation skills by answering these questions:

1. In what ways, if any, did your preconceptions lead you to misperceive or misinterpret your initial reading of this case? What did you take for granted? To what conclusions did you leap before reading the last line of the case? How did you react after reading the last line?
2. Were you amused by "Ken, Franklin, and Media Specialists, Inc."? Why? What serious implications did your initial reactions indicate about your own values and interpretations?
3. What nonverbal cues reinforced oral communication in this case? What did those nonverbal cues convey?
4. Based on the information given in this case, is Ken's promotion fair? Why? What do your answers convey about your attitudes toward the people in the case—and toward yourself?
5. In what ways is this case related to information presented in Chapters 1 and 2.

CASE B: BAILEY AND GARCIA
(Perception, Interpretation, and Multicultural Communication)

Sitting alone in his Chicago office, John Bailey reviews his recent attempts to do business with a Latin American firm. "Will I get that Garcia contract?" he wonders.

Although usually confident, Bailey feels uneasy now. "The deal I'm proposing is a good one for Garcia and for me," Bailey assures himself. "But my competitors can offer similar terms. I feel that something besides the terms themselves may influence Garcia's decision."

At that moment, thousands of miles south of Chicago, Luis Garcia is considering Bailey's offer. The terms seem agreeable. "However," Garcia reflects, "if we accept this proposal, we shall have to deal often with John Bailey.

"Frankly, Bailey's manner disturbs me. For him punctuality is an obsession. During his visit here, he seemed to be much more preoccupied with his wristwatch than with us. During our discussions, when I approached him and intended to converse quietly, he leaned away as if he meant to increase the distance between us.

"I do not wish to transact business often with a person who behaves as though time must be a tyrant. I prefer to associate with someone who considers people to be more important than hours. What do Bailey's competitors offer us? What kind of people are they?"

INSIGHTS

Test your perception and interpretation skills by answering these questions:

1. What cultural differences involving time and space influence business communication between Garcia and Bailey?
2. How do those cultural differences affect the business aspects of this case?
3. In what ways can Bailey and Garcia reconcile their cultural differences?

NATURE'S WONDERS

By completing this six-part case, you will experience communication challenges confronted by a management trainee. In this segment of "Nature's Wonders," you will be introduced to the company and your role in the organization. Additional case parts follow Chapters 8, 13, 15, 20, and 22. Each case segment requires integration and application of the communication skills you are developing by studying *Effective Communication in Business.*

Case Facts

Nature's Wonders is a large mail-order marketer of horticultural specialties. Its $75 million annual sales include nationwide shipments of garden plants, flowers, shrubs, and trees as well as a full line of gardening tools and supplies.

Established as a family-owned business in the early 1970s, Nature's Wonders rapidly became a major force in the horticulture market. It currently controls about 10 percent of that market. The company has averaged a 15 percent annual growth in net income for the past five years. Management has set a goal of a continued 15 percent annual growth rate for the next five years. The growing interest in home gardening and the company's reputation for quality and service virtually assure that the goal will be reached.

The major problem Nature's Wonders now faces is the need for new managerial talent. The president and two vice presidents will retire within five years. Strongly committed to a promotion-from-within policy, the company is grooming midlevel managers to assume those positions. The company has also launched a summer intern program for college students. The objective of that program is mutual benefit: To give promising business students an opportunity for business experience and to give Nature's Wonders an opportunity to recruit the best new talent.

Here's where you enter the scene. You have been hired as a summer intern. For ten weeks you will work in several functional areas of the firm. Your rotation among various job assignments will acquaint you with many of the firm's operations, but your tasks will always be communication related. At the end of the summer, your performance will be evaluated. If you perform well, you may be a candidate for an exciting job: Director of Corporate Communication.

Your Tasks

Your first assignment is in Information Services. This functional area coordinates the information flow within the company. It is also responsible for monitoring the quality of the company's external communication.

You have been asked to evaluate a letter that your instructor will provide. Specifically, you are to do the following:

1. Proofread carefully for possible errors in spelling, punctuation, grammar, and sentence structure. Use appropriate proofreader's symbols to identify and correct errors.
2. Identify the writer's emphasis techniques and comment about their effectiveness. Suggest appropriate changes.
3. Comment on the logical accuracy and the ethics of the appeal used in the message.

As directed by your instructor, begin a file of your Nature's Wonders case solutions. Use the file to review case data and your solutions as you complete future Nature's Wonders tasks.

PART 2

COMMUNICATION READINESS

As explained in Chapter 1, communication by objectives (CBO) is a purposeful approach to business communication. Before composing a message, the CBO speaker or writer decides on definite results which the message is to elicit.

What CBO methods are likely to produce such results? What are CBO techniques for planning, organizing, and developing messages to achieve those results? What CBO techniques convey empathy through message tones? What are appropriate message formats and layouts?

Chapters 6 through 8 give you useful answers to those questions and to these: How shall I begin my message? When and how shall I end it? What shall I put between the beginning and ending? Why should I do so?

6

PLANNING, ORGANIZATION, AND DEVELOPMENT OF BUSINESS MESSAGES

CHAPTER OUTLINE

OBJECTIVES

After completing this chapter, you should be able to:

1. Distinguish between *building-block* and *whole-into-parts* methods of planning, organizing, and developing messages.

2. Develop data lists into message outlines.
3. Develop message outlines into message drafts.
4. Revise and proofread message drafts.
5. Convey the dual purpose of a message through an appropriate corethought statement.
6. Arrange paragraphs inductively or deductively for logical coherence.
7. Relate every sentence to its paragraph topic.
8. Relate every paragraph to the message corethought.
9. Revise and edit message drafts into final version.

DECISIONS CASE

This morning R. K. Neel, personnel manager of Ruston Enterprises, Inc., interviewed you for potential employment with that firm. You realize now that something you said during the interview may have misled Neel. You telephone Ruston Enterprises to clarify what you meant but are told that Neel will be away on a business trip for several days.

What detailed procedure should you follow in writing an appropriate message to greet Neel's return? Specifically, what decisions should you make for planning, organizing, and developing this important message?

Additional questions about this decision-making case are stated at the end of this chapter. Study the chapter before answering those questions.

CHAPTER CONTEXT

Long before you were ready to plan, organize, and develop your messages, you began to express yourself. For example, your first message to the world was almost certainly a vocal and loud protest. You were reacting to eviction from nature's most protective, nourishing, and comfortable environment. You communicated your loss of nearly perfect security by your birth cry.

Soon you added other sounds to your communication repertoire. You learned that smiles, gurgles, and chuckles could also help you get what you wanted. You learned that people and things have names, that you could say those names, and that by saying them you could affect what happened to you. So you talked. Your nonsense syllables became words, phrases, sentences. Bit by bit, you learned to manage your new environment by what you did *and* by what you said.

Then you learned that what you thought, felt, or said could be written. You discovered that the letters of an alphabet stand for the sounds you had acquired. You began to print those letters. You began to write. Your writing pattern emerged also bit by bit: first, the alphabet; then words, phrases, sentences, paragraphs. Finally came the building of whole messages.

Are you still using that "building-block" approach to writing? When you compose a message, do you still try to decide upon the first word, then the next? upon the first phrase, then the next? Do you feel that you know what you want to say but just "can't" write or speak it? If so, Chapter 6 can be exceptionally valuable to you.

BUILDING-BLOCK METHOD

Visualize a child playing with a set of brightly colored plastic bits. When fitted together in various ways, those plastic pieces produce larger objects of differing shapes. The child says: "I'll put this green, round thing here. Now I'll put this yellow, square thing next to it." The result pleases the child, who continues: "Those blue, wavy pieces are pretty, too. I'll put them *there*." And so the child goes on, placing and replacing pieces to construct a pattern.

But the pattern is made of pieces that *someone else* manufactured. The child's use of creativity is restricted, in this example, to *arranging* items that she or he did not design. After completing such an arrangement, the child may try to impose meaning upon it. He or she may present the pieced-together arrangement to someone else, who is apt to respond: "That's pretty. What is it?" And the child, disappointed by the response, replies: "Don't you see? It's a . . ." Until that follow-up message is conveyed, the child may have *expressed*, but will not have *communicated*, his or her meaning.

Some people restrict themselves as adults by applying that kind of **building-block approach** to almost all of their communication efforts. Those people tend to produce pages of carefully "fitted-together" grammar, punctuation, spelling, and format, but do not provide pertinent corethoughts and supporting data. They soon earn this kind of response: "Your report looks good, Lou. Now tell me: what do you mean?"

Of course, like the child in this analogy, all of us use building blocks to some extent throughout our lives. We use bits and pieces of data that we ourselves did not discover, bits and pieces of language that we ourselves did not create. But as adults we often redesign and sometimes do invent our own communication materials. We adapt old words and linguistic styles, invent new ones, adapt messages already in a correspondence file, and create new ones.

Unlike the child in this analogy, however, adults who are effective communicators strive *first* to determine the meanings they seek to convey; *then* they select or create message patterns for those meanings. Effective *business* communicators, especially, formulate a design *before* choosing the bits and pieces that are to be its parts. They plan a message as a whole *before* choosing and fitting together its words, sentences, and paragraphs. Rather than be-

Do you restrict
yourself as a
communicator?

ing restricted to the building-block approach, effective writers and speakers profit also from the whole-into-parts concept of communication.

CBO: WHOLE-INTO-PARTS METHOD

You often perceive the totality of someone's (or something's) appearance before you notice its details. Similarly, this **whole-into-parts method** of perception can help you determine the totality of a *message* before you plan its details.

Step 1: Determine Dual Purpose of Message

Begin this nine-step method by deciding what the *whole message* is to achieve for sender *and* receiver. Your answers to these questions will help you decide about that sender-receiver, or dual, purpose:

1. What is my purpose for writing or speaking this message?
2. What is my receiver's purpose for reading or listening to this message?

As sender, *you* may wish to promote sales of a product or service—for example, group hospitalization insurance. Your *receiver's* purpose may be to acquire the product or service providing the maximum benefit at minimum cost. But whatever the business situation may be—whether sales promotion, credit extension, collection of overdue payment, etc.—your first CBO message-planning step is to determine the **dual purpose** (sender's and receiver's) for your whole message.[1]

Step 2: State Dual Purpose as Message Corethought

Your first message-planning step has been to answer the questions "What is my purpose?" and "What is my receiver's purpose?" Your second step is to combine and word your answers to those two questions so that you convey appreciation of the receiver's viewpoint as well as your own. The result is your statement of a dual-purpose **corethought** for the whole message, as shown in this example:

> To benefit from highest-quality hospitalization insurance provided at lowest fair-profit cost.

---

[1] The CBO approach (communication by objectives) is described in Chapter 1.

Step 3: Support Message Corethought with Relevant Topics

Your third message-planning step is to identify items which pertain to the corethought. At this point, do not try to decide whether one item is more or less important than another. Just be sure that all of the items pertain to the message corethought, and list them.

Assume that you are L. R. Dubach, spokesperson for Employers Insurance Associates (EIA). You are to plan, organize, and develop replies to inquiries about EIA group hospitalization programs. On your desk is an inquiry from R. B. Ramos, Jr., general manager of Ramos Foods Corporation. The type-written portion of Illustration 6−1 shows a topic list for planning your reply.

Step 4: Revise Topic List

As shown by the handwritten "Revision Notes" in Illustration 6−1, your fourth message-planning step is to revise the topic list. You review the list and decide whether other items should be added. You decide which redundant items should be consolidated into concise equivalents. You decide which items should be omitted. Your guide as you make those decisions is the dual-purpose core-thought of your message. Every item on your topic list should pertain directly or indirectly to that corethought, as shown in Illustration 6−2.

Step 5: Organize Revised Topic List into Outline

How does a list differ from an outline? A **list** does not show relative importance or logical subordination of items. As shown by Illustration 6−3, an **outline** does convey priorities by arranging items as topics, subtopics, sub-subtopics, etc. A logically developed outline is recognizable by its format and by the grammatical parallelism of its items.

The fifth step of this whole-into-parts method is to develop an appropriate message outline, as in Illustration 6−3. You do so by putting your revised topic-list items into inductive order (specific-to-general pattern) or into deductive order (general-to-specific pattern).

Here is a traditional model for a message outline:

Corethought of Message: _____

```
    I.  First Paragraph Topic
        A.  Supporting data for I
            1.  Item related to IA
                a.  Item related to IA1
                b., etc. Items related to IA1
```

Logic: I requires at least II. A requires at least B. 1 needs at least 2. a needs at least b.

Illustration 6-1   TOPIC LIST

```
                         EIA MESSAGE


Corethought:  To benefit from highest quality hospitalization

              insurance provided at lowest fair-profit cost.


      Items:   1.  Program proposal specifying cost and coverage

               2.  Outstanding features of coverage

               3.  General and maternity services

               4.  Services for children

               5.  Preferential identification of insured persons

               6.  Medical underwriting not required to join
                   program

               7.  Additional feedback needed from prospective
                   buyer

               8.  Toll-free telephone service available

               9.  Personal visit with EIA representative
                   available

              10.  Competitors of prospective buyer already insured
                   by EIA
```

Revision Notes: --Add acknowledgment of Ramos inquiry;
              establish goodwill.
            --Consolidate Items 1-6 in this order:
              --1 and 2.
              --6, 5, 3, and 4.
            --Consolidate Items 7, 8, and 9.
            --Delete Item 10.

Illustration 6-2   REVISED TOPIC LIST

```
                              EIA MESSAGE

Corethought:   To benefit from highest quality hospitalization
               insurance provided at lowest fair-profit cost.

          1.   Acknowledge Ramos inquiry while establishing
               goodwill.
          2.   Enclose program proposal; refer to it while
               emphasizing these features:
               --medical underwriting not required to join
                 program
               --preferential identification of insured
                 persons
               --general and maternity services
               --services for children.
          3.   Elicit additional feedback from Ramos:
               --reactions to enclosed proposal
               --use of personal communication
               --availability of toll-free telephone number
                 for arranging visit with EIA regional
                 representative.
```

Revision Notes:

Test this list: Do all items pertain to the dual purpose? Are they arranged logically? Do they accommodate psychologically appropriate tone?

Notes for outline:
  -- Translate "medical underwriting" into generally understood words.
  -- Use novel greeting to attract appropriate attention.
  -- Reinforce goodwill by *you* tone throughout.
  -- Use complimentary close that combines tone of reliability with tone of goodwill.

Illustration 6-3   FIRST OUTLINE

```
                          EIA MESSAGE

   I.  What are the dual purpose and the corethought of this message?
       A.  Sender's Purpose:  To promote sales of EIA group hospi-
           talization insurance.
       B.  Receiver's Purpose:  To acquire maximum-benefit/lowest-
           cost hospitalization insurance for Ramos Foods employees
           and their families.
       C.  Corethought:  To benefit from highest quality hospi-
           talization insurance provided by EIA at lowest fair-profit
           cost.
  II.  What data should be stated?  in what sequence?
       A.  Acknowledge Ramos inquiry while establishing goodwill.
       B.  Describe available services and costs; enclose program
           proposal with details.
       C.  Emphasize outstanding features of coverage for employees
           and their families.
           1.  Medical underwriting unnecessary.
           2.  Preferential identification provided.
           3.  General hospital services covered.
           4.  Maternity services supplied.
           5.  Children's services also included.
       D.  Stimulate prospective buyer to request interview with EIA
           regional representative.
           1.  Emphasize personal communication.
           2.  Make communication easy; supply toll-free telephone
               number.
           3.  Use complimentary close to reinforce goodwill and to
               suggest EIA reliability.
 III.  How should the message be unified?
       A.  Establish and reinforce tone of interest, sincerity,
           capability.
           1.  Personalize an innovative salutation ("Thank you,
               Mr. Ramos").
           2.  Convey receiver-oriented interest.
               a.  Emphasize "you" and "your" pronouns.
               b.  Repeat receiver's name before closing message.
               c.  Use a complimentary close that combines tones
                   of goodwill and reliability.
```

Illustration 6–3   FIRST OUTLINE (continued)

B. Repeat key words deliberately for coherence.
    1. State full name of seller. Employers Insurance
        Associates, Inc., in letterhead; show "EIA" as its
        abbreviation.
    2. Repeat "EIA" in relation to "Ramos Foods Corpora-
        tion." Reinforce tie between name of seller and
        name of buyer.
C. Use a list for coherence, clarity, and emphasis in
    identifying outstanding features of program proposal.
D. Refer (in the body of the message and by an enclosure
    notation below signature block) to the enclosed program
    proposal.
E. Elicit additional feedback.
    1. Invite Ramos to use toll-free telephone number.
    2. Offer Ramos a personal interview with EIA regional
        representative.
F. Summarize general tone of presentation by a complimentary
    close that combines goodwill with reliability.

*Revision Notes: Reverse order of II A and II B. When
introducing Item II c1, translate "medical
underwriting unnecessary" into "no medical
examination required, no health questions
to be answered." Delete II D3 and III A2c.*

```
          2.   Item related to IA
               a.   Item related to IA2
               b., etc. Items related to IA2
          3., etc. Items related to IA
     B., etc. Supporting data for I
          1.   Item related to IB
               a.           }
               b., etc.     }  Items related to IB1
          2.   Item related to IB
               a.           }
               b., etc.     }  Items related to IB2
 II.   Second Paragraph Topic
       (Develop as shown for I)
III., etc. (Develop as shown for I)
```

Logic: 1 needs at least
2. 1.1 needs at least
1.2. 1.11 needs at least
1.12.

You may prefer using this decimal outline model instead:

Corethought of Message: _____

_____

```
1.   First Paragraph Topic
     1.1   Supporting data for 1
           1.11   Item related to 1.1
                  1.111 Item related to 1.11
                  1.112 Item related to 1.11
           1.12   Item related to 1.1
                  1.121 Item related to 1.12
                  1.122, etc. Items related to 1.12
           1.13, etc. Items related to 1.1
     1.2, etc. Supporting data for 1
           1.21   Item related to 1.2
                  1.211
                  1.212, etc.  }  Items related to 1.21
           1.22   Item related to 1.2
                  1.221
                  1.222, etc.  }  Items related to 1.22
2.   Second Paragraph Topic
     (Develop as shown for 1)
3., etc. (Develop as shown for 1)
```

Step 6: Revise Outline

Your sixth step of this whole-into-parts method is to revise the outline. As indicated by the handwritten "Revision Notes" in Illustration 6–3, you consolidate, delete, or add items. You tie subtopics to topics. You relate topics to corethought. And you state the outline items in grammatically parallel form. Illustration 6–4 shows a revised outline.

Step 7: Write or Dictate Message Draft from Revised Outline

As shown by Illustration 6–5, you now take the seventh step of this whole-into-parts method. Using your revised outline as a detailed guide, you place receiver-oriented words, sentences, and paragraphs into the format of what will become the message you finally send. Before you achieve that final version, consider double-spacing the draft(s) to provide room for your revisions and corrections.

Step 8: Revise and Proofread Message Draft

Your eighth step of this whole-into-parts method is to revise and proofread the message draft. If necessary, you revise and proofread subsequent drafts

Illustration 6–4   REVISED OUTLINE

```
                          EIA MESSAGE

  I. What are the dual purpose and the corethought of this mes-
     sage?
     A. Sender's Purpose: To promote sales of EIA group hospi-
        talization insurance.
     B. Receiver's Purpose: To acquire maximum-benefit/lowest-cost
        hospitalization insurance for Ramos Foods employees and
        their families.
     C. Corethought: To benefit from highest quality hospitaliza-
        tion insurance provided by EIA at lowest fair-profit cost.
 II. What data should be stated? in what sequence?
     A. Describe available services and costs; enclose program
        proposal with details.
     B. Acknowledge Ramos inquiry while establishing goodwill.
     C. Emphasize outstanding features of coverage for employees
        and their families.
        1. No medical examination required; no health questions to
           be answered.
        2. Preferential identification provided.
        3. General hospital services covered.
        4. Maternity services supplied.
        5. Children's services also included.
     D. Stimulate prospective buyer to request interview with the
        EIA regional representative.
        1. Emphasize personal communication.
        2. Make communication easy; supply toll-free telephone
           number.
III. How should the message be unified?
     A. Establish and reinforce tone of interest, sincerity, capa-
        bility.
        1. Personalize an innovative salutation ("Thank you, Mr.
           Ramos").
        2. Convey receiver-oriented interest.
           a. Emphasize "you" and "your" pronouns.
           b. Repeat receiver's name before closing message.
```

Illustration 6–4   REVISED OUTLINE (continued)

```
B. Repeat key words deliberately for coherence.
   1. State full name of seller. Employers Insurance Associ-
      ates, Inc., in letterhead; show "EIA" as its abbrevia-
      tion.
   2. Repeat "EIA" in relation to "Ramos Foods Corporation."
      Reinforce tie between name of seller and name of buyer.
C. Use a list for coherence, clarity, and emphasis in identi-
   fying outstanding features of program proposal.
D. Refer (in the body of the message and by an enclosure
   notation below signature block) to the enclosed program
   proposal.
E. Elicit additional feedback.
   1. Invite Ramos to use toll-free telephone number.
   2. Offer Ramos a personal interview with EIA regional rep-
      resentative.
F. Summarize general tone of presentation by a complimentary
   close that combines goodwill with reliability.
```

until you are confident that your message fulfills the Chapter 2 criteria of effective business communication.

Within the context of this discussion, **revising** is the updating, reorganizing, rewording, or other improvement of business correspondence, memos, reports, and publications. **Proofreading** is the actual marking of a page to correct errors. Once you have learned to use proofreader's marks, you can save much time and energy in revising material that may range from a single sentence to an entire book. Examples of common proofreader's marks and their application are shown in Illustration 6–6. The use of proofreading symbols can speed accurate revision of your messages, as shown by Illustration 6–7.

Step 9: Produce Final Version

The ninth step of this whole-into-parts method is to produce the completely revised and final draft. You now have a message which is ready for signature and transmission (see Illustration 6–8).

Illustration 6–5   FIRST DRAFT OF MESSAGE

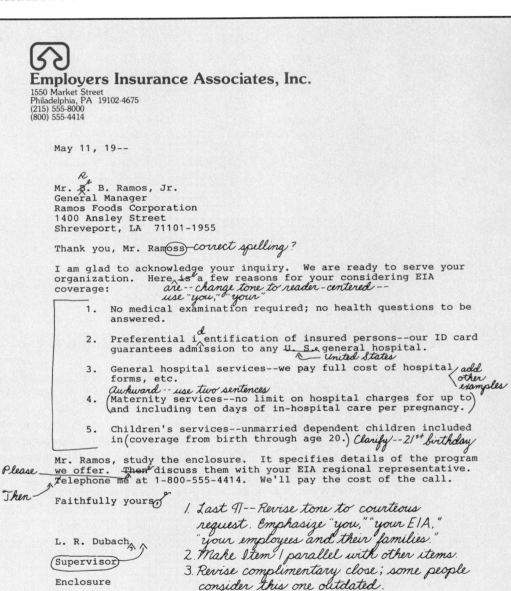

Illustration 6–6 COMMON PROOFREADER'S MARKS

∧	Insert item here.	T͗S	Triple space.
# or #/	Insert space here.	QS	Quadruple space.
tr or ∩	Transpose these items.	*cap* or ≡	Capitalize this item.
⸝	Delete this item.	*lc* or /	Use lowercase letters, not capitals.
stet	Let the original stand; disregard changes already made.	*ital* or ___	Italicize this item.
¶	Begin a paragraph here.	*no ital*	Do not italicize this item.
no new ¶	Do not begin a paragraph here.	⊙	Insert period.
⊏	Move left.	⋏	Insert comma.
⊐	Move right.	⋏	Insert colon.
⊓	Move up.	⋏	Insert semicolon.
⊔	Move down.	=	Insert hyphen.
⊃	Close up; move together.	═	Insert dash.
◯⁵	Move copy as indicated.	?	Insert question mark.
‖	Align copy.	!	Insert exclamation point.
SS	Single space.	⌄	Open a quotation.
DS	Double space.	⌄	Close a quotation.

Illustration 6–7   USE OF PROOFREADER'S MARKS TO CORRECT ERRORS

BEFORE USE OF PROOFREADER'S MARKS

Your inquiry about health-care Protection for Ramos
foods employees, and their families is welcome. EIA
staff members are ready to serve your organization.
organization. The enclosed proposal specifies ma ny
reasons for your considering EIA coverage including
these outstandign features:

WITH PROOFREADER'S MARKS

Your inquiry about health-care Protection for Ramos
foods employees, and their families is welcome. EIA
staff members are ready to serve your organization.
organization. The enclosed proposal specifies ma ny
reasons for your considering EIA coverage including
these outstandign features:

AFTER USE OF PROOFREADER'S MARKS

Your inquiry about health-care protection for Ramos
Foods employees and their families is welcome. EIA
staff members are ready to serve your organization.
The enclosed proposal specifies many reasons for your
considering EIA coverage, including these outstanding
features:

Illustration 6–8 FINAL VERSION OF MESSAGE

Employers Insurance Associates, Inc.

1550 Market Street
Philadelphia, PA 19102-4675
(215) 555-8000
(800) 555-4414

May 11, 19--

Mr. R. B. Ramos, Jr.
General Manager
Ramos Foods Corporation
1400 Ansley Street
Shreveport, LA 71101-1955

Thank you, Mr. Ramos

Your inquiry about health-care protection for Ramos Foods employees
and their families is welcome. EIA staff members are ready to
service your organization.

The enclosed proposal specifies many reasons for your considering
EIA coverage, including these outstanding features:

1. <u>No Medical Examination Required; No Health Questions to Be
   Answered</u>--All of your employees and their immediate families can
   receive EIA policy coverage without medical screening.

2. <u>Preferential Identification of Insured Persons</u>--The EIA identification card guarantees admission of Ramos employees and their
   families to any general hospital in the United States.

3. <u>General Hospital Services</u>--EIA pays full cost of hospital rooms,
   operating facilities, medicines, X rays, and the like.

4. <u>Maternity Services</u>--EIA places no limit on hospital charges for
   ten days, or less, of in-hospital care. That allowance applies
   to <u>each</u> pregnancy.

5. <u>Children's Services</u>--EIA family contracts cover unmarried
   dependent children from birth to twenty-first birthday.

Mr. Ramos, please study the enclosed program proposal, which specifies the details of insured protection for your employees and their
families. For an appointment to discuss this program personally
with your EIA regional representative, please telephone me at this
toll-free number: 1-800-555-4414.

Sincerely yours

L. R. Dubach

L. R. Dubach, Supervisor

ti

Enclosure

What are the nine
steps of the whole-
into-parts method?

In summary, the whole-into-parts method of planning, organizing, and developing a business message has these steps:

1. Determine the dual purpose of your message.
2. State that dual purpose as the message corethought.
3. Support the message corethought with a list of relevant topics.
4. Revise the topic list: Consolidate, delete, or add relevant items.
5. Rearrange the revised list into a message outline.
6. Revise the outline: Consolidate, delete, or add relevant items. Subordinate subtopics to topics. Subordinate topics to corethought. State items in grammatically parallel form.
7. Write or dictate the message draft from the revised outline.
8. Revise and proofread the draft. If necessary, revise and proofread subsequent drafts. Use proofreader's marks to speed the process.
9. Produce the final version of your message.

As you develop expertise with this method, you may find that you can condense those nine steps into six:

1. Identify dual purpose.
2. State corethought.
3. List and revise topics.
4. Write and revise outline.
5. Draft and revise message.
6. Produce final version of message.

And when you become an experienced business communicator, you may perform Steps 1−4 of that condensed method with (or, often, even without) just a few notes to guide yourself.

COLLABORATIVE WRITING (TEAM WRITING)

The whole-into-parts method accommodates one writer working alone or a writing team. When one writer uses this method, he or she is solely responsible for fulfilling the nine steps of message planning, organization, and development. When a team engages in collaborative writing, those steps are shared.

The entire team may participate in determining and stating the dual purpose of a message. One team member may then focus on topic lists and outlines. Another member may subsequently draft and revise the emerging message. Still another member may proofread and produce the final version.

Solo writing requires expertise of a single person throughout the nine-step whole-into-parts method. Collaborative writing, or team writing, requires meticulous and timely coordination of several people's expertise throughout the nine-step whole-into-parts method. Solo writing and team writing are used extensively today for the production of effective letters, reports, memos, training manuals, advertisements, and myriads of other business messages.

SPECIAL CONSIDERATIONS FOR PARAGRAPHS AND SENTENCES

How do paragraphs and sentences work in holding together all of your message? Here are guidelines and examples of paragraph/sentence use in business communication.

Paragraph Placement and Length

A paragraph may consist of a *single* sentence related to the message corethought. Or a paragraph may be a *group* of sentences related to themselves and to the message corethought.

For clarity, state the paragraph topic as a sentence. For variety and emphasis in paragraphs of more than one sentence, place the *topic statement* at the beginning or at the end of the paragraph. Finally, build the paragraph with other sentences pertaining to its topic. Remember: As a whole message should be unified by its corethought, so should a paragraph be unified by the paragraph topic. Deliberately use your paragraphs to show your reader the step-by-step sequence of topics supporting your message corethought.

Effective business writers use paragraphing to prevent formidable masses of words, to provide a change of pace in reading rate, to give a "breather" to the reader's mind and eye. But to be more than just a mechanical convenience, all of a paragraph should pertain to its topic. And the topic should pertain to the whole message corethought.

Sentences which open and close a *message* are usually better remembered than those in the middle of the message. Likewise, sentences that open or close a *paragraph* are in emphatic positions.

Expert business writers generally keep their opening and closing paragraphs relatively short. A one- to four-line opening paragraph, for instance, tends quickly to attract attention and interest. A counterpart closing paragraph tends quickly to summarize the message corethought and to elicit appropriate response.

An abundance of too long or too short paragraphs can distract your reader.

How do solo writing and team writing differ?

Where should your topic statement appear?

How can you achieve emphasis?

For example, four paragraphs of five lines each, or five paragraphs of four lines each, are often easier to read than one paragraph of twenty lines. Conversely, four paragraphs of six lines each are often easier to read than twelve paragraphs of two lines each. But effective paragraph length is more the result of empathy for the reader than of arbitrary line quotas. The same is true of sentence length and whole-message length; empathy is a reliable, profitable guide.

How long should your
paragraphs be?

Paragraph Coherence

A *paragraph* is coherently unified when all of its sentences pertain to its topic. A *message* is coherently unified when all of its sentences pertain to the message corethought. For instance, one paragraph of a persuasive message may be intended to attract attention, another to stimulate interest, a third to develop desire, and a fourth to elicit response. *Each* paragraph should relate to its respective topic (attention, interest, desire, action). *All* paragraphs should relate to the whole message corethought (persuading the receiver to think, to feel, or to do what the sender intends). Sometimes you will use more than a single paragraph to develop a complex topic. Sometimes you will use more than one message to accomplish complex communication.

These basic techniques improve coherence of paragraphs and of whole messages:

1. Use link words and phrases (*also, consequently, furthermore, however, therefore, for example, for instance, on the other hand,* and others shown in Illustration 6–9). But use them deliberately to connect the parts of your paragraphs and to connect the paragraphs of your message.

2. Repeat key words and key phrases (the names of your receiver and of her or his company, the name of your company, the name of the product or service being discussed, a phrase representing the message corethought, a phrase representing a paragraph topic). But repeat them deliberately for coherence and emphasis, taking care not to pad sentences, paragraphs, or whole messages.

3. Reinforce key data by presenting them in more than one way. Use examples, case histories, explanations, comparisons, contrasts, statistical tables, graphs, summaries, lists, or variations of spacing or typography. But use them to emphasize data and to make every part—as well as your whole message—completely understandable.

4. Use inductive order for your data. Begin the whole message or begin a particular paragraph with specific examples or reasons. End with a

How can you achieve
coherence for
paragraphs and for
entire messages?

Illustration 6–9   EXAMPLES OF LINK WORDS AND LINK PHRASES

Additions	also, and, another, as well as, besides, both . . . and, equally important as, finally, first (second, third, etc.), further, furthermore, in addition, lastly, moreover, not only . . . but also, not so obvious is, too
Alternatives	either . . . or, if, or, whether, whether . . . or not
Concessions	although, at least, despite, even, though, still, yet
Contrasts	but, by contrast, from another viewpoint, however, in contrast to, nevertheless, notwithstanding, on the contrary, on the other hand, to contrast, in another way, unlike
Emphasis	above all, especially, certainly, in detail, indeed, in fact, in particular, in truth, mainly, most importantly, particularly, principally, specifically, surely, urgently
Examples	as follows, for example, for instance, like, to illustrate
Exclusions	all but, all except, except, except that, neither . . . nor
Purpose	for, so, so that, to, to bring about, to effect, to result in
Results	accordingly, as a result, consequently, for that reason (for this reason, these reasons, those reasons), hence, so, therefore, the outcome is, the results are, thus

general principle or observation derived from those examples or reasons. Or use deductive order for your data. Begin the whole message or a particular paragraph with a general principle or observation. End with specific examples or reasons.

Opening Sentences

Use your opening sentence to get your reader's attention, keynote your message, signal your corethought, or prepare your reader for what follows.

Of all opening sentences, one that shows action favoring the reader is naturally the most welcome. Suppose, for example, that you are a retail employee who has requested time off during the peak holiday shopping season. What positive feelings would the following reply give you?

Your vacation request for the two weeks beginning December 9 has been approved.

Contrast that favorable-action opener with this wordy, self-centered one:

I have compared your vacation request with those of our other employees and have decided to authorize your time off.

Here are two more examples of favorable-action openers that come right to the point:

Yes, the St. Louis distributor will rush your shipment.

Your credit account is open and ready for your use.

The following left-hand paragraphs illustrate the effects of unnecessary wordiness. The concise paragraphs at the right attract attention.

Wordy	Concise
We desire to acknowledge the receipt of your note of January 25, in which you inquire whether you are fully protected under our policy No. 2-40378. We wish to advise that an examination of our records shows that your policy is in force and that you are protected according to the terms and stipulations therein. (55 words)	Your policy No. 2-40378 is still effective. (7 words)
We wish to acknowledge receipt of your letter of the 15th and wish to state that we appreciate the interest you have shown in our present situation. In the matter of your inquiry relative to your illustrations, we wish to advise that they have had our attention and are enclosed herewith. (51 words)	Here are the illustrations that accompanied your October 15 letter. Thank you for letting us see examples of your work. (20 words)

If you must refuse a request, reject a claim, or otherwise convey disappointing news, follow this suggestion: Begin with a relevant, neutral statement or one which is relevant and agreeable. That kind of opener will attract your reader's attention and interest, enable you to explain your reasons, and thereby prepare your reader for the disappointing news. The following left-hand examples are of openers likely to alienate a reader. The right-hand examples encourage the receiver to read on.

Relevant but Antagonistic	Relevant and Empathetic
Your vacation request is denied.	Your vacation request has been carefully considered, Lou.
I regret to inform you that we won't release your St. Louis shipment, despite your explanation of nonpayment for what is owed us.	Thank you for explaining the nonpayment of your St. Louis invoice.
We cannot supply Coretime products to you.	Your interest in Coretime products is welcome.

Closing Sentences

Use your closing sentence to reinforce goodwill, to offer a counterproposal, or to stimulate action. For example, contrast the effects of the following:

Relevant but Antagonistic	Relevant and Empathetic
Don't submit another vacation request until April.	Please resubmit your vacation request in April.
If you fail to send us at least a partial payment, you won't get that shipment.	As soon as payment, even partial, is received, the shipment will be on its way to you.
Because of a production mix-up, we don't know when those Coretime products can be sent.	Once the new production schedule is underway, we'll gladly supply you with those Coretime products.

Many business communicators, especially in the United States, consider a participial closing obsolete. Contrast the following examples. Notice that the participial closings in the left column are longer and less vigorous than the examples in the right column.

Wordy and Outdated	Concise and Current
Regretting our inability to comply, we remain . . .	May we serve you in another way?
Trusting you will give this matter your prompt attention, we are . . .	Please act promptly on this request.
Thanking you for your order, and assuring you of our careful attention, we remain . . .	Thank you for your order. It is being shipped today.

"Thanking you in advance" is an especially trite, discourteous phrase, because it implies that you take people for granted. Yes, thank people for their services. But do so *after* those services have been performed.

REVIEW AND TRANSITION

With the building-block method, you do not thoroughly plan a message before you try to compose it. You feel you need to say or write something, and you just add one word or phrase to another.

With the whole-into-parts method, you plan the entire message before choosing and fitting together the words, sentences, and paragraphs which support the corethought. You develop purpose and corethought into topic list, outline, and message draft. You revise as necessary or appropriate. Your proper use of proofreader's marks helps you to expedite revision until you produce the final version.

Continuing this discussion of planning, organization, and development, Chapter 7 focuses on appropriate message tone.

YOUR DECISIONS FOR CHAPTER 6

Your message to Neel may vitally affect your employment possibilities with Ruston Enterprises (see the Decisions Case at the beginning of this chapter). You have adequate time to plan, organize, and develop that important message based upon these communication decisions:

1. What is the dual purpose of your message to Neel?

2. What is an effective statement of that dual purpose as a message corethought?

3. What data relate the message corethought to the Neel interview, especially words and actions which may have misled Neel during the interview?

4. Which of those data should you consolidate or delete? Why? What data, if any, should you add? Why?

5. What is a logically consistent pattern for organizing the remaining data? Will you use inductive order? deductive order? Why?

6. What detailed message outline do you derive from the final form of your data list? Do minor items logically support major headings in your message outline? Do major headings logically support your message corethought? Does the outline use grammatical parallelism to show logical organization of the parts as well as the whole of your message? To what extent should you revise the outline? Why?

7. Does the first draft of your message satisfy you? Why? Is that draft likely to satisfy Neel? Why? What improvements of the draft are necessary or desirable? Why?

8. Is every sentence in the draft related to its paragraph topic? Is every paragraph related to the message corethought? Are the opening and closing paragraphs—as well as the opening and closing sentences—performing their communication functions? Specifically how, if at all, should you revise the draft? Why? If you believe you should not revise the draft, what justifies your decision?

DISCUSSION QUESTIONS

A. Within the context of Chapter 6, what are appropriate definitions and examples for these terms?

1. building-block method
2. whole-into-parts method
3. dual purpose
4. corethought
5. list
6. outline
7. revising
8. proofreading
9. *stet*
10. delete

B. In what ways does the building-block method differ from the whole-into-parts method of message planning? Why do both of those methods merit the attention of communicators?

C. What evidence supports or contradicts the following assertions?

1. Revising lists and outlines is more efficient than changing paragraphs or whole messages.
2. Effective paragraph length is more the result of empathy for the reader than of arbitrary line quotas.

D. In what ways are lists and outlines similar? How do they differ? What are the advantages of using outlines to develop messages?

E. Other than attracting attention, what are the functions of an effective opening sentence?

F. Other than ending a message, what are the functions of an effective closing sentence?

APPLICATIONS

1. Develop this list into an appropriate message outline:

   Dual-Purpose Corethought: To ensure substantial, ongoing income for an electric utility company while providing budget-control benefits for customers whose accounts may otherwise become delinquent.

   Items: 1. When your electricity bill soars, Regional Power Corporation (RPC) is ready to help you.
   2. The RPC Average Payment Program enables you to budget a *constant cost figure* every month.
   3. This program authorizes RPC to average your 12 previous monthly bills and charge you that average amount for each of the *next* 12 months.
   4. Whatever the weather and temperature extremes may be, you pay the same amount monthly.
   5. You will then be notified as to whether you have overpaid or underpaid your account.
   6. For details of how the Average Payment Program can benefit you, please visit or call your RPC Service Center.

2. Develop this list into an appropriate message outline:

   Dual-Purpose Corethought: To retain current and to acquire new bank customers by offering the convenience of automated teller service.

   Items: 1. Good news for A&E Bank customers.
   2. A&E Bank now provides access to RICA services.
   3. RICA is a network of automated teller machines that operate 24 hours daily.
   4. RICA lets you withdraw cash and determine your account balance.
   5. RICA has more than 27,000 locations in cities throughout the United States.
   6. To request your RICA access card, please visit your nearest A&E Bank office today.

3. Develop the preceding outlines into message drafts.

4. Revise—and use proofreader's marks to correct—the message drafts.

5. Plan, organize, and develop business-related examples of the following:

   a. a paragraph arranged in deductive order
   b. a paragraph arranged in inductive order
   c. a whole message arranged in deductive order
   d. a whole message arranged in inductive order

6. Plan, organize, and develop effective messages for the following situations:

    a. Assume that you are applying for financial assistance to continue your education. Your school offers Vanover Foundation scholarships, which pay the costs of tuition, books, supplies, and incidental expenses. To be considered for a Vanover scholarship, you must request written recommendations from three references (people other than members of your family) who will vouch for your intelligence, industriousness, and integrity. The recommendations are to be confidential messages sent directly by the references to M. A. Claussen, Director, Loans and Scholarships Office, at your school. Those recommendations must be received not later than two weeks from today. Prepare a recommendation request for possible use with your three references.

    b. Put yourself into the role of your business communication instructor. Write the requested recommendation.

    c. As yourself, write a follow-up letter to thank your instructor or someone else who has recommended you.

    d. You have received the Vanover Foundation scholarship. Write a letter to share the good news with your instructor.

7. Use appropriate proofreader's marks to correct the following sentences:

    a. Openning cermonies, for the new conviently located Central City Mall includes entertainment.

    b. With which recruitershave you sheduled intraviews at the campus plaemeant ofice

    c. Is the ryan company executive offices on the fortieth floor of the dalton Building?

    d. Kayle Lucas the assistant manager asked me "Is this recomendation your's or her's"?

    e. "What is the status of thos erequisitions", Lucas asked.

    f. The banker smiled and said "Thank-you Ms. Dulakis for opening you're new Account with us".

    g. Carrie's follow up thank you note impressed the inter viewer favrably.

    h. Kay's realistic detailed business plan is attracting the intrest of pro spective investor's.

8. Use appropriate proofreader's marks to correct the following paragraphs:

    a. Before you make apurchase decision, please consider the competative addvantages of our productks. Nation wide survey's rate our merchantise top sin customer statisfaction.

b.   Please authorize the atached perchase oders. They need to be processed too day, so do the Adjustment requests.

c.   Employees are required to ware protective hemets and safty glases in this area We strickly enforce this ruler please comply

d.   marketing researchers oft ten use questionaire surveys interview surveys too are important means of idenifying cutom er preferances

9.   In a written message to your instructor, summarize and illustrate these topics:

a.   paragraph placement and length
b.   paragraph coherence
c.   developing the opening sentence
d.   developing the closing sentence

MULTICULTURAL INSIGHTS

1.   What are the customary patterns of data organization for business messages composed in your native language? How are those patterns like and unlike the patterns for American English business messages?

2.   What communication techniques are used to convey the corethought of a business message in your native language? How is that corethought reinforced or emphasized with your native language?

3.   You have studied techniques for developing coherence in American English sentences, paragraphs, and entire messages. Which of those techniques are customarily used with your native language? Which are not?

4.   Are the proofreader's marks used for American English used also with your native language? If not, what symbols are used for revising and editing?

5.   Which methods and techniques discussed in this chapter apply to business uses of your native language? Which do not apply? Why?

APPROPRIATE TONES FOR BUSINESS MESSAGES

OBJECTIVES

After completing this chapter, you should be able to:

1. Identify ideas, feelings, attitudes, denotations, connotations, and contexts as ingredients of message tones.
2. Recognize message tones as products of word choice and data organization.
3. Use message tones as communication links between sender and receiver.
4. Convey informal, empathetic, and sex-fair message tones.

DECISIONS CASE

The Choudrant Company conducts annual reviews of employee performances. Intended to improve superior–subordinate communication, these reviews provide opportunities for acknowledging achievements and for deciding how to overcome deficiencies.

You have completed your first year of employment with Choudrant. Your department head is pleased with your productivity. But as your review session continues, the department head asks, "If you were sitting in my chair at this moment—if you were conducting this review session—what would you say to a sincere employee who writes like this?"

Your department head hands you copies of several memos and letters bearing the Choudrant name. You recognize those messages immediately; you wrote them.

As you skim the pages, you say, "I'm sure all of this information is accurate, and I'm certain it's organized logically."

With an encouraging smile, the department head responds: "Yes, but what if, instead of *writing* those accurate, logical messages, you had *received* them? What would your impressions have been?"

With those questions in your mind, you read the pages again. Suddenly, the messages "sound" curt, almost arrogant. They seem to misrepresent the kind of person you know yourself to be.

"What would you say to a sincere employee who writes like this?" the department head asks again, then adds: "How should that good employee improve the *tone* of what he or she writes and says?"

You realize that, before you can answer sensibly, you have important decisions to make about your attitudes toward yourself, your messages, and the people who receive your messages. You decide to define *tone*, then to learn what produces and affects it.

Additional questions about this decision-making case are stated at the end of this chapter. Study the chapter before answering those questions.

CHAPTER CONTEXT

Communication **tone** is evidence of a sender's attitude toward his or her message and its receiver. Tone is much more than an ornament for a message. Tone is an instrument with which to convey meanings.

IDEAS, FEELINGS, ATTITUDES

Your intelligence enables you to communicate logically. But you—and the interpretation of your messages—are influenced by feelings as well as ideas. The interplay of thoughts and emotions disposes you to welcome some peo-

What are the
ingredients of
message tone?

ple and some circumstances, to avoid others, to have mixed feelings, or to
remain neutral.

Reflecting that interplay of ideas and feelings, your messages convey not
only data. Through their tones, your messages also convey patterns of feelings: **attitudes.** Ideas, feelings, and attitudes are ingredients of message tones.
So are denotations, connotations, and contexts.

DENOTATIONS, CONNOTATIONS, CONTEXTS

When you plainly *state* your meaning, you are using **denotation.** To denote is
to point with your words instead of with your fingers. When you *suggest*
your meaning, you are using **connotation.** To connote is to imply (to hint
about but not to state plainly) what you think and feel.

Denotations and connotations do not operate in a vacuum. **Context—**
which is a communicative environment, a setting of words and other symbols—enables denotation and connotation to function.

As an illustration of how denotation, connotation, and context are related,
picture a school graduation ring. Visualize the total appearance of that ring.
Now, notice its parts: a gemstone, a setting for the gemstone, and an inscription on the setting. The gemstone is a principal feature of the ring. Similarly,
a corethought is the principal feature of a business message. The setting of
the ring safeguards and draws attention to the gemstone. Likewise, a context
highlights a corethought. The inscription on the ring *denotes:* it identifies a
school and a year. The inscription also *connotes:* it implies completion of an
academic program at that particular school in that given year. The ring has a
gemstone and an inscribed setting to represent meaning. A business message
has a context of words, numbers, and punctuation marks to denote data, to
connote attitudes, and to convey tones.

How can you control
your message tones?

When you change your message setting—when you change the *context—*
you are likely to change your message denotation, connotation, and tone. Obviously, you may alter the tone of a sentence by substituting one word for
another. But you may also alter tone by changing contexts without changing
words.

For example, assume that you receive this single-sentence message from
your employer:

Your work is satisfactory.

Notice how the tone changes as the context shifts:

Do contexts influence
message tones?

	Example A	Example B

Example A

Message: Your work is satisfactory.

Context: Two ratings—satisfactory and unsatisfactory—are being used.

Denotation: Your job performance fulfills the criteria set by your employer.

Connotation: Continue as you have been doing.

Example B

Message: Your work is satisfactory.

Context: Several ratings—excellent, above average, satisfactory, below average, and unacceptable—are being used.

Denotation: Your performance fulfills some criteria, not all.

Connotation: Your work is neither above nor below average; consider improving it.

The *words* of that message—*"Your/work/is/satisfactory"*—did not change. But a change of *context* did alter the message tone and thereby the meaning of that message. As you see, ideas, feelings, and attitudes—as well as denotations, connotations, and contexts—are ingredients of message tones.

WORDS AND TONES

Your messages stand for you. By their tones, your messages represent you as being formal or informal, egotistical or empathetic, hypercritical or helpful, etc. Word choice and data organization affect message tones, as the following examples show.

Formal, Informal, and Technical Tones

Business messages in the United States generally convey an informal rather than a formal tone. For instance:

Word Choice: Formal Tone	Word Choice: Informal Tone
Please elucidate.	Please clarify. *Or:* Please explain.
Parameters were ascertained.	Limits were set.
Your remittance is requested by April 10.	Please pay by April 10.

As society becomes increasingly complex, specialized vocabularies—conveying a technical tone—tend to multiply. An effective communicator, how-

When should you use—or not use—jargon?

ever, matches word choice to people and circumstances. For instance, your mentioning *capacitors* or *sintered carbides* in a message is apt to be wasted effort unless you have reason to believe your receiver knows what those terms represent. On the other hand, specialized word choice—also called **jargon**—can be valuable and precise when both the sender and the receiver understand it. "Insiders" of an occupation or a profession are often attracted to someone who "speaks their language," someone who uses "words of the trade." You may even block communication if you choose common words with someone who expects technical terms in your message. Conversely, if you use technical words with "outsiders," you may create rather than solve communication problems.

To be a successful communicator—whether you decide to convey *formal, informal, technical,* or other *tones*—fit your words to your reader or listener. Use terms that will be familiar to your receiver; explain your meaning of unfamiliar terms. As with almost every other aspect of communication, empathy is a profitable guide to your choice of words and of the tones they help to convey.

Me, We, and *You* Tones

Pronouns tend to connote a sender's egotism or, much more profitably, a sender's ability to blend self-concern with *receiver* needs.

What are the disadvantages of *me* tone?

To nourish your ego—and to risk losing rapport with your receiver—say *I, me,* or *mine* in almost all of your sentences. For example:

> I want to express my appreciation for the increase in sales reflected by the last quarterly report. I am pushing for even greater effort, but I want to emphasize that I'm pleased with last quarter's results. I expect the good work to continue; I want sales to keep increasing.

What are the effects of *we* tone?

Notice that the sender's self-centered tone is scarcely changed by pluralizing *I* into *we, me* into *us, my* into *our,* or *mine* into *ours:*

> We want to express our appreciation for the increased sales reflected by the last quarterly report. We'll push for even greater effort, but we want to emphasize that we are pleased with last quarter's results. We expect the good work to continue; we want sales to keep increasing.

What are the effects of *you* tone?

You can, however, bring sender and receiver closer together through occasional use of *you, your,* or *yours:*

> Thanks for your help in increasing our sales last quarter. All of us need to push even more; but with efforts like yours, last quarter's results have pleased and encouraged us. Let's keep up the good work; let's continue increasing those sales.

The more often *you, your,* or *yours* is used, the more involved the receiver will be with the message. This *you* tone can be reinforced by occasional use of the receiver's name, as illustrated in the following example:

> Thank you, Lee, for your help in increasing sales last quarter. All of us need to push even more; but with efforts like yours, last quarter's results have pleased and encouraged us. You and I—all of us, Lee—need to keep up the good work. Let's continue increasing those sales.

Why should you be aware of your message tones?

Certainly *I, me, my, mine* are useful and often necessary words. But when you use them, be aware of what you are doing. Recognize their representation of your self-esteem. Anticipate the attitudes they elicit as well as convey. Recognize these probabilities:

1. Making *I, me, my,* and *mine* majority pronouns in your message will connote your self-centered attitude and may elicit a self-centered attitude from your receiver. Rapport can thereby be interrupted or blocked.
2. Simply pluralizing those pronouns into *we, us,* etc., may not change their egotistical tone.
3. Placing *I, me, my,* and *mine* in a context that includes *you, your,* and *yours* will connote an attitude of sender-receiver sharing.
4. Making *you* words the majority pronouns of your message can attract your receiver's attention and develop your receiver's interest.

Destructive and Constructive Tones

Empathize with your receiver when you choose words to convey suggestions or criticism. These message-tone techniques are especially useful for such circumstances:

1. Ask a question that connotes the need for improvement and guides your receiver toward the improvement.
2. Choose words that focus attention on what is needed instead of on your receiver's failure.

How do word choice and tone interact?

Notice how word choice can produce destructive or constructive tones:

Destructive Tone	Constructive Tone	Constructive Tone
You failed to type the second line of this memo.	Did I dictate the second line of this memo?	Please insert this second line and retype this memo.
I don't like your console design. You didn't	Would your console design be improved if	Your console design would be excellent

put the control lever close enough to the power switch.	you moved the control lever closer to the power switch?	with the control lever closer to the power switch.
You've ignored those instructions.	Have you followed those instructions?	Let's review those instructions; we need to follow them.

To develop a *constructive tone,* give praise where praise is due. Acknowledge accomplishments before focusing on the need for additional improvements. Whenever you can appropriately do so, word your criticism in the form of helpful questions, suggestions, requests, recommendations, or clear directives rather than as accusations.

Sexist and Sex-Fair Tones

Your choice of pronouns may connote a sexual bias *or* a belief in equality of men and women, as these examples show:

Male-Bias Tone

Relate your words to your receiver. Use terms familiar to him, terms that he will understand quickly.

Female-Bias Tone

Relate your words to your receiver. Use terms familiar to her, terms that she will understand quickly.

Sex-Fair Tone (Singular)

Relate your words to your receiver. Use terms familiar to your receiver, terms that he or she will understand quickly.

Sex-Fair Tone (Plural)

Relate your words to your receivers. Use terms familiar to your receivers, terms they will understand quickly.

Here are other examples of *sexist* and of *sex-fair tones:*

Sexist Tone	Sex-Fair Tone
An executive knows the value of continuing education for himself and for his employees. He recognizes the need for updating infor-	Executives know the value of continuing education for themselves and for their employees. Executives recognize the need for updating

mation and modernizing office procedures.

Wanted: Manager for new day-care
center. Her credentials must include
collegiate courses in educational
psychology, and she should have
had at least two years of administrative experience.

information and modernizing office
procedures.

Wanted: Manager for new day-care
center. Required: Collegiate courses
in educational psychology and at
least two years of administrative
experience.

A business firm contradicts itself when it announces equal-opportunity
policies but conveys sexist bias in the wordings of directives, instructions, reports, or other messages. Word choice discloses such contradiction, and pronouns are an important part of word choice.

Notice that exclusion of male-female distinctions is not being advocated
here. It is realistic and appropriate for feminine pronouns to characterize a
message referring solely to women or for masculine pronouns to characterize
a message referring solely to men. But freedom from sexist bias is realistic,
appropriate, and *fair* for messages referring to people *as people.*

DATA ORGANIZATION, WORD CHOICE, AND MESSAGE TONES

As discussed earlier, induction (reasoning from specific details to a generalization) and deduction (reasoning from general to specific) are basic styles of
logic. However, effective business communication involves *psychology* as
well as logic. This discussion now focuses on *psychological* aspects of data organization, word choice, and message tones for informing, influencing, and
persuading your reader or listener.

Business messages are conveniently classified as those that say yes, no, or
maybe. But that classification usually summarizes what is conveyed by the
message *data* rather than by the message *tone.* For instance, when you deny a
request, your data *denote* no. Yet your tone may *connote* yes, maybe, or a
reinforced no to granting that request or a variation of it at another time.
Whatever data you *denote,* you may organize your information and choose
your words to *connote* positive, negative, mixed, or neutral attitudes. You can
deliberately use *tone* to convey your feelings toward your receiver, toward the
request, toward the reasons for denying the request, and so on. Your data
may say "no"; but your data *organization* and your word *choice* can safeguard
your receiver's self-respect, thereby preserving rapport for future communication. Through *combinations* of data and tone, as shown by the following
examples, you can influence your receiver's attitude and behavior.

Do data organization
+ word choice =
message tone?

Positive Data and Positive Tone

Congratulations, Terry; you've earned a 10 percent raise in salary.

Since joining the Ellerby organization last year, you have tackled hard-to-please accounts (Fedor, the Hahn Company, Joggerst Associates, among others); and you've succeeded in satisfying their requirements as well as Ellerby's.

Please accept this informal acknowledgment of your fine efforts, Terry. Clipped to it is the first of your increased paychecks.

Notice the organization of that positive-data message:

1. good news
2. justification for good news
3. acknowledgment of excellent work
4. connotation of future rewards

Positive tone is conveyed by "Congratulations," "you've earned a 10 percent raise in salary," "you have tackled hard-to-please accounts . . . and you've succeeded," "your fine efforts, Terry," "the first of your increased paychecks."

Positive Data and Negative Tone

It has come to my attention that your handling of the Fedor, Hahn, and Joggerst accounts, and others assigned to you, hasn't been unsatisfactory. You have not failed to fulfill our customers' requirements and our own during the 12 months of your employment with us.

Since your efforts should not go unrecognized, it is not without pleasure that I have authorized the 10 percent increase in your salary reflected by the enclosed paycheck, with the expectation that the quality of your work will not lessen.

The organization of that positive-data message is as follows:

1. acknowledgment of performance
2. repeated acknowledgment of performance
3. good news
4. expectation of continuing quality

Negative tone is conveyed by "hasn't been unsatisfactory," "not failed to fulfill," "not go unrecognized," "not without pleasure," "will not lessen." Opening with "It has come to my attention that" suggests the sender's sense of self-importance but scarcely suggests the good news. The phrase "during the

12 months of your employment with us" momentarily suggests that the receiver may have lost his or her job.

Negative Data and Negative Tone

Although your handling of the accounts assigned to you during the past year has been competent, I regret to inform you that there is no possibility of a salary increase for you at this time.

That negative-data message has only two main parts:

1. acknowledgment of competent performance
2. bad news

Abruptly following recognition of accomplishment with words that denote disappointment is sure to stimulate negative feelings. Those negative feelings are reinforced by "regret to inform you . . . no possibility. . . ." The phrase "at this time" weakly connotes better possibilities later, but word choice and curtness combine to emphasize negative data by negative tone.

Negative Data and Positive Tone

You're right to review your salary prospects, Terry.

As you know, when you joined Ellerby, you agreed to probationary terms for the first year of your employment. Those terms included the salary that you currently earn. Eight of the twelve probationary months have passed now, and you will be eligible for salary review in April. Continue your good work, and I'll gladly recommend a sizable increase in your paycheck then.

The negative data now are stated in four main parts:

1. mutually agreeable opening
2. summary of reasons preparing receiver for temporary disappointment
3. confirmation of present salary with reminder of possible raise soon
4. recognition and encouragement of good work

Attention to receiver's needs and *you* tone are highlighted by "You're right . . . Terry," "As you know, when you joined Ellerby, you agreed," "you currently earn," "you will be eligible," "Continue your good work," "increase in your paycheck then." The wording of the final sentence reinforces positive tone for the whole message. Data and word choice combine to remind the receiver of the employment agreement, acknowledge the receiver's performance, encourage continuing excellence of work, and reaffirm the possibility of increased reward when the probationary period ends.

As with other elements of effective business communication, the key to developing appropriate message tones is empathy.

REVIEW AND TRANSITION

Communication tone is evidence of a sender's attitude toward a message and its receiver. Besides attitudes, which result from interplay of ideas and feelings, the ingredients of tone are denotations, connotations, and contexts. Data organization and word choice affect message tones, which may be formal or informal, sender-centered or receiver-centered, destructive or constructive, sexist or sex-fair, etc. Your messages *represent* you. And a vital aspect of that representation is the tone they convey.

Continuing your study of message organization and preparation, Chapter 8 presents techniques for developing the effective appearance of business letters, memorandums, and other format patterns.

YOUR DECISIONS FOR CHAPTER 7

In your role as the Choudrant employee, what communication decisions do you make? Why should you make those decisions? What are your answers to the questions asked by your department head? What justifies those answers?

DISCUSSION QUESTIONS

A. Within the context of Chapter 7, what are appropriate definitions and examples for these terms?

1. tone
2. attitudes
3. denotation
4. connotation
5. context
6. formal tone
7. informal tone
8. technical tone
9. jargon
10. *you* tone
11. constructive tone
12. sex-fair tone

B. Attitude is an ingredient of tone. What is *your* attitude toward writing business messages? How does your attitude toward speaking resemble or differ from your attitude toward writing? Why are those attitudes similar or different? As a business communicator, which of those attitudes do you intend to change? Why? What procedure will you use for making the change? What results do you expect?

C. How are denotation, connotation, and context related to tone? How are data organization and word choice related to tone?

D. What was your attitude when you began reading about formal and informal tones? technical tone? egotistical tone? *you* tone? constructive tone? sex-fair tone? How were your attitudes changed or reinforced as you continued studying Chapter 7? What accounted for the change or for the reinforcement of your attitudes?

E. What circumstances justify the use of jargon? When does the use of jargon block communication? What are examples of terms which once were jargon and now are generally understood?

F. What real-life incident elicited a negative attitude from you because of the tone with which you or your efforts were criticized? How have you overcome—or how do you plan to overcome—that negative attitude? What insights for constructive criticism have you derived from that real-life incident and from your study of Chapter 7?

APPLICATIONS

1. Locate a recent business message. It may be a letter that you recently received, a full-page magazine or newspaper advertisement presented as a message from a corporate officer, or the like.

   a. Write an analysis of the message by answering these questions: What is the corethought? What is the pattern of data organization? What is the tone? What evidence in the message justifies your answers to those questions?
   b. If the message conveys a *me* tone, rewrite it to convey a *you* tone.
   c. If the message conveys a negative or destructive tone, rewrite it to convey a positive or constructive tone.
   d. Review your written analysis of the original business message. If necessary, rewrite your analysis to convey appropriate tone.

2. For each of the following sentences, write two paragraphs that illustrate change of meaning by change of context. For each of those paragraphs, identify denotation, connotation, and context.

   a. Thank you for your interest in employment with Metrico, Inc.
   b. Since joining this company two years ago, you have had several opportunities for advancement.
   c. The decision is based upon information accompanying your loan application.

      d.   Payment on your account was received this morning.

      e.   A refund check for $750 is enclosed.

3.   Revise the following sentences to convey informal tone:

      a.   It is the policy of Benco to strive to provide its customers with service which is the best that is available.

      b.   Earnings with reference to Region 4 have increased in the order of magnitude of approximately 2.5 percent during the last quarter.

      c.   Analysis of the data justifies the recommendation by us that purchase of additional shares in Wrenn Corporation is advisable.

      d.   Assurances are herewith given that financial information disclosed by the C&G investigation is considered to be confidential at this point in time.

      e.   It is requested that you provide the requested data on or before but not later than the ninth of July.

      f.   A downturn in the market is recognized by us to be within the realm of probability.

      g.   Immediate payment of the enclosed invoices is requested.

      h.   It has been decided that an increase of 4 percent in the amount of your commission will commence on August 1.

      i.   Should your response be not immediately forthcoming, this matter will be referred to our attorneys.

      j.   With reference to your request of April 29, please be advised that approval has been granted.

4.   Revise the following sentences to emphasize *you* tone:

      a.   It gives me pleasure to offer my congratulations.

      b.   I want to say that I appreciate your suggestion.

      c.   I checked the records, and I found that you are correct.

      d.   I have confirmed that the data in your report are correct.

      e.   I am pleased to give my opinion of your work; it is excellent.

      f.   I know that I am right, but I thought I'd ask your opinion of Newton's proposed contract.

      g.   I am happy to take this opportunity of acknowledging the assistance that I have received from you.

      h.   We expect to have your reply by noon tomorrow.

      i.   We appreciate your cooperation more than we can say.

      j.   I regret that I shall have to postpone my conference with you.

5.   Revise these sentences to emphasize positive (constructive) tone:

      a.   If you do not buy this merchandise before July 31, you won't get the 15 percent discount.

      b.   If you would like additional details of this offer, please do not hesitate to visit our office.

      c.   No, that equipment cannot be delivered before March 23.

    d.   There is no way that we can give you a definite answer, because our loan committee has not reached a decision.

    e.   It is impossible for us to inspect Plant 19, at least not until tomorrow.

    f.   Anders doesn't believe that these sales figures are inaccurate.

    g.   Please don't forget to process the work orders today.

    h.   Don't you agree that increased productivity is not undesirable?

    i.   This project will not be completed without additional funding.

    j.   It is not improbable that profits will rise this quarter.

6.   Revise these sentences to convey sex-fair tone.

    a.   A successful executive expects challenges; in fact, he welcomes them.

    b.   If a person intends to be credible, he strives to be ethical in all of his transactions.

    c.   A business student who habitually ignores due dates for class work may be creating career problems for himself.

    d.   Like other managers, an executive in the fashion industry constantly uses her decision-making skills.

    e.   Can you think of any successful businessperson who doesn't need to use his communication skills effectively?

    f.   If someone has ethical, profitable ideas and he communicates them effectively, his career opportunities are splendid.

    g.   A careless writer or speaker often causes difficulties for himself and for others.

    h.   Before he applies for a bank loan, an entrepreneur needs to have a suitable business plan.

    i.   When an applicant prepares for an employment interview, he should research the company and familiarize himself with the employer's goals.

    j.   A successful sales strategy accommodates a shopper's personality, her preferences, and her needs.

7.   Use nontechnical language to define these terms:

    a.   abstract of title

    b.   accounts payable

    c.   accounts receivable

    d.   actuary

    e.   *ad valorem*

    f.   amortization

    g.   annuity

    h.   balance sheet

    i.   bill of lading

    j.   *bona fide*

    k.   common stock

l. condominium
m. consortium
n. debenture
o. escrow
p. fiduciary
q. loan comaker
r. par value
s. power of attorney
t. preferred stock

Now compose sentences or paragraphs which demonstrate appropriate use of your "translations."

MULTICULTURAL INSIGHTS

1. What tones are customary for business messages written in your native language? How are those tones like and unlike the tones of business messages written in American English?

2. In what ways do denotation, connotation, and context affect the tones of business messages written in your native language?

3. If you were writing a business message in your native language, how would you convey a formal tone? an informal tone? a technical tone?

4. For a business message written in your native language, what tone is appropriate to convey news likely to disappoint the reader?

5. If nouns (or their equivalents) have grammatical genders in your native language, how do business messages convey a sex-fair tone?

8 EFFECTIVE APPEARANCE OF BUSINESS MESSAGES

OBJECTIVES

After completing this chapter, you should be able to:

1. Appreciate effects of message format and appearance.
2. Identify characteristics of effective message formats.
3. Recognize standard letter parts and letter formats.
4. Recognize effective design and use of memorandums.
5. Appreciate other business message formats besides those of letters and memos.
6. Choose and use appropriate message formats for various communication purposes.

DECISIONS CASE

Railco, Inc., produces railway roadbed-maintenance equipment. Railco's manufacturing plants are in the United States, Canada, Australia, and England. Serving customers throughout the world, Railco transmits most written messages by conventional surface or air mail.

1. What communication factors should Railco consider as it designs its letterhead?
2. What communication factors should Railco consider as it adopts a standard letter format for use throughout its international company?

Additional questions about this decision-making case are stated at the end of this chapter. Study the chapter before answering those questions.

CHAPTER CONTEXT

You have studied how to choose words for clear, concise, accurate, and courteous communication. While words are the primary tools for forming business messages, communication also occurs without words, or **nonverbally**. Format and appearance of written messages are nonverbal communicators.

Successful business writers recognize the guides presented in this chapter as parts of business-writing protocol. **Protocol** is a societal system of behaviors considered appropriate in a specific situation. Observing protocol serves to establish and reinforce interpersonal relationships while achieving one's purpose.

Consider these business behaviors:

A secretary answers the telephone with, "Good morning. This is Shandon Interiors."

A salesclerk says, "May I help you?"

An accountant greets a client with a handshake.

How does *protocol* apply to business communication?

Each person is observing business communication protocol—expected behaviors associated with business transactions.

Similar protocols apply to written business communication. Customary, courteous, expected behaviors include orienting the reader by providing—at the head of the message—information about the sender. Greeting the reader and using logical message format are other business-writing courtesies.

Interestingly, you may not always receive praise for behaving as expected; but when you deviate from protocol, you risk criticism. Those facts, however, should not enslave you to business communication protocol. Rather, you should learn standard message formats so that you may adapt them if necessary to achieve the emphasis or attention you desire.

BUSINESS LETTERS

The appearance of your letter is a powerful nonverbal stimulus. Stationery quality and size, letterhead and envelope design, and letter format contribute to your reader's first impression of you and your business. And first impressions often endure.

Stationery

Unruled, firm-textured paper is customary for business **correspondence** (communication by letter). The weight[1] of paper affects transparency and durability. The lighter the weight, the less costly, less durable, and more transparent the paper is likely to be. For business stationery, 20- or 24-pound paper is commonly used.

In the United States, the standard size of business stationery is 8 1/2 by 11 inches. Some firms use half-size sheets, 8 1/2 by 5 inches, for short messages. High-ranking managers and other prominent professionals in business and government may use executive-size stationery, 7 1/2 by 10 1/2 inches, for their correspondence. In many countries that use the metric system for measurement, the standard size of business stationery is 21 by 29.5 millimeters, approximately 8 1/4 by 11 5/8 inches.

Stationery colors can complement the image that the firm wishes to establish. White has traditionally been the most popular and conservative color for business use, but off-white and ivory are rapidly replacing stark white as preferred stationery colors. Some firms select brilliant colors, such as red or

---

[1]*Weight* (measured in pounds) refers to the weight of 500 17- by 22-inch sheets, which, when cut in quarters, yield the equivalent of four reams of 8 1/2- by 11-inch paper.

In what ways may stationery affect a business message?

green, to project an image of vigor or to attract attention. Others use pastels to suggest warmth or refinement.

As you select stationery, consider possible nonverbal effects. When you use the familiar 8 1/2- by 11-inch, 24-pound, white or off-white paper, the absence of distracting stimuli moves the reader quickly and comfortably into the written message. An unfamiliar weight, size, or color presents uncommon stimuli. The reader will likely react to those "touch-see" stimuli before reading the message. And that reaction—positive or negative—can influence the response to the verbal message.

Letterheads and Envelopes

Printed stationery customarily shows the name, address, and telephone number of the sender's firm. Additional features may be the firm's trademark or logotype; slogan or motto; cable, fax, or Telex II (TWX)® address; and branch addresses, often with telephone numbers.

Printed stationery is called **letterhead** because the firm's identifying information often appears at the top of the page. Creative designers also place such information at the side or the bottom of the stationery. The terms *letterside* or *letterbottom* may someday be as familiar as *letterhead*.

Since stationery design adds to or detracts from the message, all letterheads (lettersides, letterbottoms) should meet the criteria for message effectiveness presented in Chapter 2. The rating guides shown in Illustration 8–1 will help you evaluate a letterhead's effectiveness.

Business envelopes customarily match their letterhead stationery in size, quality, texture, design, and color. An envelope is more than a container for a letter. It is a vital part of the communication process. If the address is incorrect or illegible, the message may never reach its intended destination. If the

Illustration 8–1 LETTERHEAD RATING GUIDES

1. Are data correct?
2. Are items clear? legible? pleasantly arranged?
3. If a trademark or logotype appears, is it attractive? Is it relevant to the firm's purpose?
4. Are addresses complete, including postal codes?
5. Are telephone numbers complete, including area codes?
6. If colors are used, do they enhance legibility and visual appeal?

Why should you
address envelopes
according to U.S.
Postal Service
recommendations?

format differs from common business practice, the receiver may infer that the sender is careless, uninformed, or inefficient.

To speed mail delivery, most countries have adopted postal code systems. The five-digit ZIP Codes used for several years in the United States are gradually being changed to nine-digit codes. The U.S. Postal Service has also installed optical character recognition (OCR) equipment in many post offices. **OCR** equipment can sort envelopes electronically if addresses are typed within a specific *read zone* in all capital letters with no punctuation. Business writers can improve communication efficiency by addressing envelopes according to OCR requirements. (See Illustration 8–2.)

Appendix D gives specific instructions for addressing envelopes and illustrates other address formats. That appendix also includes a list of the two-letter state abbreviations recommended by the U.S. Postal Service.

Letter Formats

As the *right* frame enriches a picture, so does the proper format enhance a business letter. By using a picture-frame guide, you can present your letter in a visually appealing format.

Picture-Frame Guide. Position your message so that the margins frame it evenly. Use side and bottom margins of about the same width so that your message, under its letterhead, resembles a picture placed in an attractive frame.

The **picture-frame guide** applies to stationery of standard or of unusual shape and design. Suppose, for example, that a column of printed data extends down the left margin of a letterhead sheet. In that column may be branch office addresses, lists of executive personnel, names of committee members, or the like. With such a format, simply move your message slightly to the right and frame it in the remaining space. Or, if lines of printed data extend across the bottom of the sheet, move your message upward, again framing it in the available space.

How does use of
standard letter parts
and formats
contribute to the goal
of goodwill?

Letter Parts. Each standard letter part contributes to the writer's information-exchange and goodwill goals. Effective business writers observe the following protocols for letter parts. (See Appendix D for additional discussion of letter parts.)

Heading. The **heading** shows the place and date of message origin. On a printed letterhead, only the date is typed, usually 13 to 19 lines from the top of the sheet, depending on the length of the letter. (See Illustration 8–3.)

With plain paper (no printed letterhead), the writer's complete mailing address and the date are typed 10 to 13 lines from the top of the sheet. (See

Illustration 8–2 ENVELOPES ADDRESSED ACCORDING TO
UNITED STATES POSTAL RECOMMENDATIONS

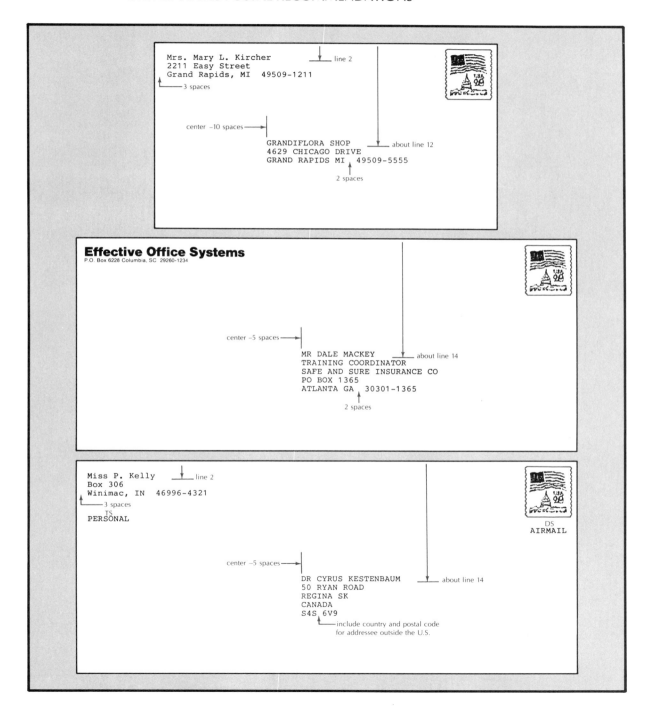

Illustration 8–3   BLOCK FORMAT, OPEN PUNCTUATION

Heading

Effective Office Systems
P.O. Box 6228 Columbia, SC 29260-1234
Telephone (803) 555-7404

line 16   April 4, 19--

Letter
address

Mr. Jose Ferreira, President
Ferreira Enterprises
1801 Wheat Street
Columbia, SC 29205-8670

Greeting   Dear Mr. Ferreira

The letter you are now reading is an example of <u>block
format</u>. Many businesses use this style today because
its format saves typing time.

Note that all lines begin at the left margin. This
practice eliminates the machine manipulations and typing
strokes required to indent the date, paragraphs, and
closing lines.

Body   This letter is punctuated in the open style, with no
punctuation following the greeting and complimentary
close. Mixed punctuation style, with a colon after the
greeting and a comma after the complimentary close, may
also be used.

We recommend that you use the block format for most of
your correspondence. It projects an image of efficiency
while retaining the standard letter parts that many
readers expect to see.

Complimentary
close

Sincerely

Priscilla Taylor

Signature
lines

Priscilla Taylor
President

Reference
initials

sk

Illustration 8–4.) In U.S. businesses, the date is commonly written in month, day, year sequence (June 5, 19—). Most U.S. military establishments use the day, month, year sequence (5 June 19—). Many European, Asian, and Latin American businesses also use that format. An emerging trend in some countries is to use the year, month, day sequence (19— May 6). Since those variations exist, avoid using only numerals to designate a date (6/5/88). The possibility of misinterpretation is too great. (In 6/5/88, is June 5 or May 6 intended?)

Letter Address. The letter address includes the receiver's name, title, company unit (if used); name of the receiver's firm; its street address; city, state, and postal code number. Include country of destination for all mail sent to a country outside the one from which the letter originated. All lines are blocked at the left margin, starting on the fourth line space below the date. (See Illustrations 8–3, 8–4, and 8–5.)

Greeting.[2] The greeting that begins a letter is typed at the left margin a double space below the last line of the letter address. The first line of the letter address governs the greeting.

When you select courtesy titles for addressees, be guided by equity and respect for others' preferences about their names and titles. For example, if a wife and husband have retained their birth names, appropriate titles and names in the address are Ms. Emily Simmons and Mr. Robert Dyer; the greeting is "Dear Ms. Simmons and Mr. Dyer" or "Dear Emily and Robert." Use the title *Mrs.* when you know a married woman prefers that title and *Miss* when you know it is an unmarried woman's preference. If you do not know the individual's preference, use *Ms.* or no title. *Ms.* and *Mr.* differentiate individuals on the basis of gender only, not marital status. When you do not know the addressee's sex, use a gender-free title and greeting. Here are examples of appropriate addressees and greetings:

Addressee	Greeting
Mr. A. B. Ross	Dear Mr. Ross
Mrs. A. B. Ross	Dear Mrs. Ross
Miss A. B. Ross	Dear Miss Ross
Ms. A. B. Ross	Dear Ms. Ross
A. B. Ross	Dear A. B. Ross
A. B. Ross, M.D.	Dear Dr. Ross
	Dear A. B. Ross

What guides should determine your selection of courtesy titles and greetings?

[2]This letter part is also called the *salutation.* The term *greeting,* instead of *salutation,* is used in this book since it is more consistent with the communication guides for message tone. *Greeting* connotes an expression of friendliness, pleasure, or respect upon meeting someone, whereas *salutation* connotes a ceremonial or military gesture.

Illustration 8–4   MODIFIED BLOCK FORMAT, MIXED PUNCTUATION

```
                                             619 Chapel Drive
                                             Gary, IN  46410-8391
                                             April 4, 19--


        Mr. James Stoll
        48 Harrington Gardens
        London SW7 4JO
        England

        Dear Mr. Stoll:

        This letter illustrates modified block format which has
        the following features:

        1.  Date, complimentary close, and signature block begin
            at the horizontal center.  Paragraphs may be in-
            dented or blocked at the left margin.

        2.  All other letter parts begin at the left margin.

        3.  Greeting and complimentary close may have either
            mixed or open punctuation.

        An advantage of modified block format is the appearance
        of balancing the message for eye appeal.  Visual balance,
        however, does require the typist to use tab stops for
        date, complimentary close, and signature block.  These
        machine manipulations increase message-production time.

                                    Cordially,

                                    Glenda Jett
                                    Miss Glenda Jett
```

Mr. H. G. Smith and Ms. A. B. Ross	Dear Mr. Smith and Ms. Ross
Ms. Ann Ross and Mr. Harry Smith	Dear Ms. Ross and Mr. Smith Dear Ann and Harry
Ross Enterprises	Ladies and Gentlemen Ladies *or* Mesdames (if an all-female enterprise) Gentlemen (if an all-male enterprise)
Personnel Manager	Dear Personnel Manager

The context may justify other greetings. Some writers use conversational openings such as "Good morning" or "Hello, (name)" to establish an informal tone.

The greeting is omitted in the simplified block letter format. (See Illustration 8–5.) Many writers use this format when they are not sure how to greet the receiver.

Body. The **body**, which contains the primary letter message, is started a double space below the greeting, single-spaced with double spacing between paragraphs. In the simplified block letter format, the body is started a double space below the subject line.

Complimentary Close. The **complimentary close** is keyed a double space below the last line of the body. The complimentary close is omitted in the simplified block format. (See Illustration 8–5.)

"Yours truly," "Yours very truly," and "Very truly yours," are considered formal closings. "Sincerely," "Sincerely yours," and "Yours sincerely," are most commonly used in U.S. business correspondence. "Cordially," "Cordially yours," and "Yours very cordially," are also used, especially when the letter tone is personal and friendly. Word your complimentary close to match the prevailing tone of your message.

Participial wordings like "Thanking you in advance, I remain" or "Hoping to receive your prompt reply, we are" were once popular transitions to the complimentary close; but such participial transitions are considered obsolete in U.S. correspondence today. Move your reader directly from the last paragraph of the letter body to your complimentary close.

Signature. The **signature line** may consist only of the name of the writer keyed on the fourth line below the complimentary close[3] or may also include the writer's official title. The title may follow the typed name and a comma; or it may be keyed on the next line space, blocked with the name and the complimentary close.

How are letter tone and complimentary close related?

---

[3]Some firms still show the company name in all capital letters a double space below the complimentary close. This practice is unnecessary when the company name appears in the letterhead.

Illustration 8-5   SIMPLIFIED BLOCK FORMAT

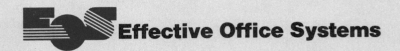

April 4, 19--

Mr. Jose Ferreira, President
Ferreira Enterprises
1801 Wheat Street
Columbia, SC 29205-8670

SIMPLIFIED BLOCK LETTER FORMAT

Does this streamlined letter format appeal to you, Mr. Ferreira?
If it does, you are one of a growing number of correspondents who
prefer the simplified block format because of its efficiency and
simplicity. Note the features of this format:

1. All lines begin at the left margin.

2. The greeting and complimentary close are omitted.

3. A subject line is required. It is typed in all capital letters
a double space below the inside address.

4. The body of the letter begins a double space below the subject
line.

5. The author's name and title are typed on one line in all capital letters four spaces below the body of the letter.

6. Typist's initials are typed a double space below the author's
name and title.

The simplified block format gives your letter a crisp, clean appearance. However, omission of the greeting and complimentary
close may suggest unintended curtness. You can offset that curtness, Mr. Ferreira, by using the reader's name within the message.

Priscilla Taylor

PRISCILLA TAYLOR, PRESIDENT

mh

P.O. Box 6228   •   Columbia, SC 29260-1234   •   Telephone (803) 555-7404

Reference Initials. The initials of the typist or transcriber, **reference initials**, are keyed in lowercase at the left margin, two lines below the keyed signature or sender's title.

Special letter parts, such as the attention line, subject line, reference line, and enclosure and copy notations, are discussed and illustrated in Appendix D.

Punctuation Styles. In *personal* letters, both the greeting and the complimentary close (placed just above the sender's signature) end with a comma. But in *business* letters either of two punctuation styles is used for the greeting and complimentary close.

How do *open* and *mixed* punctuation styles differ?

Open style omits punctuation after both the greeting and the complimentary close. **Mixed style** places a colon after the greeting and a comma after the complimentary close. Remember: If you do not put a colon after a greeting, place no comma after the complimentary close. If you put a colon after the greeting, place a comma after the complimentary close.

Letter Formats. The letter formats used most frequently in U.S. businesses are *block, modified block,* and *simplified block.* Some firms use one format in all their correspondence. Other companies permit their writers to choose any standard format. When you are allowed to select a format, consider the nonverbal message it conveys. Do the format, letterhead, and content reinforce the total message?

What nonverbal message is suggested by block format?

What nonverbal message is suggested by modified block format?

What nonverbal message is suggested by simplified block format?

1. *Block.* Since every line of the block format (see Illustration 8–3) begins at the left margin, this format saves typing time. Block format tends nonverbally to suggest efficiency. The evenness of the left margin projects a crisp, neat, orderly image.
2. *Modified Block.* The modified block format (see Illustration 8–4) is popular and moderately conservative. The positions of the date, complimentary close, and signature block provide visual balance. Paragraphs may or may not be indented in this format. Well established for many years, this format projects a more traditional image than either the block or simplified block format. The modified block format is commonly used for personal business letters.
3. *Simplified Block.* The simplified block format (see Illustration 8–5) has grown in popularity during the past decade. This is an efficient format since most lines begin at the left margin and the greeting and complimentary close are omitted. Writers often use this format to avoid awkward greetings. Some readers consider the omission of the greeting and complimentary close a breach of business etiquette, but a personal tone can be established by using the reader's name in the letter body. The simplified block format is well received by business

writers who are efficiency conscious and by those who keep abreast of new business communication practices.

MEMORANDUMS

What basic goal is to be met by memo format and tone?

Memorandums (also called *memoranda* or *memos*) differ from letters in several respects. A **memorandum** is used primarily for internal rather than external communication. Consequently, memo format and tone are directed toward efficiency within an organization.

Memos are keyed—or handwritten—on printed letterhead, printed memo forms, or plain paper. Efficient firms adopt a memo format and require its consistent use. Two memo formats, *standard* (formal) and *simplified* (informal), are shown in Illustrations 8–6 and 8–7. Notice these five features:

1. Courtesy titles (Mr., Ms., etc.) for sender and receiver are usually omitted, but job titles or department designations are sometimes used.
2. The memo does not contain a letter address, greeting, complimentary close, or signature block. The writer can personalize a memo by using the receiver's name in the memo body.
3. The standard memo heading consists of four parts. The order may vary.

   TO: (receiver's name and/or title)

   FROM: (sender's name and/or title)

   DATE: (month, day, year, even the time of day when appropriate to the message)

   SUBJECT: (message corethought or file reference)

4. In the simplified memo format, guide words (TO, FROM, DATE, SUBJECT) are omitted, and the sender's name appears at the end of the message in a signature block.
5. The picture-frame guide is rarely applied to memo format. For efficiency, memos are usually keyed with one-inch top and side margins. The body begins a double space below the heading. Paragraphs are blocked and single-spaced with a double space between.

When may signatures or initials be used on memos?

Policies of some firms require originators to initial or sign all memos. In other firms, however, the writer's initials or signature adds a nonverbal message. When the memo is intended as a routine message, the writer customarily does not sign or initial it. Memos that are to be perceived as moderately important (neither routine nor urgent) are initialed. Those the writer wishes to be recognized as of great importance are signed.

Illustration 8–6 MEMO IN STANDARD FORMAT

Safe and Sure Insurance Co.

INTEROFFICE MEMORANDUM

TO: Jack J. Kool, Region V Manager

FROM: Sally M. Skardon, Zone Underwriter *SMS*

DATE: March 15, 19--

SUBJECT: Region V Report, February, 19--

Your agents produced exceptionally well in February, Jack. We approved 91 policies in your region last month. The approvals in each state were:

Alaska	20	Montana	3
Arizona	16	Nevada	0
California	4	Oregon	1
Hawaii	17	Utah	2
Idaho	16	Washington	12

Only five individual policies were declined:

Agent	Plan	Reason
Kenneth Hayes	1752	Cancelled by applicant
Susan Keane	1752	Inspection report
Jeanne Newell	1781	Incomplete
Pedro Ross	1781	Occupation
Peter Sazehn	1752	Incomplete

We're pleased with the production in your zone, Jack; we want to help you and your agents in any way we can. Please call me if you have any questions.

mwh

Illustration 8–7   MEMO IN SIMPLIFIED FORMAT

March 15, 19--

Jack J. Kool, Region V Manager

REGION V REPORT, FEBRUARY, 19--

Your agents produced exceptionally well in February, Jack. We
approved 91 policies in your region last month. The approvals in
each state were:

Alaska	20	Montana	3
Arizona	16	Nevada	0
California	4	Oregon	1
Hawaii	17	Utah	2
Idaho	16	Washington	12

Only five individual policies were declined:

Agent	Plan	Reason
Kenneth Hayes	1752	Cancelled by applicant
Susan Keane	1752	Inspection report
Jeanne Newell	1781	Incomplete
Pedro Ross	1781	Occupation
Peter Sazehn	1752	Incomplete

We're pleased with the production in your zone, Jack; we want to
help you and your agents in any way we can. Please call me if you
have any questions.

Sally M. Skardon, Zone Underwriter   *SMS*

mwh

Businesspeople often place their initials, and sometimes their signatures, next to their typewritten names in the "FROM" space of a memo heading. But by initialing or signing at the *end* of the memorandum (as at the end of a business letter), the sender is likelier to review the message a final time and to correct errors before transmission.

A memo should be written so that the reader can extract the corethought quickly and correctly. A meaningful, concise subject line creates a context or frame of reference that helps the reader preview the message and interpret it quickly. Numbered items, columns, or lists focus the reader's attention upon key points of the message.

OTHER BUSINESS MESSAGE FORMATS

You have studied the formats of letters and memorandums. Other formats you may use in business include minutes of meetings, news releases, and postal or reply cards.

Minutes of Meetings

Minutes, which are written records of meetings or conferences, usually include these data:

1. Identification of the group that met.
2. Classification of the meeting (e.g., regular, monthly, quarterly, special, emergency).
3. Location, date, and time that the meeting began.
4. Identification of people in attendance and of the presiding officer (sometimes of other officers as well).
5. Identification of absentees and of reasons for their absence.
6. Reference to minutes of the previous meeting. (Were they accepted as read? Were they amended and then accepted?) An exception, of course, would be the case of a group that is meeting for the first time and therefore would have no previous minutes.
7. Reports of action on matters previously presented to the group; such matters sometimes are called "old business." In the case of a group meeting for the first time, the equivalent of old business would be statements of authorization for the group's existence and definitions of the group's role, scope, and administrative organization.
8. Reports of action on matters currently presented to the group (new business).
9. Notation of when the meeting ended. (If the meeting is other than a

regularly scheduled session, the place and time of the next session should be mentioned before this notation.)

10. Identification of the person responsible for preparing the minutes.

What primary
communication
objective should be
achieved by meeting
minutes?

Minutes should include only objective data and actions, not subjective generalities. For example, if during a meeting the chairperson accepts a report as "splendid work" and authorizes those words to appear in the minutes, the recorder would quote them directly. The group may also pass an official resolution of thanks, which would appear in the minutes. The recorder should not emotionalize the minutes with *brilliant, superb, antagonistic,* or similar terms. The recorder's job is to record and report the business of the meeting.

If a complimentary close is used for minutes, it customarily is either "Respectfully submitted," or "Respectfully." Minutes usually are signed by the duly authorized officer(s) of an organization—for example, by the official secretary or by another officer.

Whatever format is used, minutes should:

1. Help the reader to perceive corethoughts easily and accurately.
2. Permit the reader to make notes or corrections for a later meeting.

A *report-style format* and an *indented format* for minutes of a meeting are shown in Illustrations 8–8 and 8–9. Each format has its own advantages. The report-style format is easy to type; but, the indented format guides the reader's eyes to key points.

News Releases

Another business communication format is the **news release** (see Illustration 8–10) intended for mass-media transmission by radio/TV broadcasts, newspaper stories, and magazine articles. Effective news releases do the following:

1. Identify the sender.
2. Indicate when the message should be publicized.
3. State the corethought as a journalistic headline.
4. Cite the information source when applicable.
5. Answer the basic communication questions: *Who? What? When? Where? Why? How?* The order for answering those questions may vary (for example, *What* before *Who*).

What is the *inverted
pyramid form?*

The body of a news release is organized in what journalists call *inverted pyramid form:* Answers to the basic questions appear first; supporting de-

Illustration 8–8 MINUTES OF A MEETING: REPORT-STYLE FORMAT

```
                MINUTES OF THE EXECUTIVE COMMITTEE MEETING
                          KEUKA TEXTILES, INC.


         A regular meeting of the executive committee, Keuka Textiles,
    Inc., was called to order at corporate headquarters, New York City,
    October 16, 19--, at 10:30 a.m.  Members present were A. O. Chism,
    M. S. Dunn, J. D. Gratz, D. R. Green, M. R. Haneda, C. J. Smith,
    G. R. Raub, and E. P. Hart who presided.  R. Mendez was absent,
    representing the company at the Fiber Technology Conference in New
    Orleans.

         Minutes of the September 28, 19--, meeting were accepted as
    read.

         M. R. Haneda reported that expansion of Keuka Mills at Charlotte
    and Winston-Salem, North Carolina, and at Greenville, South Carolina,
    was proceeding as planned.  Production schedules are being maintained
    during this interim period; the expansion program is set for comple-
    tion early next year.

         E. P. Hart distributed copies of a progress report from G. W.
    Hill, manager of Carolinas Division, for study and discussion at
    the next meeting of this committee.

         J. D. Gratz and D. R. Green announced that, as authorized by
    the committee, Keuka Educational Grants-in-Aid, totaling $55,000
    for the current fiscal year, have been made available to students
    at the following schools:

             Atlantic School of Design, Providence, RI ($20,000)
             Barstow Technical Institute, Roanoke, VA ($15,000)
             Boone A&M University, Durham, SC ($5,000)
             Caycee Community College, Columbus, GA ($5,000)
             Muscogee Junior College, Columbia, SC ($5,000)
             Eufala Technical Institute, Troy, AL ($5,000)


         J. D. Gratz presented a memorandum from J. M. Walsh, manager
    of personnel recruiting department, suggesting that recipients of
    these grants be invited to visit Keuka headquarters.  A. O. Chism
    moved approval, with the stipulation that Keuka underwrite expenses
    for the visitors.  C. J. Smith seconded the motion, which passed
    unanimously.  M. S. Dunn will assign a member of the community ser-
    vices staff to plan the visit.  The plan will be reviewed at the
    next meeting on November 27, 19--, at 10:30 a.m.

         The meeting was adjourned at 11:45 a.m.

                             Respectfully submitted

                             G. R. Raub

                             G. R. Raub, Secretary
```

Illustration 8–9   MINUTES OF A MEETING: INDENTED FORMAT

```
                   MINUTES OF THE EXECUTIVE COMMITTEE MEETING
                             KEUKA TEXTILES, INC.
                              (Regular Meeting)


TIME/DATE/PLACE        10:30 a.m., October 16, 19--, corporate head-
                       quarters

PRESIDING OFFICER      E. P. Hart

ATTENDANCE             Members present:  A. O. Chism, M. S. Dunn,
                       J. D. Gratz, D. R. Green, M. R. Haneda, C. J.
                       Smith, G. R. Raub

                       Member absent:  R. Mendez, representing the
                       company at the Fiber Technology Conference in
                       New Orleans

APPROVAL OF MINUTES    Minutes of the September 28, 19--, meeting
                       were accepted as read.

COMMITTEE REPORTS      M. R. Haneda reported that expansion of the
                       plants at Charlotte and Winston-Salem, North
                       Carolina, and at Greenville, South Carolina,
                       was proceeding as planned.  Production sched-
                       ules are being maintained during this interim
                       period.  The expansion program is set for com-
                       pletion early next year.

                       E. P. Hart distributed copies of a progress
```

```
Executive Committee Meeting
Page 2
October 16, 19--

NEW BUSINESS          J. D. Gratz presented a memo from J. M. Walsh,
                      manager of personnel recruiting department,
                      suggesting that recipients of these grants be
                      invited to visit Keuka headquarters.  A. O.
                      Chism moved approval with the stipulation that
                      Keuka underwrite expenses for the visitors.
                      C. J. Smith seconded the motion, which passed
                      unanimously.  M. S. Dunn will assign a member
                      of the community services staff to plan the
                      visit.  The plan will be reviewed at the next
                      meeting.

NEXT MEETING          November 27, 19--, 10:30 a.m., corporate head-
                      quarters

ADJOURNMENT           The meeting was adjourned at 11:45 a.m.


                            G. R. Raub
                            ─────────────────────
                            G. R. Raub, Secretary
```

Illustration 8–10   NEWS RELEASE

NEWS RELEASE
Administrative Management Society Foundation
2360 Maryland Rd., Willow Grove, PA 19090   215-659-4300
Dedicated to the improvement of management through research and education

CONTACT Jeff Long

RELEASE Immediately

Willow Grove, October 10, 19--. The long-awaited "office of the future," where people and computers will work and communicate in harmony, is now predicted to arrive by 1995, according to a report on the office technologies of tomorrow recently published by the Administrative Management Society (AMS) Foundation.

The Office Technologies: Tomorrow's Tools for Automation Success reports that the technological advances emerging from research laboratories are already being incorporated into new office systems and will move business into the truly integrated and multifunctional office by the mid-1990s. The report is the third of a four-part research study by the AMS Foundation on "Managing the Office--1990 and Beyond."

Accordi...
station will
of handling
capabilities
flat display
quiet laser
text and gra
    Further
lem will be

Office of the Future
Page 2
October 10, 19--

Since information will be distributed electronically, there will be far less paper transported among offices and companies and less need for copiers. When required, printers will produce copies which can be thrown away after use, since the information will already be filed on computer. As a result, bulging file cabinets will virtually disappear.

For additional information about the survey, contact Jeff Long, Administrative Management Society, 2360 Maryland Rd., Willow Grove, PA 19090; or call 215-555-4300.

tails of the answers come later in the message. News releases are double-spaced, sometimes with additional space between paragraphs.

Postal Cards and Reply Cards

What are the values of postal and reply cards in a communication plan?

Among relatively fast and inexpensive business messages, **postal cards** and **reply cards** deserve attention. Their arrangement can be simple, allowing easy and speedy preparation. They save the cost and time of folding, sealing, and stamping a message; and, for postal cards, the mailing charge is less than that of a letter sent first class.

The heading and greeting appear on the message side of the postal card. The receiver's address need appear only on the stamped side of the card. When the heading on the message side gives the sender's address, you may omit that address from the stamped side of the card. When the sender's address is printed, you further reduce time and amount of message preparation. And to save space, the sender's address may be arranged in straight-line style. (See Illustration 8–11.)

Illustration 8–11   SAMPLE REPLY CARDS

Many business writers have learned that reply cards are inexpensive tools to get information from current or prospective customers. Affirmative answers to the questions in the rating guides shown in Illustration 8–12 will help you to design effective reply cards.

Illustration 8–12   REPLY CARD RATING GUIDES

1. Does the card contain clear, simple instructions?
2. Does the reply require a minimum of effort by the respondent?
3. Are the response spaces large enough for the requested information?
4. Is the requested information neutral and impersonal?
5. Does the card contain return postage?

Illustration 8–13   INFORMAL NOTES

Office Notes and Message Forms

What are the values of
informal office
messages in a
communication plan?

Perhaps the least formal kind of written business message is a brief note of information requiring no permanent record. Although informal, such notes are significant to the life of the business. Readers use them for decisions and actions. Therefore, the information in a note must be accurate, clear, and complete. Omission of the time of a telephone call or the date of a meeting is lost information and may result in lost business. (See Illustration 8–13.)

Interoffice messages often are on fill-in forms (see Illustration 8–14) that ask or answer questions about administrative functions or request goods and services. Copies of the forms frequently flow along multidirectional channels within the firm. Since the form may be used by several people for different purposes, careless treatment of forms can cause needless misunderstanding

Illustration 8–14   INTEROFFICE MESSAGE FORM

REPROGRAPHIC CENTER
REQUEST FOR SERVICES

Requested By: _J. L. Torres_   Phone _Ext. 187_
Date Received _4/11/- -_   Date Needed _4/13/- -_
Time Received _8:45 a.m._   Time Needed _10:30 a.m._
Number of Originals _4_ Number of Copies _100_

INSTRUCTIONS

Printing: 1 Side _____   Collate: Yes _✓_   Staple: Yes _✓_
              2 Sides _✓_   No _____   No _____
Paper Size: 8-1/2 x 11 _✓_   Reductions: 98% _____
                 8-1/2 x 14 _____   74% _____
                 Other _____   65% _____
Stock: Letterhead _____ Specify type: _____
           Plain bond _✓_ Specify color: _Buff_
           Labels _____ Transparencies _____
Instructions to operator _Adjust placement of_
page 3; move 3/4 inch to right.

Department Charged _Personnel_ Security Required: Yes _____
                                                                      No _✓_

Applied Cost _____
(To be completed by Reprographic Center)

and expense. Like other business communications, completed form messages are judged by their accuracy, clarity, coherence, and conciseness. Therefore, when you prepare form messages, be sure to insert all necessary information into appropriate blank spaces. Align your fill-in data as much as possible for easy reading. Choose your words carefully. For example, select concrete terms rather than vague expressions. Use jargon or specialized vocabulary only when it is likely to be understood by your readers. Be sure to write or type your fill-ins legibly.

REVIEW AND TRANSITION

The business writer who practices communication by objectives (CBO) is a decision maker. That writer:

1. Evaluates both verbal content and nonverbal stimuli when choosing stationery and letterhead design.

2. Considers business protocol and efficiency when choosing formats for internal and external written messages.

The successful business writer *decides* which medium and format are best suited for what he or she needs to convey.

Part 2 has presented the importance of readying yourself for your communication tasks. Effective communicators determine the dual purpose of each message and then choose message structure, tone, and format to achieve that purpose. Part 3, which presents basic message categories and patterns, will help you plan message structure and tone.

YOUR DECISIONS FOR CHAPTER 8

Review the Railco questions at the beginning of this chapter. Based on the information presented in Chapter 8, evaluate your original answers. What, if anything, do you wish to add or delete? Why? How does the international scope of Railco's operations affect its communication decisions?

DISCUSSION QUESTIONS

A. Within the context of Chapter 8, what are appropriate definitions and examples for these terms?

   1. nonverbal messages
   2. protocol
   3. OCR
   4. picture-frame guide

5. letter heading
6. greeting
7. complimentary close
8. open style
9. mixed style
10. memorandum

B. What verbal information do standard letterheads convey? What non-verbal messages accompany the letterhead design?

C. The first line of a letter address determines word choices for the greeting (salutation) in a business letter. What are appropriate greetings for letters that have letter addresses with these first lines?

1. Ms. Rita Gomez
2. Mr. J. F. Poe, Jr.
3. Mrs. Robin Moore
4. Miss Maureen Casey
5. A. L. Soo, Ed.D.
6. Lori Penn-Jeffries, M.D.
7. S. I. Tanaka, Ph.D.
8. Mr. and Mrs. J. W. Gibbs
9. Joshua and Edwin Stein
10. Mustafa Jabar
11. Customer Services Manager
12. R&D Director
13. Purchasing Agent
14. Executive Vice President
15. Perkins Industries, Inc.
16. Tamara-Drake Corporation

D. In what ways are the following letter formats similar? How do they differ from one another?

1. block
2. modified block
3. simplified block

E. Identify a situation in which the simplified block format would be more appropriate than either the block or modified block format.

F. How do the *standard* (formal) and *simplified* (informal) memo formats differ from each other? How are they similar? Which do you prefer? Why?

G. Contrast the nonverbal messages that accompany a writer's initials and a writer's signature on a memo. How do they differ? What is the advantage of placing the writer's initials or signature at the end of the memo rather than near the "FROM" part of the heading?

H. What are the advantages and disadvantages of the report-style and indented formats for minutes of meetings?

I. What communication advantages do postal cards and reply cards provide?

J. What criteria should informal office notes and message forms meet? Why?

APPLICATIONS

1. Obtain three different samples of actual business letterhead stationery. Evaluate those examples according to the criteria given in Illustration 8–1. Explain and illustrate use of the picture-frame guide with those samples.

2. Design letterheads which you believe would effectively represent at least two of the following firms. Then in a memorandum to your instructor, explain why your letterhead designs would be especially appropriate to the firms. Request constructive criticism of your designs and of your memo.

   a. Fairfax Corporation, 180 Piedmont Avenue, NE, Chicago, IL 60622-1100. In-state telephone: (312) 555-5604. Toll-free telephone: (800) 555-3636. Manufactures and markets resilient flooring materials, carpeting, and home furnishings. Has plants and branch offices at Gainesville, Macon, and Savannah, Georgia; Chattanooga and Knoxville, Tennessee; Oak Brook, Illinois; Dallas and Lubbock, Texas; San Jose, California. Established in 1885.

   b. Fulton and Samuels, Inc., 1201 Michigan Boulevard, Racine, WI 53402-1943. In-state telephone: (414) 555-7766. Toll-free telephone: (800) 555-3800. Manufactures paper and cellulose products. Has plants at Charleston, South Carolina; Green Bay, Wisconsin; St. Paul, Minnesota; Portland, Oregon; Moses Lake, Washington. Motto: Quality You Can Trust.

   c. Greater Yield Company, Inc., 1059 Sixth Avenue, Des Moines, IA 50314-1141. Telephone: (515) 555-0870. Buys, transports, stores, and sells grain; manufactures formula feeds; processes oil-bearing seeds; operates barges and boats for agribusiness transportation. Has storage elevators, processing plants, and other facilities in Iowa, Illinois, Nebraska, Kansas, Tennessee, Alabama, Mississippi, and Louisiana. Uses GYC monogram as its identifying emblem.

   d. Haidegger's, Herzog-Friedrich-Strasse 15, 6020 Innsbruck, Austria. Telephone: 0 22 52-85 1 22. Retail distributor of collectible wood-carvings and porcelain figurines. Ships worldwide.

   e. Futuro, Inc., P.O. Box 1984, Grand Rapids, MI 49501-1984. In-state telephone: (616) 555-5700. Toll-free telephone: (800) 555-4400. Manufactures and markets flexible office work stations to accommodate many types of office tasks, especially those requiring use of electronic information processing equipment. Worldwide sales and service. Has plants in Grand Rapids, Michigan; Toledo, Ohio; and Houston, Texas.

   f. The Tabor Place, P.O. Box 100, Denver, CO 80201-0100. Telephone: (303) 555-7908. Historical hotel, blending nineteenth-century elegance and twenty-first-century comforts. Located in downtown

Denver, near fine shopping and restaurant facilities. Meeting rooms, banquet facilities, and world-famous Ice Palace Dining Room.

3. For each of the businesses listed in Application 2, recommend a standard letter format to be used by the company. Using standards described in Chapter 8, justify your recommendation.

4. Illustration 8–3 shows a business letter in block format. Appropriately adapt that illustration as follows:

   a. Place some letterhead information in a letterbottom.
   b. Change the letter format to modified block.
   c. Use open punctuation for the greeting and complimentary close.
   d. Revise the message body to reflect the changes you have made.

5. Illustration 8–5 shows a business letter in simplified block format. Appropriately adapt that illustration as follows:

   a. Add these data to the letterhead: Consultants in office systems and procedures.
   b. Change the letter format to modified block.
   c. Add a greeting and complimentary close with mixed punctuation.
   d. Revise the message body to reflect the changes you have made.

6. Refer to Illustrations 8–3 and 8–5. Assume you are a conference coordinator for Ferreira Enterprises. Write a letter to Ms. Taylor in which you do the following:

   a. Thank her for sending the illustrations of letter formats.
   b. Inquire whether she is interested in conducting a seminar about message formats for your office staff.
   c. Propose a time and place for a meeting to discuss the seminar if she is interested in doing the program.
   d. Use the simplified block format for your letter to Ms. Taylor.

7. Continue the assumption that you are a conference coordinator for Ferreira Enterprises. You are planning a series of two-hour programs on various business communication topics. You plan to invite experts to speak or conduct workshops for these programs.

   a. Compose a letter to the experts whom you will invite to participate in the programs. Describe the number of people expected to attend the seminars and their educational and business backgrounds. Indicate the fee that you will pay to the speaker. Ask that the person return a reply card (which you will enclose) if he or she is interested in participating in the program. Use the simplified block letter format.
   b. Design the reply card that you will enclose in the letter. The card

must permit the respondent to indicate whether he or she will talk to you about participating in a program, a proposed time and place to discuss the details of the program, how you can contact the person, and any other information that you think is relevant.

8. Ferreira Enterprises occasionally sponsors free public-service programs. You have scheduled a lecture by Dr. Reginald Brewster, a psychologist whose specialty is nonverbal communication. Compose a news release about the lecture. Assume the necessary details about time and place.

9. You are the manager of an office supply store that employs 15 people in positions ranging from sales to graphic design. Write a memo to your employees encouraging them to attend the lecture by Dr. Brewster (Application 8).

10. Assume that you are the personnel manager for a local department store. You attended Dr. Brewster's lecture (Application 8). Write Brewster a letter acknowledging that his information was useful in your job. Ask Brewster to confer with you about a seminar on nonverbal communication for your store employees. Suggest a time and place to meet. Use any letter format illustrated in this chapter.

11. Prepare suitable minutes based on these notes of a corporate committee meeting. Use report-style format.

    a. Media Selection Committee, Bryton Corporation, met at Bryton corporate headquarters office, 60 Park Place, Chicago, September 5, 19—, 9:30 a.m. Called to order by committee chairperson, who presided throughout this meeting.

    b. Present: Chairperson W. A. Parr, Vice Chairperson C. L. Flores, Secretary M. J. Rowny, and members J. O. Blonsky, Y. I. Morita, and G. N. Rivers. Absent: member A. R. Duval, Jr.

    c. Minutes of previous meeting were accepted as read. Then Parr and Rowny reviewed the August 31 committee discussion of prime-time availabilities and costs at commercial TV networks and independent "superstations." Rowny, Duval, and Morita summarized print media availabilities and costs. Parr asked the committee whether the information is confirmed by the latest ratings/circulation reports. Flores answered affirmatively; Rowny distributed copies of updated schedules and costs (see exhibit appended to these minutes). Flores moved that the committee study the documentation provided at this meeting and that a selection decision be scheduled for the next committee meeting. Blonsky seconded the motion, which passed unanimously.

    d. New Business: Flores reported that Fremont Advertising Associates would present the new direct-mail campaign materials, highlighting Bryton Corporation's environmental concerns and safeguards, at the committee's convenience. Morita moved that the Fremont presentation be added to the agenda for the next meeting. Rivers seconded the motion, which passed unanimously. Parr asked Flores to notify Fremont.

e.   Next Meeting: Parr announced that the committee will meet again September 12, 9:30 a.m., at the same location.

f.   Adjournment: Duval moved adjournment; Morita seconded. Meeting was adjourned at 10:15 a.m.

12.   Review Application 11. To demonstrate your familiarity with message styles, use indented format (instead of report-style format) for the minutes of the September 5 Bryton Media Selection Committee meeting.

13.   Review Application 11. Following the September 5 meeting of the Bryton Media Selection Committee, C. L. Flores telephones R. M. Clark, account executive at Fremont Advertising Associates. Clark agrees to present the new direct-mail campaign materials at 10:15 a.m., September 12, during the committee meeting. Flores follows up the phone call with a letter to Clark.

Write the Flores letter to Clark. The Bryton Corporation address is 60 Park Place, Chicago, IL 60604-0006. The address of Fremont Advertising Associates is 205 Rogers Avenue, Chicago, IL 60612-0205. Use a business letter format that is illustrated in Chapter 8.

14.   Review Applications 12 and 13. In the role of C. L. Flores, compose an informal business note to W. A. Parr, chairperson of the Bryton Media Selection Committee. Inform Parr that R. M. Clark of Fremont Advertising Associates has agreed to present the direct-mail campaign materials at 10:15 a.m. during the next committee meeting. Attach a copy of the follow-up letter to Clark.

15.   Review Application 14. As Chairperson W. A. Parr, compose a standard-format memo to the Media Selection Committee. Confirm the details of Clark's scheduled presentation to the committee. Inform the committee that media-selection business, postponed from the September 5 meeting, will be decided before Clark's presentation. Urge all committee officers and members to study the documentation provided at the September 5 meeting and to attend the September 12 meeting.

16.   In a simplified-format memo to your instructor, summarize the messages required by Applications 11–15. State your understanding of how they demonstrate the importance of sharing accurate and timely information in a business situation. Explain how familiarity with message formats can facilitate effective business communication.

17.   In a standard-format memo to your instructor, discuss the intentional and unintentional effects produced by the physical appearance of a business message. Relate your discussion to your awareness of meta-

communication and of nonverbal communication. Suggestion: Review Chapters 2 and 8 before composing this memo.

18. Assume the role of corporate communication director, Belton National Bank, 50 Waverly Road, Madison, WI 53794-3604; the telephone number is (608) 555-2121. Prepare a news release to convey this information: Linda R. Duffy has joined Belton National Bank as assistant vice president for educational and civic programs. Duffy is an alumna of Morrow University. Credentials include bachelor's degree in economics, master's degree in business administration, seven years of experience in banking, and two years of volunteer work with United Community Services. Her appointment to this newly established position reflects Belton's continuing commitment to community advancement. The release date for this message is one week from today.

19. Assume the role of information services manager, Trayco Engineering, Inc., 590 Industrial Road, Minneapolis, MN 55460-3910, telephone (612) 555-3000. Prepare, for immediate release, a news item to announce these two Trayco promotions: W. F. Roberts to vice president of operations, responsible for overall direction of construction activities; R. L. Jeffers to senior project manager, responsible for construction management of the new Marston College branch campuses on Perimeter Highway and on Airline Boulevard.

20. Assume the role of communication director, Business Ventures Council, Inc., 880 Rossiter Avenue, Indianapolis, IN 46206-3726, phone (317) 555-2711. Prepare, for release one week from today, a news item to convey this information: L. D. Graff, executive director of Business Ventures Council, is in Frankfurt and Moscow to explore possibilities of new European business opportunities for Indiana-based firms. Graff joined the executive staff of Business Ventures Council in 1991 after a six-year assignment as development director with Capital Enterprises of Philadelphia, where she had specialized in overseas investments.

21. As customer relations manager, prepare the following news release for Corbett Appliance Corporation, 770 Culver Place, Paterson, NJ 07530-2410, phone (201) 555-9515: Corbett is recalling 1,750 kitchen countertop blenders, Model 9190-AT. Reason: potential electrical hazards to consumers. Toll-free telephone number for replacement or refund instructions: 1-800-555-7000. This news item is for immediate release.

22. As communication manager, prepare this news release for Brookland Savings and Loan Association, Inc., 109 East Monte Street, El Paso, TX 79910-4007, telephone (915) 555-4141: Dixon Savings and Loan has pledged 1.5 million dollars to the Home Ownership Opportunity Program for low-income and middle-income families. Brookland offers an adjustable interest rate for qualified buyers who meet credit require-

ments but whose family income is less than $19,500 annually. This news item is for release on Community Day, which is the second Saturday of next month.

23. As community services director, prepare this news release for Mountain Enterprises, Inc. (MEI), 1200 Industrial Road, Colorado Springs, CO 80935-0055, telephone (719) 555-8040: MEI is a company dedicated to conserving and improving the environment. Examples: MEI maintains recycling bins for its employees and for the public; MEI copier-toner cartridges are recharged instead of merely discarded; MEI uses recycled cardboard boxes, recycled computer paper, even recycled memo pads. MEI sponsors educational programs and events to inform the public of community-wide recycling methods and other environmental concerns. And MEI asks: What are *you* doing—at home, at work, and at school— to help win the war on waste? This public-service message is for immediate release.

24. As communication manager, prepare this customer-oriented message for Sabrina's Buffets, Inc., 3030 Culver Avenue, Norwalk, CT 06856-3917: The message is to be in the form of a printed, postage-paid reply card. Copies of the card, addressed to President V. G. Laurens, will be placed in special holders on the dinner tables of Sabrina's Buffets. Although the company operates 225 family restaurants nationwide, the reply cards will be coded so that customers need not state the precise restaurant location.

      You are authorized to use Laurens' name to do the following: Thank the customer for dining at Sabrina's. Confirm Sabrina's commitment to meriting the customer's return. Invite comments on the quality of food and beverages, service, cleanliness, courtesy, and atmosphere at Sabrina's. Request the customer's name, address, telephone number, and date/time of visit.

25. Review Application 24. As Sabrina's Buffets communication manager, prepare an informal office note for transmitting your version of the Application 24 message. Address the note to Kim Mosley, who is executive assistant to V. G. Laurens. Request Mosley's comments about your Application 24 message.

MULTICULTURAL INSIGHTS

1. What stationery sizes are most commonly used for business letters in your native country? If the stationery differs from that used in the United States, show examples to your classmates.

2. Which of the seven standard letter parts are used consistently in business correspondence composed in your native language? Which ones

are not used or differ from those explained and illustrated in this chapter?

3. What reactions would a businessperson who uses your native language have to the simplified block letter format? Why?

4. Is the tone of interoffice messages in your native country formal? informal? How are those messages like and unlike interoffice memos used by U.S. businesses?

5. In what ways has trade with U.S. businesses changed correspondence practices associated with your native language?

6. What are examples of typical greetings, opening paragraphs, closing paragraphs, and complimentary closes used for business letters written in your native language?

Cases

These case studies emphasize challenges, skills, and tasks for making decisions. You will apply your perception, interpretation, and recall skills. You will also demonstrate your ability to plan and develop messages.

CASE A: DANA DREXEL'S REQUEST
(Communication Challenges, Skills, and Tasks Related to Appropriate Decisions)

For a short time, Leonard Sommers employed Dana Drexel. Although cordial, courteous, and honest, Drexel began to cause costly communication problems within the firm. When Sommers brought these matters to Drexel's attention, the new employee grinned good-naturedly and said: "Nobody's perfect. If some folks mistake what I say or write, that's *their* problem, isn't it?"

After one of Drexel's confusing memos had caused several large shipments to be misrouted, Sommers reluctantly dismissed Drexel. "Nothing else to do," Sommers thought. "We can't keep losing money because an employee keeps miscommunicating. It's a pity, though. Drexel is hardworking and ambitious. Those qualities are fine, but we need someone who can communicate effectively."

A week has passed since Drexel left the firm. Today Sommers receives this letter:

```
117 South Dixie Drive
Vandalia, OH  45377-2142
May 3, 19--

Dear Mr. Sommers

I tried several times to telephone you today,
but was unsuccessfull.  The thing is that I am
applying for work with the Evans Company, and
need letters of recomendation from my previou
employers including you right away.

They want you to confirm the dates of my
employment with you and the duties assigned to
me and if I did them satisfactory, or not.

As you may or may not know, the Evans company
like other companys nowadays have high com-
unication standards for it's employees.  So
you might mention the speach I gave during the
Comunity Fund Drive, and also they want to
know if my memoes and reports was writen
clear.  Please keep that in mind when you
write the letter which should be adressed to
J.K. Mallory who is a personel recruiter at
Evans.

Please send me a copy of your letter Mr. Som-
mer, for my records, irregardless of what you
decide to write, but just between you and I
your letter will mean alot in determining if I
get this job, or not.  So I am sure it will be
a good one, for which I thank you in advance.

Yours truely
```

Dana Drexel

```
Dana Drexel
```

Remembering Drexel's attributes as well as deficiencies, Sommers wonders: "Ethically and fairly, what should I do?"

INSIGHTS

Test your knowledge of communication challenges, skills, tasks, and decisions by answering these questions:

1. What evidence of Drexel's attributes and deficiencies does this case disclose?
2. Do you empathize more with Drexel than with Sommers? Why?
3. Do you empathize more with Sommers than with Drexel? Why?
4. If you were Sommers, what decision would you make after reading Drexel's letter? Why? How and to whom would you communicate that decision? Why?

CASE B: SPAHR'S MONOLOGUE TO BISCOE
(Perception, Interpretation, and Message Revision)

Stacy Spahr, a junior executive at Tolby Associates, returns from a staff conference and beckons Cass Biscoe into a private office. Looking pale and harassed, Spahr rapidly says all of the following to Biscoe. The statements are presented here as a single paragraph to simulate Spahr's manner and rate of speaking.

"Am I glad *that* meeting's over! Tell me, Cass; why do some people use so many words to say so little? Never mind; we're way behind schedule now aren't we? First thing: You'd better take these notes I made on the conference. Type them for our reference file. If you have trouble deciphering my scribbles, let me know while they're still fresh in my mind. Handle them yourself, Cass; don't give them to the typing pool. A few of those items are confidential, okay? I've also got a bunch of letters and memos to dictate as soon as possible. They need to get out right away, Cass. Say, did Crandell phone? I'm expecting calls from Crandell and Breen; be sure to put them right through. And tell Ross and Yates I'll be in their office today about the Sima Imports deal. About 2:30. No, better make it 2:15, will you? Now, *this* goes to Doyle at Salt Lake City. Make it a memo. Tell Doyle we must have those sales summaries by the 15th of every month. Make it clear, Cass; the 15th is the date for delivery here, not the date for mailing them to us. But don't make it sound harsh; firm but not harsh. You know, Doyle's a little sensitive about that kind of thing. Say the sales volume is good, but we've got to have those things when they're due—and that's by the 15th of every month. The next one I want to dictate personally. It goes to Ortega at Albuquerque. Start with 'Congratulations on landing the Roswell account. I want you to know we're impressed by your efforts.' Guess that's all I really want to say, Cass, but it's too short. Add a few words of your own. Make it personal, but use executive letterhead. Which reminds me: I'm not satisfied with some of the letters and memos our people have been sending. Here are some samples; look them over and see what you can do with them, will you? I mean, see if you can come up with some models, maybe some guide forms, for routine correspondence, you know? Got another meeting now; I'll be in Bethune's office if you need me."

Here are the unsatisfactory messages which Spahr gives to Biscoe for revision:

MESSAGE 1

Unfortunately we are unable to grant your request for a refund with reference to the Tolby Industrial Marine Products that you purchased seven months ago.

The enclosed literature covering Tolby products, including the Industrial Marine line, is for your reference. It behooves you to notice that the period of time for the guarantee is six months, not seven months, for the date of sale and that, under the terms of our agreement, we are not required to provide refund, repair, or replacement at our expense beyond that date.

We solicit your interest in ordering new Tolby products to replace those concerning which you expressed dissatisfaction.

MESSAGE 2

Your failure to answer our previous reminders of your long overdue payment disappoints us.

We are entitled to full settlement for your July 15 order or to at least an explanation of why your account remains delinquent and a definite indication of when you will make payment.

MESSAGE 3

Here is my memo on justification of expansion of our Engineering Services. The purpose of this proposal is to justify the hiring of additional personnel needed to increase the efficiency and productivity of that department and to enable the department to render faster and better service to other units of our organization. Briefly stated, the current workload cannot be handled adequately and effectively with the present number of engineering personnel and support staff. We need more people as soon as they can be hired. Space requirements for the additional personnel can be handled without additional offices being assigned at this point in time.

INSIGHTS

Test your communication knowledge and skills by answering these questions:

1. What evidence in this case indicates that communication improvements are needed in the working relationship between Spahr and Biscoe? What improvements should be made? Why? Who has responsibility for achieving them? Why?
2. Exactly what tasks did Spahr give Biscoe? What priorities did Spahr

3. assign to each of those tasks? As Biscoe, in what sequence would you perform those tasks? Why?

3. If Spahr returned to find that those tasks had not been done as quickly as desired, what would you as Biscoe say to Spahr? Why? If Spahr then became disappointed or angry, how would you renew rapport in the working relationship? If Spahr demonstrated empathy instead of disappointment or anger, what constructive suggestions would you as Biscoe offer at that moment? How would you word those suggestions? Why?

4. Prepare the memo to Doyle and the letter to Ortega. What are the positive features of the Doyle and Ortega messages you prepare?

5. What are the positive and negative aspects of the three additional messages given to Spahr for revision? What would be appropriate revisions of those messages? Why?

NATURE'S WONDERS

In this segment of Nature's Wonders, you will demonstrate your knowledge of planning, developing, and formatting messages.

CASE FACTS
As you continue working in Information Services, other employees become aware of your interest in and knowledge of effective business communication. You are beginning to serve as an internal consultant on communication.

Meanwhile, the executive committee is moving ahead with plans to create a new position, Director of Corporate Communication. The Vice President for Information Services has asked you to attend a meeting in which the responsibilities of the person holding that title will be defined. You know the committee expects input from you.

YOUR TASKS
To prepare for the meeting, you will complete two tasks that the Director of Corporate Communication may be expected to perform.

1. One responsibility of the Director may be to help company correspondents improve the quality of messages sent to customers. Prepare a memo in which you explain general principles for planning, organizing, and developing business messages. Also explain ways to achieve a constructive, customer-oriented tone.

   Write this memo as though you are sending it to correspondents in the customer-service area. Remember that you will use the memo in the executive committee meeting as an example of a service that the Director of Corporate Communication could provide.

2. Another responsibility of the Director may be to design or evaluate letterhead and promotional materials. Prepare a written evaluation, in memo format, of Nature's Wonders letterhead for presentation to the executive committee.

NATURE'S WONDERS
1039 Nursery Road
Seattle, WA 98144-5632

MESSAGE PATTERNS

Parts 1 and 2 introduced the communication-by-objectives (CBO) concept, described CBO methods of message organization and preparation, and provided CBO insights to nonverbal, oral, and written communication. Part 3 applies the CBO approach to structuring and wording four kinds of business messages:

1. good-news or neutral messages (Chapter 9)
2. bad-news or mixed-news messages (Chapter 10)
3. goodwill and special-occasion messages (Chapter 11)
4. persuasive messages (Chapters 12 and 13)

Those basic categories are illustrated by:

1. inquiries, requests, and replies
2. orders, acknowledgments, and remittances
3. messages of welcome, appreciation, congratulation, or condolence
4. messages designed deliberately to influence or to convince

Part 3 provides CBO applications to help you gain goodwill, inquire, inform, and persuade. Part 3 helps you answer this question: How shall I *effectively* begin, develop, and end my business messages?

GOOD-NEWS OR NEUTRAL MESSAGES

CHAPTER OUTLINE

OBJECTIVES

After completing this chapter, you should be able to:

1.   Recognize business situations that require sharing of favorable or neutral information.
2.   Apply the communication-by-objectives (CBO) approach as you plan message structures, word choice, and communication tone to convey favorable or neutral information.
3.   Compose effective favorable or neutral business messages.

DECISIONS CASE

You are a management trainee at Hopkins Enterprises, a major distributor of import goods in the United States. As part of your employment program, you work under the supervision of J. D. McClure, Vice President of Corporate Communication. McClure challenges you to think of management *as* communication.

"Sometimes," McClure points out, "you can say 'yes' or 'Here's good news for you.' At other times you can say neither 'yes' nor 'no.' How should you organize these messages? You must convey the necessary information. You also must establish or reinforce goodwill for a continuing, profitable association with your receiver. What decisions should you make to achieve those aims?"

McClure is asking you to think about the structure and wording of messages. You begin to realize that effective messages do not just happen. They are planned, organized, developed, and transmitted with constant attention to the purposes of their senders and receivers.

Additional questions about this decision-making case are stated at the end of this chapter. Study the chapter before answering those questions.

CHAPTER CONTEXT

Messages that are apt to please your receiver are classified as **good-news** or **favorable messages**. Use them to reinforce sender-receiver *goodwill*, a feeling of mutual approval and support.

Messages that say neither yes nor no are classified as **neutral messages**. Use neutral messages to keep communication channels open until improvement of circumstances makes good-news messages possible.

BASIC STRUCTURE AND WORD CHOICE OF FAVORABLE MESSAGES

What is an appropriate structure for a good-news message?

When you grant a request, extend an agreement, or otherwise provide information likely to please your receiver, you have a ready opportunity for promoting goodwill. And goodwill *is* good business.

Structure your favorable, good-news message this way:

1. Begin with the favorable news.

    Your promotion to Assistant General Manager of Food Quality has been approved.

2. State details that support the favorable news.

    During your six years with Big K Foods, you have consistently demonstrated your determination to meet our quality standards. For your positive influence among your coworkers, you also earned the Quality Leadership Award three times.

3. Close with a statement of goodwill.

    Congratulations, Sondra. This promotion rewards your dedication to Big K Foods. We are confident you will continue to excel in your new position.

When the goal of your communication effort is to give good news, your receiver should readily accept the message. However, if you treat the message routinely, your receiver may react negatively to you and your organization. As with all forms of effective business communication, empathize with your receiver when you word a good-news message. Match the tone and structure of your message to the news you convey. Illustration 9–1 is a reply to a customer requesting a credit account. If *you* were a receiver, would Illustration 9–1 impress you as good news reinforced by a goodwill tone? Why? Would you prefer Illustration 9–2? Why? How do you rate Illustrations 9–3 and 9–4? Why?

Illustrations 9–1 through 9–4 have correct grammar, punctuation, and spelling but differ greatly in effectiveness. Illustrations 9–1 and 9–3 do not demonstrate the recommended good-news structure. They contain the words *you* and *your,* yet they do not convey a *you* attitude—an understanding of the receiver's needs and feelings. Instead of building goodwill, those messages seem almost to scold and antagonize the receiver. In contrast, Illustrations 9–2 and 9–4 reinforce the good-news structure by positive, courteous words and empathetic references to the reader. As you see, message tone is a product of structure *and* word choice.

Why should tone complement structure?

BASIC STRUCTURE AND WORD CHOICE OF NEUTRAL MESSAGES

What is an appropriate structure for a neutral message?

When you can say neither yes nor no but need to keep communication channels open, send a neutral message, structured as follows:

1. Begin with a mutually agreeable statement.

    Your application materials are being carefully reviewed.

2. Indicate neither yes nor no; reassure your receiver of continuing interest.

    If your credentials meet the requirements of the position, you will be contacted by a human resources representative for an interview.

Illustration 9–1   NEGATIVE EXAMPLE: GOOD NEWS BUT BADWILL TONE

Hewes Sawyer, Inc.

1210 River Plaza East
New York, NY 10023-1947
Telephone 212-555-3347

November 12, 19--

Mr. Alan G. Wainwright
General Manager
B & C Hardware, Inc.
1171 Burlington Road
Trenton, NJ 08650-8722

Dear Mr. Wainwright

Reasons (excuses) precede the good news

I'm sorry it took so long to process your credit request. During this quarter we received hundreds of requests like yours. That's why we couldn't respond earlier. However, B & C Hardware now has a credit line with us. You are expected to observe the terms spelled out in the enclosed brochure.

Brusque, negative, condescending tone

Our current catalog is enclosed, along with a price list that applies for November only. You might be interested in some of the items for your anniversary sale.

Negative closing paragraph

If you decide to order, do so now. Since many customers will be taking advantage of the special prices, we cannot promise immediate delivery of orders received after November 15. Once again, I'm sorry it took so long to open your account.

Yours truly

R. G. Soames

R. G. Soames
Sales Manager

Enclosures

pw

Illustration 9–2   POSITIVE EXAMPLE: GOOD NEWS AND GOODWILL TONE

Hewes Sawyer, Inc.
1210 River Plaza East
New York, NY 10023-1947
Telephone 212-555-3347

November 12, 19--

Mr. Alan G. Wainwright
General Manager
B & C Hardware, Inc.
1171 Burlington Road
Trenton, NJ 08650-8722

Dear Mr. Wainwright

Good news
reinforced
by reasons

Your Hewes Sawyer account is open and ready for use.
B & C Hardware established an outstanding sales and payment record during its first year of business. That
record entitles you to 3/10, n/60 credit terms with us.

Customer-
oriented
goodwill
closing

Thank you for mentioning your upcoming anniversary sale.
Please let us help you make it a success. Our current
catalog accompanies this letter; to help you celebrate
your anniversary, we will pay all shipping charges on
orders placed before November 30.

Sincerely yours

R. G. Soames

R. G. Soames
Sales Manager

Enclosure

pw

Illustration 9–3 NEGATIVE EXAMPLE: GOOD NEWS BUT BADWILL TONE

```
We always inspect our products carefully
before they are shipped.  We have sold
hundreds of Model D901 table saws, and
you are the first person who has com-
plained about a poorly aligned rip
fence.

However, based on the report of Rex Bar-
stow, our representative who examined
your saw, we will replace your Model
D901.

Rex will notify you when he is ready to
replace your saw.  We hope you have bet-
ter luck with the new one.
```

Illustration 9–4 POSITIVE EXAMPLE: GOOD NEWS AND GOODWILL TONE

```
You are right.  Your Model D901 table
saw is guaranteed to perform satisfac-
torily.  We're ready to justify your
faith in our word.

Rex Barstow's examination confirmed your
observation that the rip fence is not
parallel to the blade.  To ensure your
complete satisfaction, we want to re-
place the entire saw, not only the rip
fence.  Rex will call you to arrange a
convenient time to deliver and set up
your new saw.
```

3. Close with a courteous statement of goodwill.

Richards, Inc., appreciates your interest and wishes you well in your search for career opportunities.

Again, empathize as you apply that structure and as you word your message. Illustration 9–5 is a negative, writer-centered message that may jeopardize the business relationship. In contrast, Illustration 9–6 demonstrates positive, reader-oriented language. It is worded to keep communication channels open.

Your awareness of tone as a product of structure and word choice will allow you to compose effective messages to obtain or provide information, products, or services. The category of good-news or neutral messages includes routine inquiries and replies. This category also includes messages required to maintain effective buyer-seller communication, such as purchase orders, acknowledgments, and remittances. Unfavorable or mixed counterparts of such messages are discussed in Chapter 10.

INQUIRIES, REQUESTS, AND FAVORABLE OR NEUTRAL REPLIES

Routine inquiries or routine requests are queries that businesspeople expect to receive in their everyday business operations. Normally, the receiver welcomes such requests and can easily fulfill them. Routine inquiries or requests[1] may consist of single sentences in business-letter or postal-card format. Examples include "What models of Avery SLR cameras do you regularly stock?" and "Please send us your current catalog." Often, however, routine inquiries or requests may need to be quite detailed. Then it is important to let your reader know exactly *what* you seek and *when* you need it.

What are examples of routine inquiries?

An example of a detailed routine request is a request for adjustment, also called a claim.[2] An adjustment request is considered routine if businesses usually grant such requests. The message structure of detailed inquiries or requests is shown by the following example and Illustrations 9–7 and 9–8.

1. State your inquiry or request. Your statement may be worded as a question.

    Do you stock Ellenwood Career Development audiocassettes?

2. Give reasons for your inquiry or request.

    Many of our engineers have suggested that we should supply management development audiocassettes for their use while commuting. Our initial research suggests that Ellenwood cassettes may benefit our engineers.

---

[1]Special, or persuasive, requests are discussed in Chapter 12.
[2]Persuasive claims are discussed in Chapter 13.

Illustration 9–5   NEGATIVE EXAMPLE: NEUTRAL/MAYBE NEWS
BUT BADWILL TONE

Hewes Sawyer, Inc.

1210 River Plaza East
New York, NY 10023-1947
Telephone 212-555-3347

January 28, 19--

Mr. T. H. Patrick
109 Race Club Road
Summerville, SC 29483-0109

Dear Mr. Patrick

Negative
opening
suggests
negative
outcome

We will be unable to grant your request for repair or
replacement of your Model D901 table saw until one of our
authorized representatives examines it. Before making any
adjustment, we must be sure that we are responsible for
the claimed defect.

Inconsiderate,
nonreassuring
explanation
and conclusion

Our representative in your area, Mr. R. W. Barstow, will
stop at your home on February 12 to examine the saw.
Please be sure that someone is available to show him the
problem you have had.

If Mr. Barstow determines that we are at fault, we will
exercise our option to repair or replace the saw.

Yours truly

A. L. Grimes

A. L. Grimes
Customer Service Manager

pw

Illustration 9–6 POSITIVE EXAMPLE: NEUTRAL/MAYBE NEWS AND
 GOODWILL TONE

Hewes Sawyer, Inc.

1210 River Plaza East
New York, NY 10023-1947
Telephone 212-555-3347

January 28, 19--

Mr. T. H. Patrick
109 Race Club Road
Summerville, SC 29483-0109

Dear Mr. Patrick:

Agreeable, neutral opening statement

Yes, your Model D901 table saw is guaranteed to perform
satisfactorily within the terms of your purchase contract
and our warranty.

Reassurance without indicating yes or no

Mr. R. W. Barstow, the Hewes Sawyer customer service representative in your area, will call you to arrange a convenient time for him to examine the saw. Mr. Barstow is
well qualified to analyze the difficulties you are experiencing. He is also authorized to repair or replace any
Hewes Sawyer tools that do not meet our rigid quality
requirements.

Goodwill closing

Thank you for your continuing loyalty to Hewes Sawyer
tools.

Sincerely yours,

A. L. Grimes

A. L. Grimes
Customer Service Manager

pw

Illustration 9–7 ROUTINE ADJUSTMENT REQUEST

109 Race Club Road
Summerville, SC 29483-0109
June 10, 19--

Hewes Sawyer, Inc.
1210 River Plaza East
New York, NY 10023-1947

REQUEST FOR $34.98 REFUND

Statement of request

Please send me a check for $34.98 to cover the purchase price ($29.99) and shipping charges ($4.99) for the Model 24760 Drill Press Planer that I am returning.

Details to justify request

Although I was excited about the potential uses for this planer, my practice sessions demonstrated that I would have difficulty controlling it and getting the smooth cuts necessary for my workworking projects. Therefore, I'm returning the planer under your generous guarantee, which promises a full refund for any items returned within 90 days.

Courteous, goodwill closing

That guarantee, along with the superior quality of your woodworking tools, is one reason why I continue to buy from Hewes Sawyer. I always look forward to your catalogs. Through them I discover new tools to make my woodworking hobby even more enjoyable.

T. H. Patrick

T. H. PATRICK

Enclosure

Illustration 9–8   DETAILED ROUTINE INQUIRY

HAWTHORNE AND KLEBEV, INC.
3200 Anderson Avenue
Grand Rapids, MI 49509-2544
(616) 555-3232

October 20, 19--

Convention Manager
Hotel Puerto Caribbean
310 Islaverde Avenue
San Juan, PR 00914-8019

Dear Convention Manager:

Statement of inquiry	What are your hotel facilities and rates for business meetings?
Explanation	Our company has scheduled its February sales conference for your city, and I am comparing available accommodations before making a recommendation to our selection committee. J. C. Mallory of Benway Corporation has recommended your facilities and services, saying that he was most pleased with how you accommodated the Benway Exhibition held at your hotel last March.
Facts and details	Here are our requirements:

Here are our requirements:

Dates:	February 27-28
Attendance:	125 people
Bedrooms:	Sixty double-occupancy, five single-occupancy rooms
Meeting Rooms:	Four for conferences of 30-35 people each and one for meetings of the entire group of 120-125 people
Meals:	February 27--lunch and dinner
	February 28--breakfast and lunch

I understand from Mallory that your hotel observes the usual industry practice of providing a complimentary suite and complimentary coffee breaks for conventions booked at your hotel.

Cordial, courteous, action-inducing close

Our hotel selection committee will meet on November 10. Any information we receive from you, along with Mallory's recommendation, will be considered carefully at that time. We hope to sign a contract with the hotel of our choice no later than November 20.

Sincerely,

Rosalind S. Bergen

Rosalind S. Bergen
Sales Manager

fap

3.　Furnish pertinent facts and specific details to elicit a suitable response; otherwise, your receiver may not know precisely what to provide.

Specifically, please supply the title, description, length, and price for all Ellenwood Career Development audiocassettes that you stock. If you have other management development programs that may benefit our engineers, please send similar information about those programs.

4.　End your message courteously, stressing the action the receiver should take and the date you need it, if necessary.

I must submit my annual training budget on December 1. Please send this information before November 1 so that I can determine whether to include audiocassettes in next year's budget.

What is an appropriate structure for a favorable reply?

Favorable replies supply the information the receiver requested. Here is an effective structure for a favorable reply:

1.　Begin with the response to the receiver's request.

We have in stock the complete set of Ellenwood Career Development audiocassettes that you inquired about in your September 19 letter.

2.　State reasons that justify or reinforce that good news.

The enclosed brochure describes in detail the topics covered by this ten-volume set, along with the price for each cassette. Notice that the complete set comes in an attractive storage case and sells at a 15 percent discount from the individually priced tapes. The brochure also provides testimonials from satisfied users.

3.　Close with a goodwill statement.

The enclosed cassette contains excerpts from three of the career development topics. This complimentary tape will help you evaluate the training potential of Ellenwood Career Development audiocassettes. If you encounter additional questions while preparing your training program and budget, please call me at 1-800-555-4321.

What should a neutral reply achieve?

Neutral replies keep the lines of communication open until a further decision is made. Here is an effective structure for a neutral reply:

1.　Begin with a courteous but noncommittal statement.

Thank you for requesting a reprint of Dr. Ronald Wayne's article,

"Markets Today," which appeared in the April issue of *Dividends Journal.*

2. Convey awareness of your receiver's needs, desires, interests; keep the door open for further communication.

   Because of an unprecedented number of requests, our editorial board is deliberating whether to authorize another printing of this popular article.

3. Close with a goodwill statement.

   If the decision is favorable, you will be among the first to receive a reprint.

FAVORABLE AND NEUTRAL BUYER-SELLER MESSAGES

What are examples of favorable and neutral buyer-seller messages?

Many messages that pass between businesses and their suppliers or customers contain favorable or neutral information required to maintain the daily flow of business. Such messages often are handled routinely and impersonally. The positive context for these messages, however, can also be used to reinforce buyer-seller goodwill. This category of messages includes purchase orders, acknowledgments, and remittances.

Purchase Orders

Since orders for products or services stimulate business, they are good-news messages. The chief requirements of a purchase order are accuracy and clarity. Orders are often submitted on printed purchase-order forms. Whether you use a printed order form or compose a personalized order letter, verify every detail of the contents. To ensure clarity, use a separate line or, when necessary, a separate paragraph to describe every item you order. Tabulate all items and their prices.

Data organization for order forms and order letters is demonstrated in Illustrations 9–9 and 9–10. Notice these features:

1. *Order number.* Give the order number to facilitate records management as well as communication between buyer and seller.
2. *Quantity.* State number of units, sets, feet, yards, dozens, ounces, pounds, tons, reams, etc.
3. *Catalog Number.* Cite the catalog number, a shortcut to exact identification of the article.

Illustration 9–9   PURCHASE ORDER FORM

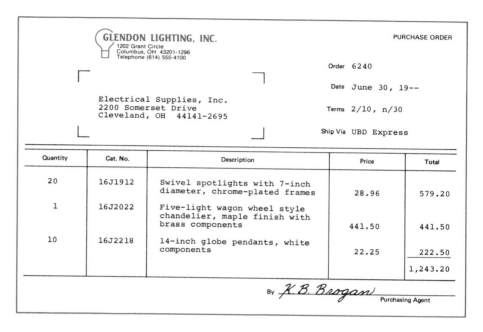

4. *Description.* Describe the item in detail (size, color, material, weight, finish, quality, style).
5. *Price.* List the individual price per item.
6. *Totals.* List the extensions (individual price × quantity); add these for the total cost of the order.
7. *Shipment.* Unless you have a special agreement with the seller, specify the shipping method (parcel post, express, air freight, or other means) and, if necessary, the shipping route. If the goods are to be sent to an address other than yours, show the destination of the shipment. Be sure to state whether the goods are to be delivered by a definite date. Specify *rush delivery* when you need especially speedy shipment. You may also speed the order by using telephone or facsimile transmission.
8. *Payment.* Describe the method of payment unless you and the seller have already agreed on a method.

Acknowledgments of Orders

Acknowledgments are good news. They assure your clients that you have received their messages. Ideally, an acknowledgment is sent the same day the order is received. Even when you ship the merchandise promptly, an acknowl-

Illustration 9–10   PURCHASE ORDER LETTER

109 Race Club Road
Summerville, SC 29483-0109
June 10, 19--

Carlyle Products, Inc.
1905 Rowland Highway South
Nashville, TN 37212-2221

PURCHASE ORDER

Begin with request: Please ship the following items by Universal Express to the address shown above:

Quantity	Catalog No.	Description	Price	Total
2	B473-175533	Pet Door, Small	$24.99	$59.98
1	B582-167763	Lawn Spreader	19.99	19.99
		Merchandise Total		79.97
		Universal Express Chge.		6.95
		Total		$86.92

Tabulate details for clarity

Specify payment method: You may charge this purchase to my All-Charge, Account No. 5220-37224-2209.

T. H. Patrick

T. H. PATRICK

edgment will reassure the customer that you appreciate the business relationship. If feasible, use electronic technology—such as facsimile transmission, voice mail, or computer messaging—to speed the acknowledgment to its destination.

The structure of an acknowledgment depends on the type being composed; for example, general or interim, new or loyal customer, large order, or declined order.

General and Interim Acknowledgments. Use **general acknowledgments** for routine orders that you can fill completely and promptly. Such orders may be acknowledged by standardized forms, such as preprinted cards or form letters. The message should reinforce goodwill by informing the customer that the order has been received and is being fulfilled.

Although delays in filling orders or in providing answers to inquiries are sometimes unavoidable, silence during such a delay may evoke doubt or suspicion. To reassure your receiver, send an **interim acknowledgment.** Here is an effective structure for that message:

1. Thank your receiver for the order, inquiry, request, etc.

   Thank you for your interest in the Seed King Spring Vegetable Catalog.

2. Explain reasons for delay.

   The catalog is currently being printed and should be available in a few weeks.

3. Tell your receiver what further response to expect and, if appropriate, when to expect it.

   Your catalog will be mailed no later than February 1, in time for your spring planting order.

4. End the message cordially.

   As in previous years, this year's Seed King catalog offers an extensive selection of seeds and plants, along with many gardening suggestions. We wish you hours of pleasant gardening and a bountiful harvest.

What should a new-customer acknowledgment achieve?

New-Customer Acknowledgments. When you receive a new customer's order, use a personalized acknowledgment to establish or reinforce goodwill. Here is a suitable message structure:

1. Thank and welcome the new customer.

Welcome to Seed King, Mother Nature's largest distributor of vegetable seeds and plants. We appreciate your order from our spring catalog.

2. Identify (sometimes you may need to restate) the order.

You ordered products that are among our customers' favorites: Green Crown Asparagus and Lamont Everbearing Raspberries. Both of these species are excellent investments. Once the plants are well established, you will enjoy delicious harvests year after year.

3. Explain exactly how you are handling and shipping (or how you are otherwise providing) what was ordered.

Your plants will be shipped on March 1 by Speedy Express. They should arrive at your home on March 2, ready for immediate planting. We encourage you to plant this stock within ten days of arrival.

4. Confirm your interest in continuing to serve the customer; reinforce rapport and promote future orders by inviting customer comments.

We look forward to serving you with top-quality Seed King products and prompt service. Remember our guarantee: If at any time within one year of your purchase you are not satisfied with a Seed King product, we will replace the product or refund your money.

Another appropriate structure for a new-customer acknowledgment is this:

1. Explain what you are doing about the order. (Be sure to identify the order here or in Step 2.)

Your copy of Graphware IV graphics software will be shipped tomorrow.

2. Thank and welcome the new customer.

Discount Software Supply appreciates your order and welcomes you to discount prices all year round.

3. Confirm your interest in continuing to serve the customer through regular or special accommodations, extended hours of operation, unusual bargains, etc.

Our most recent price list for nationally advertised discontinued software is enclosed. These products come with full documentation and standard warranties, along with discounts of up to 70 percent off retail prices. Many of our customers have found that these products fully satisfy their software requirements.

We look forward to supplying you with powerful software at substantial savings.

What should a loyal-customer acknowledgment achieve?

Loyal-Customer Acknowledgments. Inexperienced or complacent businesspeople sometimes take their customers for granted. Acknowledging loyal patronage, however, often increases business. Structure acknowledgments to loyal customers as shown here and by Illustration 9–11.

1. Thank the customer for the most recent order.

   Thank you for your May 12 order for 100 dozen FlyHigh golf balls.

2. Thank the customer for previous orders as well.

   During the past 15 years you have trusted us to provide the high-quality products your customers rightfully demand. The steady increase in the size of your orders indicates that both you and your customers have been satisfied.

3. Reinforce rapport for continuing the business relationship.

   Thank you for the long-standing partnership we have enjoyed with Golf City. We look forward to continuing as your supplier while you serve the Vista Green golfing community.

Large-Order Acknowledgments. In response to a purchase order which is large (in price *or* quantity), send an acknowledgment that reinforces the

Illustration 9–11   LOYAL-CUSTOMER ACKNOWLEDGMENT

Thanks for current order and previous business

Your March 8 order (No. 135-08-2966) was shipped this morning by KWW Express as you requested.

Your orders are always appreciated. This acknowledgment, however, is a special thank you for the pleasant ten-year association we have had with your firm.

Reinforcement of goodwill

We pledge to justify the confidence you have placed in us. Fulfilling that promise will be a pleasure.

buyer's good decision to deal with you. Structure your message as shown here and by Illustration 9–12.

1. Convey appreciation for the large order.

    Your order for the complete 20-volume set of Hawthorne Video Seminars will be shipped by Speedy Express today. Thank you for giving us this opportunity to participate in your management development program. We're sure your employees will benefit from the professional development topics included in this series.

2. "Resell" the buyer. State reasons which confirm the wisdom of the purchase decision.

    Hawthorne Video Seminars have been tested extensively both in laboratory and field settings. Industry users consistently rate the

Illustration 9–12   LARGE-ORDER ACKNOWLEDGMENT

Appreciation and justification for purchase decision

Your purchase of ten AGR-3 micro-computers is good news--good news for your firm as well as ours. Thanks for your decision to buy your computers and software from us. That purchase entitles you to six months of comprehensive follow-up services after installation of the computers.

Laurie Tyler, the AGR representative with whom you negotiated your contract, will personally supervise installation and testing of your new AGR-3 system. Laurie will also provide four on-site seminars to train your employees on the system.

Reinforced goodwill

During the next six months, Ms. Tyler and I will be readily available to ensure that you get the best possible benefits from your AGR-3 system. We will also help you explore new ways to improve office efficiency. Please call on us often as you continue with the computerization of your office operations.

highly qualified seminar leaders and the wide range of topics "Outstanding."

Remember that your purchase includes customer support. Please contact me if you need additional presentation suggestions or answers to questions raised by your participants.

3.   Reinforce goodwill. Indicate that you plan to continue developing the mutually profitable relationship established by the order.

You can continue to count on Hawthorne for top-quality, timely training aids. We are constantly developing new products and want to hear from you about your emerging training needs.

If you cannot fill all or part of a customer's order, you should send a bad-news or mixed-news acknowledgment promptly. The customer will value your honesty and may continue to purchase other products from you. Declined-order acknowledgments are described in Chapter 10, along with other bad-news or mixed-news messages.

Statements of Account, Invoices, and Remittances

Sellers normally notify credit customers when account payments are due. For personal purchases, the notification is a **statement of account**. For business purchases, the notification is an **invoice**. As shown by Illustrations 9–13 and 9–14, an invoice usually has more detailed information than does a statement of account.

Statements of account and invoices can be interpreted both as good-news and as neutral messages. Interpreted as neutral messages, statements of account and invoices routinely notify the receiver that, based upon delivery of products or provision of services, payment is due. Interpreted as good-news messages, they connote opportunities to continue doing business by paying current obligations. Payment involves remittance messages, which are also examples of good news.

Remittance is the transmission of money. The remittance message must clearly specify the amount of payment and how it is to be applied. This message is often impersonal, accomplished by sending a voucher check or a duplicate invoice (a copy of the original) with an attached check. The upper portion of Illustration 9–15 shows a voucher check; the lower portion lists invoices for which the voucher check is payment. If Illustration 9–14 were a duplicate invoice with an attached check for $919.50, it too would be a remittance.

When circumstances justify a more personal message, send a remittance

Illustration 9-13   STATEMENT OF ACCOUNT

Statement of Account

Date   August 1, 19--

New Horizons Co.
333 Granville Drive
Chicago, IL 60606-2911
Telephone (312) 555-2700

To   Mr. John Lucas
     1300 Northville Street
     Chicago, IL 60608-8620

Date	Items	Debits	Credits	Balance Due
July 1	Balance			23.10
10	Invoice 6775	32.50		55.60
15	Invoice 6823	15.25		70.85
20	Credit Memo 123		5.50	65.35
25	Payment on account		50.00	15.35

Illustration 9-14   INVOICE

INVOICE	*LUDWIG OFFICE FURNITURE* 11515 Grandin Parkway Reading, PA 19602-4188 Phone (215) 555-8388	Invoice 1650212

Sold To   MacArthur Manufacturing Company   Date   May 2, 19--
          1456 Industrial Avenue
          Reading, PA 19603-3327   Order   415673

                                                    Shipped By   Our truck

Terms   2/10, n/30

Quantity	Description	Cat. No.	Unit Price	Amount
5	Four-drawer, letter-size file cabinets, green	523J10	110.95	554.75
5	Two-drawer, letter-size file cabinets, green	523J20	72.95	364.75
				919.50

Salesperson   T. Ormsby

letter. The letter, with check enclosed, should describe the amount and form of payment and specify how the payment is to be applied. The *how* is especially important if you, as debtor, have more than one account, owe a note, or are late in payment. Unless a debtor specifies the item or account to which payment should be applied, the creditor may apply that payment as the credi-

Illustration 9–15   VOUCHER CHECK

tor sees fit. For additional security, a remittance letter also should identify the enclosed check by a definite reference—for example, "Enclosure: Check for $2,026.33."

A remittance letter may also be used to request information, assistance, or service, as shown by this example:

1.   Refer to your enclosed remittance.

     Please apply the enclosed check, No. 12204, to our Computer Accessories account, under the 2/10, net 30 terms agreed upon.

2.   Identify the amount of payment and the invoice number to which the payment should be applied.

     This check covers the following:

Invoice 06791:	$ 965.07
Invoice 06900:	844.95
Invoice 07124:	267.87
Gross	$2,077.89
Discount	41.56
Net	$2,036.33

3. State your inquiry or request; and, if appropriate, reinforce goodwill.

> Our customers are becoming more environmentally aware. Many have asked for recycled or recyclable paper products. We hope you can help us supply this growing market. Please send your Recycled Only catalog for computer paper products.

How should you respond to a customer's incorrect payment?

As a seller, you may receive remittances that misstate the amount of payment or indicate that payment terms are misunderstood. Such situations must be corrected promptly, clearly, and tactfully. The following example shows how to correct a customer's overpayment; Illustration 9–16 shows how to request correction of an underpayment.

1. Refer cordially to the reason for your message.

> This $55 check is a refund for overpayment of your account.

2. Indicate the problem or misinterpretation; request or explain appropriate action to correct it.

> Since you paid for Invoice No. 075541 within ten days of billing, you were entitled to a 2 percent discount. You may apply that discount to all future payments made within the ten-day discount period. This policy is our way of rewarding customers who pay promptly.

3. Close with a cordial, off-the-subject statement that lets the receiver know you want to continue your business relationship.

> Next month's special is a 15 percent discount on all audiotapes, a savings you can pass on to your customers. Study the enclosed brochure and order promptly to get the best selection.

REVIEW AND TRANSITION

Think about your receiver's likely reaction to your message. Will your message be viewed as good news or neutral? If so, your communication objective is to give or request information in a way that satisfies the receiver and reinforces goodwill.

To convey yes or good news, begin with information likely to please your receiver; state details which support that favorable information; and close with a courteous statement of goodwill. To convey neutral or maybe information, begin with a cordial, mutually agreeable statement; support that statement with words and tone intended to keep communication lines open; close with a courteous statement of goodwill.

Examples of favorable or neutral messages include routine inquiries, requests, and replies; orders and acknowledgments; statements of account,

Illustration 9–16   REMITTANCE-CORRECTION MESSAGE

HAMMOND AND GALLS, INC.
200 BRENDEN PLAZA
OKLAHOMA CITY, OK 73110-3741
TELEPHONE 405-555-2909

September 30, 19--

Mr. D. B. Owens, Sr.
Owens Variety Store
840 Kersfield Street
Lawton, OK 73505-6154

Dear Mr. Owens:

Reason for letter

While crediting your account for your September 25 check
($4,052.70) in payment of our August 18 invoice ($4,503),
we noticed an apparent oversight.

Explanation and requested action

It appears you applied a 10 percent discount, although your
check was dated four weeks after the discount period. To
earn the 10 percent discount under our 10/10, n/60 terms,
you must send your check within 10 days of the invoice date.

To have your account marked "Paid in full," please send us
your check for $450.30.

Goodwill, off-the-subject closing

The enclosed brochure describes unusual values on over
stocked items. We are offering discounts of up to 70 percent on this first-quality merchandise--items that should
sell well during the holiday season. While supplies last,
orders will be shipped promptly on a first-received, first-
filled basis. The standard 10/10, n/60 terms will apply to
these deeply discounted items, giving you an opportunity for
substantial profits.

Sincerely,

W. B. Rogers

W. B. Rogers
Accounts Supervisor

ml

invoices, and remittances. Unfavorable or mixed counterparts of such messages are described in Chapter 10.

YOUR DECISIONS FOR CHAPTER 9

J. D. McClure, Vice President of Corporate Communication of Hopkins Enterprises, awaits your reply. McClure smiles and says: "I'm glad you're carefully considering your communication decisions instead of giving just a glib answer." What will you now convey to McClure about your understanding of effective structures for good-news and neutral messages?

McClure continues: "Here's a request from Rugs International for information on imported Oriental rugs. And here's our latest catalog, which includes prices and other ordering information. Rugs International could become a profitable customer. I'd like you to prepare a letter of reply. Let me see the letter before you send it."

You nod confidently and return to your desk. How will you structure that message?

Write the reply to I. R. Tillman, President, Rugs International, P.O. Box 4471, Chicago, IL 60617-4471.

DISCUSSION QUESTIONS

A. In the context of Chapter 9, what are appropriate definitions and examples of these terms?

   1. good-news message
   2. neutral message
   3. interim acknowledgment
   4. remittance

B. What is the basic structure of a good-news message?

C. What is the basic structure of a neutral message?

D. Why does a message with *you/your* words not always convey a *you* attitude?

E. What should an effective purchase order specify?

F. In what ways are the items in each of these sets alike? unlike?

   1. interim, new-customer, loyal-customer, and large-order acknowledgments
   2. favorable and neutral replies
   3. routine inquiry and favorable reply

G. Which letter format (block, modified block, or simplified block) does each of these illustrations show?

      1. Illustration 9–1
      2. Illustration 9–7
      3. Illustration 9–8

H. Which punctuation style (open or mixed) does each of these illustrations show?

      1. Illustration 9–1
      2. Illustration 9–6

APPLICATIONS

1. Revise these items to convey clarity, conciseness, courtesy, *you* attitude, positive tone, and correct grammar.

    a. We do not want you to be a dissatisfied customer.

    b. We cannot ship that item to you before February 20.

    c. We have received your demand for a $318 refund, which is enclosed with this letter.

    d. No, we do not mind if you return those two items for credit to your account.

    e. We have received your employment inquiry and résumé and are reviewing them, and we thank you for your interest in our company.

    f. The Investment Committee has not decided about your May 19 proposal, but they are still studying it and will notify you of a decision as soon as they make a decision.

    g. Your recent order is acknowledged, and we are pleased you chose us as your supplier and assure you that we will always give prompt attention to your orders.

    h. We have reviewed your complaint about the HL 40 cassette player included in our shipment of May 2 (which was billed on Invoice No. 92583). Although contrary to our normal policy, we have been authorized to credit your account for the price of that item. We haven't been able to determine what might have caused the problems your customer claims to have had with that player. But to keep you happy, we will credit your account since you have already given your customer a refund.

    i. Your order for 12 dozen (one gross) of paint brushes is appreciated because it is so large. If we can supply additional merchandise for your new Super Paint Discount Center, do not fail to let us know.

    j. I expect to be employed by Corwin Industries this summer; and since I need letters of recommendation, Professor Galway, I wonder if I may ask you to write one for me to them as soon as possible. By the way, your statistics course, which I took last year, gave me enough confidence to apply for work at Corwin where I hear you have a good reputation for preparing statisticians.

k. I have been asked to give you this information: The loan application which you submitted to us on January 27 and about which you inquired on February 6 and February 13 has finally been approved. Call me to set up a time to sign the promissory note.

l. Thank you for letting me know about the problems you had during your last stay at the Lion's Head Inn. I want you to know that all employees involved have been reprimanded. If you ever visit Greenwood again, I hope you will give us another chance to serve you.

m. Not being in a position at this point in time to ascertain the definite cost of repairing your W5 light meter, the best I can do is estimate that it should cost in the vicinity of $85. For that price you might want to consider buying a new one. We have several in stock, beginning at $75 and going as high as $350, as you can see from the enclosed brochure.

n. Regretfully I must inform you that we have employed someone else with more experience for the position which you wanted, but I thank you for your interest in our firm.

o. Our policy being that our application forms must be fully completed before being considered, I must reject your application. If you want to be considered for a job, you should complete the items marked and return the form to my office immediately.

2. You have been elected to the Fund-Raising Committee of Alpha Omega (AO), the leading service society on your campus. This year AO has decided to sponsor two needy children for a one-week stay at a local summer camp. Since running, hiking, and bike riding are popular in your college community, you believe that a dependable sports watch, offered at an affordable price, would sell well and help raise funds for your summer camp project. The chairperson for this project has written the following messages. Identify the strengths and weaknesses of each and give suggestions for improvement. Rewrite each message to reflect your evaluation.

a. Letter to potential suppliers of sports watches (letter body only):

I am comparison shopping for a dependable sports watch. Alpha Omega has decided to sell sports watches as a fund-raiser so that we can send two children to summer camp. If you can give us the kind of watch we want at a good price, we'll probably order about 300 from you. Our goal is to raise $3,000, so we only have to make $10 on each to reach that goal.

Here's what we are looking for: total size of about 2-1/2 by 3-1/2 by 3/4 inches; a time display to 59 minutes, 59 99/100 seconds; readouts of lap and total elapsed time; readouts of hours/minutes/seconds and month/date/day. The watch must be available at a price that will permit us to make at least $10 profit on each one.

Please let us know soon what you can do for us.

b. Memo to Alpha Omega members (memo body only):

When you gave me this assignment, I immediately contacted three suppliers of sports watches. After waiting four weeks, I finally have answers from all three.

L. T. Knowles, Inc., from St. Louis, MO, offers the best deal. Not only that—Knowles was the first to respond. That makes me think we ought to buy from them, but I'll let you decide. Knowles can supply the LTK Exact battery-operated watch (Model No. 36-027) for $180 per dozen. That's only $15 each. If we sell 300 of those jewels at $25 each, we will have the $3,000 we're trying to raise. Surely we can sell 300 at only $25.

What's more, Knowles offers credit privileges if our order is signed by the president of AO and the AO faculty advisor.

As I said, I think we should buy from Knowles, but the information from the other suppliers is attached in case you want to look at it.

We'll vote on this at next Tuesday's meeting.

CASES

With this chapter you are introduced to cases, many of which require role playing. Try to picture yourself as the person whose role you are asked to play. When you are asked to compose a message as someone else, be sure to write your own name (or student number) on the assignment as indicated by your instructor.

1. Craig Power, Inc., a public utility company serving your community, is about to open a consumer information center at Central Shopping Mall. Beginning next month—from 10 a.m. to 4 p.m. on Tuesdays, Thursdays, and Saturdays—energy specialists will be available to confer personally with Craig customers about methods and cost effectiveness

of converting from electric to gas heating systems. Also, during these informal meetings, home appliance exhibitors will demonstrate new energy-saving products.

As program director of the Craig Consumer Information Center, invite Craig customers to attend. Format this message as a short, informal memo to be enclosed with statements of account to Craig customers.

2. The Metro Convention Office (MCO) in your city provides timely business opportunities by sending local executives a weekly newsletter. The letter announces upcoming conventions, dates, expected attendance, and meeting places. As MCO media coordinator, prepare a letter that informs local executives of the following conventions, scheduled for the second week of next month:

Monday and Tuesday—Regional Jewelers Association, 420 delegates, Tarleton Hotel

Tuesday through Thursday—Association of Industrial Managers, 455 delegates; and Society for Electronic Technology, 470 delegates. Both groups meeting at the Grand Plaza Hotel and Convention Center

Thursday and Friday—Society for Environmental Engineers, 560 delegates, Ridgecrest Lodge and Convention Center

Remembering that the Metro Convention Office is located in your city, use realistic but not actual business names, addresses, and telephone numbers to format this letter. Use the simplified block format.

3. Review Case 2. On behalf of the Metro Convention Center, prepare a business letter to welcome the convention delegates. Thank them for selecting your city as their convention site. Describe major civic and leisure-time attractions available to them. Invite the delegates to return. Copies of this letter, with your name as MCO media coordinator, will be placed with registration materials in packets that delegates receive when they arrive for their meetings. Use the simplified block format for this letter.

4. Attach the messages prepared for Cases 2 and 3 to a memorandum which reminds the MCO employees about the expected influx of convention delegates and the inquiries that the visitors probably will direct to MCO. Emphasize the good news of how these conventions benefit your city and MCO. Acknowledge and reinforce confidence in MCO employees as helpful and hospitable representatives of the community.

5. The meetings cited in Cases 2, 3, and 4 have been successful. Convention officers and many delegates have congratulated MCO for its ex-

cellent support services. In a personalized letter to MCO employees, acknowledge their work and reinforce goodwill within your organization.

6. You are public information officer of the Tidelands Mortgage Lenders Association (TMLA), 140 Congaree Plaza, Columbia, SC 29202-1002, telephone (803) 555-9030. Prepare a business letter to inform homeowners of the following: South Carolinians whose primary homes were destroyed or heavily damaged by Hurricane Hugo may be eligible for below-market mortgage loans. These loans are made possible by the Regional Disaster Recovery Program. Detailed information, including a list of participating mortgage lenders, is available from TMLA.

7. As a homeowner whose property was seriously damaged by Hurricane Hugo, you receive the TMLA letter described in Case 6. You try repeatedly to telephone the TMLA office, but you keep getting a busy signal. You need detailed information about below-market mortgage loans for the coastal community in which your home is located. Write a letter of inquiry to TMLA. Your address for this exercise is 1117 Seaside Road, Ocean View, SC 29424-1017, telephone (803) 555-6272. The TMLA address and phone number are given in Case 6.

8. As TMLA public information officer, prepare a reply to the Case 7 inquiry. Refer to enclosures that specify details of the special below-market loans and that identify participating mortgage lenders, including those in the Ocean View area.

9. To fulfill a research requirement in your academic program, you decide to explore often-overlooked career opportunities. Your research discloses that the entertainment industry employs thousands of accountants, financial analysts, marketers, managers, and other business specialists. You learn that Weston Associates, Inc. (WAI), produces syndicated television game shows, including the "Weston College Quiz" program, which offers cash prizes to defray educational expenses.

   You decide to use your research project as an opportunity to gain first-hand information about the industry and, simultaneously, to earn cash as a game-show contestant. Prepare an inquiry letter to WAI. Explain that you are a college student; identify your school, your academic program, and your expected graduation date. Ask how you can become a "Weston College Quiz" contestant. WAI's address is 800 Lombard Lane, Hollywood, CA 90029-5401.

10. As WAI contestant coordinator, prepare a reply to the Case 9 inquiry. Establish and reinforce goodwill as you convey these facts: WAI conducts contestant tryouts at its Hollywood offices from June through November only; videotapes of the program are broadcast throughout

the year. At the program producer's discretion, prospective contestants who pass an array of preliminary tests and who comply with other eligibility requirements may or may not be selected for "Weston's College Quiz." Prospective and actual contestants pay their own travel, lodging, and other expenses. Viewers who would like additional information, and who plan to be in the Los Angeles area for business or vacation purposes, are welcome to telephone WAI at (213) 555-4193. (The WAI address is given in Case 9.)

11. Review Cases 9 and 10. Prepare a letter to thank the WAI contestant coordinator for answering your first inquiry. Ask whether WAI's plans include any possibility of contestant searches in cities other than Los Angeles. Mention your willingness to audition for "Weston's College Quiz" if a contestant search is held in your geographical area. (Note: If you actually reside in or near Los Angeles, write this letter on behalf of a friend who lives elsewhere.)

12. As WAI contestant coordinator, answer the Case 11 inquiry. Explain that if WAI decides to conduct regional contestant searches, announcements will appear in local newspapers. Reinforce goodwill; thank the prospective contestant for writing; encourage the prospective contestant to keep watching "Weston's College Quiz."

13. As sales manager for Business Suppliers, Inc. (BSI), W. M. Selwyn solicits new business by sending the BSI catalog to prospective customers. Accompanying the catalog is a letter which mentions that new customers are eligible for a 5 percent discount on the first order. As W. M. Selwyn, compose that letter to L. M. Kim, purchasing agent for Larchmont Corporation, 672 Logan Place, Galveston, TX 71554-1034; telephone (409) 555-2645; fax (409) 555-1870. The address of Business Suppliers, Inc., is 1400 Sherwood Road, Houston, TX 77033-2013; telephone (713) 555-6181; fax (713) 555-8893.

14. Review Case 13. As L. M. Kim, prepare a purchase order letter to W. M. Selwyn. On behalf of Larchmont Corporation, order these items and cite the 5 percent discount: Stock Number DS 3803, Blair 3-1/2-inch diskette filing trays, with lock feature, 60-diskette capacity, 6 at $22.47 each. Stock No. DS 6260, Blair visual display terminal filters, 11-3/8 inches by 8-3/8 inches, 5 at $21.27 each. Stock No. FT 8903, Premium glass filament tape, 3/4 inches wide by 60 yards long, 1 dozen rolls at $70.20 per dozen. Stock No. PA 7402, Ecology recycled paper pads, 18-pound weight, 8-1/2 inches by 11 inches, unbleached white, 3 dozen at $22.30 per dozen. Stock No. FT 9903, Starco filament tape dispenser, 2 at $14.99 each. Remember to apply the 5 percent discount to the $408.25 total of these prices, and specify shipping instructions.

15. Review Cases 13 and 14. As W. M. Selwyn of BSI, prepare a new-customer acknowledgment of L. M. Kim's purchase order. Address your letter to Kim at Larchmont Corporation.

16. Review Cases 13 through 15. Business Suppliers, Inc., shipped the incorrect size of visual display terminal filters to Larchmont Corporation. As purchasing agent L. M. Kim, write a routine adjustment request. State that you are returning the filters to BSI. Restate the correct item description. Ask for prompt delivery of the correct filters.

17. Review Case 16. As W. M. Selwyn of BSI, grant Kim's adjustment request by expediting shipment of the correct replacement filters to Larchmont Corporation. In an appropriate letter to Kim, reinforce goodwill.

18. Last year, during a holiday trip with friends, you visited Wonderworld Theme Park in Florida. Now you are considering employment possibilities for next summer and believe that you would enjoy working at Wonderworld. You want to know the application procedure, the background requirements for working at Wonderworld, when the summer season starts and ends, and whether the park has summer lodging for employees. Prepare an inquiry letter addressed to Wonderworld's personnel recruitment office, 5700 Morrow Boulevard, Clearwater, Florida 33545-6626, telephone (813) 555-3600.

19. Review Case 18. As E. M. Ramos, Wonderworld personnel recruiter, answer that inquiry. Refer to an enclosed brochure that describes Wonderworld's summer employment opportunities for college students. Also, refer to an enclosed employment application form. Request its completion and return. Inform the potential applicant that Wonderworld has no lodging for summer employees but maintains a "roommate wanted" bulletin board. Be sure to build goodwill.

20. Review Cases 18 and 19. Prepare your reply to E. M. Ramos. Thank Ramos for the Wonderworld summer employment information. Refer to the application form which Ramos sent you. Having completed the form, you are enclosing it with this letter. Describe two or three of your special qualifications for Wonderworld employment. Close by reinforcing goodwill with Ramos and Wonderworld.

MULTICULTURAL INSIGHTS

1. How do favorable or neutral messages written in American English resemble and differ from those written in other languages with which you are familiar? Specifically, what are message structures and tones for

conveying favorable or neutral information through inquiries, requests, and replies? through purchase orders? through remittances?

2. In what ways does Chapter 9 pertain to oral as well as written business communication in the United States and in other cultures? Share with your classmates cross-cultural differences, if any, that you have observed.

BAD-NEWS OR MIXED-NEWS MESSAGES

CHAPTER OUTLINE

I. Basic Message Structures
II. Unfavorable or Mixed Replies to Inquiries and Requests
III. Unfavorable or Mixed Acknowledgments of Orders
    A. Acknowledgments of Incomplete Orders
    B. Notices of Delayed Shipments
    C. Acknowledgments That Suggest a Substitution
    D. Acknowledgments That Decline Orders
IV. Review and Transition

OBJECTIVES

After completing this chapter, you should be able to:

1. Recognize business situations that require sharing of bad news or mixed news.
2. Apply the communication-by-objectives (CBO) approach as you plan message structure, word choice, and communication tone to convey bad news or mixed news.
3. Compose effective bad-news and mixed-news business messages.

DECISIONS CASE

You are progressing as a management trainee at Hopkins Enterprises. J. D. McClure, your supervisor, ends today's meeting with these words:

"Sometimes a businessperson must say no or, in a single message, must say no to one thing and yes or maybe to another. Consider your communication objective: You need to say no and at the same time show empathy for your receiver. You want to maintain or begin a positive business relationship. How can you reinforce goodwill when your information is not what the receiver hopes to read or hear? How should you organize and word such a message to avoid its rejection?"

Additional questions about this decision-making case are stated at the end of this chapter. Study the chapter before answering those questions.

CHAPTER CONTEXT

Assume you need to convey information that will probably disappoint your receiver. If you open the message with the bad news, your reader or listener may not attend to the rest of what you say and may not forgive you for your lack of empathy. Your receiver may react negatively toward the disappointment *and toward you* because of the way you conveyed the information. Struck by bad news at the outset, your receiver may miss the important reasons you offer for the bad news— reasons that could lessen the disappointment. If confronted first by bad news, your receiver is apt to reject any helpful suggestions or counter-proposals you offer later in your message.

BASIC MESSAGE STRUCTURES

What circumstances justify a bad-news message?

Circumstances often prevent you from doing what someone hopes you will do. When you are unable to fill an order, when you cannot answer an inquiry, or when you refuse a request, you must send an **unfavorable** or **bad-news message**. In this chapter you will learn to structure and word disappointing information so that you can keep channels open for future communication.

What is a counterproposal?

When you need to say yes *and* no, or when you prefer to offer a **counter-proposal** (an alternative to what has been requested), you send a **mixed-news message**. Mixed news—like disappointing news—should be structured and worded, truthfully and ethically, to convey goodwill and maintain the business relationship.

To communicate unfavorable or mixed news bolstered by goodwill, open your message with a statement about which you and your receiver can agree. Or begin with a neutral statement, one that probably will neither please nor displease your receiver. Such openings are called **buffers**. They enable the receiver to tune in the message, and they lead to reasons that help the receiver prepare, psychologically as well as logically, for a statement of bad news.

What are
characteristics of an
effective buffer?

A buffer should be related to the central message. An off-subject buffer could confuse the receiver about the purpose of the message. And although a buffer should not be negative, neither should it mislead the receiver to think the message will be favorable. Here are examples of buffers:

Thank you for your July 9 purchase order, No. 15-8475.

Your April 12 adjustment request for Invoice 801-2607 has received prompt and thorough consideration.

Your inquiry about summer employment is appreciated.

Your September 5 loan request is receiving the careful processing that you rightly expect.

These are the basic structures of unfavorable and mixed-news messages with such openings:

1. Begin with a mutually agreeable or neutral statement (buffer).

   Your application to Redi-Cast Products for the Systems Analyst position is appreciated.

Why use inductive
order for an
unfavorable message?

2. Use inductive[1] (indirect) order to present pertinent data. Supply true and relevant reasons that prepare the receiver to expect and accept the unfavorable news, mixed news, or counterproposal.

   You were among 18 applicants who were screened for the single opening we had in that job category.

3. State the unfavorable news as a necessary consequence of the facts you have cited. If the reasons clearly imply the unfavorable news, an explicit statement may not be necessary.

   Although your qualifications fall short of our needs at this time, we will keep your materials on file for six months. During that time, if a position in which we can use your skills becomes available, we will notify you.

How should you close
a bad-news message?

4a. Close with a courteous statement of goodwill. Do not refer to the bad news.

   We wish you success in your search for new career opportunities.

---

[1]Inductive reasoning was discussed in Chapter 2.

Or:

4b. Provide a transition to the good news you can convey—say what you *can* do, not what you *can't* do. State the good news. Close cordially.

Your education and experience do qualify you for employment as a Programmer II. I have given your application file to Whitney Sutch. Please call him at 555-1145 if you are interested in that position. He will schedule an interview for you.

Or:

4c. Provide a transition to your counterproposal. Use deductive[2] (direct) order now. That is, offer the counterproposal first; then give reasons that justify it. Emphasize reasons likely to benefit the receiver. Close by courteously and confidently asking the receiver to accept the counterproposal. Add nothing else to the body of your message.

We do have openings for which you qualify in our Programming Division. Whitney Sutch is eager to interview you for one of those positions. Many of our systems analysts began in that division and moved rapidly into systems analysis after becoming familiar with our company and its information system.

Please call Whitney at 555-1145 to schedule an interview for a position in the Programming Division.

Illustrations 10−1 and 10−2 are examples of responses to an adjustment request. Which would you rather receive? To which would you respond more favorably? Illustration 10−1 demonstrates an unempathetic structure and tone for a bad-news message. In contrast, Illustration 10−2 demonstrates that even bad news can be conveyed in a positive, empathetic manner.

Illustrations 10−3 and 10−4 demonstrate positive structures and tone for mixed-news messages. Each letter denies a loan applicant the amount and terms requested, but offers a counterproposal.

U.S. government regulations require that applicants for credit be given specific reasons for denial of credit. Many lending institutions use a form message listing several possible reasons; those applicable to a particular applicant are checked. However, empathetic managers use personalized letters, such as those shown in Illustrations 10−3 and 10−4, in addition to form messages.

As with other types of business communication, empathy is essential throughout an unfavorable or a mixed-news message. One evidence of empathy is avoidance of negative language and ironic statements.

---

[2]Deductive reasoning was discussed in Chapter 2.

Illustration 10–1   NEGATIVE EXAMPLE: BAD NEWS WITH NEGATIVE TONE

> Bad-news opening; negative words
>
> Your request to replace your Model D901 table saw has been denied.
>
> Negative, condescending tone
>
> When you bought the saw it was clearly marked "Discontinued Model." Our policy is to sell discontinued merchandise on an "as is" basis. We discontinued the Model 901 in 1989 because we had received several complaints about the rip fence.
>
> Ironic close
>
> We hope to be of further service to you soon.

Illustration 10–2   POSITIVE EXAMPLE: BAD NEWS BUT EMPATHETIC TONE

> Buffer opening; positive tone
>
> Your request to replace your Model D901 table saw has been carefully reviewed.
>
> Reasons; bad news as consequence of reasons; courteous, positive close
>
> We stopped manufacturing the Model 901 in 1989 and sold the balance of our inventory to various discounters. Although we clearly inform discounters that our warranty does not apply to discontinued merchandise, some discounters offer a supplemental warranty for a small fee. Since you bought the saw from The Tool Shed in your city, I recommend that you return to that store to request an appropriate adjustment.

A negative tone is counterproductive in any message. Although you must convey bad news, you can achieve an empathetic tone by using neutral or positive words. Avoid words with negative connotations, such as those in the list on page 256. Can you add other words to the list?

Illustration 10-3   MIXED NEWS AND EMPATHETIC TONE

Buffer opening; positive tone	Your application for a $6,000 unsecured loan has been evaluated by the City Bank and Trust Co. loan committee.
Reasons leading to mixed news; positive tone	Current economic conditions have prompted the loan committee to place a $5,000 limit on unsecured loans for a single borrower. Since you already have a $2,000 unsecured loan with our bank, we can approve an additional loan for a maximum of $3,000.
Courteous, positive close	This approval is effective until November 27. If you desire the $3,000 loan, please call me before November 25 so that I can prepare the necessary forms and schedule a time for you to sign the note.

cannot send	inadequate	sorry
complain, complaint	incomplete	unable
deny	neglect	unfortunately
dissatisfied	not interested	unnecessary
do not understand	prohibit	unsatisfactory
error	refuse	wrong
fault	regret	you should/should
forgot	reject	not have

Although you cannot avoid all negative words, you can reduce their impact by subordinating them within the message. Consider the following examples:

Negative Tone

I do not understand your request.

We must deny your request for an interview.

I regret to inform you that your proposal was rejected.

Unfortunately, you supplied incomplete information. As soon as you correct the error, I will order new checks for you.

Illustration 10–4 COUNTERPROPOSAL WITH EMPATHETIC TONE

. CITY BANK AND TRUST COMPANY .
One Tower Place, Cincinnati, Ohio 45202-1390
TEL: (513) 555-6210 • FAX: (513) 555-3817

November 12, 19--

Mr. George Garrison
808 Dayton Street
Cincinnati, OH 45214-2226

Dear Mr. Garrison

Buffer opening;
positive tone

Your application for a $6,000 unsecured loan has been
evaluated by the City Bank and Trust Co. loan committee.

Reasons for
decision;
transition to
counterproposal

Current economic conditions have limited our approval of
unsecured loans, especially for applicants whose financial obligations are already heavy. Although we must
therefore decline your current request, a secured loan
may be the solution to your financial needs.

Benefits of
counterproposal

A secured loan will enable you to demonstrate your
capacity to pay while assuring City Bank and Trust Co.
that its funds are safe. Your financial statement indicates that you have assets, such as jewelry and corporate bonds, that can be used to secure the loan you
requested. If you are willing to pledge those assets as
collateral, we can supply the $6,000 you requested.

Courteous,
positive close

I'll gladly discuss the details of this offer with you.
Please call me at 555-6210.

Sincerely

R.G. Salter

R. G. Salter
Loan Officer

I am writing to complain about the unsatisfactory performance of your customer service representative.

Neutral or Positive Alternatives

Please help me understand your request.

Our spring interview schedule is completely filled.

A competing proposal has been accepted.

As soon as I receive the additional information, I will request a new order of printed checks for you.

Please let me tell you about my experience with your customer service representative.

Unfavorable Message in Dominant Position

Your application for a part-time position in our accounting department has been declined.

Unfortunately, we are unable to hire you at this time.

I'm sorry to inform you that we cannot repair your food processor.

Unfavorable Message Implied or in Subordinate Position

Although your application for a part-time position in our accounting department must be declined now, we encourage you to apply again after you have completed 12 hours of accounting courses.

Since we have filled all accounting positions, we encourage you to apply with another firm.

The Model K food processor was replaced by Model L five years ago. The production of Model K parts was discontinued one year later. Since we are unable to repair your food processor, we are returning it to you.

What is an ironic ending?

In an attempt to conclude a message in a favorable tone, some writers inadvertently use an **ironic ending**. An ironic ending is a surprising, incongruous statement that contradicts the theme of the message. For example, suppose your letter denies a job-interview request. To close with an offer of "further help" is ironic if the letter contains no helpful suggestions. Similarly, if you are unable to supply the service a customer requests, it is ironic to close with "I hope to be of service to you soon." You can avoid such irony by closing your message as indicated by the structures and examples in this chapter.

Should you always use indirect structure for unfavorable news? In most instances, that structure is likely to reinforce goodwill. A direct approach, however, may sometimes be preferable. In the interest of efficiency, some receivers prefer directness for production-related messages. Assume, for example, that you are an employment recruiter seeking a qualified candidate to direct your company's health and fitness program. You must report to the Director of Human Resources that you have found no satisfactory candidates. Even though the news is unfavorable, the manager is not likely to react negatively to the message. Therefore, a direct approach is acceptable and satisfies the manager's efficiency goal of quickly discerning the purpose of the message.

For all bad-news messages, use the CBO approach. Consider not only your purpose, but also the communication context, your receiver's goals, and your receiver's preferences. If the message—even though unfavorable—will not be received with disappointment or disfavor, use the direct approach demonstrated in Chapter 9.

As a businessperson, you will encounter two major categories of bad-news or mixed-news messages. Those categories are unfavorable or mixed replies to inquiries or requests and unfavorable or mixed acknowledgments of orders.

UNFAVORABLE OR MIXED REPLIES TO INQUIRIES AND REQUESTS

Appropriately saying no involves psychology as well as logic. People usually believe that their inquiries and requests deserve favorable responses. When your reply is other than yes, prepare your receiver for the unfavorable or mixed news while maintaining goodwill.

Avoid beginning your reply with "no," "we cannot," or other negative words. They tend to close your receiver's mind to whatever else you may say. Instead, assure your receiver that the inquiry or request has been considered carefully. Use words and phrases that prepare the receiver to anticipate and to accept the unfavorable news. Don't hide behind a vague statement of "company policy." Remember to *explain* reasons that make the unfavorable news necessary. State the bad news as a *logical consequence* of those reasons.

For unfavorable or mixed replies to inquiries or requests, use the following message structure:

1. Begin with a buffer that identifies the request and establishes goodwill.

    Your invitation to speak on "Trade Opportunities in Eastern Europe" at the upcoming Young Executives professional development seminar is an honor. I applaud your interest in this timely topic.

2. Give reasons for your refusal showing that you carefully considered the request. If the refusal is not clearly implied, state it explicitly.

I am scheduled to travel to Argentina for a meeting with one of our largest importers. Since that meeting is tentatively scheduled for May 9, I will probably be en route to Argentina on May 8, the day of your seminar.

3a. Suggest an alternative.

My business partner, Kim Do, is a dynamic speaker. She also has considerable experience in imports and exports and is knowledgeable about developments in Eastern Europe. Kim is willing to speak at your May 8 seminar. You can contact her at 555-0997.

Or:

3b. Close with a courteous statement of goodwill.

I wish you success on your seminar. If you need a speaker for a future program, please contact me again. I always enjoy sharing my experience and insights with attentive groups such as the Young Executives.

Illustrations 10–5 through 10–7 are additional examples of replies that convey unfavorable news, mixed news, and counterproposals.

What are examples of unfavorable or mixed replies?

UNFAVORABLE OR MIXED ACKNOWLEDGMENTS OF ORDERS

Chapter 9 discussed the importance of acknowledging customer orders promptly, and presented structures for good-news acknowledgments. When you cannot fulfill a customer's order as received, you must send an unfavorable or mixed-news acknowledgment. Examples of such messages are acknowledgments of incomplete orders, notices of delayed shipments, acknowledgments that suggest a substitution, and acknowledgments that decline orders.

What are examples of unfavorable or mixed acknowledgments?

Acknowledgments of Incomplete Orders

When you receive a purchase order that omits necessary data, your acknowledgment is a bad-news message. The bad news is a delay during which you must request, and the buyer needs to provide, additional information to com-

Illustration 10–5   BAD-NEWS REPLY WITH EMPATHETIC TONE

MEMORANDUM

TO: Daniel J. Wyatt

FROM: L. B. Copeland

DATE: March 13, 19--

SUBJECT: Response to Salary Increase Request

Buffer

Your March 6 memorandum requesting a salary increase has been referred to me by Robert Blakey, your department head.

Reasons; necessary consequences

All Copeland Industries employees accept a starting salary with the understanding that increases will be considered annually, if justified by a satisfactory performance review. You have been with us for eight months, and it is somewhat early to consider a salary increase now.

Positive close; reinforced goodwill

Blakey reports that your work and your attitude are praiseworthy. Continue your fine performance, and your request--reinforced by Blakey's recommendation--will certainly be reconsidered in July.

Illustration 10–6   MIXED-NEWS REPLY WITH EMPATHETIC TONE

MEMORANDUM

TO: Victor Barnes

FROM: Carol Kendricks

DATE: August 11, 19--

SUBJECT: Your EEA Inquiry

Your August 10 inquiry about additional Employees' Educational Aid payments has been carefully evaluated. The
decision criteria described in our firm's Policy and
Procedures Manual, page 32, were applied with fairness
to you and all Copeland Industries employees.

Those criteria include the stipulation that EEA
privileges require earning a grade of at least B for
every course in which the employee enrolls. The EEA
plan also requires that participants maintain at least a
B average to retain eligibility for tuition assistance.
Your grade of C in your Shaw College management course
(MGT 380) prevents EEA reimbursement of your tuition
cost for that course and puts your continued eligibility
for the EEA plan in jeopardy.

But here's good news for you: At its quarterly meeting
last week, the board of directors approved continuation
of tuition assistance for an employee in your situation.
The requirement is that you earn at least a B+ for the
next college course in which you enroll.

Copeland Industries is committed to an educated work
force and supports your efforts to complete your college
degree. You have our best wishes for success.

Illustration 10–7 COUNTERPROPOSAL WITH EMPATHETIC TONE

MEMORANDUM

TO: G. B. Sheridan

FROM: M. L. Cartaret

DATE: September 14, 19--

SUBJECT: Nomination to Head MA Committee

Buffer; sincere appreciation

Your request that I head the management advisory committee is gratifying. Thank you for the confidence you have shown in me.

Reasons; refusal as logical consequence; helpful counterproposal

This morning, however, I accepted a transfer to our Off-Shore Explorations Division in New Orleans. Since this new assignment prevents acceptance of your request, please let me suggest other candidates for the position. Seth Calloway and Mae Chung have been members of the committee for several years; either of them would be an excellent leader of that important group.

Reaffirmed goodwill

The management advisory committee is evidence of management's commitment to effective employee communication. It has been a privilege to serve on that committee.

plete the order. The delay will be especially disappointing if your receiver requested a rush order.

Your tone should be one of interest and cooperation in determining precisely what the buyer wants. Do not state or even imply that the buyer is careless or that the order is confusing. Avoid words like "you forgot," "you neglected to," or "you failed to." Instead, use positive words to emphasize your desire, on behalf of your firm, to fill the order properly and promptly. That desire can also be shown by using a speedy communication medium, such as telephone or fax.

The following examples and Illustration 10–8 demonstrate an effective message structure for acknowledging incomplete orders:

1. Thank the customer for the order.

    Thank you for your recent order (No.155698) for 12 dozen 5-1/4-inch floppy diskettes.

2. Emphasize your desire to fill the order properly by explaining your further information needs.

    We stock two types of 5-1/4-inch floppy diskettes: double sided/double density (DS/DD), and double sided/high density (DS/HD).

Illustration 10–8   INCOMPLETE-ORDER ACKNOWLEDGMENT

Dear Ms. Mullaney

Thanks; identification of order

Thank you for your June 28 mail order for three men's mesh knit shirts with pocket (No. 0790-7434); size, XL; color, blue.

Explanation, reinforced by you attitude

This shirt comes in three shades of blue. To be sure you receive exactly the shirts you want, please tell us the color or colors to send: bright blue, lapis blue, or navy blue.

Courteous, clear request

For prompt, accurate processing of your order, just complete and mail the enclosed reply card today.

Sincerely

3. Ask courteously for the needed information, and indicate how the information should be supplied (for instance, by completing and returning a special form or a reply card that you enclose with your acknowledgment).

To ensure that you receive the correct diskettes, please mark your preference on the enclosed reply card, which is already addressed to me. You may mail the card or send your message by fax (1-800-555-3621).

4. Assure the customer that prompt attention will be given to the reply.

I will ship your diskettes as soon as I receive your reply.

Notices of Delayed Shipments

What circumstances require a delayed-shipment acknowledgment?

Sometimes you may not be able to ship part or even all of an order. Extraordinary demand may have depleted your stock. Perhaps new merchandise is in production but has yet to be finished for shipping. In circumstances of partial shipment, deferred shipment, depleted stock, substitution, or the like, use this message structure, demonstrated by Illustration 10–9:

1. Thank the customer for the order.

Pedalinc appreciates your order for 3,000 bicycle pedals (Model 41).

2. Explain the cause of the delay.

To ensure the best quality possible, we have redesigned our manufacturing facility. The redesign was completed in three weeks, but during that time production was halted.

3. Stressing what you can do, promise service as promptly as circumstances allow.

We are now back at full production levels. Our high-quality bicycle pedals will be ready for shipment by February 19. The Model 41 pedals should arrive at your warehouse by February 26.

4. Request the customer's cooperation, or simply end the message cordially.

Pedalinc appreciates your patience in waiting for the Model 41 bicycle pedals—recently rated No. 1 in *Cycling World*'s consumer tests.

Illustration 10-9   DELAYED-SHIPMENT ACKNOWLEDGMENT

Dear Ms. Mullaney

Reinforcement of goodwill

Your June 28 telephone order was welcome. Thank you for your loyal
patronage.

Explanation, emphasizing can do

The demand for the men's mesh knit
shirt with pocket (No. 0790-7434) was
greater than we had anticipated,
resulting in rapid depletion of
stock. Our supplier promises we will
again be fully stocked no later than
July 15. We will ship your order by
Speedy Express as soon as our stock
is replenished.

Positive close; promise of service

The enclosed brochure shows our complete line of summer sport shirts.
Please call our 24-hour order number,
1-800-555-4104, if you want any shirt
instead of--or in addition to--your
June 28 selection.

Sincerely

Acknowledgments That Suggest a Substitution

Sometimes a customer requests an item you no longer stock, but for which you have an acceptable alternative. You must convince your customer that the substitute is as acceptable as the discontinued product. Beware, however, of using the word *substitute;* your receiver may associate that word with "second best." Also avoid apologizing. An apology connotes fault or error. Focus, instead, on the benefits of the alternative. When you must suggest a substitute product, use the following message structure:

1. Thank the customer for the order.

    Your recent order for the Antaspec Scanner Model 202 is appreciated.

2. Describe the product you *can* provide and its benefits.

We now stock exclusively the Executive line of computer scanners. These scanners come in both hand-held and tabletop models, produce exceptionally clear images with high resolution, and are compatible with all leading microcomputers.

3. Tell your customer how to order.

    The enclosed catalog provides detailed information about Executive scanners. To order the Executive, call me at 1-800-555-4321 to authorize the necessary change to your previous purchase order.

4. Close courteously.

    I look forward to shipping your new Executive scanner soon. I'm sure you will be pleased with its operating ease and high-quality output.

Acknowledgments That Decline Orders

What conditions require a declined-order acknowledgment?

Because of merchandising policies, exclusive contracts, or restricted territories, you may be required to decline or to redirect an order. For example, some manufacturers sell their products only through authorized retailers. In such circumstances, encourage the buyer to complete the transaction through proper channels, or recommend another source, as shown by this message structure and by Illustration 10–10:

1. Thank the customer for the order or the interest in your product or service.

    Thank you for your interest in Sport King shoes.

2. Explain the regulations, practices, or circumstances that prevent you from accepting the order. Decline the order explicitly if necessary.

    To ensure exact fit, the removable orthotic arch supports for each pair of Sport King shoes are made to exact measurements taken by our certified shoe consultants.

3. Decline the order, impliedly or explicitly.

    For that reason, we market these shoes only through authorized Sport King retailers.

4. Suggest, courteously and definitely, what the customer should do or what action you will take (for instance, referring the order to a local dealer).

    I have sent your inquiry to Marcela Diaz, the Sport King represen-

Ilustration 10–10   DECLINED-ORDER ACKNOWLEDGMENT

<table>
<tr>
<td>Buffer
establishing
goodwill</td>
<td>Thank you for your August 30 order and for this opportunity to help you purchase a backyard utility building.</td>
</tr>
<tr>
<td>Reasons
for denial;
helpful offer</td>
<td>Approximately six months ago we decided to limit our production of utility buildings. We now produce buildings that are 12x18 feet or smaller. Since you requested dimensions of 14x24 feet, we must refer you to another manufacturer.

Homestead Builders produces a top-quality 14x24-ft. utility building. Homestead's address is 1760 Industrial Road, Norwalk, CT 06831-7354.</td>
</tr>
<tr>
<td>Goodwill;
resale</td>
<td>If any of our smaller buildings, described in the enclosed catalog, should satisfy your needs, please call me at 1-800-555-4466. I will fill your order promptly.</td>
</tr>
</table>

tative in your area. She will contact you soon to explain the requirements for becoming an authorized Sport King retailer.

REVIEW AND TRANSITION

To convey unfavorable or mixed-news messages, including counterproposals, begin with a mutually agreeable or a neutral statement. Then use indirect order to present true and relevant reasons that prepare your receiver psychologically for what follows. If the reasons do not clearly imply the refusal, state the unfavorable news as a logical result of the facts you have stated.

Close the message in a positive manner. For an unfavorable message, simply close with a courteous statement of goodwill. For a mixed-news message, provide a transition to information that probably will please your receiver. State the good news, and close cordially. For a message that offers an alternative to what your receiver requested, provide a transition that leads to your counterproposal. Then use direct order: Offer the counterproposal and give reasons to justify it. Emphasize reasons that are to the receiver's advantage. Close by courteously and confidently asking the receiver to accept your counterproposal.

Chapter 9 discussed favorable or neutral messages; Chapter 10, unfavorable or mixed-news messages. Goodwill and special-occasion messages are described in Chapter 11.

YOUR DECISIONS FOR CHAPTER 10

"I suppose you knew I asked this question because I have an assignment for you," smiles McClure. "Remember that customer who requested information about our Oriental rugs? She has ordered seven rugs. That's good news, but she's asking for '90 days same as cash' terms. In fairness to other customers—and to protect our cash flow—we cannot approve those terms. The best terms we can offer are 2/10, net 30. Maybe she can take advantage of the discount. Please answer her request. Help her see the advantage of the discount, especially on large orders. But remember, we want her business!"

In what ways has Chapter 10 helped you to understand the communication challenges in this decision case? What kind of message—bad-news or mixed-news—is appropriate? What structure should you use? What cautions should you observe?

Write the reply to I. R. Tillman, President, Rugs International, P.O. Box 4471, Chicago, IL 60617-4471.

DISCUSSION QUESTIONS

A. Within the context of Chapter 10, what are appropriate definitions and examples for these terms?

   1. unfavorable or bad-news message
   2. mixed-news message without a counterproposal
   3. mixed-news message including a counterproposal
   4. inductive order for structuring a message
   5. deductive order for structuring a message

B. What is an effective basic structure for an unfavorable or bad-news message?

C. What is an effective basic structure for a mixed-news message without a counterproposal? for a mixed-news message with a counterproposal?

D. How can unfavorable messages be structured and worded to keep communication lines open?

E. What is a "buffer"? What are characteristics of an effective buffer?

F.   Why should an unfavorable reply use buffer-reasons-refusal-close structure instead of buffer-refusal-reasons-close structure?

G.   When may it be appropriate to begin a message with bad news?

APPLICATIONS

1.   Revise the following items to convey conciseness, goodwill, positive word choice, *you* tone, and correct grammar.

    a.   At the outset of this reply to your request, I must inform you that your loan application has been rejected.

    b.   We cannot grant you credit privileges with us, but we will not hesitate to do business with you on a C.O.D. basis.

    c.   Sorry to disappoint you, but we don't sell directly to consumers.

    d.   You failed to specify catalog numbers, and we can't fill your order without those numbers.

    e.   We don't have R500 in stock, but it won't be long until we do.

    f.   If we can help in some other way, do not hesitate to ask us.

    g.   Don't think that your orders are not appreciated by us.

    h.   No, I don't mind granting your request.

    i.   I'm not saying you're wrong; I'm saying the opposite.

    j.   Damage in shipment is not our responsibility, so we cannot grant your claim.

    k.   Our inspection of the HL 40 stereo cassette player (Invoice 92588) shows no justification for granting your claim. We cannot authorize repair, replacement, or refund for you in this case.

    l.   I cannot provide the confidential information you requested. Do not fail to let me know, however, if there isn't some other way I may be able to help you.

    m.   The job about which you inquired is not available. Although it is impossible for us to predict if we'll need people with your qualifications later on, do not neglect to inquire again in a few months.

    n.   The catalog numbers you used for your March 9 purchase order, No. 8015, are wrong. We cannot fill your order until we get the correct information from you.

    o.   A production delay makes it impossible for us to fill your complete order for three weeks or longer. But if we can fill part of your order before then, do you want us to ship it whenever we can?

    p.   I cannot accept your invitation to speak at your Employees Appreciation Day banquet June 17. But don't hesitate to ask me again.

    q.   No, we don't have additional copies of the publication you requested. Our stock has run out because of unforeseen demand. We're not sure, but we will probably print more copies. Ask us for those copies again in a few months, if you still need them then.

r.   We are not retailers. Try to get the items described in your May 30 inquiry from Jensen Stores in your region.

s.   No, we can't supply style WA 920 at the price you requested. If you want a cheaper item, substitute WA 850 for the 920.

2.   You are assistant sales manager of Elton Mail-Order Corporation, 21 Central Plaza, Youngstown, OH 44503-1285. For many years, the Elton catalog was mailed free of charge to people who requested it. Because of rising costs, Elton now charges $5 for each catalog mailed. The catalog contains a coupon for a $5 rebate on an order of $50 or more. Compose a form reply to requests that say, "Please send me your free catalog."

3.   A. E. Sanchez is purchasing agent for Martinique Salons Corporation, a new firm with headquarters at 1110 Bay Boulevard, Miami, FL 33108-8046. Sanchez requests credit privileges for the first Martinique order sent to Dale Preparations, Inc., 667 River Street, Jacksonville, FL 32220-2322. As Dale credit manager, you decide to postpone credit arrangements until Martinique proves financially reliable. But you want Martinique to buy Dale products now. Among those products is the complete line of Dale's Tropic Cosmetics, about to be marketed for the first time in the southeast United States. Answer Sanchez's request.

4.   You are district manager for Central Insurance Company, 56 Circle Drive, Salem, MD 21860-2712. You receive a message from Roberto Tonelli, 2056 Miller Avenue, Warren, PA 16365-0021, protesting cancellation of his $50,000 life insurance policy. Although a premium notice had been sent to him, Mr. Tonelli states that he did not receive it. To guard against such circumstances, Central Insurance Company usually has a local representative telephone or visit policyholders during a 30-day grace period to request the payment due. Mr. Tonelli says that this courtesy was not extended to him. On consulting the local representative, you learn that the Tonelli residence has no telephone. The agent went to the Tonelli residence twice, but no one responded when the agent knocked at the door. Write an appropriate message to Mr. Tonelli: either a no message, or an offer to continue his policy at a higher premium.

5.   As C. V. Stokely, you need to send a mixed-news memo to Tracy J. Todd, a member of the department that you head. The date is February 15. Several weeks ago, Tracy submitted a proposal for Phase 3 of the Rondex project. You forwarded the proposal to E. K. Morley, Rondex project coordinator. Concerned about costs of implementing Tracy's

proposal, Morley and Rondex have decided to reject Tracy's ideas for Phase 3. You must inform Tracy of the decision and encourage Tracy to rework the proposal for possible adoption in Phase 4 of the project. Write the appropriate memo to Tracy J. Todd.

CASES

1. As a college student who manages time efficiently, you are doing well with your academic program, extracurricular activities, and social relationships. You are an active member of several campus organizations, but today you receive a letter from Kerry Dawe, president of the Students' Social Group, a new organization that plans to meet weekly throughout the academic year. Dawe's letter invites you to join the new group, but you can't afford the time and expense involved. Compose a reply, declining Dawe's invitation. Use your actual name and address for this message. The address for Kerry Dawe is Students' Social Group, Box 1420 at your campus Student Center.

2. As a successful entrepreneur, you are well known in your community and receive many requests for assistance. This morning's mail brings a letter from the Homeless Children Foundation asking for a financial donation. You contribute often to civic and charitable organizations, but you cannot grant every request for funds. Prepare a suitable message for declining this financial request.

3. Since joining Dillon Travel Associates several years ago, you have earned substantial salary increases and have become director of the Educational Tours Department. This morning you receive a letter from R. C. Garza, an employment recruiter for Delta Manufacturing Corporation. Garza explains that Glenn Powell has applied for Delta employment and has listed you as a reference. Garza asks you to complete and return an enclosed recommendation form. You remember someone named Glenn Powell, who was a classmate and casual acquaintance during your college days, but you have not heard from or about that person for almost five years. Apparently, Powell has used your name, without your permission, as a reference. Decline Garza's request for a recommendation on Powell's behalf. Your business address is Dillon Travel Associates, Inc., 1100 Duval Plaza, Washington, DC 20014-0019, telephone (202) 555-1818. R. C. Garza's business address is Delta Manufacturing Corporation, 725 Riverbend Place, New Orleans, LA 70135-2006.

4. Review Case 3. Use the following information for a different reply to Garza: Explain why you cannot supply the requested information about

Powell, but mention that you recall Powell as a fellow student who seemed to succeed academically and who was liked by other students.

5. Review Case 3. Almost two weeks have passed since you answered Garza's inquiry. Today you receive a letter from Powell, who refers to Delta Manufacturing Corporation and asks permission to use your name as a character reference. You notice that Powell's letter used an incorrect ZIP Code for your address, explaining its delay in reaching you. Reply to Powell, whose address is 763 Chester Avenue, Monroe, LA 71229-4415. Explain the correspondence with Garza, and why you cannot be a character reference for Powell.

6. Your career as director of the Educational Tours Department at Dillon Travel Associates is flourishing. A few months ago, Lauren Grieg left Dillon for an executive position with Brazos Travel and Tours. Favorably impressed by the quality of your work, Grieg writes asking you to consider applying for an attractive employment opportunity with Brazos. You prefer, however, to continue your Dillon employment. Answer Grieg's letter and decline the offer. Your business address is stated in Case 3. Grieg's title and address are marketing vice president, Brazos Travel and Tours, Inc., 1930 Clegg Road, Dallas, TX 75265-3019.

7. The Shandon Malley accounting firm offers summer internships to college students whose overall grade point average is at least 3.5 (B+) on a 4-point scale. However, students with averages lower than 3.5 sometimes apply. As Shandon Malley internship program director, prepare a form letter to notify unqualified applicants that they are ineligible until they improve their grades. Encourage them to do so. The Shandon Malley address is 9125 Sloane Street, Boston, MA 02105-1005, telephone (617) 555-8010.

8. Review Case 7. As Shandon Malley internship program director, prepare a form letter to notify students whose grade point averages are at least 3.5 (B+) but who cannot be considered for internships because their applications arrived after the announced due date.

9. Review Cases 7 and 8. As a college student majoring in accounting, you applied for a Shandon Malley summer internship. While awaiting a reply, you accepted summer employment at another firm. Now you receive a letter from Blake Calhoun, summer internship administrator at Shandon Malley, saying that your application has been approved. Answer Calhoun's letter and decline the offer. Indicate that you cannot accept the internship offer, but keep channels open for possible employment next summer.

10. As assistant customer relations manager at Whitney Corporation, you receive a letter from Taniko Burke, who asks: "What is the procedure

for free repair or replacement of an unsatisfactory Whitney product? Fourteen months ago, before moving to Portland, I bought a Whitney electronic word processor, Model 871310, and have been unable to find a Whitney dealer who will repair or replace it at no cost to me." In your reply to Taniko Burke, explain that the limited warranty of the Whitney 871310 is for 12 months, as stated in the customer information packet accompanying the machine. Encourage Burke to consult any authorized Whitney dealer for product repair at reasonable cost. Whitney Corporation's address is 800 Clifford Road, Memphis, Tennessee 38124-3642, telephone (901) 555-7160. Taniko Burke's address is 301 Craig Avenue, Portland, OR 97206-3514.

11. You are an assistant to T. J. Malone, customer service manager, Gifts by Mail Corporation, 1470 Eastern Avenue, Wayne, PA 19022-3722, telephone (215) 555-8799. Malone tells you: "Many of our customers unintentionally omit stock numbers and detailed item descriptions. We need that information to process orders efficiently. Please prepare a form message—courteous, concise, and helpful—that we can mail to those customers who send us incomplete orders." Prepare the message.

12. Review Case 11. Pleased with your acknowledgment-of-incomplete-orders form, T. J. Malone says: "Sometimes, even when purchase orders are complete, circumstances beyond our control may prevent prompt shipment. For example, stock may be temporarily depleted because of extraordinary demand for an item, or unexpected transportation problems may occur. We need a courteous form message that informs customers of unavoidable delays but keeps their goodwill." Prepare the message.

13. Review Cases 11 and 12. To make room for new products, Gifts by Mail Corporation discontinues the sale of obsolete or outmoded merchandise. Occasionally, however, a customer orders a discontinued item. T. J. Malone asks you to prepare an acknowledgment message that declines such an order; invites the customer to purchase a new, improved version of the item; encloses a current catalog; and cites the page on which the new product description appears. Prepare this acknowledgment message.

14. Coastal Enterprises Corporation, a firm that offers a variety of boating expeditions, receives many more job inquiries than it has employment opportunities, and the number of inquiries keeps increasing. As assistant human resources manager, prepare a courteous, empathetic form letter to notify job seekers that Coastal is not currently hiring for any of its positions. The address of Coastal Enterprises Corporation is 881 Bridge Street, Jacksonville, FL 32249-2540, telephone (904) 555-7027.

15. A year ago, you offered employment to E. J. Hendrix, who courteously

declined your offer. Now Hendrix writes to you and asks if a suitable employment opportunity is available with your company. You thought highly of Hendrix when you first made an offer. You would still consider employing Hendrix, but all the jobs on your staff are currently filled. You would like to keep his credentials on file. Compose an appropriate letter to Hendrix, whose address is 3570 Archer Road, Des Moines, IA 50338-6424. Your title and address are Sales Manager, Ridgeway Beamer, Inc., 1250 Valery Street, St. Louis, MO 63122-4414, telephone (314) 555-8282.

16. Last month, to attract new customers, Electrical Suppliers, Inc., advertised a 10 percent discount on first-time orders. Although the advertisement clearly stated that this special offer was for one week only, an order arrives today from K. B. Brogan, purchasing agent, Glendon Lighting, Inc. Brogan requests the 10 percent discount. As sales representative for Electrical Suppliers, Inc., write to Brogan. Explain that you can fill the order promptly but that the 10 percent discount is no longer available. The address of Electrical Suppliers, Inc., is 2200 Somerset Drive, Cleveland, OH 44141-2695, telephone (216) 555-8218. The address of Glendon Lighting, Inc., is 1202 Grant Circle, Columbus, OH 43201-1296.

17. Review Case 16. Use the following new information for your letter to K. B. Brogan: Although the 10 percent discount period has ended, Brogan's purchase order is large enough to justify a 5 percent discount. Ask Brogan to authorize your filling the order on that basis.

18. Review Cases 16 and 17. As K. L. Brogan, decline the 5 percent discount offer. State, courteously but firmly, that you will place your first-time order only if the 10 percent discount is applied.

19. Having suffered heavy financial losses, Summit Life and Casualty Insurance Corporation announces a restructuring plan, including 2,500 employment terminations, to consolidate operations and save millions of dollars. As Summit vice president for human resources, prepare an empathetic form message to notify employees of their dismissal. Refer to an enclosure that describes Summit's free outplacement services—a wide range of services to assist in the search for new employment.

20. Review Case 19. As vice president for human resources, you receive numerous messages from Summit workers who ask you to continue their employment. This request from Dale Parker is typical: "I am a loyal employee," Parker reminds you, "who has earned three efficiency awards and two promotions during my five years of work with Summit. My career goal is tied to Summit employment." But you know these facts, also: Summit had a 51 percent drop in earnings last quarter and heavy losses in previous quarters as well. The restructuring plan re-

quires termination of Parker's job. With great reluctance, you must deny Parker's request. Compose a suitable message. Parker's home address is 3118 Newton Avenue, Hartford, CT 06135-4219.

MULTICULTURAL INSIGHTS

1. What are the customary structures and tones of unfavorable or mixed-news messages, including counterproposals, in cultures other than the United States? What are the similarities or differences between those messages and their U.S. counterparts?

2. In what ways does Chapter 10 pertain to oral as well as written business communication with American English? with other languages with which you are familiar?

GOODWILL AND SPECIAL-OCCASION MESSAGES

OBJECTIVES

After completing this chapter, you should be able to:

1.   Recognize occasions that call for special goodwill messages.
2.   Apply appropriate structures, wordings, and formats to special goodwill messages.

DECISIONS CASE

You are this year's president of the Clayton Corporation Employees Association. Kay Pryor, of the Clayton Gulf States Office, has received Clayton's outstanding sales representative award. The award includes a ten-day, expense-paid Caribbean cruise for the winner and one guest. Kay's guest will be her husband, Fred. As president of the Clayton Employees Association, you are expected to congratulate Kay. How should you structure and word your message?

Weeks later you learn that a misfortune has occurred. As Kay and Fred Pryor taxied from the Miami airport to the cruise-ship terminal, their vehicle was hit by a delivery van. While Kay and Fred were at a Miami hospital for treatment of their cuts and bruises, the cruise ship sailed without them. Disappointed, they decided to stay for a week at the Bayside Hotel in Miami. What message should you send them?

Additional questions about this decision-making case are stated at the end of this chapter. Study the chapter before answering those questions.

CHAPTER CONTEXT

When you confront difficult problems, are you grateful to people who help you solve them? When disappointment or sorrow comes to you, do you appreciate the person who offers you sympathy and encouragement? When you are a newcomer to a group or a community, are you pleased by efforts to help you become acquainted with its members? When you invest hard work in doing a job well, are you gratified by praise or congratulations? Almost certainly your answer to those questions is *yes*.

When you have opportunities to reciprocate—when you can convey goodwill in return for empathy or assistance given you—*do* you? How often? How well?

VALUE OF GOODWILL AND SPECIAL-OCCASION MESSAGES

Goodwill is value beyond the price of what is bought or sold. Goodwill is the positive feeling your associates have toward you or your firm. That feeling reflects the belief that you treat your clients, employees, suppliers, community—and even competitors—fairly and justly.

In a competitive environment, goodwill is essential to a firm's success. When a company builds a reputation for agreeable and ethical dealings, goodwill evidences itself in many ways: Customers and employees are loyal to the company; suppliers offer fair prices and prompt service; community

Why is goodwill
important to a
business?

members and competitors acknowledge the company's positive contributions
to the economy. In contrast, if a company does not build goodwill, its customers may go elsewhere, its employees are apt to be dissatisfied and dis-
loyal, and it may become the target of criticism by the community.

Chapters 9 and 10 emphasized that nearly all messages provide an opportunity to promote goodwill. This chapter emphasizes special-occasion messages whose *chief* function is to convey goodwill. The material presented
here can help you structure face-to-face and telephone conversations as well
as written messages.

PERSONALIZED GOODWILL MESSAGES

Your business career will present many opportunities to build goodwill by
demonstrating your recognition of individuals, their accomplishments, and
their concerns. Personalized goodwill messages are appropriate on such occasions. Examples of such messages are business introductions, employment
recommendations, and messages of welcome, appreciation, congratulation, or
sympathy.

Business Introductions

What is the purpose
of a business
introduction?

Introductions are messages that acquaint people with one another. Your
business career may take you to a community that is new to you but in which
your employer has business associates or friends. When you are relocated,
messages of introduction that precede or accompany you will help you to establish relationships with colleagues and customers in your new environment. Also, as your career progresses, you will need to provide introductions
for other people.

Whether the introduction is written or oral, here is a useful message
structure:

1. Identify the person being introduced.

    Please join us in welcoming Julie Muller, a new account executive
    in Global Advertising's Daytona Beach office.

2. Explain the reason for the introduction.

    Ms. Muller recently transferred to Daytona Beach from our Tampa
    office. She will be filling the position vacated by Jim Stratford
    when he was promoted to senior account executive. Ms. Muller
    will assume her duties in the Daytona Beach office on June 1.

3.   Describe the person's business relationship to you.

Ms. Muller has been with Global Advertising for two years. During that time she has demonstrated the creativity and competitive insights that you have come to expect from your account executive. Ms. Muller has worked closely with Mr. Stratford to review the accounts she will serve in Daytona Beach.

4.   Offer appreciation for courtesy or assistance.

Ms. Muller will visit you within the next month. Please welcome her as the newest member of the Global Advertising team in Daytona Beach.

That message structure is shown by Illustration 11−1.

Employment Recommend

Employment recommendations, also called **reference letters** or **references**, are messages sent in response to a request from a job seeker or a potential employer. Be aware of the potential conflict between an employee's desire for privacy and an employer's need for information.

Privacy protection is provided to employees by a combination of federal legislation, state legislation, and voluntary company policies. The Privacy Act of 1974 restricts the kinds of information that a government agency can release about its employees. That act also established a Privacy Protection Study Commission to examine the need for further legal protection of employees' privacy. The commission established three general policy goals:

1.   *Minimize intrusiveness:* Individuals who are asked for information should be informed of the need for and potential use of the information so that they can make an informed decision about whether to supply the information.
2.   *Maximize fairness:* Information that is released must be accurate, timely, complete, relevant, and used fairly.
3.   *Create a climate of confidentiality:* Limit freedom to make voluntary disclosures to third parties by:
—Keeping employees informed about the kinds of records that are kept and how the information is used.
—Permitting employees to see and obtain copies of information in their personnel files.
—Guaranteeing employees the right to challenge the accuracy, timeliness, or completeness of information and the right to correct errors or add statements to the record.

Illustration 11–1   LETTER OF INTRODUCTION

MERRICK ASSOCIATES, INC.
3190 Jefferson Avenue, NE Atlanta, GA 30314-4995
Telephone 404-555-4643

A Meridian Company

August 15, 19--

Mr. Anthony R. Caddo
Vice President, Marketing
G. V. Lutes and Co., Inc.
3400 Commerce Avenue
Tucson, AZ 85718-3144

Dear Anthony:

Identification

This letter introduces Victor Rossiter, who has been with Merrick Associates for five years.

Explanation and description

Victor is the new manager of our Sunbelt region, with offices in Tucson. He is a civic-minded businessperson who was active in two community-service organizations when he worked in our Atlanta office.

Appreciation; offer to reciprocate

If possible, please familiarize Victor with Tucson and some of its major service organizations. When I can return the favor, please let me know.

Cordially,

N. K. Harrington

N. K. Harrington
Executive Vice President

dh

—Collecting information about an employee from third-party sources only upon authorization by the employee.

—Releasing information to third parties only upon authorization by the employee.

Although variations exist, those goals are embodied in the privacy laws of many states and in the privacy policies of some organizations.

When you are asked to give an employment recommendation, recognize that the request requires your careful attention. At stake are your reputation, the reputation of the concerned employee, and the needs of the prospective employer to whom your message is sent. The information you supply should pertain to the employee's job-related attributes and behaviors. Avoid value judgments in a recommendation, such as describing an employee's performance as "good" or "bad"; rather, focus on accurate statements of objectively verifiable behaviors or events.

Although employment recommendations should identify excellent accomplishments, serious deficiencies sometimes exist. In such circumstances, you must shield the unsatisfactory employee from unfair accusations without misleading the potential employer. If an employee asks for but does not deserve a favorable recommendation from you, courteously decline the request. If, however, you decide it is appropriate to respond, send a factual but nonjudgmental message. You may, for example, provide information on how long the employee worked for you and in what capacity. Or, if someone requests information about the employee's attendance record, report objective data (tardy approximately 20 percent of the time, absent 25 days during the last six months of employment). Avoid subjective statements ("undependable," "chronically ill").

A **general employment recommendation**, which tends to omit details, is sometimes used when an employee has demonstrated few, if any, positive attributes or achievements. Illustration 11–2 shows a general recommendation. Such messages often use the simplified block format to avoid the trite "To Whom It May Concern" greeting.

When you can provide a favorable recommendation, use a **specific employment recommendation**, which is appropriately personalized and detailed. Emphasize the employee's achievements and give examples of events that demonstrate the employee's strengths. Avoid excessive praise, however; the reader may question your motives. (See Illustration 11–3.)

Illustrations 11–2 and 11–3 demonstrate this basic message structure for an employment recommendation:

1.   Identify your business relationship with the person being recom-

> What should, and should not, be included in a recommendation?

Illustration 11–2 GENERAL EMPLOYMENT RECOMMENDATION

EMPLOYMENT RECOMMENDATION FOR
CHRISTINA DANIELS

Identification; objective description   From June 1, 19-- to May 31, 19-- Ms. Christina Daniels was my administrative assistant. During that period, she performed her duties satisfactorily and cooperatively.

Neutral close   Ms. Daniels left her position voluntarily for employment with another firm.

Helen Autrey

HELEN AUTREY, COMPTROLLER

mended, and the employment period. (If you heartily recommend the employee, you may begin with your good-news recommendation.)

James Waltman served as my student assistant during his junior and senior years at State University.

2. Describe the person's work assignment and performance quality, if favorable.

As my assistant, Waltman was responsible for computer data entry, security of data files, and preliminary data analysis. He consistently completed assignments accurately and on time.

3. Close the message with a statement of goodwill.

Although I was pleased to see Waltman complete his college degree, I was sorry to lose an excellent assistant. I recommend him for employment in your administrative support unit. If I can provide further information, please call me at 555-1289.

Messages of Welcome

When you are a newcomer to a group or a community, surely you are pleased to have people greet you and make you feel at home. When circumstances change and you are able to reciprocate, you should welcome others.

Illustration 11-3   SPECIFIC EMPLOYMENT RECOMMENDATION

Good-news recommendation	I welcome this opportunity to recommend Martin G. Stewart for the position of field engineer.
Indentification	Martin Stewart, about whom you inquired November 5, was a member of my engineering team from February 1, 19--, to September 30, 19--. As a Darcy Enterprises employee, Marty was productive, reliable, and trustworthy.
Description of performance	Your inquiry mentioned Tech-Starr's concern with safety awareness as well as engineering skills. Among his other accomplishments, Marty Stewart earned three safety awards and two quality assurance awards while he worked here.
Goodwill closing	When market conditions required that we reduce our staff, I regretted having to furlough Marty. I would gladly rehire him if I could.

Welcoming a newcomer can be pleasant and profitable. Greeting a newcomer to your community is personally rewarding because it creates a climate for establishing new social or professional relationships. Welcoming a newcomer to your business establishes a favorable relationship which may lead to purchases of your products or services. You can use such messages of welcome, also, to assure the receiver that he or she is right to trust you, your organization, and the products or services that you and the company provide.

This basic structure is useful for a message of welcome:

1. Greet the newcomer cordially and sincerely.

    Welcome to Boyne City. The opening of the HealthServe emergency center and your arrival as its administrator are happy occasions for this community.

2. Identify yourself and your organization.

What are purposes of business welcomes?

> The Boyne City Merchants Association has long felt the need for an emergency medical center in this community. As president of the Association, I offer my services to help you become familiar with this community, its citizens, and its health-care needs.

3. Indicate the products/services associated with your organization, if relevant.

> A major goal of the Boyne City Merchants Association is to improve the social, cultural, and economic climate of our community. In addition to backing the medical center, we have sponsored events ranging from community picnics to concert series.

4. Close with a statement of goodwill.

> Our next dinner meeting is scheduled for June 14 at 7:30 p.m. If you are free at that time, please be my guest. I'd like to introduce you to other members. I'll call you soon to make final arrangements.

Illustration 11–4 shows a variation of this message structure which a firm may use to greet one of its new employees.

Messages of Appreciation or Gratitude

It is presumptuous, perhaps even arrogant and offensive, to thank people for things they have not yet decided to do. But business etiquette requires that you express appreciation or gratitude for things people have done favorably and well. Examples of favors that require a thank-you message include job interviews, recommendations, introductions, volunteer services, considerate actions of a client or supplier, and any other situation in which you feel gratitude.

The words *thank you* convey more than courtesy; they confirm goodwill. Messages of appreciation or gratitude—appropriately structured, worded, and timed—can be potent, constructive motivators in business relationships. Illustration 11–5 shows the kinds of paragraphs which convey gratitude and demonstrates this basic message structure:

What are appropriate structures for thank-you messages?

1. Thank the receiver.

> Thank you for introducing me to Meredith Escobar and George Chandler.

2. Explain why the receiver has merited appreciation or gratitude.

> Your efforts to acquaint me with these interior decorators have

Illustration 11–4   MEMO OF WELCOME TO NEW EMPLOYEE

```
                    INTEROFFICE MEMORANDUM

        TO: Angela DeCarlo, Sales

      FROM: Jan Webster, Personnel

      DATE: September 5, 19--

   SUBJECT: Welcome to Graphics, Inc.
```

Greeting, identification	Please add my greetings to those you have already received, Angela. We are happy that you decided to join the Graphics, Inc., team.
Relevant information	The success of this company depends on you and your coworkers. Many of the policies and procedures explained in the enclosed booklet were suggested by Graphics, Inc., employees. Please stop at my office (408) if you have any questions or suggestions about our employment policies. Your constructive suggestions will always be welcome.
Goodwill	We have confidence in your abilities, Angela. Welcome to Graphics, Inc.

Illustration 11–5 LETTER OF GRATITUDE

<table>
<tr><td>Cordial thanks</td><td>Thank you, Ms. Autrey!</td></tr>
<tr><td>Explanation</td><td>Lucille McGruder-Briggs, the Strother Associates human resources manager, has told me of your prompt and favorable recommendation on my behalf. Thanks to you, I am now her assistant for wage and salary administration.</td></tr>
<tr><td>Reinforced goodwill</td><td>Your letter and your encouragement, Ms. Autrey, helped me move to this exciting career opportunity. I intend to demonstrate that your faith in me was justified.</td></tr>
<tr><td></td><td>Cordially yours,</td></tr>
</table>

helped me establish my import business in Tucson. I hope I can return the favor some day.

3. Close by reinforcing goodwill.

I look forward to seeing you at the next meeting of the Tucson Imports Club. I'm eager to discuss our mutual interests and concerns about the importing business.

Or reverse the first and second of those steps as follows and as shown by Illustration 11–6.

1. Explain why the receiver has merited appreciation or gratitude.

Your efforts to acquaint me with Meredith Escobar and George Chandler have helped me establish Mementos of Mexico.

2. Thank the receiver.

Thank you, Shana, for your support as I launch my import business in Tucson.

3. Close by reinforcing goodwill.

I look forward to seeing you at the next meeting of the Tucson Imports Club. I'm eager to discuss our mutual interests and concerns about the importing business.

Illustration 11–6   MEMORANDUM OF APPRECIATION

Explanation
and thanks

The management committee of your group has repeatedly commented on your excellent performance since you joined DEI one year ago. The quality of your work, backed by perfect attendance and punctuality--despite frequent work-shift changes--has been noticed. Thank you, Marty, for your productivity and your loyalty to DEI.

Goodwill

A copy of this memo has been placed in your personnel record and will be available for salary and promotion considerations. I hope to be able to supply a similar commendation at your next annual review.

Messages of Congratulation

Outstanding achievements, honors, and other recognitions of merit provide opportunities for messages of congratulation. So do happy events such as marriages, anniversaries, births, birthdays, and retirement celebrations. Whether extended to an individual or to a group, congratulations promote goodwill by focusing warmly and unselfishly on the receiver. This message structure is effective for messages of congratulation:

1. Open with a personalized statement that is congratulatory.

   Congratulations on your recent Realtor of the Year Award.

2. Indicate why the congratulations are merited.

   You have been an inspiration to many "youngsters" in this profession. Your professional achievements, community service, and unselfish encouragement of those who are new to the profession are rarely seen in a single individual. You have demonstrated that hard work complemented by generosity lead to a satisfying life.

3. Close with a confirmation of goodwill.

   I'm pleased that your contributions to the Bellville community have received the recognition they deserve.

What are effective
structures for letters
of congratulation?

Or vary that structure by reversing Steps 1 and 2:

1. Begin by indicating why congratulations are merited.

   Your professional achievements, community service, and unselfish encouragement of those who are new to the profession are rarely seen in a single individual.

2. Personalize a statement that is congratulatory.

   Congratulations on your justly earned Realtor of the Year Award. You have demonstrated that hard work complemented by generosity leads to a satisfying life.

3. Close with a confirmation of goodwill.

   You have been an inspiration to many "youngsters" in the profession, including me. I am proud to be considered one of your colleagues.

Some businesses insert sales appeals into messages of congratulation. That practice, however, tends to weaken the goodwill value of the congratulations, unless the sales appeal is very low key. Messages similar to Illustration 11–7 may be printed on company letterhead to accomplish a low-key promotion of a firm's products or services (insurance, travel services, etc.).

Messages of Condolence

What are
condolences?

Condolence consists of actions or words that represent sensitivity to someone else's misfortune or grief. **Condolences** are messages of sympathy to a sorrowing person.

You may find condolence messages difficult to compose because they are associated with unhappy circumstances. You can, however, compose such messages appropriately when you recognize that they reassure the sorrowing person. Condolences remind the receivers that others care about them and empathize with them.

Instead of reminding the receiver of his or her sorrow, use words that convey empathy and encouragement. Illustration 11–8 shows this basic message structure:

1. Open with a personalized statement of sympathy.

   Please accept my sympathy, Mr. Silverberg.

Illustration 11–7   WEDDING CONGRATULATIONS TO ACTUAL OR
PROSPECTIVE CUSTOMERS

NOLEN AGENCY, INC.

Insurance for All Your Needs

1295 North Willard Road   Minneapolis, MN 55421-8224   Telephone (612) 555-0848

June 19, 19--

Congratulatory
statement   Congratulations, Mr. and Mrs. Porter:

                     Here is a keepsake for you--the matted copy of your
Explanation   wedding announcement as reported in today's Twin
                     Cities News.

                     You have our best wishes for a long and happy
Goodwill   marriage.

                     Cordially yours,

                     M. A. Wilson

---

2. Indicate your concern for the receiver, but do not stress the circumstances of his or her misfortune.

   Anita's contributions to the university, to Alpha Iota, and to the community will be remembered by many.

3. Reassure and encourage the receiver. (If you can provide means of assistance, offer them.)

   In Anita's memory, Alpha Iota will make a contribution to the College of Business Administration. That contribution will be marked by a plaque displaying Anita's name on the Donor's Wall in the lobby of the College of Business Administration.

4. Close with a reaffirmation of goodwill.

   If Alpha Iota members can help you in any way, Mr. Lawrence, please call us at 555-0981.

Although business letters usually are produced by typewriter or computer, many people prefer to send *handwritten* condolences. Both the letter and its addressed envelope are handwritten.

Illustration 11–8   MESSAGE OF CONDOLENCE

July 27, 19--

Dear Paul,

Sympathy — Please accept my condolences, Paul.

Concern and reassurance — Harry was proud of the business you helped him establish. Making a success of that business will be your best memorial to him.

Encouragement and goodwill — I always enjoyed discussing business plans with you and Harry. Please let me continue helping you in that way.

Sincerely,

Eleanor

GENERAL GOODWILL MESSAGES

Goodwill is often reinforced through personalized messages, as demonstrated by the previous illustrations in this chapter. However, goodwill can also be fostered by impersonal messages, such as general messages to employees, clients, or the public. The tone and structure of such messages must demonstrate a genuine interest in and concern for the target audience. As was indicated in Illustration 4–4 (Chapter 4), an impersonal message to a large, diverse audience may be received more positively than a message that has been "personalized" by computer.

When may impersonal goodwill messages be effective?

Appropriate uses for general goodwill messages include celebration of special events and holidays, public recognition of group or individual achievements, and community-service announcements.

Celebration of Special Events or Holidays

Local and regional festivals, national and international celebrations, and holidays provide opportunities for exchanging goodwill messages. Some businesses use such messages as low-key sales messages. Here is an effective structure for a special-event message:

1. Relate the receiver to the occasion that is being celebrated.

   Dutch Fork's 50th Anniversary is a proud occasion for all its community members. As one member to another, Surety Bank says, "Let's celebrate!"

2. Convey good wishes, linked to a low-key sales message if appropriate.

   The Dutch Fork Anniversary Gala is our way of saying "Congratulations" to a community that has demonstrated the unity and loyalty needed to preserve a heritage.

3. Close with reinforcement of goodwill.

   We hope you will join us on August 5 to launch the Anniversary Gala and the next 50 years of community cooperation.

When wording seasonal greetings, be sensitive to cultural diversity. Although people of many religious traditions celebrate their holidays at approximately the same time of the year, do not assume that all receivers of your holiday greetings celebrate as you do. For example, although Christians celebrate Christmas, Jews celebrate Hanukkah. And although Mexicans celebrate Christmas, they celebrate the eight days *before* the *navidad* (birth) rather than Christmas Day. In some Asian and Scandinavian countries, personal messages at religious and seasonal holidays are valued as signs of great respect for the receiver.

If your receiver's religion or culture differs from yours, empathize and use inclusive terms like "Holiday Greetings" or "Season's Greetings" instead of specifically naming a religious holiday in your message. Illustration 11–9 demonstrates empathetic wording for a general holiday greeting.

Illustration 11–9 SEASONAL OR HOLIDAY GOODWILL MESSAGE

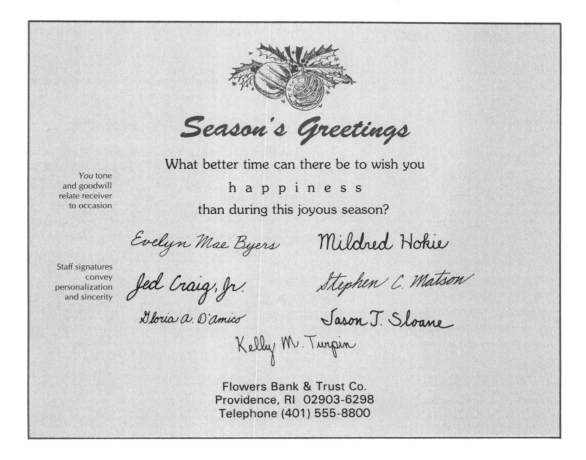

You tone and goodwill relate receiver to occasion

Staff signatures convey personalization and sincerity

Public Recognition of Achievements

Public recognition of individual or group achievements provides an opportunity to extend goodwill beyond those being recognized. For example, a public utility company provides several scholarships each year to its employees' children. Although the scholarship recipients undoubtedly receive individual announcements and letters of congratulation, an appropriately written announcement in a newspaper generates goodwill in the community served by the utility. Such public-recognition messages are often part of a company's public relations program.

An effective structure for public-recognition messages is demonstrated by this example:

1. Convey appropriate recognition (congratulations, thanks, praise).

    Thank you, Richland Fire Department.

2. Identify the reason for the recognition.

    Your prompt response to the brush-fire call on July 18 saved lives and property in the Riverbend subdivision.

3. Close with reinforcement of goodwill.

    The Riverbend Homeowners Association wants you—and others—to know we appreciate your dedication to protecting our community.

Community-Service Messages

As part of its public relations effort, a firm may periodically issue community-service messages. These messages typically provide receivers with useful information to protect themselves from harm or to enrich their lives in some way. Community-service messages are appropriately viewed as goodwill messages—they are voluntary and they do not directly promote the company's products or services.

Although varying in length and complexity, public-service messages typically follow a structure similar to the following example:

1. Identify the main topic and its relevance to the receiver.

    Telephone scams are becoming a part of life. Although many telephone callers promote legitimate products or services, every year con artists bilk consumers out of millions of dollars. We don't want you to become a victim.

2. Provide relevant information.

    Here are some tips on recognizing and avoiding a possible scam . . .

3. Suggest specific action, if appropriate.

    Call the Consumer Protection Division (555-4810) if you suspect a scam.

4. Close with a positive statement of goodwill.

    We at Surety Bank want to help you become a smart consumer. Call Anne Farrell at 555-5565 if you have comments or suggestions.

REVIEW AND TRANSITION

Chapters 9 through 11 have emphasized goodwill as a necessity for successful good-news, neutral, bad-news, mixed-news, and special-occasion messages. Personalized special-occasion messages include introductions, recommendations, welcomes, statements of appreciation or gratitude, congratulations, and condolences. General goodwill messages are often used to celebrate special events and holidays, to acknowledge achievements publicly, and to convey community-service information.

Persuasive messages, like those described in Chapters 12 and 13, also confirm that goodwill is good business.

YOUR DECISIONS FOR CHAPTER 11

Review the Decisions Case given at the beginning of Chapter 11. In what ways has the information presented in Chapter 11 changed, or reinforced, your initial answers to the questions asked in that case? Why? What structures will you use for those messages? Why?

As president of the Clayton Corporation Employees Association, compose the messages. The Clayton Corporation address is 5400 Riverside Avenue, New Orleans, LA 70130-5398. The Bayside Hotel address is 18 Ocean Parkway, Miami, FL 33112-3874.

DISCUSSION QUESTIONS

A. Within the context of Chapter 11, what are appropriate definitions and examples of these terms?

  1. goodwill
  2. reciprocate
  3. general employment recommendation
  4. specific employment recommendation
  5. condolence

B. If virtually every business situation provides opportunities to express goodwill, why do successful communicators send *special* goodwill messages?

C. What business circumstances or occasions call for personalized goodwill messages? for general (impersonal) goodwill messages?

APPLICATIONS

1. Write an opening sentence for each of these messages:

   a. Introduction of James Arends, a new sales representative for Baker Publishing, to clients whom he will serve.

    b.   A welcome letter to James Arends, who will be your new Baker Publishing sales representative.

    c.   A favorable employment recommendation for Jenny Krueger, whom you supervised for three years.

    d.   A thank-you letter to Karen Martin for a favorable employment recommendation.

    e.   A letter of congratulation to a high school classmate who has graduated from college with honors.

    f.   A letter of condolence to a friend whose teenage brother was killed in an automobile accident.

2. For the past three years, the R. G. Burton Corporation has employed you part-time while you have been attending college. You hope to have a full-time career with Burton after your college graduation, six months from now. Compose special goodwill messages (memos, letters, or informal notes, as your instructor directs) for the following situations. They involve Burton employees with whom you are acquainted.

    a.   Max G. Brandt, a systems analyst, has been recognized for his overhaul of Burton's computerized management information programs. His work saved the company time in terms of daily production and a great deal of money. (You are interested in management information systems as a career field and have assisted Brandt on some jobs.)

    b.   The current edition of *Burton Employees Newsletter* announces the marriage last week of Rosa Martino, staff assistant in the Customer Services Office, and Charles Garner, sales representative. (You have sometimes shared a table with them in the Burton lunchroom.)

3. Review Illustration 11–1. Assume you are Victor Rossiter. Mr. Caddo has graciously welcomed you, acquainted you with several members of his firm, and introduced you to the officers of Business-Community Alliance, a service organization.

    a.   Compose a letter of appreciation to Anthony R. Caddo. Your new Merrick Associates address is 3430 Commerce Avenue, Tucson, AZ 85718-3956, telephone (602) 555-3930.

    b.   Compose a letter thanking N. K. Harrington for the introduction to Caddo. Describe Caddo's helpfulness.

4. Review Illustration 11–4.

    a.   As Angela DeCarlo, compose a goodwill response to Jan Webster's memo.

    b.   You have been with Graphics, Inc., for two years; Jan Webster has continued to be thoughtful and helpful. Today you learned that Jan's sister, Donna, has died after a lingering illness. Jan is not expected to return to work for at least a week. Compose an informal but appropriate message of condolence to Jan Webster.

CASES

1. Recently promoted to the position of sales manager at Rowe Computer Products Corporation, you receive messages of congratulation from associates and customers. You recall that when you first worked as a field representative for the company, the task of introducing yourself to customers was sometimes formidable. Now that you have become sales manager, you intend to help new field representatives become acquainted, quickly and favorably, with Rowe customers.

   The first representative you want to introduce is Lorraine S. Gorman. Relevant data are: Ms. Gorman joined your St. Louis office after completing advanced training at the company's home office in Fort Wayne, Indiana. She graduated from Michigan State University with concentrations in systems analysis and Spanish. Ms. Gorman will begin calling on clients in eastern Missouri and western Illinois on June 1. She will call specific clients in advance to make appointments.

   As Rowe sales manager, prepare a message to introduce Ms. Gorman in advance of her visit. Compose the message as a form letter which can be personalized. The address of Rowe Computer Products Corporation is 2200 Larkin Street, St. Louis, MO 63142-1440, telephone (314) 555-7066.

2. Chen's Healthful Foods, Inc., will open its new Honolulu office three weeks from today. As corporate vice president for marketing, prepare a message that can be personalized and mailed to Hawaii restaurateurs and retailers. Use the message to announce the opening of Chen's new office and to introduce its manager, C. S. Mott, who has been with Chen's Healthful Foods for seven years, most recently as manager of the company's San Francisco office. The corporate address of Chen's Healthful Foods, Inc., is 620 Barrow Place, Los Angeles, CA 90040-3142, telephone (213) 555-1820. The address of Chen's new branch office is 3310 Sabo Road, Honolulu, HI 96823-4020, telephone (808) 555-4925.

3. Since joining Claremont Electronics Corporation almost three years ago, J. R. Daly has been one of your most valuable assistants. As marketing research director, you have been particularly impressed by Daly's skills in data analysis and research reporting. In addition, Daly has been absent only twice in three years. You would like to keep Daly on your staff, but family reasons require this productive employee to seek employment in a region closer to where Daly's disabled sister resides. Daly asks you for a letter of recommendation to Blair J. Saunders, research and development director at Skouras Enterprises, Inc., 3810

Frawley Avenue, Detroit, MI 48222-3329. The address of Claremont Electronics Corporation is 220 Atkins Street, Richmond, VA 23235-1830, telephone (804) 555-9383. Compose the letter of recommendation.

4. Review Case 3. As customer relations manager of Moresby National Bank, Inc., a full-service financial institution with 14 branches throughout the Greater Detroit Area, compose a form message to welcome new residents, including J. R. Daly, who now lives at 4733 Quinn Road, Detroit, MI 48235-1411. The address of Moresby National Bank is 110 Arkin Avenue, Detroit, MI 48219-1050, telephone (313) 555-8000.

5. Review Cases 3 and 4. As J. R. Daly, you are now a research assistant to Blair J. Saunders. Compose a thank-you message to your former Claremont employer, who wrote a letter of recommendation on your behalf.

6. Committed to community service as well as profits, Ferrar Corporation, publisher of the *Western Star* newspaper, encourages civic responsibility among its employees. One of your duties as employee relations manager is to commend employees who perform outstanding community service. Compose a memo to Emilio Sanchez, who delivers copies of *Western Star* to subscribers' homes. Personally acquainted with many of his customers, Sanchez noticed that newspapers delivered to the residence of a senior citizen, who lived alone at a remote location, were accumulating on her doorstep. Sanchez's repeated knocking brought no response. Looking through a window, Sanchez saw his customer huddled in a chair. Sanchez tapped on the window and called loudly, but the woman did not move. Hurrying to a neighbor's house, Sanchez telephoned 911 for emergency medical service. His customer was rushed to a hospital. She had suffered a stroke; but, thanks to Emilio Sanchez, she survived. A copy of this memo will be placed in his personnel file.

7. As general manager of Building Suppliers Corporation (BSC), you receive a letter of gratitude from C. C. Vitelli, director of Shelter for the Homeless. Vitelli thanks BSC for donations of building materials and labor provided by BSC employees. A once-dilapidated building now safely accommodates people who otherwise would have to live on the streets. In a memo to BSC employees, convey Vitelli's gratitude and your own appreciation.

8. A month ago, torrential rains caused disastrous flooding and widespread property damage, as well as injuries and deaths, throughout the region served by Webber Power Corporation (WPC). Almost a quarter of a million WPC customers were affected. In 20 days, WPC restored its entire utility system, which had taken 73 years to build and improve. Laboring strenuously under emergency conditions, WPC employees not only restored power in record-breaking time but also rescued

many people who had been stranded by the disaster. As WPC's chief executive officer, compose the body of an appreciation message to accompany the next paycheck which WPC employees will receive.

9. As communications director for Hauser Home Furnishings, Inc., you regularly scan newspapers for announcements like this: "Mr. and Mrs. Paul T. Baxter announce the engagement of their daughter, Deborah Elizabeth, and Carl Stephen Worsham, son of Mr. and Mrs. Kenneth L. Metter." Compose the body of a message that Hauser Home Furnishings, Inc., can send to congratulate newly engaged couples, whether or not they are presently Hauser customers. Include a coupon which entitles them to a 10 percent discount on their first furniture purchase.

10. As communications director for Heirloom Photographers, Inc., you notice that local hospitals are authorized to sponsor weekly television and newspaper announcements of births at their facilities. The announcements mention, with permission, the names of the parents and their newborns. Compose the body of a message that Heirloom Photographers, Inc., can send to congratulate new parents.

11. Carnera Corporation, a producer of stainless steel pipe and industrial equipment, has achieved quarterly sales of $20.2 million, up 12.5 percent from the same quarter last year. Much of this success is due to an improved quality control system designed by Carnera employees. As president of the corporation, prepare a memo to congratulate Brett Walsh, your vice president for production. Ask Walsh to share the good news by congratulating the quality control team. The address of Carnera Corporation is 950 Industrial Road, Pittsburgh, PA 15229-2110, telephone (412) 555-1711.

12. Review Case 11. As Brett Walsh, prepare the congratulatory message to members of the quality control team. Refer to the memo of appreciation that you have received from the Carnera Corporation president. Reinforce goodwill with your employees, who have made the new quality control system successful.

13. Seven years ago, Hannah Porter established Porter Associates, Inc. (PAI), a consulting firm that specializes in research to reconcile commercial and environmental needs. PAI's achievements, with Porter as founder and president, have earned worldwide attention. Today, the International Enterprise Society presents its Distinguished Leadership Award to Porter. As president of Tanos Corporation, one of PAI's client companies, compose a letter to congratulate Porter. Acknowledge the environmental benefits and cost effectiveness of the waste management system which PAI recommended for Tanos Corporation. The Tanos address is 7201 Pulaski Road, Jersey City, NJ 07349-0310, telephone (201) 555-1811. The PAI address is 405 Breen Avenue, Denver, CO 80256-3421.

14. Hannah Porter, distinguished civic leader and business executive, has suffered fatal injuries in a traffic accident. According to news media, the driver of another car, which collided with Porter's, failed a sobriety test at the accident site. Hannah Porter's husband, David, and their teenage daughter, Susan, were at home awaiting Hannah Porter's return from a business conference. The family has requested that memorial contributions be made to the Literacy Improvement Center. As manager of Bondi's travel agency, whose services the Porters have used frequently, write a condolence message to David and Susan Porter. Your address is Bondi's, Inc., 1632 Royce Avenue, Denver, CO 80219-2632, telephone (303) 555-1911. The Porter family's address is 3500 Hillcrest Road, Denver, CO 80238-0215.

15. Review Case 14. Since 1987, Hannah and David Porter had participated in programs of the Literacy Improvement Center. Besides providing financial assistance, the Porters worked faithfully as unpaid tutors. You are director of the Literacy Improvement Center. Write a message of condolence to the Porter family. The center's address is 1430 Pawley Street, Denver, CO 80225-1812, telephone (303) 555-2685.

16. You are the supervisor of accounts receivable at SkiTown, a large distributor of skiing equipment and accessories. Jeremy Wignall, manager of Mountain View Ski Outfitters, has requested a recommendation for C. R. Suskind, a former accounts receivable clerk. Suskind worked for SkiTown for eleven months (September 4, 19—, through July 31, 19—) and was absent an average of one day per week. Suskind was consistently late, worked distractedly, and did not exhibit an affinity for accounting. In fact, you found yourself correcting Suskind's customer billings weekly, sometimes to your great embarrassment. After a particularly poor performance review, Suskind voluntarily left SkiTown. You gave Suskind permission to use your name, although you mentioned at the time that you would be unable to give a favorable recommendation. Respond to Wignall's request. Send the letter to Mr. Jeremy Wignall, Manager, Mountain View Ski Outfitters, 9100 Summit Parkway, Montpelier, VT 05602-7561.

17. The management of Montrose Fashion Plaza, an 85-unit shopping mall, has decided to use the year-end retailing season as an opportunity for holiday festivities that nurture community goodwill. The theme is "Happy Holidays for You." The first in a series of special events is scheduled for 9:30 a.m., November 15, when Montrose Fashion Plaza will provide free entertainment and refreshments in its central atrium. Shoppers are requested to donate canned foods, which Plaza representatives will collect and deliver to family-assistance organizations in a four-county area. As Plaza special events coordinator, prepare a message for newspaper publication to convey seasonal greetings and to describe this

first event of the "Happy Holidays for You" program. The address of Montrose Fashion Plaza is 8300 Alton Boulevard, Charlotte, NC 28248-2012, telephone (704) 555-4022.

18. Review Case 17. The "Happy Holidays for You" program at Montrose Fashion Plaza has been launched successfully. A centerpiece of the next special event, scheduled for December 5–24, is "The Sharing Tree." Community-service organizations will have representatives and donation-collection boxes around the base of a beautifully decorated holiday tree. Visitors are encouraged to contribute gift-wrapped items with a card attached identifying the person for whom the gift is most appropriate (sex, age, size, etc.). The gifts will be distributed to families and individuals whose holidays may otherwise be cheerless. Costumed musicians and dancers will provide free entertainment. Complimentary refreshments will be available. As special events coordinator at Montrose Fashion Plaza, prepare a message for general mailing to residents of the area. Convey seasonal greetings and an invitation to enjoy these goodwill festivities at Montrose Fashion Plaza.

MULTICULTURAL INSIGHTS

1. What are examples of business goodwill customs in cultures, other than the United States, with which you are familiar? How are they like, or unlike, business goodwill customs in the United States?

2. What nonverbal aspects of communication convey business goodwill in cultures, other than the United States, with which you are familiar? How are they like, or unlike, their United States counterparts?

PERSUASIVE MESSAGES: SALES AND SPECIAL REQUESTS

IV. Preparing Special Requests
    A. Select a Central Appeal
    B. Use AIDA Structure
V. Using Ethics in Persuasion: A Reminder
VI. Review and Transition

OBJECTIVES

After completing this chapter, you should be able to:

1. Define your communication objective and analyze your audience before composing persuasive messages.
2. Use the AIDA message structure skillfully and ethically to influence receivers' actions or attitudes.
3. Recognize persuasive techniques when they are used to influence your own actions or attitudes.

DECISIONS CASE

Manager Ron Greer has summoned the Spa Health Center employees to a staff meeting. "Come on, folks," he urges. "Give me some good ideas for our summer promotion."

Ideas flow: "Let's hit on vanity—how people look in swimsuits." "How about health? 'Don't take a vacation from exercise!' " "We could mention our swimming pool and whirlpool." "Or our expanded facilities and new equipment."

"But," one timid voice offers, "wouldn't people rather be outdoors during the summer? How can we make indoor exercise sound appealing?"

What advice would you give Greer? How should he promote Spa Health Center memberships for the summer months?

Additional questions about this decision-making case are stated at the end of this chapter. Study the chapter before answering those questions.

CHAPTER CONTEXT

Observe your business and personal environments.

- ▶ Your business or school associates solicit your money or time for social and charitable organizations.
- ▶ A sales brochure tempts you with a "once-in-a-lifetime" opportunity to buy gemstones.
- ▶ Your boss urges you to put in extra hours, hours you usually spend in community service or studying for school.
- ▶ Your best friend invites you to see a movie instead of studying for an exam.
- ▶ You bargain for a new car.

What do those examples have in common? How do they differ? Why are some people successful at persuasion, others not?

Chapter 12 can help you answer those questions. This chapter provides guides for achieving positive, ethical results with your persuasive messages. And Chapter 12 may help you understand why you have not always elicited the responses you expected when you have tried to influence someone's attitudes or actions.

PERSUADING ETHICALLY

Analyze the words of this definition: Persuasion is "communication intended to influence choice."[1]

▶ *Communication:* Sender and receiver interact by words or other symbols.
▶ *Intended:* Sender has a clearly defined goal.
▶ *To Influence:* Change of attitude or behavior is desired.
▶ *Choice:* Receiver is free to accept or reject sender's proposals.

What is persuasion?

Business communication involves many attempts to influence choice: interviewing for a job, selling goods or services, requesting assistance, encouraging a delinquent customer to pay, urging passage of favorable legislation.

Persuasion is the use of communication to elicit responses you need or desire when other responses are possible. Persuasion, like other forms of communication, involves ethical responsibilities.[2] Ethical behavior demonstrates respect for the well-being and rights of others. Achieving your goals at the expense of or without regard for others constitutes **manipulation**. But when you achieve another person's goals while you achieve your own, you engage in ethical persuasion.

What constitutes ethical persuasion?

Persuasion involves both senders and receivers, who *share* the responsibility for ethical behavior. When you use communication successfully to change people's beliefs, attitudes, or actions, you are ethically accountable for the consequences of having persuaded. The people whom you convince are also accountable—for the consequences of allowing themselves to be persuaded by you.

Some behaviors are readily labeled unethical by a majority of the business

---

[1] Winston L. Brembeck and William S. Howell, *Persuasion: A Means of Social Influence,* 2d ed. (Englewood Cliffs, NJ: Prentice-Hall, 1976), p. 19.

[2] *Ethics* are principles, values, and duties of right or good conduct. Examples of ethical behavior include honesty, truthfulness, and fairness.

community. For example, in the 1980s some stockbrokers made substantial profits for themselves and selected clients through insider trading. This practice (buying and selling a corporation's stock based on information obtained from a person inside that company) was clearly illegal. When violators were apprehended, their behavior was widely condemned as unethical. Similarly, "churning" an account (recommending frequent sales and purchases so that the broker earns repeated commissions) is generally considered unethical. This practice tends to take advantage of naive investors and often unnecessarily risks their capital.

However, other behaviors fall into a "gray area" between what is clearly ethical and what is clearly unethical. For example, suppose R. J. Barnes intends to solicit money for an international organization that protects the environment and wildlife. Barnes decides to conduct a direct mail campaign. With a letter, Barnes includes a persuasively worded survey. Barnes is actually not interested in the receivers' responses to the survey; instead, the objective is to use the survey questions to stir emotions and elicit contributions. The survey includes leading questions, such as: "What is your attitude toward the senseless clubbing of baby seals?" The final question asks the respondents to indicate the amount of money they intend to contribute. Do praiseworthy ends, such as raising money for protection of the environment, justify deceptive means? What are receivers' responsibilities when they are the targets of this kind of persuasion?

As you plan persuasive messages, remember that in persuasion you convey incentives or motives that stimulate people to respond as you propose. To persuade is not to *com*pel by force. To persuade is to *im*pel, by psychology and logic, so that people appreciate the benefits of believing or acting as you propose.

PLANNING PERSUASIVE MESSAGES

What considerations should guide your planning of persuasive messages?

With the objective of influencing ethically, you begin to plan your persuasive message by answering these questions:

1. What are my needs/desires within the context of this communication?

   I must convince Dr. Clarey to accept an invitation to be the keynote speaker at the IMF annual convention. If she accepts, a large number of IMF members will likely attend the convention, satisfying my desire for a successful meeting.

2. What are my receiver's probable needs/desires within the context of this communication?

Dr. Clarey needs to expand the forum for her ideas and broaden the market for her books.

3. In what ways should my message combine the receiver's needs/ desires and mine?

I must convince Dr. Clarey that the IMF members will be a receptive audience and a new market for her books.

Successful persuasion requires that you define your objective, analyze your audience, and evaluate available media or channels.

Define Your Objective

Why should you define the objective of a persuasive message?

Clearly and precisely identify your purpose for influencing the receiver's choice. Is your objective to secure a special favor? To obtain a job interview? To get a promotion? To sell a product? By defining your objectives, you take an essential step toward gaining these communication advantages:

1. justification for the message
2. guidance for assembling relevant data
3. direction for word choice to communicate clearly and accurately
4. insight for composing follow-up messages in response to feedback from your receiver
5. stimulation of the receiver's favorable consideration of your message

Analyze Your Audience

What is the advantage of analyzing your audience?

People respond to *their* needs and desires, which, at a given moment, may differ from yours. To address your audience successfully you must analyze your receivers' needs, their desires, and the circumstances under which you are attempting to persuade.

Although group behavior can differ from one person's actions, the public consists of many individuals. Therefore, even when you use mass communication media, such as newspaper advertisements or radio commercials, realize that you are presenting your message to individuals. Consider the person and his or her motives.

Motivation is an inner urge that stimulates action. One popular theory of motivation is Abraham Maslow's need hierarchy theory. This theory suggests that people act to satisfy a set of internal needs. Maslow classified those needs in a hierarchy that progresses from basic survival needs to complex self-actualization needs. (See Illustration 12−1.)

How does Maslow's hierarchy of needs relate to persuasion?

According to Maslow, needs at the lower end of the hierarchy must be sat-

Illustration 12–1   MASLOW'S NEED HIERARCHY

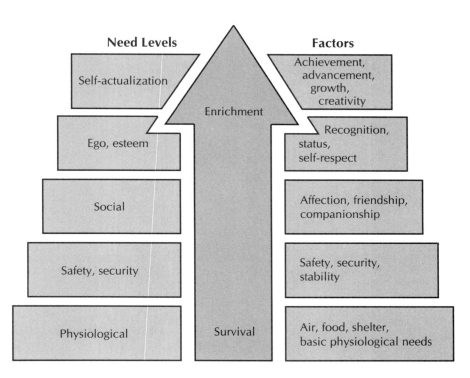

isfied before higher-level needs emerge as motivators. However, satisfaction of needs at one level is never complete. For example, although at one meal you may satisfy your need for food, you never fully eliminate that need—you become hungry again after a few hours. A need, though satisfied at one time, may emerge again as a motivator.

When a message stimulates someone's awareness of need or desire, that person becomes receptive to persuasion. A persuasive message excites receiver motivation through psychological appeals that suggest an action to satisfy the receiver's needs. The following examples of needs/desires and related psychological appeals are roughly parallel to Maslow's need hierarchy.

Needs/Desires	Psychological Appeals
curiosity	being aware, seeking, wondering, discovering
activity, being "alive"	creating, building, doing, accomplishing, achieving

self-respect, sociability	ethical responsibility, confidence, esteem, prestige, ambition, loyalty, cooperation, competition, successful interaction with others
attractiveness	personal appearance, favorable character and disposition, intellectual/emotional/physical attributes
love	personal fulfillment, protection of and devotion to others, physical and emotional gratification shared with others
pleasure	play, sport, amusement, humor, joy, intellectual/emotional/physical satisfaction, celebration of life
comfort, well-being	health, safety, warmth, coolness, exercise, relaxation, rest
appetite, hunger, food	nourishment, wholesomeness, flavor, aroma, texture

Use that list as a thought starter to which you may add other needs, desires, and appeals. Also, consider using dual or multiple appeals. For example, taking the bus to work may satisfy the need for transportation; but it may also satisfy the desires of contributing to a cleaner environment, having time to read, or meeting interesting people. As you plan your persuasive messages, select psychological appeals that satisfy multiple levels of need.

Evaluate Available Media

Awareness of needs, desires, and appeals will lead you to select appropriate media for your persuasive messages. Answers to these questions aid in choosing those media:

What are guides for selecting appropriate media?

1. *Am I likely to reach my intended audience through this medium?* A demonstration dinner party reaches potential buyers of cookware; a classified advertisement in a newspaper may not.
2. *How adaptable is this medium for the total persuasive effort?* A speech or conversation offers opportunity for immediate feedback. A letter or memo permits the receiver to contemplate and reread the message. A television or radio spot announcement allows several repetitions of the message within a brief time span.
3. *What expertise is required to use this medium?* Do I have—or can I

acquire—that expertise? A person who writes project proposals effectively may not be skilled at oral presentations, or vice versa.

4. *Can I afford the cost of this medium?* A candidate for political office may prefer to use television but may be able to afford only lawn placards.

5. *What human needs does this medium itself—not only the verbal message—satisfy?* A letter inviting membership in a gourmet club appeals to hunger and pleasure needs. A telephone invitation may satisfy the social need as well.

After you have defined your objective, analyzed your audience, evaluated and selected a medium, you are ready to prepare the persuasive message.

The remainder of Chapter 12 discusses development of sales messages and special requests. Chapter 13 focuses on claims, collections, and employee-discipline messages.

DEVELOPING SALES MESSAGES

Why do you respond to some persuasive messages and ignore others? One reason is that some are clearly focused on you and others like you. Other messages make you wonder if the sender knows or cares about you except for your ability to say yes. Still other messages are so unstructured that you may wonder what the sender wants you to do.

You can persuade by developing a central appeal, which may be reinforced with other appeals, and by structuring your message to attract attention, arouse interest, develop desire, and elicit a favorable response.

Select a Central Appeal

In a sales message, the central appeal is called the **central buying point**, the attribute of your product or service that is likely to make the strongest positive impression on a prospective purchaser. (From the supplier's viewpoint, it is the **central selling feature**.) Examples of such points include needs or desires for safety, utility, reliability, economy, comfort, or prestige of a product or service.

You may identify several persuasive appeals. But highlighting *one* appeal, and reinforcing it, is likely to accomplish these aims:

1. You can develop coherence and consistency for your message.
2. You can focus—rather than scatter—your receiver's attention and interest.

Why should you select a central appeal?

To identify a central buying point (or central selling feature), familiarize yourself with the needs or desires of your customers. Then familiarize yourself with the features of the product or service that can satisfy your customers' needs.

Buyer's Viewpoint. Project yourself into the customer's circumstances. If you were the buyer, what product benefits would help you motivate yourself to purchase? If you were the buyer, what service features would attract your attention, develop your interest, reinforce your desire, and move you to order? If you were the buyer, what other considerations would influence your purchasing decisions and behaviors?

Visualize the person who will receive your sales message. Before you plan the details of what you are going to write or say, think about and feel for that person. Associate the word *you* with that person. Create attitudes like the following toward your receiver.

- ► You like to be accepted, perhaps even popular; you would rather be in than out of style. I understand; we can communicate.
- ► You prefer safety and health to injury or illness. You dislike excessive heat and humidity or sub-zero weather and slush. At about the same time each night you yawn and become sleepy. At about the same time every morning you wonder what the rest of the day will bring. I recognize those feelings; I share them with you. We can communicate.
- ► Several times a day you are hungry. You enjoy tasting delicious foods, but somehow they taste even better in the company of other people. All of your physical sensations seem better when they are shared and appreciated. I understand, it's the same with me. We can communicate.
- ► You like to buy things to enjoy now, yet you want to save money for the future. That doesn't seem contradictory to me. I understand; we can communicate.

Such attitudes are essential to successful communication. But you need more than attitudes to make sales. You need adequate and appropriate knowledge of the product or service you offer.

Product/Service Knowledge. Continue empathizing with your prospective buyer. Anticipate the questions that the buyer would ask. Some examples are: What raw materials are used in the product? Are they safe? Strong? What are the manufacturing methods, construction designs, methods of operation and maintenance? What are the primary and related uses? How easy is your product to learn? What is its service record? In what ways does your product compare/contrast with others? What costs and prices are involved?

Know your product or service. Only then can you begin to share that knowledge with people who will pay for it. Only then should you begin to structure the sales message itself.

Structure Your Message

Sales messages are energizers of a dynamic communication process that brings together products, services, sellers, and buyers. A familiar and effective message structure for sales messages is **AIDA**: *a*ttention, *i*nterest, *d*esire, *a*ction—all from your *receiver's* viewpoint. (See Illustration 12–2.)

The AIDA message structure is designed to persuade orally or in writing. This structure is logically and psychologically consistent. Attention, once favorably attracted, arouses interest. Interest, once appropriately aroused, leads to desire. Desire, reinforced by the belief that the product or service is valuable, leads to a buying decision. The culmination of these factors produces action.

What are the components of AIDA?

Illustration 12–2   AIDA STRUCTURE FOR SALES MESSAGES AND SPECIAL REQUESTS

Attention	Refer to your *receiver's* interests, hopes, wishes, requirements.
Interest	Stimulate your *receiver's* motivation with psychological appeals to physical and emotional fulfillment.
Desire	Reinforce your *receiver's* motivation with word images of benefits and advantages attainable by what you propose.
Action	Provide a summary motive; then clearly, courteously, and confidently tell your receiver what to do.

Attract Appropriate Attention. The first paragraph of your message greatly influences the outcome of your sales effort. Learn these successful techniques to attract attention:

1. *Ask a pertinent question.*

   How long does it take you to type a one-page letter?

2. *Make an agreeable assertion.*

    Coming home should be the best part of the day.

3. *Cite a timely situation.*

    Three major airlines have slashed Houston–Miami fares.

4. *Highlight a benefit.*

    Save 30 percent on your heating bills.

5. *Visualize an event.*

    A snap of the wrist, a hum of the reel . . . and you have a strike on your Sportgear fishing line.

How can you attract the receiver's attention?

6. *Stimulate physical senses.*

    Just touch this sample of Newmark silk. Feel its kind-to-the-skin texture. Luxuriate in its softness.

7. *Summarize a case history.*

    Four years ago he was a customer service representative. Today he is vice president for communication services.

8. *Provide a testimonial.*

    "We can vouch for Weston Office Systems," says Supervisor R. A. Jensen. "They've cut our costs by 15 percent."

9. *Use a famous quotation.*

    A few folks may think they "can fool some of the people some of the time," but Renno Corporation has another philosophy. You can trust Renno products all of the time.

10. *State a startling fact.*

    Most office equipment is bought during or after a sales representative's third visit. But only 28.5 percent of the representatives make that third visit. Frankly, that's why your Raymer agent asks to see you regularly. Raymer people gladly make that third visit, and a fourth, and as many as you authorize.

Here are more examples of attention getters, distinctive in formats as well as wordings:

Suddenly
silence
except for . . .
. . . the rustle of leaves . . . the murmur of brooks . . . the music of
songbirds. Yours to enjoy at Greenmont Village.

Engineering . . .
  Durability . . .
    Dependability . . .
All these, plus many more features, are what you get when . . .

Y o u
may be
the solution.

Here is the problem:

Use your communication insights to generate and sustain attention. Offer protective rather than scare openings, and relate attention openers to the gist of your message. State novel rather than trite questions. Here are examples of attention techniques:

Scare	Protective
Thousands of lives are lost each year through house fires!	Protect your family with a Newton smoke detector.

Unrelated	Related
Have you ever wondered how you will be able to recall memories?	The Monarch SLR camera transforms special moments into lasting memories.

Trite	Novel
I would like to tell you something about taxes.	You can reduce your income taxes—the annuity way.

Develop Interest and Desire. Having attracted appropriate attention, you continue your message by providing relevant details that develop interest and stimulate desire.

Inflation, unemployment, consumer advocacy, and intense competition have made customers cautious about their purchases. Although sometimes motivated by impulse, today's customers increasingly require valid, appropriate reasons before they change their attitudes or behaviors.

For example, if as a seller you reduce price to increase sales, and thus profit on volume, you gain and the customer saves money. Your customers are interested in saving money, but they are concerned also with reasons for your actions. They know you probably would not reduce prices if losses resulted. They may interpret a lower price as reduction of quality rather than as reduction of your profit margin. Your communication work includes defining, describing, explaining *what* you do and, often, *why* you do it.

People are emotional as well as rational. Logical explanations work to satisfy information needs; words, illustrations, and demonstrations that create mental pictures may satisfy emotional needs. Therefore, to develop interest and desire, state your information clearly and vividly. Help the receiver visualize the benefits of your proposal. For example, describing the physical features of a new automobile provides basic information that the buyer needs for a rational decision. But using words that cause potential buyers to see themselves driving the car and being the object of friends' admiration can do more; it can persuade.

With descriptions and explanations, you reinforce the receiver's interest until, almost imperceptibly, that interest becomes desire. Here is an example:

> *You* relax. We do the work . . . at Timber Lodge.
>
> Enjoy your full-comfort room with its private balcony overlooking the beautiful scenes of Lake Huron. Relish the old-fashioned, home-cooked meals served at our Lakefront Restaurant. Sunbathe and swim—indoor and outdoor pools as well as a sandy beach await you. Explore woods and shoreline. Be active. Be lazy. Be happy at Timber Lodge.

To develop interest and desire, stimulate ideas as well as feelings. Factual appeals promote confidence in the worth of your proposal. Emotional appeals promote eagerness for what you offer. By using both logical and emotional appeals, you can persuasively answer the receiver's basic question: "What will your offer do for me?"

Factual (Physical) Description. Factual description represents objective details: length, breadth, height, size, shape, color, scent, sound, texture, and other specifications. Factual description may specify the materials and operations of an industrial pump, the types and extent of documentation for a new computer system, the fresh powder snow and accommodations at a ski resort, etc. Such factual description helps to develop the receiver's interest.

Psychological Description. Sensations, satisfactions, or pleasures are represented by psychological appeals that translate a proposal into fulfillment of needs and desires. Successful persuasion is the ethical blending of cold facts with warm feelings. Factually described, an electronic organ has an automatic rhythm unit; plays melodies in preset piano, banjo, mandolin, and harpsichord voices; is equipped with a 12-inch speaker, a 6-inch speaker, and a 6-inch, 2-speed rotor horn for acoustic tremolo effect. Psychologically

How can you develop the receiver's interest and desire?

described, the same electronic organ is beautifully designed to accent the furnishings of the proud homeowner who enjoys music and tranquility. The illustrations in this chapter synthesize objective and subjective images through both factual and psychological appeals.

Descriptive Evidence. To arouse attention, develop interest, and stimulate desire, you may use a variety of evidence: (1) facts and figures; (2) explanations of design or construction; (3) tests by manufacturer, independent laboratory, dealer, or customer; (4) records of the product in actual use; (5) testimonials; (6) free demonstrations, trials, samples; (7) illustrations; and other means. Here are examples:

Testimonial

How does Hiker's backpack compare with similar products? Dr. Martin Koepler, president of International Hikers' Association, gives this assurance: "The lightweight anodized aluminum frame, padded shoulder straps, moistureproof lining, and adjustable polypropylene waistband make Hiker's backpack the best that I have used."

Try-It-Yourself Offer

You like lemonade but not the calories? Lemon Light can solve that problem. Empty the contents of the enclosed trial packet into a glass. Add eight ounces of cold water; stir; add ice. Then enjoy the tangy, refreshing taste of fresh lemonade. We think you'll agree that Lemon Light is the easy way to true lemon flavor—with only four calories a glass.

Thirsty for more? Use the enclosed coupon for 50 cents off the price of a 32-ounce canister of Lemon Light—enough for five gallons of easy-to-mix, easier-to-enjoy lemonade.

Performance Guarantee

Grueling tests made by the Independent Testing Institute prove that the Beta electronic watch is the most dependable timepiece sold by fine jewelers. With this evidence, the Beta carries a five-year warranty of its precision construction and fine materials.

Free-Trial Offer

You owe it to yourself to sample the premiere issue of *Profit Magazine*. Just return the attached RSVP form to request a complimentary copy.

Then pay the invoice we will send you—and get 11 more issues. Or write "cancel" across the face of the bill, and you won't pay or owe us anything at all.

Demonstration Offer

Showing you the easy operation and efficient performance of the Osgood will be a pleasure. For a demonstration in your home, please call us at 555-2641, or complete and mail the enclosed card.

Stimulate Favorable Action. The final step in persuasion is to provide a two-part ending: First, reinforce the central appeal by stating a summary motive or reason for your receiver to respond. Then clearly, courteously, and confidently tell your receiver the action required for fulfilling that need.

To elicit appropriate responses to a sales message, offer inducements like the following:

How can you elicit appropriate response?

1. *Reward for prompt response.* Examine for (a specific number of days) on approval; act by (a certain date) and get (a gift or a discount); act now and enjoy the benefits immediately.
2. *Easy-payment plan.* Send no money in advance; use our deferred payment plan.
3. *Guarantee of satisfaction.* Be completely satisfied or payment will be refunded immediately; if dissatisfied at any time during the life of this product, return it for a full refund.
4. *Time or quantity limit.* This offer is available only until (a given date); the price will go up (a specified amount) after (a specified date); a limited supply is available, so act now.

Make responding easy. For instance:

1. *Enclose an order form.* Keep the form simple (for example, have the customer check squares or fill in spaces).
2. *Enclose a business reply card or business reply envelope.* Postage is due on business reply cards and envelopes only if they are returned.
3. *State exactly what to do.* "To enjoy this special discount, please call 1-800-555-6543 now."
4. *State a vibrant request.* "Let's win that Merit Award. Please sign and return your pledge card today."

Provide Suitable Emphasis. Stylistic methods of attracting attention and stimulating response include short sentences and paragraphs, technical devices, and prominent postscripts.

Short Units. When used for deliberate emphasis, brief paragraphs and short sentences can emphasize persuasive points. Even sentence fragments may be used deliberately for emphasis if you know this will not offend your audience. The contrast effect of the short unit placed amid longer sentences or paragraphs tends to draw the receiver's attention to the short item.

Technical Devices. "Special effects," when used sparingly, add emphasis. Colors, indentions, unique formats, and other typographical and visual aids can be used to move the reader or listener to decision and action.

Postscripts. As part of a written presentation, you may deliberately use a postscript. Since it is separated from the message body, the postscript can convey emphasis. For this reason, an important sales point is often intentionally positioned as a postscript. For example, a special offer may be postscripted: "You can save 10 percent by ordering before September 3."

Notice the AIDA structure and word choices used in Illustrations 12–3 through 12–5. Notice, also, that purposeful deviations from standard letter formats can be used effectively to attract the reader's attention and emphasize the central appeal.

Follow-Up Programs

Many products and services are sold not by single messages but by series of messages called follow-up programs. Follow-ups include the campaign system, the wear-out system, and the continuous system.

What are the major features of the campaign system of follow-up?

Campaign System. The **campaign system** is fully prepared before the first message of a series is sent. The number of messages, intervals between messages, and total length of the campaign are carefully scheduled. The campaign is based on current market research, which is expensive but indicates clearly to the seller the best approach.

As part of the planning, the sales messages are carefully coordinated with one *central buying point* as the theme. Throughout the entire campaign, attention and interest are maintained through a variety of appeals. The change of pace in the appeals freshens the customer's interest.

Early messages in the campaign attract attention and develop interest, and the later messages present powerful offers to induce action. The intervals between these mailings may be a week, ten days, or two weeks. Action is invited at the close of each message in the series, so the reader may be convinced and ready to buy long before the campaign is complete. Securing orders by early action economizes the rest of the expensive effort. Throughout the campaign, the action urge increases until it reaches its most forceful persuasion in the final message.

The campaign system is used to promote relatively expensive products or services, but it may also be intended to bring a salesperson and prospective customer together. A high-priced article with a wide profit margin may be marketed through a large number of mailings to a selective mailing list. For new

Illustration 12–3   AIDA STRUCTURE APPLIED TO SALES MESSAGE

Attract attention; receiver's concern	IS <u>YOUR</u> AUTO INSURANCE COSTING TOO MUCH? You need reliable protection for yourself and others who ride in your car. That protection is affordable and available to you through Boland. Boland Associates, Inc., can offer you money-saving discounts for:
Arouse interest; detailed information	1. completion of an accredited driver-training course 2. a no-accident driver safety record for the past two years 3. use of your car for below-average mileage
Develop desire	How can you save on car insurance? How can you get reliable protection and financial savings in one insurance package? With a Boland Preferred Motorist insurance policy.
Elicit action; easy response	Join the growing number of drivers who enjoy the security and economy provided by that policy. To get details of what Boland Associates can offer you, please complete and return the enclosed postage-paid form today. *Jason L. Briggs, Jr.* JASON L. BRIGGS, JR. MARKETING REPRESENTATIVE

and unfamiliar articles, the system must be lengthy to develop confidence. For an expensive article, a system of six to ten mailings with elaborate enclosures may be profitable.

Wear-Out System. In the **wear-out system**, each mailing piece carries its own complete message. One message after another is sent out until returns are no longer profitable. Each successive mailing may be either the same message or a different, complete presentation. The wear-out system is ordinarily used for selling inexpensive products, and the duration of the program is dependent upon when the mailing list is "worn out"—until a sufficient number of addressees buy or until the series budget is depleted.

What are the major features of the wear-out system?

The seller may purchase or rent mailing lists instead of paying for original market research. Thus, the wear-out system is less costly than the campaign system but more costly than the continuous system.

Continuous System. The **continuous system** is indefinite. Sales messages are sent at intervals, usually with monthly bills or weekly price lists. When

Illustration 12–4 AIDA SALES MESSAGE WITH DELIBERATE USE OF SENTENCE FRAGMENTS IN *ATTENTION* AND *INTEREST* STEPS

```
              Dear Mr. Kolb:

              Swimming?
Attention           Boating?
                         Fishing?
                              Sunbathing?

              Yes . . . and privacy, too . . .

              Come to Summit Lake Resort and enjoy--

                   natural beauty of lake and woodland
Interest                friendly group activities or blessed seclusion
                            gourmet cuisine and connoisseur beverages

              And more, much more, to delight you . . .

              The photographs in the enclosed brochure are complete,
              Mr. Kolb, except for you.  Put yourself into the pic-
Desire        ture.  Savor the fresh, clean mountain air as you set
              your own pace, living as you want to live, at incom-
              parable Summit Lake Resort.

              For complete rate schedules and reservations, simply
Action        complete and mail the enclosed card.  Or call this
              toll-free number:  1-800-555-7100.

              Sincerely yours,
```

sales messages are sent to established customers, a special mailing list is not necessary. And when sales messages are included with other regular mailings, the postage costs are less. For these reasons, the continuous system is the least expensive follow-up program. The continuous system is typically used to maintain customer loyalty and to stimulate additional sales among a known clientele.

What you have learned about persuasive techniques in sales messages is also applicable to special requests.

What are the major features of the continuous system?

PREPARING SPECIAL REQUESTS

A *special request* is a favor-seeking message. In a special-request situation you seek the receiver's cooperation although there appears initially to be little reason for a favorable response.

**Illustration 12–5   AIDA MESSAGE WITH INTENTIONAL USE OF POSTSCRIPT
                          AS PART OF THE *ACTION* STEP**

Aristo Corporation

400 South Salina Avenue
Syracuse, NY 13202-2224
Telephone 315-555-9191

September 15, 19--

Mrs. C. M. Sullivan
502 Greenhill Circle
Port Henry, NY 19297-4231

Dear Mrs. Sullivan

Attention

It's a cold, drizzly evening. You're late driving
home. You step out of your car to open the garage
door. The cold, damp air chills and drenches you.
The thought of who or what may lurk in the darkness
also chills you.

Interest

But what if, sitting in your car, you simply push a
button . . . and your door automatically opens to a lighted
garage? "What if" is affordable. "What if" is Aristo.

Desire

The Aristo garage door locks automatically. It cannot be
opened except by your own special key switch, button, or
receiver. Talk about personal safety and property
protection!

Action

Invest in your security. To have our representative visit
you at your convenience, please complete and return the
enclosed card.

Sincerely

Anna Martino

Anna Martino

dr

Enclosure

Action

Order before October 30 to avoid the winter rush--and get a 10
percent discount.

Effective special requests are similar to sales messages. They contain a central appeal, which is derived from an analysis of your objective and your receiver's needs; and they use the AIDA structure.

Select a Central Appeal

The International Management Federation letter (Illustration 12–6) demonstrates presentation and reinforcement of a central appeal: the desire for informed decision making. Notice the words and phrases chosen to convey that appeal—*information, knowledge, reports, seminars*—related to these persuasive factors:

- ▶ Objective: Obtain a membership application.
- ▶ Audience analysis: Business managers—eager to learn, progressive, profit oriented, rational in decision making, cost conscious, competitive.
- ▶ Possible appeals: Information value, prestige, financial value.
- ▶ Central appeal: Desire to make informed decisions.
- ▶ Secondary appeals: Costs, actions of other members of their group (managers), competition, prestige.

Use AIDA Structure

To attract attention, special requests often begin with a question. If you use this approach, word your question so it requires more than a yes or no answer. Asking your receiver to think before answering can enhance his or her interest.

Develop interest by explaining how a positive response can benefit the receiver. Your employees, customers, and associates expect answers to these questions: What is happening? Why is it happening? How can it affect my life? Describe the details of your request within the context of the receiver's self-concern. Use words that help the receiver visualize mentally the positive results of cooperating with you. Stimulate the receiver's desire to grant your request.

To promote action, ask your receiver to accommodate your request, or tell the receiver courteously and confidently what action should be taken. Use positive, confident language. You might say, for example, "Let me know which of the following two dates is more convenient for you." But avoid statements such as, "Is either of the two dates convenient for you?" Such a yes-no question not only invites an excuse for refusing your request but also indicates you are not confident of a positive answer.

Illustration 12–6   PERSUASIVE LETTER WITH CENTRAL APPEAL AND
AIDA STRUCTURE

INTERNATIONAL MANAGEMENT FEDERATION
1515 North Castle Road, Suite 100
Arlington, VA 22201-1921
(703) 555-7800

July 9, 19--

Mr. Keith O. Hoek
Regional Manager
Touro Industries, Inc.
1529 Emerson Rd.
Denver, CO 80210-3204

Dear Mr. Hoek:

Attention   As someone who makes informed decisions, please evaluate
these facts about the International Management Federation.

IMF's 50-plus years of effective service to the management
community rests upon the exchange of knowledge among experienced executives. IMF's messages and media are designed for
business leaders like you.

     IMF journal gives you original and timely management
strategies, analyses, and recommendations.

     IMF MANAGEMENT REPORTS discuss current issues of vital
importance to you. Here is a sample of titles just
released or soon to be distributed to IMF members only:

Interest   "Estate Planning for Rising Executives"
       "Communication: More Than Words or Numbers?"
       "A Systems Approach to Career Advancement"
       "CEO Profiles: Index to Leadership?"

     IMF SEMINARS bring managers together to share their
knowledge and investigate new ideas.

Desire   IMF helps companies to move ahead. IMF provides insider
information for discerning, ambitious decision makers like
you, Mr. Hoek. You need IMF; IMF needs you.

Action   To profit from IMF membership, please complete and return
the enclosed reply card today.

Sincerely,

Kyle Corbett

Kyle Corbett
Membership Manager

gj

Enclosure

When writing a favor-seeking message, be success conscious. Believe, and help your reader believe, the positive value of your request.

Here is a useful structure for special requests:

How should you structure a special request?

1. Attract attention by referring to the receiver's concerns.

   Recent requests to rezone the property on Stoneridge Road suggest that our community will soon change. The important question is: Who will direct that change?

2. Describe details of your request; make a connection between those details and the receiver's interests and desires.

   The officers of the Stoneridge Homeowners Association believe that you, the long-term residents of this community, should control the community's future. We need your contributions—ideas, time, money—so that we can wage a campaign to preserve the quality of life that has characterized Stoneridge Heights.

3. Ask the receiver to accommodate your request, or courteously and confidently state the desired action.

   Please attend a meeting to discuss how we can counteract the attempts to convert tree-lined Stoneridge Road into Used-Car Alley.

   When: May 15, 8 p.m.
   Where: Graham Elementary School Cafeteria
   Why: Because your quality of life depends on it.

Applications of those guides are shown by Illustrations 12–6 and 12–7.

USING ETHICS IN PERSUASION: A REMINDER

As stated at the beginning of this chapter, ethical questions arise when you try to influence someone's beliefs, attitudes, or behaviors. Is it right or wrong to persuade a person to buy your particular product? to contribute to your favorite charity? to join a fraternity, sorority, or club? to buy XYZ Corporation stock? to trust you and the organization you represent?

Certainly it is possible to persuade unethically and thereby to deceive or mislead people who trust you. But liars and cheats become their own worst enemies. To safeguard your integrity—and to avoid being victimized by people who try to influence you unfairly—be alert to these snares:

Illustration 12–7 PERSUASIVE REQUEST IN MEMO FORM

TO: C. J. Swensen

FROM: R. B. Starnes

DATE: August 22, 19--

SUBJECT: Request for Released Time

Attention; reader concern

The community relations goals for our firm, which you emphasized at our staff meeting yesterday, include working closely with City College administrators.

Supporting details; develop interest and desire

Dean Arlene Quinn of City College has asked me to teach a business communication course in the college's lifelong learning program. Dean Quinn hopes to reach employed adults who are in line for promotions to supervisory or managerial positions--if they demonstrate proficiency in business communication. The course will be offered on Tuesdays, 5:30-7:30 p.m., from September 5 until December 12.

Although Dean Quinn has offered me an honorarium to teach this course, I prefer to contribute my time as evidence of our commitment to community service. What I will need from Graphics, Inc., is permission to leave my office at 4:30 p.m. each Tuesday for the duration of the course.

Summary incentive; desired action

Dean Quinn's request provides a unique opportunity to achieve one of our community relations goals with little cost to the company. Please authorize my participation by initialing the approval line and returning a copy of this memo to me.

Approved _____ Date _____

1. presenting—or accepting—false or distorted information as if it were valid and reliable
2. using—or accepting—fallacies that masquerade as logical reasoning[3]

To enjoy personal and professional benefits of ethical persuasion, realize that honesty and truthfulness are themselves persuasive. When reinforced by AIDA, they are also extraordinarily rewarding. You judge other people by the results of their words and actions. *You* are judged, likewise, by the consequences of what you say and do.

[3]Review Chapter 2 for examples of fallacies.

REVIEW AND TRANSITION

Ethical persuasion is an essential business tool in democratic societies. Those societies reject compulsion or coercion in the exchange of goods or services.

Ethical and effective persuasion begins with identification of sender and receiver needs, preferences, and attitudes. The AIDA message structure unifies sender and receiver purposes by attracting appropriate attention, impelling pertinent interest, developing relevant desire, and stimulating favorable action.

When planning the *attention* step, address a person instead of a mass. Consider that person's motives; identify a need or desire that you can ethically satisfy. Focus the attention step on that person's hopes, wishes, preferences, or requirements.

When planning the *interest* and *desire* steps, stimulate your receiver's motivation with ethical appeals. Use factual appeals; they promote confidence in what you propose. Use emotional appeals; they promote eagerness for what you offer. Blend cold facts with warm feelings. Describe vividly, but do not overwhelm your receiver. Supply details, but relate them to your receiver's concerns. Reinforce your receiver's interest until it becomes desire for what you propose. Promise only what you and your firm can fulfill.

When planning the *action* step, identify a culminating motive or reason for your receiver to respond favorably. Avoid words that convey doubt; the action step is not a place for words like *if* or *maybe*. Reinforce courtesy and goodwill; *please* is a word that prevents the action step from sounding like a coercive command. To persuade is to *im*pel, not *com*pel, favorable response. Clearly, courteously, and confidently state what the receiver is to do. Make action easy. End the action step at that point. Add nothing else to the body of your message; avoid risking an anticlimax.

Chapter 12 has described ethical persuasion for sales messages and special requests. Chapter 13 focuses on persuasion strategies for claims, collections, and employee-discipline messages.

YOUR DECISIONS FOR CHAPTER 12

As an employee of Spa Health Center, what psychological appeals do you recommend for summer sales promotion of the center? Why do you recommend those appeals rather than others? What follow-up program or programs (campaign, wear-out, continuous) do you recommend? Why? What communication media do you recommend? Why?

DISCUSSION QUESTIONS

A.   Within the Chapter 12 context, what are appropriate definitions and examples of these terms?

1.   persuasion

2. manipulation
3. audience analysis
4. motivation
5. AIDA
6. descriptive evidence

B. When you plan persuasive messages, why should you define your objective and analyze your audience?

C. What factors help to determine the central appeal of a persuasive message?

D. What techniques are likely to attract appropriate attention to persuasive messages?

E. What techniques are likely to develop a receiver's interest?

F. What techniques are likely to stimulate a favorable response?

G. What are similarities and differences of campaign, wear-out, and continuous systems in follow-up programs?

H. What are similarities and differences of sales messages and persuasive requests?

I. In what ways do ethical standards influence you as you send or respond to persuasive messages?

APPLICATIONS

1. Use the following format to compare or contrast two competing products or services.

BASIC DATA STUDY CHART

Factor	Product 1	Product 2
1. Name of product or service.		
2. Materials and construction.		
3. Method of operation.		
4. Design and appearance.		
5. Uses and performance facts.		
6. Maintenance and repair record.		
7. Prices and terms.		

Orally, or in a memo to your instructor, state your findings.

2. From your findings for Application 1, define an audience for each product or service. Convert the differentiating features of the products or services into buyer benefits. Orally, or in a memo to your instructor, state those buyer benefits and identify possible appeals to use in sales messages to your audience.

3. Review your solutions to Applications 1 and 2. Write a sales message to promote *one* of the products or services.

4. Compose, or bring to class for evaluation, examples of these persuasive items:

    a. testimonials
    b. test-it-yourself offers
    c. guarantees
    d. free-trial offers
    e. home or office demonstrations

5. Orally, or in a memo to your instructor, describe and evaluate a persuasive message that you have received.

6. You believe that your community needs a "crime watch" program. Crimes have been increasing in recent months; and you want your neighbors to join you in requesting police to patrol the area frequently, post "crime watch" warnings, and sponsor meetings to inform residents about security-improvement methods. Cash contributions will be needed to pay expenses of the program. Prepare two persuasive requests:

    a. a letter encouraging your neighbors to attend an informational meeting at your home
    b. a request for a $10 contribution to get the "crime watch" program started.

7. One of your campus organizations has decided to sponsor a festival that may become an annual event. To open the festival, a parade will start at 9:30 a.m., May 12, 19—. You have been asked to persuade all campus groups to provide attractive floats for the parade. Compose a persuasive invitation. Ask your receivers to participate, to estimate the number of people their groups will provide, to identify the themes of their floats, and to answer your letter by a specific date.

8. You are a college representative for Clear Water Camp, which is supported by charitable donations. Its purpose is to provide pleasant learning experiences for teenagers who otherwise would not attend a summer camp. Clear Water Camp is located on a 40-acre site bordering Skytop Lake and Pine Ridge State Forest. Housing, food, and trained supervisors are provided. Swimming, boating, hiking, and horseback riding are featured. A $125 donation will support a teenager at camp for one

week. Write an AIDA message body for requesting donations from business firms.

CASES

1. Harkins College is suffering the effects of increased illicit drug use among students. As president of the Harkins student association, compose a message that encourages your peers to behave responsibly on and off campus. Avoid a "lecture" tone. Reinforce goodwill as you persuade all of your readers to be accountable and caring persons. The campus address of the Harkins College Student Association is Box 1000 at the Student Center, telephone 555-2121.

2. Murray Associates, Inc., a major advertising agency, offers summer internship programs to junior and senior college students. Competition for these internships, which provide valuable business experience and attractive paychecks, is keen. Using actual data concerning your own attributes and achievements, compose a persuasive message requesting consideration for a Murray internship. Address your request to Ashley Lynn Granger, director of internship programs, Murray Associates, Inc., 701 Carleton Avenue, Chicago, IL 60622-1120.

3. Review Case 2. To compete successfully for a Murray summer internship, you need to provide an original example of persuasive, sales-oriented writing. Compose the body of a message intended to increase sales of this video camera-recorder: The Unicorp compact 8-millimeter camcorder, with wireless remote control, 6:1 zoom, autofocus, title maker in 7 colors, high-quality stereo sound capability, priced at $898.98.

4. Review Cases 2 and 3. You have been selected as a Murray summer intern and are now assisting an account executive who specializes in advertising automotive products. The executive requests your ideas for promoting sales of this vehicle among college students: the Utopica X500 full-size pickup truck, available in vivid sunset colors, with 4.3-liter V-6 engine, 5-speed manual transmission, overdrive, speed control, AM-FM stereo radio, air conditioning, list priced at $11,995. In a persuasive memo to K. B. Brophy, your account executive, sell your ideas for advertising this vehicle to college students.

5. Review Cases 2 through 4. K. B. Brophy asks you to prepare the body of a persuasive letter incorporating your ideas for promoting Utopia X500 sales. Compose the message so that it will appeal to college students, especially to those on your own campus.

6. As advertising director of Electronics Stores, Inc. (ESI), prepare the first in a two-letter series addressed to ESI credit customers promoting sales of the following products: ESI Model 410 compact disc digital stereo

player, with on-track programmable memory, auto-search feature, and concert-quality engineering, priced at $149.95; ESI Model 525 VHS videocassette recorder, with on-screen prompts for 21-day and 5-event programming, 2-speed forward and reverse visual search, priced at $289.95. The ESI address is 9170 Mitchell Avenue, Wichita, KS 67241-2108, telephone (316) 555-8367.

7. Review Case 6. Compose the second letter in the ESI sales-promotion series. Higher prices for the ESI Model 410 compact disc player and Model 525 VHS videocassette recorder go into effect three weeks from today.

8. Review Cases 6 and 7. Instead of targeting all ESI credit customers, adapt the first letter in the ESI series so that it appeals especially to college students.

9. Review Cases 6 through 8. Adapt the second letter in the ESI series so that it appeals especially to college students.

10. For many years, Rawley National Bank profited from its reputation for customer satisfaction. Rawley employees were known as courteous, efficient people who made their customers feel welcome. However, as Rawley National Bank expanded, negative incidents damaged goodwill. Customers were treated brusquely, sometimes even rudely. Although Rawley salaries and working conditions were typical of the banking industry, customers could not help overhearing employees complain about being underpaid and overworked. Without being given an explanation or apology, customers were made to wait in long lines while employees chatted about plans for after-work hours. Business declined quickly as customers transferred their accounts to other financial institutions. Rawley executives decided that wholesale dismissal of employees would create additional problems; but persuasive communication, designed to improve employee performance, could be a major step toward remedying this costly situation. As the Rawley employee relations manager, you share the task of damage control. Compose a constructive, persuasive message to Rawley National Bank employees. Persuade the employees that customer treatment must improve. Customers should always be greeted cordially. Customers are to be treated courteously at all times, even if they are rude, demanding, or slow to understand. Customers need to be confident in the abilities of each employee, since bank customers may judge the security of their funds by the competence of the employees whom they meet. Maintain goodwill as you persuade.

11. Review Case 10. As employee relations manager at Rawley National Bank, compose two additional messages in a persuasive campaign series to Rawley employees. Be success conscious. Space these messages two weeks apart.

12. Review Cases 10 and 11. As vice president for customer relations at Rawley National Bank, compose a persuasive form letter (which can be personalized) to Rawley customers who have not moved their accounts to other banks. Thank these customers for their loyalty; let them know that they are appreciated. Reinforce their confidence in Rawley's financial resources and products. Assure them that Rawley is improving customer services. Invite these faithful customers to share, with Rawley officers and managers, suggestions for continuing improvement. The Rawley headquarters address is 3505 Archer Street, Seattle, WA 98019-0020, telephone (206) 555-4800.

13. Review Cases 10 through 12. As vice president for customer relations at Rawley National Bank, adapt your message for Case 12 so that it can be sent to former Rawley customers who have moved their accounts to other banking institutions.

14. The management of Hogan, Inc., a chain of full-service department stores, offers gift certificates that are available at Hogan customer service offices. These certificates may be purchased for any amount of $10 or more and are redeemable at any of the Hogan stores nationwide. Hogan gift certificates are in the form of greeting cards to help celebrate birthdays, weddings, anniversaries, holidays, and other special occasions. Recipients can use them conveniently, instead of cash, to purchase items from Hogan's array of clothing, furniture, housewares, jewelry, and other premium-quality merchandise. As the Hogan advertising director, you are asked to promote the sale of these gift certificates. Prepare the body of a persuasive message that will be sent, with monthly bills during the last quarter of this year, to Hogan credit customers.

15. Review Case 14. As Hogan advertising director, compose the body of a continuous-series sales message to promote the sale of Hogan gift certificates during May, June, and July. Relate your message to holidays and other special events associated with those months.

16. Review Cases 15 and 16. As advertising director, compose the body of a continuous-series message to promote the sale of Hogan gift certificates during November and December. Relate your message to holidays and other special events associated with those months.

17. Building on your entrepreneurship studies at college, you launched your business career by establishing Foodfest, Inc., a buffet-style restaurant near a university campus. As founder and president of this new venture, you have worked hard to secure adequate financing, competent employees, and a reputation for offering wholesome food at low prices. Recently, however, many of your customers have been unfairly jeopardizing your business success and carelessly wasting food by mis-

using the Foodfest self-serve buffet system to overload their plates. Other customers are hurting your business by paying for one buffet meal but sharing it with companions who buy only beverages. Compose the body of a brief persuasive message, which will be displayed at the restaurant entrance and at the beginning of the buffet line, to discourage these practices. But remember that, to prosper, Foodfest needs customer goodwill.

18. A recent series of thefts and assaults at Greenpark Shopping Mall has received widespread publicity and has seriously impacted Greenpark businesses. The mall has improved and expanded its security systems, appropriate arrests have been made, and Greenpark is much safer than it had been. As Greenpark general manager, prepare an open letter for publication in local newspapers. Persuade shoppers to return to Greenpark Mall. The address is 6000 Beltway Boulevard, Boston, MA 02149-0012, telephone (617) 555-9220.

19. Review Case 18. As general manager of Greenpark Shopping Mall, you observe that after publication of your open letter business has improved only slightly. Compose a second open letter in your campaign to have shoppers return to Greenpark.

20. Review Cases 18 and 19. As general manager of Greenpark Shopping Mall, compose a third letter in your campaign. Announce that the mall stores are offering customer-appreciation discounts of 25 percent off regular prices. Emphasize the attractions, conveniences, and state-of-the-art security services that are provided now for Greenpark customers.

21. Review Cases 18 through 20. As manager of security services at Greenpark Shopping Mall, compose a memo to your security employees. Congratulate them on the improved performance of their duties. Acknowledge the importance and the quality of their work. Reinforce their dedication to protecting the public and to safeguarding Greenpark.

22. With monthly bills to its customers, Minden Electric Power Corporation encloses a continuous series of consumer-protection messages. As assistant to the Minden customer relations manager, prepare the body of the next message in this series. Reassure Minden customers about enjoying the convenience and reliability of electric power, but urge every reader of your message to follow sensible precautions, including these: Be extremely careful when making house repairs, trimming tree limbs, or adjusting rooftop antennas. Avoid any contact with power lines. Especially warn children to keep kites, model airplanes, and other flying toys away from power lines. For additional information, customers may call a Minden customer service office at 1-800-555-8100.

23. As communication director of Citizens for Community Improvement, Inc., a nonprofit organization of property owners, compose a message

that persuades citizens to attend a public meeting at which a new wastewater facilities plan will be discussed. The agenda includes detailed information about wastewater health hazards, collection system alternatives, and funding sources. The meeting will begin at 7:30 p.m., two weeks from today, at the Akers Community Center, 1200 Linwood Road. The address of Citizens for Community Improvement, Inc., is 2815 Dorset Place, Baltimore, MD 21217-1019, telephone (301) 555-1948.

24. Review Case 23. Only a week remains before the public meeting to discuss the new wastewater facilities plan. As communications director of Citizens for Community Improvement, Inc., compose a second persuasive message in your campaign for public participation.

MULTICULTURAL INSIGHTS

1. Of the psychological appeals discussed in Chapter 12, which ones are frequently used with persuasive messages in cultures with which you are familiar? Which are not? Why?

2. Discuss the structure and tone of an actual persuasive message (printed advertisement, sales letter, or persuasive request) written in a language other than American English. In what ways does that example illustrate— or depart from—the AIDA message structure? What cultural values and traditions are reflected by the structure and tone of that example?

PERSUASIVE MESSAGES: CLAIMS, COLLECTIONS, AND EMPLOYEE DISCIPLINE

CHAPTER OUTLINE

OBJECTIVES

After completing this chapter, you should be able to:

1. Apply the AIDA structure to special requests, such as persuasive claims, collection messages, and employee-discipline messages.
2. Demonstrate your ability to select and apply an appropriate structure (inductive, deductive, chronological, or corethought refrain) for a specific persuasive claim.
3. Compose firm but empathetic payment requests that are appropriate to specific stages of the collection process.
4. Prepare employee-discipline messages that are appropriate for the nature of the infraction and the stage of the discipline process.
5. Observe legal and ethical standards as you compose persuasive claim, collection, and employee-discipline messages.

DECISIONS CASE

Kim Carter responds to the direct mail offer of *Rock Concert Classics:* two compact disks (CDs) of rock music favorites. The offer includes this assurance: "If, within one week of delivery, you are not satisfied with this product, just write *Cancel* on the bill. Then return that bill with the album and owe nothing."

When the CDs arrive, Kim is disappointed. The recordings have poor tone quality, and their volume levels are uneven. Kim marks *Cancel* on the bill, encloses the bill with the disks, and promptly mails the return package.

Three days later, Kim receives a duplicate of the bill with the stamped notation *"Please pay now."* The following week, Kim receives an urgent demand for payment. Another message arrives, but its tone is gentler: "This is just a reminder; your remittance for *Rock Concert Classics* is overdue. If you have already sent payment, disregard this notice."

Exasperated, Kim decides not to order anything from that company again. Thousands of other potential customers who share Kim's experience make the same decision.

Additional questions about this decision-making case are stated at the end of this chapter. Study the chapter before answering those questions.

CHAPTER CONTEXT

Sales messages and special requests (Chapter 12) are not the only categories of persuasive business communication. The success of a business—large or small—depends on many forms of persuasion. Suppliers must be influenced to correct unsatisfactory shipments, credit customers must be convinced to pay what they owe, and employees must be motivated to change behaviors that are contrary to company policies and procedures. In this chapter you will learn how to apply persuasive strategies to claim, collection, and employee-discipline messages.

CLAIMS AS ADJUSTMENT REQUESTS

The buyer or the seller—sometimes both, sometimes neither—may be responsible for dissatisfaction with a business transaction. Although intending to communicate clearly, a buyer may incorrectly state an order or may unintentionally misuse goods after they arrive. Although intending to satisfy a customer's desires, a reputable firm may unknowingly sell a defective item or may ship products too late for use.

At one time, "complaint departments" handled such situations. That name suggested—perhaps it even stimulated—irritation and negativism for seller as well as buyer. Today, business communicators recognize **claims** or **adjustment requests** as legitimate requests for satisfaction. An effective business communicator treats such claims as sources of valuable feedback to signal needed changes in products or services. Today, businesses process adjustment requests through "customer services," "adjustments," or departments with similar names which connote a goodwill effort for continuing business relationships.

How do today's attitudes about adjustments differ from earlier attitudes?

PERSUASIVE CLAIMS AS SPECIAL ADJUSTMENT REQUESTS

An ordinary adjustment request may be a neutral or mixed-news message.[1] But if such a request is unsuccessful, or if a stronger-than-usual message is needed when you first ask for adjustment, word your message as a *special* request: a **persuasive claim.**

For a persuasive claim, you will need to specify details of the problem to be resolved; ask for, or suggest, a suitable remedy; and request prompt action, preferably by an appropriate, definite date. As explained in this chapter, the necessary information can be structured logically, chronologically, or with a corethought refrain (request-details-request). Arrangement of information will vary according to which of the message structures you use, but all of them accommodate the attention, interest, desire, and action (AIDA) elements of persuasion.[2]

What information should a persuasive claim convey?

---

[1] Basic structures for neutral and for mixed-news messages are discussed in Chapters 9 and 10.
[2] AIDA is explained in Chapter 12.

Logical Structure

What is the structure
of a persuasive claim
with an inductive
pattern?

By presenting facts in logical order, you can develop support for your persuasive claim. Two logical patterns are useful for special adjustment requests. Those patterns are *induction* (reasoning from specific details to a derived conclusion) and *deduction* (reasoning from a general assumption to specific details).[3] Persuasive claims with inductive (indirect) patterns are structured as follows:

1. Explain specific details.

   On July 1, 19—, I purchased a Kelly-Black Model 8689 electric lawn edger at your store. After I had edged approximately 300 feet of grass along my sidewalks, the blade of the edger snapped in two, hurling bits of jagged steel as far as 30 feet.

2. State your requested adjustment as a logical conclusion derived from those details.

   Because of this experience, I question the safety of the Model 8689. I am, therefore, returning this edger and requesting a full refund of the purchase price, $89.98 including sales tax.

Illustration 13–1 shows inductive message structure for a persuasive claim from one business firm to another.

Persuasive claims with deductive patterns are structured as follows:

What is the structure
of a persuasive claim
with a deductive
pattern?

1. State a general assumption.

   Knowing your reputation for product safety, I believe you would want to know about my experience with a Kelly-Black lawn edger (Model 8689) that I purchased on July 1, 19—.

2. Support that assumption with specific details.

   After I had edged approximately 300 feet of grass along my sidewalks, the blade of the edger snapped, hurling bits of jagged steel as far as 30 feet. Fortunately, no one was injured. That experience, however, causes me to question the safety of the Model 8689.
   I returned the edger to Home Help Hardware, where I had purchased it. However, the manager declined my request for a refund because I could not produce the sales receipt.

3. Request the desired adjustment as a logical result.

---

[3]Induction and deduction, as well as fallacies, are discussed in Chapter 2.

Illustration 13–1   BUSINESS FIRM'S PERSUASIVE CLAIM:
INDUCTIVE STRUCTURE

BELLAMY BUILDERS, INC.
2140 Claymore Road
Biloxi, MS 39520-4991
Telephone 601-555-8540

June 18, 19--

Mr. R. B. Pawlik
Sales Manager
Alba Suppliers, Inc.
8900 Leesville Avenue
New Orleans, LA 70836-4565

Dear Mr. Pawlik

ATTENTION:
Reminder
of order

You recently received our Purchase Order 71-2860 for 40
awning window units (48x53 inches). Those units were
ordered for installation in five homes now under construction.

INTEREST AND
DESIRE:
Details to
justify request

Your truck and crew delivered the units this afternoon.
Cameron Osborne, our construction supervisor, promptly
inspected the windows. He reports that five of the
locks are defective.

ACTION:
Specific
request for
adjustment

In accordance with your reputation for customer satisfaction, please deliver five replacement windows immediately so that we can meet our contracted completion
date, July 15.

Sincerely

L. Y. Rasmussen

L. Y. Rasmussen
Project Manager

cl

pc Cameron Osborne

Please restore my confidence in Kelly-Black lawn tools and in your concern for consumer safety. I request either a refund of the purchase price ($89.98 including sales tax) or replacement of the Model 8689 edger with an equivalent model that has a protective blade guard.

Illustration 13–2 shows deductive message structure for a consumer's persuasive claim.

Illustration 13–2   CONSUMER'S PERSUASIVE CLAIM:
DEDUCTIVE STRUCTURE

```
                          1080 Fontaine Avenue
                          Springfield, MO  65823-6199
                          February 19, 19--


                          Catalog Sales Department
                          Morgan Ross, Inc.
                          2010 Bridge Street
                          Cleveland, OH  44117-8277

                          Ladies and Gentlemen

ATTENTION:    Because your company guarantees its products against
General       manufacturing defects, I confidently ordered a 12-cup
assumption    Monarch coffee maker, Model KM 930, from you a month
              ago.
INTEREST
AND DESIRE:   Following the instructions in the accompanying booklet,
Details to    I have been trying to operate the coffee maker as
support       directed.  The water temperature, however, remains
assumption    lukewarm; and the coffee is unsatisfying.
and request
              With trust in your guarantee and your excellent busi-
ACTION:       ness reputation, I am returning the coffee maker to you
Request for   in its original shipping box.  Please send a replace-
adjustment    ment or a full refund promptly so that I can again en-
              joy steaming hot coffee each morning.

                          Sincerely

                          Karen O'Donnell

                          Karen O'Donnell
```

Chronological Structure

Presenting facts in the order of their occurrence, the chronological structure is a special variation of the inductive structure. Chronological structure may enable an adjuster to appreciate details as well as total context for your persuasive claim.

A persuasive claim with chronological structure has two main parts:

1. Describe relevant, significant circumstances or events as they occurred, using exact dates or times for added emphasis.

    On July 1, 19—, I purchased a Kelly-Black lawn edger (Model 8689) at Home Help Hardware in this city.

    On July 4, after I had edged approximately 300 feet of grass along my sidewalks, the blade of the edger snapped, hurling bits of jagged steel as far as 30 feet. Fortunately, no one was injured.

    On July 5, I returned the edger to Home Help Hardware. However, the manager declined my request for a refund because I could not produce the sales receipt.

2. Request the appropriate adjustment.

    Please restore my confidence in Kelly-Black lawn tools and in your concern for consumer safety. I request either a refund of the purchase price ($89.98 including sales tax) or replacement of the Model 8689 edger with an equivalent model that has a protective blade guard.

When you use chronological structure, emphasize what you perceive as significant information. Describing all details as if they were equally important may weaken your claim. In the previous example, for instance, the writer probably unpacked and assembled the edger before using it and may have returned to the hardware store early on the morning of July 5. Those details, however, are less important than the major facts of purchase, limited use with unpleasant outcome, and immediate return to the store.

Illustration 13–3 demonstrates how the chronological structure could be used for the persuasive claim situation addressed in Illustration 13–1.

Corethought Refrain

More direct than other message patterns, the corethought refrain begins with the request for adjustment and restates the request at the end of the message. In poetry and music, a refrain repeats a theme, often at the end of a stanza. That emphasis technique is applied in this corethought refrain structure:

1. Courteously state the desired adjustment (message corethought).

    Please refund the purchase price ($89.98 including sales tax) of

If you use chronological structure, what should you emphasize? Why?

In what way is the corethought refrain more direct than other kinds of persuasive claims?

Illustration 13–3   BUSINESS FIRM'S PERSUASIVE CLAIM:
CHRONOLOGICAL STRUCTURE

ATTENTION:
Goodwill
opening
establishing
beginning of
chronology
INTEREST
AND DESIRE:
Continued
chronology
with details to
justify request
ACTION:
Request for
action with
emphasis
on time

Dear Mr. Pawlik

The 40 awning window units (48x53 inches) we ordered
from you on June 10 arrived at our construction site
yesterday, June 17. We appreciate the prompt delivery.

Upon initial inspection, the units appeared to be in
good condition. This morning, however, close inspection showed that the locks on five of the units function improperly.

Please deliver replacement windows before July 1.
Prompt replacement is necessary for us to finish construction by the contracted completion date, July 15.

Sincerely

the Kelly-Black lawn edger (Model 8689) that I purchased on July 1, 19—.

2.   Clearly explain details that justify your request.

     After I had edged approximately 300 feet of grass along my side-walks, the blade of the edger snapped, hurling bits of jagged steel as far as 30 feet. Fortunately, no one was injured. That experience, however, causes me to question the safety of the Model 8689.

     Although I returned the edger to Home Help Hardware, the manager declined my request for a refund because I could not produce the sales receipt. Therefore, I purchased another edger that had a safety shield over the blade.

3.   Courteously restate your corethought (the desired adjustment).

     I am returning the Model 8689 lawn edger for your examination. Please restore my confidence in your reputation for customer service and product safety by sending me a check for $89.98.

The corethought refrain is especially effective when you have strong support for a claim. Directness attracts the reader's attention, while the supporting explanation justifies and reinforces the restated request. Although the structure is direct, the tone should still be courteous.

Illustration 13–4 shows a persuasive claim with a corethought refrain.

Illustration 13–4 CUSTOMER'S PERSUASIVE CLAIM: CORETHOUGHT REFRAIN

```
                    CORRECTION TO ACCOUNTS

    ATTENTION:      Please correct a $200 discrepancy involving my savings
   Specific request and checking accounts.  Their numbers are 51-99088-43
                    and 23-01702-07 respectively.

     INTEREST       My employer, City Suppliers, Inc., automatically
    AND DESIRE:     deposits my salary in your bank every two weeks.  When
    Details to      selecting this pay option, I authorized your institu-
  support request   tion to deposit $50 of each paycheck into my savings
                    account.  The remainder was to be deposited in my
                    checking account.

                    On February 4, I notified your bank that my entire
                    salary was to be deposited--beginning March 15--into my
                    checking account.  My April bank statement, however,
                    shows that this transaction was not made.

     ACTION:        Please transfer $200 from Account No. 51-99088-43 to
    Courteous       Account No. 23-01702-07 immediately and discontinue
   restatement      further savings account deposits.
    of request
                    Lisa Stapleton

                    LISA STAPLETON
```

Persuasive claims tend to be variations of AIDA. The AIDA components—attention, interest, desire, action—also build effective collection messages.

COLLECTION MESSAGES AS PAYMENT REQUESTS

What are three categories for classifying credit customers?

In today's economy, the success of a business often depends upon its willingness to extend credit and its ability to collect amounts due from credit customers. For example, 1990 credit sales for the May Department Stores Company totaled $5.8 billion, 66.9 percent of its total department store sales. For the same year, that company reported bad debt expense of $82 million, approximately 1.4 percent of credit sales.[4] For that company, if bad debts were to increase only slightly—perhaps to 2 percent of credit sales—profits would decline an additional $34 million. Similarly, if collection attempts were to alienate 1 percent of the company's retail credit customers, the company's sales could decline as much as $58 million. A proficient business communica-

---

[4]The May Department Stores Company Annual Report, 1990, p. 22.

tor is one who can collect past-due payments while preserving goodwill for future transactions.

Collection treatments tend to vary with a customer's credit classification. Merchants often classify credit customers into three categories representing patterns of payment. The category may change as the customer's payment behavior changes. Some customers generally pay when first notified; they are classified as *good pay*. These people are eager to maintain credit privileges and cooperate with the collection department when payment is delayed. Other customers may lack self-management or may be careless about due dates; they are classified as *slow pay*. Customers in the slow-pay category cause the collection department most of its work, but they respond to increasingly persuasive messages and eventually pay what they owe. Customers who pay only under pressure are classified as *uncertain*. Eventually, they may lose their credit privileges.

To secure payment from credit customers who are in the slow-pay or uncertain categories, collection messages must become increasingly persuasive through the stages of the collection procedure.

Collection Stages

Collection messages are usually prepared in a series of four general stages: reminder, stronger reminder, discussion, urgency. The four general stages may include more than four messages. For example, customers with good payment histories may receive several reminders and more than one discussion message. For uncertain accounts, however, the collection stages may be condensed, with brief intervals between messages, to emphasize the need for immediate payment.

Most customers pay when they receive a statement of account or an invoice. Many others respond to the first reminder. Increasing persuasiveness, with empathetic but firm tone, characterizes later stages of the collection series.

Reminder. At this stage, you may assume that the customer has overlooked the bill and will pay on receipt of your second notice. To stimulate appreciation of benefits associated with payment, you may enclose new sales-promotion material.

Reminder stage messages are often impersonal notices. Some firms send a duplicate of the original bill with the notation "This is a reminder" or equivalent wording. Other firms place reminder stickers on the duplicate bills. Still others send printed cards—often amusing although their intent is clearly serious—to jog awareness of the financial obligation.

This modified AIDA structure is effective for a reminder-stage message:

What are four general stages for collecting overdue payments?

What characterizes a reminder-stage message?

1. Attract favorable attention by reinforcing rapport.

   We don't mean to hound you, but . . .

2. Refer to customer's payment obligation.

   The enclosed bill for veterinarian services is past due.

3. Resell advantages of doing business with your firm.

   St. Andrews Pet Center has added a complete line of nutritionally balanced pet foods. At your convenience, please pick up a free sample of the product that Dr. Lee especially recommends for your pet.

4. Request payment.

   To ensure that we can continue to provide the care you want for your pet, please send your check for $85.50 today.

That structure is demonstrated in Illustration 13–5.

Illustration 13–5   REMINDER-STAGE COLLECTION MESSAGE

Dear Ms. Squiers

Reinforcement of rapport

Now that the back-to-school shopping rush has ended, surely you are planning to introduce your winter line of merchandise. Please include us in your plans.

Reminders: Customer's obligation; advantages of doing business with seller

This note conveys best wishes for another successful season--and a reminder. Payment on your Purchase Order 171, shipped under our Invoice 8210, is 30 days past due. Your payment for that order will enable us to offer you special discounts on the items described in the enclosed brochure.

Courteous, specific request

To take full advantage of those discounts, please send your $1,675 check today.

Sincerely

Stronger Reminder. When you compose a subsequent reminder, you may assume the customer has again overlooked your payment request or other circumstances are preventing payment. In either of those cases, whether addressed to business firms or to consumers, the message becomes more personal, and the tone becomes firmly persuasive. Here is an effective message structure for stronger reminders:

How does stronger reminder differ from reminder?

1. Focus attention on buyer's obligation to pay.

    You recognized your obligation to your pet and took Archi to St. Andrews Pet Center for the high-quality pet care you wanted. Now we ask you to recognize also your obligation to St. Andrews Pet Center.

2. Request immediate payment.

    To ensure that we can continue to monitor Archi's health, we need payment on your account, which is now 60 days past due.

3. Encourage prompt response.

    Please send your $85.50 check today.

That structure is demonstrated in Illustration 13–6.

Illustration 13–6   STRONGER REMINDER COLLECTION MESSAGE

Dear Ms. Squiers

Reminder of obligation to pay

The attached statement is another reminder that payment for your account is past due.

Request for, advantage of payment

By sending us your $1,675 check, you will bring your account up-to-date and protect your credit rating.

Encourage payment

A reply envelope is enclosed. Please use it today to send a check that will clear your account and reinstate your full credit privileges.

Sincerely

Discussion. If you receive no response to the reminder and stronger reminder stages, use the discussion stage to obtain (1) full payment, (2) partial payment as a temporary stopgap, or (3) at least an explanation for the customer's delay. At this stage you not only present relevant facts for the customer's consideration, you may also invite the customer's presentation of facts that you need for fair, reasonable treatment of the account.

Illustration 13–7 shows this AIDA structure for the discussion stage:

What characterizes a discussion-stage message?

1. Attract attention with a firm opening that retains a goodwill tone.

    Until recently we have enjoyed monitoring Archi's health so that you could enjoy his companionship. Now is the time to ensure

Illustration 13–7   DISCUSSION-STAGE COLLECTION MESSAGE

LANCASTER SUPPLIERS, INC.
1912 Gateway Boulevard   St. Louis, MO 63130-7144   Telephone 314-555-7210

May 9, 19--

Ms. Katherine R. Burleigh
Purchasing Officer
Halston and Gibbs, Inc.
3390 Brighton Avenue
Peoria, IL 61621-3387

Dear Ms. Burleigh

<table>
<tr><td>Attention</td><td>Serving your business needs on a credit basis has been mutually advantageous for you and for us. Until now, your payments have been prompt, and your firm has been among our top-rated customers.</td></tr>
<tr><td>Interest</td><td>However, six weeks have passed since the last payment was due; and we have had no reply to our reminders of April 18, April 25, and May 2. Have extraordinary circumstances prevented your payment? If full payment of your account is impossible now, would partial payment today and payment of the balance next month help you?</td></tr>
<tr><td></td><td>To preserve your credit privileges, please do one of the following:</td></tr>
<tr><td>Interest, desire, and action</td><td>1. Remit the full amount of $3,200 today.

2. Send us $1,600 today as partial payment, with the balance payable by June 5.

3. Explain your situation and tell us what you can do to meet your obligation.</td></tr>
<tr><td>Action emphasized</td><td>Your immediate response is necessary. Please reply by May 16.</td></tr>
</table>

Sincerely

Elaine R. Jordan

Elaine R. Jordan
Collection Manager

ar

Archi's access to high-quality veterinarian care and your peace of mind.

2. Stimulate interest by reviewing the facts of the case.

    We have sent you two reminders that your account balance ($85.50) is past due, but we have had no response from you.

3. Develop or reinforce desire to cooperate with you. Use appropriate logical and psychological appeals (impact on credit record, loss of service, loss of credit privileges, etc.) to obtain payment or an explanation.

    Archi trusts you to choose a competent veterinarian, which you have done by selecting the services of St. Andrews Pet Center. Don't betray Archi's trust by losing those services.

4. Elicit action. Firmly request payment or, at the very least, an explanation.

    Please send your check for $85.50 before October 10; or, for Archi's sake, call us to say when we can expect payment.

Urgency. The tone of an urgency-stage message may suggest reluctance at having to take more drastic measures to collect the amount due. That tone, however, should be strong, definite, unapologetic, and free of anger. The corethought of the urgency stage is that now credit privileges must be curtailed. Moreover, in many cases the effort to secure payment must be referred to a collection agency or an attorney. The customer may be offered a final opportunity to pay before such referral is made or credit privileges are ended.

Illustration 13–8 shows this structure for an urgency-stage message:

1. Review the pertinent facts.

    For the past three months we have sent notices reminding you of your overdue account for veterinarian services. Regretfully, we have had no reply.

2. State necessary action as a consequence of those facts.

    Because we have had no response, we can no longer supply you with veterinarian services on a credit basis.

3. Close the message at this point; offer the customer a final opportunity to pay before legally compelling action is taken.

    On November 30 our accountant will mark "Provide No Service;

How does an urgency-stage message differ from a discussion-stage message?

Illustration 13–8   URGENCY-STAGE COLLECTION MESSAGE

LANCASTER SUPPLIERS, INC.

1912 Gateway Boulevard   St. Louis, MO 63130-7144   Telephone 314-555-7210

May 23, 19--

Ms. Katherine R. Burleigh
Purchasing Officer
Halston and Gibbs, Inc.
3390 Brighton Avenue
Peoria, IL 61621-3387

Dear Ms. Burleigh

Attention
and
interest

Although this message is necessary, it is sent with regret
that previous efforts to obtain payment of your account have
been unsuccessful. The attached statement specifies the exact amount owed and the full period of its delinquency.

Desire
and
action

Unless full payment of your account is received by June 5,
your file will be referred to Garvey Associates for collection. To prevent this action, please send us your payment
for $3,200 immediately.

Sincerely

Elaine R. Jordan

Elaine R. Jordan
Collection Manager

ar

Attachment

Allow No Credit" on your file, unless we receive your check for
$85.50 before then.

Collection Timing

What factors affect
collection timing?

Many factors influence the timing of collection messages. For a buyer with a
good-pay credit record, intervals between collection stages—and between
messages at a particular stage—may exceed those for a customer in the uncertain category. The nature of a business enterprise may also affect collection timing. For example, farm implement dealers often allow extended collection periods, aware that farm income is seasonal. Conversely, a specialty
manufacturer operating on small capital and fast turnover may condense collection efforts and move quickly from reminder to urgency stage. Moreover,
general economic conditions may affect collection timing. During prosperous
periods, payments tend to be prompt. During recessions, payments lag.

The stage of business development may also affect collection timing.
Owners of small businesses must be especially attentive to the collection process during the early stages of business development. Many small businesses
fail within the first few years of operation. In the years 1984 to 1986, for example, the birth rate for small businesses in the United States was 9.0, but
the death rate was 9.9.[5] Frequently the owner-managers of small businesses
focus most of their attention on the day-to-day tasks of attracting customers
and providing them with goods or services. If those entrepreneurs do not follow through with a carefully planned collection system, they find themselves
with a cash-flow problem, unable to meet their own financial obligations.
Business closure soon follows.

The concept exemplified in the collections process—increasingly persuasive messages at intervals that are appropriate to the circumstances—can
also be applied effectively to the employee-discipline process.

EMPLOYEE DISCIPLINE AS PERSUASIVE REQUESTS

A positive approach to employee discipline demonstrates a desire to rehabilitate problem employees and turn them into productive workers. The objective of employee-discipline messages is to correct unacceptable behavior.

---

[5]U.S. Bureau of the Census, *Statistical Abstract of the United States: 1990* (110th ed.), Washington, DC,
1990, p. 532. Business birth rate represents the number of establishments formed during a specified period relative to the number in the initial year. Business death rate represents the number of establishments discontinued during a specified period relative to the number in the initial year.

Employees who respond positively to disciplinary messages will become valued employees; those who do not respond will be terminated.

Discipline Stages

What are the stages of progressive discipline?

An ideal disciplinary process uses a sequence of progressively persuasive messages and increasingly severe penalties for infractions. Progressive discipline typically includes some or all of the following stages.

Oral Warning. The supervisor warns the employee that a behavior (any violation of company policy or procedure) is unacceptable. The purpose of the warning is to ensure that the employee knows what is expected and what is not condoned. Usually no formal written record is made, but the supervisor may make an informal notation in a personal file and refer to the warning in the employee's performance appraisal. This stage is similar to the reminder stage of the collection process.

Oral Reprimand. At this stronger-reminder stage, the supervisor firmly explains the rules, clearly identifies the unacceptable behavior, and informs the employee that improvement is required. Since the purpose of the reprimand is correction, the supervisor must be sure that the employee knows the problem and how to correct it. Although the reprimand is oral, the supervisor typically places in the employee's file a written record of the conversation.

Written Reprimand. This discipline stage is similar to the discussion stage for collection messages. In this stage the supervisor prepares a written description of the problem, the previous attempts to correct it, the corrective action the employee must take, a target date for correction of the problem, and a warning of the consequences if the employee's behavior does not improve. Message tone should be firm but empathetic, encouraging the employee to change so that he or she can remain on the job.

After discussing a written reprimand with an employee, the supervisor should sign that document. The employee should sign it also as evidence of having read and understood the message. Typically, the supervisor, employee, and personnel office retain copies of the reprimand. In a unionized organization, a copy may also be given to the union steward.

Suspension. An employee who has not responded to previous disciplinary action is suspended—not allowed to work for a period of time. The suspension message specifies the length of suspension and the conditions for the employee's return to work. Message tone should be unapologetic and unemotional.

The suspension message is similar to the urgency-stage message for collections; it is the employee's last chance to correct the unacceptable behavior. The employee is told that certain things must be done to prevent the final action: discharge.

Discharge. The discharge message is issued after reasonable attempts to change the employee's behavior have failed. Discharge messages must be firm, unemotional, and unconditional. They should contain a review of the relevant evidence and a clear statement of the discharge terms.

Discipline Timing

Effective discipline messages are prompt; that is, little time passes between an infraction and the disciplinary communication. Promptness promotes objectivity by ensuring that relevant facts are fresh in the minds of employee and supervisor. Prompt correction may also protect the company from liability if the infraction has a potential impact on employee safety or public health and security.

The nature of the problem and company policies determine how many disciplinary stages are used and the time lapse from warning to termination. For example, many companies have rules that prohibit employee gambling on company premises. If an employee organizes a company football pool, most supervisors would issue the oral warning, oral reprimand, written reprimand, and suspension messages before discharging the employee. In contrast, an employee proven to be involved in an organized gambling ring might well be discharged without having received previous warning or reprimand messages.

To compose effective claims, collection, or employee-discipline messages, business communicators must constantly evaluate the communication context to make appropriate decisions about the severity and timing of those messages. Other decisions, too, are necessary for properly persuading sellers to fulfill their promises, buyers to pay what they owe, and employees to change unacceptable behavior. Those decisions involve ethical, logical, and legal dimensions of business communication.

How are collection and employee-discipline messages alike?

ETHICS AND PERSUASIVE REQUESTS

Business communicators need to be ethical as well as persuasive. You are right to use persuasion to seek replacement or refund for defective merchandise and unsatisfactory service. You are right to use persuasion for collecting overdue payment. You are right to use persuasion to improve the working environment for you and your employees. But you are wrong—in fact, you risk heavy legal penalties for yourself and for the firm that employs you—if your messages are vehicles for maliciously injuring someone's reputation, illegally coercing payment, or unjustifiably terminating someone's employment.

Ethically persuasive claimants seek justice through their requests. An ethical buyer does not take undue advantage of the seller. Instead, that buyer expects ethical business establishments to satisfy reasonable customer expectations while enjoying a fair profit on goods or services. In that spirit, you will supply evidence to support each claim and use a confident, courteous, respectful message tone.

Ethically persuasive collectors word their oral and written payment requests with the guidance of legal experts. Guard yourself against making false assumptions or jumping to conclusions. For example, assume that you are tempted to make statements like these:

This is the third reminder of payment you owe us. Why do you refuse to pay?

Your failure to pay what you owe us has jeopardized your account.

Why do you ignore your financial obligations?

Can you prove that the debtor did not send payment? Are you certain that the check was not lost or misrouted in transit? In this example, all you can prove—and can legally say—is that the payment has not reached you.

Ethically persuasive supervisors acknowledge employee discipline as a process whereby worthy individuals are helped to become satisfied, productive employees. As that kind of supervisor you will avoid emotional outbursts and irrational threats. The ethical supervisor also acts legally. You must be aware of—or seek advice about—legal aspects of employer-employee relations. Federal and state laws, as well as specific labor-management agreements, affect the kinds of actions you can take to change employee behavior.

Do you begin now to appreciate the care, insight, and skill required for ethical persuasion?

REVIEW AND TRANSITION

Using the components of AIDA—attention, interest, desire, action—you can build persuasive claim, collection, and employee-discipline messages.

Claims are adjustment requests that are made persuasive by logical, chronological, and corethought refrain message structures. Collection messages are payment requests that become increasingly persuasive through stages of reminder, stronger reminder, discussion, and urgency. More than one message may be sent at any of those collection stages. The stages may be condensed or expanded according to the customer's credit classification, nature of the business enterprise, and general economic conditions. Employee-discipline messages become increasingly persuasive as they progress through oral reminder, oral reprimand, written reprimand, suspension, and termination stages. Those stages, too, may be condensed or expanded according to company policy and the severity of the problem.

By studying Parts 1 and 2 of this book, you have heightened your awareness of—and developed your readiness for—effective business communication. With Part 3, you have acquired techniques for applying your awareness and readiness to recurring kinds of business messages. Your study of Part 4 will focus on visual and oral media for transmitting your messages successfully.

YOUR DECISIONS FOR CHAPTER 13

Review the Decisions Case at the beginning of this chapter. What violations of standard collection procedure are evident—especially related to the timing and sequence of collection stages? In what ways are those violations counterproductive for the company offering *Rock Concert Classics?*

DISCUSSION QUESTIONS

A. Within the Chapter 13 context, what are appropriate definitions and examples for these terms?

   1. logical structure
   2. chronological structure
   3. corethought refrain
   4. stronger reminder
   5. discussion-stage message
   6. urgency-stage message
   7. oral reprimand
   8. written reprimand
   9. suspension

B. What communication values do these names connote?

   1. complaint department
   2. adjustments department
   3. customer services department

C. What are advantages and disadvantages of these message structures for persuasive claims?

1. logical structure
2. chronological structure
3. corethought refrain

D. What kinds of business messages *other* than persuasive claims would benefit from logical structure, chronological structure, or corethought refrain? Why?

E. In what respects are collection messages and employee-discipline messages similar?

F. How does the ethical standard of fairness apply to adjustment requests?

G. How does the ethical standard of respecting the rights of others apply to collection messages?

APPLICATIONS

1. Appropriately revise these items:

    a. Sirs: The merchandise that I recently ordered from you is unsatisfactory. I want my money back. Cordially, J. Smith.
    b. This is the third time I've written to you for adjustment of your Invoice 12801. When we received the merchandise ordered from you February 11, we found errors in size and defects in construction as noted on the enclosed copy of the claim report I sent you last week. We need a credit memo from you promptly.
    c. We wrote to you about your unpaid balance twice in August and again on September 9. Why do you refuse to pay?
    d. Our records indicate two persons with similar names at your address. If you are the person in question, it is imperative that we have some payment on your overdue account. If you are not the person in question, please disregard this notice.
    e. As indicated by our previous reminders of your unpaid balance, we have really tried to avoid this. But we have referred your account to our attorneys for collection. If you have already mailed your check, disregard this ultimatum.
    f. Yesterday someone told me that you took a 90-minute lunch hour instead of 60 minutes. Surely you know the company rules. If you do that again, don't come back.

2. Revise the following messages. Make each message appropriate for its stage in the collection process.

a.   Reminder

> ### *May we remind you . . .*
>
> that payment on your account was due several weeks ago and has not yet been received.
>
> ### *May we urge you . . .*
>
> to send the past-due amount shown on the enclosed statement together with the installment currently due.
>
> ### *May we encourage you . . .*
>
> to send payments each month upon receipt of your regular statement so that your record will remain clear.
>
> Your Friendly Fulton Store
Kansas City

b.   Stronger Reminder

The new Toddman, which you purchased from us on October 6, is one of the better suits that is on the market today. You will enjoy the satisfaction and confidence of the well-dressed as you wear it.

We also have confidence that this message will remind you to pay the balance due on your account. May we have a check for $350 so that we can mark your account "Paid in full."

A new shipment of spring suits arrived this past week. Why not stop in and see them?

c.   Discussion

Serving your business needs on a credit basis has always been a pleasure. You have always been punctual in making your payments, and we have appreciated that effort. That's why we can't understand why you have let six weeks pass without making a payment. We have had no answer to our notices of April 15 and May 1, calling attention to the evident oversight.

Knowing that you value your good credit reputation, the only conclusion we can reach is that some extraordinary circumstances have prevented you from making your payment. Is there anything we can do to help? Won't you let us know?

Of course, we would like to have full payment of your account; but, if this is not possible, perhaps sending a partial payment now and the balance next month will make things easier for you. We sincerely want to work with you in protecting your credit, but our hands are tied unless you let us know the problem.

Help us to help you in preserving your good credit by letting us hear from you now. Please use the enclosed reply envelope to do one of three things: (1) enclose your check for the full amount—$1,250; (2) enclose a check for part of that amount—and we will assume you will send the balance next month; or (3) explain your situation and let us know what you can do to meet your obligation. We need a response from you immediately. If we don't hear from you by May 30, we will be forced to take drastic action against you.

d. Urgency

We have had no response to all our efforts to reach a mutually acceptable, friendly solution to your indebtedness, which is indeed unfortunate. The attached statement indicates the exact amount of your account, Mr. Saunders, and the full period of its delinquency. Justice to other customers prevents further delay of your payment.

Unless your check for full payment of your account is received by June 15, your account will be transferred to a collection agency. Such action—as you well know—will inevitably lower your credit rating.

To prevent this unpleasant action, your check must be in our hands by June 15. Please send us your check today.

CASES

1. Last week you bought four Wearwell tires for your car. Two of those tires now have ply separation. The local Wearwell dealer agrees that your limited warranty provides for replacement, then says: "Your warranty does not stipulate *immediate* replacement. You'll get the tires, but that size is in short supply right now. Check back with me in two or three weeks. Of course, if you can't wait that long, I can make you a good deal on buying two other tires today."

   You want immediate replacement or refund and decide to write A. J. Marshak, customer services manager at the corporate headquarters of Wearwell Tire Company, 75 E. Kramer Road, Akron, OH 44308-3297.

a. Write three versions of a persuasive claim to Marshak: logical, chronological, and corethought refrain. Be sure to consider where you live. Your specific request must be one that Marshak in Akron, Ohio, can feasibly fulfill for you at your current address.

b. Select the version you believe is the most effective and, in a memo addressed to your instructor, explain why your selection is more persuasive than the other two versions.

2. You own the Land O'Music Shop, 107 S. Pinckney Street, Madison, WI 53703-5482. You recently placed a $4,500 order at Upbeat Merchandisers, 511 Peak Street, Nashville, TN 37211-2345. You specified delivery before the first day of this month so that the merchandise would arrive in time for special promotion of Land O'Music's first anniversary sale.

The shipment arrived four days late. You returned it and asked that the $4,500 be credited to the Land O'Music account. Today, you receive a letter from S. A. Cadiz, Upbeat accounts manager, who politely but firmly declines your request and offers to send the merchandise back to you.

a. Write one version (logical, chronological, or corethought refrain) of a persuasive claim to S. A. Cadiz. Remember that this is your second adjustment request.

b. In a memo addressed to your instructor, justify your choice of message structure.

3 Shortly after purchasing her condominium, Ms. Rosa Perez installed a new dishwasher that was covered by a one-year warranty. She bought the dishwasher from Capitol Appliances, from whom she had made other purchases of major appliances. Returning from a business trip approximately 13 months later, Ms. Perez was dismayed to discover that the dishwasher had sprung a leak while she was away. Water had apparently covered the kitchen floor for most of the three days that she was away. Consequently, the floor was damaged also. Since Ms. Perez lives alone, she had operated the dishwasher two or three times a week, not two or three times a day as a larger family might. She thinks the defect in the appliance might have been discovered earlier if the washer had been subjected to normal family wear and tear.

As Rosa Perez (or Ramos Perez if you are male) write a persuasive claim letter to the dealer from whom you bought the dishwasher, Arthur Compton, Capitol Appliances, 845 North Main, Columbia, SC 29201-2304. Request repair or replacement of the dishwasher. Persuade Compton to grant your request even though the appliance is no longer under warranty. Perez's address is 155 Jefferson Place, Columbia, SC 29212-1203.

4. Review Case 3. Ms. Perez's insurance agent has viewed the damage to the kitchen floor. The agent agrees that the company should pay for repair of the sub-floor and replacement of the vinyl floor covering in the kitchen. However, the agent balks at Ms. Perez's request to replace the floor covering in the utility room, which is adjacent to the kitchen and currently has the same kind of flooring as the kitchen. The agent refers Ms. Perez to Warren Grover at the regional adjustments office to make that request. Write a persuasive claim to Home Insurance Company, 3600 Forest Drive, Columbia, SC 29206-4304. Convince Grover that the insurance company should pay to restore the kitchen-utility room area to its former condition.

5. Review Case 3. To maintain the goodwill of an excellent customer, Arthur Compton has agreed to replace Ms. Perez's dishwasher at no charge. Now, however, Compton wants to recover that cost from the manufacturer. As Compton's administrative assistant, write a persuasive claim to Kitchen Help Appliances, P.O. Box 2500, Woodbury, NJ 08096-2500. Since Capitol Appliances regularly purchases appliances from Kitchen Help, Capitol has an account with that manufacturer. Therefore, request credit to the account for the dealer's cost of the replacement dishwasher ($485) and labor ($75) to install it in Ms. Perez's home.

6. Wilma Able is owner-manager of Able Maintenance, specializing in general cleaning and maintenance of business offices. After a contract is signed, Able rarely sees her clients. Able's employees do most of the work at night after offices have closed. Aware of the need for timely collections, Able bills all clients monthly. However, approximately 5 percent of her customers require a reminder notice. Of that group, half require a second reminder. Most customers eventually pay their accounts, but approximately 1 percent do not pay even after several reminders. Able's billings average $35,000 a month. Her policy has been to carry customers for 6 months before discontinuing services and referring their accounts to a collection agency.

    As a consultant to Ms. Able do the following:

    a. Propose a collection strategy for Ms. Able. How many collection stages should she use? What intervals between stages do you recommend? Present your strategy in a letter to Ms. Able. The address for Able Maintenance is 5520 Haverly Avenue, Birmingham, AL 35228-8165; telephone (205) 555-9080.

    b. Write a model letter for each collection stage you recommended.

7. Your employer, Classic Renovators, is a construction firm that specializes in remodeling old houses, restoring them to their classic beauty. The company has a strict substance abuse policy that forbids employees

to use alcohol or drugs while on the job or to report to a job site while under the influence of those substances. The objective of the policy is threefold: to protect employees and clients from injury by coworkers who are under the influence of alcohol or drugs, to ensure that employee performance—and contract fulfillment—is not impaired, and to encourage employees with substance abuse problems to seek rehabilitative services. The policy, which is published in the employee handbook, includes only two discipline stages: written reprimand for the first offense and termination for a second offense.

As project manager, you are responsible for supervision of several remodeling projects. Although each project has an on-site supervisor, you typically visit each site daily to confirm progress on the contracts and help supervisors resolve problems with suppliers or employees.

One day you arrive at a construction site shortly after 1 p.m. You notice construction supervisor Adam Ellerby in heated discussion with employee Harold Johnston. As you approach the two, you hear Johnston acknowledge, somewhat belligerently, that he drank two beers for lunch; but he insists he is not "under the influence" and did not drink them at the job site. Therefore, he contends, he has not violated the policy.

What advice will you give Ellerby for handling this situation? What should be his goals? Should Ellerby prepare any written messages?

a.   If you answered yes to the last question, write those messages for Ellerby.
b.   If you answered no, justify your decision in a memo to your instructor.

8.   As communications director for Reliable Casualty Company, you have noticed that some employees seldom send messages by facsimile transmission (fax). Other employees use this transmission method frequently, often unnecessarily. To improve Reliable's external communication, do the following:

a.   Write a persuasive memo to employees who have never used the fax system. Encourage appropriate use.
b.   Write a persuasive memo to employees who have used the fax system excessively. Encourage appropriate use.

MULTICULTURAL INSIGHTS

1.   Share with your classmates your knowledge of claims and collection strategies used in cultures other than the United States. What are customary message structures and tones for persuasive claims? for persuasive collection messages?

2. What employee-discipline practices are common in other cultures with which you are familiar? In what ways, if any, do they differ from the employee-discipline approach described in Chapter 13? What cultural characteristics account for those differences?

Cases

The communication challenges represented by these cases include perception, interpretation, empathy, and message structure.

CASE A: SHANNON, KERRY, AND VAUCLUSE INDUSTRIES
(Empathy and Message Structure)

Shannon and Kerry have been friends since their college days. After receiving their business degrees two years ago, both of them were employed by Vaucluse Industries, Inc. The two friends share a career goal: advancement to managerial positions within the company.

This afternoon, as they leave work and head for their cars in the Vaucluse parking lot, the following conversation takes place:

SHANNON: Is Miller leaving?

KERRY: Yep. Transferred to the Los Angeles office. It's supposed to be a good opportunity from what I hear.

SHANNON: Good for Miller. And maybe good for one of us, too.

KERRY: What do you mean, Shannon?

SHANNON: Well, someone has to fill Miller's shoes as assistant manager here. The job was posted this morning. Interviews begin next week. I wouldn't mind having that job.

KERRY: Think you could handle it?

SHANNON: Sure. Why not?

KERRY: Being assistant manager involves "people problems," you know.

SHANNON: The heck it does. You just sit behind that big desk. You tell people what to do. And they do it.

KERRY: What were your grades in our management and communication courses back at college, Shannon?

SHANNON: Don't rub salt in a wound, friend. You know darned well I didn't mind repeating a couple of those courses.

KERRY: You repeated four of them, didn't you?

SHANNON: Only three, Kerry, not four. Don't make it worse than it was. Anyhow, I finally scraped through them; that's the important thing. Besides, grades don't have anything to do with what we were discussing.

KERRY: Don't they?

SHANNON: Nah. Remember how our instructors used to grade us on empathy and *you* tone and all that jazz? That stuff may sell textbooks, but I don't believe in it.

KERRY: Why not, Shannon?

SHANNON: I just don't, that's all.

KERRY: Well, it works well at Vaucluse Industries. Empathy and *you* tone reinforce the Vaucluse management style. Effective communication is good business, Shannon; just look at the profitable effects on productivity and morale.

SHANNON: I don't care, Kerry. When I get to be a manager, there'll be some changes around here. I'm going to treat people the way *I* want to be treated. Direct and to the point; that's the way.

KERRY: Always?

SHANNON: Always, Kerry.

KERRY: Even if there's bad news?

SHANNON: Bad news, good news, mixed news—what's the difference?

KERRY: Well, I'm not sure that philosophy will get you the promotion.

Two weeks later, Shannon and Kerry again meet in the Vaucluse parking lot.

KERRY: Remember our conversation about communication style?

SHANNON: Yeah?

KERRY: Well, look at it this way: What if someone—a friend, let's say—has news that is good for the firm but bad for *you*. How should the friend tell you?

SHANNON: Haven't you been listening, Kerry? I'm telling you that every message should be direct and to the point.

KERRY: *Every* message? Even bad news? Wouldn't you want a buffer

first? Wouldn't you want reasons that help you prepare for disappointment?

SHANNON: No, not me. "Direct and to the point always"—that's my motto.
KERRY: Okay, Shannon. I'm the new assistant manager.

INSIGHTS

Empathy involves psychologically projecting yourself into someone else's circumstances without surrendering your own identity, needs, and obligations.
Test your knowledge of empathetic message tone by answering these
questions:

1. Shannon and Kerry have been friends for years. They are also coworkers and competitors for advancement at Vaucluse. In what ways
   do those facts influence communication in this case?
2. At what points in Shannon and Kerry's conversation does Kerry try
   to use buffers? When does Kerry try to move the conversation from
   "buffer" to "reasons" stage?
3. Was it ethical for Kerry to apply for the position without telling
   Shannon?
4. Assume that you are Shannon. You value your friendship with Kerry
   and your employment at Vaucluse. When you learn of Kerry's promotion, you are glad for Kerry but disappointed for yourself. What do
   you say to Kerry after hearing: "Okay, Shannon. I'm the new assistant
   manager"?

CASE B: LUCY ANN STEDSEN AND THE DIEMER COMPANY
(Perception, Interpretation, and Recall)

A month ago, Miss Lucy Ann Stedsen, a senior citizen, ordered merchandise
totaling $58.96 from the Diemer Company catalog. Instead of using her
Diemer credit account, she decided to enclose her personal check with the
mail-order form from the catalog.

Lucy Stedsen received all of the ordered items except a Companion AM—FM
transistorized pocket radio, Catalog No. 38A, price $24.95. She promptly tele-
phoned the Diemer Customer Service Office about the missing radio and
was told it probably would reach her in a separate shipment.

Three days later, still waiting for the radio, Miss Stedsen telephoned
Diemer again and was promised that the Adjustment Office would trace the
shipment immediately. On the following Monday she telephoned Diemer

once more and was told: "Mrs. Fuentes is the adjuster. She isn't here today. Please call tomorrow."

The next morning, this postal card message reached Miss Stedsen:

```
We have been trying to contact you by
telephone but have been unsuccessful. At
your convenience, please call me con-
cerning your adjustment request.

                               C. L. Fuentes
     555-0200, Ext. 1821   The Diemer Co., Inc.
```

Miss Stedsen phoned and was told: "Mrs. Fuentes is on vacation. I'll ring Mr. Harit's office for you." After having her call transferred, without satisfaction, to both Harit and another employee, Miss Stedsen asked the Diemer switchboard operator: "Who is your general manager?" She was given the name of S. J. Gantry, vice president of operations.

Disappointed by her attempts at telephone communication, Miss Stedsen wrote to Gantry, specifying the details of her experience and demanding a refund for the price of the undelivered radio. She severely criticized Diemer and its staff members. In her letter, Miss Stedsen explained that being elderly and afflicted with arthritis, she depended on the telephone and the mail for ordering special merchandise. Finally, she instructed Gantry to close her Diemer credit account.

After mailing the letter, Lucy Ann Stedsen returned to her apartment and found a Diemer Company box at her door. Inside the box, carefully wrapped, was the Companion radio.

INSIGHTS

Test your perception, interpretation, and understanding of collection messages.

1. What miscommunications occurred in this case? What were their causes? What were their consequences?
2. Which of Miss Stedsen's actions would you have taken? Why? In what ways would your actions have differed from hers? Why?
3. What are your recommendations for improving communication procedures of the Customer Service Office in this case?

NATURE'S WONDERS

The Customer Services and Collections departments have requested that you work in those areas. On this assignment you will demonstrate your knowledge of appropriate content, structure, and tone for customer correspondence.

CASE FACTS

To ensure customer satisfaction and promote prompt payment, Nature's Wonders has a generous product guarantee. The company will refund the price of or replace any bulbs or plants that do not grow to the customer's satisfaction. Management also insists that all customer correspondence be positive and reader-oriented.

YOUR TASKS

Your assignment is to demonstrate company policy and your communication skills in letters related to filling orders, adjusting accounts, and collecting overdue accounts.

1. Although Nature's Wonders mails its garden catalogs in January, some customers delay their orders until shortly before planting time. Compose a promotional letter to be mailed in February. In this letter refer to the catalog sent in January. Encourage early orders to assure that the customer will receive requested stock. Reinforce desire by emphasizing the company's guaranteed-to-grow policy. Use the simplified block letter format.

2. Unfortunately, the company is not always able to fill late orders. Compose a model message to be used when part or all of a customer's order cannot be filled. The objectives of the message are to inform, to suggest an alternate product, and to maintain goodwill.

3. Since Nature's Wonders works hard to ensure customer satisfaction, most customers settle their accounts promptly. How-

ever, the company must encourage some customers to pay. Write a series of three collection letters: (a) reminder, (b) stronger reminder, and (c) discussion stages. Each letter must be positive and customer-oriented, yet the request for payment must be progressively more insistent.

VISUAL AND ORAL MEDIA

Part 3 illustrated practical applications of communication by objectives for inquiring, informing, persuading, and gaining goodwill. You learned to plan every aspect of the message—content, data organization, tone, and format—to reflect empathy with the receiver.

Studying the memos and letters illustrated in Part 3 may leave the impression that business is conducted primarily through written messages. Many written messages, however, are enhanced by visual aids. Moreover, many business activities depend on nonwritten communication. Oral instructions, telephone transactions, meetings, presentations—these are daily business events. Each requires that you possess verbal and nonverbal communication skills.

Part 4 introduces you to such skills. Chapter 14 presents guides for construction and use of visual aids to accompany your verbal messages. Chapter 15 examines physiological, psychological, and nonverbal aspects of oral communication. That chapter also unites concepts concerning oral communication and effective use of visual aids.

14

COMMUNICATING WITH VISUAL AIDS

CHAPTER OUTLINE

OBJECTIVES

After completing this chapter, you should be able to:

1. Select visual aids that are appropriate for the data to be displayed.

2. Construct visual aids that effectively clarify, emphasize, or condense data.
3. Integrate visual aids into the report by introducing, displaying, and discussing each aid.

DECISIONS CASE

"Today I'll convince you that we should buy a Model BC729 copier from Scribex," Maria declared as she opened her presentation to the vice president and assistant vice president for administration. Maria felt confident they would agree with her recommendation. It was supported by extensive analysis of objective data. As she continued with her presentation—copy volume, comparative costs and benefits of various copiers, suppliers' reputations and service records—Maria's confidence waned. She noticed her audience looking at the clock, shifting in their chairs, or staring into space.

When the presentation ended, the VP thanked Maria routinely for the report. Maria had hoped for some enthusiasm.

"What more could I have done?" she asks you. "I collected relevant data and analyzed them thoroughly. I wrote and rewrote my report. I rehearsed that oral presentation. I even used a table to display some of the data."

Based on your experience as a report receiver, what advice do you have for Maria?

Additional questions about this decision-making case are stated at the end of this chapter. Study the chapter before answering those questions.

CHAPTER CONTEXT

Modern business communicators use nonverbal media to increase the effectiveness of their verbal messages. Appearance, timing, distance, body movement, etc., influence oral communication. Similarly, paper quality and format complement or detract from the words of a written message. In addition, business communicators frequently use visual aids such as tables, charts, pictures, or diagrams to improve communication effectiveness.

PURPOSE OF VISUAL AIDS

Effective visual aids increase understanding and retention of message content. **Visual aids** (also called *visuals, graphic aids,* or *graphics*) clarify complex data, emphasize points that deserve special attention, or condense voluminous data. Graphics may also be used to provide contrast or visual appeal in a document—a satisfying break from a mass of words.

PLANNING AND CONSTRUCTING VISUAL AIDS

Visual aids work if, as part of the communication-by-objectives approach, they are used purposefully. You must choose a table, graph, chart, or other illustration for its ability to provide the specific clarity, emphasis, condensation, or contrast you desire.

General Guides for Effective Visual Aids

For each visual aid, you must make decisions related to appearance, placement, identification, headnotes, source acknowledgments, and footnotes. The following general guides will help you make effective decisions.

Appearance. A visual aid should appeal to the eye. As a general rule, simple aids are more effective than complex, cluttered ones. To focus your reader's attention, include only essential information. Identify all variables clearly. Use color, shading, column headings, etc., as communication cues.

Placement. If a visual aid is to clarify, support, or emphasize the narrative, it must be integrated into that narrative. An effective integrating strategy is *introduce, display, discuss*.

How and why should visuals be integrated into the narrative?

Introduce the visual aid by referring to pertinent information transmitted by the aid. To enhance understanding, emphasize the *content* of the aid rather than the *device* itself. Key your visual aids to the report narrative. An introductory statement about the content lets you make a subordinate or parenthetical reference to the aid, as shown in the following example.

> Although the average weekly earnings of nonfarm workers rose rapidly from 1978 to 1988, the purchasing power of those workers was unchanged (Figure 2).

If space permits, display the visual aid immediately after the introductory statement. In written messages, avoid unnecessary division of an aid. If an aid cannot be placed on the page containing the introductory statement, place it at the top of the next page. Insert a full-page visual aid on the page following your first reference to the graphic.

Provide enough interpretive discussion to help viewers understand the content of the graphic. Remember that the illustration is an *aid* to understanding; do not assume that your viewers will extract the information you want them to receive. Let the visual aid complement, not substitute for, your words.

Applications of the introduce-display-discuss strategy in written reports are sketched in Illustration 14–1. That strategy is demonstrated in the comprehensive report presented in Chapter 20.

Some writers place all visual aids in a report appendix. That practice is discouraged since it requires the reader to leaf through the appendix to find the illustration. A visual aid may be placed in an appendix if it presents supplementary data or if you refer to the aid in several segments of the document. However, if you must cite a single aid frequently, consider displaying its content in several less comprehensive forms. Those visuals can then be incorporated appropriately into the narrative.

Identification. For easy reference and communication clarity, visual aids are often identified by number and title. A title summarizes the content of the visual aid. A title should contain the relevant *who, what, why, when, where* data whenever possible.

A **table** is a columnar arrangement of words and numbers. If more than one table is used, the title is preceded by the word *Table* and an appropriate number. When your document contains more than one chapter, you may number tables sequentially throughout the document (Table 1, Table 2, etc.); or you may number tables sequentially by chapters (Table 1–1, Table 1–2, Table 2–1, Table 2–2, etc.). Although Roman numerals are acceptable, today's trend is to use Arabic numerals.

All visual aids other than tables may be referred to as **figures** or **illustrations**. If more than one of those visuals are used, the title is preceded by the word *Figure* or *Illustration* and an appropriate Arabic numeral (1, 2, etc.; or 1–1, 1–2, 2–1, etc.).

Traditionally, identification of a visual aid is shown at the top of tables and at the bottom of figures. Current practice, however, permits identification at either the top or the bottom of tables and figures. The number and title may be centered or placed to begin at the left margin of the graphic. Several identification styles are demonstrated in Illustrations 14–2 through 14–15. For visual appeal, be consistent. Use the identification style you or your superiors prefer for all tables and all figures in a single message.

Headnote. Information required for accurate interpretation of the entire visual aid is placed in parentheses below the title (or subtitle, if used). Units of measurement (e.g., in thousands) or index bases (e.g., 1960 = 100) are examples of information placed in headnotes.

Source Acknowledgment. Acknowledging data sources establishes your credibility as a communicator. Source acknowledgments are customarily placed

---

Sidebar margin notes:

Why and how should visuals be identified?

What is a headnote?

Illustration 14–1   INCORPORATING VISUAL AIDS INTO WRITTEN REPORTS

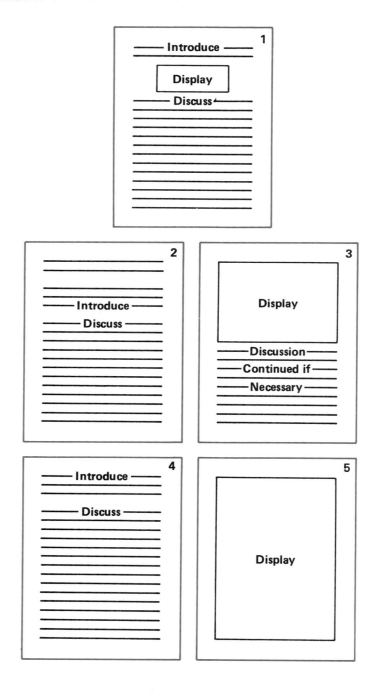

Why and how are
data sources
identified?

at the bottom of visual aids, with the word *Source* introducing the acknowledgment. An alternative placement is below the title. If the data source has been identified clearly in the report text, the source notation may be omitted from the visual aid.

If the data source is a book or other publication, identify it as for a footnote. For common business references, a simplified source notation is adequate. The following styles are acceptable in business writing.

Source: J. A. Lee, *Business Tomorrow* (New York: S–W Books, 1991), p. 40.

Source: *Statistical Abstract of the United States,* 1990, p. 429.

Source: Company annual reports

If the data are from a primary source that has been fully identified in your narrative, the source notation may be omitted or indicated by a brief notation (e.g., Source: Primary). For primary data sources that are not identified in the narrative, the following procedures are recommended:

1. If the data source is your personal observation, give the circumstances, location(s), and date(s) of the observation.

    Source: Personal, on-site observation, West Shopping Mall, Atlanta, Georgia, 12 p.m. – 2 p.m. and 5 p.m. – 7 p.m., May 8–9, 19—

2. For conversations, speeches, and the like, also give circumstances, location(s), and date(s).

    Source: Keynote address by W. P. Morris, National Convention of Business Communicators, Bergdorf Civic Center, Chicago, July 21, 19—

3. For interview surveys, give the name of the survey, the location(s), and the date(s).

    Source: MGA Marketing Survey, 335 face-to-face interviews, Lawson's Supermarket, Westmont Shopping Mall, Bridgeport, CT, March 12–15, 19—

    Source: MGA Marketing Survey, 355 telephone interviews, Greater Bridgeport Area, CT, March 12–15, 19—

4. For questionnaire surveys, give the name of the survey, distribution date(s) and area(s), and collection date(s).

Source: Lohre and Lee Questionnaire Survey; 4,500 questionnaires mailed to residents of Stimmons County, NJ, February 29. 19—; 1,112 usable returns by due date of March 10, 19—

Footnotes. When any part of a visual aid requires explanation, place a footnote below the source notation and key it with an asterisk or superscript to the item being explained.

The general guides for appearance, placement, identification, source acknowledgment, and footnoting are incorporated into the illustrations in this chapter.

Specific Guides for Effective Visual Aids

The following guides will help you construct effective tables, charts, and other visual aids.

Tables. Tables are used to compare exact numbers within and among categories. To construct tables that communicate effectively, familiarize yourself with the special parts that are identified in Illustration 14–2. Whereas a *stub* identifies information in a row (horizontal plane), a *column head* identifies data in a column (vertical plane). A *stub head* describes the stubs, and a *spanner head* describes the column heads. The information appearing in the columns and rows of the table is the *field* or *body*.

Informal tables (brief tabulations) may be inserted into the report text, without number or title. The following examples illustrate appropriate techniques for use of informal tables:

The major reasons given by new customers for opening a checking account with C&B Bank are:

Location	60.2%
Availability of automatic teller machines	15.1%
Referral by another customer	10.5%
Distinctive services	5.1%
Favorable hours	4.9%
Other	4.2%

The National Automobile Theft Bureau reported that Newark, New Jersey's 1988 auto theft rate was the highest among cities of over 50,000 population. The five cities with the highest theft rates were:[1]

What are the parts of a table?

In what ways are formal and informal tables similar? dissimilar?

---

[1]*Insurance Review,* January 1990.

Illustration 14–2   FORMAL TABLE

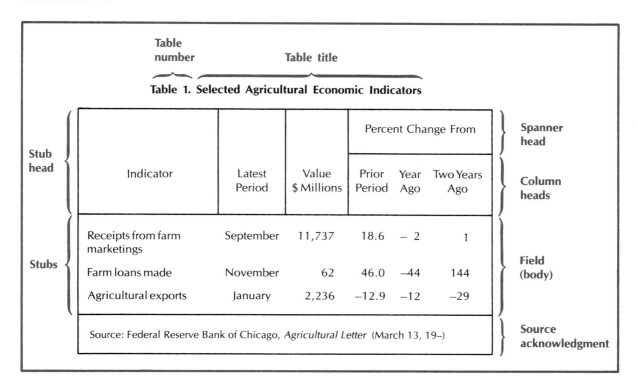

Table number

Table title

Table 1. Selected Agricultural Economic Indicators

| Indicator | Latest Period | Value $ Millions | Percent Change From | | |
			Prior Period	Year Ago	Two Years Ago
Receipts from farm marketings	September	11,737	18.6	– 2	1
Farm loans made	November	62	46.0	–44	144
Agricultural exports	January	2,236	–12.9	–12	–29

Source: Federal Reserve Bank of Chicago, *Agricultural Letter* (March 13, 19–)

Stub head

Stubs

Spanner head

Column heads

Field (body)

Source acknowledgment

City	Thefts per 100,000 Population
Newark, NJ	4,561
Irvington, NJ	3,493
East Orange, NJ	3,009
Camden, NJ	2,937
Boston, MA	2,879

In what ways are various line charts similar? dissimilar?

Line Charts. When you want to show changes over time in a continuous series of data, a line chart is more dramatic than a table. A **simple line chart** (Illustration 14–3) illustrates the movement of one variable; a **multiple line chart** (Illustration 14–4) shows changes in more than one variable. These guides for preparing line charts are demonstrated in Illustrations 14–3 through 14–6:

Illustration 14–3   SIMPLE LINE CHART

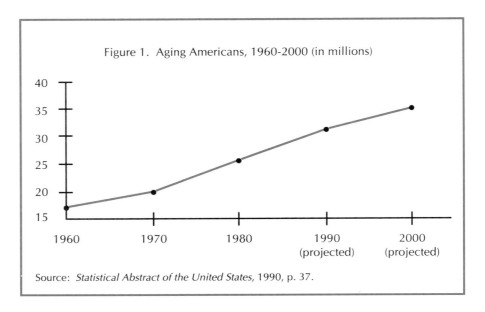

Figure 1. Aging Americans, 1960-2000 (in millions)

Source: *Statistical Abstract of the United States,* 1990, p. 37.

1. Place time on the horizontal (*X*) axis. Identify time spans clearly.
2. Place unit of measurement on the vertical (*Y*) axis. Identify measurement unit clearly.
3. For an arithmetic progression, begin the Y axis at 0. The axis may be broken if the break does not distort the data. (See Illustration 14−4.)
4. Use color, broken lines, etc., to differentiate variables. Place identifying captions inside the boundaries of the chart.

A **bilateral line chart** (Illustration 14−5) demonstrates movement of a data series relative to a base point. Both positive and negative values appear on the vertical axis of such a chart, which may show percentages or quantities.

The **belt chart** (also called *component-parts line chart*) illustrates the progression of a total and the parts comprising the total. Determine plot points for such a chart by adding each component quantity to the sum of the quantities already plotted. For example, the plot points for the first year shown in Illustration 14−6 were computed as follows:

Parts & Accessories	14,004	*plot point*
add Trucks & Buses (new)	+ 2,789	
	16,793	*plot point*
add Passenger Cars (new)	+ 6,027	
Total	22,820	*plot point*

Illustration 14–4   MULTIPLE LINE CHART

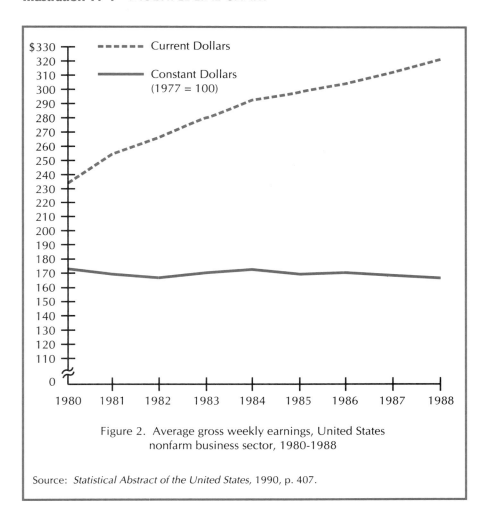

Figure 2. Average gross weekly earnings, United States
nonfarm business sector, 1980-1988

Source: *Statistical Abstract of the United States,* 1990, p. 407.

How do bar charts
differ from line
charts?

Bar Charts. Bar charts facilitate comparison of discrete (discontinuous) data. Bars may be placed vertically or horizontally.

The **simple bar chart** compares identified factors (geographic units, salespersons, years, etc.) on one dimension (Illustration 14–7), whereas a **multiple bar chart** (Illustration 14–8) compares factors on more than one dimension. To avoid confusion, many reporters restrict multiple bar charts to no more than four dimensions.

Other variations of the bar chart are the bilateral bar chart and the subdivided bar chart. Similar to the bilateral line chart, the **bilateral bar chart**

Illustration 14–5   BILATERAL LINE CHART

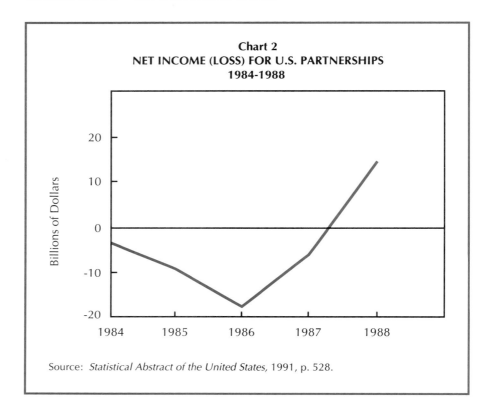

Chart 2
NET INCOME (LOSS) FOR U.S. PARTNERSHIPS
1984-1988

Source: *Statistical Abstract of the United States,* 1991, p. 528.

shows positive or negative deviations from a fixed reference point. (See Illustration 14–9.) **A subdivided bar chart** illustrates components of variables being compared. Those components may be shown as parts comprising a total (Illustration 14–10) or as percentage breakdowns (Illustration 14–11).

Shading or color distinguishes the variables or segments in bar charts. Place the identifying caption (legend) within the boundaries of the chart.

What are appropriate and inappropriate uses of pie charts?

Pie Charts. Pie charts dramatize percentage components of a single factor. (See Illustration 14–12.) To avoid distorting the data, observe these guides as you construct pie charts:

1.   Place the segment you most want to emphasize at the top of the pie or begin it at the "twelve o'clock" position. Viewers in Western cul-

Illustration 14–6   BELT CHART

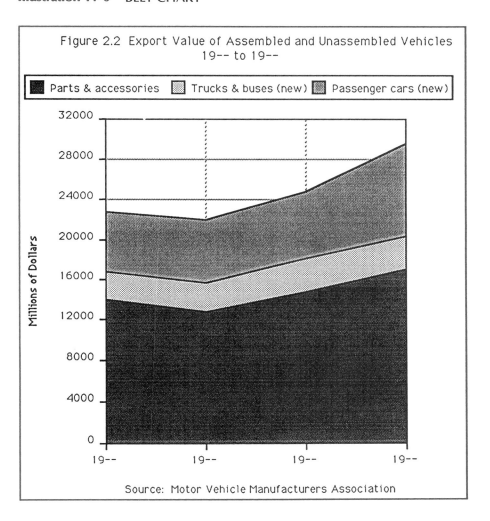

Figure 2.2 Export Value of Assembled and Unassembled Vehicles 19-- to 19--

Source: Motor Vehicle Manufacturers Association

tures tend to read a pie chart in a clockwise direction; hence, they will note first the item in the top or twelve o'clock position.

2. Arrange subsequent items clockwise in the desired order of emphasis, usually in large-to-small sequence.
3. Identify each segment and the percentage it represents.
4. Be sure all segments total 100 percent.
5. Avoid comparing two items with different-sized pie charts (e.g., 1950 and 1990 national debts). Viewers are rarely able to perceive the exact comparisons intended.

For emphasis, you may "explode" (pull out) one section of the pie, as was done for the lower chart in Illustration 14–12. The exploding technique is most effective when used sparingly. Avoid exploding two contiguous segments of a pie.

Other Visual Aids. Creative communicators reach beyond traditional tables and charts to clarify or emphasize their report messages. **Diagrams, drawings,** or **flow charts** may simplify complicated procedures or instructions. **Pictograms** are variations of bar charts which employ images of items compared (e.g., coins, people, automobiles) instead of bars. **Statistical maps** can effectively dramatize differences among geographic regions with respect to the variable being considered. **Pictures** of products, employees, facilities, or production processes add a personal touch or a sense of reality to reports. Examples of miscellaneous visual aids appear in Illustrations 14–13 through 14–15.

Illustration 14–7   SIMPLE BAR CHART

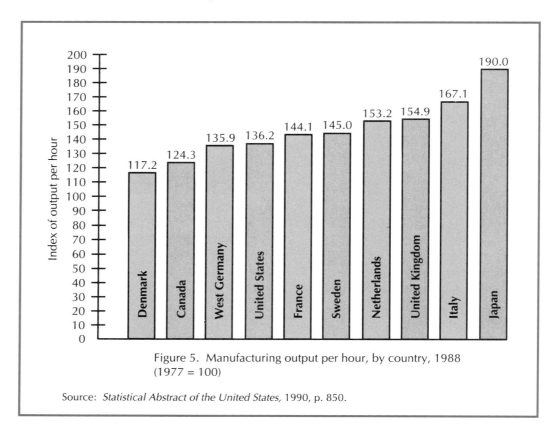

Figure 5. Manufacturing output per hour, by country, 1988 (1977 = 100)

Source: *Statistical Abstract of the United States,* 1990, p. 850.

Illustration 14-8   MULTIPLE BAR CHART

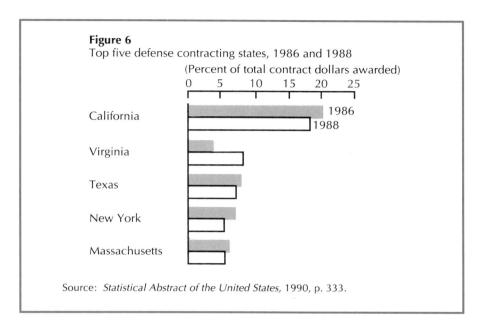

Figure 6
Top five defense contracting states, 1986 and 1988
(Percent of total contract dollars awarded)

Source: *Statistical Abstract of the United States,* 1990, p. 333.

Illustration 14-9   BILATERAL BAR CHART

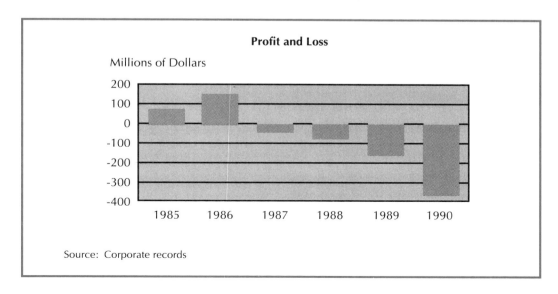

Profit and Loss

Millions of Dollars

Source: Corporate records

Illustration 14-10   SUBDIVIDED BAR CHART—QUANTITIES

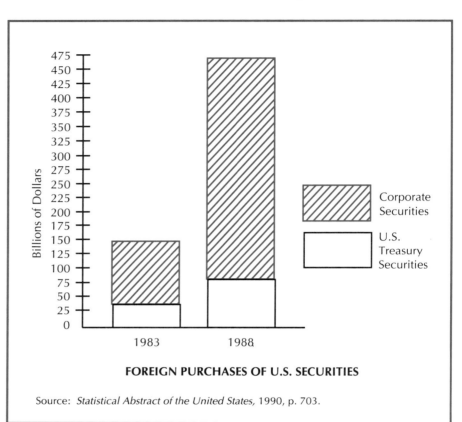

FOREIGN PURCHASES OF U.S. SECURITIES

Source: *Statistical Abstract of the United States,* 1990, p. 703.

COMPUTER GRAPHICS

Through advances in electronic technology, attractive—and unattractive—graphics can be generated quickly by computer. Although **computer graphics** (the term used for this aspect of computer technology) can facilitate graphics construction, the decision about what visual aid best serves your interests still rests with *you,* the message originator. Defining your objective—what you hope to accomplish—for each graphic aid will become increasingly important as you use computer resources.

Whether constructed manually or by computer, visual aids must be simple, complete, readable, and uncluttered. Evaluate your computer output on those criteria. An example of a computer-generated belt chart appeared in Illustra-

Illustration 14-11 SUBDIVIDED BAR CHART—PERCENTAGES

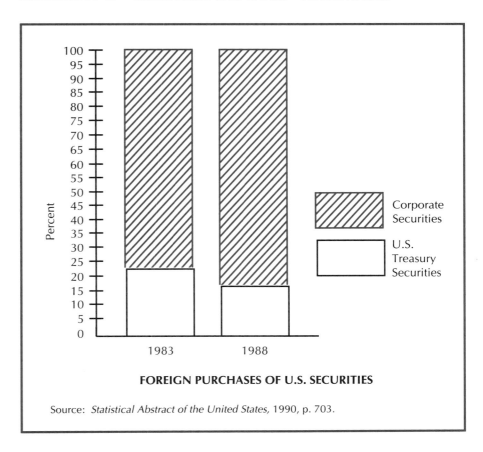

FOREIGN PURCHASES OF U.S. SECURITIES

Source: *Statistical Abstract of the United States,* 1990, p. 703.

tion 14-6. The software used to produce that chart permits full identification of the data: title, variables, plot values, and source notation. This software produces attractive, legible charts on a laser printer.

The same software was used for the pie charts in Illustration 14-12. Since the software does not accommodate text at the bottom of a pie chart, the writer must decide whether to omit the source notation or to place it below the title.

As a user of computer graphics, you must make several choices. You must first choose the graphic form that best displays your data, and you must then choose the graphics features that enhance rather than detract from your display. The quality of your graphics depends on the quality of your choices. Compare the following examples of ineffective and effective choices.

Ineffective: Pie chart incorrectly used to display discontinuous data; nearly illegible title.

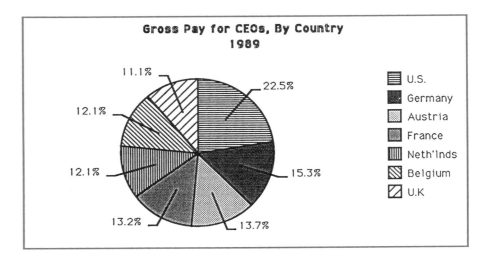

Effective: Bar chart correctly used for discontinuous data; easy-to-read labels; proportionate dimensions.

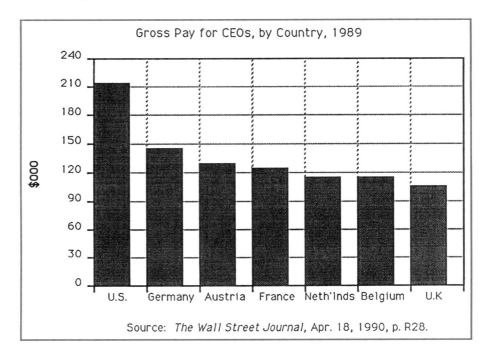

Ineffective: Bar chart with too many variables, difficult-to-read labels.

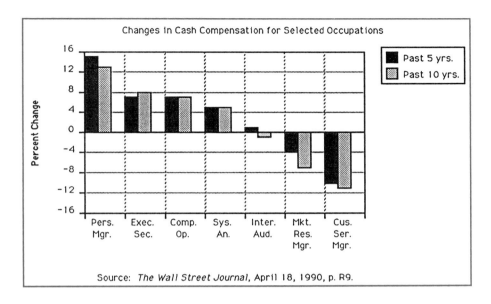

Effective: Bar chart for limited number of discontinuous variables; easy-to read title and labels.

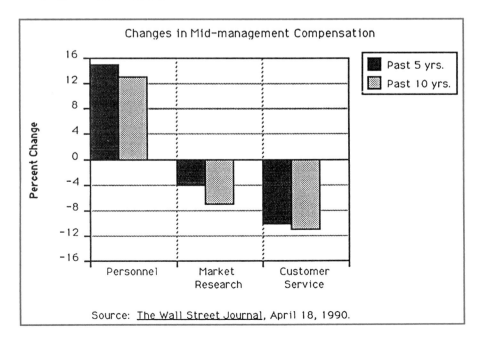

Illustration 14–12   PIE CHARTS

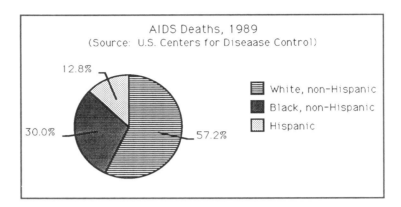

AIDS Deaths, 1989
(Source: U.S. Centers for Diseaase Control)

12.8%

White, non-Hispanic
Black, non-Hispanic
Hispanic

30.0%   57.2%

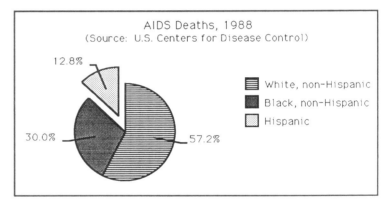

AIDS Deaths, 1988
(Source: U.S. Centers for Disease Control)

12.8%

White, non-Hispanic
Black, non-Hispanic
Hispanic

30.0%   57.2%

REVIEW AND TRANSITION

Effective business communicators select visual aids to complement communication objectives. Visual aids clarify, condense, or emphasize data. They also supply pleasing visual contrast for the receiver.

The most common visual aids and their appropriate uses are:

► *Tables*—compare exact data within and across categories
► *Line charts*—show movement of one or more continuous variables over time
► *Bar charts*—compare one or more discontinuous (discrete) variables
► *Pie charts*—show percentage components of an item

Other aids that clarify or dramatize data are diagrams, pictograms, drawings, flowcharts, maps, and pictures.

Illustration 14–13   STATISTICAL MAP

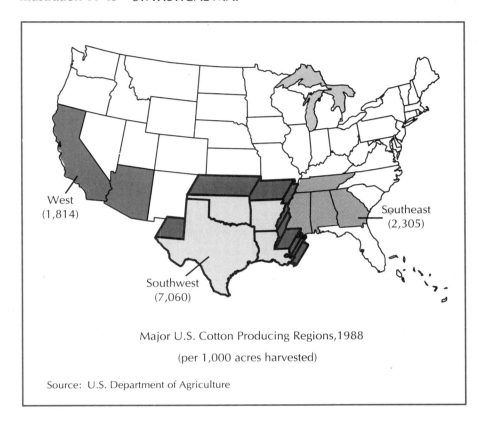

Major U.S. Cotton Producing Regions,1988

(per 1,000 acres harvested)

Source: U.S. Department of Agriculture

Effective use of computer graphics requires the user to define the desired objective for each computer-generated visual aid and to evaluate software and printer options.

You will have an opportunity to apply your knowledge of visual aids as you prepare audiovisual presentations (Chapter 15) and written reports (Chapters 19 and 20).

YOUR DECISIONS FOR CHAPTER 14

Did your advice to Maria include suggestions about using visual aids? What visual aids, other than a table, could have improved the presentation?

DISCUSSION QUESTIONS

A.   Within the context of Chapter 14, what are appropriate definitions and examples for these terms?

Illustration 14–14 GANTT CHART: TIME FRAME FOR CONSTRUCTION PHASES

SOUTHFIELD OFFICE BUILDING

Item	June	July	August	Sept.	Oct.	Nov.	Dec.	Jan.	Feb.	March	April
	4 11 18 25	2 9 16 23 30	6 13 20 27	3 10 17 24	1 8 15 22 29	5 12 19 26	3 10 17 24 31	7 14 21 28	5 12 19 26	4 11 18 25	1 8 15 22 29
Building Excavation											
Conc. Ftg & Fdn. Wall											
Structural Steel											
Metal Decking											
Conc. Lower Floor											
Conc. First Floor											
Conc. Second Floor											
Sprayed on Fireproofing											
Conc. Roof Deck											
Exterior Masonry											
Interior Masonry											
Roofing and Sheetmetal											
Aluminum Windows & Ent.											
Wall Finish Lower Floor											
Wall Finish First Floor											
Wall Finish Second Floor											
Acoustic Ceilings											
Hydraulic Elevator											
Rough in First Floor											
Rough in Second Floor											
Ductwork – Lower Floor											
Ductwork – First Floor											
Ductwork – Second Floor											
Plumbing Fixtures											
Mechanical Room Equipment											
Underground Conduit											
First Floor Conduit											
Second Floor Conduit											
Feeders											
Branch Circuits – Lower											
Branch Circuits – First											
Branch Circuits – Second											
Lighting – Lower											
Lighting – First											
Lighting – Second											
Switchgear & Trans.											

Illustration 14–15 PICTOGRAM

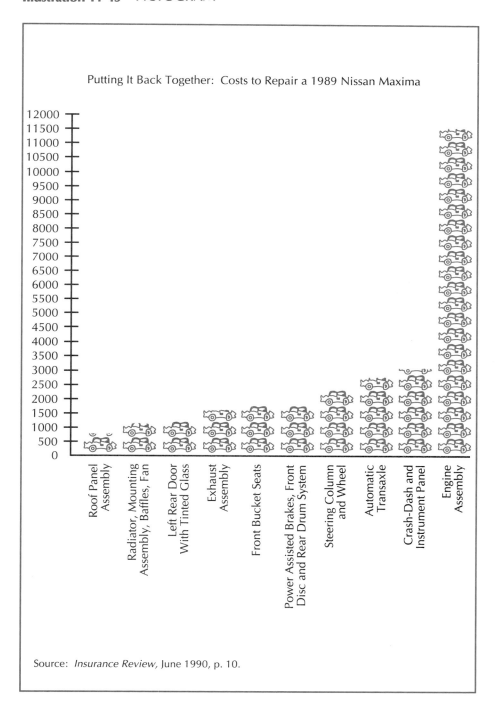

Putting It Back Together: Costs to Repair a 1989 Nissan Maxima

Source: *Insurance Review,* June 1990, p. 10.

1. visual aid
2. headnote
3. table
4. line chart
5. bar chart
6. pie chart

B. How does an informal table differ from a formal table?

C. How does a simple line chart differ from a simple bar chart?

D. How does a belt chart differ from a multiple line chart?

E. What circumstance requires the use of a bilateral line chart instead of a simple line chart?

F. What are computer graphics?

APPLICATIONS

1. Select two visual aids from a current newspaper or magazine. Using the information presented in Chapter 14, compare their effectiveness. Present your evaluation orally or in a memo to your instructor.

2. Examine a corporate annual report. Write a memo to your instructor assessing the effectiveness of the visual aids used in the report. Include recommendations for changing, adding, or deleting specific visual aids.

3. Construct an appropriate visual aid for each of these sets of data. Justify your choice.

   a. U.S. residents below poverty level, 1988

	1988	
Race	Number (1,000s)	Percent
White	21,409	65.8
Black	9,683	29.8
Other	1,454	4.5

   Source: *Statistical Abstract of the United States,* 1990, p. 38.

   b. Annual rate of return on Standard & Poor common stocks, 1981 through 1987.

   1981: -4.9%   1985: 32.2%
   1982: 21.4%   1986: 18.5%
   1983: 22.5%   1987: 5.2%
   1984: 6.3%

   Source: *Cross Sections,* vol. 6, no. 3 (Fall 1989), p. 3.

c. U.S. Labor Force Distribution, 1988:

Managerial and professional: 25.4%
Technical, sales, and administrative support: 30.9%
Service occupations: 13.3%
Precision production, craft, and repair: 11.9%
Operators, fabricators, and laborers: 15.5%
Farming, forestry, and fishing: 3.0%

Source: U.S. Bureau of Labor Statistics, *Employment and Earnings*, January 1989.

d. Changes in Department of Defense payroll for major defense contracting states, 1987 and 1988:

State	% Change 1986 to 1987	% Change 1987 to 1988
California	1.0	2.9
Virginia	3.2	6.6
Texas	5.6	.3
Florida	26.4	−17.5
North Carolina	6.1	9.9
Georgia	2.7	−0.7
Maryland	3.3	−1.3

Source: *Statistical Abstract of the United States*, 1990, p. 333.

e. Credit card debt, 1980, 1985, and 1988 (billions of dollars):

	1980	1985	1988
Bank	25.0	65.6	113.5
Travel and entertainment	2.7	6.4	12.3
Retail store	47.3	50.5	41.8
Oil company	2.2	2.7	2.5
Other*	4.0	2.8	9.9

*Includes airline, automobile rental, telephone company, hotel, motel, and other
miscellaneous credit cards
Source: *Statistical Abstract of the United States*, 1990, p. 506.

f. Pollution abatement and control expenditures, 1975–1985

Kinds of expenditures	Amounts (millions of dollars)		
	1975	1980	1985
Pollution abatement	28,420	50,491	70,945
Regulation and monitoring	653	1,296	1,279
Research and development	1,104	1,751	2,412

Source: *Statistical Abstract of the United States*, 1990, p. 207.

g.   U.S. family structures, 1988

Family Unit	Percent
Married couple, no children	41.7
Married couple, with own children	37.8
Female householder, no spouse present, no children	6.7
Female householder, no spouse present, with own children	9.6
Male householder, no spouse present, no children	2.6
Male householder, no spouse present, with own children	1.6

Source: *Statistical Abstract of the United States,* 1990, p. 38.

h.   Distribution of contributions to United Way of the Midlands

Expenditure	Percent
Health and rehabilitation	20
Family services	18
Youth services	16
Education, job training, placement	10
Disaster relief, safety, crime prevention	11
Volunteer & social service coordination	11
Food & shelter	9
Fundraising costs	5

Source: United Way of the Midlands, 1991.

4.   Select one of the visual aids for Application 3. In a memo to your instructor, interpret the data. Use the introduce-display-discuss technique.

5.   In a memo to your instructor, discuss the following data. Include at least one visual aid in the memo.

Fastest growing and fastest declining occupations, 1988 to 2000
(Based on low and high trend assumptions)

Occupations	Projected percent change, 1988-2000	
	Lo	Hi
Fastest growing		
Medical assistants	60	74
Home health aides	58	73
Radiologic technologists and technicians	57	70
Medical secretaries	49	61
Securities and financial services sales workers	45	63
Travel agents	43	66
Fastest declining		
Electrical and electronic assemblers	-50	-39
Farmers	-30	-18

Stenographers	-27	-18
Telephone and cable TV line installers and repairers	-25	-16
Sewing machine operators, garment	-21	-9
Crushing and mixing machine operators and tenders	-21	-7

Source: *Statistical Abstract of the United States*, 1990, p. 392.

6. Construct two different visual aids to display all or some of the following data. In a memo to your instructor, explain which of the two would be better for a written report. Justify your choice by including your assumptions about the report's purpose and audience. Attach both visual aids to your memo.

Foreign (nonimmigrant) student enrollment in U.S. institutions of higher education, by region of origin and field of study, 1980 and 1988:

Region	Enrollment (1,000)		Percent enrolled in					
			Engineering		Science		Business	
	1980	1988	1980	1988	1980	1988	1980	1988
Africa	36	28	20	15	9	7	19	19
Asia	165	224	32	25	8	10	16	18
Europe	23	39	15	12	9	9	14	18
Latin America	42	45	20	14	8	6	14	17
North America	16	16	8	9	6	7	13	16
Oceania	4	4	5	6	7	4	16	20

Source: *Statistical Abstract of the United States*, 1990, p. 155.

7. In a memo to your instructor, discuss the following data. Include at least one visual aid in the memo.

Percent of cardiologists who do the following things to avoid heart disease:

Don't smoke	97.5
Know their cholesterol level	96.0
Have changed diet to reduce cholesterol	72.2
Limit intake of salt	69.7
Work out at least 20 minutes, 3 times per week	63.4
Have taken treadmill test	61.6
Take aspirin at least once every other day	40.6
Eat oat bran	33.8

Source: Survey of 400 cardiologists reported in *The Wall Street Journal*, May 11, 1990, p. R27.

MULTICULTURAL INSIGHTS

1. Based on your experience and observation, describe the use of visual aids for messages presented in your native language. How does that practice resemble or differ from uses described in Chapter 14?

2. What characteristics of your native language, if any, would increase or decrease the need for visual aids in oral or written messages?

3. Present a visual aid constructed in your native language. Explain the aid orally to your classmates.

ORAL COMMUNICATION IN BUSINESS

OBJECTIVES

After completing this chapter, you should be able to:

1. Appreciate and begin to control the physiological, psychological, and metacommunication aspects of effective speech.
2. Participate effectively in business conversations and interviews.
3. Construct and deliver business presentations that meet speaker's and listener's needs.
4. Participate in or assist others with these special communication modes: audiovisual, group, and videotaped presentations; question-answer sessions; statements to the media; speechwriting.

DECISIONS CASE

"I'm worried about this presentation," says your coworker Andre. "We worked hard on that project—objective data, comprehensive analysis—and the written report was clear and convincing. Ms. Luciano was satisfied. Now she wants us to present our findings and recommendations to the division managers next week. What are we going to do? Who will be responsible for what? What if they ask questions after our presentation—or worse yet, what if they interrupt to ask a question during the presentation?"

"Relax," you say. "We can handle it. Let me make some suggestions."
How will you relieve your friend's fears?

Additional questions about this decision-making case are stated at the end of this chapter. Study the chapter before answering those questions.

CHAPTER CONTEXT

Oral communication involves much more than uttering words. Picture yourself arriving at your office or plant. Your coworkers greet you. Your supervisor asks about a revised production procedure. Your secretary reminds you of an important meeting. A customer telephones you. You participate in a decision-making conference. You are interviewed by a local reporter. These circumstances are typical of your need to communicate orally.

"So what?" you say. "I've been talking for years, and talk is easy." You are right; talk is easy. *Talk* is casual, largely undirected, often expressive; but communication transcends expression. Many people talk. In business, however, you need to *speak*—intelligently, clearly, informatively, and persuasively. A classic study of how executives spend their time revealed that American business leaders spend an average of 78 percent of their working day in oral communication.[1] Business clearly needs employees who use this medium effectively.

THE SPEECH PROCESS

What is oral communication? How is speaking related to you and to your career? How do breaths become messages? Unless you appreciate and apply the answers to those questions, you risk misusing a remarkable instrument of personal fulfillment and of business success. Effective speakers skillfully control the physiological, psychological, and metacommunication aspects of speech.

Physiological Aspects

To communicate orally, you produce sounds that stand for meanings. Production of these sounds involves four physiological phases: inhalation, phonation, resonation, modification. Understanding these phases can help you consciously to control and improve your oral communication.

---

[1]Henry Mintzberg, "The Manager's Job: Folklore and Fact," *Harvard Business Review,* July-August 1975, pp. 49–61.

Inhalation. To obtain the raw material of speech, you introduce air through your nostrils and your mouth. That air proceeds to your lungs where it is temporarily stored in tiny sacs called **alveoli**, which function as reservoirs. Consciously or unconsciously, you cause your stomach muscles and your diaphragm to act so that the air moves out of the alveoli. (See Illustration 15–1.)

Phonation. Moving upward along its escape route, the air that has become your breath passes through your **larynx** (voice box). The larynx contains two

Illustration 15–1   THE ORGANS OF SPEECH

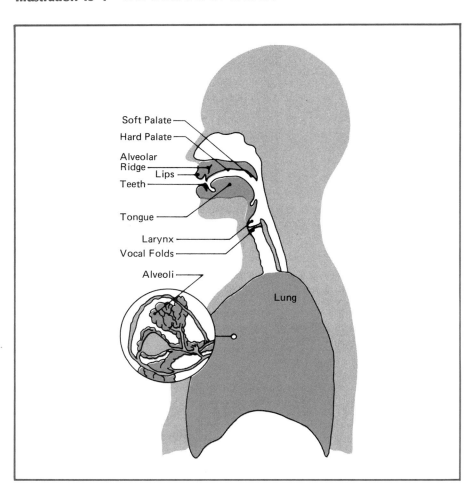

What is the function
of each phase?

membranous surfaces, the vocal folds, which impart **pitch** (highness or low-ness of sound) to your breath. When your vocal folds vibrate quickly, the pitch of your voice is high. When they vibrate slowly, your vocal pitch is low. Your breath thus becomes voice but not yet speech.

Resonation. Continuing its escape, the breath imbued with pitch moves into your head. The cavities of your nose, throat, and mouth amplify and enrich that breath, which reverberates within them. The greater the reverberation, the richer the **timbre** (quality or warmth) of your voice. In effect, your throat and head cavities act as natural echo chambers, or resonators, creating overtones that enhance your voice. You can control your use of these echo chambers. By swallowing to relax your throat muscles, by flaring your nostrils, or by slightly protruding your lips, you adjust the resonators to add warmth and richness.

Air has become breath in the alveoli of your lungs. Breath has become voice between the folds of your larynx. Voice has gained resonance in the cavities of your head. You have created sounds but not yet speech. Now you proceed to shape those sounds into spoken words that represent meanings.

Modification. You shape sounds into words with your lips (*w*ish, *wh*ere), your teeth (*f*riend, tele*ph*one), the ridge in back of your upper teeth (*h*ow, *wh*o), the hard palate above and behind the teeth ridge (*c*ool, *g*et), the soft palate extending in back of the hard palate (bri*ng*, thi*ng*), and your tongue acting with your teeth (*th*ere, *th*in) or acting with your teeth ridge (*t*o, *d*o). The speech sounds you produce are classified as vowels, diphthongs, and consonants. They are the elements of syllables, words, and phrases.[2]

The process of oral communication is especially remarkable. You transform air into breath. You give that breath pitch and resonance. Then, using lips that obtain your food, teeth that chew your food, a tongue that moves your food so that your body may be nourished, you speak. You use your body to transcend itself, to communicate. Surely this wonderful process merits your awareness, your appreciation, and your care.

Why should you be
aware of the speech
process?

People who habitually mumble or shout, who elocute without saying, who chatter without communicating may exhale noises; but they rarely speak. The rest of this chapter shows how you can master the *speech* process and use it to fulfill personal and business goals.

---

[2]Appendix F contains a list of words using the common vowels, diphthongs, and consonants of the English language. If you have difficulty enunciating certain American English words, say the listed words aloud until you recognize the spellings and pronunciations of the sounds.

Psychological Aspects

Oral communication is more than a physical process. It also has psychological aspects. Appropriate attention to those aspects can reduce **stage fright**, the tension and apprehension felt by many speakers, whether in conversation or during a public presentation.

Stage fright is often nothing more than a speaker's misdirected awareness. For example, when you speak with your supervisor, participate in a meeting, or address a group, you may sense a nervousness, a tensing of your muscles, a quavering of your voice. Such signs usually indicate that you are directing your attention excessively to yourself instead of to your message and its receivers.

What is stage fright?

The first step in overcoming fear of oral communication is to justify that communication. The effective business speaker, like the effective business writer, establishes definite reasons for exchanging messages. Those reasons involve answers to basic communication questions: What potential value does the oral message have for the speaker and for the listener? What results is the oral message likely to produce? Why does the communication merit the investment of time, money, and other resources? By determining appropriate need for your oral communication, you can begin building confidence in yourself as a business speaker.

These techniques can help you develop confidence:

How can you develop confidence?

1. Recognize why you are asked to speak. Whether you are invited to participate in a conversation or to address a large audience, you are asked to speak because your knowledge and opinions are respected.
2. Prepare yourself. Look for and use opportunities to speak—in school, on the job, in your community. These opportunities provide experience for improving your oral communication skills. Familiarize yourself with your listener's traits, needs, desires, and behaviors. Whether your audience is one person or a large group, determine the purpose of your oral communication. For a formal presentation, acquire a thorough understanding of the topic, organize your information carefully, and rehearse until you know the sequence for presenting that information. Adopt a positive attitude toward this preparatory work. Thorough preparation can be your most effective safeguard against stage fright.
3. Assume your audience is friendly. Expect empathy from your receivers. They are likely to be less critical of you than you are of yourself.
4. Review your performance. Whenever possible, review your oral communication with the aid of a constructive critic, a videotape recording, or both. You may be pleasantly surprised to learn that you appear less

nervous than you feel. After each review, concentrate on improving at least one specific aspect of your oral communication.

Metacommunication Aspects

Physiological and psychological aspects of oral communication are inseparable. Their interrelatedness is partially explained by metacommunication. Through metacommunication, communicators reveal perceptions of their relationships to one another.[3]

How is
metacommunication
related to oral
messages?

Metacommunication is sometimes oral, but most often it is accomplished through the many nonverbal, tonal, and contextual clues accompanying the verbal message. Compare the following messages, each spoken by a supervisor requesting a report from an assistant:

- ▶ "I need this report by 3 o'clock this afternoon. That's an order."
- ▶ "I need this report in ten minutes. Just kidding! Three o'clock will be fine."
- ▶ (Stern tone) "I need this report by three o'clock."
- ▶ (Cordial smile) "I need this report by three o'clock."

The basic message content is the same in each situation, but the verbal and nonverbal accompaniments say something about the relationship between the communicators. "That's an order" is not only a comment about the basic message, but also about the speaker's perception of a superior-subordinate relationship. Similarly, "just kidding," the stern tone, and the smile are metacommunications defining relationships.

When relationship is the central issue of a communication, denotations are often disregarded. For example, in a strong, positive relationship, an adult female may not object to being called "baby" by a male friend; but if the relationship weakens, she may interpret the word denotatively and resentfully.

Communication breakdowns often occur because people disagree at the relationship level even though no disagreement exists at the content level. Consider this example:

Boss to assistant: "Where is the Bruce file?"

Assistant to boss: "I'll get it immediately!"

---

[3]To refresh your knowledge of metacommunication, review the information about metacommunication and nonverbal communication that appeared in Chapters 1, 3, and 5.

The two may agree about the words and the boss's need for the file. But they could well disagree about their relationship. The boss's metacommunication, revealed through tone of voice or gestures, may be "you are an incompetent assistant. You don't provide timely support for my important work." The assistant's metacommunication may be "you are a demanding egotist. You won't condescend to open a file drawer even when I'm busy." The relationship may deteriorate and even be ended unless such people improve their metacommunications.

Effective oral communicators analyze their nonverbal behaviors and avoid those that detract from their verbal messages. For example, when you make an oral presentation, you must judge the audience's time expectations. If you use less than the expected time, the audience may question your credibility. If your message is longer than expected, your audience may become restless and inattentive.

As you develop your communication behaviors, observe nonverbal cues of other speakers. Notice, for example, that when a speaker is rooted rigidly to one spot for a long time, or rocks and swings constantly, you pay little attention to that speaker's words and much attention to the disconcerting behavior. If speakers habitually place their elbows or forearms on lecterns, those speakers seem to diminish their body heights; and diminished height tends to project diminished authority. If speakers slouch constantly, they nonverbally communicate feelings of fatigue or stress to their viewers. If speakers shuffle aimlessly, they suggest a lack of organization that viewers may attribute to a lack of logic in what is being said.

As we tend to be distracted by no movement or by too much movement of a speaker, so we may be distracted by too few or too many hand-and-arm gestures and facial expressions. But when gestures and facial expressions seem genuine rather than contrived, relevant to the message purpose, and integrated with the speaker's total body balance, nonverbal communication greatly enhances what is spoken.

As a business communicator you will use many languages—among them the languages of words, numbers, appearances, timings and distances, postures and movements, gestures, and facial expressions. Using complementary verbal and nonverbal languages will increase your communication effectiveness, whether in conversation or other forms of business communication.

BUSINESS CONVERSATION

Conversing designates relatively informal and impromptu speaking that may range from a friendly chat to a casual discussion. Business conversation includes face-to-face verbal exchange and telephone conversation.

Conversing Face to Face

How can you
stimulate
conversation?

Because it is usually spontaneous, conversing requires you to perceive and to interpret circumstances quickly. For proper relevance and timing of your remarks, you need to detect purposes and interests; to evaluate events, statements, and implications; to relate people, things, actions, and words. You may be expected to respond and to help direct the course of conversation by questions, explanations, descriptions, transitions, comparisons, or contrasts.

By using your listening and speaking skills and your knowledge of nonverbal behaviors, you can encourage reciprocal conversation that especially enhances social gatherings and business transactions. If timidity or unfamiliarity blocks conversation, you can introduce topics of common interest dealing with mutual friends or acquaintances, sports, travel, entertainment, or the like. When conversation lags, you can ask about the individual's interests, concerns, or attitudes toward current events. And you can respond to comments or reinforce your own remarks nonverbally as well as orally. A smile, a nod, or a gesture can be a potent stimulus to further conversation.

Conversing by Telephone

How is the *you*
attitude evidenced in
telephone
conversation?

Telephone conversation requires special awareness and care. When you speak with someone by telephone, visualize the person. Instead of talking at a disembodied voice, converse with a person. Successful telephone conversation demands empathy. When your phone rings, answer promptly and courteously. Although you may be busy at the moment, resist the temptation to snap "Hold on" or "Just a minute." Begin by identifying your office and yourself, thereby personalizing the communication and promoting rapport. Let the caller identify himself or herself. Then, if you must ask the caller to wait, do so pleasantly. When you resume the conversation, thank your caller for being patient.

Before you place a telephone call, gather pertinent correspondence, reports, or other references for the conversation. Have note-taking materials ready for your use. Give your party enough time to answer—approximately one minute. When your party answers, ask if this is a good time to call. If it isn't, determine when you should call back.

When you speak into a telephone, place the receiver against your ear and keep the mouthpiece about an inch from your lips. That is the distance recommended for a regular telephone handset. For a headset, the distance between lips and transmitter should be about half an inch. Speak clearly; neither shout nor whisper. Speak slowly enough to be understandable, rapidly enough to be interesting. Strive to be as brief as thoroughness permits. And when you are the one to end a conversation, do so courteously but definitely.

The communication interaction skills used in conversation are also useful in an interview.

BUSINESS INTERVIEWS

An **interview** is a conversation directed toward an objective other than the satisfaction derived from conversation itself. Although the interviewer may direct the conversation, an interview is most successful when it fosters interaction between interviewer and interviewee. Your business roles will provide opportunities for many kinds of interviews. These guides will help you perform effectively, whether as interviewer or interviewee.

Before the Interview

Why and how should you plan an interview?

Plan your interview carefully. Define the purpose, identify the information to be obtained or given to accomplish that purpose, and structure specific questions to elicit that information.

State the goal as specifically as possible. For example, the goal statement "to determine the Wilsons' readiness to buy a house" will focus a realtor-client interview more effectively than the general statement "to talk to the Wilsons about buying a house." Specific questions might be: "How long have you rented?" "What made you think of buying a house?" "Have you considered taxes and maintenance costs?" As you plan specific questions, anticipate possible answers from your interviewee and follow-up responses or questions that will keep the interview moving toward your goal.

As an interviewee you should also prepare. Try to determine the interviewer's objective and whether it complements or conflicts with your goals. Anticipate likely questions and appropriate responses from the interviewer as well as from yourself.

During the Interview

How can you foster an effective interview environment?

Your first task as an interviewer is to establish a positive, trusting communication environment. In most cases, trust can be established by identifying the purpose of the interview and how the data will be used. Most interviewees will cooperate when they feel that they are not being tricked into giving information, that their opinions are appreciated and respected, and that the questions are relevant to their objectives. A relaxed, attentive posture and appropriate eye contact (neither staring at nor avoiding the interviewee's gaze) also contribute to a comfortable interview environment.

You can keep the interview on track by listening attentively and observing nonverbal cues. Attempt to control your biases as you interpret and summarize the interviewee's responses. Rephrasing the question or probing for further information may be necessary if the interviewee does not answer adequately. When nonverbal cues contradict verbal responses, avoid jumping to conclusions. Instead, use additional questions and further observations to clarify the responses.

As an interviewee, you increase interview effectiveness by active listening. If you do not understand a question, ask the interviewer for restatement or clarification. Answer questions completely, but avoid volunteering additional information, unless you think the information is necessary to ensure that the interviewer interprets your response accurately. If you prefer not to answer a question, courteously inform the interviewer and encourage progression to another question.

After the Interview

To improve your interviewing skills, evaluate each interview soon after its completion. What were its strengths and weaknesses? Was the goal accomplished? Plan and monitor any follow-up activities required to achieve the goal. A written summary of the interview results may be useful—or required— as confirmation of information obtained and agreements reached.

BUSINESS PRESENTATIONS

During your business career, you will likely be required to make formal or semiformal business presentations. Those presentations may be independent of or complements to written messages.

When you transmit a written message to your receiver, control of the communication process shifts from you to others. Factors in the environment, for example, may prevent the receiver from giving the message full attention. To extend your control of the communication process, you may present the message orally. To heighten its impact, you may supplement your oral message with visual aids.

Your oral presentation may serve one of many objectives. The message may be primarily informative, offering data without recommendations. It may be analytical, offering investigation and recommendations for solving a problem. Or the presentation may be persuasive, encouraging changes in action or attitudes and providing justification for those changes. In each case, you are responsible for showing relationships between your message and management objectives. You may need to convince your listeners that your data are pertinent, accurate, and useful to the organization and the people it serves.

Immediacy of feedback in an oral presentation benefits both the sender and the receiver. The sender can clarify, amplify, or condense data in response to the audience's verbal and nonverbal feedback. Receivers benefit from immediate clarification or assurances that they are interpreting the message appropriately. By interacting with other members of the audience, receivers often acquire needed reinforcement for understanding the message and making decisions.

Successful business presentations result from preliminary analysis of the event, coherent message structure, appropriate delivery style, and practice.

Preliminary Analysis

The first step to a successful presentation is to define the event. That definition includes the purpose of the presentation, the anticipated audience, and the likely conditions under which you will make the presentation.

Determine Purpose. To enhance your presentation, establish a twofold purpose for the message: What is *your* purpose? What is the *audience's* purpose? Is your purpose mainly to transmit or receive information? to stimulate awareness, affect attitude, elicit feedback? What complementary purpose do you provide your receivers? Is it fulfillment of an obligation? satisfaction of a desire or need? Determine the twofold purpose of your message; then translate that purpose into listener as well as speaker contexts. One way of having people listen is to tell them about themselves and their needs in relation to whatever else you say.

Why should you establish the purpose of your oral message?

Analyze Audience. Determining message purpose requires awareness of your receivers' traits. The number and nature of your listeners should influence your planning as well as your presentation. Are you to address one person during an employment interview, five at a department meeting, hundreds of people at a shareholders' meeting, or thousands at an industrial convention?

Often the only way to develop audience awareness is to ask questions about your listeners' needs, interests, education, and experience. Recognize occupational, social, and cultural influences that can block or aid your communication. Consider *why* your listeners have assembled, their awareness of one another, their awareness of you, and their familiarity with your topic.

Hollingworth, a pioneer investigator of audience psychology, developed a useful guide for audience analysis.[4] That still-relevant guide suggests five

---

[4]Harry L. Hollingworth, *The Psychology of the Audience* (New York: American Book Company, 1935).

In what ways do the general audience types differ?

types of audiences: casual, passive, selected, concerted, and organized. Each type differs from the others in the members' orientation to one another, to the speaker, and to the speaker's topic.

A **casual** or **pedestrian audience** consists of transient persons who are intent on their own objectives. No common ties or lines of communication exist among audience members or between audience and speaker. The audience has no immediate interest in being addressed formally by anyone. (Examples: employees leaving the parking lot at the end of a work day; shoppers in a store.)

Members of a **passive audience** initially have little orientation to one another and a very preliminary orientation to the speaker and the topic. (Examples: new employees at an orientation meeting; students attending the first session of a course; employees from several departments assigned to a committee.)

Members of a **selected audience** have a common purpose but are not initially linked to one another or the speaker. (Examples: accountants attending a seminar on new tax law provisions; delegates to a convention.)

Members of a **concerted audience** are closely united in purpose. Those not interested in the purpose of the gathering have likely not been invited or have declined to attend. The audience has a strong interest in the topic and is often eager to hear the particular speaker's views. (Examples: managers who have chosen to attend a motivation seminar conducted by a nationally known management consultant; members of a professional organization attending its annual convention workshops.)

The **organized audience** is strongly oriented toward the speaker and seeks her or his help in achieving its goals. The members are eager to receive specific direction for action. (Examples: members of an athletic team listening to their coach; members of a sales team listening to a "super salesperson.")

Recognizing the general audience type and evaluating specifics of the situation will help you relate your presentation to your listeners.

Evaluate Situation. Anticipate the circumstances of your communication effort. In what ways are your timing, content, location, and presentation apt to affect your listeners' responsibilities, ideas, and feelings? Is the authority of your listeners subordinate, equal, or superior to yours? What other personal and organizational factors are likely to affect their responses? In what ways do you expect the acoustics, the lighting and furniture arrangements, or the size and shape of the room to affect your presentation? What kind, shape, and size of charts, tables, diagrams, maps, or models would reinforce your oral message? What type of microphone, public address system, lectern, chalkboard, or visual projection equipment should you use?

Answering these and kindred questions can help you familiarize yourself with the psychological and physical situation for your message. You then can work toward uniting people and purposes in that setting, through an effectively structured message.

Message Structure

A simple yet effective message structure is:

What is the function of a partition statement?

1. *Opening.* Reach out; draw listeners into the message by establishing its relevance for them.
2. *Preview or partition statement.* Tell the audience where you are going—what points will be covered.
3. *Body.* Discuss those points; use them as signposts to guide listeners; provide coherence through appropriate transitions and summaries.
4. *Conclusion.* Clinch the message: Summarize; request action; use an illustration or anecdote to reinforce the message purpose.

Arrange your data according to your knowledge of particular purposes involving a specific audience in a given situation. Hollingworth[5] suggested that the type of audience should guide the speaker's relative emphasis on five elements of the message: attention, interest, impression, conviction, and direction. (See Illustration 15−2.)

How does knowledge of audience affect organization of speech data?

Attention. As a business communicator, you may not often face a *casual* audience. When you do, however, you must divert attention from many separate purposes to those that you and your audience share. Usually some action or object providing a dramatic contrast with the environment is effective. For example, a colorful display with moving parts or a person stepping forward to offer a sample may entice shoppers to stop and listen.

With other types of audiences—those already inclined to listen—you may not need dramatic attention-getting strategies. In fact, those audiences may consider such strategies insulting or obtrusive.

Interest. Your first task with a *passive* audience (and your second task with a casual audience) is to establish interest in the specific topic and in you as a presenter. You can do so in several ways:

1. Mention a subject, especially a problem, that affects your listeners; but do not yet describe it.

---

[5]Ibid., p. 25.

Illustration 15–2   ORGANIZING MESSAGE BY TYPE OF AUDIENCE

Audience Type	Speaker's Tasks				
Casual	Attention	Interest	Impression	Conviction	Direction
Passive		Interest	Impression	Conviction	Direction
Selected			Impression	Conviction	Direction
Concerted				Conviction	Direction
Organized					Direction

Source: Adapted from Harry L. Hollingworth, *The Psychology of the Audience* (New York: American Book Company, 1935), p. 25

2. Tell an anecdote, but relate it to the twofold communication purpose in terms that your listeners will appreciate.
3. Say or do something that startles or puzzles, but that neither terrifies nor antagonizes your listeners.
4. Begin with deliberate or emphatic silence. For a few seconds, without saying a word, look directly at your listeners. When appropriate, nod or smile during this initial phase.

Avoid such curiosity-killing openings as "today I'd like to talk to you about investing in mutual funds" or "the topic of my speech is mutual funds." Instead, stimulate interest by involving your audience in the message: "Today you will learn how you can build a $1 million retirement fund."

Impression. With a *selected* audience, attention and interest are already provided by the common purpose that has drawn the group together. Your primary purpose is to reinforce that interest and impress the audience with your ability to satisfy their needs.

You can impress by involving your listeners in what you say and do. Emphasize those parts of your presentation that appeal to your audience's wishes and wants. Add variety by examples, comparisons, contrasts, statistics, testimonials, restatements, demonstrations, or audiovisual aids. Nourish your listeners' logical and psychological appetites for ideas and for feelings.

If you spend too much time on the attention and interest stages, you may alienate a selected audience. For example, accountants attending a tax seminar are ready to listen because of their interest in the topic. The speaker's first task is to assure them that they will get the information they seek from a credible source.

Conviction. A *concerted* audience typically has a keen interest in the topic and is already favorably impressed by the speaker. Members of this audience come primarily to gain from interaction with the speaker and one another. They expect substantive listener-oriented discussion with little time spent on attracting attention to the speaker or the topic.

For other audiences (pedestrian, passive, selected), conviction is a reinforcement of the impression stage. Identify, explain, and describe your core-thoughts and details; but do so while emphasizing their relevance to your listeners' concerns. Use transitions to move your listeners from the familiar to the new, from the simple to the complex. For persuading rather than merely informing, describe anticipated benefits of what you propose. Also describe negative consequences of rejecting your proposal. Use words that stimulate your listeners to visualize what you explain. Then summarize your discussion.

Direction. The *organized* audience is ready to act and assembles primarily to get specific direction from a respected speaker. For such an audience the major portion of your speech should focus on listeners' goals and ways to achieve them.

With other audiences you may need to stimulate action by eliciting pertinent questions or comments, requesting a specific action, or giving explicit instructions for subsequent behavior. Observe how your listeners use your information. In speaking as in writing, communication should elicit responses from receivers.

Unify the total message by continually relating data to the dual communication purpose that integrates the listeners' needs and yours. Emphasize key data with appropriate examples and comments. Acknowledge your listeners' abilities and accomplishments. By suitable personal references, demonstrate your appreciation of individuals or of groups that listen to you.

While structuring your message, consider also an appropriate delivery style. Your choice of delivery style must be guided by your preliminary analysis of purpose, audience, and situation.

Delivery Style

The four general types of oral message delivery are impromptu, extemporaneous, textual, and memorized. A fifth type, combined delivery, blends techniques of two or more styles. By acquainting yourself with the advantages and disadvantages of each, you can appropriately develop your own presentation techniques.

Impromptu Delivery. Impromptu delivery is the only type that omits rehearsal. When you speak on the spur of the moment, without text, notes, or memorized script, you are speaking impromptu.

Since this type of presentation typifies conversations and casual meetings, its significance in business is sometimes underestimated. However, more than 50 percent of a manager's or supervisor's time is spent in contacts that last less than nine minutes and involve brief conversational exchanges of information.[6] The advantages of impromptu delivery include timeliness, immediate pertinence, enthusiasm, and sincerity.

Although you cannot rehearse impromptu delivery, you can and should anticipate situations that elicit your impromptu participation. Prepare by considering possible and probable messages for those situations. Develop effective listening habits to increase your confidence in impromptu participation.

Impromptu messages are usually brief. If you prolong impromptu speaking, you may tempt yourself into digressions. When asked for an impromptu contribution, pause long enough to organize a brief, pertinent message. Then say it simply, clearly, completely, and without distracting mannerisms.

The other delivery types—extemporaneous, textual, and memorized—require preparation and rehearsal.

Extemporaneous Delivery. Extemporaneous delivery gives the appearance of spontaneity but involves the use of notes, often on cards. Reassured by the presence of your notes, you tend to be confident. With those notes on the lectern or in your hand, you can establish and maintain eye contact with your listeners. You can adjust your physical position relatively freely. You can benefit from the outlined order of your presentation; but you must keep your notes in order and avoid impulses to flip or sort them as you speak.

Notes should be used as prompts, not crutches. Useful prompting materials are:

1. The opening statement. Review it just before standing to speak so that it is fresh in mind. Maintain eye contact as you deliver it.
2. The partition statement. Deliver it clearly and with appropriate emphasis to prepare the listeners for your main points.
3. An outline of key data and transition words or sentences. Use the out-

In what respects are the message delivery types similar? dissimilar?

6Mintzberg, "The Manager's Job," p. 50.

line to reassure yourself that you can—and will—present necessary facts, completely and coherently.

4. The closing statement. Review it just before standing to speak. Remind yourself: Maintain eye contact; neither speed up nor hesitate; don't whisper or shout.

Textual Delivery. Reading complete sentences aloud from a typescript, manuscript, or other verbatim material is **textual delivery.**

Although textual delivery is not recommended for most business presentations, speakers use textual delivery when they want to ensure that technical or controversial information is presented and received accurately. Some situations that may warrant textual delivery are presenting scientific data to managers or to other scientists, reporting company operations to shareholders, or releasing a statement about company plans to the media. An advantage of textual delivery is that the availability of every word in your message tends to bolster your confidence. Also, as soon as you complete this kind of delivery, the text itself becomes a record of what you have said.

When you speak textually, however, your delivery runs the risk of becoming monotonous, mechanical, or obviously formal. This risk becomes great if you assemble your audience, distribute word-for-word copies of your complete text, recite the text, and expect your listeners to be attentive. They will read your copies faster than you can speak, and you will therefore disturb rather than promote rapport. Consider these alternatives instead: Before beginning your textual delivery, distribute concise summaries or condensed outlines to guide your listeners. Or first present your textual message orally; then distribute copies of the text, a summary, or an outline. Enable your listeners to use such handout material for discussion with you and among themselves as well as for their own future reference.

Memorized Delivery. When you use **memorized delivery,** you repeat what you have stored in your mind—paragraph by paragraph, sentence by sentence, word by word. Memorized delivery gives you maximum freedom for posture, movement, and eye contact. Another advantage is that you convey expertise; your audience sees that you need no notes or text to assist your communication.

Memorized delivery has serious disadvantages, however. Anxiety or interruption may cause you to forget the words and the organization of your message. You must also avoid the tendency to speak too rapidly and to orate rather than communicate.

Combined Delivery. Combinations of these oral delivery techniques are frequent in business communication. For example, imagine that you are a salesperson speaking to a prospective buyer. You use memorized statements to attract favorable attention, develop interest, reinforce desire, and stimulate action. You intersperse impromptu remarks based on what the buyer asks or states. To emphasize key topics or to verify details, you read verbatim from a typewritten or printed text. You also use extemporaneous delivery by referring to notes taken from your research file or made during the present conversation with the buyer.

You can enjoy the advantages of these delivery types, separately or combined. However, whether you choose extemporaneous, textual, memorized, or combination delivery, you will improve the impact of your presentations by purposeful practice.

Practice

You will benefit most by practicing aloud, in the standing or sitting position you will occupy during the actual delivery. If possible, use an audience of one or two people or a videotape recording for feedback.

These techniques will aid you during rehearsal and delivery of your oral message:

1. Thoroughly familiarize yourself with the data and with your statement of that data.
2. Underline words and phrases that you wish to emphasize. Stress those items with adjustments of volume and pitch during rehearsal as well as delivery. Underline once for slight, twice for moderate, and three times for heavy emphasis.
3. Draw a rising arrow when you particularly want the pitch of your voice to go up, as at the end of a question. Draw a falling arrow where you want your vocal pitch to drop, as at the end of a declaration.
4. Place vertical or diagonal lines in your text where you want to pause. Draw one line for a brief pause, two lines for a moderate pause, and three for emphatic silence. If you prefer using colors instead of repeating those line cues, let one color stand for slight or brief, a second color for moderate, and a third color for heavy or long.
5. When you prepare to speak from notes or text, number your cards or pages consecutively. Keep the cards or pages bound appropriately to avoid loss or mix-up. Before final rehearsal and actual delivery, verify the numbering sequence; be sure those cards or pages are in proper order.

For memorized delivery, here is a method to offset mental blocks. Instead of rehearsing your message word by word or sentence by sentence, begin to memorize the text as a whole. At the beginning of your rehearsal, avoid trying to remember every bit. Rehearse by speaking aloud several times the entire message from start to finish. Each repetition will imprint more of the message upon your memory. By learning the message as a whole, you will reduce possibilities of forgetting a part. Finally, on a single page, summarize the entire message in outline form. Look at that page as if you were examining a photograph or a painting. Let the total appearance of that page impress itself upon your memory. Then, if a lapse occurs during your memorized delivery, your mental picture of the outline will help you complete your presentation.

As you deliver your message, focus your attention where it belongs—not on yourself, but on your message and your listeners. Remind yourself of your listeners' need to receive data that only your message, at the moment of its delivery, can give them. If you make an error, correct it and continue the delivery. Everyone makes a mistake now and then; why should you be different? The important thing is to correct errors and go on.

Trembling is merely evidence that your body is generating energy. Use that natural energy for appropriate adjustments of your posture or movements, for relevant facial expressions, for pertinent gestures. If you must remain at one spot because of microphone location, lectern position, or furniture arrangement, release the extra energy you feel. For instance, press your fingertips against the sides of the lectern momentarily. Or press your thumb against the reading surface of the lectern. If you are seated, just touch the side of your chair.

Remember that your listeners are human beings, no more, no less. If you need to relax, notice their appearance as they listen to you. Imagine how they look when they first awaken in the morning. Invent your own preposterous images if you need them to help you relax. Continue speaking confidently, but be careful: You may have so much fun that you overlook the serious business of your message!

Contemporary business communicators often enhance their presentations with audiovisual aids and question-answer sessions. Group presentations are also common in today's collaborative communication environment. Guides for enhanced business presentations are discussed next.

ENHANCED BUSINESS PRESENTATIONS

Using audiovisual aids, question-answer sessions, and collaboration are current methods for enhancing business presentations. Each of these methods tends to increase listeners' interest and participation in the presentation.

Audiovisual Presentations

By adding visual or audio presentation aids, effective speakers deliberately use the dynamics of change, contrast, and multisensory learning. Effective users of audiovisual aids recognize the advantages and limitations of those media.

Advantages and Limitations. Several factors within the speaker's control can increase the informative and persuasive impact of an audiovisual presentation. Through speech dynamics and appropriately selected visuals, the speaker can emphasize points, project enthusiasm, and convey a sense of urgency when desired. The speaker's nonverbal behaviors may heighten that emphasis, enthusiasm, and urgency. The speaker also controls the time devoted to various aspects of the presentation and can return easily to selected visuals if audience feedback indicates the need for repetition or further explanation.

Potential limitations of audiovisual presentations are cost and impermanence. Well-constructed, effective visual aids can be expensive. Often those aids are useful for one presentation only. Moreover, an oral message often has a short life. Listeners may remember the main points, but forget supporting data, even if those data were displayed by charts or slides. Consequently, if information is needed for later reference, the message should be totally or partially written.

To overcome the limitation of impermanence, many contemporary managers videotape important presentations. That practice permits the audience—or absentees—to review the message as often as necessary. However, videotaping adds to expense.

Preparation and Delivery. When you decide that an audiovisual presentation will improve the effectiveness of your message, refresh your comprehension of what the planning, development, and presentation of an oral message generally require. Determine the purpose of your presentation from your standpoint and that of your listeners. Evaluate the situation that involves you with your audience. Accommodate your data organization, visual aids, and delivery style to the type of audience you will address.

Early in the presentation, clearly state its subject and purpose. You may begin with a concise statement of transmittal and authorization: "This is a report comparing the XYZ and UNI proposals to automate our internal communication. You asked me on March 7 to compare the proposals and recommend which one to accept." Or you may stimulate interest by appealing to your listeners' motives: "Today I'll show you how to save 20 percent on your telecommunication expenses." Relate your data to the aims and resources of

---

What are the advantages and limitations of audiovisual presentations?

your company and to the responsibilities of your listeners. As evidence of accuracy, describe the data sources and the research methods used. Basing your discussion on your data, state your logical conclusions. Also, when appropriate to do so, offer your recommendations. Invite pertinent questions and comments concerning your presentation; they can supply valuable feedback.

As with other forms of communication, audiovisual presentations are flexible. Adjust your own to the preferences of your listeners and to the policies of your company.

Use of Presentation Aids. Presentation aids are audio or visual aids that support your oral presentation. Besides traditional visual aids such as charts, tables, or pictures, consider using others. Audiotape, videotape, or disk recordings can give your audience a vicarious experience that has more impact than your narration alone. Flip charts are useful to present visual aids prepared in advance and to outline or summarize data as your report progresses. Slide or motion film presentations, with or without audio support, as well as models and demonstrations, are useful to increase the realism of a presentation.

Those aids are effective *if* they are skillfully integrated into your oral narrative. These guides will help you gain the benefits of presentation aids:

> How should you prepare for an audiovisual presentation?

1. Whenever possible, do not reveal a visual aid until it is needed. Then use the introduce-display-discuss technique suggested in Chapter 14. That strategy tends to direct attention toward you and your words until you wish the audience to direct its attention to your presentation aid.

2. Use colors for emphasis and contrast. Against a dark background, try white, light green, or light yellow. Against a white or gray background, try black, red, dark blue, or dark green.

3. Be sure the audience can see your visual aids and hear your audio aids. Stand at the side of visuals and use a pointer if necessary to avoid blocking your audience's line of vision. Observe nonverbal feedback to detect when people cannot see or hear the aid.

4. Speak toward your audience, not toward the visual aid, as you explain its contents.

5. Keep visual aids simple and uncluttered. Make seeing, understanding, and remembering easy for your audience. (See Illustration 15-3.)

6. When using handout materials, try to distribute them as they are needed or at the end of the presentation. If the room arrangement or audience size prevents that practice, a cover message or an oral reminder may deter the audience from studying the materials while you are speaking. The most effective deterrent, however, is the interest-

Illustration 15–3 USING A FLIP CHART

ing nature of your presentation. With appropriate attention-getting and interest-arousing statements, you can prevent your audience from looking at handouts until you direct attention to those aids.

7. Before the presentation, familiarize yourself with the equipment. Be sure that all equipment is operational.

8. When using an overhead projector, verify before the presentation that the image is in focus and within the boundaries of the projection surface. During the presentation, face your audience as you discuss the aid. Directing a pencil or a pointer to selected items on the transparency itself (rather than to the screen) is an effective emphasis technique. Turn off the projector when you want attention directed toward you.

The prevalence of videotaping in contemporary business and school environments requires that you learn how to communicate effectively when that medium is used.

How can you ensure
success of a
videotaped
presentation?

Videotaped Presentations

To achieve your communication objectives in a videotaped presentation, you must be in control of your presentation. To maintain professional control of a videotaped presentation, follow these guides:

1. Before the presentation, consult with the technician who will do the taping. Determine the best locations for the lectern and microphone, your visual aids, the audience, and the camera. If the camera is fixed on a tripod, determine the range within which you can move.

2. Dress to accommodate video requirements. Avoid clothing with bold or checked patterns. Such patterns tend to create distracting images on videotape. To avoid fading into the background, wear a color that contrasts with the wall or studio backdrop.

3. Avoid using an overhead projector in your presentation. The light projected on the screen tends to create a "washed out" image on the videotape. Visuals projected are rarely visible on the tape.

4. Don't drift too far from the microphone for the video recorder. If possible, use a cordless microphone that permits easy movement without loss of audio input to the recorder.

5. Remember that your primary responsibility is to the people who attend your presentation. Speak to the audience, not to the camera. If, however, you have no audience at the taping session, maintain "eye contact" with the red light on the camera and use your best speaking voice. Avoid speaking too rapidly or too loudly.

6. Relax. Remind yourself that a camera is not a hostile audience!

To increase audience participation or to obtain feedback in a presentation, you will often solicit questions from your audience.

Question-Answer Sessions

When you plan to use a question-answer session, inform your audience at the outset whether you will answer questions during your presentation or only at its conclusion.

Answering questions as they arise has the advantage of immediacy. Both listeners and speaker can verify audience understanding of a point before progressing to another. That verification is especially important when one point in your speech builds upon a previous point. When you accept questions during a speech, keep your objective in mind. Do not permit the audience to channel the presentation in another direction. Answer questions clearly but briefly so that later you need not rush to complete your presentation within the allotted time.

What are the
disadvantages of a
question-answer
session? How can they
be overcome?

If you prefer that questions be held until you have completed the presentation, suggest that listeners jot down their questions as the presentation progresses. That practice helps to focus audience questions and improves the productivity of the question-answer session.

These guides will help you handle questions comfortably and effectively:

1. Prepare for questions. As you plan and rehearse your presentation, use a critic or be your own critic. Anticipate controversial or difficult-to-understand points. Plan possible answers to anticipated questions.

2. Be sure the audience hears the question. If necessary, repeat the question or ask the questioner to use a microphone.

3. Be sure you and the audience understand the question. When in doubt, rephrase the question, define terms, or ask the questioner "Do you mean . . . ?" before answering.

4. Speak to the entire audience—not only to the questioner. You can include all by looking at other members of the audience as well as at the questioner.

5. Seek feedback from the questioner to determine whether he or she is satisfied. Frequently, nonverbal cues will tell you whether further explanation is necessary.

6. Limit the time devoted to a single questioner. If a person monopolizes the questioning period, suggest that others be given a turn. When someone tries to make a speech or becomes argumentative, suggest that you will continue the discussion with that person after the session.

7. Be ready to begin the question period if no one raises a question. Say something like "Some of you may wonder why . . ." and answer that posed question. Your comments may stimulate another question.

8. Stimulate discussion by posing your own *who, what, why, where,* or *how* question. Responses to such questions often stimulate other questions or comments.

9. Stop the questioning courteously when you approach the end of your allotted time. You can signal the end of questioning by suggesting that you will accept one, two, or three more questions.

10. End the session when your audience has no more questions. To reinforce goodwill at the conclusion of your oral presentation, thank the listeners for their questions and tell them how to contact you if questions arise later.

A question-answer session is an excellent way to build rapport with your audience. Even if a part of your presentation was weak, by demonstrating confidence, honesty, and knowledge in your responses, you can leave a favorable final impression with your audience. Question-answer sessions are effective in both solo and group presentations.

Group Presentations

How can you ensure
success of a group
presentation?

As a member of a project group, you will participate frequently in team presentations. An objective of such presentations is to give the audience the experience of a single, unified message—not the sense of several individual speeches.

This chapter's principles apply to team as well as solo presentations. In addition, following these guides will unify your presentation:

1. Establish each person's responsibility for various sections of the message or for coordinating the presentation.
2. Familiarize yourself—and be sure others do so—with the entire presentation.
3. Plan seating arrangements and placement of presentation aids to facilitate smooth transition from one speaker to another.
4. Rehearse the presentation until all team members are confident about its effectiveness. Give constructive criticism to one another. Be sure the presentation fits within the time allocation.
5. Anticipate questions. Determine who is best able to answer specific categories of questions.

A team presentation is a shared responsibility. By planning together, becoming familiar with the entire project, and critically rehearsing the presentation, team members fulfill responsibilities to one another and to their audience.

As your skills at oral business communication are recognized, your job responsibilities may expand to writing speeches for other members of your organization.

SPEECHWRITING

A 1989 survey revealed that almost one-third of the Fortune 250 companies employ a speechwriter whose primary responsibility is preparing speeches for the chief executive officer. Moreover, in nearly half of the companies that did not have an executive speechwriter, employees in corporate communications, public relations, or editorial services undertook speechwriting duties.

Some speechwriters have achieved senior management level and hold positions of genuine power in the organization.[7]

Speechwriting is a unique communication task requiring the speechwriter and the speaker to communicate with two audiences. The writer must empathize with the speaker for whom the speech is written and the audience to whom it will be delivered—in effect conveying a dual *you* attitude. Likewise, the speaker must communicate effectively with the writer and the audience. The speaker conveys to the writer key ideas and style preferences for the speech; the writer clarifies, amplifies, and organizes those ideas and presents them in a style that honestly and convincingly projects the speaker's personality to the audience.

The following guides contribute to effective speaker-speechwriter relationships.

What are the mutual responsibilities of speechwriter and speaker?

1. Allow ample time for the speechwriting process. Time must be allotted for exchange of ideas between speaker and writer, research, drafting, and rewriting. The speaker must also allow time to read, possibly edit, and rehearse the speech. Although time will vary with situations, executive speechwriters spend an average of 50 hours on a major address: 20 on research, 15 writing the first draft, 10 rewriting, and 5 getting approvals.[8]

2. Agree on these factors at an initial meeting of speaker and writer:

   a. Main point of the speech. The speaker should establish the main point. The writer's task is to develop it and provide supporting data.

   b. Audience characteristics. The speaker and the writer should share their knowledge about the audience and the context for the speech. If possible, examine the meeting agenda to determine what activities or speakers will precede or follow this speaker.

3. Identify and project the speaker's values and personality. The speaker should share personal preferences with the writer. Does the speaker like humor? If so, what kind? Does the speaker like quotations? If so, whom does the speaker find quotable? What are the speaker's vocabulary preferences, speech patterns, and knowledge of history or current events? Can he or she comfortably speak—and answer questions—

---

[7]"Survey: CEO Speechwriters' Median Salary Is $75,000," *Public Relations Journal,* February 1990, p. 12.
[8]Ibid.

about "white knights"? "golden parachutes"? "Europe 1992"? "perestroika"? If the speaker does not readily share information about values and preferences, the writer may find clues by asking questions, listening keenly, and reading other speeches given by that person.

4. Establish specific times to review speech development and the final product. As the writing progresses, the speaker must maintain quality control. Scheduled meetings enable the speechwriter to get additional information, if necessary, and let the speaker provide essential feedback about speech content or style. The speaker should read the speech aloud before the final text is prepared. That reading is especially useful to identify needed changes in sentence structure and word choice.

Both speaker and speechwriter must recognize the speaker's personal responsibility for the speech. A speechwriter's task is to make the speaker look good. If that goal is achieved, the speaker gains the praise; if that goal is not achieved, the speaker also receives the criticism. Some of the most-quoted political leaders are remembered because they had creative but anonymous speechwriters.

A final oral communication task that deserves your consideration is that of media relations.

MEETING THE MEDIA

Media relations encompasses an organization's full range of communication—or lack thereof—with print and broadcast journalists. Press releases, press conferences, exclusive interviews, and on-the-spot interviews are aspects of media relations. Whereas effective use of those communication forums can benefit an organization, silence or press avoidance often damages credibility.

CBO and Media Relations

Communication by objectives (CBO) applies to media relations as to other areas of business communication. Ideally, a company's strategic plan includes a media relations plan. Executives should decide what the company wants to accomplish in media relations, how to reach those goals, what has been done, and what is still needed.

To promote effective media relations, managers must recognize what constitutes a good news story. Exceptionally good or poor company performance; conflicts between the company and its employees, competitors, or the government; internal power struggles; breakthrough developments or new products; substantial expansions; plant closings; industrial accidents; environmental problems—these are newsworthy events that draw reporters seeking interviews and press releases. In contrast, continued steady earnings with a proven product line, routine promotions within the company, expanding plant capacity, or opening a second office in a city are the kinds of events that—although important to the company and its employees—often receive little newspaper, radio, or television coverage. The company itself must promote coverage of such news.

Since the most newsworthy events often deal with sensitive issues, an effective media relations strategy includes techniques for communicating with the press about such issues. One guide applies to all aspects of media relations. Never lie to the press. Both you and your organization will lose a priceless asset—your credibility.

Here are additional guides for effective media relations:

1. Involve management in communication planning. A media relations plan should answer questions such as:

   a. Who will be the company's primary spokesperson during crisis situations? Since the spokesperson must be highly credible, many companies assign that task to the chief executive officer.

   <aside>What are guides for crisis communication?</aside>

   b. What procedures will be followed when the company confronts a disaster or potential disaster? Although no company can foresee the exact nature of a crisis, answers to key questions will help managers deal with a crisis when it arises. Who will be involved in decisions about news releases? Who, besides the primary spokesperson, may be authorized to speak? What actions will be taken to correct problems?

2. Speak with one voice. All spokespeople must be fully informed so that they can perform credibly and with confidence that their statements will not be contradicted.

3. Avoid "no comment" positions. This response often suggests a coverup. Reporters will likely seek information from other—often less reliable—sources or may report the "no comment" in a negative context.

4. Speak soon and tell the complete story. The less people know about something, the more receptive they are to rumors. Cover all important subjects to the extent possible at the first news release. Releasing information in stages prolongs the story and jeopardizes the company's credibility.

5. Provide regular updates, particularly about damage control. Company

credibility can be restored if the public is assured that a responsible corrective program is in operation.[9]

6. Keep employees informed. If an impending event, such as a plant closing, affects employees, inform them fully before or as the news is released to the press.

The procedures for press releases presented in Chapter 7 and the oral communication guides given in this chapter will promote effective communication with print and broadcast media. In addition, specific guides pertain to participation in press conferences and media interviews.

Press Conferences

A press conference is called by someone who wants to get information to the news media. To gain maximum benefits from a press conference, follow these guides:

1. Schedule the conference carefully. Try to avoid a heavy news day, such as an election day. Unless the subject matter is urgent and must be released immediately, avoid scheduling a conference in the late afternoon. Broadcast journalists may be unable to cover the event and edit their film in time for the evening prime-time newscasts.

2. Select a broadcast-friendly location for the conference. The space must be large enough for all reporters and their equipment. Provide chairs for newspaper reporters and an unobstructed view of the podium for photographers. Avoid placing the podium in front of windows; if TV cameras do not adjust well to backlighting, the speaker will look blurred.

3. Distribute a written text of the press statement. The text saves reporters time and increases the chances of being quoted accurately. Have enough copies for all reporters. Double-spaced copy with extra space between sentences permits reporters to add their notes and to indicate when the speaker deviates from the prepared text.

4. Be available for follow-up. When writing a story, even the best reporter sometimes needs to clarify conflicting information or fill in missing facts. The story may be dropped or shortened if a reporter cannot reach someone to resolve the problem.

5. Maintain control of the conference. State in advance whether you will

What actions contribute to effective press conferences?

---

[9]For interesting accounts about companies dealing with crises, see Marion K. Pinsdorf, *Communicating When Your Company Is Under Siege* (Lexington, MA: D. C. Heath and Company, 1987).

answer questions after the prepared statement. If you do allow questions, confine them to the topic of the news conference; don't let reporters lead you into discussions of other issues. The following guides for requested interviews also apply to answering questions during a press conference.

Requested Interviews

Interviews requested by reporters fall into two general categories: impromptu and exclusive. In an *impromptu interview,* often at the site of a newsworthy event, the reporter seeks immediate answers to questions for which the interviewee has had no time to prepare. In an *exclusive interview,* a company representative agrees to discuss an issue with a reporter from only one news agency. The reporter may or may not supply questions in advance of the interview. Even when the interviewee previews the questions, he or she must anticipate and prepare for other routes the interview may take.

The following techniques can help you deal with sensitive questions during interviews. Each avoids a direct answer, while providing a reporter with quotable material.

How can you avoid direct answers to sensitive questions?

1. Tell why you cannot discuss an issue in detail: information that you don't want to divulge to competitors; in the midst of labor negotiations; too soon after an accident to know exactly what happened.
2. Don't overreact to criticism. Overreacting can be more damaging than the criticism itself.
3. Offer constructive responses to negative issues: the company will release damage estimates after its investigation; management and labor both want to avoid a strike; management is considering several options, but no decision has yet been made.
4. Use humor when it is appropriate. Humor, especially if directed at oneself, can defuse a sensitive situation.

REVIEW AND TRANSITION

Effective oral communication begins with a knowledge of physiological, psychological, nonverbal, and metacommunicative factors. Inhalation, phonation, resonation, and modification are controllable physiological aspects of oral communication. Psychological aspects involve developing confidence to overcome stage fright. Metacommunication explains the interrelatedness of physiological, psychological, and nonverbal factors. Metacommunication consists of words and nonverbal behaviors that give evidence of perceived relationships between communicators.

These basic preparation and presentation steps apply to all oral communication: determine purpose, analyze audience, evaluate situation, structure message, and plan delivery. Often combined for maximum effectiveness, the types of oral delivery are impromptu, extemporaneous, textual, and memorized. A final preparation step, practice, applies to all but impromptu delivery.

Categories of oral communication used in business include conversing, interviewing, business presentations (including audiovisual, videotaped, and group presentations, and use of question-answer sessions). In addition, your career uses of oral communication skills may include writing speeches for others and making presentations to media representatives. In each communication mode, verbal and nonverbal messages should complement one another to achieve the communicators' objectives.

In Chapters 14 and 15, you have considered principles of oral communication as well as use of visual aids to enhance message effectiveness. As a business decision maker, you will need investigative skills to supplement your communicative skills. Part 5 acquaints you with research techniques and reporting strategies—the bases for effective decisions.

YOUR DECISIONS FOR CHAPTER 15

Review your advice to Andre. What information should your friend acquire from the boss before preparing the presentation? How may that information relieve the apparent anxiety? What Chapter 15 guides for business presentations will assist this group?

DISCUSSION QUESTIONS

A. Within the context of Chapter 15, what are appropriate definitions and examples for these terms?

1. inhalation
2. phonation
3. resonation
4. modification
5. impromptu delivery
6. extemporaneous delivery
7. presentation aids
8. media relations

B. What techniques seem especially useful to you in overcoming stage fright?

C. How might metacommunication alter these messages?

1. Instructor to student: "Please come to my office to discuss your work."
2. Sales manager to sales representative: "Look at that January sales record! Are you trying to get my job?"

D. In what ways do preparing and presenting oral communication resemble and differ from preparing and presenting written communication?

E. How does audience analysis influence decisions about the relative importance of attention, interest, impression, conviction, and direction in a speech?

F. What should a speaker achieve in each of these parts of a business presentation: opening, partition statement, body, conclusion?

G. What advantages and disadvantages are associated with these types of oral delivery: impromptu, extemporaneous, textual, memorized? In what ways can you minimize the disadvantages?

H. How is communication by objectives applicable to the following?

1. conversing face to face
2. conversing by telephone
3. interviewing
4. speechwriting
5. media relations

I. What contributes to effective videotaped presentations?

J. In what ways may a question-answer session increase the effectiveness of a business presentation?

K. What responsibilities do members of a team presentation have to one another? to their audience?

APPLICATIONS

If a videotape recorder is available, use it for playback of these exercises. Use the tapes to evaluate yourself and your classmates.

1. As an application exercise for Chapter 1, you prepared a written introduction of yourself. Using that material for reference, introduce yourself orally now to your instructor and your classmates. Limit your oral introduction to a maximum of three minutes. Invite written evaluations of your presentation; introduce yourself orally again.

2. If your introduction (Application 1) was taped, do the following:

a. View the tape using video only. Observe your nonverbal behaviors. Are they natural, comfortable? How can you improve your nonverbal behaviors?

b. Play the tape again, using audio and video. Observe your nonverbal behaviors. Do they complement the verbal message?

3. With all members of the class as a team, say aloud the sounds represented by the underlined letters in Appendix F. Then individually pronounce those sounds.

4. Select a current issue that has business or economic implications. In an audiovisual presentation, relate the background to the problem, your position on the issue, and information to support your position. Invite constructive criticism from your instructor and classmates. Orally present the material again. (Your instructor will assign a time limit for this activity.)

5. If you have access to videotaping equipment, record a ten-minute segment of a television drama, talk show, or quiz show. Play the tape a few times using video only. Analyze the nonverbal aspects of the message. Then play the tape using video and sound. Observe whether verbal and nonverbal aspects complement or contradict one another. Present your analysis to the class extemporaneously.

6. Form a seven-student team (a team leader and six presenters) to discuss preparing and presenting oral communication. Each presenter is responsible for one of these topics:

   determine purpose   structure message
   analyze audience   plan delivery
   evaluate situation   practice

   a. The coordinator will introduce the team and its topics and will end the team presentation by inviting questions and comments from the audience. All students will communicate their assigned topics by extemporaneous delivery. Follow the presentation with constructive criticism by the other students in the class and by the instructor.
   b. Form a second team of seven students. This team will use memorized delivery and invite constructive criticism of its performance.
   c. Following the two presentations, discuss the relative advantages and disadvantages of extemporaneous and memorized delivery.

7. Identify the task-oriented, process-oriented, and/or dysfunctional behaviors practiced by each team member with whom you worked as you completed Application 6. (Refer to Chapter 5 to review small-group communication behaviors.)

8. Critique any speaker whom you have an opportunity to hear and observe (e.g., a campus lecturer, a televised speaker). Identify the techniques, if any, the speaker uses effectively. Identify the delivery weaknesses, if any, that you observe. As directed by your instructor, report your observations in a memo to your instructor or in an oral presentation to your class.

9. Form teams of two students—an interviewer and an interviewee. Role-play the following situations using Chapter 15 concepts about interviewing and Chapters 9 and 10 concepts about good-news, bad-news, mixed-news messages. Alternate as interviewer and interviewee.

   a. Supervisor warns a frequently tardy employee that lateness is cause for dismissal. Employee explains that tardiness occurs only when the regular baby sitter cannot care for the employee's child and another sitter must be found.

   b. Supervisor reviews an employee's outstanding performance record and plans expanded job responsibilities. Employee is reluctant to accept new responsibilities.

   c. Accounting supervisor interviews employee who wants a transfer from the payroll area to accounts payable. Employee thinks accounts payables offers greater opportunities for advancement. Grant the transfer.

   d. Repeat c; deny the transfer.

10. Form teams of two to four students. Each team will do the following:

   a. Select a visual aid and prepare a presentation to discuss criteria for its construction and use.

   b. Videotape the presentation.

   c. View another team's tape. Prepare a critical analysis of that presentation. Present the analysis in a memo to the instructor or in an oral presentation to the class.

11. Form teams of two students to interview a technician who videotapes student or faculty presentations on your campus. In the interview solicit clues for effective video presentations. Present the findings orally to the class and have the presentation videotaped. As directed by your instructor, use one of these presentation and evaluation techniques:

   a. Student 1 presents findings orally; Student 2 replays the tape and orally evaluates that speech before the class.

   b. Student 1 and Student 2 give a team presentation of the findings; the class orally evaluates the presentation as it is replayed.

12. Select a newspaper story about a sensitive issue involving a business or prominent not-for-profit organization. In a memorandum to your instructor or an oral report to your class, do the following:

   a. Identify the issue

   b. Describe how the newspaper got the information (news release? interview? combinations of techniques?)

   c. Evaluate the effectiveness of the company's media relationships. Support your evaluation with evidence from the story.

13.   Find information about one of the following corporate crises (or another approved by your instructor). In a five-minute speech, share your findings with your classmates. Summarize facts about the crisis and the company's communication with the public during the crisis.

▶   Eastern Airlines: Criminal indictment; 1990.
▶   Exxon: Valdez tanker spilling 260,000 barrels of crude oil into Alaska's Prince William Sound; 1989.
▶   Johnson & Johnson: Tylenol tampering; 1982.
▶   A. H. Robins: Dalkon Shield case; approximately 1980–85.
▶   Union Carbide: Leak of methylisocyanate gas into atmosphere; Bhopal, India; 1984.
▶   Any other crisis situation, as assigned or approved by your instructor.

CASES

1.   The American Lung Association is the oldest voluntary health organization in the United States. Its twofold mission is the promotion of lung health and the conquest of lung disease. You are the president of the volunteer advisory board for a regional chapter of that association. In that capacity, you frequently address civic and religious organizations to solicit funds for special projects, such as a summer camp for children who suffer from asthma or other breathing disorders. Prepare a speech that you can use repeatedly, requiring only minor changes for various audiences. Since you usually are given limited program time, your speech should be seven to ten minutes long. Consult your library or contact the office of your local lung association for information to include in your speech. Deliver the speech to your classmates, assuming that they are members of a campus organization that undertakes one major community project each year.

2.   The Humphries Corp. training department sponsors the Lunch and Learn program. This program provides free sack lunches and lectures of interest to employees during the lunch hour every Friday. The lectures are held in the company's auditorium, and approximately 50 employees, primarily supervisors and office employees, attend. As a personnel associate you have noticed that many employees seem uncertain about business etiquette. You have suggested to the training director that the topic would be appropriate for the Lunch and Learn program. The director agreed and immediately asked you to be the lecturer. Prepare and give the speech (about 15 minutes followed by audience questions). Assume your classmates are the Lunch and Learn

audience. Include protocols for such things as handshakes, introductions, forms of address, opening doors, entering and exiting elevators, transferring telephone calls.

3. Lynn Westman, a sales manager for Humphries Corp., has heard about your Lunch and Learn lecture on business etiquette (Case 2). Ms. Westman thinks her sales representatives need some reminders about business etiquette, and has asked you to give a speech about that topic at one of the weekly sales meetings. Adapt the speech you prepared for Case 2 to this audience. Since some of the female sales representatives have complained that they or their contributions are frequently ignored during staff meetings, Ms. Westman has asked that you include information about effective, courteous behavior during problem-solving conferences. Your presentation, including a question-answer session, should be no longer than 20 minutes.

4. A local television station is presenting a series of one-minute public-service messages on money management. The program director has asked you, as manager of a local credit union, to do one of the messages. Select a topic from the following list; prepare a one-minute message and deliver it in person or by videotape to your classmates.

   a. Dangers of co-signing a note for a friend or relative
   b. How to evaluate special options on a new car
   c. Steps to effective household budgeting
   d. Importance of having a will
   e. Energy conservation in the home
   f. Turning castoffs into cash
   g. Buying in bulk—boon or bane?
   h. How to select a bank
   i. Is credit-card insurance necessary?
   j. Inexpensive, environmentally safe alternatives to household cleaning products

5. The director of student services for your college thinks that first-year students need mid-year reorientation sessions. The director plans to set up informal discussion groups in which upper division students talk with freshmen about choosing an academic major. Each session will include a five- to seven-minute presentation by an upper division student from each of three different majors. After the presentations, the freshmen will be given an opportunity to ask questions and to converse informally with the upper division students. You have been asked to represent your major. Prepare your formal speech and prepare for the conversations. Appropriate information includes why you chose your academic major, most interesting courses, possible minor or cognate courses, perceived job opportunities. Two of your classmates should

represent other academic majors, and the remainder of the class should assume the roles of freshmen who need reorientation.

6. You are a management trainee for a major oil company and have been identified as a person who writes effectively. Noticing your interest in the company's programs to protect the environment, your supervisor suggests that your skills and interests may qualify you to become one of the company's speechwriters. To demonstrate your qualifications, write a speech for the company president to deliver at the beginning of the annual stockholders' meeting. The press will be invited to cover that meeting. The president wishes to set a positive tone for the meeting by emphasizing the socially responsible actions the company has taken to protect the environment. To prepare to write this speech, consult your library for information about environmental-protection activities of any of the major oil companies.

7. Assume that you are the director of media relations for a small private college. A student has brought a sexual harassment suit against a professor. Although the college's administrators subscribe to the principle that a person is innocent until proven guilty, the professor has been suspended (with pay) pending the outcome of the trial. You realize that protecting your college's reputation requires you to make a statement to the press. You also have a responsibility to protect the reputations of the professor, if innocent, and of the student, if victim. Conduct a meeting of your staff to decide what information should be included in a written or oral statement to the press. Ask two of your classmates to assume the roles of staff members. Demonstrate the meeting before your class.

8. The director of media relations (Case 7) has agreed to give an exclusive interview to a reporter from a local television station. Assume that you are either (a) the reporter or (b) the director of media relations. (Your instructor will assign the role you are to assume.)

    a. As the television reporter, your task is to obtain as much information as possible during the interview without antagonizing your viewers, many of whom are staunch supporters of the college. Although the college is a private institution, you believe in the public's right to know what is happening in any organization that influences the lives of people in your community.
    b. As the director of media relations, you need to satisfy the interviewer's desire for information while revealing nothing that may jeopardize the outcome of the trial or your institution's reputation.

    Prepare for a two-minute television interview. Demonstrate the interview to your classmates or videotape it for viewing by your classmates.

MULTICULTURAL INSIGHTS

1. Which sounds in the English language are most difficult for you? Why? (Refer to Appendix F if necessary.) What sounds in your native language would be difficult for a person whose native language is English? What physiological speech adjustments should the English-speaking person make to master those sounds?

2. What advantages, if any, exist in making an audiovisual presentation to an audience whose native language differs from yours? disadvantages?

3. Based on your reading, observation, or experience, what presentation practices are common among firms that conduct business in your native language?

4. In what ways, if any, does the structure of your native language affect use of presentation aids?

5. What protocols or customs should U.S. businesspeople be aware of when they prepare to meet with representatives of news media in your native culture?

Cases

As you complete these cases you will continue to demonstrate your understanding of communication challenges confronted by business people. Part 4 challenges include telephone communication and assisting someone with an audiovisual presentation.

CASE A: COMMUNICATION TEAMWORK AT BAUER
(Preparing an Audiovisual Presentation)

C. W. Brenner is marketing vice president of Bauer Corporation, a large agribusiness firm headquartered in Minneapolis. Recognized nationally as a knowledgeable communicator, Brenner often accepts speaking engagements on behalf of the Bauer organization.

Ordinarily, Brenner schedules adequate preparation time for those important speeches, but there are unexpected circumstances on this occasion. At 11 a.m. today, Brenner concludes a marketing staff conference. Scheduled to leave Minneapolis at 11:45 a.m. and to address the National Farmers and Bankers Convention in Chicago at 2:30 this afternoon, Brenner hurries from the conference room. A staff assistant, Leslie Taro, is at Brenner's side.

"You've just enough time to get to the airport," Taro remarks.

"Right," says Brenner as they approach the elevators. "Thanks for pitching in, Les."

"Glad to do it," Taro replies, "especially since Atkins is ill. Now, here's the manuscript for your Chicago speech."

Quickly leafing through the pages, Brenner exclaims: "They're not here!"
"What's missing?"

"Those pages with comparative data for 1990 and 1992. I need them to
clinch my recommendations at the convention. I made longhand notes of
those statistics. Atkins was going to edit the notes and add a summary
chart—something I can use for quick reference at the convention. But Atkins'
illness came on so suddenly that—"

An elevator door opens as Taro says, "If you miss your plane, there'll be no
Chicago speech at all. Let me see what I can do."

Stepping into the elevator, Brenner urges Leslie Taro to locate the missing
materials. "Get them to me through our Chicago branch as soon as you can,
Les. I need that part of the speech and a summary chart."

The elevator door closes. Returning to the Marketing Department suite of
offices, Taro locates the following notes in Atkins' file.

<u>Corethought</u>: Bauer Research Reports 85-014 and 87-052
cite the decrease in Region IV farmers net incomes
between January 1, 1985, and January 1, 1987.

<u>Comparative Data for Region IV</u>:
1. As of January 1, 1990, Region IV farm assets were
   valued at $59.4 billion, down from $64.8 billion
   recorded January 1, 1988.

2. Net farm income (i.e., what remained after
   farmers had paid their bills) dropped from
   $2.3 billion (January 1, 1988) to $1.6 billion
   (January 7, 1990).

3. Farm debt was reported on January 1, 1990 as $10.6
   billion, up from $9.8 billion (January 1, 1988).

4. Farm real estate accounted for 85 percent of total farm
   assets reported January 1, 1990. But money owed on
   farm real estate accounted for about 57 percent
   of the farm debt reported January 1, 1990.

<u>Special Notes</u>: Use visual aids for those data.
Emphasize that the data pertain to
Bauer Region IV only.

"Well," Taro muses, "we need to convert those notes into effective speech copy, do the visual aids, get the results to Brenner in Chicago—and all in less than three hours. No problem; here we go."

INSIGHTS

In the role of Taro, test your communication skills by answering these questions:

1. Specifically what communication challenges and tasks do you face? What sequence do you propose to follow in meeting them? Why? What teamwork do you expect from other Bauer employees? How do you expect to elicit and manage that necessary teamwork?
2. Knowing that Bauer has both electronic and traditional communication equipment at its Minneapolis office and at its branches, what media will you use to do this job for Brenner? Why?
3. What is your revised version of the notes for Brenner's speech? In what ways does your revision fulfill effective communication criteria? Timing is critical in this case. How long did you need to complete the revision? What, if anything, would have expedited the revision?
4. What is your visual aid for Brenner's speech? How is your visual aid likely to be appropriate and effective for Brenner's use at the Chicago convention?

CASE B: KHAMCO ISN'T KIRBY'S
(Telephone Communication)

Cast:

- ▶ Caller
- ▶ Voice on Tape Recording
- ▶ Switchboard Operator
- ▶ Salesperson
- ▶ Answering Service Operator

Seated at a table or desk on which there is a telephone, CALLER studies a wrinkled bit of note paper.

CALLER: Hmmm, let's see now . . . Khamco Industries, 555-1010. (*Dials the telephone number.*) 5-5-5 . . . one-oh . . . one-oh.

VOICE ON TAPE RECORDING:	The number you have reached is not in service. We cannot complete your call as dialed. Please consult your telephone directory before placing the call again. (*CALLER hangs up the telephone, looks at note again.*)
CALLER:	Khamco Industries . . . 555-1010. (*Looks more closely at note.*) Or is that *seven*-oh, *seven*-oh? (*Rubs eyes, looks at note once more.*) Whoever wrote this was in some kind of a hurry. Well . . . I'll try 7070. (*The call goes through, and we hear:*)
SWITCHBOARD OPERATOR:	Hold, please. (*Puts the call on hold. Music plays.*)
CALLER:	I don't believe this. Hello? Helloooooh! I want to talk to someone! I don't want to listen to music!
SWITCHBOARD OPERATOR:	Thank you for holding. I can connect you with Housewares now.
CALLER:	Connect me with what?
SWITCHBOARD OPERATOR:	Aren't you the party who wants Housewares? That line is clear now; I'll connect you.
CALLER:	Don't connect me!
SALESPERSON:	Housewares. May I help you?
CALLER:	Is this Khamco?
SALESPERSON:	This is Perkins. Pat Perkins in Housewares.
CALLER:	What's your phone number?
SALESPERSON:	I beg your pardon?
CALLER:	What telephone number have I reached?
SALESPERSON:	This is Extension 1214.
CALLER:	I mean, what's your *company* telephone number?
SALESPERSON:	555-7060.
CALLER:	Seven-oh-*six*-oh? Aren't you Khamco Industries?
SALESPERSON:	I'm Pat Perkins. And this is Kirby's.
CALLER:	Kirby's what?
SALESPERSON:	Kirby's Department Store.
CALLER:	Wrong number. (*Hangs up the phone abruptly.*) One more time . . . (*Dials again.*)
ANSWERING SERVICE OPERATOR:	Khamco Industries . . . .
CALLER:	Listen, I'm returning an important call from (*looks at note*) J. B. Dorsey, or Darcey, or—
ANSWERING SERVICE OPERATOR:	It's after five o'clock; the offices have just closed for the weekend. They'll open again at 8:30, Monday morning . . . . Excuse me; Monday's a holiday. They'll be closed until Tues-

CALLER: day. This is the answering service. Would you care to leave a message?

CALLER: Never mind. Have a good weekend. (*Hangs up the phone, looks at the note, shrugs shoulders, and tosses the note into the wastebasket.*) It probably wasn't important anyway.

INSIGHTS

Test your ability to communicate by telephone. Answer these questions:

1. At what points in this minidrama did miscommunications occur? What were their causes and consequences?
2. What techniques would you use for preventing or resolving those miscommunications?

Revise the minidrama script to demonstrate your recommendations.

NATURE'S WONDERS

Your most recent assignment at Nature's Wonders places you with the Director of Training and Development. Your tasks require application of knowledge gained as you studied Parts 1 through 4 of your textbook.

CASE FACTS

New employees participate in a program that emphasizes the company's commitment to customer satisfaction. You will assist in development of communication training programs that will contribute to the customer-satisfaction goal.

YOUR TASKS

The Director of Training and Development has asked you to evaluate messages written by other Nature's Wonders employees, identify weaknesses, and develop training materials that will address those weaknesses.

1. A customer services representative designed the following form to use when a customer makes a claim against the com-

pany's satisfaction-guaranteed policy. Evaluate the message and revise it as necessary. Justify all revisions. Your evaluation and revision will be used in the training program for new employees.

We're sorry to learn that you were disappointed with the (product) we sent you on (date) . But we're glad you told us so that we can prove that we didn't lie when we made a satisfaction-guaranteed sale.

Please deduct (amount) from the total amount shown on Invoice (No.) , and mail us a check for (amount) , the remaining balance due.

Be sure to enclose this note with your check.

Cordially,

2.   Evaluate this reminder-stage collection message that is enclosed with a statement for the overdue payment. Revise the message as necessary. Justify all revisions. Your evaluation and revision will be used in the training program for new employees.

I'm sure, (Name) , that you intend to pay your Nature's Wonders bill for the merchandise that we shipped to you on (date) , but we haven't heard from you and your account is now 30 days past due.

Maybe you wanted to see if the plants would grow before you paid the bill. Surely you've had enough time to prove that we shipped healthy plants that will grow if planted and cared for properly.

But if you aren't satisfied, remember our guarantee. We'll gladly replace any defective plants. Fair enough?

Please be fair with us, too. Use the enclosed envelope and send us your check today.

3.   Assume your classmates are a group of trainees. Orally present your evaluation of the letters and your suggested revisions. Since the trainees are not familiar with your word processing software, include a brief explanation of the reasons for using form messages and how to produce such messages efficiently on your word processing system. Include appropriate visual aids in the presentation.

COMMUNICATING WITH REPORTS

Reports stimulate decisions; reports summarize decisions. As your business career advances, your responsibilities for reporting—orally or in writing—will increase.

All communication concepts and criteria presented in Chapters 1 through 15 apply to the reporting process. But you need additional research and writing skills to produce effective reports. Part 5 helps you to develop those skills. Chapters 17 through 20 present guides for planning reports, explain procedures for collecting and analyzing relevant data, and provide strategies for effective presentation of written reports.

REPORTS AS DECISION AIDS

OBJECTIVES

After completing this chapter, you should be able to:

1. Explain the significance of reports in the business decision-making process.
2. Identify business reports by dominant characteristics.
3. Describe trends in business reporting.
4. Explain the relationship of report function to report structure.

DECISIONS CASE

Your friend, J. B. Gunn, has recently started working as an administrative assistant to the dean of Best Business College. One of Gunn's first assignments was to prepare a report on placement of graduates who have received bachelor's or master's degrees in business from BBC since 1980.

While visiting the Best campus, you step into Gunn's office. "How's the job?" you ask.

Proudly Gunn places a ten-page report on the desk. "I just finished this—my first big assignment. Dean Jones should really be pleased with this. Our placement record is outstanding. Ninety-five percent of our graduates are employed within three months of graduation. And they get good jobs too."

You leaf through the pages and reluctantly begin to read. Masses of statistical data are presented in single-spaced narrative style. After reading one page, you realize that extracting information from that report will be tedious.

Reluctantly, you look at your friend and shake your head. "There's great stuff in this report, Gunn. But let's look at how you've presented it—from Dean Jones's perspective."

What will you suggest to Gunn? Why?

Additional questions about this decision-making case are stated at the end of this chapter. Study the chapter before answering those questions.

CHAPTER CONTEXT

Employees at all job levels rely on reports. Managers develop the firm's strategy in response to internal and external reports. Supervisory, technical, and staff personnel base daily operating decisions on reports. Effective business decisions require objective, understandable reports. The communication-by-objectives approach, which you have been encouraged to use throughout this book, will serve you well as you plan and write business reports.

PURPOSE OF BUSINESS REPORTS

What characteristic is
common to all
reports?

The primary purpose of a business report is to convey information for decision making. Report styles and formats vary greatly; reports may be written, oral, or multimedia messages. But whatever their manner or means of communication, **business reports** share this characteristic: They are objective, factual messages used in the decision process.

Several kinds of reports may be generated in a series of related decisions. Illustration 16–1 shows a typical report-decision sequence. Although the reports suggested by that sequence differ in many respects, each report helps managers or employees make decisions.

Illustration 16–1   BUSINESS REPORT–DECISION SEQUENCE

Memorial Hospital Employees Request Child Care as Employee Benefit

Report: Personnel Director Conveys Request to Hospital Administrator.

Decision: Hospital Administrator Requests More Information.

Report: Personnel Department Presents Written Analysis of Pros and Cons of Child Care as Optional Employee Benefit.

Decision: Hospital Administrator Defers Action for Memorial Hospital; Decides to Request Study by Southeast Association of Hospital Administrators.

Report: Hospital Administrator Tells Personnel Manager of Decisions; Requests that Employees Be Informed.

Report: Memo from Personnel Director to Memorial Hospital Employees Tells About Administrator's Decisions.

Decision: Individual Employees Decide Whether to Continue Working for Memorial Hospital.

CLASSIFICATION OF REPORTS

How may reports be classified?

Business reports can be classified according to dominant characteristics or traits. The first seven traits described here influence decisions about the eighth—formality.

Predominance of Words or Numbers

Narrative reports use more words than numbers. **Statistical reports** use more numbers than words.

Intervals of Transmission

Periodic reports are issued regularly (for example, weekly, monthly, annually). **Progress** or **interim reports** occur occasionally between start and finish of a project or an operation. **Special reports** are sent irregularly in response to nonroutine requests or needs.

Direction of Transmission Flow

Horizontal reports move among levels of equal authority within an organization. **Vertical reports** move between superior and subordinate levels. **Radial reports** cut across levels of authority and may move within or outside an organization.

Context

Technical reports use specialized vocabularies to convey information among specialists with similar training and experience. **Nontechnical reports** use simpler words to convey information to people with dissimilar training and experience. Classification by field or subject (e.g., production report, sales report) also characterizes the message according to its context.

Message Structure

Chronological structure presents information according to the sequence in which events occurred. **Logical structure** arranges information in patterns of deliberate reasoning (e.g., patterns of induction, deduction, comparison, contrast, elimination of alternatives). **Psychological structure** accommodates the receiver's preferences or idiosyncrasies by arranging information according to her or his special demands, needs, or wishes.

Message Purpose

The purpose of **informational** or **fact-finding reports** is to present data with little or no interpretation. In contrast, **analytical reports**—including examination, investigation, and recommendation reports—formulate an issue or identify a problem; analyze, synthesize, and interpret pertinent data; present logical conclusions; and often offer recommendations for appropriate action. **Research reports** are analytical reports that deal with the quest for knowledge (basic or pure research) or with practical uses of knowledge (applied research).

Length

Some writers consider three or four pages as a dividing line between a **short report** and a **long report**. Reports cannot, however, be placed arbitrarily into those categories. Periodic production reports, for example, are often one or two pages in length; but annual reports, also periodic reports, are considerably longer. Depending on the context, a short report may be presented in letter, memorandum, or manuscript format. Reports of more than three or four pages most frequently appear in manuscript format, often accompanied by a letter or memo addressed to the receiver.

Formality of Tone and Structure

Context, direction of transmission flow, interval of transmission, message function, and length may all influence the formality of a report. **Formal reports** employ an impersonal tone and follow protocols for structure and format. Formal reports may be written in memo or letter format. Frequently, however, they are presented as self-contained documents including such preliminaries as a title page, a table of contents, and an executive summary. Supplementary parts, such as bibliography, appendix, and index, may also be included. The sample report in Chapter 20 exemplifies formal report structure. The following section of a progress report demonstrates formal tone:

> Eleazer and Associates offers the following information in response to your request to be kept abreast of the litigation pending for fiscal years 19— and 19—. On August 24, 19—, Judge Ellen Jones signed an order to dismiss our case. Motions to reconsider the case have been filed. If relief is not rendered via this avenue, an appeal will be filed with the United States Court of Appeals for the Fourth Circuit in Richmond, Virginia.

Informal reports project a personal tone, often using first- and second-person pronouns, contractions, and other conversational qualities. Memo or letter format is common for informal reports, but variations of the manuscript format are also used. Informal tone and format are illustrated in this example showing a portion of the Inco Corporation annual report, employees' edition.

TO ALL INCO EMPLOYEES AND THEIR FAMILIES

You did it again! You manufactured and sold almost $548 million worth of paper, paperboard, and converted products. That's 8 percent higher than last year.

Your efforts showed up even more in our earnings picture—up 15 percent to $20.6 million. And wages, salaries, and benefits for employees were up too, to a new high of $127 million. I'm proud of our record last year, and I want to thank all of you for your efforts in achieving this excellent showing.

In previous progress reports, you were told where Inco stands and how each of us can contribute to its growth. This year we are going to tell you about our benefits program, our safety record, our efforts in air and water quality, and other important aspects of our company.

When You Need It, It's There

Last year the Inco group insurance plan paid $3,518,338 for employees and dependents who met medical and other emergencies. The Inco retirement plan added 175 new names to make a total of 1,350 receiving monthly checks. When you need help, it's there: "The operation I had last September put me back in good health, but it also ran up a lot of bills. The Inco group insurance came through in a big way to pay the expenses."

TRENDS IN BUSINESS REPORTING

Although classifications are diverse, several trends are prominent in modern business reporting. Awareness of these trends can help you plan, produce, and use reports effectively.

What is an advantage of each trend in business reporting?

Informal Tone

Increasingly, modern managers require clearly understandable language rather than stilted language for reports. Informal tone tends to make reports more "user friendly," thereby contributing to prompt, effective decisions.

Suggestions for achieving an informal tone were presented in Chapters 2 and 7. The degree of formality may be varied to accommodate report content, reader expectation, or company policy.

Visual Aids

Today's business reports use charts, graphs, diagrams, and tables to picture ideas. Some companies also enliven the pages of their reports with photographs of what is underway in manufacturing, sales promotion, and research. Chapter 14 contains guides for use of visual aids.

Deductive Order

Summary, conclusions, and/or recommendations are often placed at the beginning of the report, followed by supporting data. This direct structure quickly directs the reader's attention to the main point of the report.

If a report of more than three pages is written in the inductive order, the trend is to preface the report with an **executive summary**. This concise abstract of the report is often written in deductive order. The comprehensive report model in Chapter 20 displays a deductive-order executive summary. (See Illustration 20–1.)

Informative vs. Structural Captions

Informative captions emphasize the content of report sections; **structural captions** emphasize the report structure. Captions such as "Summary" and "Recommendation" are structural captions. "Work Completed," "Work in Progress," and "Anticipated Problems" are informative captions.

Informative captions increase reader comprehension. They also serve as tests for writers who verify that all content presented in a report section is logically related.

Single-Spaced Format

Many businesses today use single-spaced format for all reports. The crisp, businesslike appearance and paper-saving potential of this format have contributed to its popularity. Although single spacing permits effective display of text, some report users prefer the reading ease of double spacing. Use your reader's preferences as guides to developing your report.

Whatever style you follow for a particular report, be consistent in your use of that style. Use margins of at least one inch on all sides. If the report is to be bound, allow an extra one-half inch at the binding edge (left or top). Use white space liberally; it tends to emphasize section headings and subheadings, thereby guiding your reader quickly to the content and relative importance of your message parts. You may place headings and subheadings in the center of the page, flush with the left margin or otherwise; but be consistent.

If you capitalize every word in the first major heading, do so with every major heading. If you underline the first subheading of a group, do so with every equivalent subheading.

Collaborative Production

Business reports are often produced in collaboration with other employees. Collaborative report writing includes collective planning, drafting, revising, and final production of the report. Successful collaboration requires that persons assigned to a project be skilled at group problem solving (Chapter 5). Much of the group writing is accomplished by working together in the same room. But collaborators today also accomplish tasks by computer networks, whereby writers share their writing and give or receive feedback electronically.

Group members must ultimately agree on the content, structure, and language of a report. To reach that agreement, each member must participate actively in all phases of planning, research, and report production. Chapters 17 through 20 discuss those phases.

REPORT FUNCTION AND STRUCTURE

Whether informational or analytical, an effective business report fulfills one of three primary functions: production, innovation, or maintenance.[1]

Production Messages

The primary objective of **production messages** is to accomplish the organization's work. In most business environments, efficiency is a prime production concern. Furthermore, the receiver of a production-oriented message frequently needs little psychological preparation for the message. Therefore, efficient—and empathetic—structures for such messages tend to be direct. An appropriate structure for a production-related report is:

1. Use a **directed subject line**, which reveals your intention and embodies the main point of the message (e.g., Overtime Hours Required in Finishing Unit Through June 30).[2]

Marginal notes:

What structure is appropriate for a production message?

What is a directed subject line?

---

[1]This discussion of function builds on work of Richard V. Farace and Donald MacDonald, "New Directions in the Study of Organizational Communication," *Personnel Psychology,* vol. 27 (Spring 1974), pp. 1–15.

[2]See Priscilla S. Rogers, "A Taxonomy for the Composition of Memorandum Subject Lines: Facilitating

2. Begin with the main point of your message: a recommendation, a conclusion, a summary, a question, or an answer.
3. Provide supporting details, listed or enumerated, whenever possible to improve clarity.
4. Conclude with a statement of goodwill relevant to this situation (optional).

Innovation Messages

The primary objective of **innovation messages** is to foster a change in organization behavior or structure. When the receiver needs no psychological preparation for the proposal, the direct structure of production messages is appropriate. Frequently, however, the receiver requires preparation for the proposed change. In such situations, an indirect structure is appropriate. Here is a suggested structure for innovation messages:

1. Use a **neutral-topical subject line,** which provides a broad-label identification of the report content but does not reveal the writer's intention (e.g., Overtime Schedules in Finishing Unit).
2. Use induction by stating details that justify the proposal.
3. State the proposal clearly and positively.
4. Conclude with a statement of goodwill relevant to this situation.

Maintenance Messages

The primary objective of a **maintenance message** is to promote the receiver's feelings of self-worth and worth to the organization. Maintenance of human resources may be achieved through goodwill messages. The following structure is appropriate for a maintenance message:

1. Use a directed or a neutral-talking subject line. **A neutral-talking subject line** uses descriptive words that suggest message content but do not reveal the writer's intent (e.g., Success of Overtime Operations in Finishing Unit).
2. Begin with a positive statement that reinforces the receiver's feelings of self-worth.

What structure is appropriate for an innovation message?

What is a neutral-topical subject line?

What structure is appropriate for a maintenance message?

What is a neutral-talking subject line?

Writer Choice in Managerial Contexts," *Journal of Business and Technical Communication*, vol. 4, no. 2 (September, 1990), pp. 21–43 for a discussion of directed, neutral-talking, and neutral-topical subject lines.

3. Provide details that support or validate those feelings. End the message here.

Or:

4. Close with an additional goodwill statement.

The following example demonstrates that structure. Goodwill-message structures given in Chapter 11 are also appropriate for reports that serve the maintenance function.

TO: All Employees
FROM: A. E. Bay, President
DATE: August 19, 19—
SUBJECT: Bay Electric Employees Are Community Benefactors

Your generous participation in the blood donor program has placed Bay Electric Co. in the "Community Benefactors" category for this summer's blood drive. Eighty-five percent of our employees participated in the donor drive last week—a new record for Bay Electric.

Thank you for responding to a community need. Employees like you have helped maintain Bay's reputation as a socially responsible company.

REVIEW AND TRANSITION

Reports are decision aids. Since businesses require many types of decisions, businesses also require many kinds of reports. Your career progress will be influenced by your ability to adapt your research and writing practices for various contents, intervals of transmission, directions of transmission, contexts, and message purposes.

Your report writing should reflect awareness and appropriate use of these contemporary trends: informal tone, visual aids, deductive order, informative captions, and single-spaced format. Moreover, you will likely find yourself participating in the trend toward collaborative production of business reports. The structure of a report, whether produced by one person or collaboratively, should complement the report's function. Three primary functions of business reports are production, innovation, and maintenance.

Effective reports begin with a coherent plan for acquiring information and communicating the results of a project. Chapter 17 presents processes for planning and producing effective reports.

YOUR DECISIONS FOR CHAPTER 16

Which of your initial suggestions to Gunn, if any, were reinforced by your study of Chapter 16? What additional advice will you now give Gunn? How may the classifications of reports guide Gunn's decisions about this report?

How can you use the trends in business reporting to help Gunn improve the report?

DISCUSSION QUESTIONS

A. In the context of Chapter 16, what are appropriate definitions for these terms?

1. business report
2. chronological structure
3. logical structure
4. psychological structure
5. narrative reports
6. statistical reports
7. horizontal reports
8. vertical reports
9. radial reports
10. production message
11. innovation message
12. maintenance message

B. What trends are evident in current business reports?

C. Refer again to the opening Decisions Case. Which of the report classifications apply to Gunn's report of Best Business College graduate placements?

D. What is an appropriate use for a directed subject line? neutral-topical? neutral-talking?

E. Share with your classmates a report that you have received in your role as student or employee. Using Chapter 16 report classifications, how do you classify the report? Which trends does the report exemplify? What function (production, innovation, or maintenance) was served by the report?

APPLICATIONS

A list of suggested report topics follows these Applications. Use those topics, or others approved by your instructor, to complete Applications 1 and 2. As directed by your instructor, these applications may be continued in Chapters 17 through 20.

1. Review the list of topics. Select three topics that interest you for a term project. In a memo to your instructor, report your choices. Use the message structure suggested for a production message. Include the following in your report:

a. The topics you have selected.

b. Your reasons for selecting each topic (e.g. relevance to career preparation, previous experience, access to data, etc.).

c. A request for tentative approval of the topic list and/or further guidance in defining a topic.

2. In work groups of four or five students, select a topic for a term project. Specifically, do the following:

a. Each student selects a general topic in which he or she is interested.

b. Group members discuss mutual areas of interest and select a general topic in which all members of the group have an interest.

c. Group members collaboratively write a memo to the instructor to report the outcome of the meeting. State the topic and request approval to continue developing a term project focused on that topic. Use the message structure suggested for a production message.

3. Refer to Application 2 and review Chapter 5, Collaborative Communication. In a memo to your instructor, report your assessment of the group's performance. Identify group members and the communication behaviors exhibited by each. Conclude the memo with a request to remain with this group or to be transferred to another group as you continue this term project.

BUSINESS REPORTS: SUGGESTED TOPICS

The following topics are clustered in two groups. The first group is a sample of research projects that involve data sources easily available to you at your school. Your selection or adaptation of a topic from this first group requires authorization by your instructor and by other persons whom your instructor may designate.

The second group is a sample of problems often confronting a business firm (identified here as "XYZ Company"). If you are employed while attending school, consider using or adapting topics from this second group. Projects based upon this group require authorization by your instructor, by other campus authorities concerned, and by your employer.

As you select a topic, follow these suggestions:

1. Reword the topic to suit your circumstances. Because this book is used by many people in various situations, the topics are worded somewhat generally. As you progress to Chapter 17, limit the scope of your topic so that your research will be valid and reliable but manageable.

2. For controlling data-source use, your instructor may restrict you to published materials only. Otherwise, as indicated by Chapters 17 and 19, consider using publications and other valuable aids, such as the following:

a. unpublished documents—e.g., relevant master's theses, doctoral dissertations, records or reports supplied by your employer and which you get permission to use
b. interviews and questionnaires that you design, pretest, and, if necessary, revise before using—but only with permission of all people concerned
c. your own scientifically controlled observations or experiments—again only with permission of all people concerned

Group A Topics: Campus Issues

1. Specifically, how am I managing my time, effort, and other resources while attending school? What, if anything, should I do to improve that management? Why? What challenges to my communication abilities are disclosed by my answers to those questions?

2. What role does stress play in my life as a student? How can stress affect me in my career? What resources are available at my school to help me learn stress-management skills? How are communication skills—or lack thereof—related to stress management?

3. In what ways should I improve my ability to perceive, interpret, recall, or evaluate my own and other people's communications?

4. In what ways should I improve my ability to observe, listen, read, speak, write, or communicate nonverbally?

5. What career should I follow after earning my diploma or degree? Why? What employment opportunities probably will be available to me then? What employment opportunities are available to me while I attend school? What placement services does my school offer me? What other forms of career assistance (aptitude tests, other psychological inventories, etc.) does my school provide? Which of these aids should I use? Why?

6. In what ways are academic needs similar and different for students who are unemployed, employed part-time, or employed full-time? To what extent do, or should, the needs of working students affect academic requirements at my school? What communications do I perceive as necessary among working students and their employers, professors, and academic administrators?

7. In what ways are academic or social needs of students who live off campus like or unlike those of students who live on campus? What special services, if any, do off-campus students desire? What special services, if any, does my school provide to off-campus students?

8. What child-care needs exist among faculty, staff, and students at my school? What services, if any, does the school provide? What services,

if any, do faculty, staff, and students desire from the school? How can (should) those services be funded?

9. Of total costs for educating students at my school, how much is actually provided by tuition or student fees? What sources provide additional necessary funds? What effect does this information have upon my evaluation of my education? What changes of attitude, if any, does that evaluation produce within me?

10. How are athletic programs—intramural and intercollegiate—funded at my college? What impact does such funding have on other college activities?

11. Which campus organizations, if any, should I join? In what organizational programs or projects should I participate? to what extent? Why?

12. To what extent does my school demonstrate concern for the environment? What recycling and pollution-control policies and practices exist? What are the costs and benefits of those policies?

13. What has my college or university done to increase educational opportunities for persons with physical disabilities? What, if anything, should be done—as perceived by students? by faculty? by administrators? What legal and ethical issues are involved?

14. What has my school done to assist students with learning disabilities? What, if anything, should be done—as perceived by students? by faculty? by administrators? What legal and ethical issues are involved?

15. What communication problems do international students encounter at my school? What, if anything, has the school done to assist international students who experience communication problems? What are the attitudes of students whose native language is English toward differential treatment of students whose native language is other than English?

16. What research and/or instruction related to new communication technology is being conducted at my school? What plans exist to expand or reduce that research and/or instruction? Why?

17. What attitudes do students, faculty, and administrators have toward the practice of granting academic credit for experiences outside the classroom (e.g., work, travel)? What policies and procedures has my school adopted for such credit? What changes can/should be made in those policies/procedures?

18. What is the feasibility of a student credit union at my school? What experiences have other colleges and universities had with such credit unions?

19. What is the feasibility of a student book exchange at my school? What are possible advantages? problems?

20. In what ways, if any, is my school serving the non-traditional student (over age 25; retired persons; "empty-nest" homemakers, etc.)? What attempts are made to recruit such students? How are they assimilated into the school community? What special services exist for them? What unique problems do they face? Are deviations allowed in admission and progression standards?

21. What ethical and legal issues are associated with the purchase and use of computer software? What are student attitudes toward those issues? Do students in different major fields of study evidence different attitudes?

22. What collaborative writing experiences are required or encouraged at my school? What instruction and resources are available to facilitate collaborative writing? What problems do students encounter? How are those problems resolved?

23. What kinds of courses or programs does my school offer to prepare students for working in an international business environment? How effective are those offerings? What plans does the school have to expand those offerings? How does my school's efforts at internationalizing the curriculum compare with X school's efforts?

24. What efforts has my school made to incorporate a study of business ethics into the business curriculum? How effective are those efforts? How does my school compare with X school in this regard?

25. What is my school doing to prepare students for work in a technological environment? How do graduates of my school rate that preparation? How does my school compare with X school in computer instruction and other aspects of working in a technological environment?

Group B Topics: Business Problems

1. Where, when, why, and how is unofficial communication within XYZ Company more effective than official communication? What are the consequences? What communication changes, if any, should be made? by whom? involving whom?

2. What electronic communication technologies should XYZ Company incorporate into its communication system? Why? What will be the likely costs and benefits? What training will be required? What protocols for use must be defined?

3. What communication training needs exist at XYZ? How were they

identified? What training options are available? What criteria should be used to evaluate those options? How should training be provided?

4. Where should XYZ Company locate its plant? its offices? its other facilities? When? Why?

5. When and why should XYZ Company expand, add, reduce, or close organizational units?

6. What has XYZ Company done to prepare its employees for merger with ABC Company? What communication problems or successes are evident in that preparation?

7. When should XYZ Company introduce a new product or service to a particular market? How? Why?

8. Why did XYZ Company profits decline, rise, or remain stable during a given period?

9. Why should XYZ Company own rather than lease, or why should it lease rather than own, particular equipment or facilities?

10. What is the feasibility of an entrepreneurial venture (e.g., maternity clothing store, catering service) in X location (e.g., your home town, your college town, your favorite resort town)?

11. Specifically, how should XYZ Company minimize its maintenance and repair costs? expand its customer services? improve its safety practices? its merchandising programs? inventory controls? sales promotions? collection procedures? purchasing procedures? production procedures? information management? administrative services? communication systems?

12. What, if anything, has XYZ done to promote awareness of the arts in your community? What, if anything, has the company done to communicate with the public about its interest in the arts? What commendation or criticism has XYZ management received from its stockholders and members of the arts community for its support of the arts?

13. XYZ is a retail firm that operates a store near your campus. Conduct a research-and-report project that enables you to accomplish the following:

    a. Compare, contrast, and evaluate the local advertising practices of XYZ and its chief competitor.
    b. Offer suitable recommendations to XYZ management.

14. XYZ must decide whether to advertise through local mass-communication media. Research and report the relative advantages and disadvantages of advertising by AM radio, FM radio, TV, newspapers, and outdoor media.

15. XYZ must expand its word processing capabilities. Besides WP, what communication technology should XYZ evaluate now? What criteria for purchase and use should XYZ adopt?

16. What employment opportunities exist at XYZ for persons with physical disabilities? What benefits have accrued to XYZ from hiring persons with disabilities? What problems, if any, accompany such hirings?

17. What can (should) XYZ do to rehabilitate employees who incur work-related disabilities? What advantages accrue to the company from rehabilitation programs? to employees? to society? Should XYZ communicate its rehabilitation efforts to the public? If so, how?

18. What can (should) XYZ Company do to assist employees with child-care responsibilities? What advantages or disadvantages might accrue to the company by providing child-care services? What form(s) of services, if any, should be considered?

19. What has XYZ Company done to demonstrate concern for the environment? What recycling and pollution-control policies and practices exist? What are the costs and benefits of those practices? In what ways, if any, has the company communicated its environmental awareness to the public?

20. What policies, if any, has XYZ established for communicating with the public following a company crisis? What stimulated the development of those policies? Compare XYZ's policies with those of another major corporation such as Procter and Gamble or Exxon.

21. What international communication challenges has XYZ Company confronted in recent years? Why? What has the company done to meet those challenges?

22. In what ways, if any, does XYZ Corporation encourage its employees to participate in community activities? What benefits, if any, have accrued to the company and to its employees for community participation? What are employees' attitudes about involving themselves in community activities or issues?

23. XYZ management has been encouraged to join a trade association. Investigate and report to management the possible benefits and disadvantages of membership in a trade association.

24. XYZ Company currently produces both gas-powered and electric-powered furnaces, air conditioners, and hot water heaters. XYZ wants to expand its operations and is considering the manufacture and sale of solar-powered heating and cooling devices. What is the feasibility of entering the solar market?

25. What ethical challenges have XYZ Company employees confronted

while employed with that company? How did they deal with those challenges? What XYZ Company policies/procedures facilitate resolution of ethical issues?

CASES

1. As chairperson of your department's Safety and Health Committee, you conducted a survey of employees to determine their competence in lifesaving skills. You discovered that 85 percent of your associates have had no instruction in lifesaving skills of cardiopulmonary resuscitation (CPR), and 75 percent have not completed a basic first-aid course. The survey also showed that 50 percent of the respondents would likely participate in company-sponsored CPR and first-aid training courses. Moreover, 5 percent of the employees reported job-related incidents, suggesting that employee safety could be improved if a greater number of employees possessed those lifesaving skills. Report this information in a memorandum to Austin Mitchell, Director of Personnel. Use the message structure recommended for production messages.

2. Refer to Case 1. You are a certified CPR instructor. Austin Mitchell has asked you to conduct CPR training sessions for the employees. In a memo to employees, announce the company's plan to provide free instruction. Provide realistic details about time, place, number of sessions, etc. Each training group will be limited to 12 participants. Encourage employees to participate. Ask them to call the Personnel Office to sign up for the training sessions. Use the message structure recommended for innovation messages.

3. Refer to Cases 1 and 2. Twelve employees successfully completed the first CPR training session. In a memo to all employees, report this achievement and its impact on workplace safety. Remind employees that the next session begins in two weeks and space is still available. Use the message structure recommended for maintenance messages.

MULTICULTURAL INSIGHTS

1. Are the trends described in Chapter 16 characteristic of business reporting in your native country? Why or why not? What cultural characteristics may account for different practices?

2. Are the production, innovation, and maintenance classifications and structures discussed in Chapter 16 relevant for reports used in your native culture? Why or why not? What cultural characteristics may account for acceptance or rejection of those classifications and structures?

PROCESSES FOR PLANNING RESEARCH AND WRITING REPORTS

        G.   Edit Drafts
        H.   Produce Final Copy
  III.   Review and Transition

OBJECTIVES

After completing this chapter, you should be able to:

1. Develop a plan for business research.
2. Convert that plan into a research proposal.
3. Analyze your objectives before writing a report.
4. Explain the primary tasks of each phase in the report-writing process.
5. Apply the steps of the report-writing process as you compose reports.

DECISIONS CASE

Six months ago you became sales manager of Nymeyer Music Mart, a family-owned business in a university town 150 miles from Chicago, Illinois. Your third-quarter report shows that net sales of orchestra and band instruments were 30 percent higher than for the same quarter a year ago. But sales of music supplies were down 15 percent.

"If we can move musical instruments, why not the other merchandise?" President Nymeyer asks. "Churches, schools, colleges, universities—they're all around us. They need music supplies. Why isn't our inventory moving? Please investigate that problem and give me a report—within a month."

What will you do first to fulfill that assignment? What will you do last? What communication guides from Chapters 1 through 16 will help you? What unanswered questions do you have?

Additional questions about this decision-making case are stated at the end of this chapter. Study the chapter before answering those questions.

CHAPTER CONTEXT

A report may be as short as a single sentence or as long as a complete book. Whatever its length, an effective report begins with a plan. Moreover, when your report deals with a complex problem, you may need to conduct extensive research before you can begin writing the report. That research also must follow a plan.

Once again, the communication-by-objectives approach applies: Decide what you want to achieve by your research and your report. Then design a strategy to reach your objectives.

PLANNING BUSINESS RESEARCH

What is business
research?

All reports—whether long or short, formal or informal—rely on research. **Business research** is an organized, thorough search for decision-relevant information.

The temptation to begin writing a report without adequate research planning can be strong. But surrendering to that temptation may cause needless waste of time, money, and effort. Guide yourself with these insights:

1. The complexity of the problem tends to dictate the complexity of the research. Some reports are based upon research as simple as recalling and analyzing observations or experiences. Other reports require much more extensive data collection and analysis.
2. Your research and your report are not identical. Each must be planned separately. Business research is an *activity;* business reports *communicate the nature and results of that activity.* Plan the details of your research first. After your plan has been approved or modified, apply it to data collection, analysis, synthesis, interpretation, and evaluation. Then—and, logically, not until then—will you be prepared to outline the first draft of your report.

Some reports are concerned with easily defined problems and present easily obtained data. An example of such a report is a sales representative's weekly summary of contacts made and sales volume. The sales representative may be able to write an effective report after briefly searching for and organizing relevant papers. The report plan may be no more than a mental or informal written outline; the report may even follow a prescribed format. Other reports deal with much more complex problems, require considerable data collection and analysis, and involve extensive outlining, drafting, and revision before a final report can be produced.

What are the ten parts
of an effective
research work plan?

Whether your report is as simple as a sales summary or as complex as a market analysis, the ten-part work plan summarized in Illustration 17–1 will guide you toward effective research. The following paragraphs describe those ten parts individually.

Authorization

To avoid needless duplication of effort and resources, you and your coworkers need to know the source and the context of a request for a report. Knowledge of that authorization enables you to channel your research efforts productively.

Authorization for some reports exists as part of your normal job assignment. As a sales representative, for example, you would likely be authorized (required) to prepare periodic sales reports. But your superior may also make special research assignments. If you do not receive an authorization message with your research assignment, ask your superior to tell you for whom the research and the report are to be prepared.

Identification

Early in your research plan—unless someone has already done so for you—you should identify the principal topic and the tentative title of your report. In formal research projects, the topic is called the **problem** to be investigated. Precise identification of the topic (the *what*) of your report will direct your data collection efforts.

A report topic or problem may be so complex that paragraphs of concise wording are necessary to describe it properly. The title, however, summarizes the topic. A report topic may also be as simple as "Greer Plant Production, March, 19—." In that case, the title (or the subject line of a memo report) may be identical to the topic.

Purpose

As with every other effective communication effort, you need to determine the objectives that your proposed research will accomplish. *Why* are you doing the research? What do you intend to disclose, establish, describe, explain, prove, disprove, or recommend?

Scope

After determining your research purposes, decide upon the range of your research efforts. By analyzing your topic and purpose, you detect subtopics and issues. Then you can logically decide what to include within the scope of your research. To define the **scope**, you state where your research will begin, what it will include, and where it will stop—all in relation to the purpose you have stated.

Delimitations

In research terms, **delimitations** or **restrictions** are statements that reveal the controls placed on your research. Scope and delimitations are related in these ways: Whereas scope is a commitment of what your research will in-

Illustration 17–1   A WORK PLAN FOR EFFECTIVE RESEARCH *

1. **Authorization**—What people, policies, regulations, or circumstances permit you to undertake your research project?
2. **Identification**—What is the topic of your study? the tentative title of your project?
3. **Purpose**—What is (are) the objective(s) of your project?
4. **Scope**—What are the major areas of your study?
5. **Delimitations**—How do you propose to confine your scope? What factors will you deliberately exclude?
6. **Limitations**—What factors, beyond your own control, probably will modify or restrict your study?
7. **Design**—How do you intend to build and conduct your study?
   a. *Assumptions:* What ideas or concepts do you hypothesize initially without proof?
   b. *Methodology:* What kinds of data do you seek? How do you plan to collect and evaluate the data?
      (1) *Sources.* What people, publications, records, and other references pertain to your study? Which of the pertinent references are available to you? Which of the available, pertinent references do you intend to use?
      (2) *Data collection.* How do you intend to acquire information from available, pertinent sources—readings, observations, interviews, questionnaires, experiments, other means? In what sequence do you expect to use the methods of acquiring information?

clude, delimitations are statements of related aspects that you deliberately will exclude. Scope represents the proposed direction and extent of your research. Delimitations include definitely set boundaries that keep the scope of a research project from becoming too broad to be significant.

How do limitations differ from delimitations?

Limitations

Factors beyond your control, such as time, money, or availability of data, may restrict your research. Those factors are **limitations**. Similarly, delimitations

Illustration 17-1 A WORK PLAN FOR EFFECTIVE RESEARCH (continued)*

---

    (3) *Previous findings.* What earlier work, if any, is related—directly or indirectly—to your project? What have earlier studies revealed?

    (4) *Data processing.* How do you plan to organize the data that you collect? How do you propose to analyze, synthesize, and interpret the information?

  c. *Report format.* What kind of message do you expect to produce? Is your report to be written—a memorandum, a letter, a multi-page document, a publication? Is your report to be oral—an extemporaneous, a textual, a memorized message? What style and tone of writing or speaking do you intend to use?

8. **Schedule and Budget**—What are the due dates for intermediate phases of your study? What is the deadline for presenting your final report? How much time, money, and other resources does every major phase of your proposal require? How much of these resources does your total project require?

9. **Justification**—Of what potential value is your project? Who is apt to benefit from your report? What kinds of benefits are likely to result? Why does your project merit the investment of time, money, and other resources?

10. **Additional Remarks**—What relevant considerations are omitted from the preceding categories of your work plan?

*According to writer and reader preferences, the parts of this plan may easily be rearranged while retaining logical unity. For example: authorization, identification, purpose, justification, scope, limitations, delimitations, design, schedule and budget, additional remarks.

---

imposed upon the research may restrict the outcome. By acknowledging limitations, you recognize that a gap may exist between the ideal research plan and the practical realities you confront in the business world.

Scope, delimitations, and *limitations* are technical terms that emphasize this important concept: Effective business researchers and reporters practice communication by objectives. They plan what *will* and *will not* be included in a project.

Typical steps in narrowing the scope of a project are suggested in Illustration 17–2. The topic evolves from a broad statement, "Employees' Needs for

Illustration 17–2   NARROWING THE SCOPE OF THE PROJECT

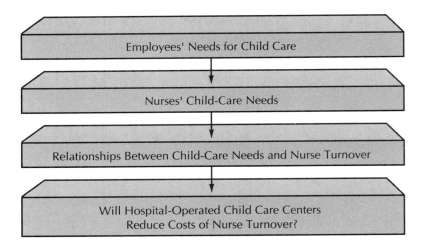

Child Care," to a statement restricted by needs of specific employees (nurses) and benefits to a specific industry (hospitals).

Design

Having determined authorization, identification, purpose, and boundaries, you are ready to plan your research design.

Except perhaps for a chronologically arranged project and message—like the journal accompanying a laboratory experiment—your research design for the work plan may not coincide with the subsequent content outline for your report. Often, the research design contains many more planning details than the final report requires. The **design** is a description of a logical pattern of activities by which you will achieve your purpose. The design may include a statement of your assumptions, hypotheses, and tentative conclusions, as well as your proposed study order.

Assumptions. An **assumption** is acceptance of something as true without proof. For example, an information systems analyst who samples documents prepared by word processing users assumes that the sampled work accurately represents all word processing production. **Hypotheses** are conjectures or beliefs that can be tested empirically. If you are studying users' satisfaction with your word processing system, one hypothesis might be that satisfaction is related to "user friendliness" of the word processing software. Your design begins with statements of assumptions and/or hypotheses to be tested.

What is included in
research design?

Methodology. Stating your proposed methodology involves this procedure:

1. *Identify and locate relevant data sources.* People, publications, records, previous reports concerning the *what* and *why* of your research are potential data sources. Select from among all the available and appropriate sources those that you will actually use for your project. Let your precisely stated topic and purpose guide you as you evaluate and select data sources. Chapter 18 discusses primary and secondary data sources for business research.

2. *Review previous studies or company files.* Discover what has already been learned from earlier studies that pertain, directly or indirectly, to your project. Usually you will report these insights under one of these headings: "Review of Previous Findings," "Review of Pertinent Sources," "Review of Relevant Literature," or the like.

3. *Decide upon data-collection methods (through readings, interviews, questionnaires, experiments, observations).* Determine what resources are available or must be developed for the methods you choose. For example, will you need to conduct a survey? Are interviewers available? Must they be specially trained? Who will develop, distribute, and collect questionnaires? Who will tabulate the responses?

4. *Determine data-processing techniques.* Data processing (analysis, synthesis, interpretation) will yield information for the discussion, conclusions, and recommendations sections of your report. When you analyze, you separate data into parts. When you synthesize, you arrange those parts into patterns that pertain to your research purpose, scope, and limitations. When you interpret, you relate your research discoveries to information that is already known. Chapter 2 of this book (which discusses analysis, synthesis, and logical reasoning) will help you with nonquantitative analysis. A business statistics book can assist you with quantitative data analysis.

Report Format. The final step of your research design is anticipation of the message to be produced—the report itself. You are not yet at the stage of outlining—certainly not of drafting—the report. You are still engaged in planning the complete research process.

At this point, however, part of your research design is to anticipate the format of that final report. Is the format to be written? If so, in what style? Is the format to be written and oral? Again, in what style? Is it to be primarily narrative? mostly explanatory? mainly persuasive? Will it include statistics? computer printouts? charts, graphs, tables, other exhibits? Will the format be that of a business letter, memorandum, semiformal report, full-length research document, audiovisual presentation? What message style, tone, and medium will be appropriate for your audience? As you see, the concept being advanced here is that research is not complete until it has been communicated.

Schedule and Budget

Often the authorization message from your superior will indicate how much time, money, personnel, and other resources are to be invested in your project. But if a schedule and a budget are not specified, you need to set your own deadlines and determine the necessary resources for completing the entire project, including its final report.

A useful strategy is to plan your work schedule in reverse chronological order. Plan your project from the anticipated completion date to the starting date. Set intermediate due dates for completing phases of the work in this way:

1. Deadline for delivering final report:
   Resources required:
2. Due dates for revising and editing:
   Resources required:
3. Due dates for outlining and drafting:
   Resources required:
4. Periods for data analysis, interpretation, evaluation:
   Resources required:
5. Periods for data collection and tabulation:
   Resources required:

Why are a research schedule and budget important?

By scheduling your work in reverse chronological order, you can realistically pace your research efforts, step by step, without having to race the clock for the final deadline. Instead of submitting a late report, you can use your timetable and budget guide to monitor your progress as you work. If one phase of the project requires more or less time and resources than scheduled, you can adjust other phases as you move along. If necessary, you can request your superior to authorize additional time and resources well before the final deadline.

Justification

Communication by objectives implies that authors justify every report—for themselves and their superiors. Defining the report purpose often provides adequate justification. A research proposal, however, sometimes involves selling the value of your work plan. Therefore, be prepared to identify people, units, or operations likely to benefit from the results of your project; and describe the nature of those benefits when appropriate to do so. The justification may be combined with the purpose or may be stated separately.

Additional Considerations

If your work plan requires information that does not logically suit the preceding headings, state that information in a section headed "Additional Remarks," "Other Considerations," or the like. A statement about your qualifications to do what is proposed may be included here or in a section headed "Qualifications of Researcher."

Before beginning the work represented by your research plan, you will be wise to get feedback from your superiors. As you communicate your work plan, include a specific or implied request for approval. That request may be made under "Additional Remarks," highlighted in a separate section, "Request for Approval," or conveyed in an accompanying letter or memorandum.

For some projects, an outline of your work plan will suffice. Frequently, however, your superior will require a formal document. A formal, written version of the ten-part work plan is a **research proposal**, as exemplified by Illustration 17–5 at the end of this chapter. Examples of other business proposals appear in Chapter 19.

THE REPORT-WRITING PROCESS[1]

As an effective researcher, you will use your work plan to guide your data gathering and analysis. But data analysis rarely marks the end of your responsibility. You must communicate that analysis, orally or in writing.

The preceding discussion of the work plan emphasized the importance of clarifying the problem and purpose. Illustration 17–4 suggests, however, that to navigate the route from problem identification to production of a final report, you must complete—and probably repeat—many steps. An effective written report is the product of a multiphase process involving these steps:

1. Clarify problem and purpose.
2. Analyze audience.
3. Assemble, evaluate, organize data.

---

[1]Description of the process and guides for different phases of the process are synthesized from the following: Jeanne W. Halpern, "What Should We Be Teaching Students in Business Writing?" *The Journal of Business Communication,* vol. 18, no. 3 (Summer 1981), pp. 39–53; Linda Flower, *Problem-Solving Strategies for Writing,* 2d edition (Orlando: Harcourt Brace Jovanovich, 1985); Linda Flower, John R. Hayes, Linda Carey, Karen Schriver, and James Stratman, "Detection, Diagnosis, and the Strategies of Revision," *College Composition and Communication,* vol. 37, no. 1 (February 1986), pp. 16–55.

Illustration 17–3   A RECURSIVE REPORT-WRITING MODEL

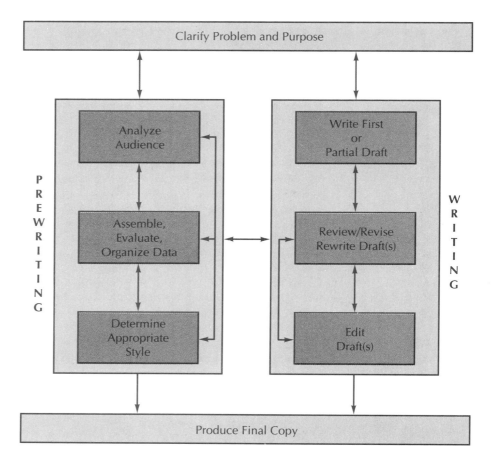

4. Determine appropriate style.
5. Write first or partial draft.
6. Review/revise/rewrite draft(s).
7. Edit draft(s).
8. Produce final copy.

The steps are not necessarily performed in sequence. In fact, most skilled writers follow a **recursive** pattern, returning to and repeating steps until a desired objective is met. The arrows in Illustration 17–3 indicate the recursive nature of the report-writing process. The following guides will help you in each stage of the process.

What is the meaning of *recursive*?

Clarify Problem and Purpose

Why review report problem and purpose before writing?

If you prepared a research plan, you have already identified the report problem (what was studied) and the purpose (why the study was conducted). Review those parts of your research plan before you begin to write the report. Knowledge of the problem and purpose will help you choose relevant content and appropriate structure for your report.

If you had no formal research plan, answering these questions will help you clarify the problem and purpose:

1. What is the context?
2. What is the specific conflict, difficulty, question, or assignment?
3. What are the significant features, parts, or elements of the problem?
4. Who is involved?
5. When or how did the problem begin?
6. What alternative solutions should be considered?
7. What criteria should a solution meet?

Problem clarification is a prewriting step. So too are the three tasks shown in the left-hand box of Illustration 17–3. Appropriate answers to some of the questions about problem and purpose require that you define your audience and consider how you will collect and present data to satisfy your reader's needs. As you engage in those prewriting tasks, you may revise your concept of the report problem and purpose.

Analyze Audience

What is included in audience analysis?

Audience analysis includes determining who will read the report and what effect you want to achieve with that audience. Answers to these questions can guide your audience analysis:

1. Who is my primary audience? Is it internal? external?
2. What effects do I want to achieve with this audience?
3. How will the audience use my writing?
4. What content should I add, condense, change, or omit to adapt my message for my audience?
5. Will there be a secondary audience? Is it internal? external?
6. Does the answer to Question 5 change any of my decisions about the audience?

As the two-directional arrows in Illustration 17–3 indicate, decisions about your audience will affect your collection and presentation of data.

Assemble, Evaluate, Organize Data

Before writing, assemble your data and evaluate their adequacy in terms of the problem, purpose, and desired audience effect. Arranging the data into an outline will reveal data gaps or overlaps and can assist you in data-organization decisions.[2]

As you prepare your outline, answer these questions:

What questions should guide your outlining activity?

1. Am I outlining with a real reader in mind?
2. How can I organize my writing to help that reader understand and use it?
3. Does this organizational plan include all that my reader needs to know?

Before you use that outline as a guide for writing, you must answer one more question: What tone, style, or voice should I adopt for my audience?

Determine Appropriate Style

Style is a manner of expression. Your communication style results from your choice of language components—words, punctuation, structure (sentence, paragraph, document), etc. By conscious choices of language, you should adapt your style to accommodate your analysis of the reader's needs, desires, knowledge, and status. Answers to these questions will help you achieve appropriate style:

How can you evaluate style?

1. Is my language appropriate to my audience? too complicated? too abstract? too ambiguous? too technical?
2. Is my language appropriate for my purpose? too formal? too casual?
3. Have I selected sentence structure, words, and punctuation to convey my desired style?

As the arrow connecting the left and right sides of Illustration 17–3 suggests, those questions must be posed before and while you write. After completing the prewriting steps, you are ready to begin writing. Be reminded, however, that the connecting arrows between the two sides of the illustration suggests that you may return to the prewriting steps repeatedly, even as you progress through several stages of writing.

---

[2]Review outline techniques presented in Chapter 6.

Write First or Partial Draft

With your outline as a guide, you can capture your ideas on paper. Many writing-process experts recommend that you write the first draft of your report freely, without excessive concern for technical precision. Some writers find it constructive to break that drafting task into small units such as outline sections. Completion of each unit provides a sense of achievement and marks a point for constructive review.

Expert writers seldom accept the content and structure of the first draft. Skilled writers revise their first drafts to produce a second, third, or fourth draft of the document.

Review/Revise/Rewrite Draft(s)

Draft revision requires intense review of the document in terms of your purpose and audience. During the revision stage you should not attend merely to surface problems, such as spelling, grammar, and style. The goal of revision is substantial change. It can lead to re-seeing, restructuring, and even rethinking the entire report.[3]

What comprises revision?

Effective revision consists of three elements: detecting problems in the text, diagnosing those problems, and selecting a strategy for improvement.[4]

Detecting Problems. Problem detection requires that you read the text and compare it with your intentions. Try to approach the text as your reader would. Avoid the tendency to blithely "read" what you intended to say. A sentence or paragraph or larger section may seem clear to you because you come to the revision with an internal "set," or expectation of what is there. Since your reader will not have that internal representation of the text, you must scrutinize your writing for problems of logic, organization, and meaning.

Diagnosing Problems. If you detect a problem, take a few minutes to diagnose it before rewriting. Did you lose sight of the purpose? Did you forget your audience? Did you include irrelevant data simply because it was interesting? Is the text confusing?

One way to approach problem diagnosis is to remind yourself of what you wanted to do. ("The main point of this section is . . . .") Use that statement to test your text. If the text seems confused, outline it to determine where it

---

[3]Flower, et al., p. 16.
[4]Ibid., pp. 27–51.

fails to fulfill your intent. If a statement seems awkward, go beyond a superficial diagnosis ("This doesn't sound right"). Identify *why* it doesn't sound right: not parallel? too forceful? too passive? unclear subject? indefinite pronoun? faulty logic? Then use the diagnosis to plan the revision, just as you planned your original writing.

Improving the Text. Diagnosis of problems should suggest ways to improve the text. You will paraphrase, redraft, reorganize, add to, or subtract from parts of the text. Always compare your output with your intent—as modified during the writing process—and your reader's likely response.

Revision is not a one-time step in the writing process. In all likelihood, you will have to go through a series of write-and-test loops. And revision must be followed or complemented by editing and proofreading.

Edit Drafts

Whereas revision tends to be a *macro* approach to text improvement, editing and proofreading are *micro* approaches. During revision you will scrutinize larger units to determine if content and structure fulfill your goals. In the editing phase you will scrutinize smaller units (words, phrases, sentences) for clarity and accuracy.

The goal of editing is to write:

> ▶ economical prose that says exactly what you mean
> ▶ forceful prose that holds your reader's attention
> ▶ logical prose that expresses the hierarchical structure of your ideas[5]

You will achieve those goals if you apply the Chapter 2 guides for appropriate use of logic and the criteria for communication effectiveness (accuracy, coherence, clarity, conciseness, and courtesy).

A communication-by-objectives approach will help you manage your revision and editing: The guide presented in Illustration 17–4 suggests content, structure, and style objectives. Also review and apply the suggestions for revising and proofreading presented in Chapter 6.

Produce Final Copy

Your final copy should be a polished product of which you are justifiably proud. Many report writers wait a day or more between revisions. That time lag permits the writer to approach each revision with fresh mind and eyes.

What is the goal of editing?

---

[5]Flower, op. cit., p. 191.

Illustration 17–4 REVISING/EDITING BY OBJECTIVES

Content	1.	Does the information under each heading or subheading logically belong there?
	2.	Are the data accurate? adequate? relevant?
	3.	Should a visual aid be used?
	4.	Are summaries used for complex sections?
	5.	Are conclusions logical?
Structure	1.	Is the opening paragraph precise? relevant?
	2.	Are the report sections sequenced in the most effective order?
	3.	Do section heads aid communication?
Style	1.	Is sentence structure correct? clear?
	2.	Have I eliminated vagueness? wordiness? grammatical errors? clichés?
	3.	Are transitions clear?

Answer these questions as you prepare your final copy:

1. Does my format signal the message structure?
2. Has my revision clarified the communication for my audience?
3. Has my editing removed distractions such as needless words, clichés, and mechanical errors?
4. Does this communication represent my best writing?
5. Does the appearance of the report complement its content and purpose? Is the appearance of the report complimentary to the reader and the writer?

Your career success may well be influenced by the quality of your reports. Chapter 17 offers two stepping stones to success:

1. Plan your research.
2. Take a process approach to your report writing.

Professional researchers and writers have used those strategies successfully for many years.

Illustration 17-5   RESEARCH PROPOSAL IN REPORT FORMAT

```
                        RESEARCH PROPOSAL

            WILL HOSPITAL-OPERATED CHILD CARE CENTERS
                 REDUCE COSTS OF NURSE TURNOVER?









                            Prepared for
                   Dr. P. E. Shaughnessy, President
            Southeast Association of Hospital Administrators
                        222 Medical Center
                 Columbia, South Carolina  29202-4218









                            Prepared by
                   Susan B. Booth, President
                        Booth and Associates
                        One Watermark Plaza
                      Columbia, SC  29210-3291
                         October 10, 19--
```

Illustration 17–5 RESEARCH PROPOSAL IN REPORT FORMAT (continued)

RESEARCH PROPOSAL

WILL HOSPITAL-OPERATED CHILD CARE CENTERS
REDUCE COSTS OF NURSE TURNOVER?

1. <u>Background and Authorization</u>

A critical shortage of nurses who are willing to work in hospitals
poses serious problems for the hospital industry. At its September
25, 19--, meeting, the Southeast Association of Hospital Administrators discussed ways to reduce the high turnover rate among nurses,
particularly those with young children. Hospital administrators
observed that nurses who have difficulty finding high-quality child
care tend to drop out of the labor force until their children enter
school. Moreover, absentee rates are high among workers on the
evening and night shifts. Administrators suspect that high absenteeism on evening shifts is related to lack of adequate child care.

You requested that I submit a proposal to investigate the relationship between availability of child care and turnover rates among
hospital nurses.

2. <u>Identification of Problem</u>

I propose to investigate the potential for hospital-operated child
care centers to reduce the costs associated with nurse turnover. The
working title is "Will Hospital-Operated Child Care Centers Reduce
Costs of Nurse Turnover?"

3. <u>Scope</u>

This study will include analysis and projections of the following
factors related to child care and nurse turnover:

a. What proportion of the nurse shortage is related to
    lack of adequate child care facilities?

b. What are the costs associated with nurse turnover?

c. What is the cost of a hospital-operated child care center?

4. <u>Purpose</u>

The purpose of this study is to identify a feasible solution to the
critical shortage of hospital nurses. If inadequate child care is a
major factor in nurse turnover, removing that barrier may attract a
greater number of nurses to long-term careers as hospital nurses.

Illustration 17–5   RESEARCH PROPOSAL IN REPORT FORMAT (continued)

5. <u>Delimitations</u>

The following factors are not within the scope of analysis:

a. The effects of turnover on the quality of nursing care.

b. The physical capabilities of hospitals to provide space for a child care center.

c. The assessment of needs for child care services at a particular hospital.

d. The costs related to absenteeism and extended maternity leave.

6. <u>Limitation</u>

One factor may limit the interpretation of data. Since no hospitals in the Southeast currently operate a child care center, estimated costs must be based on expenses incurred by private or state-operated centers. Costs of a hospital-operated child care center may not be fully comparable to those of a private or public center.

7. <u>Design</u>

The study requires identification, evaluation, and projection of child care needs among nurses in the Southeast, the costs to hospitals of nurse turnover, and the costs to hospitals of operating a child care center for nurses.

a. Assumptions. Initial beliefs include these:

  (1) Statistics contained in national studies of the nursing shortage may be used confidently to estimate similar conditions in the Southeast.
  (2) Information derived from interviews with nurses and child care providers in Columbia, South Carolina, may be used confidently to estimate similar data for the Southeast.

b. Methodology. The proposed project will use primary and secondary data sources. Both quantitative and qualitative data-analysis techniques will be used.

  (1) Sources. Secondary data will be collected from recently published reports about company-operated child care services, the costs of nurse turnover, and the shortage of hospital nurses. State licensing requirements for child care centers will also be reviewed. Primary data will be sought from hospital administrators, directors of child care centers, and hospital administration consultants.

Illustration 17–5 RESEARCH PROPOSAL IN REPORT FORMAT (continued)

(2) Data collection. The probable sequence for data collection
     is:
     (a) Conduct computerized literature search to identify
          relevant secondary data sources. Analyze and
          synthesize data from those sources.
     (b) Identify needs for primary data. Develop interview
          guides. Conduct interviews. Analyze and synthesize
          data from those sources.
(3) Data analysis. Information about nurse shortages will be
     used to determine the proportion of the shortage related to
     child care problems. That percentage will be applied to the
     shortage in the Greater Columbia area to project a potential
     increase in working nurses for that area if child care prob-
     lems are resolved.

     Detailed operating budgets from public and private child
     care centers will be used to project costs for a hospital-
     operated center. Direct and indirect costs of nurse turn-
     over (recruiting and hiring, orientation and training,
     separation) will be used to calculate an average per-nurse
     turnover cost. That cost will be compared with the average
     cost per child for operating a child care center.
(4) Report format. A written report of this proposed research
     will be presented to you on December 8, 19--. A team from
     our research staff will also present the findings, conclu-
     sions, and recommendations orally at your executive board
     meeting on that date. The tentative time and place for that
     presentation are 2:30 p.m. at the Association's head-
     quarters, Suite 13, Rogers Office Park, 116 Park Lane,
     Columbia, SC.

8. Schedule and Budget

Assuming proposal approval on or before October 17, 19--, target
dates for major phases of the project are:

October 31:   Analysis of secondary sources completed
November 7:   Interview guides written, tested, and
               printed
November 21:   Interviews completed
November 30:   Data analysis completed
December 5:   First draft of report completed
December 8:   Transmittal of written report and oral
               presentation of findings to Executive Board

The total cost for the project is $6,750. This cost reflects our
standard consulting fee of $75 per hour and an estimate of 90 employ-
ee hours to be devoted to data collection, data analysis, report
preparation, and report presentation.

Illustration 17–5   RESEARCH PROPOSAL IN REPORT FORMAT (continued)

9.   Justification

Results of this study should indicate one way that members of the
Southeast Association of Hospital Administrators can address the
critical shortage of hospital nurses. If a hospital-operated child
care center proves to be feasible, hospital administrators will be
able to reduce operating costs and hospital nurses will be able to
maintain a steadier career pattern than they currently experience.
More important, however, hospital patients may experience better-
quality care by nurses who have removed a major source of stress from
their own lives.

10.   Request for Approval

Thank you for inviting this proposal. My staff and I are ready to
begin the project as soon as the proposal is accepted. Approval on
or before October 17 will ensure completion in time for the December 8 meeting of your Executive Board.

REVIEW AND TRANSITION

Effective reports begin with a coherent plan for acquiring information and communicating the results of a project. The plan, which can be used for simple or complex research, includes the following: acquire authorization; identify topic; state purpose; define scope, delimitations, and limitations; design the study; develop time schedule and budget; justify the project; and recognize other relevant facts.

Research is not complete until its results are communicated. That communication often is by written report. Effective report writers use this recursive writing process:

1. Clarify problem and purpose.
2. Analyze audience.
3. Assemble, evaluate, organize data.
4. Determine appropriate style.
5. Write first or partial draft.
6. Review, revise, rewrite draft(s).
7. Edit draft(s).
8. Produce final copy.

Researchers frequently formalize the work plan into a written research proposal, as shown by Illustration 17–5. After receiving approval for a research proposal, you will progress to data collection and analysis. Chapter 18 presents guides for those steps. You may need to submit progress or interim reports as you collect and process your data. Chapter 19 presents examples of those reports.

YOUR DECISIONS FOR CHAPTER 17

Which, if any, of the ten planning steps presented in Chapter 17 did you suggest for the Nymeyer Music Mart report? Which, if any, did you not suggest? Why? What is the communication value of each step? How may the recursive model for producing a report help you complete the Nymeyer report?

DISCUSSION QUESTIONS

A. In the context of Chapter 17, what are appropriate definitions for these terms?

1. business research
2. business report
3. research or report problem
4. research or report purpose
5. recursive

           6.   revision
           7.   editing

B.   In what ways is the communication-by-objectives concept related to Chapter 17?

C.   In what ways are topic and purpose related?

D.   How are scope, delimitations, and limitations related?

E.   What is the relationship of a research work plan to a research proposal?

F.   How does the comprehensive model of a work plan, as presented in Chapter 17, apply to your actual research assignments for an employer or an instructor?

G.   Explain these statements:

    1.   Data analysis rarely marks the end of your responsibility. You must communicate that analysis, orally or in writing.
    2.   Decisions about your audience will affect the presentation of your data.

H.   Based on your previous writing experience, in which phases of the process (as represented by Illustration 17–3) do you encounter the most difficulty? What tips for overcoming those problems can you share with your classmates? In which phases of the process would collaboration be most helpful?

APPLICATIONS

1.   For Application 1 of Chapter 16, you identified three general topics for a term project. Based on your instructor's feedback to that application, do the following:

    a.   Select one of those broad topics.
    b.   Define the problem, purpose, and scope of a research project that can be completed within the time span specified by your instructor. If applicable, also identify delimitations and limitations.
    c.   In a memo to your instructor, report your proposed project as you defined it in 1b. Include a tentative title for a report based on the proposed research. Request approval to continue developing a work plan for the research.

2.   For Application 2 of Chapter 16, your group identified a topic for a term project. Based on your instructor's feedback to that application, do the following:

    a. Define the problem, purpose, and scope of a research project that can be completed within the time span specified by your instructor. If applicable, also identify delimitations and limitations.

    b. In a memo to your instructor, report your proposed project as your group defined it in 2a. Include a tentative title for a report based on the proposed research. Request approval to continue developing a work plan for the research.

3. As directed by your instructor, form work groups of two or three persons. In a memo to your instructor, evaluate the content, structure, tone, and format of the following report to employees.

TO: All Department of Transportation Employees
FROM: James Jenro, Director
DATE: October 31, 19—
SUBJECT: Recycling Policy

On May 30, 19—, Governor Hanks signed into law the Clean Environment Act. The purpose of the act is to ensure that all state agencies actively contribute to promotion of a clean environment. One provision of the Act requires that each state agency demonstrate "active, constructive, measurable efforts to reduce environmental pollution." Evidence of compliance must be reported to the Division of Environmental Control annually.

To comply with that provision, I mandate the following recycling policy:

▶ Each operational unit shall maintain bins for collection and separation of recyclable aluminum, plastic, and paper materials. Bins shall be placed at convenient locations throughout the unit and shall be clearly labeled.

▶ Employees shall be instructed to deposit all recyclable materials that they encounter during the course of their working day.

▶ The Department's Maintenance staff shall collect the deposited materials daily and transport them weekly to Grove's Recycling Center.

▶ Monies obtained from Grove's shall be deposited into a separate account. The total amount received annually shall be reported to the Division of Environmental Control as evidence of DOT's compliance with the Act. Those funds shall be disbursed annually to a local charity designated by a committee consisting of one representative from each operating unit.

I expect full compliance with this policy. Please do not hesitate to call me if you need further information about its implementation.

4. Based on your analysis for Application 3, revise the memo.

5. Refer to Applications 3 and 4. In a memo to your instructor, describe how your group used the various phases of the report-writing process described in Chapter 17.

CASES

1. You are a customer services representative for Things of Beauty, a nationwide mail-order distributor of nursery plants. Your money-back-guarantee policy urges customers to report any dissatisfaction with their shipments of plants. You have noticed that the number of complaints about slow deliveries—and consequently dead or dying nursery stock—has increased. You have further noticed that all complaints relate to shipments that were picked up by Driver No. 48 of the express company you use. Write a letter report in which you present the problem and request appropriate action to relieve it. Address the report to J. Adamek, Manager, Presto Express, 6809 Balsam Ave., St. Louis, MO 63143-6809.

2. You are the supervisor of SMP Corporation's graphics department. The function of the department is to provide advice and technical assistance for company employees who need graphics for internal or external communication. One of your employees, Hugh Paque, has been using SMP supplies and time to make graphics for his personal use. After his first violation of company policy—which forbids that practice—you orally reprimanded Mr. Paque and asked him to pay for the supplies he had used. He has not yet reimbursed the company, and now you have discovered him violating the policy again. Write a report, in memo format, to Personnel Director, E. E. Overstreet; report the policy violation and request advice about further disciplinary action.

MULTICULTURAL INSIGHTS

1. Is the ten-step work plan described in Chapter 17 a useful planning guide for writers who compose reports in your native language? Why or why not? Which steps, if any, are more important than others?

2. What authorization procedures are typical in firms that conduct business in your native culture? From your observation, experience, or reading, tell how those procedures differ from or are similar to those used in U.S. firms.

COLLECTING AND ANALYZING DATA

CHAPTER OUTLINE

A. Editing
B. Classifying
   1. Appropriate to the Research Problem and Purpose
   2. Exhaustive
   3. Mutually Exclusive
   4. One Dimensional
C. Interpreting
IV. Review and Transition

OBJECTIVES

After completing this chapter, you should be able to:

1. Use primary and secondary data sources efficiently, effectively, and ethically to fulfill research objectives.
2. Understand why, when, and how to acknowledge data sources.
3. Carry data analysis through to logical, defensible conclusions and recommendations.

DECISIONS CASE

Brenda Nymeyer, president of Nymeyer Music Mart, has given you another difficult assignment.

"We have been in the music market for 20 years, but we've never sold pianos. Please prepare a report that will help us decide whether to add pianos to our inventory."

What kinds of data will you need? What are potential sources for those data? What methods will you use to get the data?

Additional questions about this decision-making case are stated at the end of this chapter. Study the chapter before answering those questions.

CHAPTER CONTEXT

Business reports convey information for decision making at all levels of the organization. Vast information needs in business require that you be able to extract information from a variety of primary and secondary data sources.

Your work-plan statements of authorization, scope, purpose, limitations, schedule, and budget will help you decide upon the kinds and numbers of sources to use. By constantly reminding yourself of those factors, you will gather and process only pertinent data. The data processing for your project may include manual, mechanical, or electronic techniques. But whatever the techniques may be, your research requires these actions: analysis, synthesis, and interpretation.

USING SECONDARY DATA SOURCES

Efficient data collection begins with an examination of **secondary data**—information compiled and made accessible by other researchers. Effective use of secondary data sources includes three factors:

1. knowledge of business data sources
2. acknowledgment of secondary data sources
3. procedures for collecting secondary data

Business Data Sources

The business library is a rich source for many categories of data, including general business, industrial, company, and miscellaneous statistical data.

General Business Data. A productive first step in your data search is to examine *Business Information Sources*[1] or *Encyclopedia of Business Information Sources.*[2] Those comprehensive annotated bibliographies will direct you to sources most likely to contain the data you seek.

Guides to current business information include these indexes:

Business Periodicals Index and its on-line counterpart, *WILSONLINE*
Canadian Business Periodicals Index
Management Contents
New York Times Index
Predicasts F & S Index United States
Predicasts F & S Index Europe
Predicasts F & S Index International
Public Affairs Information Service Bulletin
Public Affairs Information Service: Foreign Language Index
Wall Street Journal Index

Each of those indexes is arranged by subject, author, or standard industrial classification (SIC) numbers to facilitate your search.

The **SIC system**, developed by the U.S. Census Bureau, assigns a four-digit classification number to all manufacturing and nonmanufacturing industries. This classification system is used in many government and nongovernment

---

[1]Lorna M. Daniells, *Business Information Sources,* rev. ed. (Berkeley: Univ. of California Press, 1985).
[2]Paul Wasserman et al., eds., *Encyclopedia of Business Information Sources,* 6th ed. (Detroit: Gale Research Co., 1988).

What is the SIC
system?

sources, such as market guides, directories, and indexes. Consequently, familiarity with SIC numbers enables you to locate industry and product data efficiently.

Industry and Company Data. As you continue your data search, you may want to focus on a particular industry, company, product, or individual. These directories and handbooks will assist you.

What sources supply
industry and company
data?

Annual reports of specific companies

Directory of American Firms Operating in Foreign Countries
Directory of Foreign Manufacturers in the United States
Dow Jones Investor's Handbook

Dun and Bradstreet directories and handbooks:

American Corporate Families: The Billion Dollar Directory
America's Corporate Families and International Affiliates
Canadian Key Business Directory
Guide to Key British Enterprises
International Market Guide—Continental Europe
International Market Guide—Latin America
Middle Market Directory
Million Dollar Directory
Principal International Businesses

Local directories:

Classified Directory of Wisconsin Manufacturers
Directory of New England Manufacturers
South Carolina Industrial Directory

Moody's manuals:

Moody's Bank and Finance Manual
Moody's Industrial Manual
Moody's International Manual
Moody's Municipal & Government Manual
Moody's OTC Industrial Manual
Moody's Public Utilities Manual
Moody's Transportation Manual
Moody's Complete Corporate Index

Standard & Poor's directories and handbooks:

Industry Surveys
Outlook
Register of Corporations, Directors and Executives
Stock Reports

Thomas' Register of American Manufacturers
U.S. Industrial Outlook
Value Line Investment Survey
Who Owns Whom: Continental Europe
Who Owns Whom: North America

What sources supply
statistical data?

Statistical Data. When you require statistical data, these sources will provide general social and economic statistics as well as specific industrial or commodity data.

County Business Patterns
Dun and Bradstreet Credit Service: Industry Norms and Key Business Ratios
Economic Indicators
Federal Reserve Bulletin
Historical Statistics of the United States
Monthly Labor Review
Predicasts Forecasts
Statistical Abstract of the United States
Statistical Service
Survey of Current Business

Special Business Periodicals Issues. Several business periodicals publish special reference issues annually. Those that are especially useful for business research include:

Business Week Corporate Scoreboard Issues
Forbes Annual Directory Issue
Forbes Annual Report on American Industry
Fortune Annual Directory Issues
Sales and Marketing Management Survey of Buying Power Issues

Computer Information Services. Locating business information has become much easier in recent years, thanks to electronic aids such as on-line and CD–ROM (Compact Disc–Read Only Memory) reference services.

If your college or business library subscribes to on-line information services, you will use a computer and telecommunications connections to access a database or reference service at a remote location. Typically, a user fee is charged for each search, often based on search time and the number of abstracts printed. Two useful on-line reference sources are *PTS F & S Indexes,* which contains statistical data and forecasts as well as an index to the sources of those data; and *WILSONLINE,* the computer version of *Business Periodicals Index.*

CD–ROM reference services consist of databases stored on compact discs that are accessed through personal computers. If your library subscribes to this service, there is no additional user fee. Two useful CD–ROM business databases are COMPACT DISCLOSURE and ABI/INFORM ONDISC.

COMPACT DISCLOSURE, which is updated monthly, contains detailed financial data on 12,000 publicly traded corporations. The information includes:

- ▶ five years of balance sheet and income statement data
- ▶ quarterly balance sheet and income statement data for the most recent three quarters
- ▶ three years of key annual financial ratios
- ▶ Zack's Corporate Earnings Estimates
- ▶ Company profiles, including complete description of the business and the relevant SIC Codes
- ▶ the president's letter and management discussion sections of annual reports
- ▶ full text of the financial footnotes to the 10-K reports for New York and American Stock Exchange companies and all Fortune 500 companies

All of that financial information for the 12,000 companies is stored on a single CD–ROM disc, measuring only 4.75 inches in diameter!

ABI/INFORM is a database covering business periodicals. It contains abstracts and indexes to business articles in 800 different journals, covering a five-year period. The database is updated monthly, adding the most recent month's information and dropping the oldest month, thereby maintaining a uniform five years of data. A companion to ABI/INFORM is BUSINESS PERIODICALS ONDISC (BPO). BPO provides the full text from 382 of the 800 journals indexed by ABI/INFORM.

Whether using an on-line or a CD-ROM information service, you can locate information quickly by entering search terms, key words or phrases, that describe your topic. From then on, the computer does the work of searching stored documents and identifying those in which your key words appear. For example, COMPACT DISCLOSURE can be searched by such variables as company name, geographic area, type of business, financial information, or number of employees. Using appropriate commands, you can design your search to match your data needs: for example, companies in the electronics industry, headquartered in the Southwest, with long-term debt greater than $100 million.

The key to an effective search is to select search terms that are neither too broad nor too narrow. Assume, for example, that you are conducting research about environmental ethics. Using *ethics* as your search term yields over

What are advantages of a CD–ROM search?

2,300 titles in an ABI/INFORM search—an unmanageable number. Combining *ethics* with *environment* narrows that search to four titles. (These numbers were valid when this text was written. Since ABI/INFORM is updated monthly, the numbers may change; but the principle remains: An effective data search requires purposeful selection of search terms.)

After locating relevant documents, you have various options for recording the information. For an on-line search, you can request a paper printout of the citations list and abstracts of articles you select. With most CD–ROM services, you can get a paper printout or you can download the information to a floppy disk for use in a spreadsheet or word processing program.

Acknowledging Secondary Data Sources

Appropriate acknowledgment of data sources (documenting) requires an understanding of why, when, and how to document.

Why. Acknowledging the sources from which you obtain report data is justified on three bases: ethics, courtesy, credibility. Ethical standards require that you give credit to whom credit is due. *Plagiarism* (using another's words or ideas without crediting the source) is literary theft, sometimes resulting in serious professional or legal consequences. Hence, you will use footnotes or other acceptable reference notations to credit contributors of unique data.

Acknowledging data sources is also a courtesy to your report readers. Your list of sources is a valuable aid to those who wish to conduct research in areas related to your study.

Fully as significant as ethics and courtesy is the opportunity to establish your credibility as a researcher and your contributions to the report. By inference, any information that is not attributed to a secondary source may be credited to you. Excessive documentation suggests that you contributed little to the analysis. Appropriate documentation identifies your reliance on others for data along with your ability to analyze, synthesize, and interpret data.

When. Dependence upon others for words, ideas, and style should be acknowledged. As specificity increases, the need for documentation increases. These examples may guide your decisions about source acknowledgments:

Exact quotation (acknowledge source)

"Since 1963, money given to the arts by corporations, foundations, and federal, state, and local government has increased more than 2,000 percent."[3]

Why should you acknowledge secondary data sources?

---

[3]Marshall Doswell, "Business and the Arts," *Business and Economic Review* (October 1984), p. 16.

When should you
acknowledge second-
ary data sources?

Paraphrase of one or more authors—not general knowledge (acknowledge source)

In 1982, nearly 75 percent of support for the arts came from corporations or foundations.[4]

Paraphrase of several sources—general knowledge (no documentation
required)

Many corporate executives consider a company's support of the arts a
legitimate business expense.

How. Standard documentation procedure includes a **bibliography** (list of
sources, references) and an **in-text reference** (footnote or other accepted notation) for specific information.

Technically, *bibliography* refers only to published material—books, magazines, newspapers, etc. Some writers prefer to place all sources—including
interviews, broadcasts, lectures, etc.—in a single list. If you follow that practice, an appropriate heading for the list is *Sources* or *References.* The list
should include all relevant sources consulted, even though your report does
not contain specific citations from each. The list is normally placed at the end
of the report. (Appendix E and Illustration 20–1, Comprehensive Report
Model, demonstrate source lists.)

A bibliographic citation includes the *who, what, when,* and *where* of a
publication. Consult any standard reference manual for format and punctuation style. One acceptable style is shown here and in Appendix E.

How does a
bibliography differ
from sources or
references?

Book

Harris, Philip R., and Robert T. Moran. *Managing Cultural Differences,*
3d ed. Houston: Gulf Publishing Company, 1991.

Journal article

Carroll, E. Ruth. "Improved Interpersonal Relationships a Result of
Group Learning." *Journal of Business and Technical Communication*
vol. 5, no. 3 (July 1991), pp. 285–299.

Footnotes are used to acknowledge sources of information, to amplify or
validate statements in the text, and to refer the reader to other parts of the
report. A raised, or superscript, Arabic numeral usually is placed in the text
immediately after the statement or the part of a statement to which the footnote pertains. (Asterisks, daggers, or other symbols are used instead of

---

[4]Ibid.

Arabic numerals occasionally, particularly in statistical tables.) Footnotes may be numbered consecutively for each chapter of a very long report or numbered consecutively throughout the whole of a relatively short report. When more than one source is cited for a fact, the several sources may be mentioned in a single footnote, with a semicolon separating one source from another.

A footnote traditionally is placed at the bottom of the page to which it pertains and is separated from the text by a one-inch line beginning flush with the left margin. That style was used to give source acknowledgments for the exact quotation and paraphrase used in the previous section. Many writers today use an in-text citation instead of the traditional footnote. Here are examples of an in-text citation for the paraphrase. (No page number is used for a paraphrase that captures the gist of an entire article.)

Author's name and page number following cited material

In 1982, nearly 75 percent of support for the arts came from corporations or foundations (Doswell 16).

Or:

Author's name, year of publication, and page number following cited material:

In 1982, nearly 75 percent of support for the arts came from corporations or foundations (Doswell, 1984, p. 16).

What are acceptable substitutes for footnotes?

Another variation for source acknowledgments is to place all citations at the end of the report. Ways to acknowledge sources are presented in Appendix E. Any of those styles may be used if used consistently within a single report.

For efficiency, your data collection procedure should include techniques for exact recording of bibliographic information. Keeping exact records of data sources eliminates the need to return to the source as you prepare your footnotes and bibliography.

Procedures for Collecting Secondary Data

A useful procedure for collecting secondary data employs index cards and a subject-numeric indexing system. These guides will help you develop such a system for your research.

1.   Identify the major subtopics or factors about which you are seeking information.

What are the
advantages of using
both data and
bibliography cards?

2. As you locate information about a subtopic, prepare a bibliography card and a data card. (See Illustration 18–1.)
    a. *Bibliography card.* Write complete, accurate bibliographic data on the card. Number the cards consecutively as you prepare them.
    b. *Data card.* Identify the factor or topic at the top-left position on the card and the source number at the top right. Record all information accurately, including page numbers. Use quotation marks to differentiate exact quotations from paraphrases. Use a separate card for each item of information.
3. File data cards by topic. These cards can easily be accessed and rearranged for data analysis and synthesis.
4. File bibliography cards numerically. The numerical system facilitates easy identification of sources and construction of footnotes. You can later alphabetize the cards as you construct your bibliography.

USING PRIMARY DATA SOURCES

Information acquired at or from its point of origin is **primary** or **original data**. Although the data may already exist—in people's minds, in companies' files—they have not been assembled. You, as a researcher and report writer, will develop plans and procedures for assembling such data.

Acquiring Primary Data

Primary data are acquired from many sources and through various methods. The major **sources** are people, events, and organization records. The major **methods** are questioning, observation, and examination or search. In some contemporary businesses, application of CD–ROM technology simplifies the search of company records.[5]

The quality of a report can be no better than the quality of the data on which it is based. Researchers exercise care to ensure the validity and reliability of sources and tools used to tap those sources.

Validity is a concept referring to the accuracy or truthfulness of a data source, the ways the source was used, and the resulting conclusions and recommendations. For example, company records are a more valid data source about employee productivity in Department A than is the department supervisor's memory. Similarly, systematically recording output at the production

What is data validity?
reliability?

---

[5]Paul Bonner, "CD–ROM Power: Knowledge in Hand," *PC Computing,* vol. 3, no. 2 (February 1990), pp. 64–75.

Illustration 18–1 BIBLIOGRAPHY AND DATA CARDS

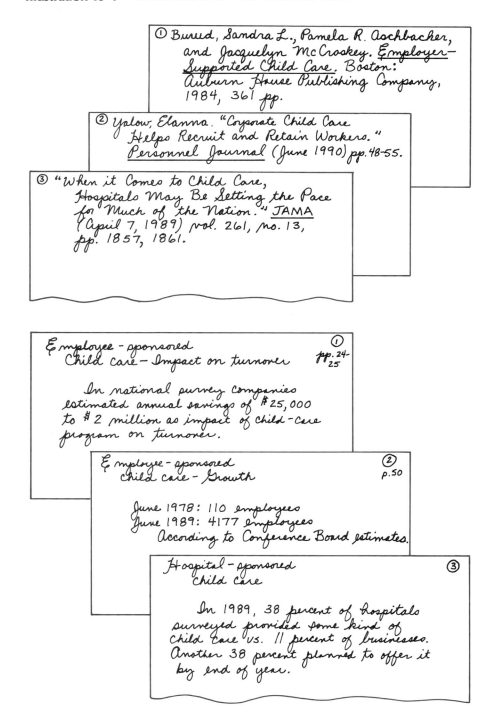

site is a more valid data-collection method than is questioning employees at a later date.

Reliability is a component of validity. **Reliability** is the extent of variation in a data source or the instruments used to collect data. A reliable instrument gives consistent measurements when used repeatedly or by different people. For example, a properly operating indicator on a machine will give a consistent measurement of that machine's output. Such a measurement is likely to be more reliable than an employee's manual count of output.

Questionnaires and interview guides, transmittal messages, and observation forms are commonly used data collection tools. Each must be designed and used carefully for valid research.

Questionnaires and Interview Guides

To question effectively, a researcher first selects a questioning procedure. Then the researcher decides upon the content and structure of the questions.

Questioning Procedures. When questioning people is the only way—or the only practical way—to obtain desired data, you will use a survey or interview technique. A **questionnaire** is a form on which respondents record solicited information. An **interview guide** is a similar form used by an interviewer while questioning interviewees. The form guides the questioner and provides space to record responses.

Questionnaire surveys have several advantages over interviews. The written questionnaire is usually less expensive to use than is its oral counterpart. The questionnaire is easy to administer, merely handed or mailed to intended respondents. In contrast, face-to-face or telephone interviews require considerable time to conduct, and time is costly in business.

Interviews have these advantages over use of questionnaires:

1. Because many people consider speaking to be easier than writing, they may respond more freely to an interview than to a questionnaire.
2. When a question or a response needs clarifying, interviews can permit such clarification immediately.
3. Especially during a face-to-face interview, not only the respondent's words but also the behavior while responding can be perceived, thereby enhancing evaluation of the information given to the researcher.

Questioning—whether by interview or questionnaire—has some shortcomings. Respondents may provide inaccurate or unreliable data. For example, they may recall an event as they wish that event had happened instead of as it actually happened. Moreover, because people are apt to report their

How does a
questionnaire differ
from an interview
guide?

values and behaviors favorably at the expense of accuracy, questionnaires and interviews rarely yield completely objective data. However, when designed and administered by communicators who are knowledgeable about people and words, questionnaires and interviews can elicit data that might otherwise be unobtainable or prohibitively expensive to collect.

The procedures identified in Illustration 18–2 can be used for questionnaires or interview guides. To develop an interview guide, substitute *interview* for *questionnaire* in Steps 1–9. Then relate Step 10 to your oral presentation of the transmittal message as well as to the questions you ask.

Illustration 18–2   GUIDES FOR QUESTIONNAIRE AND
                        TRANSMITTAL MESSAGE

STEPS FOR DEVELOPING AN EFFECTIVE QUESTIONNAIRE AND TRANSMITTAL MESSAGE

(This procedure can be easily modified for an interview guide.)

1. **Identify** the purpose of the questionnaire. (What is my objective for asking the questions? What is my respondent's objective for answering?)
2. **Justify** the use of the questionnaire. (Why should I use this kind of data-collection instrument? Why should my respondent invest time and effort in answering?)
3. **Anticipate** the kinds of data that the questionnaire should elicit. (What kind of data am I seeking? What kind of data is my respondent likely to give?)
4. **Design** an appropriate questionnaire format. (How should I arrange the items so that they are convenient to answer? How should I word the items so that they are pertinent and clear? How should I logically and psychologically move the reader from simple to complex issues? How should I organize the items so that answers are easy to classify, record, and analyze?)
5. **Draft** the questionnaire and transmittal message. (What written statements should represent effective answers for Steps 1–4 in this procedure?)
6. **Revise** the draft of the questionnaire and transmittal message. (What logical, psychological, and linguistic aspects of the draft should be corrected or refined?)

7. **Pretest** the draft of the questionnaire and transmittal message. (What changes should I make after trying the revised draft with people who resemble the intended respondents?)
8. **Revise** the pretested draft. (Which of the changes that Step 7 disclosed as necessary or appropriate should I incorporate into my materials?)
9. **Produce and proofread** the pretested and revised materials. (What attributes, derived from Steps 1–8, should the copies of the final questionnaire and transmittal message convey?)
10. **Distribute** copies of the final questionnaire and transmittal message. (What schedule should I follow so that respondents can answer in time for me to use their information effectively? What postage medium—first class, special delivery, certified mail, registered mail—should I use? Should I include a postage-paid, addressed return envelope? If I am not mailing the materials, when and how should I otherwise distribute and collect them?)

Item Content. As you write items for your questionnaire or interview guide, examine the relevance, scope, and adequacy of each. Include only those items related to your research purpose and scope (defined in your work plan). Furthermore, if you can obtain the requested data elsewhere, consider whether to omit the item.

Questions that are too broad or too narrow often yield invalid data. The broad question "In what type of restaurant do you prefer to eat?" may yield varied responses such as "clean," "Chinese," or "fast food." Conversely, a question that is too narrow may lead respondents to answers that do not truly reflect their attitudes or experiences (e.g., "Is full-flavored coffee your favorite after-dinner beverage?").

Item Structure. Questionnaire items are written in closed or open style. **Closed items** provide responses from which respondents choose. **Open items** give no suggested responses.

Some researchers favor closed style because, if written well, the items are easy to answer and easy to process. Other researchers favor the open mode because such items allow much latitude for response. Ideally, a style is chosen for its potential to extract valid data from respondents. For that reason, questionnaires often contain both open and closed items. (See Illustration 18–3.)

As you construct items, evaluate their relevancy, scope, and adequacy against

---

When may a question be too broad? too narrow?

How do open items differ from closed items?

Illustration 18–3 CONSUMER QUESTIONNAIRE

RIVER HILLS PLANTATION

Banking-Shopping Questionnaire

Instructions: Please select one adult (age 18 or older) from your household to complete this questionnaire. That person should answer each question as it applies to her or him.

1. Who is answering this questionnaire?

   Unmarried head of household ( )   Wife   ( )
   Husband   ( )   Other (specify) _____

2. What is your age?

   18 to 24   ( )   35 to 44   ( )   55 to 64   ( )
   25 to 34   ( )   45 to 54   ( )   65 or over ( )

3. How long have you lived in River Hills Plantation?

   Less than 1 year   ( )   Over 3, under 5 years   ( )
   Over 1, under 3 years   ( )   Over 5 years   ( )

4. Where did you live before moving to River Hills Plantation?

   _____

5. How many adults (age 18 or older) live in your household?   _____

6. How many full-time wage earners live in your household?   _____

7. In what city or town do you do most of your shopping? (Please check only one.)

   Bowen   ( )   Hamilton   ( )   Macomb   ( )
   Carthage   ( )   Keokuk   ( )   Nauvoo   ( )
   Ft. Madison ( )   Lima   ( )   Other (specify) _____

8. In what city or town do you bank most frequently? (Please check only one.)

   Bowen   ( )   Hamilton   ( )   Macomb   ( )
   Carthage   ( )   Keokuk   ( )   Nauvoo   ( )
   Ft. Madison ( )   Lima   ( )   Other (specify) _____

9. What banking services do you use? (Check any that apply.)

   Automatic Teller Machine   ( )   Drive-Up Window   ( )
   Certificate of Deposit   ( )   Individual Retirement Account ( )
   Checking Account   ( )   Loan   ( )
   Credit Card   ( )   Safe Deposit Box   ( )
   Deposit by Mail   ( )   Savings Account   ( )
   Direct Payroll Deposit   ( )   Trust Services   ( )
   Other (specify) _____

Illustration 18–3   CONSUMER QUESTIONNAIRE (continued)

10. When do you usually do your banking? (Please check no more than <u>two items.</u>)

    Going to or from work   ( )   While shopping   ( )
    During working day (e.g., lunch)   ( )   On a special banking trip   ( )
    Other (specify)   _____

11. What would be your reaction to the establishment of a 24-hour, 7-days-a-week automatic teller machine at the River Hills Plantation entrance?

    Very pleased   ( )
    Somewhat pleased   ( )   ⟩ Go to Item 12.
    Indifferent   ( )
    Somewhat displeased   ( )
    Very displeased   ( )   ⟩ Go to Item 13.

12. If you did not already have a banking relationship with the financial institution that established the automatic teller machine at River Hills, how likely would you be to change your banking business to that institution?

    Very likely   ( )
    Somewhat likely   ( )
    Unsure   ( )   ⟩ Go to Item 15.
    Would open a checking account,
      for convenience, but keep
      other business as it is.   ( )
    Somewhat unlikely   ( )
    Very unlikely   ( )   ⟩ Go to Item 14.

13. Please explain why you would be displeased.

    _____

    _____

                                Go to Item 15.

14. Please explain why you would be unlikely to change.

    _____

    _____

15. Thank you for your cooperation. Please return your completed questionnaire in the enclosed envelope to:

                            Ms. Anne J. Jarrell
                            P.O. Box 123
                            Hamilton, IL 62341-1008

the criteria shown in Illustration 18–4. A yes answer to each question indicates that your questionnaire meets the criteria for content effectiveness.

Illustration 18–4   CRITERIA FOR ITEM CONSTRUCTION

1. Is this item necessary? Does it relate to my research topic? Can (should) I get the information from another source?
2. Have I chosen appropriate style—open or closed—for this item?
3. Are all options included for closed items?
4. Is the language clear, unambiguous?
5. Is the item unbiased? Have I avoided leading questions?

What does effective questionnaire format accomplish?

Questionnaire Format. The appearance of a questionnaire may attract or distract respondents. Effective format prompts participants to respond without biasing or distorting their answers. Cautious researchers avoid a layout that promotes **response set**, the tendency to give similar answers to all items. Grouping related items, along with brief instructions for each group, is an effective way to make a long questionnaire seem less burdensome.

When a respondent need not answer all items, branching techniques (instructions to guide the respondent appropriately through the questionnaire) should be used. Illustration 18–3 (Items 11, 12, and 13) demonstrates branching techniques.

After constructing a questionnaire, evaluate its format by applying the criteria for questionnaire format shown in Illustration 18–5. A yes answer for each question indicates that your questionnaire meets the criteria for format effectiveness.

Illustration 18–5   CRITERIA FOR QUESTIONNAIRE FORMAT

1. Have I used white space to enhance readability and relieve tedium?
2. Are answer spaces (lines, blocks) placed near the items to prevent a respondent's giving an unintended answer?
3. Is adequate space provided for open items?

Illustration 18–5   CRITERIA FOR QUESTIONNAIRE FORMAT (continued)

> 4. Are items grouped logically? psychologically? to prevent response set?
> 5. If a respondent need not answer all items, are logical branching instructions given?
> 6. Have I given instructions for returning the completed questionnaire?
> 7. Does the format help me classify and analyze the data?

Illustration 18–3 demonstrates the criteria for item construction and questionnaire format.

Transmittal Messages

What is a transmittal message?

A **transmittal message** presents the questionnaire or introduces the interview. Effective transmittal messages, as demonstrated by Illustration 18–6, are usually arranged according to the familiar AIDA sequence of attention-interest-desire-action:

1. Attract the respondent's appropriate attention to the questionnaire or interview.
2. Stimulate relevant interest.
3. Develop desire to respond.
4. Request, confidently and courteously, the desired action by the respondent (completion and return of the questionnaire or participation in an interview).

A written transmittal message may be placed at the head of the questionnaire, or the message may be an accompanying letter or memo. When the transmittal message is separate from the questionnaire, cautious researchers end the questionnaire with instructions for its return. That practice ensures that—even if the transmittal message or the return envelope is misplaced—the respondent knows what to do with the questionnaire.

For an interview guide, the transmittal message may consist of instructions to the interviewer as well as instructions to the interviewee. The format of the guide must clearly indicate which information is intended for the interviewer and which is to be said or read to the interviewee. (See Illustration 18–7.)

Illustration 18–6   TRANSMITTAL MESSAGE

Jackson and Jackson, Inc.
11266 South 46th Avenue
Chicago, Illinois 60658-2779
(312) 555-4617

July 30, 19--

Dear River Hills Resident:

Your decision to live in River Hills Plantation shows your appreciation for a gracious yet convenient lifestyle. By sharing information about your shopping and banking attitudes, you may be able to make life at River Hills Plantation even more pleasing.

A major financial institution is deciding whether to expand services into the River Hills area. By answering the enclosed questionnaire, you may influence that decision.

If we receive your answers before August 15, they will be included in our analysis. Please take a few minutes now to complete the questionnaire and mail it in the enclosed envelope.

Sincerely,

anne J. Jarrell

Anne J. Jarrell
Project Manager

tm

Enclosures

RESEARCHING FINANCIAL MARKETS SINCE 1955

Illustration 18–7   INTERVIEW GUIDE

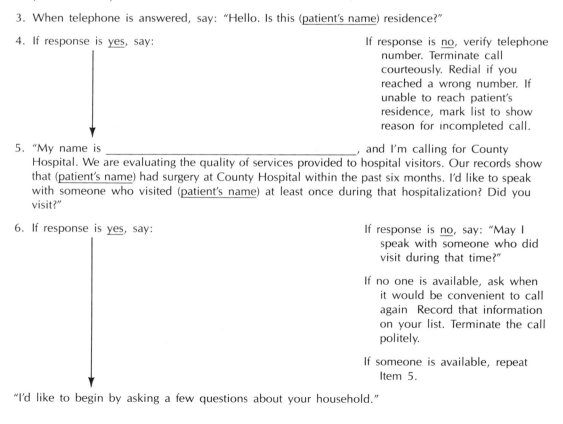

INTERVIEW GUIDE

County Hospital Visitors Survey

Directions for Interviewer:

1. Do all interviewing between 4:00 and 5:30 p.m.

2. Check list for former patient's name and telephone number. Be sure patient's name is fresh in your mind as you dial the number.

3. When telephone is answered, say: "Hello. Is this (patient's name) residence?"

4. If response is <u>yes</u>, say: If response is <u>no</u>, verify telephone
                                                                        number. Terminate call
                                                                        courteously. Redial if you
                                                                        reached a wrong number. If
                                                                        unable to reach patient's
                                                                        residence, mark list to show
                                                                        reason for incompleted call.

5. "My name is _____, and I'm calling for County Hospital. We are evaluating the quality of services provided to hospital visitors. Our records show that (patient's name) had surgery at County Hospital within the past six months. I'd like to speak with someone who visited (patient's name) at least once during that hospitalization? Did you visit?"

6. If response is <u>yes</u>, say: If response is <u>no</u>, say: "May I
                                                                        speak with someone who did
                                                                        visit during that time?"

                                                                        If no one is available, ask when
                                                                        it would be convenient to call
                                                                        again Record that information
                                                                        on your list. Terminate the call
                                                                        politely.

                                                                        If someone is available, repeat
                                                                        Item 5.

"I'd like to begin by asking a few questions about your household."

(READ QUESTIONS AND COMMENTS FROM PAGE 2 AND RECORD ANSWERS)

Illustration 18–7   INTERVIEW GUIDE (continued)

2

A. What is your relationship to (patient's name)?

Husband _____   Father _____   Brother _____   Son _____

Wife _____   Mother _____   Sister _____   Daughter _____

Other (specify) _____

B. How many adults, over age 18, live in your household? _____

C. How many children, under age 18, live in your household? _____

D. How many members of your household visited (patient's name) at County Hospital? _____

E. Approximately how often did someone from your household visit?

Once a day _____   More than once a day _____   Less than once a day _____

F. Now I'm going to ask you to evaluate some of our services for visitors. I'll read a series of items. Please rate each one Very Good, Good, Poor, or Don't Know.

	Very Good	Good	Poor	Don't Know
a. parking facilities				
b. visiting hours/rules				
c. reception area				
d. receptionist services				
e. elevators				
f. cafeteria				
g. visiting/waiting areas				
h. in-room visiting comfort				
i. courtesy of hospital personnel				

G. I have only two more questions for you.

1. What changes, if any, would you recommend in visitor policies or procedures?

2. If you had to choose a hospital for yourself or someone else, would you choose County Hospital?   Yes _____   No _____   Why?

That's my last question. County Hospital appreciates your responses. Thank you.

Observation Forms

Using structured forms facilitates collection and enhances the validity of data obtained by observing an event or examining company records. To design such forms, identify anticipated observations. Use a format that fosters easy, accurate recording of data. An example appears in Illustration 18–8.

ANALYZING DATA

Your research work plan guides you to collect data related to factors falling within the scope of your project. The data collection process—perhaps involving both secondary and primary sources—yields many relevant facts. **Data analysis** is the process whereby you, using induction, deduction, and/or statistical analysis, assign meaning to the collected data.[6] Data analysis requires editing, classifying, and interpreting your data.

Editing

Editing is the process of inspecting the data to identify errors and omissions. Data must be edited to ensure that they are accurate, consistent, complete, and arranged to facilitate classification and interpretation.

You may do some editing during or immediately after collection. For example, immediately after an interview you can check the interview guide to determine whether all items have been covered and whether any obvious inconsistencies exist. If you detect errors or inconsistencies, you may be able to schedule a prompt follow-up interview to improve the quality of your data.

As you evaluate your data, retain only the data that are clearly related to your research purpose and whose validity is not questioned. Although you may have invested much time and energy to gather your data, the validity and ultimate usefulness of your report depend upon your willingness to discard irrelevant or doubtful data. The evaluation process may also reveal the need to collect more or different kinds of data.

Why should data be edited?

Classifying

Classifying data is a **data-reduction** process by which you reduce many pieces of information to fewer categories. Skillful questionnaire construction can simplify this process.

What is data reduction?

---

[6]Review the "Interpretive Skills" section of Chapter 2.

Illustration 18–8   OBSERVATION FORM

OBSERVATION FORM

Consumer Response to Free Sample of Munchies

Instructions: Observer should stand unobtrusively about 20 feet from distributor. Distributor should offer a Munchies sample pack to a pedestrian approximately every 90 seconds. Observer is to record subject's response to the sample offer.

A. Location: Briefly describe where the samples were distributed. (e.g., in front of Student Union on State University campus, at intersection of Main and Richland)

B. Observations: Examples of "other behaviors" are avoidance, stop/look, stop/talk, taste, discard on street, discard in trash receptacle, place into pocket or purse, etc.

No.	Subject's Response			Other Behaviors
	Accept	Reject	Ignore	

Your data-classification categories must meet four criteria: appropriate to the research problem and purpose, exhaustive, mutually exclusive, one-dimensional.

Appropriate to the Research Problem and Purpose. The purpose and scope of your project define the classification categories. For example, assume your task is to determine whether female and male business students in your school hold work values similar to those of students in other business schools. Classifying questionnaire responses by sex of respondent is essential. Further classification of data to indicate work values (e.g., achievement, independence, economic reward) would be required. Data acquired from secondary sources (reporting studies conducted on campuses other than yours, for instance) would be classified similarly.

Exhaustive. The classification categories must capture the full range of information. Consider the following categories:

Under $50; $50–$99; $100–$149; $150 and up.

In a survey of career women, those classifications may adequately represent the range of answers to this question: "What price range characterizes most of your shoe purchases?" However, the same categories would likely not capture the range of answers to this question: "How much is your monthly rent or mortgage payment?" The majority of responses to that question might fall into the last category. Little would be learned other than that most career women spend at least $150 monthly for housing.

Mutually Exclusive. The data classifications must not overlap. The categories in the previous example are mutually exclusive. A response logically fits into only one of the four categories. As you establish numerical categories, avoid ambiguity at the extremes of each category (e.g., $50–$100; $100–$150; $150 and up).

For non-quantitative categories, a description of each category may clarify correct placement. Assume you have conducted a survey of professional writers. The survey included this open-ended item: "Describe how you compose your original draft." As you classify information obtained from the interview, you may be interested in several aspects of composition, one of which is the kinds of writing tools used. The categories "computers" and "word processing" are not mutually exclusive. More precise descriptions (e.g., microcomputer equipped with word processing software; dedicated word processor) are needed for adequate data classification.

What are criteria for data classification?

One Dimensional. All items in a classification set must pertain to the same concept. Consider this classification of business students' majors:

Accounting
Finance
International Business
Management
Management Information Systems
Marketing
Dual Major

The classification scheme is faulty. The first six items suggest that a student can be classified by a major area of study. But the last item, dual major, suggests another dimension. It is best handled separately.

Interpreting

Data classification and editing are preliminary data-interpretation steps. Further steps include reporting and summarizing findings, drawing conclusions, and making recommendations.

The **findings** of your study are discoveries contained within the data. **Conclusions** are inferences based on the findings. **Recommendations** are proposed actions to take or attitudes to adopt as a result of the research. In each step you move further from the objectivity of the raw (unprocessed) data. By guarding against the fallacies described in Chapter 2, you can assure your audience of the objectivity of your analysis.

The relationship of findings, conclusions, and recommendations is demonstrated in Illustration 18–9.

Differentiate: findings, conclusions, recommendations.

REVIEW AND TRANSITION

Chapter 17 explained how to plan your research process. Chapter 18 has described how to complete two elements of that process: collecting and analyzing data.

To use secondary data sources effectively, you will become familiar with the resources of your business library. You will also design an efficient procedure for collecting secondary data and will appropriately acknowledge your use of secondary sources. Using primary data sources requires application of communication skills to develop questionnaires, interview guides, transmittal messages, and observation forms.

The communication-by-objectives concept can guide you as you collect data; you will direct your efforts to gather only data relevant to your topic. CBO can also help you as you analyze data; guided by the objectives of your

Illustration 18–9   FINDINGS, CONCLUSIONS, RECOMMENDATIONS

Goal: To determine whether small changes in wording of a message produce differences in how tone and context of the message are perceived.

Findings

1. Differences in wording of a hypothetical organization's orientation statement significantly related to interpretations of organization's climate.

2. Readers of "flexible" company's statement reported positive perceptions of company's social responsibility and labor relations.

3. Readers of "strict" company's statement reported negative perceptions of company's social responsibility and labor relations.

Conclusions

1. Small change in tone of a written communication directly affects reader's perceptions of the organization.

2. Tone of a message influences impressions of organizational elements not intended as content of the message.

Recommendation

Organizations should pay close attention to nuances of seemingly neutral reports and statements

Source: Based on Raymond W. Kulhavy and Neil H. Schwartz, "Tone of Communication and Climate Perceptions," Journal of Business Communication (Winter 1981), pp. 17-24.

research work plan, you will edit and classify data, derive findings, draw conclusions, and make recommendations.

Chapters 19 and 20 will guide you toward effective written presentations of your research findings, conclusions, and recommendations.

YOUR DECISIONS FOR CHAPTER 18

In what ways, if any, did Chapter 17 help you with the Decisions Case for Chapter 18? How can knowledge of the SIC system help you with that case? Did you propose to use both primary and secondary data sources? Why? In what ways could computer technology help you with this task?

DISCUSSION QUESTIONS

A.   In the context of Chapter 18, what are appropriate definitions and examples for these terms?

1.   secondary data
2.   SIC system
3.   primary or original data
4.   validity
5.   interview guide
6.   findings
7.   conclusions
8.   recommendations

B.   Why is acknowledging secondary data sources important?

C.   What are the advantages and disadvantages of using questionnaires and interviews as data-collection tools?

D.   In what ways are the purpose and scope of a project related to data collection and analysis?

E.   What is the purpose of editing data?

F.   What criteria should data-classification categories satisfy? Why?

APPLICATIONS

1.   Refer to Application 1, Chapters 16 and 17. Based on your instructor's feedback for those applications, write a formal research proposal. Include a description of your proposed data collection techniques.

2.   Refer to Application 2, Chapters 16 and 17. Based on your instructor's feedback for those applications, write a formal research proposal. Include a description of your proposed data collection techniques.

3.   Based on an approved proposal that you developed for Application 1 or 2, complete the research you proposed.

4.   As directed by your instructor, select one or more of the business information sources listed in Chapter 18. Familiarize yourself with the

source(s). In a memo to your instructor, report what you have learned about the source(s).

5. Refer to the Chapter 16 list of suggested topics for business reports. Select one of those topics. Using a CD–ROM information service (such as ABI/INFORM) locate five recent journal articles related to that topic. In a memo to your instructor, give the titles of those articles and describe the process you used to locate them.

6. Skim the pages of a current business news source, such as the *Wall Street Journal, Business Week,* or *Fortune.* Select any company that appears in the current news. Prepare a profile of that company. Use the sources listed in Chapter 18 to find information about the company's officers, major products, industry position, financial condition, etc. Present your findings in a memo to your instructor. Attach to the memo a list of your sources. Model the source list shown in Appendix E, Illustration E–2.

7. Using the AIDA structure and criteria for effective communication as guides, analyze the following transmittal message. Report, orally or in writing, your findings and conclusions.

Dear Member:

As a member of the Women in Management Division of the Management Association, we would appreciate your completing the enclosed survey.

The purpose of the survey is to gather information about interests of division members in order to plan future programs and prepare a directory of interest.

Would you please fill out the enclosed form and return it (in the enclosed self-addressed envelope) within the next three weeks?

If you have any questions concerning the above, please feel free to call me at (803) 555–7471.

Thank you for your cooperation.

Sincerely,

8. Using the criteria presented on pages 501 and 502, evaluate the Transcon Airways questionnaire. In a memo to your instructor, report your evaluation.

9. Using the business information sources listed in Chapter 18, obtain data and prepare visual aids to illustrate the following:

   a. consumer price indexes for food, by country, 1985 and 1990 (or most recent year available)

↔↕ **Transcon Airways**

Flight No.: _____

Date: _____

I am traveling via Transcon Airways from _____

_____ to _____

Scheduled departure time: _____

Actual departure time: _____

Estimated arrival time: _____

Purpose of trip:

Business ☐   Pleasure ☐   Other (please specify)

_____

I learned of Transcon service from:

Travel Agent ☐   TV ☐   Radio ☐   Newspaper ☐

Magazine ☐   Other (please specify) _____

I rate your service as:

Excellent ☐   Good ☐   Fair ☐   Poor ☐

My name, address, and telephone no.: _____

_____

Additional comments: _____

_____

_____

(Please complete and give this card to your flight attendant.)

Thank You for Flying Transcon!

b. hourly earnings in selected U.S. industries, 1985 and 1990 (or most recent year available)
c. components of gross income for a selected corporation, 1985 to most recent year
d. net income of selected corporations in an industry of your choice, 1985 to most recent year
e. other data assigned by your instructor

CASES

1. Dalton Shoemaker is a registered nurse who senses the need for adult day-care services in your community. Mr. Shoemaker wants informa-

tion that will help him evaluate the feasibility of his opening an adult day-care center.

    a.   Locate secondary data sources for Mr. Shoemaker. Prepare an annotated bibliography of those sources. (See Appendix E, Illustration E–3 for an example of an annotated bibliography.)

    b.   Prepare a questionnaire for Mr. Shoemaker's use in a survey to determine the need for adult day care.

2.   You are a student intern assigned to your campus Chief of Security, P. Haskins. Because of serious crimes against students on many campuses, Chief Haskins is developing a crime awareness and prevention program for your college. The chief has asked you to conduct related research.

    a.   Locate secondary data about actions colleges have taken to improve campus safety. In a memo to Chief Haskins, summarize your findings. Attach a list of your data sources, compiled in correct bibliographic style. (See Appendix E, Illustration E–1.)

    b.   Prepare a questionnaire for use in a campus survey. The objective of your survey is to determine students' attitudes about campus safety and what students are doing to protect themselves against crime.

    c.   Using your questionnaire, collect data from a sample of students on your campus. Analyze the data. In a memo to Chief Haskins, present your findings, conclusions, and recommendations.

3.   During the past 20 years, U.S. citizens have confronted economic, social, political, and military crises because of U.S. dependence on foreign oil. You are an aide to the senior U.S. senator from your state. Prepare a questionnaire to be sent to the senator's constituency. The objective of your survey is to determine citizens' actions to reduce oil consumption, citizens' attitudes toward steps that the federal government has taken to decrease oil consumption, and citizens' suggestions for ways that the United States can reduce its dependence on foreign oil.

4.   The Free Trade Agreement (FTA), effective January 1, 1989, lowered or eliminated trade and investment barriers between the United States and Canada. An objective of the FTA was to enable businesses in both countries to build long-term relationships that would not easily be disrupted. You are an assistant to the Director of Research for a U.S. manufacturer of microcomputers. The director, R. D. Allardice, has asked you to determine what effect, if any, the FTA has had in stabilizing or improving U.S.–Canada trade in microcomputers and related products. Locate relevant secondary data. In a memo to Director Allardice, summarize your findings.

5. You are an assistant to J. McKay, director of Leisure Life, a residential center for elderly persons who want relief from daily housekeeping tasks. Your community provides private apartments for its residents. Lodging options are a one- or two-bedroom apartment with kitchenette and sitting room or a bed-sitting room with no kitchenette. Two meal-plan options are available: all meals in the central dining room; dinner only in the central dining room. Residents are entitled to weekly cleaning and laundry services, use of the recreation center and golf course, and 24-hour on-call emergency medical care.

Leisure Life has apparently underpriced its services; it has a long waiting list of persons who want to enter the center, yet it shows only a small profit each month. Director McKay, has asked you to determine what similar centers in communities comparable to yours charge for their services.

Collect and analyze relevant primary and secondary data. In a memorandum to Director McKay, summarize your findings and recommend a monthly fee for each of the lodging and meal options offered at Leisure Life.

MULTICULTURAL INSIGHTS

1. What secondary data sources would you recommend to someone who desires information about a firm that conducts business in your native culture? Briefly describe each source.

2. Is questioning, via questionnaire or interviews, a common business research method among firms that do business in your native culture? Why?

3. In your opinion, are the principles of data analysis presented in Chapter 18 applicable in all cultures? Why?

SHORT REPORTS AND BUSINESS PROPOSALS

CHAPTER OUTLINE

I. Planning and Writing Short Reports
II. Types of Short Reports
    A. Periodic Reports
    B. Progress Reports
    C. Special Reports
        1. Exception Reports
        2. Trip Reports
        3. Information Reports
        4. Recommendation Reports
        5. Policy and Procedure Statements
III. Business Proposals
    A. Persuasive Aspects of Proposals
    B. Types of Proposals
IV. Review and Transition

OBJECTIVES

After completing this chapter, you should be able to:

1. Identify typical short reports used in business.
2. Vary the structure and format of your short reports to meet the requirements of your reader and the report content.
3. Apply the criteria for appearance, accuracy, coherence, clarity, conciseness, and courtesy to proposals and short reports.

516

4. Explain the purposes and types of proposals used in business.
5. Prepare effective business proposals.

DECISIONS CASE

Two weeks have passed since Ms. Nymeyer gave you the assignment to investigate why Nymeyer Music Mart has not been successful in the music supplies market. You have gathered preliminary data about Nymeyer's competition, past marketing strategies, and numbers of area churches and schools that are potential consumers of music supplies. You are considering conducting a survey of those potential customers to determine what they look for in a music supplier. You feel good about what you have accomplished. You should be able to finish your report within the month's time Ms. Nymeyer gave you.

But as you are working with the data, Ms. Nymeyer steps into your office. "How's that report coming along? Are you going to be able to complete it before our next staff meeting? I'm eager to find out what you've learned. Do you need any extra help with it?"

You look up in confusion. "Doesn't she trust me?" you wonder. "How shall I assure her that I can—and will—do the job she asked for?"

How can you satisfy Ms. Nymeyer's desire for information? What could you have done to forestall her questions?

Additional questions about this decision-making case are stated at the end of this chapter. Study the chapter before answering those questions.

CHAPTER CONTEXT

Some business reports or proposals are relatively brief, ranging in length from one or two sentences to a few pages. Whatever the length or type of your report, try to discover and accommodate the preferences of your employer or instructor. Remember that your job in business communication is to inform or persuade your readers or listeners. Try to determine their expectations about message timing, message content, and message format. Those expectations often vary with circumstances. By accommodating reader preferences, you are likely to establish a climate for acceptance of your message.

Chapter 19 presents several options for short reports and business proposals. Those options demonstrate diverse ways to meet your reader's needs or desires.

PLANNING AND WRITING SHORT REPORTS

Each report-writing situation is unique. For that reason, it is important that you use an analytical approach to planning and writing short reports. Apply the guides presented by the Chapter 17 model of the report-writing process: clarify the problem and purpose; analyze your audience; assemble, evaluate, and organize your data; determine an appropriate style; write, revise, and edit drafts. Then—and only then—will you be ready to produce a final copy.

Although each situation is unique, through experience you will observe similarities of context, purpose, content, and audience. Those similarities permit classification of reports and the development of guides to simplify your report writing.

TYPES OF SHORT REPORTS

Three categories of short reports are periodic reports, progress reports, and special reports.

Periodic Reports

What are examples of periodic reports?

Reports issued at regular intervals are **periodic reports**. Unit production reports, such as sales or manufacturing, are the most common examples of periodic reports. A company's annual report is also a periodic report.

Most internal periodic reports are production related. Therefore, characteristics of those reports are deductive order, summary tables or figures, and concise style aided by captions, enumerations, or tabulations. Those characteristics are evident in the reports shown in Illustrations 19–1 and 19–2. Since authorization for periodic reports usually exists in the job description or in company policy, authorization facts are rarely included in periodic reports.

Progress Reports

What is the purpose of a progress report?

As the name implies, a **progress report** presents the status of a project or progress toward a goal. Appropriate content includes problems encountered or resolved as well as progress achieved. The report may also request special assistance or additional instructions. The following example demonstrates a progress report.

TO: A. J. Bowers
FROM: D. A. Phillips
DATE: December 3, 19—
SUBJECT: Progress Report, Bayfield Office

November work was on schedule, as summarized here.

Illustration 19-1 PERIODIC REPORT IN LETTER FORMAT

LAMAR & LEONARD, INC.
INVESTMENT ADVISERS
SUITE 1127, FAIRFIELD BUILDING
19 SIMMONS SQUARE NORTH
BOSTON, MA 02115-4368
(617) 555-7073

August 12, 19--

Mrs. Corrine V. Martin
220 Lorraine Avenue
Orono, ME 04473-6928

Dear Mrs. Martin

Here is our biweekly report of established firms offering attractive
investment opportunities. Supporting financial details concerning
these companies, as well as today's NYSE or AMEX closing quotations,
are enclosed.

1. AMB Corporation, 659 Mellon Plaza, Pittsburgh, PA 15230-3744

   Manufactures alloys, forgings, valves, oil-tool products. Has
   production and repair facilities in Erie, Pennsylvania;
   Charleston, West Virginia; Gary, Indiana; Flint, Michigan;
   Tulsa, Oklahoma; Dallas, Texas. Has announced plans for new
   maintenance and repair installations.

2. ANCON, Inc., 1010 Market Street, Wilmington, DE 19898-4412

   Produces industrial control systems and electronic components.
   Has plants in New Castle, Delaware; St. Louis, Missouri; Long
   Beach, California. May establish branch operation in Waterbury,
   Connecticut.

3. C&D Clark Company, Inc., 211 Broad Street, Philadelphia, PA
   19107-5314

   Manufactures agricultural and industrial equipment. Has plants
   in Allentown, Pennsylvania; Moline, Illinois; Louisville, Ken-
   tucky. Negotiating for additional site in Omaha, Nebraska.

To discuss details of these issues, please call me at your convenience.

Sincerely

R. A. Shaw, Vice President

sk

Enclosures

Illustration 19–2   PERIODIC PRODUCTION REPORT IN MEMO FORMAT

Safe and Sure Insurance Co.

INTEROFFICE MEMORANDUM

TO: Jack J. Kool

FROM: Kelli Carona

DATE: March 10, 19--

SUBJECT: Region V Report, February 19--

Region V agents did well in February, Jack. We underwrote 90 percent of the applications submitted from the Western zone.

ACCIDENT POLICIES APPROVED

Alaska	14	Montana	7
Arizona	6	Nevada	2
California	24	Oregon	11
Hawaii	15	Utah	12
Idaho	3	Washington	7

INDIVIDUAL APPLICATIONS REJECTED

Agent	Plan	Reason
Diane Johnson	1781 and L85	Occupation
Robert Kellner	1752	Incomplete--need
	Intensive care rider	bank card
Kenneth Martin	1752	Inspection report--
		confidential
Joan Silvers	1752	Canceled by appli-
	Intensive care rider	cant
	Cancer	

LIFE POLICIES DECLINED

Agent	Plan	Reason
Donna Compton	L65	Canceled by
		applicant
Albert Fung	DP65	Health
John Hill	5-year renewable and	Canceled by
	convertible term	applicant

Jack, I hope you are as pleased as I am with the work of our Region V agents. Their participation in the January sales conference and training seminars has really paid off.

Work Completed

1. Concrete floors on the first and second levels were mixed and placed.
2. Mechanical room equipment was installed.
3. First floor conduit was installed.

Work in Progress

1. The concrete roof deck was begun on November 26; completion is scheduled for December 7.
2. Exterior masonry was begun on November 12; completion is scheduled for February 19.

Anticipated Problem

Contract negotiations with bricklayers seem to be running into difficulties. Should a strike materialize, both exterior and interior masonry will be delayed.

Additional Remarks

The October progress report cited delay in delivery of air-conditioning equipment. When the equipment arrived, the subcontractor assigned additional workers to the project; they completed the installation on schedule.

Special Reports

What are examples of special reports?

Nonroutine activities, requests, or needs give rise to a variety of special reports.

Exception Reports. An exception report calls attention to an activity that deviates from expectations. Reports of equipment malfunctions, accidents, violations of company policies or procedures, and unusual behaviors of customers or suppliers are examples of exception reports.

Under a management-by-exception policy, subordinates make all decisions about deviations from standards within specified tolerance ranges. Only those deviations that exceed the tolerance ranges are referred to a manager for decisions. Such a policy reduces the number of exception reports. Minor deviations may be summarized in periodic reports.

Since exception reports are production-related messages, the trend is to write them in deductive order. Captions or other creative formats—even incomplete sentences—may be used to facilitate rapid comprehension of the message. The following examples demonstrate effective structures for exception reports.

Example 1. Policy violation

TO: Yvette Panella, Security
FROM: Edie Harrison, Industrial Relations
DATE: November 2, 19—
SUBJECT: Parking Facilities for the Disabled

REFERENCE: Policy Statement 20-155

SUMMARY: Corporate headquarters maintains a parking lot for visitors and company personnel. Although space is available to accommodate all vehicles, unauthorized drivers are using the parking spaces reserved for handicapped people.

RECOMMENDATIONS: To correct this situation, Security should do the following:

1. Notify all personnel about this violation.
2. Assign security personnel to enforce parking regulations, especially between 7 a.m. and 10 a.m.

DISCUSSION: During the last two weeks, I have observed 15 instances of unauthorized use of these spaces. These violations forced disabled employees and visitors to park far from the building.

Example 2. Problem with service contractor

TO: J. Lowe
FROM: D. Weaver
DATE: January 31, 19—
SUBJECT: Problem with EX-30 Maintenance Contract

Our service contract with EX-Main no longer meets our needs. Here is an example of the kind of problem we have encountered.

On January 30 I had difficulty getting service for our EX-30 printer.

8:10 a.m.	Discovered printer not functioning
8:15 a.m.	Called EX-Main and requested service
9:30 a.m.	Placed second call to EX-Main; spoke with Walter Burke, who said field engineer was serving a larger account and could not come until 11:30
10:20 a.m.	Field engineer arrived
11:05 a.m.	Printer repaired

We should meet with the EX-Main account representative and insist on fulfillment of our service contract. We cannot afford to have our system down for most of a morning.

Trip Reports. When an employee takes a trip on company expense—to fulfill a special assignment; to attend a conference, meeting, or seminar—the employer often requests a **trip report**. Trip reports should be informative messages which help others evaluate the value of the trip for the employer and employee. Avoid lengthy descriptions about travel details and social amenities that may have been part of the trip. The following example demonstrates a trip report.

TO: Claire Kane
FROM: Susan Cooper
DATE: November 15, 19—
SUBJECT: Trip to Fibertech and Riteweave; Evaluation of Thread-waste Reworking

Summary

On Wednesday, November 14, Jim Logan, Ted DeCotis, and I visited the Fibertech plant to see how that company reworks thread waste.

In an experimental lab, employees were processing hard thread waste through a Black & Taylor cutter, followed by a run through a Shredsall. The slivers produced were completely free of strings.

We also visited Riteweave, where a Shredsall is in operation. Riteweave was running 70 percent polyester/25 percent rayon. The cut thread waste made up about 10 percent of this blend. We were told the cut waste has no ill effect on yarn quality, and our inspection confirmed that evaluation.

Recommendation

Considering the cost of fibers and the little we get from the sale of thread waste, I believe we should experiment with reworking our thread waste. Although this operation could be profitable for our company as a whole, I don't think we need a Shredsall at each plant.

We should install a Shredsall at the Bamburg plant and rework thread waste into our yarn at that location first. If we are satisfied with the yarn quality, we could shred each plant's waste at the Bamburg site and return the bales to the originating plant for reworking into its yarn.

Information Reports. A report that presents facts only, with no analysis or interpretation of the data and no recommendation or request for action, is an **information report**. Announcements and responses to requests for information are examples of such reports.

Since information reports often cover nonroutine situations, you may need to provide more background information than is required in a periodic report or an exception report. Illustration 19–3 provides an example of an information report sent to a client. The following example illustrates a brief internal information report.

Illustration 19-3 INFORMATION REPORT IN LETTER FORMAT

Bay Electric Co.   Twenty Circle Drive ■ Duluth, Minnesota 55801-2177
218-555-4691

April 19, 19--

Mr. James Stark
1020 Applewood Lane
Hibbing, MN 55746-0213

Dear Mr. Stark

As you requested, your building plans have been reviewed to determine the electrical service capacity your cottage will require.
These suggestions are based upon a floor area of 1,800 square feet.

<u>Service Entrance Panel</u>

A 100-ampere fuseless service panel is suggested to provide these
circuits for present and future needs:

1. Five 15-ampere, general-purpose circuits to be used for bed-
    rooms, bath, living room, basement, and kitchen lights; one
    15-ampere circuit for oil furnace.
2. Two 20-ampere circuits for kitchen appliances.
3. One 30-ampere circuit for electric washer and dryer; one 30-
    ampere circuit for electric water heater.
4. One 50-ampere circuit for electric range.

<u>Wiring Requirements</u>

The following suggestions will help you wire your cottage properly:

1. <u>Convenience outlets</u>. Use No. 14 wire with ground for all
    15-ampere outlets; however, use No. 12 wire with ground for all
    20-ampere outlets.
2. <u>Electric range</u>. Use a separate 3-wire No. 6 cable from a 50-
    ampere circuit to a heavy-duty wall receptacle.
3. <u>Clothes dryer</u>. Use a separate 3-wire No. 6 cable from a 30-
    ampere circuit to a heavy-duty wall receptacle.

When you are ready to wire, please let us know. We will gladly
supply you with a cost estimate.

Sincerely

Laurie Yetter

Laurie Yetter
Customer Services

kb

TO: J. O. Albrecht
FROM: M. J. Miller
DATE: August 19, 19—
SUBJECT: Vacation Time Survey

Here are the results of the survey you requested on July 3. I contacted 50 local firms to ask about their vacation policies: 39 responded.

VACATION TIME
(Percent of Firms Granting)

Years of Service	Weeks Off Annually				
	2	3	4	5	6
5	28	69	3	—	—
10	1	72	26	1	—
20	—	1	68	30	1
30	—	1	32	46	21

I hope these data are useful to you in your revision of the employee benefits package.

Recommendation Reports. A recommendation report consists primarily of recommendations, with only minimal presentation of supporting data. A recommendation report may be used when the receiver is already aware of the conditions warranting the recommendations. A written recommendation report often accompanies an oral presentation of findings. Illustration 19–4 demonstrates a recommendation report. A model for a comprehensive report, which presents recommendations and extensive analysis of data to support those recommendations, is presented in Chapter 20.

Policy and Procedure Statements. Policy statements and procedure statements instruct employees or customers about expected behaviors. **Policies** are general guides; **procedures**, specific guides.

Routine policies or procedures can be conveyed with directness. New or radically changed policies or procedures, however, may meet resistance. In such situations an indirect style is effective. Provide information that justifies the policy or procedure before stating the details.

The following example demonstrates a direct (deductive) style for a routine procedure. This style typically appears in procedures manuals.

DISPLAY PROCEDURES: SHORT REPORTS

Give proper display to a short report. Display is the effective use of white space and captions to improve readability.

Margins   In manuscript format, use a 1-1/2-inch top margin on the first page and a 1-inch top margin on following pages. For

Illustration 19–4   RECOMMENDATION REPORT IN MANUSCRIPT FORMAT

RECOMMENDATION REPORT

JONES PIPE COMPANY, INC.

This report presents the results of a study of Jones Pipe Company, Inc., to determine what action should be taken to reduce costs and put the company on a profitable basis. The report outlines a plan that will enable you to recover your investment within four years.

Current Condition

Rarely have we encountered a company that needed improvement in so many areas. Facilities are antiquated, methods are costly, labor is inefficient, and the existing management is ineffective.

Fortunately, such weaknesses are at the same time opportunities for great improvement. By using modern management techniques, you can correct these weaknesses, earn a handsome return on your investment, and demonstrate your keen judgment in buying a company that appeared destined for the auction block.

Recommendations

Here are the changes that should be implemented:

1. Make building alterations. These alterations are essential to provide adequate housing for modernized operations.

2. Modernize pipe-threading equipment. This modernization is necessary to bring plant efficiency and labor costs in line with those of competing manufacturers.

3. Clean up the plant. Sell all parts for unused machines and other scrap in the warehouse and about the plant. In addition, paint the plant and install new lighting fixtures.

4. Mechanize the unloading and handling of pipe. A small electric hoist mounted on a rail running from the railroad siding across the pipe storage shed should eliminate most of the present manual unloading.

5. Install mechanical equipment for the movement of pipe and finished nipples. If the lengths of pipe coming from the cutters are dropped into properly designed tote boxes, they can easily be moved by a small forklift truck from the cutters to the threading machines.

6. Establish a system of inventory control and production scheduling. Such a system is needed to avoid partial shipment to

Illustration 19–4 RECOMMENDATION REPORT (continued)

```
                                                                    2

    customers, rush production orders, and an irregular volume of
    work in the shop itself.

7.  Establish output standards and financial incentives for plant
    workers.  All the preceding steps will contribute to a reduc-
    tion of labor costs.  Setting individual output standards
    with financial incentives will assure that savings are real-
    ized.

If those changes are made, your labor costs can be reduced to ap-
proximately 20 percent of selling price, compared with your cur-
rent 25 percent of selling price.  At the same time, you will im-
prove your service to customers and your employees will receive
more take-home pay because of their bonuses.

Comments

The changes will require a capital investment of approximately
$88,000.  Based on labor-cost reductions alone, you should
recover the investment within four years.  A detailed cost-
benefit analysis is available in our office.
```

unbound reports, use 1-inch left, right, and bottom margins. For bound reports, allow an additional 1/2 inch at the binding edge (left or top).

In letter or memorandum format, use AMCO's standard letter and memo margins.

Spacing Use single spacing for all reports. Double space between paragraphs.

Captions Double-space before and after captions. Key main captions in all capitals, centered on the page or even with the left margin. Key subcaptions in uppercase and lowercase letters. Place each subcaption at the left margin preceding the section to which it refers or insert it at the beginning of the first paragraph of that section. Subcaptions may also be placed at the left margin opposite the sections to which they refer, as demonstrated in this procedure statement.

Here is an example of an indirect (inductive) style for a procedure statement.

TO: All Office Personnel
FROM: Ed Lombardi
DATE: May 18, 19—
SUBJECT: Use of fax transmission

Increased demand for fax transmission has caused long delays for some users. Since our business depends on rapid transmission of critical data to our customers, delays in fax transmission may result in lost sales. To reduce our fax load, please follow these procedures:

1. Restrict fax messages to critical sales data only.
2. Complete the FAX REQUEST (Form FR100). The form requires full identification of sender, receiver, and purpose of message. Transmission costs for nonessential messages will be charged to the user.
3. Write concisely. Avoid using a separate cover message. Whenever feasible, combine transmittal information and essential data into a single document, preferably one page.

An example of a policy statement appears in Illustration 19–5. Is its style inductive or deductive?

BUSINESS PROPOSALS

A **business proposal** presents plans, actions, or alternatives for consideration and implementation. Written proposals are presented in letter, memo, or manuscript format. Some writers classify proposals as special reports. However, since proposals are always persuasive—never strictly informative—it is useful to consider them in a separate category.

Persuasive Aspects of Proposals

A business proposal is fundamentally a persuasive message. Consequently, variations of the AIDA structure (Chapter 12) will serve you well as you write proposals.

Successful proposal writers sell their projects by:

1. demonstrating need satisfaction
2. specifying relevant objectives and methods
3. highlighting qualifications of proposer

How can a proposal be made persuasive?

If a proposal is *unsolicited*—that is, if you initiate the idea—your first objective is to draw attention to the merits of what you propose. Thus, you may place a justification section near the beginning of the document to attract attention and build interest. The clarity and precision with which you state the terms of your proposal further stimulate desire and prompt favorable action.

Illustration 19–5   POLICY STATEMENT IN MEMO FORMAT

MEMORANDUM

TO: All Employees

FROM: Ray Robbins   *R.R.*

DATE: October 18, 19--

SUBJECT: Designated Smoking Areas

Background

Several employees have requested a review of our smoking policy. The September survey of employee attitudes toward tobacco use revealed the following:

1. Sixty percent of respondents indicated concern about effects of passive smoke on nonsmokers.

2. Seventy-two percent of respondents participate in the employee wellness program.

3. Fifty-four percent of respondents support smoking <u>restrictions</u>, but only thirty-one percent support smoking <u>prohibitions</u> during working hours.

Policy Change

To establish a working environment that complements employee attitudes, management has approved a change in our smoking policy.

<u>Policy 8-49326</u> now reads:

> Employees are permitted to smoke in desig-
>
> nated smoking areas only. Designated smoking
>
> areas are smoking sections of dining rooms
>
> and private offices (if approved by office
>
> occupant).

am

Your entire proposal should be designed to persuade the reader that the project is justified and—in many instances—that you are the person to do what is proposed.

If a proposal is *solicited* (requested by the reader), the need to draw attention to the project is reduced. But the need to draw attention to your abilities and understanding of the project may be increased, particularly if your competitors are also submitting proposals.

Types of Proposals

Proposals related to business decisions fit into three categories:

What types of proposals are used in business?

1. investigative/research
2. product/service
3. organizational/operational

As Chapter 17 indicates, an **investigative** or **research proposal** presents a plan to examine a problem. This type of proposal usually contains the ten parts listed in Illustration 17–1, although the headings that identify those factors may vary. The research proposal shown in Illustration 17–3 was built on those ten parts. That ten-part work plan can also guide your preparation of other business proposals.

A **product** or **service proposal** gives details of a product or service to be provided by one person or organization to another. A **bid** is a special form of this proposal.

A product/service proposal may be solicited by a formal **request for proposal (RFP)**. RFPs often state the required content, structure, and format for the proposal. To ensure consideration of your proposal, always follow the specifications of the RFP. A consultant's proposal for services is shown in Illustration 19–6.

A recommendation to initiate or to change an organizational policy, practice, procedure, or structure is an **organizational** or **operational proposal**. This kind of proposal generally follows formal or informal research related to an issue or problem. The proposal may contain a review of the problem and the investigation, but primary emphasis is on the proposed changes and their justification. An operational proposal is shown in Illustration 19–7.

REVIEW AND TRANSITION

Content and structure of short reports vary according to the receiver's need and psychological readiness for information. Short reports commonly used

Illustration 19–6   SERVICE PROPOSAL IN LETTER FORMAT

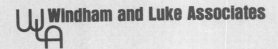

Windham and Luke Associates

1025 Foothills Boulevard
Boulder, CO 80302-3636
(303) 555-5337

July 10, 19--

Mr. Luis Garces
Training Coordinator
Huber Industries
3396 Tanforan Drive
Englewood, CO 80020-7225

Dear Mr. Garces

In response to your June 24 request, here is the proposal for an
in-house training program to improve correspondence effectiveness
and efficiency.

<u>Background and Justification</u>

A recent study of correspondence generated in your firm revealed
both a need and a desire for correspondence training. You have
further requested that the training program be tailored to the
specific needs of your employees.

<u>Procedure</u>

The following steps will be taken to develop and deliver our proposed program.

1. You will provide us with a minimum of ten letters from each
    participating department for our analysis.
2. Using our analysis of your correspondence and criteria for
    effective communication, we will design instructional materials
    for your employees, including a pretest and posttest.
3. We will conduct a program consisting of four 90-minute sessions,
    spaced at two-week intervals. The program will be conducted in
    your training rooms. We will provide all instructional materials.

<u>Cost</u>

The cost for the program is $3,000 (one-time development fee)
plus $75 per participant. The program is limited to 20 partici-
pants, but it may be repeated according to demand.

<u>Request for Approval</u>

Please call me if you have any questions about this proposal. Your
approval before August 10 will permit you to place the program on
your fall training schedule. We guarantee the program will be ready
for delivery on September 10 if we receive your sample correspondence
before August 15.

Sincerely

Beverly A. Windham

Beverly A. Windham, President

bb

Illustration 19–7   OPERATIONAL PROPOSAL IN MEMO FORMAT

HUBER INDUSTRIES

TO: John Werder

FROM: Luis Garces LG

DATE: July 15, 19--

SUBJECT: Proposed Correspondence Training Program

<u>Proposal</u>

We should contract with Windham and Luke Associates to provide an in-house correspondence training program.

<u>Justification</u>

Cosmos Consultants (CC) recently analyzed a random sample of correspondence from all departments in our company. Major findings in that study were:

1. Eighty percent of our employees have had no formal instruction in business communication.

2. Eighty-seven percent of our employees expressed a desire for training to improve correspondence effectiveness and efficiency.

3. Ninety percent of the sampled documents contained violations of criteria for effective correspondence.

Following CC's recommendation to solicit bids for an in-house training program, I have evaluated proposals from three organizations. Windham and Luke Associates appears to offer the best program at least cost.

<u>Procedure</u>

Windham and Luke Associates will do the following:

1. Design instructional materials based upon an analysis of our correspondence and criteria for effective communication.

2. Prepare and administer pretests and posttests.

3. Conduct a program consisting of a series of four sessions spaced at two-week intervals. Number of program cycles will be determined by employee demand.

<u>Cost</u>

The fee for this program will be $3,000 for development plus $75 per participant. The participant's fee covers all instruction and materials for the four sessions.

Illustration 19–7 OPERATIONAL PROPOSAL IN MEMO FORMAT (continued)

```
John Werder
Page 2
July 15, 19--

Time

Windham and Luke Associates guarantees ability to develop and
deliver the program within one month of approval.

Additional Information

Copies of the following items are available in my office:

1.  Cosmos Consultants report.

2.  Proposals from Windham and Luke Associates, Technical
    Trainers, and Gloria Closson, Inc.

Request for Approval

Your approval of this program before August 1 will permit us to
put the program into our fall training schedule, which begins
September 15.

bb
```

in business fall into three categories: periodic, progress, and special reports. Examples of special reports are exception, trip, information, and recommendation reports, as well as policy or procedure statements.

In addition to the investigative or research proposal presented in Chapter 17, you may be asked to write product/service and organizational/operational proposals. The work plan that guides the preparation of a research proposal is also useful to direct the preparation of other business proposals.

Some report data are so lengthy or complex that they cannot be presented effectively in the short report styles demonstrated in this chapter. Chapter 20 presents a comprehensive report model for effective presentation and analysis of more complex data.

YOUR DECISIONS FOR CHAPTER 19

Based on your reading of Chapter 19, what kind of report should you give Ms. Nymeyer even though you have not completed the research she requested? What could you have included in your research proposal to forestall her questions?

DISCUSSION QUESTIONS

A. In the context of Chapter 19, what are appropriate definitions and ex-
    amples for these terms?

    1. periodic report
    2. progress report
    3. special report
    4. policy statement
    5. solicited proposal
    6. unsolicited proposal
    7. product/service proposal
    8. organizational/operational proposal

B. How does the recursive report-writing model of Chapter 17 apply to
    short reports?

C. In what ways are these reports alike and unlike: production report,
    progress report, trip report, exception report, information report, rec-
    ommendation report, policy statement, and procedure statement?

D. In what ways are the three types of proposals discussed in Chapter 19
    similar? dissimilar?

APPLICATIONS

1. Refer to Application 1, Chapters 16 through 18. If you are working on
    the project designated by those applications, prepare a status report for
    that project. Direct the report to your instructor.

2. Refer to Application 2, Chapters 16 through 18. If you are working on
    the project designated by those applications, prepare a status report for
    that project. Direct the report to your instructor.

3. Using the Gantt chart shown in Illustration 14–14, write a progress re-
    port to A. J. Bowers concerning the status of the Southfield Office
    Building construction at the end of August. These data are pertinent:
    Heavy rains caused a two-week delay of work with concrete footings
    and foundation walls. Consequently, this construction phase cannot be
    completed before the second week of September. Underground con-
    duit installation is on schedule, but an electricians' strike is pending
    and may cause additional delays.

4. Think of a meeting that you attended recently either in your town of
    residence or out of town. Assume you attended the meeting on your

employer's time. Write a trip report to your supervisor in which you state the purpose of the meeting and summarize its major outcomes.

CASES

1. Assume you are a sales representative for Good Workers, a temporary help agency. Each week you must report your sales activity for the past week and your sales plan for the coming week to your supervisor. Write a report in memo format to D. G. Purdy, regional sales director. Include the following data. You may add other reasonable information.
   This week:

   a. visits to old clients: 5
   b. visits to potential clients: 15
   c. temporaries placed with old clients: 15
   d. temporaries placed with new clients: 9
   e. billings (old clients): $3,600
   f. billings (new clients): $2,000
   g. applicants screened: 12
   h. applicants accepted: 8

   Next week:

   a. appointment with conference director at new Executive Suite Hotel to discuss supplying temporary office workers for conferences
   b. appointment with dispatcher at Bronte Movers to discuss supplying temporary workers for loading and unloading vans

2. As sales representative for Contemporary Signs, Inc., you must write a report to your client, Wallace Stores. Wallace is a major department store chain in the Southeast, with headquarters in Charlotte, North Carolina. Here's what happened:

   Tuesday, January 28, 19—: At your Greenville, North Carolina, plant, Randy Goodman and Jesse Chavis loaded signs for Wallace's St. Augustine, Florida, store. They drove to St. Augustine, arriving late at night.

   Wednesday, January 29, 19—: Randy and Jesse arrived at the job site at 7:00 a.m. and began installing one set of the Wallace letters. (Each lowercase letter was eight feet high, and the *W* was ten feet high.) They finished installing the first set and had prepared to do the second set. At this point, they were stopped and told that the store name was to be changed to Wallace–Tate.

Thursday, January 30, 19—: Randy tried to find a small warehouse to store the remaining sign letters. He was unable to find a warehouse in St. Augustine or Jacksonville that had a large enough door to get the *W* in. He and Jesse returned to Greenville with the remaining letters.

You had scheduled enough time, including travel, to fulfill the original contract, but Randy and Jesse were prevented from installing the signs. You feel justified in billing Wallace for the total of the original contract.

Write your report in letter format. Send it to Mr. Bob Glasser, Architectural Department, Wallace Store Services, P.O. Box 8034, Charlotte, NC 28216-8034.

3. Assume the role of assistant to Luisa Morales, training director for Citizens Bank. Citizens hires recent college graduates as management trainees. Successful completion of the management trainee program leads to appointment as a branch manager. Citizens requires that all branch managers be able to use the bank's computer system and standard microcomputer software applications efficiently. You conducted a survey to determine the level of computer readiness in your current group of 58 management trainees. This is what you learned.

    a. Percent of trainees who have had college instruction in software applications:

Word processing	84.9
Spreadsheet	90.6
Database	50.9
Graphics	50.9
Desktop publishing	13.2
Electronic mail	30.2
Electronic calendar	15.1

    b. Percent of trainees who expect to use software applications in their banking careers:

Word processing	100.0
Spreadsheet	96.2
Database	84.9
Graphics	75.5
Desktop publishing	56.6
Electronic mail	71.7
Electronic calendar	62.3

Write a recommendation report to Director Morales. In that report suggest priorities for computer training. Include enough data to justify your recommendations.

4. Luisa Morales (Case 3) sent you on October 20 to San Diego, California, to determine what Fail-Safe Software Trainers could do to help Citizens Bank with its computer training program. Write a trip report for Morales. Include these facts:

   ► Owner Marie Victor accompanied you on a tour of the Fail-Safe facility and permitted you to observe training sessions in progress.
   ► You observed five training sessions; facilities and equipment were attractive and up to date; trainers were skilled and used the most recent versions of software applications.
   ► You interviewed 15 trainees; all expressed great satisfaction with the thoroughness of the training.
   ► Ms. Victor gave you names of three banks that have used Fail-Safe training and authorized you to contact them to inquire about their satisfaction with the training.
   ► Ms. Victor agreed to submit a proposal to train 20 of your management trainees in spreadsheet, database, and graphics applications. You should receive that proposal before November 1.

5. Ms. Rhonda Miller, an operations officer at a local bank, has told you that she wants a constructive, critical review of ten form letters that the bank uses to welcome new checking account customers and to sell additional bank services. Write a proposal in letter format. Offer to review the letters. Identify the review procedures you will use, cost, time required, reporting method, etc.

6. You are the sales manager for the Independent Brokers Division of Insure-Safe, a company that develops computer software for the insurance industry. You want to motivate your sales representatives to increase their sales efforts among small independent insurance brokers. Such brokers are able to insure their clients with several insurance underwriters. The brokers typically have a loyal clientele, who trust the broker's judgment to locate the best insurance protection at the lowest price. Many independent brokers use computers for word processing, but they have not yet developed integrated information systems to easily match their clients' needs with the many insurance products offered by the underwriters they represent. You have a new policy management software product that will do just that.

   Prepare a proposal for a new sales incentive program. Address the proposal to your superior, J. R. Cassidy, Vice President for Marketing. Include the following information. Supply additional data, if requested by your instructor.

   a. Need for new incentive program.
   b. Details of proposed incentive plan: Seven-night cruise vacation for two, all expenses paid; contest dates, January 1–December 1,

19—; all representatives who exceed their annual independent-broker sales quotas by at least 10 percent will be eligible for the competition; award winner will be the person who has the greatest percentage increase in sales to independent brokers; award winner will be announced at Insure-Safe's annual employee-recognition dinner in December; approximate cost to the company is $2,000 for the award and $100 for publicity to the sales representatives; $250,000 projected additional revenue to Insure-Safe if sales to independent brokers increase by 10 percent.

c.   Request for approval of proposal.

7.   You are a sales representative for Insure-Safe (Case 4). You want to win that cruise. Prepare a proposal for presentation to the independent brokers in your sales territory. In the proposal you will present the information management features of the policy management software, the training and service provided by Insure-Safe, the cost of the product, and a request for an appointment to demonstrate the product in the broker's office. You will provide your own portable computer and modem for the demonstration, but you are also willing to demonstrate the software on the broker's computer.

To complete this assignment you may make reasonable assumptions about software capability, cost, etc. If possible, verify the accuracy of your assumptions by consulting a professor in your school's insurance program, a vendor of software for the insurance industry, or an insurance industry trade journal.

8.   You are the manager of information systems for Petroleum Frontiers, Inc. You want to purchase 75 portable cellular phones for use by your field engineers. You will solicit bids for those units from local communications equipment companies. Write a request for proposal (RFP). Include the following information in your RFP.

a.   Equipment specifications: One-button dialing; 30-number memory; call timer; electronic lock; last-number redial; hands-free operation; shoulder-hung carrying case; maximum weight, including carrying case, 1.5 pounds; warranty, minimum of three years.

b.   Proposal deadline: February 1, 19—.

c.   Proposal destination: Petroleum Frontiers, Inc., P.O. Box 431, Ruston, LA 71270-0431.

d.   Proposal format: Specify the format in which you want the proposal.

MULTICULTURAL INSIGHTS

1.   Which of the reports illustrated in Chapter 19 are most commonly used for business reporting in other cultures with which you are familiar? Which, if any, of the reports would be oral rather than written?

2. Does the structure of any report illustrated in Chapter 19 differ if composed for use in another culture and in a language other than U.S. English? If so, which report(s)? What structure is used? Why?

COMPREHENSIVE REPORTS

OBJECTIVES

After completing this chapter, you should be able to:

1. Apply the steps of the report-writing process to the production of a comprehensive report
2. Identify and prepare each part of a comprehensive report.
3. Apply criteria for appearance, accuracy, coherence, clarity, con-

ciseness, and courtesy as you write comprehensive reports.

4. Adapt the comprehensive report model to satisfy reader requirements or preferences.

DECISIONS CASE

In response to Ms. Nymeyer's request (Decisions Case, Chapter 19), you have gathered adequate and relevant data. Your data analysis has led to interesting conclusions and recommendations. You sit down to write your report, but many questions arise:

1. How can I get Ms. Nymeyer to accept my recommendations?
2. How much detail should I provide?
3. Should I use tables, charts, maps?
4. Should I use formal or informal tone?
5. How can I convey my excitement about the results without showing bias?
6. How shall I begin?

As time passes, you become nervous. "Oh, well," you mutter, "I guess I'll just begin at the beginning."

How do you evaluate that decision?

Additional questions about this decision-making case are stated at the end of this chapter. Study the chapter before answering those questions.

CHAPTER CONTEXT

Although the short-report models presented in Chapter 18 will accommodate many reporting needs, report content and context may require a more comprehensive presentation than those models provide. Readers of analytical and research reports often require a review of the problem and how it was analyzed. Moreover, to ensure reader understanding and acceptance of your recommendations, you may need to display and discuss much of the data that support those recommendations.

NEED FOR COMPREHENSIVE REPORTS

A **comprehensive report** presents all information required to understand a problem and its proposed solution. A comprehensive report is justified whenever any reader is not fully aware of the nature of the problem and the steps taken to resolve it. The person who authorized the report may be familiar with the report problem and purpose. However, many business reports are used by people who are not familiar with the authorization facts. Those readers benefit from a comprehensive report.

When may a comprehensive report be justified?

To promote reader understanding, a comprehensive report includes identification of the problem and the purpose of the report, description of the techniques for data gathering and data analysis, and presentation of the findings. For an informational report, the presentation may end with a summary of findings; for an analytical report, however, analysis must be carried through conclusions and recommendations.

THE WRITING PROCESS AND THE COMPREHENSIVE REPORT

In Chapter 17 you saw how effective researchers use a ten-step plan for their research. The report-writing model presented in Chapter 17 also reminded you that successful writers move through several phases of planning and writing in a recursive manner—they repeat any phase of the process as often as is necessary to achieve the writer's objective for a particular audience. Consider again the phases of that process as they apply to the production of a comprehensive report.

Clarify Problem and Purpose

When you prepared your research plan, you identified the problem and the purpose of your study. Review your research proposal before writing your report. Although the person who authorized the research may be familiar with the problem and purpose, other readers of your report may not know the facts that stimulated the study. Be prepared to put that information in your report.

Analyze Audience

The person who authorized the study will likely read your report, but your audience may well include additional readers. Verify who will use the report and for what purposes.

Assemble, Evaluate, Organize Data

With your research completed, you should have ample data at hand. Evaluate what should—and should not—be included in your report. Consider how to organize the data, always reminding yourself of your audience and what you intend to achieve with that audience.

Is the report-writing model of Chapter 17 relevant when you write a comprehensive report?

Determine Appropriate Style

Your report must satisfy the criteria for message effectiveness: appearance, accuracy, coherence, clarity, conciseness, and courtesy. Those criteria were first presented in Chapter 2 and have been emphasized throughout this book.

Often, writers of analytical reports do not know all of their readers personally. For that reason, those reports may be written in an impersonal style. Do not, however, confuse impersonal with passive or pompous writing. The following examples compare a passive and pompous style with personal and impersonal writing styles.

Passive/pompous: This report shall be introduced with a generalized discussion of the parameters of the problem. The psychological aspects, both cognitive and affective, particularly as they pertain to management and the employee, shall then be discussed in depth.

Personal: I will first discuss the problem. Next I will explain the cognitive and affective aspects of the problem for managers and employees.

Impersonal: After a general discussion of the problem, the report specifies cognitive and affective aspects for managers and employees.

You must also choose the level of formality you wish to convey in your report. Formality is evidenced by language and report structure. Informal writing tends to use features of conversation, such as contractions, first- and second-person pronouns, short (sometimes deliberately incomplete) sentences. Formal writing avoids those linguistic features, as demonstrated by these examples:

Informal: You have a winner here. I think we'll top last year's sales if we go with this plan.

Formal: Projections show that this plan should contribute a 20 percent increase in sales.

Structurally, the most formal reports include parts that are not included in less formal reports. The comprehensive report model presented in this chapter includes the parts used for most formal reports. Suggestions for adapting that model to less formal situations are also given.

Write, Revise, Edit Drafts

Since a comprehensive report tends to be a lengthy document, you can expect to write several drafts before you achieve a satisfactory end product. As you draft your report, use the comprehensive report model of this chapter as a guide. However, adapt that model to satisfy the demands of your audience and your data. Then apply the guides for revision and editing that were presented in Chapter 17.

Produce Final Copy

Your final copy must meet your readers' expectations for content, structure, style, and appearance. An analysis of the comprehensive report model will help you meet those expectations.

COMPREHENSIVE REPORT MODEL

Analytical and research reports frequently follow a formal structure. Although you may modify or adapt these guides, the comprehensive model of a complete, formal report has the following parts:

A. Preliminaries
   1. Cover or binder
   2. Flyleaves
   3. Title fly
   4. Title page
   5. Authorization message
   6. Acceptance message
   7. Transmittal message
   8. Receipt or approval message
   9. Table of contents
  10. List of tables or figures
  11. Foreword or preface
  12. Acknowledgments
  13. Synopsis or executive summary
B. Body
   1. Introduction
   2. Discussion of findings
   3. Conclusions (when appropriate)
   4. Recommendations (when appropriate)
C. Supplements
   1. Endnotes
   2. Bibliography
   3. Glossary

4. Appendix
5. Index

Preliminaries

Report preliminaries are those items that supply a physical vehicle for the message and establish a context for fully appreciating the body as well as the supplements.

The **cover** or **binder**, which holds and protects the pages of the report, should show at least the report title and the author's name. If the title is necessarily long, an abbreviated version may appear on the cover or binder. Often the title is completely capitalized.

Flyleaves, which protect the other pages and provide room for the reader's comments or notes, consist of one blank sheet at the front and another blank sheet at the back of the report. Flyleaves need not be included in less formal reports.

In the most formal reports, the front flyleaf is followed by a **title fly**. This page contains the report title only. The title fly is omitted for less formal reporting situations.

The **title page** shows the full name of the report, identifies the principal reader as well as the author, and dates the submission of the report. A copyright notice appears, when necessary, on the front or back of the title page.

The **authorization message** (letter or memorandum) gives evidence of permission for the report project. The authorization message may be circulated separately from the report.

The **acceptance message** (letter or memorandum) gives evidence of agreement to undertake the project. The acceptance message may be circulated separately from the report.

The **transmittal message** (letter or memorandum) presents the report and reinforces goodwill with the reader.

The **receipt** or **approval message** (letter, memorandum, or even a stamped notation on the front flyleaf or title page) gives evidence of the report's delivery or endorsement.

The **table of contents**, which occupies at least one page, represents the chapter or section titles, headings, or subheadings.

The **list of tables** or **figures** (including illustrations), which occupies at least one page, represents the visual aids that the report contains. Customarily, the list of tables precedes the list of figures. If your report contains relatively few visual aids, you may call this page "List of Illustrations" and divide the list, with one part for tables and one part for figures.

The **foreword** or **preface**, which often is omitted when the transmittal

What is the purpose of report preliminaries?

message is bound with the rest of the report, supplies special details that may stimulate the reader's attention and interest.

Like the foreword or preface, the acknowledgments section, which gives credit to persons or groups that have particularly aided the researcher, is often replaced today by the bound transmittal message.

The **executive summary** recapitulates the purpose, methods, and results of the full study. Although copies of the executive summary may be circulated separately from the full document, a formal business report also contains that summary immediately preceding the body. The summary allows recipients to develop a context for appreciating the complete report and to decide whether or when to read the entire document. In academic settings, the summary may be called an abstract, a synopsis, a précis, a digest, or an epitome.

Body

What is included in the report body?

The **body** of a report supplies specific and definite details of the study's introduction, discussion of findings, conclusions, and (when appropriate) recommendations.

The **introduction**, which may require at least a chapter in a long report or at least a paragraph in a short report, customarily states purpose, scope, limitations, design, methodology, and justification of the study. It may include definitions of special terms and a review of previous research that contributes to the context for this report.

The **discussion**, which constitutes the bulk of the report, provides analysis, synthesis, and interpretation. If the introduction omits a review of previous research, the discussion may present that review as well as a description and explanation of the present project. The discussion often ends with a **summary**. Interim summaries may be presented if warranted by report length or complexity.

In an analytical report, **conclusions** (which are not merely endings) present logical inferences supported by the analysis. **Recommendations**, which appear when they have been requested or are otherwise appropriate, state how the conclusions should be used. Recommendations may also propose that other studies be undertaken or continued.

Supplements

What is the purpose of report supplements?

Report supplements are materials that identify data sources and provide exhibits that, although related to the study, are less than essential or too cumbersome to be included elsewhere in the report.

If footnotes are grouped at the end of the report, they are usually called **endnotes**. Endnotes generally precede the bibliography.

The **bibliography** lists the data sources upon which the study rests. Literally, a bibliography is a list of books; but this term often is used in business reporting to designate all relevant sources, including published and unpublished materials as well as respondents to questionnaires and interviews. In business reports, the word *sources* or *references* is replacing the traditional term *bibliography.*

A **glossary** presents specialized terms with their meanings. This report supplement is especially useful in a technical report presented to a nontechnical audience.

The **appendix** presents comments, tables, figures, exhibits, and other relevant materials that are referred to but are not displayed elsewhere in the report. If the appendix contains more than one item, the items may be called Exhibit 1, Exhibit 2, etc. If the supplements contain appendixes, the first may be called Appendix A; the second, Appendix B; etc. (Some readers prefer that the appendix precede the bibliography.)

The **index**, which is used especially in long and published reports, helps the reader to find specific data quickly. The table of contents lists names and page numbers of major sections, but the index lists names and page numbers of minor items as well.

Several of those preliminary, body, and supplementary parts are included in the report shown in Illustration 20–1, Comprehensive Report Model (pages 548–563).

ADAPTING THE COMPREHENSIVE MODEL

The comprehensive model can be adapted easily to accommodate variations in reader preferences or data complexity. In less formal situations, for example, you may combine the transmittal message and executive summary. A report may not require a table of contents, particularly if it has few sections.

Although the report shown in Illustration 20–1 is written in inductive style, some readers may prefer deductive style. If that style were used, the first page of the report would be similar to Illustration 20–2.

Another variation used in business is to place the details about data collection and analysis in an appendix. That modification accommodates readers who are primarily interested in the results of the study, while also supplying the information about methodology for readers who want to know how the study was conducted.

Reader preference and report content, not arbitrary guides, must determine when and how you deviate from the comprehensive model.

Illustration 20–1   COMPREHENSIVE REPORT MODEL: TITLE PAGE

WILL HOSPITAL-OPERATED CHILD CARE CENTERS REDUCE
COSTS OF NURSE TURNOVER?

_____

Research Report
Prepared for
Dr. P. E. Shaughnessy, President
Southeast Association of Hospital Administrators
Columbia, South Carolina

_____

Prepared by
Booth and Associates
One Watermark Plaza
Columbia, SC 29210-3291
December 8, 19--

COMPREHENSIVE REPORT MODEL: LETTER OF TRANSMITTAL

BOOTH and ASSOCIATES

One Watermark Plaza   Columbia, SC   29210-3291

(803) 555-4590

Consultants in Medical Administration

December 8, 19--

Dr. P. E. Shaughnessy, President
Southeast Association of Hospital Administrators
222 Medical Center
Columbia, SC 29202-4218

Dear Dr. Shaughnessy

This report summarizes the study of the costs and benefits of a
hospital-operated child care center. The report confirms that a
hospital-operated child care center can be a cost-effective way
of reducing nurse turnover costs.

The recommendation to Columbia hospital administrators is that
they cooperate in establishing a child care center to serve their
nurses.

Thank you for the opportunity to conduct the study. We will be
happy to assist you or your members in further investigations of
ways to reduce hospital operating costs.

Sincerely

Susan B. Booth

Susan B. Booth
Project Coordinator

bw

President: Susan B. Booth
Associates: Carey Bryan, Edmond Furman, Grover Richards, Olsen Naven

COMPREHENSIVE REPORT MODEL: TABLE OF CONTENTS

TABLE OF CONTENTS

iii

COMPREHENSIVE REPORT MODEL: LIST OF ILLUSTRATIONS

iv

COMPREHENSIVE REPORT MODEL: EXECUTIVE SUMMARY (DEDUCTIVE ORDER)

EXECUTIVE SUMMARY

A hospital-operated child care center can be a cost-effective
method of reducing nurse turnover. Based on estimates of one
child per retained nurse, the hospital would save $7,156 per year
per nurse. If the retained nurse has two children, the hospital
would save $4,113 per year.

The objective of this research was to evaluate the potential
impact of a hospital-operated child care center on costs related
to nurse turnover. The factors investigated were the proportion
of nurse shortage related to lack of adequate child care, costs
associated with nurse turnover, and cost to the hospital of
operating a child care center.

Data were collected through a review of related literature and
interviews with experts in hospital administration and directors
of child care centers.

The purpose of the study was to find a feasible way to alleviate
the critical shortage of nurses who are willing to work in
hospitals. Nationwide, 100,000 vacancies exist in hospital
nursing positions. Approximately 200 vacancies exist in the four
Columbia hospitals.

v

COMPREHENSIVE REPORT MODEL: REPORT BODY

WILL HOSPITAL-OPERATED CHILD CARE CENTERS REDUCE
COSTS OF NURSE TURNOVER?

Background Information

A critical shortage of nurses who are willing to work in
hospitals poses serious problems for the hospital industry.
Nationwide, approximately 100,000 vacancies in hospital nursing
positions exist; Columbia hospitals have at least 200 nursing
vacancies. (Jones, p. 39) An American Hospital Association
Nursing Personnel Survey indicated that about 18 percent of urban
hospitals are closing beds for lack of a sufficient nursing
staff. Moreover, the supply of nurses is decreasing. Eighty
percent of hospital staffs are women; but less than 4 percent of
women entering college in the '80s chose nursing careers,
compared with 26 percent for business and 6 percent for medical
careers. (De Crosta, p. 171)

A decrease in the supply of nurses accompanied by increased
vacancies in hospital nursing positions suggests the need to
reduce the turnover of nurses. Nationwide, 20 percent of nurses
quit their jobs every year. In some metropolitan areas, turnover
rates are as high as 200 percent. Such turnover rates reduce the
quantity and quality of patient care. In addition, the costs
associated with losing and replacing a nurse can be as high as
$20,000 per nurse. (De Crosta, p. 170)

A factor contributing to nurse turnover may be the lack of
adequate child care. Hospitals must provide competent patient
care 24 hours a day, 7 days a week. These 24 hours are typically
divided into three 8-hour shifts: 7 a.m. to 3 p.m., 3 p.m. to 11
p.m., and 11 p.m. to 7 a.m. Many hospitals require nurses to
work all shifts on a rotating basis, to work two or three
weekends a month and to work some holidays. Typically, a day-
care center operates from 6:30 or 7:00 a.m. until 6:00 or 6:30
p.m., Monday through Friday. Most close on holidays.
Consequently, nurses must coordinate several sources for adequate
child care. Failure of one of the sources frequently requires
the nurse to leave work to attend the child. If the nurse cannot
arrange satisfactory child care, he or she may forego involvement
in the work force. By so doing, the nurse sacrifices well-
developed skills and career aspirations temporarily, if not
permanently.

COMPREHENSIVE REPORT MODEL: REPORT BODY (continued)

2

One survey of inactive nurses indicated that low pay was not the
primary reason for the nursing shortage. Nurses cited pregnancy
and family responsibilities, not low pay, as the chief reasons
for leaving their jobs. ("Hospitals Struggle...")

The Research Problem

The goal of this study was to determine the potential for
hospital-operated child care centers to reduce hospital operating
costs associated with nurse turnover. The purpose of the study
was to find a feasible way to alleviate the critical shortage of
hospital nurses in Columbia.

Factors examined. Three questions were investigated:

1. What proportion of the nurse shortage is related to the lack
    of adequate child care?
2. What are the costs of nurse turnover?
3. What is the cost of operating a child care center?

Delimitations. The following factors were not within the scope
of the project:

1. The effects of turnover on the quality of nursing care.
2. The physical capabilities of hospitals to provide space for a
    child care center.
3. The assessment of need for child care services at a
    particular hospital.
4. The costs related to absenteeism and extended maternity
    leave.

Limitation. One factor limits the interpretation of data
presented in this report. Since cost data related to hospital-
operated child care facilities were not readily available, cost
projections were derived from estimated expenses incurred by
private or state-operated centers. Those centers typically
operate approximately 12 hours per day. Projections of costs to
a hospital-operated center open 24 hours per day included
assumptions of full occupancy during those 24 hours. Less-than-
full occupancy will affect total costs and cost per child.

Definitions. The following definitions will facilitate the
understanding of this report:

1. **Turnover cost.** The cost of replacing the set of services an
    individual will provide. This cost includes both direct and
    indirect costs.
2. **Direct costs.** Costs that can be directly associated with
    replacing the services of a nurse who leaves a hospital
    position. Direct costs include advertising and recruitment
    costs, unfilled position costs, termination costs, and hiring
    costs.

COMPREHENSIVE REPORT MODEL: REPORT BODY (continued)

3

3.   **Indirect costs.** Cost associated with bringing a new hospital nurse up to expected productivity levels. Indirect costs include orientation and training costs and decreased productivity of a new nurse.

Data Collection

Data study were collected by a literature search and face-to-face interviews. The literature search included a review of professional journals and newspaper articles, the state regulations for licensing child care centers, and pamphlets provided by child care centers.

Face-to-face interviews were conducted with hospital administrators, directors of public and privately operated child care centers, directors of hospital in-service training programs, and university faculty members who specialize in hospital administration. The interviews were formal, and interviewees understood the purposes of the interviews.

Data Analysis

Information gathered on nurse shortages was used to determine the proportion of the nurse shortage related to child care problems. That percentage was then applied to the shortage in the Columbia hospitals to project a potential increase in the working nurses in this area.

The direct and indirect costs of nurse turnover were determined to calculate an average per-nurse turnover cost. That figure was compared with the average cost per child for operating a child care center.

Detailed operating budgets from two child care centers were analyzed along with a model budget from an independent consultant. The detailed budgets were for centers operating five days a week. Those budgets were adjusted for seven-day, around-the-clock operation. Revenues and total costs per center were based on full occupancy.

The analysis yielded insights about the proportion of nurse shortage related to lack of adequate child care, the cost associated with nurse turnover, and the cost to the hospital of operating a child care center.

Proportion of Nurse Shortage Related to Lack of Child Care

The four Columbia hospitals reported a total shortage of 200 registered nurses. Although the national average turnover rate for registered nurses has been estimated at 20 percent, Columbia hospitals have been experiencing a turnover rate of approximately 26 percent. (See Table 1.)

COMPREHENSIVE REPORT MODEL: REPORT BODY (continued)

4

Table 1. Registered Nurses in Four Columbia Hospitals, 19--

Employment Factor	Mean	Range
RN Employees	341	232-439
RN Turnovers	88	53-109
RN Hires	133	75-192
Mean Number of RNs, 19--	49	28-96
RN Vacancies, 1/1/--	45	23-90

Source: Jones, p. 39.

Hospitals participating in child-care programs have reported turnover rates 10 percentage points lower than the national average. At some facilities that provide child care, as few as 5 percent of the nursing slots are unfilled. (Wolf, p. 234) If such conditions were to hold true in Columbia, hospitals might anticipate turnover rates of 10-16 percent instead of the current 26 percent.

Link and Settle investigated the extent to which the supply of nursing services would increase in response to higher nurse compensation and other employment inducements. The economic analysis indicated that the presence of young children in the nurse's household creates a major disincentive for working. According to this analysis, child-care programs capable of offsetting the work disincentive created by children between ages two and five should increase the current supply of nurses by approximately 11 percent. (Link and Settle, p. 242)

A significant proportion of the nursing shortage appears to be directly related to child-care problems. The four Columbia area hospitals employ approximately 1,365 nurses. If adequate child care were available, those hospitals could experience an 11 percent increase in the nursing supply or reduction in the nurse turnover rate to 16 percent. The supply of hospital nurses could be increased by 134 to 150, resulting in a 66-75 percent reduction in the current nurse shortage. (See Table 2.)

Table 2. Projected Increase in Registered Nurse Supply
With Availability of Child Care

Projection Method	Current Supply	Projected Increase
Increase supply 11 percent	1,365	150
Reduce turnover to 16 percent	1,365	134

COMPREHENSIVE REPORT MODEL: REPORT BODY (continued)

5

Costs Associated With Nurse Turnover

Turnover of registered nurses affects both direct and indirect costs. A recent study showed that Columbia hospitals absorb $10,199 of direct and indirect costs for each nurse that leaves a hospital. (See Table 3.)

Table 3. Turnover Costs Per Nurse

Category	Mean	Range
Direct		
Advertising/Recruiting	$1,887	$1,181-2,688
Unfilled Positions	4,101	1,358-7,794
Hiring	655	448-1,006
Termination	163	118- 193
Indirect		
Orientation/Training	2,117	1,518-3,316
Decreased New RN Productivity	1,276	915-1,543
Total	$10,199	$6,886-15,152

Source: Jones, p. 59.

1. Advertising and recruiting. Over 10 percent of the total cost of nurse turnover is the direct cost of advertising and recruitment. Advertising alone constitutes 28 percent of this cost category. Other costs are distributed as follows: recruiter salaries, 17 percent; supplies, 5 percent; student-nurse hiring programs, 26 percent; miscellaneous recruitment, 23 percent. The miscellaneous charges include costs for scholarships, creative writing consultants, school visits, and job fairs.

2. Unfilled positions. The largest direct cost is associated with unfilled positions, $4,101 per nurse; and the largest portion of that cost (78 percent) is lost revenue from closed beds. Columbia hospitals estimate an average revenue loss of $273,331 per hospital resulting from closed beds because of insufficient nursing staffs. Other costs of an unfilled position are hiring of temporary RNs (6 percent) and overtime pay for RNs (16 percent).

3. Hiring. The average cost to hire a single RN for a Columbia hospital is $655. That cost covers interviews (4 percent);

COMPREHENSIVE REPORT MODEL: REPORT BODY (continued)

6

secretarial processing (2 percent); payroll processing (2 percent); and employment processing (91 percent). Employment processing includes uniforms and supplies provided to nurses, pre-employment physical examinations, moving and travel expenses, recruitment bonuses, and internal referral bonuses. When a nurse leaves, the hospital loses the benefits those costs were intended to purchase, making hiring costs an expensive component of nurse turnover.

4. Termination. Hospitals reported paying unused vacation and sick leave to nurses upon employment termination. This factor accounted for 89 percent of termination costs. The remaining 11 percent was attributed to exit interviews. Average termination cost per nurse is $163.

5. Orientation and training. Orientation and training varies among hospitals. Total annual orientation and training costs range from $80,463 to $278,546 in Columbia hospitals. The average cost per RN turnover is $2,117, which covers staff time and salaries (66 percent), supplies and equipment (1 percent), and the nurse-preceptor system (33 percent).

6. Decreased productivity of the new RN. A substantial turnover cost results from a new employee's being less efficient than the one who is replaced. Turnover of personnel may also affect staff morale, resulting in lower group productivity. Columbia hospital administrators estimate that the average nurse needs 6.7 weeks to become 90 percent as productive as an experienced employee. Estimated annual costs per hospital for decreased productivity range from $60,991 to $168,216. The average cost per RN turnover is estimated at $1,276.

In summary, the cost to replace one full-time registered nurse can be conservatively estimated as $10,199. This figure represents direct costs of $6,806 and indirect costs of $3,393.

Cost to Hospital of Operating a Child Care Center

Operating budgets for three child care centers were analyzed to project costs a hospital would incur if it provided child care. These costs were compared with operating budgets provided by a national consultant. Projections assume around-the-clock operation for an infants-toddlers center and 6:30 a.m.–6:30 p.m. Monday-Friday operation for a pre-school facility. The infants-toddlers facility should be equipped to receive pre-school children when their parents are working evening or weekend hospital shifts.

The estimated annual budget for an infants-toddlers center is $331,670, with an estimated cost per child of $3,685. (See Table 4, page 7.) The budget is for a facility equipped and staffed to serve a maximum of 45 clients at any time. However, a 24-hour

COMPREHENSIVE REPORT MODEL: REPORT BODY (continued)

7

```
                Table 4.  Annual Budget and Costs Per Child
                     for Operating a Child Care Center
```

Cost Factor	Infants and Toddlers (90 clients)*	Pre-Schoolers (20 clients)
Staff		
Director/Teacher	$ 46,000	$ 23,000
Teachers @ $17,000 ea.	68,000	34,000
Assistants @ $12,000 ea.	48,000	24,000
Aides @ $10,000 ea.	20,000	
Substitutes (Part Time)	4,000	5,000
Secretaries (Part Time)	14,000	7,000
Cooks (Part Time)	16,000	7,000
Fringe Benefits (17%)	36,720	17,000
Total Staff	**252,720**	**117,000**
Food	32,850	5,200
Toys, Crafts, Ed. Materials	4,500	8,400
Conference Fees	600	360
Supplies		
Disposables	1,000	600
Maintenance/Cleaning	500	600
Office	500	600
Medical	150	125
Kitchen	400	200
Other Expenses		
Postage	250	500
Insurance	5,000	5,000
Printing	1,000	1,500
Rent	28,000	40,000
Utilities	4,200	6,000
Total Non-Staff	**78,950**	**69,085**
TOTAL	$331,670	$186,085

```
Annual cost per child:        $  3,685   $  9,304
Avg. annual cost per child:   $  4,707 ($331,670 + 186,085/110)
```

*Operating 24 hours per day/7 days per week; maximum capacity at any time = 45 children.

Source: Primary.

center could serve as many as 90 clients per day. Rarely would a child be in the center for the full 24 hours.

COMPREHENSIVE REPORT MODEL: REPORT BODY (continued)

8

The estimated annual budget for a 20-client pre-school facility is $186,085, with an average cost per child of $9,304. The higher cost per child is attributable to two factors: increased space requirements for pre-school activities, and higher fixed costs per child with 12-hour use of facilities.

Personnel costs, including fringe benefits, account for a high percentage of total costs, averaging $2,808 per child in the infants-toddlers center and $5,850 in the pre-school facility. Rent and utilities are based on the minimum state requirements for infant-toddler and pre-school facilities. The rental costs are more than adequate to cover the average rate in the Columbia area for rentals of this type. Food cost also varies with the number of children served, but it averages $1 per child per day, the standard rate of the U.S. Department of Agriculture.

At current market rates, a hospital-operated child care center could expect revenues to average $32 per week per child, or $1,664 per child-year. Compared to average costs, therefore, the infants-toddlers center must absorb $2,021 per child annually, in effect subsidizing child care for nurses. The annual subsidy for pre-school users would be $7,640 per child. If costs of operating both facilities are combined, the average cost per child at full occupancy is $4,707, requiring a $3,043 subsidy to users. That figure may be considered the cost to the hospital to provide child care. Based on estimates of one child per retained nurse, a hospital would save $7,156 per year per nurse by paying a child-care subsidy instead of nurse-replacement costs. If the retained nurse has two children, the hospital would save $4,113 per year per nurse. (See Figure 1.)

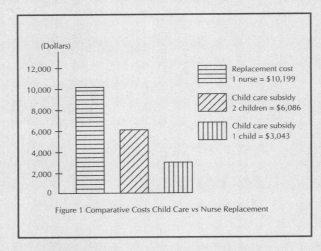

Figure 1 Comparative Costs Child Care vs Nurse Replacement

COMPREHENSIVE REPORT MODEL: REPORT BODY (continued)

9

Summary, Conclusions, and Recommendations

The findings of this study support two conclusions and two recommendations.

Summary of findings. Major findings are:

1. Each Columbia hospital loses an average of 88 nurses per year. A significant proportion of nurse turnover is related to inadequate child care facilities.
2. The supply of hospital nurses in the Columbia area would increase by 134-150 if hospitals provided child care.
3. The cost of replacing one full-time registered nurse is approximately $10,199. This figure represents direct costs of $6,806 and indirect costs of $3,393.
4. The annual cost per child incurred by a hospital in operating a child care center would be approximately $4,707.

Conclusions. Conclusions drawn from this analysis are as follows:

1. A hospital-operated child care center can be a cost-effective method of reducing nurse turnover.
2. Turnover rates and child-care needs in a single hospital may not justify establishment of a child care center. Turnover rates for the four Columbia hospitals suggest, however, that a center for use by nurses of all hospitals may be cost effective.

Recommendations. Two recommendations are made to Columbia hospital administrators.

1. Jointly sponsor a centrally located child care facility to serve nurses of the four Columbia hospitals.
2. Evaluate whether operating child care facilities has an impact on the following factors:

    a. Absenteeism
    b. Length of maternity leave
    c. Quality of nursing care
    d. Morale of nurses

COMPREHENSIVE REPORT MODEL: SOURCES

10

SOURCES

Adolf, Barbara, and Karol Rose. The Employer's Guide to Child
    Care, 2d ed. (New York: Praeger, 1988).

Bergsven, Richard, Professor, College of Business
    Administration, University of South Carolina, Columbia,
    SC, personal interview, October 5, 19--.

Burud, Sandra L., Pamela R. Aschbacher, and Jacquelyn
    McCroskey. Employer-Supported Child Care (Boston:
    Auburn House Publishing Company, 1984).

Collins, Patricia R., Paul Krause, and Sandra Machida. "Making
    Child Care an Employee Benefit." Management Accounting,
    vol. 71 (April 1990), pp. 26-29.

De Crosta, Anthony A. "Meeting the Nurse Retention Challenge."
    Nursing, vol. 19 (May 1989), pp. 170-171.

Hicks, Georgene, and Charles H. White. "The Cost of
    Orienting--and Retaining Nurses." CHA Insight, vol. 15
    (June 4, 1981), pp. 1-4.

Hiller, Marianne, Director, Spartanburg General Hospital Child
    Development, Spartanburg, SC, personal interview,
    September 19, 19--.

"Hospitals Struggle to Keep Nurses." The Washington Post
    (August 13, 1981), sec. Va, pp. 1, 6.

Jones, Cheryl B. Hospital Staff Nurse Turnover Costs: Model
    and Measurement, unpublished master's thesis, College of
    Nursing, The University of South Carolina, 1989.

Link, Charles R., and Russell F. Settle. "Financial Incentive
    and Labor Supply of Married Nurses: An Economic
    Analysis." Nursing Research, vol. 29 (July-August 1980),
    pp. 238-243.

Lund, David, Associate Professor, College of Business
    Administration, University of South Carolina, Columbia,
    SC, personal interview, October 5, 19--.

MacKenzie, Sue, Licensing Division, South Carolina Department
    of Social Services, personal interview, October 5, 19--.

Moore, Lawrence, Administrator, Presbyterian Hospital,
    Charlotte, NC, personal interview, October 20, 19--.

COMPREHENSIVE REPORT MODEL: SOURCES (continued)

11

Palmer, Marilyn, Director, Presbyterian Hospital Child
    Development Center, Charlotte, NC, personal interview,
    Fall 19--.

Ransom, Cynthia, Pamela Aschbacher, and Sandra Burud. "The
    Return on the Child-Care Investment." Personnel
    Administrator, vol. 34 (October 1989), pp. 54-58.

Reverman, Carol, Director, Booker T. Washington Child Care
    Center, Columbia, SC, personal interview, October 25, 19--.

Ritter, Anne. "Dependent Care Proves Profitable." Personnel,
    vol. 67 (March 1990), pp. 12-16.

Thornburg, Linda. "On-Site Child Care Works for the Health-
    Care Industry." HRMagazine, vol. 35 (August 1990), pp.
    39-40.

"When It Comes to Child Care, Hospitals May Be Setting the Pace
    for Much of the Nation." JAMA, vol. 261, no. 13 (April 7,
    1989), pp. 1857, 1861.

Wolf, Gail A. "Nursing Turnover: Some Causes and Solutions."
    Nursing Outlook (April 29, 1981), pp. 233-235.

Yalow, Elanna. "Corporate Child Care Helps Recruit and Retain
    Workers." Personnel Journal, vol. 69 (June 1990), pp. 48-
    55.

Illustration 20–2   FIRST PAGE OF REPORT, DEDUCTIVE STRUCTURE

WILL HOSPITAL-OPERATED CHILD CARE CENTERS REDUCE
COSTS OF NURSE TURNOVER?

Conclusions and Recommendations

A hospital-operated child care center can be a cost-
effective method of reducing nurse turnover. Although turnover rates and child-care needs in a single hospital may not
justify establishment of a child care center, nurse turnover
in the four Columbia hospitals suggest that a center for use
by nurses of all hospitals may be cost effective.

Columbia area hospital administrators are advised to do two
things:

1. Jointly sponsor a centrally located child care facility
    to serve nurses of the four Columbia hospitals.
2. Evaluate whether operating child care facilities has an
    impact on the following factors:
    a. Absenteeism
    b. Length of maternity leave
    c. Quality of nursing care
    d. Morale of nurses

Summary of Findings

Major findings of this study are:

1. Each Columbia hospital loses an average of 88 nurses per
    year. A significant proportion of nurse turnover is
    related to inadequate child care facilities.
2. The supply of hospital nurses in the Columbia area would
    be increased by 134-150 if hospitals provided child
    care.
3. The cost of replacing one full-time registered nurse is
    approximately $10,199. This figure represents direct
    costs of $6,806 and indirect costs of $3,393.
4. The annual cost per child incurred by a hospital in
    operating a child care center would be approximately
    $4,707.

Background Information

A critical shortage of nurses who are willing to work in
hospitals poses serious problems for the hospital industry.
Nationwide, approximately 100,000 vacancies in hospital
nursing positions exist; Columbia hospitals have at least
200 nursing vacancies. (Jones, p. 39). . . . . .

REVIEW AND TRANSITION

The structure of the comprehensive report model is frequently used for analytical or research reports. That structure includes these parts: report preliminaries, report body, and report supplements. Report preliminaries establish a context for full appreciation and easy use of the report. The report body supplies details of the report's problem and purpose; data presentation and discussion; and (when appropriate) conclusions and recommendations. Report supplements identify data sources and provide exhibits that are too cumbersome to be included elsewhere in the report. Using the recursive planning and writing process described in Chapter 17 and the report model presented in this chapter, you can produce effective comprehensive reports.

In your study of Chapters 1 through 20, you have developed communication skills demanded in the business environment. Those skills can also help you acquire a job that matches your interests and abilities. Chapters 21 and 22 show you how to apply research, writing, and speaking skills in your employment search.

YOUR DECISIONS FOR CHAPTER 20

Review your decisions regarding the Nymeyer report. How has your study of Chapters 19 and 20 led you to approach a report-writing task? In what ways can knowledge of the report-writing process and familiarity with the comprehensive report model develop confidence for writing a report?

DISCUSSION QUESTIONS

A. In the context of Chapter 20, what are appropriate definitions and examples for these terms?

1. report preliminaries
2. authorization message
3. transmittal message
4. executive summary
5. conclusions
6. recommendations
7. report supplements
8. endnotes
9. appendix

B. In what ways (other than length) is the comprehensive report model similar to and different from short reports?

C.   What justifies deductive structure for an executive summary in an inductive-structure report?

D.   In what ways does the information presented by Chapters 17 through 20 pertain to oral as well as written business reports?

APPLICATIONS

1.   Appropriately revise these statements to demonstrate impersonal yet vigorous, active writing style. Also apply the criteria of accuracy, coherence, clarity, and conciseness.

a.   The annuity plan was established by ABC Company to encourage employees to provide systematically for their own financial security in the years after retirement.

b.   This research involved projection of demand for business graduates and the skills these graduates will need to have acquired for filling the projected positions.

c.   This procedure permits customers to be prepared to pay their bills with promptness at a fairly regular time each and every month. On the other hand it would be, practically speaking, impossible for us to bill all of our customers on any one day of a month. But the previously mentioned procedure merits attention. Especially in reference to the situation that recurs in some of the areas with very high delinquency which on a large scale requires firm collection methods.

d.   A purposive sample was used to select the stocks instead of a random sample. Using this method the research found nine industries to use in the study.

e.   By glancing at Table II, the trend can be easily determined.

f.   Downtown merchants have solved the parking problem by building parking garages in close proximity to their stores. They have been especially successful as business people because they provide convenient parking.

g.   Incoming calls are handled by pushing the blinking light asking the particular party who they want, push the hold button, push station or extension wanted, every thing else is automatic.

h.   It was concluded that so long as the customer's order is satisfactorily handled it matters little to the customer the manner in which it is accomplished.

i.   The weight of the results of this study requires a recommendation that Metrico, Inc., forgo employment of another secretary at this time due to the simple reason that the cost does not justify the convenience.

2. Based upon an approved proposal that you developed for Application 1 or 2 of Chapter 18, conduct the research you proposed. Then present a written report of your research.

3. Examine a corporate annual report or a report in a technical journal, such as *Economic Review* or *The Journal of Business Communication*. Orally or in writing, identify how closely the report patterns the comprehensive report model presented in Chapter 20.

4. Form work groups of three or four students. Revise the comprehensive report given in Illustration 20–1. Make these changes:

   a. Use deductive structure
   b. Place the definitions, data collection, and data analysis sections in an appendix.
   c. Evaluate transitions between sections. Make necessary revisions to ensure a smooth flow between sections.

CASES

1. You are the chairperson of your college's curriculum committee. That committee is trying to find ways to improve students' writing skills. One suggested teaching technique is to incorporate writing instruction into selected undergraduate business courses. To determine the potential feasibility of such a method, a management professor and a business communication professor cooperated in an experimental study. Here are the facts about that study.

   a. Research problem: To evaluate effectiveness of incorporating writing requirements into a principles of management course.
   b. Research purpose: To assess feasibility of integrating communication instruction into required business courses.
   c. Methods used: Two classes in principles of management were used as an experimental group and two as a control group.
      Instruction in the experimental group consisted of lectures and discussion of management principles, oral case analyses, lectures and discussions of writing style and structure for written case analyses, limited reviews of writing mechanics, written case analyses followed by prompt feedback on quality of writing and application of management principles, multiple-choice examinations covering management principles.
      Instruction in the control group consisted of lectures and discussion of management principles, oral case analyses, and multiple-choice examinations covering management principles. Students

were not assigned written case analyses and received no instruction about writing principles.

Both groups were given two standardized tests of basic writing skills: Form A at the beginning of the semester and Form B at the end of the semester. Students' grade point ratios (beginning of semester) and SAT verbal scores were also obtained.

d.   Summary of findings:

Variables	Experimental Group	Control Group
Mean, GPR	2.94	2.90
Mean, SAT verbal	3.75	3.73
Test A, Mean	46.93	45.91
Range	21–63	25–62
Number	118	120
Test B, Mean	50.82	45.32
Range	33–70	21–63

As directed by your instructor, supplement the data with information obtained from primary or secondary sources. Examples of appropriate additional data are:

(1)   need of writing skills in entry-level positions for business graduates

(2)   attitudes of business students toward writing requirements in business courses

Prepare a written report incorporating your data with that given in this case. Use the comprehensive report model as a guide, including the parts requested by your instructor. Direct the report to Dr. J. A. Gossage, Academic Dean, Your College.

2.   You are an assistant to H. Algonac, the administrator of Valley Manor, a 200-resident retirement home. All resident facilities are private rooms with bath. Valley Manor also has a central dining room and twelve common-use areas, such as library, crafts room, recreation room, lounges, beauty and barber shops, and a small general store.

Valley Manor uses approximately 14,000 100-watt incandescent light bulbs each year. Each resident facility has at least five bulb sockets, and the 12 common areas average 20 bulb sockets each. Your administrator has asked you to determine the most cost-effective light bulbs to purchase. Collect data about bulb life and bulb costs, including any discounts available for bulk purchases. Cost projections must include estimated labor required to replace bulbs.

Present your findings, conclusions, and recommendations in a comprehensive report to Director Algonac. Include the preliminary and supplementary parts requested by your instructor.

MULTICULTURAL INSIGHTS

1. Based on your observation or experience, what formats are most commonly used for business reports composed for use in your native culture?

2. Discuss the significance of each of the following items for reporting in your native culture: authorization message, acceptance message, transmittal message, footnotes (or endnotes), and bibliography (or sources).

Cases

As you complete these cases you will continue to demonstrate your understanding of communication challenges confronted by business people. Part 5 challenges include ethical issues, report content, and report structure.

CASE A: WHAT SHALL I TELL THE BOSS? Part 1
(Ethical Issues, Report Content, Report Structure)

To demonstrate its social responsibility, Linton Enterprises has adopted an employee sabbatical leave program. Here's how the program works.

1. The employee must submit a proposal to provide specific services as a volunteer in a community agency. For example, an employee could propose to work for a year as an employment adviser in a center for homeless, unemployed persons. The proposal must be submitted to the agency and to the employee's immediate supervisor.
2. Upon acceptance of the proposal by the agency and approval by the supervisor, the employee is granted a sabbatical leave for up to one year. During that time, the employee has no job responsibilities at Linton Enterprises, but Linton pays the employee 50 percent of her

or his normal salary. The employee must fulfill the terms of the proposal and write two reports to the supervisor: a status report midway through the sabbatical experience and a final report within one month of completing the sabbatical leave. The employee is expected to return to Linton Enterprises at the end of the leave.

Adrian Soto and James Balch comprise a sales and technical support team for Linton Enterprises. Soto is the sales representative who obtains orders for the company's specialized accounting software; Balch installs the software on the purchaser's computer system, trains the users, and supplies technical assistance for 12 months after the initial installation.

Balch has submitted a proposal for a sabbatical year with County Hospital, offering to assist in the reorganization of the hospital's patient information system. Balch has confided to Soto that he intends to use the year to demonstrate the hospital's need for a full-time Director of Patient Information Systems, and Balch hopes to get that job.

Soto faces a dilemma. He knows that his sales presentations have been successful, in part, because of his confidence in Balch's technical support. Soto fears that his sales—and sales commissions—will suffer if Balch is not available to back him up. Soto also knows that his supervisor, Yoko Inazo, will ask for his recommendations about action on Balch's proposal and assignment of someone to fill the technical support position during Balch's absence. To complicate the issue even further, Soto suspects that Inazo wants to replace Balch, perhaps permanently, with a technical support person in whom Soto has little confidence.

INSIGHTS

To gain insights into ethical reporting, answer these questions:

1. What should Soto recommend to Inazo regarding Balch's request for a sabbatical leave? What should Soto recommend regarding a replacement for Balch if the leave is granted? What data should be included to support those recommendations. Why?
2. What structure, inductive or deductive, should Soto use for the report? Why?

Acting as Soto, write the report in memorandum format. Supply reasonable data, based on the facts given in this case and your answers to Question 1.

CASE B: WHAT SHALL I TELL THE BOSS? Part 2
(Ethical Issues, Report Content, Report Structure)

Adrian Soto and James Balch (Case A) have met periodically for lunch during Balch's sabbatical leave. Soto's goals for these meetings have been to reinforce a valued friendship and to maintain Balch's interest in returning to Linton Enterprises in his technical support role.

During those meetings, Soto has learned that Balch is unhappy with his volunteer activities at County Hospital. The hospital administrator has not drawn on Balch's technical expertise; instead the administrator often gives Balch relatively unskilled tasks, such as data input. The volunteer work will obviously not result in a lucrative job offer as Director of Patient Information Systems. Balch would like to end the experience as soon as possible and return to his former position at Linton Enterprises.

Meanwhile, Soto's worst fears about the technical support person assigned to work with him have been confirmed. That individual has neither the technical nor the communication skills needed to service Soto's clients. Two major contracts were canceled when the support person was unable to supply the promised training and technical assistance. Soto lost valuable time and substantial commissions when the contracts were canceled. Supervisor Inazo has acknowledged that the technical support team member must be replaced soon.

INSIGHTS

To further your insights into ethical reporting, answer these questions:

1. What ethical issues surround the continuance or discontinuance of the sabbatical agreement? Answer this question from the perspective of the hospital administrator, Inazo, Soto, Balch, and the employee who has replaced Balch.
2. What, if anything, should Soto report to Balch about his experience with the new technical support person? What, if anything, should Soto report to Inazo about Balch's desire to discontinue the volunteer work at County Hospital? Why?
3. What should Balch include in his midyear status report about the volunteer experience at County Hospital? What structure should he use? Why?

Acting as Balch, write that status report. Supply reasonable data based on the facts given in this case and your answers to Questions 1 through 3.

NATURE'S WONDERS

This assignment places you in the Research and Development Division of Nature's Wonders. The division's responsibilities include market and financial research.

CASE FACTS

The management team at Nature's Wonders has a goal of 15 percent annual growth, as measured by gross sales, adjusted for inflation. To reach that goal, management must be fully aware of its market and its competition.

YOUR TASKS

Your research will provide market information for management.

1. Do a comprehensive analysis of the horticultural specialties industry (SIC Number 018). Identify the two industry leaders in the United States. Collect basic financial and market data about each. Include current information about market trends, new products, etc.

2. Present your findings in a formal written report for presentation to management. Include appropriate visual aids.

3. Write an abbreviated version of the report for inclusion in the company's monthly newsletter to employees. Select information that will especially interest employees.

4. Write the script of the president's opening statement for a news conference. The president will announce that Nature's Wonders has acquired the No. 2 company in the industry (as identified in Task 1). Supply pertinent data from your research and make reasonable assumptions about the acquisition.

**P
A
R
T
6**
▼

THE EMPLOYMENT PROCESS

Selecting a career is one of the major decisions you will make during your lifetime. Moreover, changes in technology, in personal experiences, or in economic conditions may compel you to modify your job preferences during your career. With much of your adult life devoted to employment, the work you choose should be enjoyable, challenging, and rewarding. How can you determine and obtain this type of work?

Securing employment is similar to marketing a product. Product and market research precede creative promotion. The *research phase* reveals information about yourself as a prospective worker and about the job market. The *creative phase,* based on your research, yields messages whereby you fulfill your objective of obtaining work that you desire.

Part 6 demonstrates communication by objectives: combining research and creativity as you plan your career profile and the communications required to get the job you want. Chapter 21 describes the research phase: analyzing yourself, your career potential, and specific jobs; analyzing the job market; and preparing a personal career history. The creative phase is presented in Chapter 22: matching your attributes to employment requirements through messages that are logically and psychologically effective. Chapter 22 also presents the employer's perspective in the employment-communication process.

EMPLOYMENT MESSAGES: RESEARCH PHASE

CHAPTER OUTLINE

I. Using Research to Ensure Employment Success
II. Analyzing Yourself, Your Career Potential, and Specific Jobs
    A. Self-Appraisal
    B. Career Appraisal
    C. Specific Position Analysis
III. Analyzing the Job Market
    A. Preparing a Prospect List
    B. Analyzing the Prospect List
    C. Assembling Position Information
IV. Preparing a Personal Career History
V. Review and Transition

OBJECTIVES

After completing this chapter, you should be able to:

1. Appreciate the importance of preemployment research.
2. Conduct a rigorous examination of your employment strengths and weaknesses.
3. Analyze specific positions that will satisfy your employment goals.
4. Identify and analyze companies likely to need your knowledge and skills.
5. Prepare a personal career history.

DECISIONS CASE

Jeff Bult and Terry Novak will receive their college degrees soon. They are eager to apply their business knowledge and skills in challenging jobs, but they are apprehensive about the job search. Jeff wants to use his accounting degree but prefers to live in Denver, Colorado, so that he will be near excellent ski slopes. Terry wants a job that will satisfy her interests in finance and world travel.

"How do we begin?" they ask.

What is your advice? How may their initially stated goals help or hinder them in finding the right jobs?

Additional questions about this decision-making case are stated at the end of this chapter. Study the chapter before answering those questions.

CHAPTER CONTEXT

Obtaining the right job—one that is interesting, challenging, and rewarding—depends upon (1) knowing yourself, (2) knowing your career potential, and (3) relating your knowledge to specific employment opportunities. This effort focuses upon the most exciting research subject imaginable—you.

USING RESEARCH TO ENSURE EMPLOYMENT SUCCESS

What are benefits of employment research?

Only through in-depth knowledge of yourself—your ambitions, attributes, abilities—can you effectively present your qualifications to a prospective employer. How well you relate specific qualifications to a likely employer depends upon your knowledge of the requirements and responsibilities involved.

To possess this information requires research: digging for facts about yourself, your career field, and specific positions; sifting, resifting, and organizing those facts to fit a basic plan. This preliminary research is necessary for the preparation of your application message and for your success in the interview.

Many applicants handicap themselves by being concerned only with what the job can do for them. But this is a fact of life: Before you are hired, the employer must be convinced that your skills can serve the company.

Personnel executives often receive application messages that contain incomplete information and inappropriate tone. These messages may imply that the applicant does not know herself or himself, does not understand the prospective employer's needs, or lacks the communication skills that are vital to business success.

Statements of facts alone may not be enough to win a job. Creativity in communicating those facts can give you a competitive advantage in attracting attention to your talents, arousing interest in your skills, stimulating desire for your services, and producing action. Therefore, recognize your research as a foundation for your communication.

ANALYZING YOURSELF, YOUR CAREER POTENTIAL, AND SPECIFIC JOBS

Your self-study is a rigorous examination of who you are and what you can do. Knowing yourself requires a truthful appraisal—strengths and weaknesses—of your personal characteristics and work abilities. Use this appraisal to guide the preparation of your application messages and the conduct of your interviews.

Self-Appraisal

What is the purpose of self-appraisal?

A **self-appraisal** is a research activity in which you identify careers, their work requirements, and your ambitions. An appropriate starting point is to ask yourself questions that interviewers are likely to ask you.

Interviewers attempt to determine your ability and willingness to do the work and your compatibility with the organization. Prepare now to answer questions like these:

1. Why do you want to work for our company?
2. What do you know about our firm and its work?
3. What kind of work do you really enjoy? Why?
4. What other kinds of work interest you? Why?
5. Which of your academic courses did you enjoy most? Why?
6. Which of your academic courses did you not enjoy? Why?
7. What books—other than textbooks—have you read recently?
8. What are your favorite hobbies or avocational interests?
9. What do you feel most confident doing?
10. If we employ you, what salary do you expect?
11. If we employ you, how long do you intend to stay with us?
12. Are you free to travel or relocate if the job requires it?
13. What geographic location, if any, do you prefer? Why?
14. What information, other than that on your résumé, should be considered in evaluating your application?
15. What information on your résumé do you think is *especially* important for successful work with our company?

16. In what ways have you grown in the past two or three years?
17. Give an example of an important goal you have set for yourself in the past. What did you do to reach that goal? How successful were you?
18. What questions do you have?

If you know the type of career you wish to pursue, begin now to assess your personal characteristics, your general knowledge and abilities, your specific skills and competencies as they relate to that career. If you have not selected a career, use this research opportunity to identify careers, their work requirements, and your ambitions.

Consider accomplishments in all aspects of your life—for instance, in your academic work, full- and part-time experience, organizational activities, and sports or hobbies. Analyze those accomplishments to determine the skills and traits that are accountable for your success.

The following characteristics are thought starters to help you begin your self-appraisal:

accuracy	leadership
ambition	neatness
communication skills	objectiveness
cooperation	perseverance
decisiveness	personal integrity
dependability	punctuality
efficiency	responsibility
enthusiasm	self-control
good judgment	tactfulness
initiative	

Additional data for your self-study may come from aptitude or achievement tests, from your performance in academic courses, and from your continued interest in particular areas of study.

The computer-based aid SIGI PLUS®[1] can help you examine combinations of your values, interests, abilities, perceptions, preferences, and plans in relation to specific occupations. SIGI is an acronym for Systems of Interactive Guidance and Information. This career-guidance aid is available in many college career planning offices.

With these and similar data sources, you can get to know yourself privately. You can also discover the ways in which your attributes and those of successful workers apparently coincide.

In your self-appraisal, include these categories of information:

---

[1]SIGI PLUS is a registered trademark of Educational Testing Service.

What information
should be included in
a self-appraisal?

1. ratings of your personality traits, interests, and aptitudes (as deter-
    mined by yourself and tests)
2. your education (completed, in progress, and planned)
3. your work experience (completed, in progress, and desired)

From your research you can then identify, emphasize, or minimize facts
and insights for your employment applications, résumés, and interviews. The
following example illustrates a possible outcome of the self-appraisal process.

A PRIVATE SELF-APPRAISAL

I.   Personality
     A. Ambitious—I possess strong desires for personal advance-
         ment. At times these desires interfere with my personal rela-
         tionships. I make friends easily but sometimes lose them
         quickly. I admit my need to learn more about human rela-
         tions.
     B. Conscientious—I strive to fulfill obligations but recognize a
         need to attend more carefully to details.
     C. Dominant—I enjoy influencing others but realize that influ-
         ence can be reciprocal. I like to lead.
     D. Enthusiastic—My eagerness "comes on strong"; I can ener-
         gize other people's efforts as well as my own.
     E. Gregarious—I enjoy meeting people and participating in so-
         cial and service organizations. I am sometimes more inter-
         ested in making new friends than in helping old ones. I'm
         learning not to take people for granted.
     F. Self-reliant—Holding a part-time job throughout my high
         school and college education has contributed to my inde-
         pendence. I can study both sides of an issue and arrive at a
         relatively unbiased solution. However, I welcome advice from
         qualified and experienced people in an effort to draw accu-
         rate conclusions.
II. Interests
     A. Social—I enjoy these activities:
         1. Meeting people, associating with friends, and working
             with others
         2. Attending social functions on campus
         3. Participating in college activities; serving as vice presi-
             dent of Business Administration Club on campus.
         4. Participating in community recreation programs
     B. Academic—My favorite study areas are:
         1. Management
         2. Psychology
         3. Communication

4. Accounting
5. Finance
6. Mathematics
C. Career—I would enjoy a career that provides:
1. Broad experience rather than specialization in one area
2. Opportunity to work with top management
3. Advancement to leadership
4. Equitable financial rewards
D. Other—I enjoy these activities:
1. Foreign travel
2. Snow skiing
3. Swimming
III. Aptitudes
A. According to academic achievement in college:
1. Excellent—management, public speaking, business communication
2. Good—psychology, economics, foreign languages
3. Poor—physical science
B. According to psychological tests:
1. Interests
a. High—general problem solving
b. Low—mechanical
2. Aptitudes
a. High—verbal
b. Average—quantitative
c. Low—mechanical
IV. Education
A. High School—graduated June 1, 19—; ranked 20 in class of 250
B. College—Program in progress (junior year); plan to work for bachelor of business administration degree with management major and marketing cognate
V. Experience
A. Summer employment, during school, with City Parks and Recreation Department
B. Cooperative education program at City College; employed in the accounting department of a large chemical company; am being rotated to various accounting jobs

Career Appraisal

Having completed a self-appraisal, you proceed to the next phase of your employment research—the *career appraisal*.

Various careers require different preparations, attributes, skills, and interests. Also, job satisfactions—advancement possibilities, opportunities for personal growth, and professional and personal rewards—vary from one career to another. By comparing your self-appraisal with your career appraisal, you will guide yourself toward suitable employment decisions.

Your career appraisal and your self-appraisal are private records. Make your appraisals truthful, candid, and detailed. Those appraisals are your messages to yourself and the basis of your messages to prospective employers.

When preparing your career appraisal, consider the following factors:

1. responsibilities, rewards, and demands of the career field
2. education and training (nature, cost, time, location)
3. personal characteristics considered essential or highly desirable for success
4. model history of a person in this career (your evaluation of this person's professional, social, and personal success; what the career has demanded; what limitations the career has imposed upon the person; satisfactions and disappointments of the career; stages of employment from initial job to top position)
5. relation of career to your values, goals, and qualifications

For career information, visit your college library or your school career planning and placement center. An excellent source of information is the *Occupational Outlook Handbook,*[2] which provides occupational briefs grouped into clusters. Each occupation is described in these ways: nature of the work; working conditions; places of employment; training, other qualifications, and advancement; employment outlook; earnings; related occupations; sources of additional information.

Another useful source of information is *The Encyclopedia of Careers and Vocational Guidance,* Volumes I, II, and III.[3] Volume I provides general information about career planning and discussions of major career fields. Volume II gives detailed information about more than 200 specific careers and occupations. Discussions of each occupation include definition, history, nature of the work, general requirements, specific requirements, opportunities for experience and exploration, methods of entering, advancement, employment outlook, earnings, conditions of work, and social and psychological factors. Sources for additional information are also provided. Volume III focuses on careers in technical areas. The section "Emerging Technician Occupations"

---

[2]Published by the Bureau of Labor Statistics, U.S. Department of Labor (Washington: U.S. Government Printing Office, updated every two years.)

[3]William E. Hopke, ed., *The Encyclopedia of Careers and Vocational Guidance,* Vols I, II, and III, 8th ed. (Chicago: J. G. Ferguson Publishing Company, 1980).

describes some of the newest jobs available to people with technical qualifications.

The following example illustrates a possible outcome of the career appraisal process.

BUSINESS MANAGEMENT CAREER APPRAISAL

I. Career profile
  A. Responsibilities
    1. Establish unit objectives to contribute to organizational goals
    2. Organize human and material resources to achieve objectives
    3. Direct activities of subordinates
    4. Monitor activities of unit; correct deviations from plan
    5. Report results to superiors and subordinates
  B. Rewards
    1. Advancement opportunities
    2. Satisfaction from interaction with people
    3. Opportunities for financial success
  C. Demands
    1. May require long hours
    2. May require relocation
II. Requirements
  A. Education
    1. College degree, preferably in business administration
    2. Major emphasis in management courses
    3. Basic courses in finance, accounting, marketing, production, and communication
  B. Experience
    1. Familiarity with the general business environment
    2. Work in the specific area of interest
III. Personal characteristics
  A. Creativity—develop new ideas applicable to specific business situations and recognize good ideas presented by others
  B. Decision-making ability—recognize facts, develop alternative courses of action, foresee possible consequences, reach accurate decisions, evaluate results
  C. Flexibility—adapt to changing circumstances
  D. Initiative—plan and execute ideas and programs within the framework of broad company policy
  E. Persuasiveness—influence others, directly and indirectly
  F. Verbal ability—communicate effectively, orally and in writing, with superiors, peers, subordinates, and people outside the organization

> Observations of a successful person in a management career: Arnold Babcock
>
> A.   Brief history—Mr. Babcock was graduated from City College with a business administration degree (management major, cognate in marketing).
>
>   Upon graduation, Babcock was employed as a management trainee by a national building-supply company. During a 15-month training program, Babcock received intensive training for major departments of the company.
>
>   After the training program, Babcock was appointed assistant manager of the company's retail outlet in San Jose, California. During Babcock's four years as assistant manager, profits of the San Jose store doubled.
>
>   Babcock was then appointed manager of the Toledo, Ohio, store and is now completing his sixth year in this position. The Toledo store has markedly increased its sales volume and has been designated a management training center for the company.
>
> B.   Job demands—Babcock's work required long hours during peak retail buying periods. Rewards have included advancement and above-average income for a person his age. A negative factor has been occasional conflict of time needed for career and family responsibilities.
>
> V.   Relation of career to values, goals, and qualifications
>
> A.   Ambitions—I want to pursue a career offering opportunities for advancement. I also want to work for a company that encourages and rewards individual initiative. Babcock's experience demonstrates that a general management career can provide such opportunities.
>
> B.   Qualifications—I must complete my bachelor of business administration degree and supplement my cooperative work experience with additional on-job management training. My summer vacation work experiences and my vice presidency of the Business Administration Club have helped me develop necessary leadership and supervisory skills.

Specific Position Analysis

What should you include in a specific position analysis?

Your self-analysis led to a career appraisal. The next step is to prepare a specific position analysis in which you identify these factors:

1.   how well you understand the requirements for the position
2.   how your education fits those requirements
3.   how your experience fits those requirements
4.   other qualifications you possess for the position

The following example demonstrates an analysis of a specific position, sales management, that builds on the previous self-analysis and career appraisal.

SPECIFIC POSITION ANALYSIS—SALES MANAGER

I. How well I understand the requirements
   A. Plans and directs sales activities
   B. Employs, trains, supervises, evaluates sales personnel
   C. Develops and controls sales department budget
   D. Develops programs and techniques to increase sales volume and profits
   E. Prepares regular sales reports and makes recommendations regarding unprofitable items
   F. Makes sales forecasts
   G. Assigns sales territories and provides assistance to sales representatives
   H. Conducts periodic meetings with sales representatives
   I. Represents the sales department at management meetings
   J. Assists other departments when sales expertise is needed.

II. How my education fits these requirements
   A. Will have completed four years of study at City College and earned a bachelor of business administration degree with a management major, June 19—
   B. Supplemented my major area of study with a marketing cognate and advanced courses in accounting, finance, and business communication
   C. Attended several workshops sponsored by the American Marketing Association:
      1. Controlling inventory shrinkage
      2. Managing and motivating sales representatives
      3. Developing a sales strategy
   D. Visited three companies and interviewed their sales managers as a partial requirement for my marketing strategy course

III. How my experience fits these requirements
   A. Under the cooperative education program, my job in the accounting department of a large company enabled me to:
      1. Work with department heads and observe supervision techniques.
      2. Obtain a general background in many phases of accounting.
      3. Gain experience in determining customer credit terms.
   B. Summer employment with the City Parks and Recreation Department has improved my communication and supervisory effectiveness.

> C.   Experience as vice president of Business Administration Club has developed my leadership ability.

ANALYZING THE JOB MARKET

What are the three phases of analyzing the job market?

After analyzing yourself, a potential career field, and specific position opportunities, your next step is to analyze the job market. To launch your job campaign successfully, conduct your job-market investigation in three phases: prepare a prospect list, analyze the prospect list, assemble position information.

Preparing a Prospect List

Instead of haphazardly collecting names of companies, research the particular markets. Seek out prospective employers by following this kind of systematic procedure:

1.   Examine the most recent *CPC Annual.*[4] This three-volume directory gives information about positions customarily offered to college graduates. Volume 1 provides general guides to career planning and job search; Volume 2 covers employment opportunities in administration, business, and other nontechnical areas; and Volume 3 provides information about employers seeking graduates in engineering sciences, the computer field, and other technical disciplines. Specific employers are indexed by occupations, geographic areas, and experience/ education requirements. Narratives describe each organization's locations, history, products or services, types of candidates sought, plans for the future, and benefits.

2.   If you are interested in an international business career, examine *International Jobs.*[5] This directory of the international job market gives names and addresses of profit and nonprofit organizations (including government), along with a description of each agency and the education/experience background it seeks in job applicants. The book also presents strategies for getting a job in the international market.

---

[4]Published annually by College Placement Council, 62 Highland Ave., Bethlehem, PA 18017.
[5]Eric Kocher, *International Jobs* (Reading, MA: Addison-Wesley Publishing Company, 1984).

3. Examine industrial directories or directories of trade associations for information about companies in industries you have chosen.
4. Contact your state employment service. In most states, this agency maintains computerized job banks and employer files. The state employment service also has information on state and local government jobs.
5. Communicate with bankers, your local Chamber of Commerce, and government agencies to determine industrial and commercial development.
6. Examine employment advertisements in your local newspaper or the Sunday editions of major city newspapers.
7. Obtain a list of prospective interviewers from your college career center.

From these sources you can get a valuable list of prospective employers with whose needs you can match your own.

Analyzing the Prospect List

Thorough job research includes determining the history, character, products, and services of prospective employers. You can use such information profitably in your job applications and interviews. Company information may be obtained by following these suggestions:

1. Use your business library to obtain information about the company.
2. Speak with people who know the company.
3. Visit a branch office of the company if you can.
4. Identify the person who does the hiring.
5. Study relevant company publications and trade papers.
6. Familiarize yourself with current business issues concerning your field and the companies in which you are interested.

Assembling Position Information

To assemble pertinent data for each prospect that interests you, follow these steps:

1. Appraise the company's position within its industry or field.
2. Consider the company's reputation among its employees, customers, and competitors.

3. Define the nature of the products and the types of services.
4. Note whether the company promotes from within its ranks.
5. Define the qualities that the employer probably will seek in applicants: tact, conscientiousness, precision, ability, initiative, etc.
6. Determine the specific needs of available positions.
7. Request interviews with people who can acquaint you with the requirements of jobs for which you are preparing. Interview people who work at the specific job you are seeking, people who work in similar jobs but in different firms, and people who work in different jobs within your area of specialization. Ask your instructor or major professor to help you find people, perhaps recent graduates, who will talk with you about their careers.

Before you ask for interviews, however, plan your questions so that you will include these and similar topics:

▶ nature of the position
▶ duties and responsibilities
▶ usual entry-level position
▶ special training required
▶ favorable features of position
▶ unfavorable features of position
▶ opportunities for promotion
▶ places where this type of employment is likely to be found
▶ general information about salary and other benefits

PREPARING A PERSONAL CAREER HISTORY

How does a résumé differ from a *curriculum vitae*?

Executives may advise you to prepare a personal career history, adding to it as new experiences broaden your viewpoint and increase your qualifications for more responsible positions. This kind of record (sometimes called a *curriculum vitae* or "course of life") is valuable in preparing a biographical summary, called a **résumé** or **data sheet**. A **curriculum vitae** is a comprehensive career history from which you will select appropriate data as you prepare a résumé.[6]

---

[6]Curriculum vitae is sometimes abbreviated to *vitae* ("of life") or *vita* ("life").

Use the outline shown in Illustration 21–1 to guide your preparation of your personal career history. Add to that career history as your experience and responsibilities grow.

Illustration 21–1   PERSONAL CAREER HISTORY GUIDE

Personal
► Your full name, address, telephone number (home and office)
► Date and place of your birth (optional)
► Date, place of birth, and present addresses of nearest relative (This information may be needed if you are applying for a position involving national security or responsibility for large sums of money.)
► Other personal details that are relevant to your career development

Education
► Names of educational institutions attended
► Degrees, diplomas, or certificates granted (include dates, majors, minors, concentration)
► Records of academic work
► Other records, such as vocational interest and aptitude test results, special awards, and honors
► List of extracurricular activities: service on committees; offices held, stating specifically what you did and any special programs in which you participated; names of persons with whom you worked on special projects

Work and Military Experience
► Full name and address of each company, organization, or unit
► Detailed description of duties and responsibilities for each major assignment
► Dates for each job or assignment
► Salary history, promotions, and other recognitions

Community or Social Group Participation
► Activities or services that are important to you
► Church membership, leadership in groups, other services

Illustration 21–1   PERSONAL CAREER HISTORY GUIDE (continued)

Avocational and Recreational Interests
▶   Activities and hobbies you enjoy
▶   Volunteer work you perform

Clippings from Newspapers or Periodicals
▶   Items describing your activities
▶   Copies of your writings that have been published

Listing of People Willing to Recommend You
▶   Names, professional titles, business addresses, and telephone
     numbers of persons who will vouch for your abilities if their
     names are used as references—persons who have observed
     your behavior with others at school, at work, in social activi-
     ties, in community service, or with your family

REVIEW AND TRANSITION

Chapter 21 has described research methods for prospective employment:
how to prepare a self-appraisal that seriously examines your strengths, weaknesses, values, and goals; how to develop a general career appraisal that can
be converted later to a specific position analysis; how to analyze the job
market; and how to prepare a personal career history.

Chapter 22 describes the creative phase of employment communication,
the composition of messages that direct attention to you as a prospective
employee. Besides composition of the application message and the résumé,
suggestions will be given to help you participate successfully in interviews
and their follow-ups.

YOUR DECISIONS FOR CHAPTER 21

Review your advice to Jeff and Terry. Based on your study of Chapter 21,
evaluate that advice. What specific suggestions, if any, will you add?

DISCUSSION QUESTIONS

A.   In the context of Chapter 21, what are appropriate definitions and ex-
      amples for these terms?

1. self-appraisal
2. career appraisal
3. specific position analysis
4. prospect list
5. *curriculum vitae*
6. résumé

B. Explain the following statement: To be successful in acquiring the right job, you must first know yourself.

C. How can past and present accomplishments help you to determine personal characteristics that are positive factors for employment?

D. What are several similarities between a self-appraisal and a career appraisal? What important factors should be included in each? How will these factors help you in determining your career area?

E. Explain the importance of a specific position analysis.

F. What are the competitive advantages of preparing and analyzing a prospect list?

G. What data sources and research methods can help you identify and locate prospective employers?

H. What are the advantages of preparing and maintaining a personal career history?

I. In what ways is the research phase of employment messages similar to the research phase of sales messages?

APPLICATIONS

1. Prepare a self-appraisal that includes an assessment of your personal characteristics, interests, aptitudes, education, and experience.

2. Prepare a career appraisal within a career area in which you have an interest. Consider including the following information: general requirements, responsibilities, and rewards; personal characteristics considered essential; personal attributes considered highly desirable; education and training requirements; and relationship of career to your goals and qualifications.

3. By using references in your library, prepare a bibliography of sources that can be used to analyze companies and describe each source briefly. As directed by your instructor, make an oral presentation about one of the sources.

4. Using the source material in Application 3, obtain the headquarters location, annual sales, principal product manufactured, approximate

number of employees, and any additional information you think is essential regarding the following companies (or others assigned by your instructor):

a.	Allied–Signal	f.	General Mills
b.	Apple Computer	g.	La-Z-Boy Chair
c.	Black & Decker	h.	Mid-America Dairymen
d.	Bristol–Myers Squibb	i.	Morton Thiokol
e.	Eli Lilly	j.	Springs Industries

As directed by your instructor, make an oral presentation about one of the companies.

5. Prepare an analysis for a position in which you are interested. In preparing your analysis, use the career appraisal you completed in Application 2.

6. Prepare your own up-to-date personal career history.

7. Prepare a report about career stages and patterns. Include contributions of one or more of these theorists. Cite your data sources.

S. Feinstein
D. C. Feldman
D. T. Hall
F. S. Hall
R. M. Kantor
D. J. Levinson
J. Near
J. Rosenbaum
E. H. Schein
F. N. Schwartz

8. Interview a person whose native country differs from yours. Ask these questions about the employment process: How important is preemployment research? How do employment research strategies resemble or differ from those recommended in Chapter 21? What impact, if any, does the country's economic structure have upon employment-seeking techniques?

   In a brief oral report, present your findings to your class.

MULTICULTURAL INSIGHTS

1. From your experience, observation, or reading, compare the ease or difficulty of obtaining information about employment opportunities in countries other than your native country.

2. Discuss with your classmates possible strategies for obtaining employment as a foreign national in a country of your choice.

EMPLOYMENT MESSAGES: CREATIVE PHASE

OBJECTIVES

After completing this chapter, you should be able to:

1. Appreciate the persuasive context for employment messages.
2. Develop an effectively focused résumé.
3. Compose an application letter that will secure a job interview.
4. Conduct yourself confidently in an interview.
5. Practice appropriate follow-up communication.
6. As an employer, demonstrate empathy in communications with applicants.

DECISIONS CASE

Jeff and Terry (Chapter 21) have done their employment research. Each has identified prospective employers.

Jeff has composed a letter asking for an interview and has sent it to five firms in Denver. Terry has sent a short letter and her personal career history to three multinational firms with offices in the United States.

Your friends again solicit your advice. "We sent our letters a month ago but have had no responses. We're interested in those firms. How do we get them interested in us?"

What is your advice? Evaluate the actions Jeff and Terry have taken and suggest future actions.

Additional questions about this decision-making case are stated at the end of this chapter. Study the chapter before answering those questions.

CHAPTER CONTEXT

The research phase of employment messages provides you with information about yourself, your potential, and the job market. In the creative phase you apply guides for persuasive communication to convince prospective employers that your attributes fit their needs. In this chapter you will learn how applying the techniques of persuasion to employment messages can help you compete successfully for work opportunities.

CREATIVE EMPLOYMENT MESSAGES

In the competitive job market, your major challenge is to make yourself stand out from the crowd. Effective communication skills will help you compete successfully, even if you are in a large group of applicants.

Your campaign to get the job you want may include several separate but related messages: a résumé, an application letter, an interview, and follow-up messages. Each employment message should be creative. It should represent you as an individual and gently persuade your reader by attracting favorable attention, arousing interest, stimulating desire, and producing action—AIDA.

THE RÉSUMÉ

How do the résumé and application letter complement each other?

The résumé (also called the data sheet) and application letter complement each other. The résumé describes your qualifications; the *application letter,* along with the résumé, persuades the reader to grant you an interview.

Résumé Styles

What are three commonly used résumé styles?

A résumé should be tailored to a person's specific employment search. Consequently, a single style cannot satisfy all needs. The three most common styles are *chronological* (or *reverse chronological*), *functional,* and *combination* (chronological and functional). The **chronological** résumé is essentially a fact sheet, arranged according to dates, usually in reverse chronological order. A **functional** résumé highlights skills and experience in order of importance to the résumé writer. This style can effectively emphasize growth potential or the significance of unpaid work. The **combination** résumé includes the best of both the functional and chronological styles. In the combination style, the résumé writer emphasizes transferable skills but also shows an education or work-experience chronology.

Résumé Content

Your personal career history (*curriculum vitae*) is the data source for your résumé. An effective résumé is more than a catalog of your experiences and accomplishments. Think of it as a picture of yourself. A good picture has a focal point—a feature that captures the viewer's eye and gives unity and coherence to the picture. The factor that provides a focal point in your résumé is a statement of your job objective.

Job Objective. Stating your **job objective** disciplines you to:

What is the purpose
of stating your job
objective?

1. Select from your *curriculum vitae* the information most likely to attract favorable attention when presented in your résumé.
2. Focus on your future rather than your past.

Define an objective that is neither too broad nor too restrictive. Since job titles differ among firms, stating a job category or two related areas of interest is preferable to stating a specific job title. A desire for advancement may be incorporated into your objective through a phrase such as "which ultimately leads to . . . ."

Objective Too Broad

A position with a large full-service bank.

Objective Too Narrow

Operations officer with a large full-service bank.

Appropriate Objective

A position requiring use of financial analysis skills, preferably in commercial or consumer loan department of a full-service bank.

After stating your job objective, select data that demonstrate you can achieve that objective. Items traditionally included are personal data, educational qualifications, work experience, special aptitudes, and references.[1]

Why might you
choose to omit
personal data from
your résumé? Why
include those data?

Personal Data. Provide your name, address, and telephone number (including area code) so that interested employers can contact you. Other personal data such as date of birth, marital status, number of dependents, health status, religion, national origin, hobbies, and nonbusiness associations are optional. If given, those optional data often appear near the end of the résumé. Some guidelines to follow are:

1. Omit personal data if:

   ▶ The space can better be used to emphasize more job-relevant information.
   ▶ The data are not job relevant, and you suspect that they may prejudice the reviewer.

---

[1]For relative importance of these categories, see Nelda Spinks and Barron Wells, "Letters of Application and Résumés," *The Bulletin of the Association for Business Communication*, vol. 50, no. 3 (September 1987), pp. 9–16.

2.   Include personal data if:

▶   Some special-interest items will arouse the reader's curiosity.
▶   The data complement other information about you and demonstrate your competence for your job objective.

Educational Qualifications. If you are a recent graduate or approaching graduation and have limited work experience, your education may be your strongest selling point. Select educational facts that are most relevant to your job objective. Such information may include degree(s) earned or to be earned; major areas of study or some specific courses; significant extracurricular activities; offices held; scholarships received; and special research projects, internships, or field studies. Details about your high school education are unnecessary unless you have had limited postsecondary education. Reference to special seminars or industrial training programs may also be included.

Be selective. If your objective is to be a management trainee in a healthcare institution, your experience as a volunteer in a crisis intervention program may be more significant than your exact grade-point average. You may, of course, also include your grade-point average, especially if it is high.

Work Experience. Your work experience along with your education should account for all the years since you completed high school. However, you need not emphasize each job equally.

Part-time and summer work, as well as military experience, should be included, especially if your work experience is limited. If you have had little work experience since high school, you may include earlier relevant work experience. The fact that you organized and managed a lawn-service crew or supervised the play of preschool children may be the evidence of ambition, responsibility, and entrepreneurship that an employer is seeking.

Extracurricular Activities, Memberships, Honors, Volunteer Work. The major purpose of information about voluntary activities is to demonstrate your job competence. You may be credited with work experience if your volunteer activities demonstrate skills required in the job for which you are applying.

Why might you include special aptitudes on your résumé?

Special Aptitudes. Special aptitudes such as fluency in a foreign language, computer keyboarding skill, knowledge of a computer language, or artistic talent may relate directly or indirectly to your job objective. Such talents may also suggest your ability to take on new demands as organizational requirements change.

References. Supply, or be prepared to supply, the names of people who can speak knowledgeably about your abilities and character. Typical references are professors, former employers, or sponsors of organizations in which you have been active. Choose references wisely, using those who are able to speak credibly about your professional competence. As a courtesy, you should obtain permission before using anyone's name as a reference.

Attitudes differ about listing names of references on your résumé. By not listing the names, you shield your sponsors from unnecessary calls. Although some employers prefer to see two or three references named on the résumé, all employers are initially more interested in data about your education and experience. Therefore, you should first allocate résumé space to cover those factors. If you have adequate space, list references also. Otherwise, the statement "references available upon request" should be adequate; then only those employers who are sincerely interested in you will contact your references.

Another strategy is to file recommendations with a placement service such as your college placement office. Indicating on your résumé the availability of those references and the name, address, and telephone number of the placement service gives interested employers the opportunity to check references.

Résumé Structure

Your résumé presents much more than your past. It is evidence of your ability to analyze a business problem, to organize, to communicate. It reflects your respect for yourself and your consideration of others. A messy, poorly organized résumé suggests a messy, poorly organized worker.

Order of Information. A heading consisting of your name, address, and telephone number should appear first on your résumé. Other personal data, if presented at all, are usually placed near the end of the résumé. Your job objective should appear immediately after your identification, giving focus to your entire résumé.

Arrange other information, chronologically or functionally, in the order that best emphasizes your qualifications for the job you seek. If your education is the strongest point, present it next; if your experience is impressive, give it a prominent position.

Length and Appearance. Most employers prefer a one- or two-page résumé. Defining your job objective and including only data related to that objective should help you observe the two-page guideline.

You can also control length with professional formatting techniques. Use at least one-inch margins to give an attractive picture-frame effect. Use white space to separate sections for attractive appearance and reader convenience.

What is the significance of careful formatting?

Use—but don't overuse—underscoring, bold lettering, asterisks, bars, or other visual devices to separate and to emphasize data. Careful formatting directs the reader to vital information about you. For a professional appearance, or to enable inclusion of more data on a one- or two-page résumé, use computer software and a laser printer that produce variable type styles and sizes.

In what ways do the chronological, functional, and combination résumés differ?

Experiment with creative captions. The traditional captions—"education," "experience," "personal"—may suffice. (See Illustration 22–1.) You may, however, attract more attention with captions that draw attention to special competencies, as is done in a functional or combination résumé. (See Illustrations 22–2 and 22–3.)

Use white or ivory bond paper and a printing or copy process that produces clear, sharp images. Avoid a commercial look that suggests someone else "packaged" you. Let the résumé assure prospective employers of the fine work *you* will do.

THE APPLICATION LETTER

The purpose of the application letter is to get an interview. Your objective is to arouse the reader's interest and stimulate a desire to know more about you. As a courtesy to the reader, be brief. Demonstrate your writing skills by using every word purposefully.

What is a solicited letter? a prospecting letter?

Job seekers use both solicited and prospecting letters. A **solicited letter** is one written in response to an advertisement. A **prospecting letter** is sent to a firm that has not advertised vacancies. When you respond to an advertisement or a placement notice, you have the advantage of knowing what kind of employee the firm is seeking. The disadvantage is that other applicants also possess that information. Your challenge is to use the information to present yourself persuasively. Many employers welcome prospecting letters—if the letters demonstrate that applicants know the company and have skills the company needs.

What message structure is appropriate for the application letter?

By using a central theme and following the AIDA structure, you can write effective application letters. Attract attention to yourself with a creative opening that introduces your central theme. Avoid dull, trite openings. Subordinate reference to an advertisement:

Dull and Trite

Please consider this letter my application for a position in your marketing department.

I am writing in response to your advertisement in the December 3, 19—, edition of the *Charlotte Daily*.

Illustration 22–1   CHRONOLOGICAL RÉSUMÉ WITH
TRADITIONAL CAPTIONS

ARTHUR M. THOMAS

N-1 Colony Apartments
Ephesus Church Road
Chapel Hill, NC 27514-2750
(919) 555-4220

CAREER OBJECTIVE

To develop and conduct communication programs and related activities in a health
care setting. Long-term goal: To be director of training in a health care facility or a
pharmaceutical firm.

EDUCATION

Undergraduate: Bachelor of Science—Business Administration, May 1992 (anticipated)
                 Virginia Polytechnic Institute and State University
                 Blacksburg, VA 24061-8926

Certification: "Interaction Management"—Instructor and Program Director
                 Development Dimensions International
                 Pittsburgh, PA 15234-5764

EMPLOYMENT

September 1988- Virginia Polytechnic Institute and State University, Blacksburg, VA
May 1991   24061-8926
                 Held several positions while attending college:
                     Undergraduate research assistant: September 1990-May 1991
                     Public Relations: Summer 1990
                     Head resident advisor: September 1989-May 1990
                     Media Services: September 1988-May 1989

Summer 1987   Westwind Country Club, Raleigh, NC 27601-4544
                 Water safety instructor and swim teach coach

COLLEGE ACTIVITIES

Student personnel project: Revised student-life policy manual; completed May 1991.

Campus Judicial Committee: Served on student/administration council designed to
    uphold university policies, 1990-1991.

Resident Advisor Trainer: Helped direct and teach two-month training program for
    new resident advisors, September-October 1991.

Class of 1992: Class officer-at-large; headed class publicity committee and participated
    on decision-making council for class, 1990-1991.

Omega Omega Sigma: Active member of this service-oriented honor society,
    1988-1991.

Illustration 22–1 CHRONOLOGICAL RÉSUMÉ (continued)

ARTHUR M. THOMAS

COMMUNITY SERVICE

Campus Ministries: Conducted leadership workshops and coordinated special activities for Episcopal/Presbyterian/Lutheran Student Center, November 1990-May 1991.

Patient Education Volunteer: Montgomery County Hospital, Blacksburg. Taught patients about diseases and hospital procedures, 1989-1991.

Red Cross Volunteer: Filled a variety of positions, including nurse's aide, in biannual Blacksburg Blood Bank Drive, 1989-1990.

Rescue Squad: Served on ambulance unit of Blacksburg Volunteer Rescue Squad, Fall 1987-Spring 1989.

HONORS AND PROFESSIONAL ACTIVITIES

Dean's Honor List: Graduated Cum Laude

Honors Thesis: "Public Relations: A Case Study at the Student Health Service of Virginia Polytechnic Institute and State University."

Student Business Association: Active member, 1990-1991.

Virginia Association of Broadcasters: Selected to sit on panel of students which addressed annual statewide meeting, February 1987.

Virginia Folklore Society: Active member; assisted in program at annual meeting, 1986-1989.

RECOMMENDATIONS

File available from: Office of Career Planning and Placement
                         University of North Carolina
                         Chapel Hill, NC 27514-4312
                         (919) 555-7526

Illustration 22–2   FUNCTIONAL RÉSUMÉ

T. F. HOUSTON, JR.
P.O. Box 8291
Jacksonville, FL 32308-8291
(904) 555-9268

OBJECTIVE	Executive director of a volunteer-membership, service-oriented association. Special interest in coordinating local, state, or federal government advocacy programs for benefit of members.
QUALIFICATIONS	Sixteen years in association management, providing a background that reflects competence in recruiting, training, and motivating both paid staff and volunteer members; ability to maintain excellent client relationships.
STRENGTHS	Oral and written communication, budget and finance, client services, leadership, problem solving, supervision
ABILITIES	*Communication/Client Services:* Directed effective membership recruitment programs; maintained strong, effective advocacy programs regarding issues affecting members; acted as liaison between staff, local and state business leaders, local and state government officials; lectured nationally on chamber of commerce role in government.
	Leadership/Supervision: Worked with members to develop organization policies; established long- and short-range objectives; recruited, trained, and supervised staff members; coordinated activities of staff and volunteers to accomplish organization's objectives; doubled membership within four years; maintained high level of membership participation in program activities.
	Budget and Finance: Doubled membership income within four years; initiated use of computers for financial and membership records; responsible for annual budgets ranging from $300,000 to $1,500,000; oversaw facilities expansion (doubled in size).
MILITARY SERVICE	*U.S. Army Artillery:* Drafted as a private; graduated Officer Candidate School; discharged as an officer
EDUCATION	Bachelor of Science—Industrial Management, Auburn University, Auburn, Alabama
MAJOR EMPLOYERS	Chamber of Commerce, Tampa, FL Chamber of Commerce, Sarasota, FL Chamber of Commerce, Jacksonville, FL
REFERENCES	Personal and professional references will be provided on request.

Illustration 22–3 COMBINATION RÉSUMÉ

NANCY G. SIMONS
3101 Danford Creek Drive
Kalamazoo, MI 49009-0009
(616) 555-3952

PREPARED FOR: Management of a company day-care center, providing supervised learning experiences for employees' children.

QUALIFIED BY:

A background in education and related experiences that demonstrates ability to manage both the educational and business aspects of a day-care center.

AREAS OF COMPETENCY INCLUDE:

Organization and Supervision—Designed and implemented early childhood instructional programs in private and public schools; designed and supervised summer day-camp program for private agency; chaired curriculum committee responsible for major changes in K-4 curriculum.

Training—Interviewed, selected, and trained counselors for day camp; taught early childhood classes for five years; explained program objectives and evaluative criteria to clients.

Client Services—Maintained contact with established clients; reported student progress regularly; increased day-camp clientele 20 percent in first year; modified programs in response to demonstrated client needs.

Oral and Written Communication—Presented oral and written reports of student progress to parents; made frequent oral presentations to community groups; handled correspondence and telephone communication related to program.

Budget and Finance—Managed all funds for several programs; stayed within budget; increased revenues through effective promotion and client satisfaction; obtained accounting experience in industry while attending college.

EDUCATIONAL PREPARATION:

A.B. Degree, Calvin College, Grand Rapids, Michigan
M.S. Degree, Western Michigan University, Kalamazoo, Michigan
Currently enrolled in MBA program with emphasis on management of social service agencies.

PLACES OF EMPLOYMENT:

Kalamazoo Christian Schools, Kalamazoo, MI	Full time, 1987-Present
Kal-Kids Day Camp, Kalamazoo, MI	Summer 1987
Waupun Schools, Waupun, WI	Full time, 1985-1987
Wyoming Community Programs, Wyoming, MI	Summers, 1983-1985
Harvey Distributors, Grand Rapids, MI	Part-time, 1983-1985
X-L Engineers, Grand Rapids, MI	Part-time, 1981-1983

REFERENCES:

Ms. Carolyn Lowe, Director	Mr. Harold Wilson, Accounting Supervisor
Kal-Kids Day Camp	Harvey Distributors
P.O. Box 8053	351 Rosemary Drive
Kalamazoo, MI 49001-8053	Grand Rapids, MI 49507-0002
(616) 555-1257	(616) 555-9450

Creative

> You presented a management-trainee challenge in the December 3 edition of the *Charlotte Daily*. I believe my sales experience, leadership ability, and college degree in marketing qualify me to accept that challenge.

A creative opening attracts favorable attention and prepares the reader for the rest of your presentation. Concentrate on one or two points that relate to the employer's needs. Stimulate the reader's interest and desire to know more—to invite you for an interview.

> As a management trainee I can bring to CROSSROADS four years of part-time sales experience in one of Michigan's most prestigious clothing stores. That sales experience and my college degree in marketing taught me much about meeting the challenges of the retail clothing market in which CROSSROADS operates.

Refer to your résumé, but avoid the routine "a résumé is enclosed for your examination." Make a relevant, interpretive statement about the résumé.

> The enclosed résumé shows success in handling the challenge of a busy schedule that included collegiate studies, part-time employment, and extracurricular activities. My presidency of Pi Sigma Epsilon provides evidence of another trait required in marketing: the ability to inform and to persuade.

Move smoothly and quickly to a request for an interview. Ask directly and make response easy.

> Your name—CROSSROADS—conveys images of exciting choices and up-to-the-moment decisions about fashion. I'd like to work in that kind of environment. Will you permit a demonstration of the qualities that you rightly demand of your management trainees? For an interview at your convenience, please call (616) 555-1160 or write to my home address.

The solicited letter (Illustration 22–4) and the prospecting letter (Illustration 22–5) illustrate the AIDA structure applied to employment-seeking messages.

THE INTERVIEW

An interview invitation indicates you have favorably impressed your prospective employer. Recognize the interview as an opportunity to confirm interest and to develop desire for hiring you.

Illustration 22–4 SOLICITED APPLICATION LETTER

524 Linden Lane
Ann Arbor, MI 48104-8165
December 4, 19--

Personnel Officer
CROSSROADS
City Center Plaza
Charlotte, NC 28280-1820

Dear Personnel Officer

As a management trainee I can bring to CROSSROADS four years
of part-time sales experience in one of Michigan's most
prestigious clothing stores. That sales experience and my
college degree in marketing taught me much about meeting the
challenges of the retail clothing market in which CROSSROADS
operates.

The enclosed resume shows success in handling the challenge
of a busy schedule that included collegiate studies, part-
time employment, and extracurricular activities. My presi-
dency of Pi Sigma Epsilon provides evidence of another trait
required in marketing: the ability to inform and to persuade.

Your name--CROSSROADS--conveys images of exciting choices
and up-to-the-moment decisions about fashion. I'd like to
work in that kind of environment. Will you permit a
demonstration of the qualities that you rightly demand of
your management trainees? For an interview at your convenience, please call (616) 555-1160 or write to my home
address.

Sincerely,

Michael J. Drexel

Michael J. Drexel

Enclosure: Resume

Illustration 22–5   PROSPECTING APPLICATION LETTER

P.O. Box 811
Melbourne, FL   32901-0811
July 20, 19--

Ms. R. L. Kaufmann, Sales Director
Seaside Developments, Inc.
P.O. Box 11506
Los Angeles, CA   90065-4914

Dear Ms. Kaufmann

Attention   Your company's reputation as a leading developer of
interval-ownership villas in California prompts this offer
of sales skills:

--Ability to work independently or on a team: to prospect
  for new customers or to manage a project

--Effective oral and written communication skills: to
  deal effectively with your clients, contractors, and
Interest   financial agents
and
desire   --Proven sales record and California license: to
  complement your current sales team.

Many of those qualities were developed during the year I
served in sales and administration with a successful
developer of resort condominiums in Florida. The enclosed
resume lists additional experience in the real estate
industry.

Action   To discuss how that experience can benefit Seaside
Developments, please write or telephone me (305-555-6082).

Sincerely

Darlene Ferguson

Darlene Ferguson

Enclosure

Someone from the human resources department may conduct the initial interview. Additional interviews may then be held with the prospective supervisor and possibly that person's superior. The judgment of the immediate supervisor (the person who has the position to fill) often weighs heaviest in a final hiring decision.

What does an interview invitation signify?

Remind yourself that the interview signifies an employer's interest in you. You have sought an opportunity to be considered. Your application letter and your résumé have helped you achieve that opportunity. Now approach the interview with what the employer expects of you—competence, confidence, and courtesy.[2]

The Interviewer and You

Since first impressions are important to your success, be sure to appear properly dressed and groomed at the time and place set for your interview. Prepare yourself for the interview as you would prepare yourself for a business photograph. Wear suitable business attire that, rather than drawing attention to itself, encourages the interviewer to concentrate on you and on what you say. Be prepared to present a copy of your résumé and a list of references if you are asked for such items.

How may you make a good impression during an interview?

Consider your nonverbal behaviors; what you *do,* as well as what you *say,* will affect the interviewer's impression of you. When the interviewer extends a hand to you, establish eye contact and shake hands firmly. Know and correctly pronounce the name of your interviewer. If you are not sure, inquire before entering the interviewer's office. When offered a chair, sit down and assume a posture that reflects self-confidence and alertness. Square your shoulders; keep your hands in a relaxed position. Clenching your hands or placing your feet firmly together may give the impression of tenseness. Slouching or slumping may suggest carelessness. Try to give a relaxed but attentive appearance.

Your interviewer may begin by chatting with you about topics of incidental or mutual interest in an effort to help you relax. Besides asking questions related to your application message, the interviewer will attempt to determine your knowledge of the company. Be ready especially to answer this favorite: "Why do you want to work for our firm?" Also, expect opportunities to develop a topic of conversation, such as "Give an example of a problem you faced in school or on the job and tell me how you solved it." Your inter-

---

[2]For trends in employment interviews, see Nelda Spinks and Barron Wells, "Employment Interviews: Trends in the Fortune 500 Companies—1980–1988," *The Bulletin of the Association for Business Communication,* vol. 51, no. 4 (December 1988), pp. 15–21.

viewer has two purposes for inviting you to pick up the discussion: (1) to estimate your knowledge and (2) to determine your proficiency in communicating that knowledge.

Follow these guides to increase your confidence during an interview:

1. *Make a reasonable effort to learn the interviewer's needs.* What jobs must be filled? What skills is the company looking for? What salary limits are likely?
2. *Define your needs or expectations.* What jobs will you consider? For what salary range are you aiming? What working conditions (hours, travel, etc.) will you accept? What conditions will you not accept? Are your expectations reasonable for the job and the geographic area?
3. *Listen carefully.* Interviewers often give clues about their companies and about themselves in their conversations. Use those opportunities to show how your qualifications match the company's needs. Build upon or refer to statements made by the interviewer: "That reminds me of a time when I was asked to resolve a similar problem. May I explain how I handled the situation?"
4. *Be calm.* If necessary, pause and indicate thoughtful consideration before you answer a complex or an unexpected question. If you do not understand a question, courteously ask the interviewer to rephrase it. If you cannot answer—or if you wish to clarify an earlier answer—say so. Word your answers and comments so that they pertain to the employer's requirements for the job.

Difficult Interview Situations

Effective interviewers observe federal and state legislation pertaining to the interview process. The Equal Employment Opportunity Commission looks with disfavor upon inquiries concerning race, color, religion, or national origin. Such inquiries may suggest indefensible prejudice. So may questions that focus unduly upon the age, marital status, or sex of the applicant.

If an interviewer asks questions that you feel are irrelevant, remain calm and try to direct the conversation back to job-relevant information. Do not become defensive or argumentative. The following examples suggest ways to respond to difficult questions.

How should you handle inappropriate interview questions or comments?

Question	Response
How will you handle your home responsibilities when you must travel?	My wife (husband) and I have developed a system for sharing home responsibilities. How much travel is required in this job?

It would be nice to have such a pretty lady (handsome man) on our sales force.	Thank you. I'm really eager to sell your excellent line of microcomputers. I'm sure my office experience will help me understand the needs of my customers.
Do you think you can keep up with the other folks here? Most of them are older (younger) than you are.	My experience and education enable me to work efficiently with your other employees.
Why do you want this job? I didn't expect a man (woman) to apply.	I have the required skills, and the work is challenging.

OTHER EMPLOYMENT MESSAGES

Several additional messages may be transmitted during the employment process.

Acknowledgment

When you receive a response to your application message, acknowledge that response immediately. When you are invited for an interview, accept that invitation; confirm the meeting details concisely and accurately. Impress the employer at this stage with a meticulous, businesslike letter that does not undo any good impressions you made with your application letter and résumé. Since your acknowledgment is a good-news message, the structures for positive or goodwill messages are appropriate.

Thanks

Why should you send a thank-you letter after an interview?

A prompt *thank-you letter* after the interview not only demonstrates courtesy but also reminds the interviewer of your interest and your qualifications. Follow these guides for an effective thank-you letter:

1. Get the exact name, address, and title of the interviewer. Use that information in your thank-you letter.
2. Learn how the job fits into the firm's organizational structure. Read company-related material given to you during an interview. Include some comment about the company and the job in your letter.
3. Learn the names of the people you meet. Show your appreciation by asking to have your thanks extended to others who added to your enjoyment of the interview.
4. Be observant if you are taken on a plant or city tour. Make suitable comments when you write the thank-you letter.

The thank-you letter should reinforce the application, résumé, and interview. Since your interview expanded your knowledge of the company's needs, adding information that was not presented in the application letter or the résumé may be advantageous. A thank-you letter similar to this example was followed by a job offer.

> Meeting you and your staff last Wednesday was a pleasure, Ms. Clark. I enjoyed learning about the department and discussing possibilities of joining your staff as a communications trainer/consultant.
>
> The scope and quality of your work are impressive. Your media-development program to improve communication among hospital employees is especially exciting.
>
> I remain interested in the position you described. My communication degree, teaching experience, and health-care work relate directly to that position.
>
> I look forward to hearing from you, Ms. Clark, and to maintaining professional contact with you.

Follow-Up

When are follow-up messages appropriate?

If your application and résumé do not elicit a prompt reply, send a follow-up message two or three weeks after your first mailing. The follow-up should not be a duplicate of your original message. Refer to your first letter, but don't suggest that someone may have misplaced your original mailing. Enclose a photocopy of the résumé as well as of the first letter, and repeat your request for an interview. Your initiative and assertiveness may be qualities the company is seeking.

The On-Campus Interview and Follow-Up

Many large firms send interview teams to discuss employment with students who are about to receive their degrees. In these cases, the college placement center usually arranges the interview.

Although the interview is held on your campus, your preparation, your appearance, and your physical mannerisms are as important as they would be in the company office. All interview information described earlier applies to on-campus interviews.

Only rarely are specially composed application letters required for the on-campus interview. However, you should send a thank-you message. Employers often invite their best prospects to a follow-up interview at the company.

Carefully written confirmation and thank-you letters at each stage improve your chances of being hired.

Declining a Job Offer

What message structure is appropriate for declining a job offer? accepting a job offer?

As you consider a job offer, you may decide that you should not accept the position. While informing the employer about your decision, you will want to maintain goodwill for possible future business relationships. Since the prospective employer has invested resources in evaluating you as a job candidate, your refusal will be an unfavorable or mixed-news message. The following example demonstrates the structure for a mixed-news message to decline a job offer.

> Your offer of the position as senior technical writer was very attractive. Writing technical manuals in understandable language for end users is indeed challenging work. Since visiting your Chicago office, however, I have discussed relocation with my family; and the consensus is that relocation is not desirable at this time.
>
> Tech-Com will surely maintain—or improve—its already strong market position as a vital link between innovative engineers and users of technological innovations. I shall continue to watch your progress with interest. When my family circumstances change, you will likely receive another application from me.

Accepting a Job Offer

Goodwill is also a major objective as you accept a job offer. Your acceptance message can set the tone for the employment relationship that you are about to enter. Using the structure for good-news and goodwill messages, convey your enthusiasm for the job and reinforce the employer's decision that you are the right person for the job. Acceptance formalities usually include repeating the terms of the offer, such as position, starting date, and salary. Here is an example of an acceptance message.

> I accept with pleasure your offer of a position as senior technical writer at an annual salary of $42,000.
>
> Tech-Com has enjoyed a strong market position as a vital link between innovative engineers and users of technological innovations. I'm eager to begin the challenging work of writing technical manuals in understandable language for end users.
>
> I will report to Jorgen Waldermo at 8:30 a.m. on July 1 to begin my work with Tech-Com. I look forward to the orientation sessions to be presented at that time.

THE EMPLOYER'S PERSPECTIVE

You may soon find yourself in a position requiring you to write letters to job applicants.

Acknowledgment

What employment messages are commonly written by employers?

Company policy dictates whether all applications or only those from likely job candidates are acknowledged. If many applications are received, a form acknowledgment is appropriate. Most applicants prefer to receive a form letter than to receive no word at all. The structure for neutral messages is appropriate for application acknowledgments, as demonstrated in the following example.

YOUR APPLICATION FOR EMPLOYMENT

Thank you for inquiring about employment with Southern Texas Company. We are always eager to hear from qualified applicants.

All applications are screened when they arrive in our office. If we have openings that match your qualifications, you will be contacted within one month.

Information from your application has been entered into our computerized database of potential employees. Your name will remain in that database for one year. During that time you will be considered for any openings that require your skills.

Invitation to Interview

Interview invitations are extended orally or in writing. Oral invitations should be followed by a written confirmation.

Present clearly all details about the interview plans. Clarify the applicant's and the company's respective responsibilities for travel, food, and lodging. Explain arrangements made by the company.

To reinforce goodwill, you may express pleasure about being able to interview the candidate. However, avoid any statements that may be interpreted as a commitment to hire the applicant. The following example demonstrates appropriate content and structure for an interview invitation.

You will be welcome when you visit A & K Wholesale Distributors on January 15, 19—, Mr. Faris.

Reservations have been made for your flight on Trans-Air 198, leaving Atlanta at 7:25 a.m. on January 15. Please pick up your prepaid ticket at the Trans-Air counter before 7:10 that morning. Gene Hetzler will meet you at your arrival gate and drive you to our offices. Your return flight leaves San Antonio at 4:15 p.m. and arrives in Atlanta at 7:39 p.m.

You will be reimbursed for all expenses related to your trip. Please save all receipts for meals, parking, etc., and send them to me after your visit.

We look forward to talking with you about a position in our Professional Training Department, Mr. Faris. Please call me collect at (512) 555-1249 if you have any questions about the day's activities outlined on the enclosed agenda.

Job Offer

As a good-news message, a job offer may follow the pattern for good-news or good-will messages. However, the applicant may have received other offers as well as yours. In that case, consider using persuasive strategies in the job-offer letter. Include all information the candidate needs for evaluating your offer and replying to it. Emphasize the information that best appeals to the applicant's needs and desires. The following example is a job offer that focuses on the reader, begins with good news, provides information to maintain interest, and encourages a positive response.

OFFER FOR POSITION OF PROGRAMMER/ANALYST

You have the qualifications we're looking for, Toni. I'm pleased to offer you the position of programmer/analyst with a starting salary of $30,000.

As we expand, database management will become an increasingly important part of our operations. Since we have a policy of promoting competent employees, your career opportunities with us are excellent.

Please respond to this offer before July 15. We hope your response will be, "I accept." You may call me collect at (312) 555-1374 if you have further questions about the job or Gibbs Associates.

Rejection

Job applicants look for honesty in a rejection letter. You need not give all reasons that led to a decision not to hire a candidate; but do not mislead the applicant with a long, flattering description of her or his qualifications followed by the fatal "but" or "however." A suitable pattern for a rejection letter is similar to that for all bad-news letters. The following example demonstrates that pattern.

Thank you for visiting us to discuss the programmer/analyst position. You were one of three excellent applicants interviewed for that opening.

Since we are establishing a centralized database for our home office and subsidiaries, we have employed a candidate who has had several years of experience in database management.

Your qualifications in systems analysis are excellent, Ms. Heemstra. Your application and interview record will be retained. As we add subsidiaries to our system, database management operations will expand. You will be considered when we need additional systems analysts.

REVIEW AND TRANSITION

Chapter 21 describes employment research; Chapter 22 explains how to use that research to prepare the employment application letter, résumé, interview, and follow-up messages.

Your application letter should attract attention, arouse interest, stimulate desire, and produce action. The résumé gives detailed evidence of what the application letter describes. Because an interview allows you to prove that you are the kind of person your application has represented you to be, preparation for that interview is essential to your success. After the interview, send a follow-up message to convey appreciation and continuing interest.

Your job responsibilities may soon require you to respond to job applicants. Courtesy, conciseness, and honesty characterize acknowledgments, interview invitations, job offers, and rejections.

By studying Chapters 1 through 22, you have learned the principles and purposes of business communicators. You have perceived applications of logic, psychology, and ethics to informing and persuading through written–oral–visual media. You have acquired techniques of planning, composing, transmitting, and evaluating messages that range from a simple inquiry to a fully documented report. You have examined numerous communication models and illustrations offered as guides to your own appropriate creativity, and you have considered the application of electronic technology to increase communication efficiency.

The remaining parts of this book will help you refine your communication skills. Appendices A–H comprise a reference section for review or reinforcement of language skills and business communication protocols.

To help you with your continuing progress toward successful communication, we ask you now to consider the basic question suggested throughout this book: Unless a person masters linguistic skills that make it possible to perceive, process, and react to the evidence of thoughts and of feelings, how can one expect—whatever the marvels of technology—to communicate effectively?

YOUR DECISIONS FOR CHAPTER 22

Evaluate the advice you gave Jeff and Terry at the beginning of this chapter. Did you include recommendations about use of the résumé, application letter, interviewing, and follow-up messages? If not, what advice will you now give? If you did make recommendations about each of those message types, what—if anything—will you now modify?

DISCUSSION QUESTIONS

A. In the context of Chapter 22, what are appropriate definitions and examples for these terms?

    1. résumé
    2. job objective
    3. reverse chronological style
    4. functional style
    5. solicited letter
    6. prospecting letter

B. Why is the AIDA structure an appropriate guide for an application letter?

C. What is the function of the résumé? the application letter?

D. What is the advantage of stating a job objective on a résumé?

E. What communication benefits are realized when you categorize résumé data?

F. If you have had no previous work experience, what should you emphasize in your application message?

G. What are the advantages and disadvantages of including the following data on your résumé?

    1. personal data other than name, address, telephone number
    2. references
    3. volunteer activities, memberships
    4. high school education, activities

H. How does federal or state legislation on equal employment opportunities affect the information presented in the résumé? How does this legislation affect the interviewing process?

I. What preparations should you make for an employment interview?

J. Why should you send a thank-you message promptly after the first interview?

K. Your college placement service probably arranges employment interviews on campus. How are messages for on-campus interviews like or unlike messages for your independent job search?

L. The following sentences have been used as opening statements in application messages. Discuss the effectiveness of each statement. Revise ineffective statements.

1. This letter is in response to your ad in the *Mayville News* on August 22 for assistant to the executive director.
2. In regards to your April 1 advertisement, I am interested in employment with your firm.
3. How can someone with secretarial experience, a college degree in administrative management, and experience with advanced office technologies benefit your company? May I visit you to discuss how I would apply such experience and knowledge as an office manager?
4. The ad in the *Freeland Press* appealed to my overall prerequisite for a challenging and growth-oriented business career.
5. The job of systems analyst seems to be from all indications a job with which I could be comfortable in most every respect.
6. I would like to submit to you information that makes me believe I am qualified for the position you have recently advertised.
7. I am interested in the possibility of a position in your company at the present time or in the near future.
8. I am writing to inquire and apply for a position with your company.
9. I have chosen to send this letter to see if you have any job openings.
10. Adco's reputation for setting trends is well known in the advertising industry. As promotions chairperson for CMC's Phi Beta Lambda chapter, I applied some of your advertising strategies to raise over $5,000 for local charities in 19—.

M. What are appropriate responses to these interview questions and comments?

1. Tell me what you know about our company.
2. Why should I hire you?
3. Why did you go to City College? I'm a graduate of State University myself.
4. Do you plan to have a family?
5. What will you do if your child is ill and needs you at home?
6. Have you ever been married?
7. Do you think you'll fit in with the men (women) in the office?
8. Why do you want to work for *our* firm?

N. Discuss the strengths and weaknesses of each of the following messages. What changes do you recommend?

1. Application letter

Personnel Director
Evans Engineering
P.O. Box 8093
Grand Rapids, MI 49590-8093

Dear Manager:

I don't know if you have any openings, but I'm looking for a job as a civil engineer in your part of the city. Someone told me you do a lot of government work.

I have worked for three years. Most of my experience is in road work. My résumé will tell you something about my education and work experience, if you are interested.

If you have any openings, I would appreciate an interview.

Sincerely,

2. Thank-you letter

Personnel Director
Evans Engineering
P. O. Box 8093
Grand Rapids, MI 49590-8093

Dear Personnel Director

Thank you for interviewing me on June 10, 19—. I was really impressed with your company. Your receptionist, engineers, surveyors, and officers all seem like really great people to work with.

If you need more information about me, please do not hesitate to call. I'll try to answer your questions.

Once again, thank you.

Cordially

3. Follow-up application letter

D & H Transmission
4657 E. First
Tucson, AZ 85711-2810

Dear Manager:

On July 1, 19—, I sent a copy of my résumé to you with a letter inquiring about a possible sales job with you.

I'm still eager to work for you. I've heard many good reports about your work from consumers in this area. Since I've had experience selling parts to truck service centers, I believe I can reach an important market segment to help you expand your transmission repair service.

Please give me an opportunity to discuss some ideas about selling your services to truck service centers.

Sincerely,

APPLICATIONS

1. As assigned by your instructor, revise one, several, or all messages given in Discussion Question N.

2. Study the employment advertisements in a major newspaper or those posted by your college placement office. Select two positions that interest you and that fit the qualifications you expect to have upon graduation. Prepare two résumés—one tailored for each position. Select information from your personal career history that is most relevant for the specific positions you chose.

3. Select one of the advertisements you chose for Application 2. Write an application message.

4. Assume the personnel manager has responded to your message in Application 3. You have been invited to be in that manager's office next week for an interview—Thursday at 10:00 a.m. Prepare a suitable reply.

5. As a result of your interview (Application 4):

   a. You are very interested in the position. Write a suitable follow-up message.
   b. You are offered the position. Write an acceptance letter.
   c. You are offered the position. Write a letter declining the offer.

6. Assume you are the personnel director in Application 4.

   a. Write a job-offer letter to the candidate who was selected.
   b. Write a rejection letter to a candidate not selected. (Attach a note to your paper explaining any assumptions you have made about the candidate and your future needs.)

7. Write a prospecting letter to a company of your choice. When composing your message, request an interview for a position related to your major area of study.

8. Prepare and present an oral–visual report on interviewing techniques.

9. Write a report summarizing highlights of federal legislation and your state's legislation concerning equal employment opportunities.

MULTICULTURAL INSIGHTS

1. In what ways, if any, do résumés written in countries other than the United States differ from the guides given in Chapter 22?

2. Is the AIDA structure an appropriate model for application letters sent to firms that conduct business in your native country? What modifications in that structure, if any, do you recommend for students who wish to be employed by a firm in your native country? Why?

PART

6

Cases

As you complete these cases you will demonstrate your understanding of communication challenges related to the employment process. Part 6 challenges include preparation for and participation in the hiring process.

CASE A: IS MABRY CORPORATION HIRING?
(Telephone Communication, Employment Communication, Case Writing)

This minidrama is a variation on the theme of communicating by telephone. If a tape recorder is available, use it for playback evaluation and constructive criticism of the presentation.

Cast:

▶ Switchboard Operator
▶ Caller
▶ Shaw

SWITCHBOARD OPERATOR:	Good morning. Mabry Corporation . . .
CALLER:	I'm phoning about job opportunities with your company.
SWITCHBOARD OPERATOR:	Thank you; I'll ring Dale Shaw's office for you. (*The call is transferred.*)

SHAW: Personnel Recruiting.

CALLER: Mr. Daleshaw, please. Or maybe it's *Miss* Daleshaw?

SHAW: This is Dale Shaw.

CALLER: Oh. Well, I'm inquiring about possible employment with Mabry.

SHAW: Do we have a file on you? Have you contacted us before?

CALLER: No.

SHAW: What kind of work are you interested in? What's your background? Tell me something about yourself.

INSIGHTS

Continue testing your ability to communicate by telephone. Answer these questions:

1. What communication deficiencies does this brief dialogue illustrate? Although the dialogue takes only a few seconds, what communication problems, if any, do you recognize as developing between Caller and Shaw? Rewrite the dialogue to minimize or to prevent misunderstandings. Include directions concerning the tone that you believe these speakers should use. In what ways is your revised version superior to the original minidrama as an illustration of effective telephone communication? To what extent do your fellow students and your instructor share your judgments of the original minidrama and of your revision?

2. To illustrate additional communication skills, write (or improvise) the rest of the minidrama using these data:

    a. Mabry Corporation has mail-out materials for job seekers. Besides application forms, these materials include descriptions of Mabry's history, scope, organization, work classifications, and job requirements. The materials are costly; usually they are not sent in response to merely casual inquiries.

    b. As the telephone conversation continues, Shaw should begin to determine whether Caller's qualifications and Mabry's needs coincide. With this initial "screening" by phone, elicit answers to unspoken questions, including these:

        (1) Is Caller's inquiry legitimate?

        (2) Should Mabry invest time and money in having Caller complete an employment application form? in reviewing the completed form and perhaps an accompanying résumé? in interviewing Caller? Should Mabry mail its re-

cruiting materials to Caller? If so, which of those materials should be sent?

3. Write or improvise the rest of the minidrama to demonstrate each of these possibilities:

    a. Caller impresses Shaw favorably. Shaw decides to mail appropriate materials and to schedule an interview appointment for Caller.

    b. Shaw determines during the initial telephone conversation that Mabry's needs and Caller's qualifications do not match. Both Shaw and Caller know, however, that goodwill is good business; and Mabry may need Caller's services in the future.

    c. Shaw has mixed feelings about Caller's qualifications; but as the telephone conversation continues, Caller persuades Shaw favorably.

4. What communication insights have you derived by writing or improvising the rest of "Is Mabry Corporation Hiring?" How do you plan to use those insights for your continuing development as a business communicator? Discuss your insights with your classmates. What additional benefits does that discussion provide?

CASE B: WHY DO THESE THINGS ALWAYS HAPPEN TO ME?
(Interview Preparation, Communication Responsibilities)

Cast:

▶ Lee
▶ Ticket Agent
▶ Voice from Public Address System
▶ Gate Agent

After a promising on-campus interview for the position of Benefits Analyst, Lee Whaley has been invited for an on-site interview at the Tampa, Florida, office of Consolidated Products, Inc. Consolidated has reserved round-trip airplane travel via Sun Airlines for Lee's interview trip. Lee must pick up the tickets at the Indianapolis, Indiana, airport. The flight is scheduled to leave Indianapolis at 7:30 a.m and arrive in Tampa at 1:30 p.m. on Tuesday, January 22, 19—. Lee will be met at the Tampa airport by Cary Stein, Administrative Assistant to the Director of Human Resources.

On the morning of January 22, Lee awakens to cloudy, snow-threatening weather. The thought of a trip to sunny Florida cheers her (him) as she (he) rushes to pack bags. A bit late—as usual—Lee skips breakfast and begins the drive to the airport.

LEE: I can't believe this. Look at the traffic! (*To the cars ahead*) Move! Please move! Don't make me miss that plane! (*Traffic moves slowly but steadily. Lee arrives at the airport, parks the car, grabs the bags from the trunk, and checks the time.*) Fifteen minutes. I can easily make that flight. (*Reaches the Sun Airlines check-in counter.*) There's supposed to be a ticket here for me.

TICKET AGENT: Your name, please?

LEE: Oh, yeah, I guess you do need that. I'm Lee Whaley.

TICKET AGENT: Is that *W-a-i-l-e-y?*

LEE: No. *W-h-a-l-e-y.*

TICKET AGENT: Here you are. Flight 271 to Tampa. That flight will leave in five minutes from Concourse A, Gate 10. Any bags to check?

LEE: Yes, these two; no, I'll carry one. Did you say Gate 5 in ten minutes?

TICKET AGENT: No. Gate 10 in five minutes. Now what about those bags?

LEE: I'd better carry both. Want to be sure they arrive when I do. What way to Concourse B?

TICKET AGENT: Right to Concourse B; but if you want to get Flight 271, you'd better go left to Concourse A . . . and HURRY!

LEE: Thanks, I will. (*Begins to run, awkwardly carrying a garment bag and an attaché case. Nearing Gate 10, Lee drops the attaché case, and its contents spill on the floor. While stooping to repack the case, Lee hears . . .*)

VOICE FROM PUBLIC ADDRESS SYSTEM: Your attention, please. Sun Airlines announces this change in departure gate and time: Flight 271 will depart from Concourse B, Gate 7. There will be a 30-minute delay in departure time. The flight is now scheduled to leave at 8 a.m. We repeat: Sun Airlines Flight 271 for Tampa will depart at 8 a.m. from Concourse B, Gate 7. ◆

LEE: (*Drops shoulders, sighs, looks at wristwatch.*) Well, at least I don't have to run! I might even have time for a cup of coffee. (*Turns and walks in the direction of Concourse B. Spots a snack bar. As Lee enters the snack bar, the public address system comes alive again.*)

VOICE FROM PUBLIC ADDRESS SYSTEM: Your attention, please. Please ignore the previous announcement about Sun Airlines Flight 271. This is the final boarding call for Sun Airlines Flight 271 departing from Concourse A, Gate 10. (*Lee reels and dashes to Gate 10.*)

GATE AGENT: *(Raises eyebrows.)* I'm sorry. That seat has been given to another passenger. You must claim your reserved seat at least ten minutes before departure time. Our next flight to Tampa leaves at 10 a.m. and arrives at 4:05 p.m. The flight is fully booked, but I can put you on stand-by status.

LEE: Why do these things always happen to me?

INSIGHTS

Test your awareness of preparation for a job interview and oral/written/multi-media communication by answering these questions.

1. When should preparation for a job interview begin? What could Lee have done to avoid the experiences enacted in the minidrama?
2. If you were Lee, what would you do now? Why? Continue the script, showing Lee communicating effectively with the Tampa office.

NATURE'S WONDERS

Your final assignment at Nature's Wonders places you in the Human Resources Division.

CASE FACTS

Because of the success of the summer intern program, the company receives hundreds of applications for that program each year. Company policy requires that all applicants be informed about the progress being made in selecting summer interns. However, the volume of applications necessitates the use of form messages.

YOUR TASKS

Write form letters to cover the following situations. Each letter must permit personalization as it is produced by word processing. Demonstrate the company's goodwill policy in each letter.

1. Acknowledge receipt of an application for internship. Indicate that a preliminary review of applicants' qualifications will be completed by March 10. Applicants will be informed of decisions at that time.

2. Inform an applicant he or she did not pass the initial screening.

3. Inform an applicant he or she is among ten individuals selected as final candidates for the internship. Their files will be circulated to all department managers. Final selection of five interns will be based on department managers' recommendations. Decisions will be announced after April 30.

4. Inform an applicant he or she is not among the final five selected for the internship. The applicant may still be considered if one of those selected does not accept the offer.

5. Inform the applicant he or she has been selected for the internship. An acceptance or rejection of the internship offer is needed by May 1. Nature's Wonders will pay round-trip coach airfare for out-of-town interns. Interns are expected to make their own lodging arrangements (list of recommended apartments and hotels enclosed) and to pay for all living expenses. The salary for the ten-week internship is $5,000. Interns must report to the Personnel Office at 8:30 a.m. on June 1.

WORDS AND WORD GROUPS

NOUNS

Nouns, or name words, are classified as follows:

1. **Proper nouns** are capitalized to show that they are particular names (Jan Jones, Miami, Concorde).
2. **Common nouns** are not capitalized (person, city, aircraft); they are general names.
3. **Concrete nouns** identify what our physical senses can perceive (rocket, computer, fragrance).

4. **Abstract nouns** identify qualities beyond physical sensing (courage, honor, initiative).
5. **Collective nouns** identify groups (committee, company, family). In American English, collective nouns usually take singular number, as with "The committee is deciding," "Yates and Rawls is an advertising agency," "Horizons, Inc., manufactures modular office furniture."
6. **Verbal nouns** are discussed on page 633.

A noun may be used as a subject, an object, or a possessor. An apostrophe must be used in the possessive form of a noun. (See page 648.)

PRONOUNS

Pronouns are noun substitutes. Like a noun, a pronoun may be used as subject (nominative case), object (objective case), or possessor (possessive case), as shown here:

Nominative Case	Objective Case	Possessive Case
I	me	my
we	us	our
you	you	your
he	him	his
she	her	her
it	it	its

Nominative Case	Objective Case	Possessive Case
they	them	their
who	whom	whose

A pronoun functioning as subject usually takes the nominative case. (Exception: A pronoun immediately following *to be* takes the case of the preceding noun or pronoun. Example: "I know you to be him who outbid us." Such a sentence is grammatically correct but awkward. A more businesslike version would be "I know you outbid us.")

The pronouns *yours, mine, ours,* and *theirs* often take the nominative case ("Yours is the better proposal") or the objective case ("Of all those offers, I selected yours").

To indicate ownership, pronouns take the possessive case, as with these examples: "Your proposal is better; my proposal is too costly." "Our offer was accepted; their offer was declined." Notice the spelling of each possessive pronoun. An apostrophe should not be used with a possessive pronoun. A pronoun in the possessive case functions as an adjective.

ADJECTIVES

Adjectives contract or expand the scope of nouns and pronouns; thus, **adjectives** are said to *modify* nouns or pronouns. **Proper adjectives** are derived from proper nouns and therefore are capitalized.

Proper Noun

We sell silverware made in *Denmark*.

This furniture style is named for Queen *Victoria*.

Proper Adjective

Do you sell *Danish* silverware?

That shop sells modern as well as *Victorian* furniture.

The basic form of an adjective is called its **positive degree**. **Comparative degree** is used when an adjective modifies one of two items. **Superlative degree** is used when an adjective modifies one of more than two items.

Adjectives with only one syllable in their positive degree generally add -*r* or -*er* for the comparative and -*st* or -*est* for the superlative.

Positive	Comparative	Superlative
close	closer	closest
near	nearer	nearest

Adjectives with more than one syllable in their positive degree generally use *more* or *less* for the comparative and *most* or *least* for the superlative.

Positive	Comparative	Superlative
efficient	more efficient	most efficient
	less efficient	least efficient
profitable	more profitable	most profitable
	less profitable	least profitable

A few adjectives have special comparative and superlative forms.

Positive	Comparative	Superlative
good	better	best
bad	worse	worst
little	less	least
much	more	most
some	less	least
many	more	most

And several adjectives have only the positive degree.

Positive	Comparative	Superlative
excellent		
unique		
full		
empty		

Logically, nothing can be "more excellent" than *excellent*. Logically, something may be "less than unique" or "not quite unique"; it cannot be "less unique" or "more unique," because *unique* is "one of a kind." Logically, if something could be "fuller" or "fullest," it would not be *full;* it would be *overflowing*. And how can something logically be "emptier" than *empty*?

This and *that* are the only English adjectives with plural forms; the plurals *these* and *those* should modify only plural nouns. For example, instead of "these kind," "those kind," or "them kind," say or write "this kind," "these kinds," or "those kinds."

Either is used with *or. Neither* is used with *nor.*

Either you or I will attend.

Not: You or either I will attend.

Not: Either you nor I will attend.

I don't believe that either you or I can accept that order.

Neither you nor I shipped those goods.

This, that, these, those, either, and *neither* are adjectives when they modify nouns or pronouns. *This, that, these, those, either,* and *neither* are pronouns when they do not modify other words.

Adjectives

This plan looks good. That memo is incomplete.

These people are industrious. Those ideas are good.

Either applicant probably would be an effective employee.

Neither applicant has been interviewed yet.

Pronouns

This is exactly what I wanted. That looks good.

These are good; those are better.

Of the two purchase requests, either can be approved quickly; neither is extravagant.

A, an, and *the* are adjectives that sometimes are called **articles**. *A* and *an* are indefinite (a memo, an interview). The indefinite article *a* is used immediately before words that begin with a consonant sound (a bargain, a sale, a union). *A* is usually pronounced "uh"; only for extraordinary emphasis (or before an intentional pause) is it pronounced like the name of the first alphabet letter ("ayy"). The indefinite article *an* is used immediately before words that begin with a vowel, a diphthong, or a silent *h* (an office, an aisle, an hour.)

The is definite (the memo, the interview); it is used to particularize a reference (the memo you dictated this morning, the interview scheduled for 3:00 p.m.). *The* is pronounced "thuh" immediately before words beginning with consonants ("thuh" bargain, "thuh" sale). *The* is pronounced "thee" immediately before words beginning with vowels or diphthongs ("thee" office, "thee" aisle), immediately before intentional pauses in speaking, and for extraordinary emphasis before any word.

VERBS

Verbs represent actions or states of being.

Action	State of Being
do	is
communicate	seems
produce	appears

Verbs are controlled by their grammatical subjects. By composing a sentence with a grammatical subject that originates action or asserts a state of being, you put the accompanying verb into **active voice**. By composing your sentence so that its grammatical subject receives action, you put the accompanying verb into **passive voice**.

Active Voice

Pat wrote that memo. (subject *Pat* originates action)

They shipped the merchandise. (subject *they* originates action)

Passive Voice

That memo was written by Pat. (subject *memo* receives action)

The merchandise was shipped by them. (subject *merchandise* receives action)

Besides having active or passive voice, verbs possess grammatical tense, grammatical number, and grammatical person. **Tense** communicates timing. **Number** distinguishes between one (singular) and more than one (plural). **Person** distinguishes among sender (first person), receiver (second person), and others (third person).

The charts on pages 630–631 show tense, number, and person in typical verb forms. The first chart is for active voice; the second is for passive voice.

The past tense of most verbs is formed by adding *-d* or *-ed* to the simple verb form; for example, the past of *use* is used, the past of *add* is added. However, the half-million words of English also include verbs with irregular formation of past tense. When in doubt, check your dictionary for the past form of a verb.

Most verbs may be used with or without grammatical objects. A **direct object** identifies who or what receives the verb action. An **indirect object** identifies for or to whom (which) the verb action is directed.

Hoyt telephoned. (no grammatical object)

Hoyt telephoned early. (no grammatical object)

Hoyt telephoned that order early. (object: *order*)

They will deliver. (no grammatical object)

They will deliver tomorrow. (no grammatical object)

Certainly they will deliver it. (object: *it*)

They sent us the order yesterday. (indirect object: *us;* direct object: *order*)

TIME GUIDE FOR VERBS
ACTIVE VOICE

Tense	No.	Simple	Progressive	Emphatic
Present	Singular	1. I pay 2. you pay 3. he (she or it) pays	1. I am paying 2. you are paying 3. he is paying	1. I do pay 2. you do pay 3. he does pay
	Plural	1. we pay 2. you pay 3. they pay	1. we are paying 2. you are paying 3. they are paying	1. we do pay 2. you do pay 3. they do pay
Past	Singular	1. I paid 2. you paid 3. he paid	1. I was paying 2. you were paying 3. he was paying	1. I did pay 2. you did pay 3. he did pay
	Plural	1. we paid 2. you paid 3. they paid	1. we were paying 2. you were paying 3. they were paying	1. we did pay 2. you did pay 3. they did pay
Future	Singular	1. I shall pay 2. you will pay 3. he will pay	1. I shall be paying 2. you will be paying 3. he will be paying	1. I will pay 2. you shall pay 3. he shall pay
	Plural	1. we shall pay 2. you will pay 3. they will pay	1. we shall be paying 2. you will be paying 3. they will be paying	1. we will pay 2. you shall pay 3. they shall pay
Present Perfect	Singular	1. I have paid 2. you have paid 3. he has paid	1. I have been paying 2. you have been paying 3. he has been paying	
	Plural	1. we have paid 2. you have paid 3. they have paid	1. we have been paying 2. you have been paying 3. they have been paying	
Past Perfect	Singular	1. I had paid 2. you had paid 3. he had paid	1. I had been paying 2. you had been paying 3. he had been paying	
	Plural	1. we had paid 2. you had paid 3. they had paid	1. we had been paying 2. you had been paying 3. they had been paying	
Future Perfect	Singular	1. I shall have paid 2. you will have paid 3. he will have paid	2. I shall have been paying 2. you will have been paying 3. he will have been paying	
	Plural	1. we shall have paid 2. you will have paid 3. they will have paid	1. we shall have been paying 2. you will have been paying 3. they will have been paying	

TIME GUIDE FOR VERBS
PASSIVE VOICE

Tense	No.	Simple		Progressive	
Present	*Singular*	1.	I am paid	1.	I am being paid
		2.	you are paid	2.	you are being paid
		3.	He (she *or* it) is paid	3.	he is being paid
	Plural	1.	we are paid	1.	we are being paid
		2.	you are paid	2.	you are being paid
		3.	they are paid	3.	they are being paid
Past	*Singular*	1.	I was paid	1.	I was being paid
		2.	you were paid	2.	you were being paid
		3.	he was paid	3.	he was being paid
	Plural	1.	we were paid	2.	we were being paid
		2.	you were paid	2.	you were being paid
		3.	they were paid	3.	they were being paid
Future	*Singular*	1.	I shall be paid		
		2.	you will be paid		
		3.	he will be paid		
	Plural	1.	we shall be paid		
		2.	you will be paid		
		3.	they will be paid		
Present Perfect	*Singular*	1.	I have been paid		
		2.	you have been paid		
		3.	he has been paid		
	Plural	1.	we have been paid		
		2.	you have been paid		
		3.	they have been paid		
Past Perfect	*Singular*	1.	I had been paid		
		2.	you had been paid		
		3.	he had been paid		
	Plural	1.	we had been paid		
		2.	you had been paid		
		3.	they had been paid		
Future Perfect	*Singular*	1.	I shall have been paid		
		2.	you will have been paid		
		3.	he will have been paid		
	Plural	1.	we shall have been paid		
		2.	you will have been paid		
		3.	they will have been paid		

When used without a grammatical object, a verb is said to be **intransitive**. When used with a grammatical object, a verb is said to be **transitive**. Transitive verbs take objects; intransitive verbs do not. *Note:* Grammatical agreement of subjects and verbs is discussed on pages 641–642.

ADVERBS

Adjectives modify nouns and pronouns; **adverbs** modify verbs, adjectives, and other adverbs.

Adverbs Modify Verbs

We must decide here and now. (verb: *must decide;* adverbs: *here, now*)

Our employees work efficiently. (verb: *work;* adverb: *efficiently*)

That shipment has been sent east. (verb: *has been sent;* adverb: *east*)

Adverbs Modify Adjectives

This agreement is altogether legal. (adverb: *altogether;* adjective: *legal*)

Our employees are quite courteous. (adverb: *quite;* adjective: *courteous*)

Your meaning is really clear. (adverb: *really;* adjective: *clear*)

Adverbs Modify Adverbs

They filled those orders very fast. (adverbs: *very, fast*)

Our employees work quite efficiently. (adverbs: *quite, efficiently*)

Can anyone write too clearly (adverbs: *too, clearly*)

As shown by those examples, adverbs are modifiers that answer these questions: when? where? which kind? how much? how?

Many adverbs end in *-ly;* others, like the following, do not: *also, too, quite, very, here, there, where, how, then.*

Some words function either as adjectives or as adverbs:

A fast car (*Car* is a noun; *fast* modifies that noun; since nouns are modified by adjectives, *fast* functions as an adjective in this example.)

Move fast (*Move* is a verb; *fast* modifies that verb; since verbs are modified by adverbs, *fast* functions as an adverb here.)

To determine whether a modifier should take adjective or adverb form, identify the grammatical job of that modifier in what you plan to write or speak. For instance, if you want to modify a noun or pronoun, use an *adjective* as modifier. If you want to modify a verb, an adjective, or an adverb, use an *adverb* as modifier.

Quick (Adjective) or *Quickly* (Adverb)?

That's quick service. (noun modified by adjective)

That service is quick. (noun modified by adjective)

It is quick. (pronoun modified by adjective)

They work quickly. (verb modified by adverb)

This service is usually quick. (adjective modified by adverb)

It can be done very quickly. (adverb modified by adverb)

PREPOSITIONS AND CONJUNCTIONS

Prepositions and **conjunctions** are connectors; they join individual words and groups of words. A preposition requires a grammatical object. The preposition defines the relationship of its object to a noun, pronoun, adjective, adverb, or verb in the sentence. The entire **prepositional phrase** (preposition, object, and modifiers of the object) acts as an adjectival or adverbial modifier.

The next two sentences have common prepositions printed in boldface type; the objects of those prepositions are italicized. The chart beneath each sentence indicates how each prepositional phrase functions.

Among the *messages* you prepared **for** my *review* was this summary **of** a *report* **from** *Davis* **to** *Cory*.

Word Modified	Prepositional Phrase	Function
was	among the messages	adverb
prepared	for my review	adverb

Word Modified	Prepositional Phrase	Function
summary	of a report	adjective
report	from Davis	adjective
report	to Cory	adjective

Before *noon* today please verify the totals **on** this *contract* **with** *Jay Company.*

Word Modified	Prepositional Phrase	Function
verify	before noon	adverb
totals	on this contract	adjective
contract	with Jay Company	adjective

A conjunction has no grammatical object. **Subordinating conjunctions** make a grammatical element depend upon another for meaning; **coordinating conjunctions** do not.

The next sentence shows three common subordinating conjunctions:

Although those totals seem correct *because* you updated them, verify them again *since* they are so important.

This sentence shows three common coordinating conjunctions:

I received the Davis *and* Cory reports *but* have not finished editing *or* summarizing them.

INTERJECTIONS

Interjections are sounds of emotion in written form. Interjections are grammatically independent of other words or word groups. Examples: *ah, ha, O, oh, ho, uh, huh.*

Ah, I certainly enjoyed that discussion.

Oh, did you?

I—uh—I'm not too sure now.

Ha! I thought so!

VERBALS

Verbal nouns (also called **gerunds**) end with *-ing.* Like ordinary nouns, gerunds do the jobs of subject, complement, or object.

But being verbal nouns, gerunds can take objects (as transitive verbs do).

Communicating is essential to business. (Verbal noun *communicating* functions as subject.)

Writing reports is common in business. (Verbal noun *writing* functions as subject; *reports* is object of verbal noun.)

What media does XYZ Company use for communicating market quotations? (Verbal noun *communicating* is object of preposition *for; quotations* is object of verbal noun *communicating.*)

Verbal adjectives (also called **participles**) end with *-ing* or a past-tense sign; like ordinary adjectives, participles modify nouns or pronouns. But being *verbal* adjectives, participles can take objects (as transitive verbs do).

Hurrying, they reached the airport just in time. (verbal adjective modifying subject pronoun *they*)

Written reports are common in business. (verbal adjective, in past tense, modifying subject noun *reports*)

The display case, *swept* clean and *shined* to a luster, attracted buyers. (verbal adjectives modifying subject noun *case*)

When did Acme Company build the bridge *spanning* Grand River? (verbal adjective *spanning* modifying common noun *bridge;* proper noun *Grand River* functioning as object of verbal adjective *spanning*)

Marcos Diaz is the person *directing* this project. (verbal adjective *directing* modifying common noun *person;* common noun *project* functioning as object of verbal adjective *directing*)

Gerunds and present participles are verbals that end with *-ing.* **Infinitives** are verbals that begin with the word *to* and that do not end with *-ing.* An infinitive is versatile; it can function as noun, as adjective, or as adverb. And being a *verbal* the infinitive can take an object (as a transitive verb does).

To succeed is our general objective. (Infinitive *to succeed* is being used here as subject; therefore it is a verbal *noun.*)

We want to improve our efficiency. (Infinitive *to improve* is being used here as direct object of transitive verb *want;* therefore, this infinitive is functioning as a verbal noun.)

The desire to succeed is essential in business. (Infinitive *to succeed* modifies *desire; desire* is a common noun; nouns are modified by adjectives; therefore the infinitive *to succeed* functions as a verbal adjective here.)

These notes seem ready to transcribe. (Infinitive *to transcribe* modifies *ready; ready* is used here as an adjective modifying the noun *notes;* adjectives are modified by adverbs; since *to transcribe* modifies *ready,* the infinitive functions as a verbal *adverb* here.)

SENTENCE COMPONENTS

A verb and the sentence elements tied directly to it constitute a **complete predicate;** the main verb of a complete predicate is called the **predicate verb.**

Sentence elements not in the complete predicate constitute the **complete subject.** The main nouns or main pronouns of a complete subject are called the **subject words.**

Complete subjects grammatically control complete predicates. Subject words grammatically control predicate verbs.

These press and lathe operators generally work late. (complete subject: *these press and lathe operators;* subject word: *operators;* complete predicate: *generally work late;* predicate verb: *work*)

Jan, Lee, and the other supervisors sent their reports to Lou's office. (complete subject: *Jan, Lee, and the other supervisors;* subject words: *Jan, Lee, supervisors;* complete predicate: *sent their reports to Lou's office;* predicate verb: *sent*)

Subject words take these grammatical forms: common nouns, proper nouns, pronouns, gerunds, infinitives functioning as nouns.

A **complete subject** consists of subject word(s) plus any or all of these companions: modifiers(s), conjunction(s), preposition(s).

A **complete predicate** consists of predicate verb(s) plus any or all of these: modifier(s), conjunction(s), preposition(s), complement(s)—words and word groups that complete the intended sense of the verb.

These press and lathe operators generally work late. (complete subject: *These press and lathe operators;* subject word: *operators;* modifiers of *operators: These, press, lathe;* coordinating conjunction joining *press, lathe: and;* complete predicate: *generally work late;* predicate verb: *work;* modifiers of *work: generally, late.*)

Jan, Lee, and the other supervisors sent their reports to Lou's office. (complete subject: *Jan, Lee, and the other supervisors;* subject words: *Jan, Lee, supervisors;* coordinating conjunction linking subject words: *and;* modifiers of subject words: *the, other;* complete predicate: *sent their reports to Lou's office;* predicate verb: *sent;* direct object (complement) of transitive verb: *reports;* modifier of *reports: their;* preposition linking *reports, office: to;* object (complement) of preposition *to: office;* modifier of *office: Lou's.*)

Consider this version of the last example:

The supervisors sent their to Lou's.

What missing words are needed to make sense? *Reports* and *office* complete the intended meaning. Words and word groups used that way are called **complements** because they complete the intended sense of verbs.

Complements are of these types: subject complements, direct objects, indirect objects, objects of prepositions, and objective complements.

1. **Subject complements** are so called because, although they are part of a complete predicate, they refer to a *subject word.* There are basically two kinds of subject complements: predicate adjectives and predicate nominatives.

    Predicate adjectives follow a special group of intransitive verbs, called linking verbs (e.g., *appears, becomes, seems, am, is, are, was, were, looks, hears, smells, feels, sounds*).

    Your decision seems appropriate.

    Our bakery products smell good.

    That fabric feels rough.

(predicate adjectives: *appropriate, good, rough*)

Predicate nominatives (sometimes called predicate nouns or predicate pronouns) also follow linking verbs. Although part of the complete predicate, predicate nominatives—like predicate adjectives—refer to *subject words*.

Chris is the marketing manager.

Pat, Lee, and Lou are our supervisors.

You asked for the manager; I am she.

(predicate nominatives: *manager, supervisors, she*)

Note that predicate nominatives, as implied by their name, take nominative case, not objective case: "I am she" instead of "her"; "I am he" instead of "him"; "good friends are we" instead of "good friends are us"; etc.

2. **Direct objects** have these traits:

a. Direct objects are nouns or noun equivalents (pronouns, gerunds, infinitives, or word groups functioning as nouns).

b. Direct objects complete the intended sense of *transitive* verbs.

Finish those reports before you go. (transitive verb: *finish;* noun used as direct object: *reports*)

Who dictated them? (transitive verb: *dictated;* pronoun used as direct object: *them*)

They require careful editing. (transitive verb: *require;* gerund used as direct object: *editing*)

I intend to edit them. (transitive verb: *intend;* infinitive used as direct object of *intend: to edit;* pronoun used as direct object of the infinitive *to edit: them*)·

Send whoever is available. (transitive verb: *send;* word group used as direct object: *whoever is available*)

3. Indirect objects have these traits:

a. Indirect objects are nouns or noun equivalents.

b. Indirect objects are placed between transitive verbs and direct objects.

c. Indirect objects imply the sense of *to* or *for.*

Send Benson that report. (transitive verb: *send;* indirect object: *Benson;* direct object: *report*)

They've bought us new personal computers. (transitive verb: *bought;* indirect object: *us;* direct object: *personal computers*)

We mailed whoever inquired a copy of that news release. (transitive verb: *mailed;* indirect object: *whoever inquired;* direct object: *copy*)

4. **Objects of prepositions** have these traits:

a. They are nouns or noun equivalents.

b. They complete the connections that prepositions begin.

You asked for the manager. (object of preposition *for: manager*)

With whom did you speak about it? (object of preposition *with: whom;* object of preposition *about: it*)

Please send questions about your order to him or me. (object of preposition *about: order;* objects of preposition *to: him, me*)

Note that as their name implies, objects take *objective* case, not nominative case: "With whom did you speak" not "With who did you speak"; "send questions to him or me," not "to he or I"; etc.

5. **Objective complements** are adjectives or nouns used with and placed immediately after direct objects.

We painted the storefront green. (transitive verb: *painted;* direct object: *storefront;* adjective used as objective complement to *storefront: green*)

The committee members have elected you chairperson. (transitive verb: *have elected;* direct object: *you;* noun used as objective complement to *you: chairperson*)

They named the company Rualco. (transitive verb: *named;* direct object: *company;* noun used as objective complement to company: *Rualco*)

PHRASES

Phrases and clauses are word groups that do the jobs of individual words. The basic difference between phrases and clauses is that a *phrase* does not contain a verb and subject, whereas a *clause* does contain a verb and subject. Conjunctions, if used, are also parts of a phrase or clause.

The chart "Phrases: Ingredients and Functions" summarizes types of phrases, how they are formed, and how they function in sentences. Here are examples of each type of phrase.

Prepositional Phrases

Various kinds *of phrases* are used *in business writing*. (*of phrases*: adjective modifying the noun *kinds*; *in business writing*: adverb modifying the verb *are used*)

Impressive *in their size and design*, these engines are known *for reliability*. (*in their size and design*: adverb modifying the adjective *impressive*; *for reliability*: adverb modifying the verb *are known*)

Participial Phrases

Your memo *summarizing the new sales campaign* is well written. (adjective modifying noun *memo*)

Having considered the data carefully, I endorsed the merger proposal. (adjective modifying the pronoun *I*)

Gerund Phrases

Succeeding in business often requires skill at *writing messages*. (*Succeeding in business*: noun as complete subject; *writing messages*: noun as object of preposition *at*)

Business success involves *communicating thoughts and ideas*. (noun as direct object of transitive verb *involves*)

Communicating is *exchanging the evidence of ideas and feelings*. (subject complement: a predicate nominative; specifically, a predicate noun follow-

---

Phrases: Ingredients and Functions

Type of Phrase	Ingredients	Functions
Prepositional	Preposition + its object (and modifiers, if any)	Adjective or adverb
Participial	Participle + its object (and/or modifiers)	Adjective
Gerund	Gerund + its object (and/or modifiers)	Noun
Infinitive	Infinitive + its object (and/or modifiers)	Noun, adjective, or adverb
Absolute	Noun or noun equivalent + participle (and modifiers, if any)	Grammatically independent unit separated from the rest of a sentence by a comma
Appositive	Usually noun, pronoun, modifier, verb, or verbal (with or without modifiers for itself)	Reidentifies, explains, or elaborates the immediately preceding sentence element
Verb	Verb + modifiers or helpers (e.g., *shall, will, has, have, had, is*)	Verb

ing the linking verb *is* and referring to the subject *communicating*)

Infinitive Phrases

We are beginning *to understand the interaction among words and word groups.* (Direct object of transitive verb *are beginning.* Note: The prepositional phrase *among words and word groups* functions here as an adjective because it modifies the noun *interaction.* The noun *interaction* functions here as object of the infinitive *to understand.*)

To communicate is *to exchange the evidence of ideas and feelings.* (Subject complement/predicate nominative. Note: *To communicate* is an infinitive but not an infinitive phrase because it shows no grammatical object here. The basic ingredients of an infinitive phrase are infinitive + object. Also notice that *to exchange the evidence of ideas and feelings* is an infinitive phrase that contains a prepositional phrase. The prepositional phrase *of ideas and feelings* functions here as an adjective because it modifies the noun *evidence.* The noun *evidence,* in turn, functions as a direct object of the infinitive *to exchange.*)

It is easy *to understand management's need to communicate a proper image.* (Adverb modifying subject complement/predicate adjective *easy.* Note: The long infinitive phrase contains another infinitive phrase; *to communicate a proper image* functions here as an adjective because it modifies the noun *need; need,* in turn, functions as object of the infinitive *to understand.* Also notice that this example shows a noun in possessive case [*management's*], which modifies a common noun [*need*]. Insight: Nouns and pronouns in possessive case function as adjectives.)

Absolute Phrases

The conference having ended, we returned to our own offices.

The session being longer than anticipated, we revised our travel plans.

I believe the future looks really bright, *everything considered.*

Absolute phrases are grammatically independent; they do not perform the functions of nouns, adjectives, adverbs, etc. No-

tice also that an absolute phrase is separated from the rest of a sentence by a comma.

Appositive Phrases

This recommendation is sent on behalf of Emily Doyle, *a former student of mine.* (Proper noun *Emily Doyle* functions as object of the preposition *of;* so does the appositive phrase *a former student of mine.*)

Management's purposes—*to plan and to achieve*—are the themes of this book. (Common noun *purposes* functions as subject; so does the appositive phrase *to plan and to achieve.*)

Three employees (*Kenada, Brandt, and Adams*) have been promoted. (Common noun *employees* functions as subject; so does appositive series *Kenada, Brandt, and Adams.*)

As these examples indicate, appositives are often set off by commas, by dashes, or by parentheses. Exception: An appositive that is absolutely necessary to the intended meaning of a whole sentence is not set off by punctuation. Examples of such restrictive appositives:

My brother *John* works with me.

Theories of the economist *Keynes* have been influential.

The colors *red, white, and blue* are on our corporate emblem.

Verb Phrases

I *shall gladly share* my opinions with you. (verb *share* with helper *shall* together functioning as predicate verb; *shall share* modified by adverb *gladly*)

If you *had arrived earlier,* you *would have enjoyed* meeting Yates. (verb *arrived* with helper *had* functioning as predicate verb for subject *you;* verb *enjoyed* with helpers *would have* functioning as predicate verb for subject *you*)

CLAUSES AND SENTENCE STRUCTURES

Knowledge of the structure of clauses helps a writer develop effective sentences.

Clauses

A clause contains a verb and a subject. If it is equivalent to a completely stated sentence, the clause is independent. Otherwise, the clause is dependent. **Dependent clauses** need other sentence elements to make sense. **Independent clauses,** by themselves, would make sense as complete sentences. Within sentences, dependent clauses function as nouns, adjectives, or adverbs.

Independent Clauses

You telephoned me.

You telephoned me at noon last Friday.

I was busy.

I was busy with employment interviews on that day.

You probably could tell.

You probably could tell interesting stories about your experiences.

As shown by the second, fourth, and sixth of these examples, independent clauses may contain phrases (*at noon last Friday, with employment interviews on that day, about your experiences*).

Dependent Clauses

When you telephoned me at noon, I was busy, *as you could probably tell.*

Although employment interviews are often brief, I find *that they often reveal interesting stories about work-related experiences.*

Like independent clauses, dependent clauses may contain phrases (*at noon, about work-related experiences* in these examples).

Independent clauses often are linked by coordinating conjunctions (*and, but, or,* etc.) Dependent clauses may also be linked by those conjunctions. But dependent clauses are introduced by subordinating conjunctions (*as, after, although, because, before, despite, if, since,* etc.) or relative pronouns (*which, what, who, whom, whoever,* etc.). Reminder: Independent clauses are equivalent to completely stated sentences; dependent clauses function as nouns, adjectives, or adverbs.

Noun Clauses

What you recommend determines *which policy we follow.*

What you recommend has *you* as subject word, *recommend* as transitive verb, and *what* as direct object of that verb. Since this word group has subject and verb, it is a clause (not a phrase). Because the word group functions as complete subject of the sentence and because functioning as a subject is the job of a noun, we have a noun clause.

Which policy we follow has *we* as subject word, *follow* as transitive verb, *policy* as direct object of that verb, and *which* as modifier (adjective) for the noun *policy*. Since this word group has subject *and* verb, it is a clause. Because this clause functions as direct object of the transitive verb/predicate verb *determines,* and because being a direct object is one of the jobs of a noun, we have a noun clause.

Adjective Clauses

You are someone *who has a bright future with this company.* (modifier of predicate pronoun *someone;* pronouns are modified by adjectives; therefore, an adjective clause)

That's the office *where I work.* (modifier of noun *office;* nouns are modified by adjectives; therefore, an adjective clause)

Adverb Clauses

The customers returned *after you had left.* (modifier of verb *returned;* verbs are modified by adverbs; therefore, an adverb clause).

Although delivery was delayed, Hargraves accepted the merchandise. (modifier of verb *accepted;* verbs are modified by adverbs; therefore, an adverb clause)

Clauses can contain not only phrases but also other clauses.

What you recommend when you submit this report will determine which of the policies we adopt for this organization.

The basic formula of that long sentence is *complete subject + predicate verb + complement.*

The complete subject is a noun clause (*What you recommend when you submit this report*). That noun clause contains a smaller noun clause (*What you recommend*); the subject of that smaller clause is *you;* the verb of that smaller clause is *recommend;* the complement of that smaller clause is *What,* functioning as direct object of *recommend.* The clause *when you submit this report* modifies the verb *recommend,* functioning, therefore, as an adverb.

The predicate verb *will determine* is transitive. Transitive verbs take indirect objects and direct objects as complements. The long clause beginning with the word *which* and completing the sentence does the job of complement (direct object) for the transitive verb/predicate verb *will determine*. This is the structure of that ending clause:

which of the policies we adopt for this organization.

we: subject of the clause

adopt: verb of the clause

which: direct object of transitive verb *adopt*

of the policies: prepositional phrase modifying *which; which* functions as direct object of this clause; direct objects are nouns or noun equivalents, and *which* does the job of a noun equivalent (pronoun) here. Pronouns are modified by adjectives; the prepositional phrase *of the policies* functions here as an adjective modifying the pronoun *which.*

for this organization: prepositional phrase modifying *adopt. Adopt* is a verb; adverbs modify verbs; the prepositional phrase *for this organization* functions as an adverb because it modifies the verb *adopt.*

Reminder: *for this organization* is a phrase because it does not have a subject and verb. It is a prepositional phrase because it consists of a preposition (*for*), the object of that preposition (*organization*), and an adjective (*this*) modifying a noun (*organization*).

Phrases and clauses provide clarity, variety, emphasis. For *conciseness*, however, phrases and clauses often can be condensed into single words.

Phrases	Equivalents
in the event that sales increase	if sales increase
in all probability	probably
provide them with an explanation	explain it to them
starting at this (that) point in time	starting now (then)
stopping at this (that) point in space	stopping here (there)
with reference to requirements of the job	concerning the job requirements
in the order of magnitude of 2 percent	about 2 percent

Clauses	Concise Equivalents
the policy that is recommended	the recommended policy
a person who has responsibility for	a person responsible for
shipments that are delayed	delayed shipments
When seasonal trends are in effect, sales volume reflects them.	Sales volume reflects seasonal trends.
a message that is completely informative but which is briefly stated	a concise message
While you are at the Chicago office, telephone me.	Telephone me from the Chicago office.
What I want to know is whether you have received that shipment.	Have you received that shipment?
Your business messages should be accurate, complete, clear, and courteous; and you also need to write or say them concisely.	Your business messages should be accurate, complete, clear, courteous, and concise.

Sentence Structures

A **simple sentence** has one independent clause but no dependent clause.

A **compound sentence** has at least two independent clauses but no dependent clause.

A **complex sentence** has not more than one independent clause and at least one dependent clause.

A **compound-complex sentence** consists of at least two independent clauses and at least one dependent clause.

Knowing those patterns will help you vary your sentence structures, thereby providing interesting changes of pace for your readers and listeners.

Simple Sentences

Stop. (The subject is *you,* not stated but clearly understood.)

We start and stop machinery. (subject: *we;* predicate verbs: *start, stop;* coordinating conjunction for predicate verbs: *and;* direct object of the two predicate verbs: *machinery;* one independent clause; therefore, a simple sentence)

Garcia and Duval start the machinery at 8:00 a.m. and stop it at 4:00 p.m. daily. (complete subject: *Garcia and Duval;* complete predicate: the rest of the sentence; subject words: *Garcia, Duval;* predicate verbs: *start, stop;* one independent clause; therefore, a simple sentence)

Garcia, Duval, and Claussen start the machinery at eight in the morning and stop it at four in the afternoon. (complete subject: *Garcia, Duval, and Claussen;* complete predicate: the rest of the sentence; subject words: *Garcia, Duval, Claussen;* predicate verbs: *start, stop;* one independent clause; therefore, a simple sentence)

Note: Simple sentences need not be short; the number of words does not determine the kind of sentence. Each of those four sentences has one independent clause and no dependent clause. Therefore, they are simple sentences.

Compound Sentences

Garcia starts; Duval stops.

Garcia starts the machinery; Duval stops it.

Garcia starts the machinery, and Duval stops it.

Garcia starts the machinery at 8:00 a.m., but Duval stops it at 4:00 p.m.

Garcia and Phillips start the machinery at 8:00 a.m.; Duval and Ryan stop it at 5:00 p.m.; all of them leave by 5:15 p.m.

Note: Each of those five sentences consists of at least two independent clauses but no dependent clause. Therefore, they are compound sentences.

Complex Sentences
(Dependent clauses are italicized here.)

We *who write* must observe.

We *who write business messages* must develop observation skills.

Writing business messages *that are effective* requires many skills.

Writing effective business messages requires obser-

vation skills *that facilitate detection of patterns of human behavior* and linguistic skills *that enable one to influence human behavior constructively.*

Writing business messages *that get results* requires people *who understand human behavior.*

Because we are business communicators, we must observe human behavior, *which is sometimes difficult to interpret*

Note: Each of those six sentences contains one independent clause and at least one dependent clause. Therefore, they are complex sentences.

Compound-Complex Sentences
(Dependent clauses are italicized here.)

At 8:00 a.m. Garcia starts the machinery *that laminates these products,* and at 5:00 p.m. Duval stops it.

At 8:00 a.m. Garcia starts the machinery *that laminates these products,* at 5:00 p.m. Duval stops it, and at 5:15 p.m. the shop closes for the day.

The machines start at 8:00 a.m.; they stop at 5:00 p.m.; the shop closes at 5:15 p.m., *after the guards have reported for duty.*

Whoever starts the machinery checks the first run, and *whoever stops the machinery* prepares it for the next run.

Note: Each of those examples contains at least two independent clauses and at least one dependent clause. Therefore, they are compound-complex sentences.

REFERENCE OF PRONOUNS

The noun for which a pronoun substitutes is called an antecedent (from Latin "that which comes before"). A pronoun should refer unmistakably to its antecedent; otherwise, the antecedent should be repeated, or the entire sentence should be rewritten for clarity.

Vague Reference

I saw Bette, Lucy, and Georgia today; she mentioned her being recognized as Executive of the Year. (Is "she" Bette or Lucy or Georgia?)

Clear Reference

I saw Bette, Lucy, and Georgia today; Bette mentioned Lucy's being recognized as Executive of the Year.

Lucy mentioned Bette's being recognized as Executive of the Year.

Bette told me that Lucy is Executive of the Year.

Lucy told me that Bette is Executive of the Year.

"Lucy is Executive of the Year," Bette said.

Lucy said, "Bette is Executive of the Year."

Vague Reference

We successfully closed that deal, which pleased us. (What pleased us? the deal? or the successful close?)

Clear Reference

Successfully closing that deal pleased us.

Our success in closing that deal pleased us.

That deal, which we closed successfully, pleased us.

AGREEMENT OF PRONOUNS AND ANTECEDENTS

A pronoun and its antecedent must share the same grammatical gender, person, and number. Grammatical **gender** is masculine (as with *son*), feminine (*daughter*), or neuter (*home*). The grammatical **first person** "speaks," **second person** "is spoken to," **third person** "is spoken about." Grammatical **number** is either singular (one) or plural (more than one).

The noun *typewriter,* for example, has neuter gender (neither masculine nor feminine), third person (it neither "speaks" nor "is spoken to"), and singular number (one). A pronoun substituting for *typewriter* also must have neuter gender, third person, and singular number; the pronoun therefore would be *it.*

A pronoun and its antecedent should agree in gender, person, and number but need not share the same grammatical case.

That typewriter is new; take good care of it. (The subject noun *typewriter* is in nominative case, but the pronoun *it* is in objective case because that pronoun is the object of the preposition *of.*)

Disagreement

When someone communicates, it is exchanging evidence of ideas and feelings.

Whenever an executive dictates a message, you should speak clearly.

Either Pablo or Jim can change their own schedules.

Neither Sue nor Marie is casual about their own work.

Both Sue and Marie take her own work seriously.

Alcon Corporation plans to expand their facilities.

Alcon management expressed their approval.

Agreement

When humans communicate *they* exchange evidence of ideas and feelings.

Whenever an executive dictates a message, *she or he* should speak clearly.

Either Pablo or Jim can change *his* own schedule.

Neither Sue nor Marie is casual about *her* own work.

Both Sue and Marie take *their* own work seriously.

Alcon Corporation plans to expand *its* facilities.

Alcon management expressed *its* approval.

AGREEMENT OF SUBJECTS AND VERBS

A verb and its subject need to share the same grammatical person and number. (Grammatical gender and case do not apply to verbs.)

Disagreement

You instead of Lynn is scheduled for overtime work.

Salaries has been rising.

Either Evans or Ross are concerned.

Neither Evans nor Ross are concerned.

One of our employees have a master's degree.

Where is the supervisors' offices located?

Each of us hope to succeed.

All of us tries to succeed.

Agreement

You instead of Lynn are scheduled for overtime work.

Salaries have been rising.

Either Evans or Ross is concerned.

Neither Evans nor Ross is concerned.

One of our employees has a master's degree.

Where are the supervisors' offices located?

Each of us hopes to succeed.

All of us try to succeed.

SELECTION AND PLACEMENT OF MODIFIERS

Choose and position **modifiers** (words and word groups functioning as adjectives or as adverbs) so that their intended effect is clear.

Unclear Modification

The telephone rang as I dictated again and again. (Dictated again and again? Rang again and again?)

The executive who dictated that memo efficiently manages this department. (Dictated efficiently? Manages efficiently?)

I ordered a new typewriter for my secretary with all the latest features. (Does your secretary have disk storage?)

Walking into this office for the first time, that furniture looks impressive. (Although desks and chairs have legs, can furniture walk?)

I almost used a ream of paper for that report. (If you "almost used," you did not use.)

Before submitting this report, two months were spent in research. (Did those months submit the report?)

Clear Modification

The telephone rang again and again as I dictated.
OR
As I dictated, the telephone rang again and again.

The executive who dictated that memo manages this department efficiently.
OR
The executive who efficiently dictated that memo is manager of this department.

I ordered a new typewriter with all the latest features for my secretary.
OR
I ordered my secretary a new typewriter with all the latest features.

That furniture impresses people who walk into this office for the first time.
OR
Walking into this office for the first time, people are impressed by that furniture.

I used almost a ream of paper for that report.

Before submitting this report, I spent two months doing research.
OR
Two months of research went into this report.

Suggestion: Place adverbs between the parts of an infinitive only for unusual emphasis. Otherwise, do not split the infinitive.

Regular Infinitive

I intend to work efficiently.

We seem to agree absolutely.

The purpose is certainly to improve this process.

Split Infinitive

I intend to efficiently work.

We seem to absolutely agree.

The purpose is to certainly improve this process.

PARALLELISM

Parallelism indicates equality of ideas and of words that represent those ideas. To achieve parallelism of individual words, balance nouns with nouns, adjectives with adjectives, verbs with verbs, adverbs with adverbs, prepositions with prepositions, conjunctions with conjunctions, and verbals with verbals.

Nonparallel

This job requires skills in management and also communicating.

I enjoy learning to write and speaking effectively.

I expect the next shipment to be as big or bigger than this one.

I. Two Sending Skills
   A. Writing
   B. To speak
II. Two Skills for Receiving
   A. Observing
   B. By reading
      1. listening

Parallel

This job requires skills in both management and communication.

OR

This job requires skills in both managing and communicating.

I enjoy learning to write and speak effectively.

OR

I enjoy learning to write effectively and to speak clearly.

I expect the next shipment to be as big as or bigger than this one.

I. Sending Skills
   A. Writing
   B. Speaking
II. Receiving Skills
   A. Observing
   B. Reading
   C. Listening

PUNCTUATION MARKS, NUMBERS, AND WORD DIVISION

PUNCTUATION

Punctuation consists of cue marks for joining and separating words, phrases, clauses, and sentences. The purpose of punctuation is to clarify what otherwise would seem vague or confusing to a reader.

Punctuation marks control the flow of written language. Except for experimental or deliberately unconventional purposes (as, occasionally, with innovative advertisements), punctuation of business messages is systematic rather than impulsive or decorative. Punctuation is an integral part of effective writing.

Notice that punctuation itself can change a message even though the words of that message remain constant:

Pat Jones said you're correct.

Pat Jones said you're correct!

Pat Jones said you're correct?

Pat Jones said, "You're correct."

Pat Jones said, "You're correct!"

Pat Jones said, "You're correct?"

Pat, Jones said you're correct.

Pat, Jones said: "You're correct!"

"Pat," Jones said. "You're correct?"

"Pat? Jones said, 'You're correct.'"

As you see from those examples, punctuation is not an ornament but a tool for writing effectively. This section of Appendix B is designed to help you use that tool skillfully.

Period .

A period signals full stop for the following:

1. Declarative sentences (as in ordinary assertions)

   Our central office is in Milwaukee.

   Your order was filled yesterday.

2. Mildly imperative sentences (as in routine commands)

   Issue the refund.

   Make two copies of this memo.

3. Most personal initials as well as most abbreviations

R. G. Salas, Jr.	B.B.A., M.Ed., Ph.D.
Mr. L. N. Travis	a.m., p.m.
Ms. Foster	f.o.b., c.o.d.
Foster, Inc.	

   Acronyms (abbreviated names consisting entirely of initial letters or syllables) often are written in all capitals and without periods.

NASA	National Aeronautics and Space Administration
ESOP	Employee Stock Ownership Plan

   Initials of famous personalities sometimes are written in all capitals without periods.

FDR	Franklin Delano Roosevelt
JFK	John Fitzgerald Kennedy
LBJ	Lyndon Baines Johnson

4. Decimal point for dollars-and-cents amounts stated in figures

   The invoice totals $87.50, not $8.75.

Notice that a dollars-without-cents figure does not require the period as decimal point.

This $875 invoice needs correction.

SPACING CUE: When using a typewriter or microcomputer, space twice after a period ending a sentence. Space once after a period following an initial (R. G. Salas) or an abbreviation (Ms. Foster). Do not space after a period within an abbreviation (Ph.D.; f.o.b.) or a number (50.3).

Question Mark ?

The question mark punctuates direct queries.

How many pages have you revised?

I asked, "Where has the Wesco report been filed?"

The question mark does not punctuate indirect queries.

We asked if they will finish this work today.

When a sentence seems to be a query but is actually a request or a command, the question mark need not be used; a period replaces it.

Will you report to my office at once.

To convey emphasis, a question mark may punctuate each item in a series.

What is our market segment in Iowa? in Kansas? in Nebraska?

SPACING CUE: Space twice after a question mark at the end of a sentence, once after a question mark within a sentence; do not space after a question mark if other punctuation immediately follows.

Exclamation Point !

The exclamation point punctuates an urgent command, extraordinary emotion, or exceptional emphasis.

Stop! Look! Listen!

Note: Sentences normally end with only one of these punctuation marks: period or question mark or exclamation point.

Comma ,

The comma is used for these purposes:

1. To introduce a short or informal quotation

   Pat said, "Meet me in Jensen's office."

   Kim asked, "When can you ship those goods?"

2. To punctuate a dependent clause that precedes an independent clause

   If your report is accurate, we should buy those shares.

3. To set off a *non*restrictive clause (i.e., to set off a clause that may be omitted without changing the corethought of the sentence)

   This stock, which has a good dividend record, is highly recommended.

4. To set off a *non*restrictive appositive (but not a restrictive appositive)

   Boise, the capital, is our headquarters city for Idaho. (nonrestrictive appositive)

   Business leaders Ryan and Biggs are quoted in this article. (restrictive appositive)

5. To punctuate independent clauses joined by a coordinating conjunction

   They have met our terms, and we should sign the contract.

6. To punctuate a long introductory phrase or an introductory phrase containing a verbal

   With the comprehensive survey completed well before that due date, the contractor had time to develop detailed cost estimates.

   After completing the survey, the contractor had time to develop detailed cost estimates.

7. To punctuate parenthetical terms

   Consider, for example, the Patel offer.

   As you know, the work is on schedule.

8. To punctuate a series of at least three words or word groups that do not already have a comma

   Essential commodities include oil, coal, and steel.

   Note: See Semicolon, Rule 4, for punctuation when at least one item in a series contains a comma.

9. To imply (but not state) the word *and* between two adjectives modifying the same noun

   Lakelands is a strong, progressive firm.

   Ortega is an honest, industrious employee.

   Note: Do not use a comma if the word *and* would seem awkward or illogical.

   a new jet aircraft

   a former advertising executive

10. To punctuate terms of direct address

    Margaret, this information is confidential.

    This information, Margaret, is confidential.

11. To clarify sentence elements that otherwise might be misunderstood

    ### Unclear

    This branch opened in 1957; ever since it has been our most profitable unit.

    ### Clear

    This branch opened in 1957; ever since, it has been our most profitable unit.

12. To imply omitted words

    Ruth and Jay attended the sales meeting; Ann and Bill, the marketing session.

    We plan to inspect Plant A this month, Plant B in July.

13. To separate whole numbers into groups of three digits each (Exception: room numbers, many policy numbers, telephone numbers)

    Policy 18250 covers 1,875 employees.

14. To separate state from city and day from year

    Jeremy signed the contract on January 27, 1987, in Passaic, New Jersey, his hometown.

SPACING CUE: Space once after a comma except when used to divide a number into three-digit groups (1,875).

Semicolon ;

The semicolon is used in these ways:

1. To punctuate independent clauses of a compound sentence when no coordinating conjunction links those clauses

   The inspectors have been here; they will return tomorrow.

2. To punctuate transitions, a semicolon is often used before—and a comma is used after—terms such as *that is, i.e., for example, e.g.,* and the like.

   Bartok is an auditor; i.e., someone who verifies accounting records.

   I've requested three people to attend; namely, Lucas, Kaplan, and Griggs.

   Nonverbal messages have many aspects; for example, gestures, postures, timings, distances.

3. To separate independent clauses of a compound sentence if at least one of those clauses already contains a comma

   That policy, my friend, is official; be sure to follow it.

   However, this report is confidential; handle it carefully.

4. To separate items of a series when at least one of those items already contains a comma

   The crew members are Smythe, not Smith; Halsey; and Ruiz.

   Our branch offices are in Los Angeles; Chicago; and Columbus, Georgia.

   Those reports were filed on June 30, 1976; June 29, 1977; and July 1, 1978.

5. To emphasize every item in a series of at least three independent clauses

   We perceive; we interpret; we apply.

   For less emphasis, the comma replaces the semicolon

   We perceive, we interpret, we apply.

   Effective communicators notice, they read, they listen.

   SPACING CUE: Space once after a semicolon.

Colon :

The colon is used for these purposes:

1. To present a sentence element emphatically

   I have just one word to say to you: Congratulations!

2. To introduce a series or a list

   These are traditional management functions: to plan, to organize, to direct, and to control.

   Note: Do not use a colon when the list is preceded by a verb or a preposition.

   Traditional management functions are to plan, to organize, to direct, and to control.

   I have proofread everything except Chapter 20, Chapter 25, and Appendix C.

3. To introduce a long or a formal quotation

   The certificate reads as follows:

   The second paragraph of our agreement states: "You are obligated under this contract to return unused items."

4. To separate hours, minutes, and seconds when time is stated in figures instead of in words

   The conference began at 8:30 a.m.

5. To punctuate the greeting of a business letter (mixed punctuation style) or the heading of a memo

   Dear Mrs. Rossi:

TO:	L. A. McNair
FROM:	B. R. Ming
DATE:	April 3, 19—
SUBJECT:	Project 1422

   SPACING CUE: Space twice after a colon within a sentence. Do not space after a colon used in a time notation

(8:30 a.m.). Never space before a colon. Space two or more times to align items following colons in a memo heading.

Apostrophe '

Use the apostrophe for these purposes:

1. To indicate possession—*except* for words that are already shown in possessive form

   We need to protect our patent rights.

   This steel mill is operating at its peak capacity. (*Not:* it's peak capacity)

   These reports are his; those, hers; these, yours; and the rest, ours. (*Not:* his's, her's, or hers'; your's or yours'; our's or ours')

   The possessive of a singular noun may always be formed by adding *'s* to the noun. To form the possessive of a plural noun, add only an apostrophe if the plural ends in *s*; add *'s* if the plural does not end in *s*.

   The firm's patent rights are those of one firm.

   The firms' patent rights are those of more than one firm.

   Hotchkin's office is where Hotchkin works.

   Hotchkins's office is where Hotchkins works.
   OR
   Hotchkins' office is where Hotchkins works. (Acceptable formation of singular possessive when multisyllable singular form ends in *s*)
   OR
   The Hotchkins' office is where the Hotchkin brothers work. (Plural possessive when plural noun ends in *s*)

   Adele's and Dale's reports are more than one message.

   Adele and Dale's report is one message.

   The woman's report is a report by or about one woman.

   The women's report is a report by or about more than one woman.

   Bradley's home is where Bradley lives.

   The Bradleys' home is where the Bradley family lives.

2. To indicate omitted letters of a contraction (i.e., to indicate omissions that occur when two words are combined into one word)

I am	I'm
I should, I would	I'd
I shall, I will	I'll
you are	you're
you could, you would	you'd
you will	you'll
he will	he'll
she will	she'll
it will	it'll
he could, he would	he'd
she could, she would	she'd
it could, it would	it'd
we are	we're
we should, we would	we'd
we shall, we will	we'll
they will	they'll
they could, they would	they'd
are not	aren't
cannot	can't
could not	couldn't
did not	didn't
do not	don't
has not	hasn't
is not	isn't
it is	it's
was not	wasn't
were not	weren't
will not	won't
would have	would've
would not	wouldn't

3. To show the plurals of abbreviations, figures, letters, and words

   Ph.D.'s head our research programs; Ed.D.'s supervise our training programs. (also acceptable: Ph.D.s, Ed.D.s and PhDs, EdDs)

   The 4's, 6's, and 8's on this typewriter are clogged. (also acceptable: 4s, 6s, 8s)

   Remember: There are two *c*'s and two *m*'s in *accommodate*. (apostrophes required)

Too many *and*'s, *but*'s, or *also*'s may needlessly lengthen a message. (apostrophes required)

SPACING CUE: Do not space after an apostrophe unless it ends a word.

Italics (Underscoring)

In keyboarded messages, italicized words are indicated by underscoring. Use italics for these purposes:

1. For emphasis if the emphasis might otherwise be lost (use sparingly)

   He *said* he was ready. Why am I still waiting?

2. To show words as words, letters as letters, and figures as figures

   There are two *c*'s and two *m*'s in *accommodate*.

   Some typists erroneously use the *q* in place of the *g*.

   Please align the *7* with the *4* in this column.

3. For titles of complete works such as books, newspapers, magazines, motion pictures, musical works, plays, long poems, paintings, sculptures

   A picture of Rodin's *The Thinker* appears in *Art Treasures of the World*.

   Business Week is indexed in *Business Periodicals Index*.

Quotation Marks " " ' '

Use quotation marks for these purposes:

1. To enclose direct quotations

   I asked, "Who is the manager of the Collection Department?"

   "Who," I asked, "is your manager?"

   If a direct quotation has more than a single sentence and is not interrupted, use opening quotation marks only at the beginning and closing quotation marks only at the end.

I asked, "Who are your managers? What are their names?"

For typewriting of a quotation that has more than one paragraph, use opening quotation marks to begin each paragraph but closing quotation marks to end only the last paragraph.

The transmittal memo was worded as follows:

"Here is the report you authorized May 12 for submission today.

"Both historical and current data support recommendations to lease rather than to purchase Site 43. Cost figures are itemized on the following pages and summarized in the appended charts.

"Your response to this report will be welcome."

For a message that is otherwise double-spaced, you may keyboard a quotation of more than three lines with single spacing and double indention, but with no beginning or ending quotation marks.

The transmittal memo for the Site 43

recommendation report was prepared by

O. A. Rashad and worded as follows:

   Here is the report you authorized May 12 for submission today.

   Both historical and current data support recommendations to lease rather than to purchase Site 43. Cost figures are itemized on the following pages and summarized in the appended charts.

   Your response to this report will be welcome.

To enclose a quotation within a quotation, use single instead of double marks.

The minutes of the Executive Committee contain this statement:

"Evans proposed and Roswell seconded a motion 'to accept with regret the resignation of Chairperson B. K. Schuyler.' The motion passed unanimously."

For a message that is otherwise double-spaced, you may type a quotation within a quotation of more than three lines with single spacing, with double indention, and with double quotation marks at the beginning and at the end of the second quote.

The transmittal memo for the Site 43 recommen-

dation report was prepared by O. A. Rashad and

worded as follows:

> Here is the report authorized for submission today.
>
> Our research confirms this statement in Marley's September 25 letter to you: "Both historical and current data support recommendations to lease rather than to purchase Site 43." Cost figures are itemized on the following pages and summarized in the appended charts.
>
> Your response to this report and to Waley's urging "immediate action on this matter" will be welcome.

2. To enclose titles of book chapters, magazine articles, newspaper items, and other named parts of complete works. But italicize the titles of complete works (i.e., books, magazines, newspapers, etc.). Titles of their parts are quoted.

Have you read "Financial Forecasts" in today's *Manhattan Journal?*

"Ten Top Firms," the first chapter of Cory's newly published book, includes a history of Excel, Inc.

3. To enclose slang terms in an otherwise formal message, unusual words, or words used for special effect

In personnel jargon of the entertainment industry, a "gopher" is someone whose job is to "go for" coffee and to do other errands. "Gophering" is sometimes a way of "getting a foot inside the door" of that industry. As you know, jargon and slang change quickly; *gopher*, for example, is becoming *gofer*. This example shows how old words are given new definitions as well as new spellings.

Hyphen - and Dash —

Follow these guides for **hyphen** use:

1. Use a hyphen to divide a word at the end of a line. Rules for word division are given on pages 656–657.

2. The hyphen often follows these prefixes: *ex, self, vice.*

    ex-mayor
    self-centered
    vice-chairperson

3. A hyphen is often used between two adjectives that modify and that come before a noun (they are called compound adjectives).

    first-class work
    well-known resort
    up-to-date report

    But when such adjectives follow a noun, they usually are not hyphenated.

    The quality of your work is first class.

    That resort is well known.

    Please bring these figures up to date.

    Usually, a hyphen does not appear between an adverb and an adjective.

    a highly effective presentation

    their quite profitable undertakings

4. A hyphen is used in compound numbers written as words.

    ninety-eight, one hundred twenty-nine, seventy-seven, etc.

    However, a one-third share is one third of the total.

5. The hyphen can be used to clarify intended meanings.

    Vague

    They are junior high school students.

    Clear

    They are junior high-school students (in their third year).

OR

They are junior-high school students (still in seventh, eighth, or ninth grade).

To typewrite a **dash**, strike the hyphen key twice without spacing. Use the dash for these purposes:

1. To show a sudden interruption or shift of thought

   They should arrive at the Denver office by 2:00 p.m.—better make that 2:30 p.m., to be sure.

2. To convey momentary suspense for emphasis

   Congratulations, Lee—you've been promoted!

3. To emphasize an appositive

   That important document—the Bramco contract—is in the safe.

   I was asked to safeguard an important document—the Bramco contract.

4. To replace commas for emphasis

   Those who first opposed us—and they were many—supported our ideas later.

   Consider the probable consequences before you decide—not just afterwards.

Caution: If you overuse the dash, you will lose its quality of emphasis and suggest that you are unfamiliar with other punctuation marks. Use the dash sparingly and deliberately; reserve it for the purposes stated here.

Parentheses ( ) and Brackets [ ]

The functions of dashes also are those of parentheses. **Parentheses**, however, are less emphatic than dashes and are used more often than dashes for supplementary explanations.

They should be at the Denver office about 2:30 this afternoon. (Better make that 2:45 p.m., to be sure.)

Legal documents (contracts, etc.) often show money amounts in words and in parenthesized figures; e.g., one hundred fifty dollars ($150).

Use **brackets** to enclose material already in parentheses.

This parenthetical reference is directly quoted from our agreement: "The hourly rental (one hundred fifty dollars [$150]) may be applied toward purchase of said machine."

Use **brackets** to identify material that you insert into a direct quotation made by another person.

"Official protests against that regulation were filed by five corporations [the actual number was six] on April 10."

The Latin word *sic* ("thus") is bracketed to identify but not to correct an error in a direct quotation; [*sic*] stands for "thus it is in the original statement."

"Official protests against that regulation were filed by five [*sic*] corporations."

Ellipses . . .

Ellipses, or omission marks, signal deletions from quoted material. An **ellipsis** consists of three spaced periods plus a period, a question mark, or an exclamation point when the ellipsis ends a sentence.

Original Quotations

"For the time being, delete from this confidential statement the names of Croyden and Sklar; but mention that negotiations are still in the preliminary stage."

"Their purchase offer is $20 million."

Ellipses

"For the time being . . . negotiations are still in the preliminary stage."

"Their purchase offer is. . . ."

Placement of Punctuation

Observe these standards for placement of punctuation:

1. Periods for abbreviations are placed before any other punctuation mark. When an abbreviation occurs at the end of a declarative sentence, the period is not doubled.

Metrico needs two Ed.D.'s and a Ph.D.

Will you send that shipment C.O.D.?

2. Follow these American English rules of order for closing quotation marks:

    a. Place the period or the comma *inside* closing quotation marks.

        Gomez wrote "Economic Trends of Tomorrow."

        When you speak of "improving the sales picture," do you mean in terms of volume or, rather, of gross profit?

    b. Place the colon or the semicolon *outside* closing quotation marks.

        Gomez emphasized this fact in "Economic Trends": P/E ratios are the key.

        You mentioned "improving the sales picture"; did you mean in terms of volume or, rather, of gross profit?

    c. Place the question mark, exclamation point, or dash (1) *inside* when it is part of a quotation but (2) *outside* when it refers to the entire sentence of which the quote is a part.

        Should your slogan simply be "Buy now"?

        The investor asked, "Buy now?"

        Walters ordered 750 copies of the magazine containing "We Should Invest"!

        "Cancel that order!" she insisted.

        "I'm so busy that—" is all she said as she rushed by.

        Two words—"Please wait"—were all she had time to say.

    d. Punctuate a quotation within a quotation according to the preceding rules. Notice the sequence of single and double quotation marks:

        She said, "I've read 'Economic Trends of Tomorrow.' "

        I asked, "When did you read 'Economic Trends'?"

I asked, "Have you also read 'Should We Invest?' "

He exclaimed, "Cancel that order for 'Economic Trends'!"

" 'Buy now!' is Jay's idea of a slogan," I remarked.

3. Use parentheses with other punctuation as follows:

    a. If punctuation applies to the entire sentence and not just to the parenthetical material, the punctuation mark goes *outside* the closing parenthesis:

        This research confirms our prediction (see Formula 32).

        When I was introduced to Gomez (who wrote "Economic Trends of Tomorrow"), I was tempted to ask for an autograph.

    b. If a question mark or an exclamation point applies only to parenthetical material, place the punctuation inside the closing parenthesis.

        That slogan ("Buy Today!") is overused.

        Those people (are they shareholders?) have been waiting to see you.

Spacing for Punctuation—Summary

Space once after a punctuation mark—except for the following:

1. Do *not* space immediately before or immediately after

    a. a period inside an abbreviation

        Kenneth Lowry, M.B.A., will join us at 3:00 p.m.

    b. a period used as a decimal

        That percentage should be 3.15, not 3.51.

    c. a hyphen or a dash

        Can you build an up-to-date model of that process?

        Yes, we can—but not by the date you mentioned.

Note: Space *once* after a suspended hyphen when it is not followed by another punctuation mark.

Please write a one- or two-page abstract of this report.

OR

Please write a one-, two-, or three-line description of your job.

d. an apostrophe

Tyler's design is unique, isn't it?

e. a colon used in a statement of time of day

Bill Fairey needs your report for the 3:30 staff meeting this afternoon.

f. a comma within a number

Net income for 1987 was $1,200,185.

2. Do *not* space immediately after opening or immediately before closing quotation marks, parentheses, or brackets.

He announced: "We have been awarded the contract."

That price is firm (see page 37 of the catalog).

"This advertisement has typographical errors; for example, it mentions Frankln [Franklin] stoves."

3. Do not space *before* a colon in a sentence.

Please order these supplies: paper, pens, paper clips.

4. Space twice for the following:

a. immediately after a colon within a sentence

The messages began with this formal statement: "When signed by you and by us, this letter will constitute a contract."

b. immediately after a period used with itemized numbers or letters

1. Traditional Management Purposes
   a. to decide
   b. to achieve
2. Traditional Management Functions
   a. to plan
   b. to organize

c. to direct
d. to control

c. between the end of one sentence and the beginning of another sentence typed on the same line

Please transcribe this message now. It's a special directive.

That's good news! Thanks for telling me.

NUMBERS

Many writers are sometimes puzzled by whether a number should be written in words or in figures. With business forms such as invoices, sales tickets, or purchase orders, figures are used almost entirely. But with messages written in paragraph form, numbers are sometimes expressed in figures and sometimes in words.

General Rules

1. Write a number at the beginning of a sentence as a word. If the number is very large, rewrite the sentence so that the number appears later as a figure.

Fourteen dozen pairs of gloves were ordered last month.

Twenty thousand dollars is the goal of the drive.

The goal is $20,000.

2. In general business style, use words for the numbers 1–10; use figures for numbers greater than 10.

We will hire three additional employees in the Claims Department this year.

The Finance Department projects the need for 12 new employees over the next five years.

3. In formal style, use words for the numbers 1–100; use figures for numbers greater than 100 except in the case of isolated round numbers.

The Promotions Committee requests that twenty-five rooms be allocated for use in weekend promotional packages.

They registered 375 at the first convention; 1,237 at the second; and 2,119 at the third.

They shipped nine thousand carloads in the first month.

4. Round numbers (numbers in even units, such as tens, hundreds, or thousands) should be spelled in full, except when they are used with other numbers expressed as figures.

We saw him ten days ago.

These machines range in price from $10 to $23,500.

Large round numbers may be written in words or figures or both according to the writer's preference or the nature of the copy. For example, if only one large round number is used, it may be written in words. But if many figures are used in other sentences or paragraphs, a large round number should be written in figures.

fifteen million dollars
$15,000,000
$15 million

5. If several numbers are used in parallel construction, write them in figures, unless all are small or all are round numbers that can be written easily in words. A number at the beginning of a sentence should be written out even though later numbers are written in figures. You may improve the sentence by rewriting it so that the first word is not a number.

She ordered 45 management books, 125 economics books, and 68 law books.

He bought three ties, six shirts, and ten handkerchiefs.

Seventy-seven men, 725 women, and 196 children were called in the poll.

In the poll 77 men, 725 women, and 196 children were called.

When a small number is used with a large number but not in a similar context, the small number may be written as a word.

I asked the two auditors about the $652,890 deficit.

Those three men use a $750,000 machine.

6. When one number immediately follows another, spell out the smaller number and express the larger one in figures.

She purchased 75 twenty-cent stamps.

He bought four 50-cent notebooks.

7. When one unrelated number immediately follows another, separate the two numbers by a comma.

In 1982, 654 new charge customers were granted credit.

Addresses

1. Write house numbers in figures, except for house number One.

Roberts lives at One Riverside Drive; Marshall, at 2185 Sutton Avenue; and McKie, at 8 Maple Terrace.

2. Spell out a number naming a street if the number is *less* than eleven. When a street has a number as its name, you may separate the building number from the street number by a hyphen preceded and followed by a space. The letters *d, st,* or *th* may be added to the number that represents a street name.

He moved from 438 West Fifth Street to 867 - 66 Street.

Our office is located at 104 - 131st Street.

Deliver the equipment to 210 West Tenth Street.

Dates

1. After the name of a month, use figures to express the day.

Your inquiries of June 2, 6, and 9 were answered in full on June 14.

2. When the day of the month stands alone or when it precedes the month, it may be written in figures with *d, nd, rd, st,* or *th* added, or it may be spelled out.

In your inquiry of the 6th, you asked for our catalog.

In your inquiry of the sixth, you asked for our catalog.

We sent a check for $200 on the 3d of August.

Amounts of Money

1. Sums of money, whether in dollars, in cents, or in foreign denominations, should be typed in figures except for legal documents.

   The total amount of the equipment recently purchased was $769.33.

   The British firm may invest £50,000 in our project.

2. In legal papers capitalize and spell out sums of money; write figures in parentheses. Do not do so in most other business writing.

   I agree to pay the sum of Five Hundred Sixty Dollars ($560).

   I agree to pay a weekly rental of One Hundred Ten (110) dollars.

3. Even sums of money are written without the decimal and zeros.

   She mailed a check for $45 in full payment of her bill.

   Is that service charge $15?

4. When stating cents, use the figures without the decimal and spell out cents.

   The little girl purchased a small toy for 89 cents.

   Note: The ¢ sign often appears on orders and invoices.

   Two dozen @ 98¢ per doz.

Fractions and Decimals

Simple fractions that stand alone are usually written in words. Mixed numbers and decimals are written in figures. When a decimal fraction is not preceded by a whole number, a zero may be used before it.

   He bought one-half dozen erasers.

   The average age of secretaries in our department is 24½.

   The average age of secretaries in our department is 24.5.

   The quotient, 0.758, was obtained swiftly on the calculator.

Quantities and Measurements

Quantities and measurements should usually be written in figures, as in the following examples:

1. Age (*exact*)

   He was 37 years old on his last birthday.

   But use words in expressing *approximate* age:

   Richard is about twenty years old.

2. Balloting results

   There were 6,756 votes in favor of the amendment and 3,310 votes against it.

3. Dimensions

   They bought bond paper of a standard size, 8½ by 11 inches.

   Note: Spell *by* in full, except in technical matter where *x* is used for *by*.

4. Distance

   It is 13 miles from my office to my home.

   It is 2,098 miles from San Francisco to Honolulu.

5. Financial quotations

   They bought Monarch Utilities at 100 5/8%.

   Note: In financial quotations it is customary to express the plural of figures by adding the *s* without the apostrophe.

   James invested $20,000 in United Plywood 12s, issued in April 1983, and due in April 1993.

6. Mathematical expressions

   We found the total as follows: 125 plus 68 minus 38.

7. Measures

   We produced 200 bushels from every 4 acres.

   The chart showed that 231 cubic inches equal 1 standard liquid gallon.

8. Percentages

   Interest on the note was computed at 9 percent.

Note: In business writing the % sign is often used to express percent:

She purchased three 5-year, 4% bonds.

9.   Serial Numbers

Policy 622147, a new life insurance policy, is discussed in Bulletin #3.

10. Temperature

The highest official temperature record for this city is 110°.

11. Time

The plane leaves at 11:45 p.m.

But spell the hour in full when *o'clock* is used in stating time:

The office closes at five o'clock.

12. Weights

It takes 2,240 pounds to make a long ton.

DIVISION OF WORDS

When a word is divided at the end of a line, the division is indicated by a hyphen at the end of a syllable. Sometimes it is necessary to separate the parts of dates, names, and addresses even though these sentence elements are expressed as units. Such separations, however, should be avoided when possible.

Guides for dividing words and separating other sentence elements are given here. The dictionary is the authority for dividing words into syllables.

1.   Divide words only between syllables. Do not divide one-syllable words (*through, filed, missed*).

2.   Write more than one letter with the first part of the word and more than two letters with the last part of the word.

Acceptable	Not Acceptable
above	a-bove
steady	stead-y
teacher	teach-er

Thus, no four-letter word should be divided. And it is preferred that five- and six-letter words not be divided.

Acceptable	Not Acceptable
inter	in-ter
little	lit-tle
inform	in-form

3.   A syllable that is separated from the rest of a word must contain a vowel.

Acceptable	Not Acceptable
con-trol	could-n't
doc-trine	does-n't

4.   When a final consonant preceded by a single vowel is doubled before adding a suffix, divide between the two consonants.

Acceptable	Not Acceptable
step-ping	stepp-ing
run-ning	runn-ing

But when a root word ends in a double consonant before a suffix is added, divide between the root word and the suffix.

Acceptable	Not Acceptable
tell-ing	tel-ling
assess-ing	asses-sing

5.   A single-letter syllable within a word should generally be written with the first part of the word.

Acceptable	Not Acceptable
sepa-rate	sep-arate
busi-ness	bus-iness

Exceptions:

a.   When two one-letter syllables occur together within a word, divide between the one-letter syllables.

Acceptable	Not Acceptable
gradu-ation	gradua-tion
medi-ation	media-tion

b.   When the single-letter syllable *a, i,* or *u* is followed by the ending syllable *ble, bly, cle,* or *cal,* join the two ending syllables to be carried over to the next line.

Acceptable	Not Acceptable
depend-able	dependa-ble
agree-ably	agreea-bly
divis-ible	divisi-ble
mir-acle	mira-cle
cler-ical	cleri-cal

Note that this rule applies only when the vowel is correctly written as a syllable by itself. In the following examples the vowels *a* and *i* are not single-letter syllables.

Acceptable	Not Acceptable
dura-ble	du-rable
possi-ble	pos-sible
musi-cal	mu-sical

6. Divide hyphenated words and compounds—such as *three-fourths, record-breaking, self-explanatory,* and *brother-in-law*—only at the hyphen that connects the words.
7. Put on the first line enough of the divided material to suggest what the complete word will be.

Acceptable	Not Acceptable
clearing-house	clear-inghouse
diffi-cult	dif-ficult
gentle-men	gen-tlemen
recom-mend	rec-ommend
stenog-rapher	ste-nographer

8. Avoid dividing a surname. Separate titles, initials, or degrees from the surname only when it is impossible to avoid such separation.

Acceptable	Not Acceptable
Cunningham	Cunning-ham
John A. Link	John A. Link

Acceptable	Not Acceptable
Mr. Link	Mr. Link

9. Try to avoid dividing words at the ends of more than two or three successive lines, the final word on a page, or the word at the end of the last complete line of a paragraph.
10. Avoid the division of figures and abbreviations.

Acceptable	Not Acceptable
$3,500	$3,-500
A.T. & S.F.	A.T.-& S.F.

11. Separate the parts of an address only when unavoidable and then as illustrated here.

Acceptable	Not Acceptable
2143 Market Street	2143 Market Street
987 North Bridgeport	987 North Bridge-port
1741 - 16th Street	1741-16th Street
New York, New York	New York, New York

12. If separating the parts of a date is unavoidable, separate the day of the month from the year, not the month from the day.

Acceptable	Not Acceptable
August 20, 19—	August 20, 19—

QUICK PUNCTUATION GUIDE

PERIOD .

Page 645

1. To end a declarative or mildly imperative sentence
2. For most initials and abbreviations (*C.O.D., Inc., A. B. Hyer,* but *SEC*)

QUESTION MARK ?

Page 645

1. After a direct question
2. After a question in abbreviated form (Who is the em-

ployment interviewer? the advertising manager? the marketing vice president?)

EXCLAMATION POINT !

Page 645

   To indicate strong emotion or heavy emphasis

COMMA ,

Pages 646–647

1. For a subordinate clause preceding a principal clause
2. For a nonrestrictive clause
3. For a nonrestrictive appositive but not a restrictive appositive
4. To separate clauses joined by a coordinating conjunction
5. For an introductory phrase containing a verbal
6. For parenthetic words, phrases, clauses
7. For words or word groups used in a series of at least three items that have no commas
8. For words used in direct address or in explaining other words
9. For sentence elements that might be misunderstood if there were no commas
10. To indicate the omission of words that are clearly implied
11. To separate numbers (*7,892,000*)
12. To introduce a short quotation

SEMICOLON ;

Page 647

1. Between the clauses of a compound sentence if no coordinating conjunction joins those clauses
2. Before *as, that is, namely, i.e., e.g., to wit,* and *viz.* when introducing a complete clause or a series of several items
3. To separate the clauses of a compound sentence when at least one of those clauses has a comma
4. To punctuate a series of items that have at least one comma

COLON :

Pages 647–648

1. To introduce a series of items
2. To introduce a long or formal quotation
3. To separate hours and minutes in figures (*10:15 a.m.*)
4. To punctuate the greeting of a business message

APOSTROPHE '

Pages 648–649

1. To indicate possession
2. To show omission in a contraction
3. For the plural of abbreviations, letters, figures, and words

QUOTATION MARKS

Page 649–650

Double " "

1. To enclose direct quotations
2. To show titles of subdivisions of published works and titles of magazine articles, reports, lectures, and the like
3. To indicate unusual terms, words used in a special sense, slang, or jargon

Single ' '

To enclose a quotation within a quotation

   To position closing quotation marks and other punctuation, the following rules apply:

a.   Place the period or comma inside the quotation mark.
b.   Place the colon or the semicolon outside the quotation mark.
c.   Put any other punctuation mark inside when it is part of the quotation and outside when it refers to the entire sentence of which the quotation is only a part.

HYPHEN -

Pages 650–651

1. To divide a word at the end of a line
2. To join the parts of compound words

DASH —

Page 650

1. To show a sudden break or transition in thought
2. To emphasize an appositive
3. To replace a comma for heavy emphasis

PARENTHESES ( )

Page 651

1. To enclose figures following amounts in words
2. To enclose numbers or letters in enumerations, series, or lists
3. To set off nonrestrictive appositives

BRACKETS [ ]

Page 651

1. To enclose items that you insert into a direct quotation
2. To enclose a parenthetical item within material already in parentheses

ELLIPSES . . .

Page 651

   To signify omissions from quoted material

BUSINESS LETTERS AND ENVELOPES: FORMATS AND PARTS

FORMATS AND PARTS OF A BUSINESS LETTER

These guides will help you conform to contemporary business-letter protocol.

Formats

Letters may be arranged in a variety of formats, the most common of which are the block, the modified block, and the simplified block.

In the **block format** (page 184), each line begins at the left margin. This format interferes with picture-frame symmetry but saves production time.

The **modified block format** (page 186) takes a little more keying time but gives a more nearly balanced appearance.

The **simplified block format** (page 188) differs from block format in the following details:

1. The greeting is omitted.
2. A subject line is keyed in all capital letters or in capital and lower case letters a double space below the address.
3. All lines begin at the left margin.
4. The complimentary close is omitted.
5. The writer's name and title are keyed in capital letters or in capital and lower case letters at the left margin at least three blank spaces below the end of the letter.

Punctuation Styles

Open punctuation omits punctuation after the date, address, greeting, and complimentary close unless a line ends in an abbreviation requiring a period. Current usage tends toward open punctuation.

Mixed punctuation requires a colon after the greeting and a comma after the complimentary close. No other end-of-line punctuation is used in the opening and closing lines except for periods required by abbreviations.

Spacing

Businesspeople prefer single spacing for the body of a letter. More words can be put on a page keyed with single spacing, and less stationery may be required. Paragraphs have greater visual unity when keyed in single-spaced blocks with double spacing between paragraphs. Their darker mass is better displayed against the light background of the stationery.

Introductory Parts of the Letter

The introductory parts of the letter provide information about the sender and appropriately direct the message to a receiver.

Heading. The **heading** (also called the return address) shows from where the message comes and when it was written. The longest line of the heading should not run into the right margin of the letter. In block and simplified block formats, the heading is keyed flush with the left margin. Normally the heading of a modified block letter begins at the approximate center of the sheet. The preferred order of information is room and building (if they are included) on the first line, otherwise number and street on the first line; city, state, and postal code on the next line; date on the last line.

> 25 Standish Hall
> 201 College Place
> Des Moines, IA 50308-8647
> May 1, 19--

Dateline. Write the date in full: *August 23, 1992.* A legal decision may depend on the accuracy of the date. Figures alone, like *8/3/92, 8-3-92, 8:3:92,* invite misunderstanding. Avoid their use except in office memorandums. Avoid also the needless additions of *st, d, nd, rd,* and *th* after the day of the month.

Armed Forces Dateline. The Armed Forces favor writing the date with number of the day in Arabic numerals first, the name of the month second, and the figures for the year third—*3 August 1992.* This procedure is logical, and it has come into civilian use as an approved form. Correspondents in European, Asian, and Latin countries commonly use this style.

Preferred Positions for the Dateline. The date of a letter is a part of the reference material, much of which is supplied by the printed letterhead. The date gives information in terms of *time,* while the address printed on the letterhead gives information in terms of *place.* As time and place information are related, it is a good practice to place the date on the second line below the city and state names printed on the letterhead. In block and simplified block formats the dateline is started at the left margin; in the modified block format it is acceptable practice to begin the date at center or key it so that it ends at the right margin. If the letterhead is unusual in arrangement, the dateline may be placed in relation to the body of the letter to achieve an impression of balance.

Mailing Instructions. When a special postal service is to be used (airmail, special delivery, registered mail), a notation to that effect should be typed in capital letters even with the left margin a double space below the dateline.

SPECIAL DELIVERY
REGISTERED MAIL

Address. The address (also called the inside address) states (1) the name of the person or the business to which the letter is to be sent, (2) the street address, (3) the city, state, and postal code. Each line of the address is typed even with the left margin. At least three lines are normally used. When a title or a descriptive phrase is used with the name of the person or the business, four or more lines may be necessary to prevent the use of a long line that would mar the layout. A two-line address may be used when the address consists of name, city, state, and postal code.

Miss Janice McKinsey
South Ft. Mitchell, KY 41017-2920

Mrs. Edward Andrews
1521 Bond Avenue
Flint, MI 48506-2214

Mr. Ralph Johnson
Executive Secretary
Automatic Processes, Inc.
204 Woodlawn Avenue
Flushing, NY 11001-4598

Ms. J. R. Newcombe, Vice President
Evan K. Menninger Company
312 Crescentville Road
New Orleans, LA 70108-1364

The address is typed four spaces below the date. Double spacing is used between the last line of the address and the greeting.

If window envelopes are used, the address must be carefully positioned so that it will show in full through the envelope window when the sheet is folded and inserted.

Handling Numbers in the Address. Follow the guides given on page 654 for numbers in addresses.

Selecting the Correct Title. Use the correct title before the name of the person addressed, both in the address on the letter and in the address on the envelope. The correct general titles for the first line of the address when addressing an individual are *Mr., Miss, Mrs.,* or *Ms.*

Messrs. (the abbreviated form of the French *Messieurs*) may be used in addressing men; *Mmes.* (the abbreviated form of the French *Mesdames*) is used in addressing women. Contemporary usage tends to omit these two titles and to use instead the name of the firm as it appears on the letterhead. When you are unsure whether the addressee is male or female, contemporary usage is

to omit the title, using the name only (e.g., J. R. Newcombe), or to use the name of the firm.

Some writers propose use of *M.* as a title for both females and males; however, that practice has not yet been widely adopted.

To determine whether to use *The, &* (called *ampersand*), or *and,* in the corporation name, follow the exact style used on the letterhead of the company to which you are writing.

Punctuating Titles. The period is used with each of the following abbreviated titles:

M.	man or woman
Mr.	man
Messrs.	more than one man
Mmes.	more than one woman
Mrs.	married woman
Ms.	married or single woman

The period is not used with the following forms:

Miss	unmarried woman
Misses	two or more unmarried women
Mesdames	two or more married women

Special Titles. Certain titles, in addition to those already given, often occur in written correspondence.

Doctor (Dr.) is the title of one who holds a doctor's degree, whether in philosophy, law, literature, theology, education, or medicine.

Professor (Prof.) is usually written in full, but its abbreviation is becoming common.

The Reverend (Rev.) is a title for clergy.

The Honorable (Hon.) is a title for someone who holds, or has held, a prominent governmental position. It is used with the names of cabinet officers, ambassadors, members of Congress, governors, mayors, and judges. Courtesy often extends it to others. Guides for addressing elected and appointed government officials are presented on pages 670–672. Observe these protocols for special titles:

1. *The,* as an article preceding *Reverend* or *Honorable,* is traditional usage, but the growing practice in America (as distinguished from that in England) is to use the title *Reverend* or *Honorable* alone. In the case of direct *oral* address *the* is dropped.

    The Reverend Mr. Bradshaw
                    OR
    Reverend Bradshaw

    The Honorable Georgia Sherwood
                    OR
    Honorable Georgia Sherwood

2. Although abbreviation is common, many prefer to write and to read such titles in full.

3. When preceded by *the*, such titles should *not* be abbreviated.

4. Conventional addresses do not use *Reverend* or *Honorable* with the last name alone. Avoid *The Reverend Crane*, *The Honorable Towne*.

5. When *the* is not the only word used with *Reverend* or *Honorable*, *the* should not be capitalized.

We sent this suggestion to the Reverend Father Nicholas Towne and to the Honorable N. W. Johnson.

Double Titles. Double titles are justifiable when the second title adds new information or distinction and does not merely duplicate the first.

Appropriate

Mr. Richard E. Crawford, Manager
Dr. W. L. McGregor, Director
The Honorable K. L. Cameron, Chairperson
The Reverend H. H. Davenport, Moderator
Mrs. M. J. Anders, Superintendent

Inappropriate

Dr. Benjamin Contreras, M.D.
Dr. R. N. Barnes, Ph.D.

Typing the Official Title. The official title in an address may be placed on the first line following the personal name, with a comma separating the name and the title. The title may also be placed at the beginning of the second line followed by a comma and a space if the company name appears. This title indicates the official position in relation to the company named in the second line.

Mr. Carl Harrison
Manager, Ross Company
399 King Avenue
Camden, NJ 08108-4830

Mr. C. F. Wells, Vice President
Petroleum Refining Corporation
899 Kearny Road
San Francisco, CA 98104-8420

If the title is long, it may be placed on the second line by itself.

Mr. C. D. Nelson
Chairman of the Board
The Donovan Corporation
315 Randolph Street
Chicago, IL 60610-5670

Handling Names Properly. Do not alter names. In the address of the letter and elsewhere, write a name exactly as it is written by its owner.

Attention Line. If you know only the last name or position of your receiver, you may address his or her firm and follow that address with an attention line. The attention line is the second item of the address. It begins at the left margin.

Michaels and Cox, Inc.
Attention Mr. Cox
General Contractors
6300 Decatur Place
Dallas, TX 75260-1298

Michaels & Cox, Inc.
Attention Office Manager
General Contractor
6300 Decatur Place
Dallas, TX 75260-1298

On the envelope, place the attention line immediately below the company name in the address. (See the formats illustrated on page 674.)

A letter carrying an attention line will often be opened at once, along with general correspondence. If the person specified is absent and a prompt answer is required, the letter is referred without delay to another member of the staff. In larger companies, however, *all* letters—except those marked *Personal* or *Confidential*—are usually opened regardless of the address format.

Subject Line. The content of a message is sometimes emphasized with a subject line, thus: *Subject: Unions* or *Subject: Order No. 3572.* The subject line is placed on the second line below the greeting and begins at the left margin.

The word *Subject* should be followed by a colon. The word *Subject* is not necessary if the position of the subject line makes its nature clear. The body of the message begins on the second line below the subject line.

Beech Corporation
2913 Drexel Road
Austin, TX 78710-3178

Ladies and Gentlemen:

Subject: Unions

Beech Corporation
2913 Drexel Road
Austin, TX 78710-3178

Ladies and Gentlemen:

Order No. 3572

If the same message has subject and attention lines, follow this procedure:

1. Place the attention line on the second line of the address.
2. Place the greeting on the second line below the address.
3. Place the subject line on the second line below the greeting, beginning at the left margin.

Beech Corporation
Attention Office Manager
2913 Drexel Road
Austin, TX 78710-3178

Ladies and Gentlemen

Subject: Unions

Reference Line. Occasionally at the top of a letter a request like this appears: "In your reply please refer to File 586." You should then respond with the following reference line, placed at the point normally occupied by the subject line.

Reference: Your File 586
               OR
Your File 586

Greeting. Place the greeting on the second line space below the address and flush with the left margin. Double-space between the greeting and the first line of the letter body.

Common Greetings. The most common greetings are:

Men	Women
Dear Mr. Brock	Dear Ms. (Mrs., Miss) Brock
Dear Paul	Dear Ruth

Other greetings occasionally used to fit special circumstances are:

Men	Women
Sir	Madam
My dear Sir	My dear Madam

Dear Sir	Dear Madam
My dear Mr. Jones	My dear Ms. (Mrs., Miss) Jones
My dear Jones	Jones
My dear Andrew	My dear Alice

Plural greetings are:

Gentlemen—This greeting is for addressing an organization made up entirely of men.

Ladies—This greeting is for addressing an organization made up exclusively of women. *Mesdames* is an alternate greeting.

Ladies and Gentlemen—This greeting is gaining popularity for addressing an organization consisting of men and women.

How Well Do You Know Your Correspondent? Choose the greeting that represents the person addressed and that matches the tone of your message. For those whom you have never met, the formal *Sir* or *Madam* may be used, although in such instances the less formal *Dear Mr. Brock* (or whatever the name may be) is much more popular.

How to Capitalize a Greeting. Capitalize the first word of a greeting. The word *dear* is not capitalized unless it is the first word. The following words are always capitalized for greetings: *Sir, Mr., Madam, Mrs., Ms., Miss,* every surname, every first name, and all titles (President, Superintendent, Director, Doctor, and the like).

How to Punctuate a Greeting. In the mixed punctuation style, a colon punctuates the greeting of a business letter.

Dear Mr. Morris:

Do not use a comma to punctuate a *business* greeting. The comma is for *personal* correspondence. If open punctuation is used, the colon is omitted.

Special Greetings Involving Familiar Titles. It is permissible to abbreviate these titles in a greeting, but many people prefer them written in full:

Doctor (Dr.)	Dear Dr. Sterling
	OR
	Dear Doctor Sterling
Professor (Prof.)	Dear Prof. Bell:
	OR
	Dear Professor Bell:
Reverend (Rev.)	Dear Rev. Father:
	OR
	Dear Reverend Father:

Omitting Greetings. The simplified block format drops the greeting (see page 188) and puts a subject heading in its place.

A few firms have also experimented by dropping the greeting and substituting such forms as:

Mr. Rand, please . . .
Greetings, Mr. Randolph
Good morning, Mrs. Rankin
How do you do, Mr. Randall

A variation lifts the opening words of the first paragraph into the greeting position or address position:

Here, Ms. Washington,

is our idea of how you should proceed. Schedule your shipments for the first month . . .

OR

So You May
Get Acquainted
With An Extraordinary New . . .

Still another variant launches the message abruptly without using the introductory words:

Ms. Carmen Quintero
987 Waverly Drive
Louisville, KY 40209-3915

Here, Ms. Quintero, is the brochure which you recently requested . . .

Body of the Letter

Business writers follow these protocols for the body of a letter.

Paragraphs. The paragraphs in the message are indented or are in block form according to the format used. No paragraph indention is used for block or simplified block format. Indention may or may not be used for modified block. When indented paragraphs are used, the first line of each paragraph is commonly indented five or ten spaces. Paragraphs are usually single-spaced with double spacing between paragraphs.

As a rule, paragraphs in business messages are shorter than those in other forms of writing. An opening paragraph of two to five lines, for example, is easy to grasp. It is easier to read four paragraphs of six lines each than one solid paragraph of twenty-four lines. But do not overparagraph. It is easier to read four paragraphs of six lines each than twelve paragraphs of two

lines each. Strike a happy medium. In general, vary later paragraphs from four to eight lines or so.

Abbreviations. Use abbreviations sparingly. To write names, titles, and expressions in full is a courtesy that many well-known firms thoughtfully extend. Certain abbreviations should be especially avoided in business letters.

Use	Avoid
account	acc't, acct., a/c
amount	am't, amt.
received	rec'd
Philadelphia	Phila.
San Francisco	S.F.
Dear Sir	D'r S'r
Gentlemen	Gents
Secretary	Sec'y
Yours	Y'rs
March 6, 19--	3/6/--

But in routine communication when the addressees are familiar with the terms used, shortened forms are permissible. In such cases communicators often standardize their abbreviations according to the *Style Manual* of the U.S. Government Printing Office.

Second Sheets. Contrasted to pica, elite type permits more copy on a single page and makes possible more one-page messages. *But do not crowd one page merely to avoid the use of a second.*

Side margins on the second page should match those on the first. The heading of the second page is preferably written in one of the styles illustrated, approximately one inch (or six spaces) below the top edge of the sheet.

```
Mr. James K. Lamas
Page 2
January 3, 19--
```

```
Mr. James K. Lamas     2        January 3, 19--
```

Double-space between the second-page heading and the continuation of the letter.

Stationery used for second pages should *exactly match* the first sheet in quality, weight, color, and size.

Concluding Parts of the Letter

Follow these guides for the closing parts of a letter.

Complimentary Close. Like the greeting, the complimentary close is controlled by (1) good taste, (2) the practice of leading business organizations, and (3) the degree of acquaintance you have with the reader.

Choose the complimentary close to match the tone of the greeting and the message body. If the greeting is familiar because of a long-standing acquaintance, the complimentary close should be so. If the greeting is directed to a person of high position or to someone with whom you have not previously corresponded, the complimentary close should be relatively formal. Commonly used closings are listed here:

Faithfully yours Yours faithfully	Close personal friendship with or without business
Faithfully	Close confidential relations involving business
Cordially yours	Daily business contacts
Yours cordially	Close business friendship
Cordially	Informal business relations
Very sincerely yours	Semiformal Ordinary business matters
Yours very sincerely Sincerely yours Yours sincerely Sincerely	Business acquaintance Ordinary business friendship
Very truly yours Yours very truly	Formal, but widely used
Respectfully yours Yours respectfully Respectfully submitted	Severely formal or for use in official messages, reports, or communication to indicate special respect

Follow these guides for the form of the complimentary close:

1. Type the complimentary close on the second line below the last line of the body.
2. Begin it (a) flush with the left margin in the block format,

or (b) at a point even with the dateline in the modified block format.
3. Capitalize only the first word of the close.
4. When the colon is not used after the greeting, use no comma after the complimentary close. If the colon is used after the greeting, put a comma after the complimentary close.

Signature. In its usual form, the signature block of a business letter has three parts:

1. dictator's signature (penwritten)
2. dictator's name (keyed)
3. dictator's title in the organization (keyed)

Company Name. The company name, if used, is keyed in capital letters on the second line below the complimentary close. If the company name is long, it must begin far enough to the left so that it will not extend noticeably into the right margin. The company name is generally not used with the signature when the name appears on the letterhead.

Penwritten Signature. Standardize your signature for business matters. In legal disputes signatures are scrutinized, so sign consistently.

Dictator's Name and Title. The dictator's name is keyed on the fourth line below the complimentary close when a company signature line is not used. An acceptable optional arrangement is to type only the dictator's official title on the fourth or fifth line below the company name or the complimentary close and to combine the full name of the dictator with the stenographic reference initials.

If the name of the signer appears on the letterhead in such a line as "Office of A. B. Horton, Executive Director," it is unnecessary to type an identification; initials are sufficient.

If only the dictator's name appears in the typed signature position, the official title is usually placed on the line below the dictator's name.

When both the name and title are short, combine these two items on the same line.

Sincerely

Henry J. Erickson

Henry J. Erickson
Vice President

Cordially

L. V. Simms

L. V. Simms, Manager

Indicating the Status of Women. Women may identify their marital status as shown here:

Sincerely yours

Kathryn D. Lynn

Mrs. Kathryn D. Lynn

Sincerely yours

Carla M. Vargas

Miss Carla M. Vargas

Women who prefer not to identify their marital status may use *Ms.* or omit the courtesy title.

Sincerely yours

Kathryn D. Lynn

Ms. Kathryn D. Lynn

Sincerely yours

Carla M. Vargas

Carla M. Vargas
Vice President

Multiple Signatures. When more than one person is to sign a letter, the names may be typed below one another, allowing four blank lines for each signature. If several signatures are required, the names may be typed in two columns with sufficient space for the signatures.

Sincerely yours

T. Rakes

T. Rakes, Project Manager

J. Galgano

J. Galgano, Assistant Project Manager

Notations. As circumstances warrant, one or more of these notations may follow the signature.

Reference Initials. If the dictator's name appears in the closing lines, the typist's identification is typed at the left margin, thus: *bw.*

Although the preferred style identifies the typist only, some firms require use of the dictator's initials also: *cml:bw.*

If the dictator's name does not appear in the signature line, the name of the dictator is typed at the left margin, followed by the typist's initials, as shown in the following example. The reference line is placed on the second line space below the signature block, flush with the left margin.

Sincerely yours

TRI-STATE, INC.

P. A. Leed

Vice President

PALeeds/ld

Enclosures. Call attention, in the body of the letter, to enclosures. Add a notation (usually the word *Enclosure,* or the abbreviation *Enc.* or *Encl.*) at the left margin, on the second line below the reference initials.

WFK:jao

Enclosures 2
          OR
Encs. 2

Double-spacing below the reference initials causes the word *Enclosure* or the abbreviation *Enc.* to stand out clearly. When the letters have been signed by the dictator and are being folded and prepared for the mail, the enclosure reference guards against failure to include the required enclosure.

Separate-Cover Notations. When the letter refers to items sent in a separate envelope or package, an appropriate notation should appear at the left margin a double space below the last enclosure line (or below the reference initials, if there is no enclosure line). The notation should indicate the method of transportation used in sending the separate-cover material and the number of envelopes or packages.

Separate Cover—Express
Separate Cover—Mail 2

Copies. A copy of each typewritten letter is usually filed for reference. Additional copies are sometimes made for special purposes, such as conveying information to others interested in the correspondence. In such instances it is correct to sign the copy. If the copy is used under circumstances that make a personal tone desirable (for example, an identical message to several committee members), the signature should be placed on each as if it were an original.

If you wish to indicate on the original letter those to whom copies are being sent, you may write *Copy to* or *Copies to* (optionally, *c* for copy, *cc* for carbon copy, or *pc* for photocopy) on the second line below the reference, enclosure, or separate-cover notation (whichever is last) flush with the left margin, with the names of the copy recipients on the spaces immediately following, thus:

MVH/ac

Copy to John C. Halterman
           OR
MVH/ac

cc Ms. Mary Robertson
           OR
ab

pc Dr. W. G. Sprague

When copies are sent to a number of persons in an organization, the names may be arranged (a) alphabetically, (b) according to rank (highest on down), or (c) according to the relative degree of interest in the particular subject. The alphabetical arrangement is used most often.

If the information regarding copies is not for the benefit of the addressee, this notation may be placed on the copies only. If this is the case, it may be placed at the top of the sheet rather than at the bottom.

Postscripts. A postscript may be used to cover a point thought of after the message has been typed or to give special emphasis to some particular point. The postscript is seldom used in business. Logical construction of the message makes most postscripts unnecessary, except for those few cases in which deliberate special emphasis is wanted.

A postscript is the last item to be typed on the letter. It is typed on the second line below the last notation in the same form as any other paragraph of the message. The postscript should not be preceded by the letters *P.S.* (abbreviation for *post script*) or *N.B.* (abbreviation for *nota bene,* "Note well"). The position and format identify a postscript as such.

ILLUSTRATED LETTER

Illustration D–1 on page 669 shows the punctuation and placement guides presented in this appendix. As you examine the letter, refer to the following numbered explanations:

1. Make the format look like a picture in a frame.
2. A postal code appears on the same line as the names of the city and state. Leave one to two spaces between the state (or the two-letter state abbreviation) and the postal code. Do not place parentheses around the postal code or a comma before it. Some firms now use a nine-digit postal code, which is typed in a similar manner: 01021-1234.
3. Place the dateline so that it conforms to the letter format used or to the letterhead itself. The dateline may be blocked at the left margin, typed at center, or placed so that it ends even with the right margin.
4. Spell names of months in full, both in the dateline and in the body of the letter.
5. Place a comma between the day of the month and the year.
6. Omit punctuation after the year except within a sentence.
7. Type the address in block form even with the left margin; leave three spaces between the date and the address; vary the space before the date, depending on the length of the letter.
8. Make the lines of the address as nearly equal as possible. For this purpose you may place the addressee's title: (a) on the same line as the addressee's name; (b) on the next line, preceding the name of the firm; or (c) on a line by itself. Base your decision on the length of the title, the length of the addressee's name, and the length of the firm's name.
9. Place a comma between the addressee's name and official title when they appear on the same line.
10. Capitalize the principal words of titles and the names of departments (*President, Sales Promotion Department*).
11. Use no punctuation after the lines in the address except after permissible abbreviations.
12. Write the firm's name as it appears on the firm's letterhead.
13. Write in full the words *North, South, East,* and *West* in street directions. Spell out the number naming a street if it is ten or below; for 11 or above, use figures. For postal sections of a city (NE, SE, NW, SW); initials do not include periods; avoid abbreviating *Avenue, Boulevard,* or *Street* (e.g., 711-14th Street NW).
14. Type the name of the state on the same line as the name of the city in the address. Place a comma between the

Illustration D–1   ILLUSTRATED LETTER

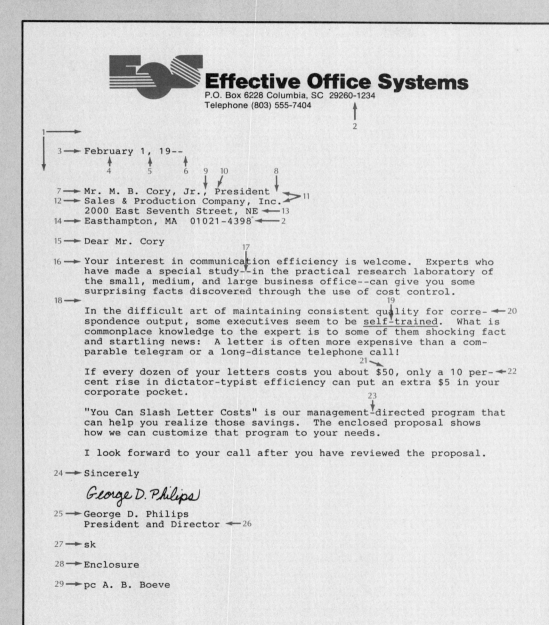

names of the city and state. Use two-letter abbreviations for identification of the state (see page 673). Type the abbreviation in capital letters with no punctuation. Type the postal code on the same line as the city and state.

15. Capitalize the first word of a greeting. Type the greeting even with the left margin two single spaces below the last line of the address. The greeting is followed by a colon in mixed punctuation.

16. Begin the body of the letter two single spaces below the greeting. For block format, begin the body even with the left margin. Single space the paragraphs.

17. Make a dash (—) by keying the hyphen twice, without spacing.

18. Double-space between paragraphs.

19. Use the hyphen (-) to link compound words.

20. Divide a word only when necessary. An even right margin may require occasional hyphenation. Avoid frequent hyphens.

21. Express even sums of money without the decimal point and zeros.

22. Express percentages in figures. Many business people prefer to spell *percent* rather than use %.

23. Use a hyphen to connect compound adjectives *before* a noun.

24. Begin the complimentary close two single spaces below the last line of the body of the letter. In block format, begin the complimentary close flush with the left margin of the letter. In modified block format, begin the complimentary close at center or so that the longest line in the complimentary close and signature ends even with the right margin.

25. Key the dictator's name four or five single spaces below the complimentary close.

26. Key the dictator's title on the same line as or directly below the name.

27. Key the reference initials flush with the left margin two single spaces below the dictator's title.

28. Key the word *Enclosure,* or the abbreviation *Enc.* or *Encl.* (if this notation is necessary), flush with the left margin two single spaces below the signature identification.

29. Use *Copy to, Copies to,* or the letters *c, cc,* or *pc* before the name or names of those to whom copies are being sent. The notation is placed two single spaces below the item it follows, flush with the left margin.

PROTOCOLS FOR CORRESPONDENCE TO PUBLIC OFFICIALS

Use this guide when corresponding with individuals in elected or appointed public offices. Use a directory for current postal codes.

FEDERAL OFFICES

Addressee	Address	Greeting and Complimentary Close
The President of the United States	The President The White House Washington, DC	Dear Mr. (Madam) President Respectfully
President's Spouse	Mrs. (Mr.) (full name) The White House Washington, DC	Dear Mrs. (Mr.) (surname) Sincerely
Assistants to the President	Honorable (full name) Assistant to the President The White House Washington, DC	Dear Mr. (Ms.) (surname) Sincerely

(continued)

FEDERAL OFFICES

Addressee	Address	Greeting and Complimentary Close
Secretary to the President	Honorable (full name) Secretary to the President The White House Washington, DC	Dear Mr. (Ms.) (surname) Sincerely
The Vice President	The Vice President The White House Washington, DC	Dear Mr. (Madam) Vice President Sincerely
The President of the Senate	Honorable (full name) President of the Senate Washington, DC	Dear Mr. (Madam) President Sincerely
Members of the Cabinet addressed as "Secretary"	Honorable (full name) Secretary of (department) Washington, DC	Dear Mr. (Madam) Secretary Sincerely
The Attorney General	Honorable (full name) Attorney General Washington, DC	Dear Mr. (Madam) Attorney General Sincerely
Under or Assistant Secretary	Honorable (full name) Under (Assistant) Secretary of (department) Washington, DC	Dear Mr. (Ms.) (surname) Sincerely
Head of a Federal Agency	Honorable (full name) (title, name of agency) Washington, DC	Dear Mr. (Ms.) (surname) Sincerely
President pro Tempore of the Senate	Honorable (full name) President pro Tempore of the Senate United States Senate Washington, DC	Dear Senator (surname) Sincerely
Committee Chairman, U.S. Senate	Honorable (full name) Chairman, Committee on (name) United States Senate Washington, DC	Dear Mr. (Madam) Chairman Sincerely
Senator	Honorable (full name) United States Senate Washington, DC	Dear Senator (surname) Sincerely
Representative	Honorable (full name) House of Representatives Washington, DC	Dear Mr. (Ms.) (surname) Sincerely

FEDERAL OFFICES

Addressee	Address	Greeting and Complimentary Close
Librarian of Congress	Honorable (full name) Librarian of Congress Washington, DC	Dear Mr. (Ms.) (surname) Sincerely
Judge of a Court	Honorable (full name) Judge of the (name of court; if a U.S. District court, give district) (local address)	Dear Judge (surname) Sincerely
Clerk of a Court	Mr. (Ms.) (full name) Clerk of the (name of court; if a U.S. District court, give district) (local address)	Dear Mr. (Ms.) (surname) Sincerely
Governor of a State	Honorable (full name) Governor of (State) (City, State)	Dear Governor (surname) Sincerely
Lieutenant Governor of a State	Honorable (full name) Lieutenant Governor of (name) (City, State)	Dear Governor (surname) Sincerely
Attorney General of a State	Honorable (full name) Attorney General State of (name) (City, State)	Dear Mr. (Madam) Attorney General Sincerely
State Senator	Honorable (full name) (Name of State) Senate (City, State)	Dear Senator (surname) Sincerely
State Representative, Assemblyman, or Delegate	Honorable (full name) (Name of State) House of Representatives (House of Delegates; Assembly) (City, State)	Dear Mr. (Ms.) (surname) Sincerely
Mayor	Honorable (full name) Mayor of (City) (City, State)	Dear Mayor (surname) Sincerely

ENVELOPES

Appropriately addressed envelopes facilitate message transmission.

Addressing the Envelope

On envelopes, the return address is typed a double space from the top edge and three spaces from the left edge. Address placement is as follows:

Envelope	From Top	From Side
Small envelope	2″	2½″
Large envelope	2½″	4″

The U.S. Postal Service recommends these guides:

1. Use all capital letters and no punctuation.
2. Block all lines of the address.
3. Single-space all lines.
4. Place city, state, and postal code (in that order) on the bottom line. The Postal Service prefers the use of two-letter state abbreviations with the postal code. Two-letter state abbreviations are shown in the chart below.

When an attention line is part of the address, it should be placed on the line immediately following the company name.

Other special lines, such as *Hold for Arrival* and *Please Forward,* are usually placed a triple space below the return address.

TWO-LETTER STATE ABBREVIATIONS

State	Abbr.	State	Abbr.
Alabama	AL	Montana	MT
Alaska	AK	Nebraska	NE
Arizona	AZ	Nevada	NV
Arkansas	AR	New Hampshire	NH
California	CA	New Jersey	NJ
Colorado	CO	New Mexico	NM
Connecticut	CT	New York	NY
Delaware	DE	North Carolina	NC
District of Columbia	DC	North Dakota	ND
Florida	FL	Ohio	OH
Georgia	GA	Oklahoma	OK
Guam	GU	Oregon	OR
Hawaii	HI	Pennsylvania	PA
Idaho	ID	Puerto Rico	PR
Illinois	IL	Rhode Island	RI
Indiana	IN	South Carolina	SC
Iowa	IA	South Dakota	SD
Kansas	KS	Tennessee	TN
Kentucky	KY	Texas	TX
Louisiana	LA	Utah	UT
Maine	ME	Vermont	VT
Maryland	MD	Virginia	VA
Massachusetts	MA	Virgin Islands	VI
Michigan	MI	Washington	WA
Minnesota	MN	West Virginia	WV
Mississippi	MS	Wisconsin	WI
Missouri	MO	Wyoming	WY

Illustration D–2   FORMATS OF ENVELOPE ADDRESSES

1. Four-line address. Note single spacing for typed return address.
2. Three-line address.
3. Four-line address. Note placement of *Hold for Arrival* notation.
4. Four-line address. Note placement of *attention line*.

Formats of Envelopes

Illustration D–2 on page 674 shows various formats of envelope addresses.

Window Envelopes

The window envelope has a transparent pane of cellophane or an opening at or near the center of its face, permitting the address on the letter itself to show through. The advantage of the window is that it cuts the cost of addressing the envelope by letting the address on the letter serve the purpose. This kind of envelope is popular for sending checks, invoices, bills, and similar items. Its chief disadvantage for use with letters is that it requires special framing, spacing, and folding which, in turn, may unbalance the letter layout.

BUSINESS REPORTS: ABBREVIATIONS AND SOURCE ACKNOWLEDGMENTS

STANDARD ABBREVIATIONS

To save writing and reading time, the following abbreviations are used in reports:

c. or ca.	about (from Latin *circa;* used in contexts of time—for example, c. 1900)
cf.	compare (from Latin *confer*)
chap. or chaps.	chapter or chapters (followed by numbers)
ed. or eds.	edited by, editor, or editors
ed. or edd.	edition or editions
e.g.	for example (from Latin *exempli gratia*)
et al.	and others (from Latin *et alii*)
etc.	and other things (from Latin *et cetera*)
ff.	and the following pages (for instance, p. 5ff.)
ibid.	the same (from Latin *ibidem*—used, especially in footnotes, to repeat an immediately preceding source)
i.e.	that is (from Latin *id est*)
l. or ll.	line or lines
loc. cit.	in the place cited (from Latin *loco citato*)
n.d.	no date (used especially concerning the details of publication)
n.n.	no name (used especially concerning the details of publication)
n.p.	no place (used especially concerning the details of publication)
n. pub.	no publisher (used especially concerning details of publication)
no. or nos.	number or numbers
op. cit.	in the work cited (from Latin *opere citato*)
p. or pp.	page or pages
par. or pars.	paragraph or paragraphs
passim	here and there (or throughout)
q.v.	which see (from Latin *quod vide*)
rev.	revised or revision
sec. or secs.	section or sections
sic	thus (usually placed within brackets, not parentheses, to in-

	dicate "thus it is in the original document or statement")
trans.	translator or translated
vol. or vols.	volume or volumes

SOURCE ACKNOWLEDGMENTS

Traditionally, source acknowledgments in a business report consist of footnotes placed at the bottom of the page and a bibliography. Footnotes cite the exact location of evidence or authority for specific statements. Bibliographical entries cite sources as whole entities. Current business practice also permits variations that effectively combine footnote and bibliographic references.

Bibliography or Source List

A bibliography should list at least the references cited in the body of the report; it may also list other pertinent references of potential benefit to the reader. Technically, **bibliography** refers to writings on a particular subject; hence, interviews, speeches, and radio or television broadcasts would not logically be part of a bibliography. To overcome that semantic difficulty, some writers use the designation *sources* or *references* to identify the list of data sources. Others use *bibliography* but categorize the sources.

An example of a categorized bibliography appears in Illustration E—1. An example of a noncategorized source list appears in Illustration E—2.

Observe these guides when preparing a bibliography or source list:

1. Alphabetize entries within categories or within the entire list if it is not categorized.
2. Use "hanging indentions" for bibliographical entries.
3. Use a solid seven-space line to avoid repeating an author's name. (See Illustration E—1. The first two books were written by Martin O. Atkins, Jr.)
4. Be consistent in preparing your bibliography or source list. Follow the sequence, capitalization, and punctuation illustrated in this text or any standard reference book.

Annotated Bibliography

A bibliography is sometimes prepared to direct the reader to useful sources of information about a subject. An **annotated bibliography**, a list of books or other publications with appropriate comments about each entry, is useful in such instances. Illustration E—3 shows an annotated bibliography.

Footnotes, Endnotes, or In-Text Citations

Footnotes are citations for specific statements. Traditional footnote style requires a superscript (number placed slightly above the line of type) at the citation point along with a footnote at the bottom of the page.

Text Citation

Managers should meet with employees at least once a month to communicate—in straight talk—about anything that has an impact on their work.[1]

Footnote

[1]Roger D'Aprix, "The Oldest (and Best) Way to Communicate with Employees," *Harvard Business Review* (September–October 1982), p. 32.

Footnotes may be grouped at the end of a report. When that practice is followed, the list is more appropriately called endnotes (see Illustration E—4).

Observe these guides when preparing footnotes or endnotes:

1. Number the notes consecutively throughout the manuscript or its chapters.
2. Indent the first line of each footnote or endnote.
3. Use standard abbreviations (ibid., op. cit., loc. cit.) for convenience and economy.
4. Be consistent in data sequence, capitalization, and punctuation. Follow the style illustrated in this text or any standard reference book.

Two variations of source acknowledgments require a complete bibliography but eliminate the need for formal footnotes. The American Psychological Association style (used in many technical and professional fields) requires an alphabetized bibliography and parenthetical placement of the publication date or the author's surname and the publication date within the text.

D'Aprix (1982) encourages frequent face-to-face communication between management and employees.

OR

Frequent face-to-face communication between management and employees improves productivity (Franklin, 1982).

A simple numerical system requires a numbered bibliography (usually numbered sequentially after having been alphabetized). In-text numerical citations then replace traditional footnotes. In the example on page 682, *1* refers to the first item in the bibliography; *32* refers to page *32* of that journal article.

Illustration E–1 BIBLIOGRAPHY

BIBLIOGRAPHY

A. BOOKS

Atkins, Martin O., Jr. <u>Canadian Markets and U.S. Producers</u>.
     Chicago: Business Publishers, Inc., 19--.

-------. <u>International Aspects of Marketing</u>. New York: Milford
     Book Company, Inc., 19--.

Foster, Samuel C., ed. <u>Development of Electronic Enterprises</u>.
     Toronto: Associated Science Publishers, 19--.

Kaplan, David G., and Doris Stewart Pierce. <u>Marketing Annual</u>,
     3d ed. Cincinnati: W. P. Denton and Sons, 19--.

B. PERIODICAL ARTICLES

Benson, Robert D. "Business TV: New Success Story." <u>National
     Business Review</u>, January 12, 19--, pp. 16-20, 22, 24.

Dalton, Arthur B. "TV Tomorrow?" <u>Manufacturers' Weekly Digest</u>,
     March 10, 19--, pp. 7-11; March 17, 19--, pp. 12-14.

"New Products, New Profits!" <u>Business Views</u>, February 3, 19--,
     p. 7.

C. INTERVIEWS

Allbright, Lawrence L., Executive Director, North American Trade
     Alliance, 500 Commerce Street, Detroit, MI 48503-8413
     (April 12, 19--).

Richardson, Wayne T., Information Officer, International Business
     Association, 717 Jefferson Avenue, Washington, DC 20008-
     2145 (April 15, 19--).

Taylor, Albert B., Secretary General, Canadian Trade Society,
     World Commerce Building, Toronto 5, Ontario (April 5, 7, 10,
     19--).

D. OTHER SOURCES

EPC Records. Annual Reports to EPC Stockholders, 19-- and
     19--; R&D Confidential File S-30; Research and Development
     Reports 125, 126, 140.

Illustration E–2   SOURCE LIST

SOURCES

Aiken, Linda H. "Nursing Priorities for the 1980s: Hospitals
     and Nursing Homes." _American Journal of Nursing_, vol. 8
     (February 1981), pp. 324-330.

Bergsven, Richard, Professor, College of Business Administration,
     University of South Carolina, personal interview, Fall 1981.

Hicks, Georgene, and Charles H. White. "The Cost of Orienting--
     and Retaining Nurses." _CHA Insight_, vol. 15 (June 4, 1981),
     pp. 1-4.

Hiller, Marianne, Director, Spartanburg General Hospital Child
     Development, Spartanburg, South Carolina, personal interview,
     Fall 1981.

"Hospitals Seeking Nurses." _The State_ (Columbia, South Caro-
     lina), March 13, 1980, sec. B, p. 11.

"Hospitals Struggle to Keep Nurses." The Washington Post, August
     13, 1981, sec. Va, pp. 1, 6.

Link, Charles R., and Russell F. Settle. "Financial Incentive
     and Labor Supply of Married Nurses: An Economic Analysis."
     Nursing Research, vol. 29 (July-August 1980), pp. 238-243.

Lund, David, Associate Professor, College of Business Administra-
     tion, University of South Carolina, personal interview, Fall
     1981.

MacKenzie, Sue, Licensing Division, South Carolina Department of
     Social Services, personal interview, Fall 1981.

Moore, Lawrence, Administrator, Presbyterian Hospital, Charlotte,
     North Carolina, personal interview, Fall 1981.

Ober, Earl, Director, Russell House, University of South Carolina,
     personal interview, Fall 1981.

Palmer, Marilyn, Director, Presbyterian Hospital Child Development
     Center, Charlotte, North Carolina, personal interview, Fall
     1981.

Registered Nurses and Licensed Practical Nurses, South Carolina
     Health Statistics, South Carolina Health Manpower Report,
     1981, pp. 63, 76, 79.

Reverman, Carol, Director, Booker T. Washington Child Care Center,
     University of South Carolina, personal interview, Fall 1981.

Wolf, Gail A. "Nursing Turnover: Some Causes and Solutions."
     Nursing Outlook, April 29, 1981, pp. 233-235.

Illustration E–3   ANNOTATED BIBLIOGRAPHY

ANNOTATED BIBLIOGRAPHY

International Banking

Badrud-Din, Abdul-Amir. <u>The Bank of Lebanon: Central Banking in a Financial Centre and Entrepot</u>. Dover, NH: Frances Pinter (Publishers), 1984.

An overview of Lebanon's economy and banking system since World War I, with emphasis on the Bank of Lebanon and the central position of Lebanon in the financial world; in-depth treatment of bank issues, such as organization and policy; comparison of central banking in Switzerland and Lebanon; discussion of Lebanon's role in wartime banking. Includes numerous tables.

Crabbe, Matthew. "Clinging to the Dear Old Hausbank." <u>Euromoney</u>, November 1986, pp. 96 ff.

Banking in Germany since partial deregulation of capital markets in May 1986.

Davis, Steven I. <u>Excellence in Banking</u>. New York: St. Martin's Press, 1985.

An attempt to identify patterns of exceptional management in commercial banking. Work is based on in-depth interviews with representatives of 16 of the world's top banks. Topics covered range from human resources, values, and cultures to leadership, education, and risk control. Indexed by bankers and by subject.

Mufson, Steve. "Barclays' Pullout Could Start the British Running." <u>Business Week</u>, December 8, 1986, p. 54.

Causes and implications of the Barclays Bank PLC pullout from South Africa in November 1986--an indication that not only U.S. businesses are leaving.

Illustration E–4   ENDNOTES IN BUSINESS REPORTS

ENDNOTES

[1]Carl J. Stone, <u>Managerial Communication</u> (Chicago: Consolidated Book Company, 129--), p. 32.

[2]Ibid.

[3]Ibid., pp. 71-73.

[4]Sara Carlson and J. Robert Anders, <u>Industrial Tomorrows</u>
(New York: Hamilton Press, 19--), p. 110.

[5]Stone, <u>Managerial Communication</u>, p. 84.

[6]Patricia J. Hart, ed., <u>Modern Managerial Practices</u>
(Boston: Thomas Budding and Sons, 19--), pp. 5, 12.

[7]Harold O. Allen, et al., <u>Legal Aspects of Business Commu-
nications</u> (Richmond, CA: Technibooks, 19--), p. 212.

[8]Leslie R. Montrose, "Cybernetics--Old or New?" <u>Admini-
strative News</u>, vol. XX, no. 12 (June 10, 19--), pp. 33-37.

[9]"News and Notes," <u>Business Management Quarterly</u>, March 23,
19--, p. 41.

[10]"Business Reports," <u>Encyclopedia of Business Administra-
tion</u> (New York: University Publishers, 19--), III, 429-432.

[11]George L. Sanders, Jr., President, Altomar Corporation,
telephone conversation, April 2, 19--.

[12]Edith S. Nachman, Dean of Women, Atlantic University,
keynote address to the national convention, Women in Administration, New Orleans, December 3, 19--.

Text Citation

Managers should meet with employees at least once a month to communicate—in straight talk—about anything that has an impact on their work. (1:32)

Bibliography

1.   D'Aprix, Roger. "The Oldest (and Best) Way to Communicate with Employees." *Harvard Business Review* (September–October 1982), pp. 30, 32.

2.   Driver, Russell W. "A Determination of the Relative Efficacy of Different Techniques for Employee Benefit Communication." *The Journal of Business Communication* (Fall 1980), pp. 23–37.

3.   Franklin, William H., Jr. "Six Critical Issues for the Eighties." *Administrative Management* (January 1982), pp. 24-27, 54.

COMMON VOWEL, DIPHTHONG, AND CONSONANT SOUNDS

The alphabetical letters *a, e, i, o, u,* and sometimes *y* are vowels in written communication. But oral communication has these definitions: A **vowel** is any sound that, if given sufficient breath, continues indefinitely. A **diphthong** is any combination of two vowels, rapidly blending into what seems to be one sound, with the first vowel stressed and the second vowel slighted. A **consonant** is any sound that, regardless of breath supply, seems to interrupt itself.

Examples of vowels, diphthongs, and consonants include sounds represented by underlined letters in the following lists. Notice that almost every sound has more than one spelling. Say the listed words aloud until you recognize the particular sounds represented by the italicized letters.

Vowels

1. b*e*, b*ee*t, b*ea*t, p*eo*ple, k*ey*, p*ie*ce, perce*i*ve, sk*i*, qu*ay*, amoeb*a*
2. *i*t, pr*e*tty, b*ee*n, wom*e*n, b*u*siness, b*ui*ld, syllab*le*
3. *ah*, *o*n, *a*re, p*a*lm, h*ea*rt, kn*o*wledge, se*r*geant, *ho*nest
4. *a*t, pl*ai*d, s*a*lve, l*au*gh
5. *ea*rn, *u*rn, h*e*r, s*i*r, c*o*lonel, w*o*rst, c*ou*rage, m*y*rrh
6. *a*bout, occ*u*r, probl*e*m, *u*pon
7. l*o*ve, d*oe*s (verb), fl*oo*d, m*u*ch, t*o*ngue, *u*s
8. t*o*, t*oo*, tw*o*, st*u*dent, kn*ew*, l*ie*u, q*ueue*, tr*u*e, y*ou*
9. l*oo*k, w*o*man, w*ou*ld, w*o*rsted, f*u*ll
10. *a*ll, *aw*l, br*oa*d, t*a*lk, v*au*lt, t*au*ght, *o*ffice, *ough*t
11. *e*gg, h*ea*d, d*e*bt, m*a*ny, *ae*sthetic, s*ai*d, w*ea*ther, h*ei*fer, l*eo*pard, b*u*ry, g*ue*ss

Diphthongs

1. *ou*r, h*ou*r, d*ou*bt, br*ow*, kr*au*t
2. *oh*, *owe*, s*o*, s*ew*, c*oa*t, r*oe*, r*ow*, d*ough*, b*eau*, y*eo*man, s*ou*l, br*oo*ch, apr*o*pos (When slighted or unstressed, this sound assumes the characteristics of a vowel.)
3. *I*, *aye*, *eye*, t*ie*, b*uy*, b*y*, h*igh*, *ai*sle, *i*sle, *eye*, g*ui*de, h*ei*ght
4. *a*ble, m*ai*n, s*ay*, m*e*sa, gr*ey*, st*ea*k, th*ey*, n*eigh*, g*au*ge, b*ou*quet (When slighted or unstressed, this sound assumes the characteristics of a vowel.)
5. b*oy*, c*oi*n
6. *ai*r, *e'e*r, c*a*re, th*e*re, th*ei*r, w*ea*r
7. *ea*r, p*ee*r, p*ie*r, h*e*re

Consonants

1. *p*ay, ha*pp*y, she*p*herd, hiccou*gh*
2. *b*est, ri*bb*on, cu*pb*oard

683

3. tip, letter, thyme, asked
4. desk, add
5. kiss, cool, occur, echo, clock, khaki
6. give, rigging, ghetto
7. five, safe, cuff, soften, diphthong, laugh
8. vote, of, flivver
9. think
10. this, breathe
11. see, success, science, psychology
12. zest, buzz, as, because, xylophone
13. shop, passion, sugar, conscience, addition, appreciate, chic
14. pleasure, azure, regime, prestige
15. chat, catch, righteous
16. joke, manager, wage
17. wear, quiet, choir
18. where
19. may, limb, name, comment, hymn
20. now, funny, gnat, know, mnemonic, pneumatic
21. think, sing
22. like, will
23. right, arrive, rhythm, write
24. you, million, hallelujah (also combined with vowel in use)
25. hello, who

asterisk–asterisks
cannon–canning
garden–gardening
cash owed–cash showed

we'll own–we'll loan
you'll end–you'll lend
will buy–wheel by

Because successful speech involves clear enunciation, practice aloud the following word sets; request constructive criticism of your speech from your classmates and your instructor.

steel–still
deep–dip
bean–bin
seen–sin
head–hid
bell–bill
caught–cot
court–cart
form–farm
store–star
coal–call
bowl–ball
sell–sill
pen–pin
real–rill
heal–hill
deal–dill
fell–fill
flows–flaws
pose–pause

rod–rode
con–cone
on–own
ah–oh
lips–lisps
gaps–gasps
mitts–mists
boats–boasts
ax–asks
tax–tasks
be in–being
see in–seeing
do in–doing
bacon–baking
taken–taking
tacks–tasks
tucks–tusks
peaks–speaks
Pacific–specific
grasp–grasps

FREQUENTLY MISSPELLED OR MISUSED WORDS

The accuracy criterion for business writing demands attention to spelling and word use. Mastery of the material in this appendix will help you avoid the most common spelling and diction errors. When in doubt about spelling or word use, check a current dictionary.

FREQUENTLY MISSPELLED WORDS

Here is a list of words frequently misspelled by business communicators. Memorize it or consult it frequently to verify your spelling.

accelerate	aggravate	ascend	corporation
accessory	all right	assignment	correspondence
accidentally	allegiance	attendance	correspondent
accommodate	already	attorneys	courteous
accompanying	altogether	auditorium	deceive
acknowledge	amateur	bargain	decision
acknowledging	among	beginning	definite
accumulate	analysis	belief	delicious
across	analyze	believe	descend
advertise	apparent	beneficial	desirable
advertisement	appointment	benefited	desperate
advertising	approximately	chief	determined
advisable	alignment	circumstance	development
		committee	dialogue, dialog
		comparison	dining
		competent	discrepancy
		competition	distinguish
		competitive	document
		computer	eighth
		congratulate	eighty
		conscientious	eligible
		consequently	embarrass
		controlled	embarrassing
		convenience	emphasize
		convenient	enthusiastically
		cooperation	environment
		cordially	equipped

essential
eventually
exaggerate
exceed
excess
excessive
existence
extraordinary
feasible
February
forfeit
forty
fourth
freight
fulfil, fulfill
gauge
grammar
guaranteed
hesitate
immediate
incidentally
indispensable
initiative
interfere
interfered
interference
interpret
interrupt
irresistible
journeys
judgment
knowledgeable
legible
leisure
library
license
lieutenant
loneliness
management
marvelous
memos
messenger
miscellaneous
mischievous
misspell
mortgage
mysterious
ninety
ninth

noticeable
nuisance
occasion
occasionally
occur
occurred
occurrence
opportunity
organized
pamphlet
parallel
parliament
particular
pastime
peculiar
perceive
permissible
personnel
politician
possession
precede
precedent
preferred
preparation
privilege
procedure
proceed
prominent
properly
prosperous
publicity
pursuing
quantitative
quantity
questionnaire
receipt
receive
recipe
recognize
recollect
recommend
referred
relevant
reliable
relieve
ridiculous
seize
separate
sergeant

significant
similar
sincerely
sincerity
solder
soldier
speech
statistics
straighten
substitute
successful
successfully
supersede
surgeon
syllable
sympathetic
tentative
tongue

transfer
transferred
transferring
traveling
tremendous
truly
unanimous
unconscious
unnecessary
valuable
view
villain
Wednesday
weird
writer
writing
written

FREQUENTLY MISUSED WORDS

Many word-use errors occur when writers confuse words that sound alike or nearly alike but have different spellings and meanings. Other word-use errors involve selection of an incorrect part of speech, such as adverb-adjective or noun-verb confusion. Using an incorrect word form may confuse your reader or mark you as a careless writer. Improve your writing by mastering this list of commonly misused words.

Word	Definition or Use
accept	to receive willingly
except	to exclude; with the exclusion of
adapt	to adjust or accommodate
adopt	to take as one's own
advice	a recommendation regarding a decision or action
advise	to give advice
affect (v)	to influence; to put on a pretense of
effect (v)	to bring about
affect (n)	the conscious, subjective aspect of an emotion
effect (n)	a consequence, result
aggravate	to make more severe

exasperate	to irritate or annoy; to incite or inflame to anger
all together	everyone or everything in one place
altogether	wholly, completely
all ready	everyone or everything in a state of readiness
already	by this time; previously
altar	a structure used in worship
alter	to change
among	in company with (used in reference to more than two)
between	in company with (used when referring to two)
analysis	separation of a whole into its parts
analyze	to do an analysis; break down
anxious	filled with anxiety or apprehension
eager	filled with keen enthusiasm, interest, desire
ascent	a climb
assent	to agree; act of agreeing
boar	the male of many mammals
boor	a rude or insensitive person
bore	a tiresome person; to drill; to make uneasy by being tedious
brake	something used to slow movement; to slow by applying a brake
break	to separate into parts; a separation
calvary	an experience of intense mental suffering
cavalry	a horseback–mounted army component
cannon	a big gun
canon	a regulation or dogma
capital	accumulated wealth; seat of government
capitol	a building in which a legislature meets
cell	a small room; a microscopic mass of protoplasm
sell	to offer for sale
cereal	a prepared foodstuff of grain
serial	arranged in series
cite	to quote, refer to
sight	something that is seen; to get a view of; to take aim

site	a place or location; to locate
complement	something that completes; to complete
compliment	an expression of admiration; to express admiration
continual	in rapid succession
continuous	without interruption
cooperation	common effort
corporation	a body formed and authorized by law to act as a single person
council	a governing body
counsel	advice; to advise
credible	offering reasonable grounds for belief
creditable	sufficiently good to bring esteem or praise; worthy of commercial credit
currant	an acidic edible fruit
current	most recent; a flow of water or electrical charge
deceased	no longer living
diseased	ill; suffering from a malady
deviate	to stray from a norm; one who departs from a norm
deviant	deviating from an accepted norm
discreet	showing good judgment in conduct
discrete	consisting of distinct or unconnected elements
disinterested	free from selfish motive or interest
uninterested	not having the mind or feelings engaged
each	one of two or more distinct elements having a similar relation
every	complete, entire, without exception
emigrant	one who leaves a place of residence
immigrant	a person who comes to a country to take permanent residence
envelop	to enclose or enfold completely
envelope	something that envelops
fare	price charged for transportation
fair	just; equitable
farther	at or to a greater distance; to a greater degree or extent
further	to a greater degree or extent; to promote

foul	offensive to the senses; an infringement of rules	prophet	a predictor
fowl	a bird of any kind	quarts	plural of *quart*, one fourth of a gallon
human	characteristic of people; a human being	quartz	a mineral, silicon dioxide
humane	marked by compassion	quiet	tranquil; free from noise
incidence	rate of occurrence	quite	wholly, completely
incident	an occurrence	respectfully	showing respect or deference
incidents	plural of *incident*	respectively	separately; in the order given
incite	to stir up	sail	a sheet of material spread to catch the wind and propel a ship or other vehicle; to travel in a ship
insight	penetration; discernment		
it's	contraction of *it is*		
its	possessive pronoun	sale	a transfer of property ownership for a price
lead	heavy, soft, malleable metal		
led	past tense of the verb *lead*	scene	locale, situation, view
lose	to part with in an accidental manner	seen	past participle of *see*, to perceive by eye
loose	not rigidly fastened or securely attached	seize	to take possession of
		siege	a persistent attack
moral	relating to principles of right or wrong	stationary	immobile
		stationery	materials for writing or typing
morale	emotional condition of an individual or a group	statue	a three-dimensional representation of a person or thing
pain	suffering distress; to cause distress	stature	natural height; status gained by achievement
pane	piece, section, side of something	statute	a rule or law enacted by a governing body
passed	past tense of *pass*, to go by		
past	gone by or elapsed	than	a function word to indicate a difference or comparison
persecute	to harass, cause to suffer		
prosecute	to bring legal action against	then	at that time; soon after
personal	of a person; private	their	of or relating to them
personnel	employees of an organization	there	in that place
perspective	point of view	they're	contraction for *they are*
prospective	likely to be or become	to	a preposition to be followed by an object
physical	having material existence		
fiscal	relating to financial matters	too	also; an adverb used to intensify an adjective (*too* cold)
plain	level, treeless country; simple or clear; unornamented		
		two	one more than *one*
plane	flat or level surface; to make smooth or even	waist	narrowed part of the body between the thorax and hips
precede	to go or come ahead of	waste	unwanted by-product; to destroy or wear away
proceed	to move along		
principal	most important, consequential, or influential; a chief or head person; a sum of money placed at interest or due as a debt	ware	an article of merchandise
		wear	to bear or have on the person
		where	at, in, or to what place
		who's	contraction for *who is*
principle	a fundamental law, doctrine, or assumption	whose	of or relating to *who* or *whom*
		your	possessive form of *you*
profit	gain, to gain	you're	contraction for *you are*

GRADING SYMBOLS

GENERAL COMMENTS

1.	✓ +	This item is excellent.
2.	✓ −	This item is defective.
3.	DDC	Discuss this item during class meeting.
4.	DWM	Discuss this item with me (during office hours).
5.	INSTRUX	Review instructions for this assignment.
6.	RR	Revise and resubmit this message.
7.	STET	Disregard earlier comment; do not change your original version.

DATA USE, MESSAGE ORGANIZATION, WORD CHOICE

8.	ACC	Is the information accurate? Is your *statement* of the information correct?

9.	CLAR	Clarify the word choice, pronoun use, or relationship to a neighboring item.
10.	COND	Condense your wording; state this item concisely.
11.	M?	What do you mean?
12.	DICT	Your diction (word choice) is inappropriate.
13.	FACT?	Is this assertion true?
14.	LOG	Are the organization, word choice, and word order logical? Are your statements free of fallacies?
15.	¶	Begin a paragraph here.
16.	No new ¶	Do not begin a paragraph here.
17.	SPEC	Specify; state precisely what you mean.
18.	TONE	Your message conveys doubt, timidity, arrogance, conceit, or other inappropriate tone.

| 19. | VAR | Vary your word choice; do not repeat one word unnecessarily. |

APPEARANCE, FORMAT, LAYOUT

20.	APP	Improve the message appearance. Is your message clean, attractive, and properly formatted?
21.	PERCEP	Your perception seems faulty. Please notice and correct mistypings, omissions, or repetitions.
22.	⊏	Move left.
23.	⊐	Move right.
24.	⊔	Move down.
25.	⊓	Move up.
26.	SS	Single space.
27.	DS	Double space.
28.	TS	Triple space.
29.	⟡	Move copy as indicated.
30.	*tr* or ∿	Transpose these items; reverse their positions.
31.	*cap* or ≡	Capitalize this item.
32.	*lc* or /	Use lowercase letters, not capitals.
33.	ℐ	Delete this item.
34.	∧	Insert item here.
35.	*ital* or ___	Italicize this item.
36.	# or #/	Insert space here.
37.	⌒	Close up; move together.
38.	SPC	Correct the spacing.

GRAMMAR, PUNCTUATION, SPELLING

| 39. | GN | Correct the grammatical number of this item. |

40.	GP	Demonstrate grammatical parallelism; use identical parts of speech.
41.	MOD	Place this word, phrase, or clause next to what it describes (modifies).
42.	SF	This item is a sentence fragment. If you intend to use a fragment for special effect, print SF in the margin before your instructor does.
43.	SI	This item is a split infinitive. If you intend to split the infinitive for special effect, print SI before your instructor does.
44.	PUNC	Correct the punctuation.
45.	,"	Put the comma inside closing quotation marks.
46.	."	Put the period inside closing quotation marks.
47.	":	Put the colon outside closing quotation marks.
48.	";	Put the semicolon outside closing quotation marks.
49.	⊙	Insert period.
50.	∧	Insert comma.
51.	∧:	Insert colon.
52.	∧;	Insert semicolon.
53.	⸗	Insert hyphen.
54.	=	Insert dash.
55.	" "	Insert double quotation marks.
56.	' '	Insert single quotation marks.
57.	'	Insert apostrophe.
58.	?	Insert question mark.
59.	!	Insert exclamation point.
60.	SPL	Correct the spelling of this item.

A